ARCHIVES
D'ÉTUDES ORIENTALES

PUBLIÉES AU FRAIS

des Forges et Aciéries d'AVESTA (MM. A. Johnson & C:ie, Stockholm), Propriétaire-Directeur M. Axel Ax:son Johnson

de M. FRANS KEMPE, Phil. D:r, à Hernösand=Stockholm

de la Fabrique Suédoise des Roulements à billes, Soc. anon. (A. B. SVENSKA KULLAGER-FABRIKEN) à Gotembourg

de la Fabrique de Cuir de L. A. MATTON à Gefle

de la Soc. anon. NORDSTJERNAN, Armateurs à Stockholm (Johnson Lignes: Suède—Brésil—La Plata, Suède—Chili—Sud Pacific, Suède—San Francisco—Nord Pacific), Administrateur-Directeur M. Axel Ax:son Johnson

PAR **J.=A. LUNDELL**

N:o 17

THE AKAMBA IN BRITISH EAST AFRICA
AN ETHNOLOGICAL MONOGRAPH
BY **GERHARD LINDBLOM**

UPPSALA 1918—1920. APPELBERGS BOKTRYCKERI AKTIEBOLAG

THE AKAMBA

IN BRITISH EAST AFRICA

AN ETHNOLOGICAL MONOGRAPH

BY

GERHARD LINDBLOM

2d EDITION, ENLARGED

NEGRO UNIVERSITIES PRESS
NEW YORK

The first edition of this monograph was published as a university dissertation (discussed publicly at Upsala, May 27th, 1916). This treatise comprised Chaps. I—XII, corresponding to Chaps. I—V, VII—XI, XIII in this edition. In the second edition numerous additions are made to the text of the first edition, and Chaps. VI, XII, XIV ff. are quite new.

Originally published in 1920

Reprinted 1969 by
Negro Universities Press
A DIVISION OF GREENWOOD PUBLISHING CORP.
NEW YORK

SBN 8371-2625-8

PRINTED IN UNITED STATES OF AMERICA

TO

COUNT ERIC von ROSEN

IN GRATEFUL AFFECTION

Contents.

P. III. Belief and Science.

INTRODUCTION.

During my linguistic and ethnographical researches in East Africa, which covered the period December 1910 to June 1912, my work was centred on the Akamba, a Bantu people living by agriculture, cattle-raising, and hunting, in the highlands south of Mount Kenia. I lived among these people from January to November 1911 and from January to March 1912, and found among them a practically untrodden field of work.

It is true that the Akamba were not discovered yesterday; Dr Krapf was the first European to visit them (in 1849), but the many travellers who have hurried through the country have not given themselves time to stay there, since they have had more interesting goals before their eyes, generally Kenia or Lake Victoria. Thus, although the Akamba are mentioned in many Travels, they have not hitherto been the object of systematic study (the literature in which the people is dealt with will be mentioned below). My endeavour has therefore been to collect the material for as complete a monograph on the Kamba people as possible, dealing with material and intellectual culture (language, folk-lore, &c), and also taking into consideration anthropological conditions. The present treatise includes the results of my investigations into the subject of the Akamba's intellectual and material culture. At the risk of seeming pretentious I consider that I may claim that, when once it is worked up, my total material will be sufficient for one of the more complete monographs that has been written about a people of the Bantu race.

Anyone who has been engaged in practical ethnological research work knows how warily one must go to work in order to gain reliable information. As often as it has been possible, I have with my own eyes been a witness of most of the practical occupations, as well as of different customs and ceremonies. In cases when I have been driven to fall back on oral statements, I have made a special point of obtaining them from reliable authorities. Information which has been obtained from one quarter has assiduously been verified by enquiries in other quarters. This is essential, for it happens all too often that one and the same individual returns different answers to the same question on different occasions.

The putting of leading questions has been avoided, for the native easily guesses what answer his interrogator would have, and if he is on good terms with him, he gives the desired answer in order to please. Even when leading questions are avoided, caution must be observed, for it often happens that the interrogated individual answers at random, in order to get rid of the troublesome questioner as quickly as possible. Further, I have only in exceptional cases turned for information to people from missionary stations, since the native unconsciously incorporates a good deal of what he hears there with his own conceptions; or else he is, or pretends to be, superior to the customs and traditions of his own people, with the consequence that he does not give a true picture of their beliefs and ideas. If, for example, he is questioned upon a matter which, from our moral standpoint, is condemnable, he perhaps feels embarrassed, and conveys the impression that the natives themselves also regard the custom in question as something repugnant, which is often by no means the case.

Finally, it is important in any study of primitive conceptions, to abandon one's own standpoint and try to assume that of the natives, endeavouring to see things through their eyes. The author commenced his work with a somewhat limited acquaintance with general ethnology; but on the other hand, he set to work without the encumbrance of preconceived opinions and theories, and this I think has facilitated his efforts to grasp the natives' way of thinking.

If it can be managed, linguistic and ethnological studies ought to proceed side by side. From my own experience, I know how much nearer one comes to the natives when one knows their language. Especially in East Africa, there is a great temptation not to trouble oneself about learning any other language than Kisuaheli, the »lingua franca» of East Africa. But even the most intelligent and skilful interpreter is not always able to interpret exactly, for the corresponding expression perhaps does not exist in Kisuaheli, and the interpreter finds himself driven to resort to other words, through which the original meaning is lost. I have had opportunities of making this observation more than once at the English government stations, when questions concerning the natives were under consideration.

It is of special difficulty to elicit the reason for a custom. Sometimes one succeeds after many if's and but's, but in most cases the stereotyped answer is: »It is a custom handed down from our fathers» (*ni maundu ma andu ala ma tæŋə*). Of course the natives themselves very often do not know why they do this or that, but the African is very conservative and does not offend against time-honoured custom, even though he feels it to be troublesome and oppressive; if he did so, misfortune would come upon him. Often, indeed, when the original reason for a custom has been lost sight of, a native will give secondary reasons, or even his own explanation. Ordinarily, it hardily occurs to him to reflect upon the reason for a certain custom, any more than it occurs to us to ask why it is considered impolite to shake hands without first drawing off the glove, the explanation of which is, of course, that many centuries ago the warrior used to protect his hands with iron gauntlets. However, the enquiring ethnologist is often helped by a comparative study of peoples; it often happens that the solution of a problem, which has to be abandoned for the time being as insoluble, is met with far away in another quarter of the world.

The following works embrace all the literature of value that has been written about the Akamba, as far as I am aware. They are given in chronological order, since none of them can really be considered as quite scientific sources, and it would not be worth while to try to make any distinctions. On the whole rather few scientifically trained observers have ever been among the African negroes:

J. L. Krapf, Reisen in Ost-Afrika 1837—55. Stuttgart 1858. Translated into English under the title of »Travels, Researches, and Missionary Labours» London 1860.
J. M. Hildebrandt, Ethnographische Notizen über Wakamba und ihre Nachbarn. Zeitschrift für Ethnologie 1878 (pp. 347—406).
G. Kolb, Im Lande der Wakamba. Luth. Miss. Blatt 1898.
G. Säuberlich in Jahrbuch der Sächsischen Missionskonferenz. Leipzig 1899.

L. Decle, Three years in savage Africa. London 1900.
J. Hofmann, Geburt, Heirat und Tod bei den Wakamba. Leipzig
1901. Verlag der Ev.-Luth. Mission. 24 pp.
E. Brutzer, Begegnungen mit Wakamba. Leipzig 1902. Verlag
der Ev.-Luth. Mission. 32 pp.
E. Brutzer, Der Geisterglaube bei den Kamba. Leipzig 1905.
Verlag der Ev.-Luth. Mission. 16 pp.
E. Brutzer, Tierfabeln der Akamba. Archiv für Anthropologie 1910,
pp. 523—542.
C. V. Hobley, The Akamba and other East-African Tribes.
Cambridge 1910 (pp. 1—117). In »Totemism and Exogamy»
Frazer has a chapter on »Totemism among the A-Kamba»
(vol. II, p. 420), which is a reproduction of Hobley's account
in The Akamba etc.
C. V. Hobley, Further Researches into Kikuyu and Kamba Reli-
gious Beliefs and Customs. Journ. Anthropol. Institute 1911,
pp. 406—457.
C. V. Hobley, Kamba Protective Magic. Man 1912.
C. V. Hobley, Kamba Game. Man 1912, pp. 179—180.
Ch. Dundas, History of the Kitui District. Journ. Anthr. Inst.
1913, pp. 480—549.
Ch. Dundas, The Organization and Law of some Bantu Tribes
in East Africa. J. A. I. 1915, pp. 234—306.

The reports of the German Mission work in East Africa contain
various things of ethnological value, both on the Akamba and on
other tribes[1]:

Evangel. Luth. Missionsblatt, Leipzig, from 1898.
Nürnberger Missionsblatt, from 1887.

There are a considerable number of works in which the
Akamba are mentioned more or less in passing:

L. v. Höhnel, Zum Rudolph-See und Stephanie-See. Vienna 1892.
J. W. Gregory, The Great Rift Valley. London 1896, pp. 346—351.
H. B. Johnstone, Notes on the Customs of the Tribes occupying
Mombasa Sub-District. Journ. Anthropol. Inst. 1902, pp. 263—272.
H. R. Tate, Notes on the Kikuyu and Kamba Tribes of British East
Africa, ibid. 1904, pp. 130—148.

A short estimate of the respective values of the above-mentioned books will not be out of place here.

Mr Hobley, who is commissioner for the province of Ukamba

---

[1] According to information kindly given to the author by Herr
G. Säuberlich, missionary, late of the Ikutha station, Leipziger Mission,
East Ukamba.

and a prominent expert in matters connected with various East African peoples, gives a certainly brief, but fairly comprehensive, account of both the intellectual and the material culture of the Kamba people. For a highly-placed official, who can only visit the natives for short periods at a time and can seldom associate freely with them, it is clearly difficult to obtain all the necessary information. It is therefore scarcely to be wondered at that Mr Hobley's book contains a number of inaccuracies and mistakes; to these attention will be drawn in the following pages. Further, his ignorance of the language has the result that the native terms and other expressions he has collected are often incorrectly reproduced phonetically, or misunderstood. In spite of that, the work is of great importance as a starting point and foundation for further investigations.

Hildebrandt's work is interesting, as it describes the Akamba of over 35 years ago, but his work, too, contains much incorrect information. In spite of their popular style, the pamphlets of the Leipziger Mission contain much that is valuable and interesting; it is seen at once that Messrs Hofmann and Brutzer are well acquainted with the subjects they deal with.

From many points of view, especially for the description of native law, the best of all the works mentioned is that of the Hon. Charles Dundas. As shown by the title, he deals chiefly with the Akamba of the Kitui district, where he stayed some time as District Commissioner and where I had the pleasure of making his acquaintance in 1911 and getting to know of his studies, then in manuscript. As my own exposition lays the chief stress on the Akamba of Machakos, Mr Dundas's paper is valuable as completing it. One reads his reliable and accurate description with great pleasure and notes that the author has tried and succeeded to get into close contact with the natives and understands them better than many other officials. Some points of detail, such as »the rite of Etumo», are unknown to me, and perhaps are not found in the Machakos district. On the other hand it is only in some few unessential cases that I should venture to assert that the author has come to a wrong conclusion. If there is any other criticism to make, it is only about the title of the work, as the essay can scarcely be said to deal with the »History of Kitui», but with the Kitui Akamba of the present time. The best chapter, certainly on account of the author's profession, is that on Kamba Law, which is in many respects more thorough than my own exposition of the same subject (Chap. XI).

For information as to existing literature on the Kamba language, reference may be made to my work, »Notes on the Kamba Language», Archives d'études Orientales, Vol. 10, Upsala 1919.

Perhaps I may also be allowed to mention the principal natives who have been of assistance to me in my work.

In the first place comes my servant and language teacher *Kıoko wa Malata* of the Machakos district. He showed great interest in the work, and I trained him systematically, until he understood exactly what I wanted. He is one of the most intelligent natives I ever met, and had served as an *askari* (soldier) in the English police troops, during which time he had learnt to associate with Europeans and to grasp their way of thinking.

Malata wa Kıambı, the father of the former, an old man who is a specialist in ceremonial purification processes, of which he knows at least one that but few Akamba are acquainted with.

Mboŋgɔ wa Kıpome, an *ıtıma*, i. e. a medicine-man, who differs from the usual type of medicine-men in that he confines his activities to the curing of diseases (Machakos).

Mulındɔ, an old man of great repute (Machakos).

Vındʒa, a *mundu muɔ*, i. e. an ordinary medicine-man from the district of Kibwezi. I pitched my tent near his village, and we were together every day. He conceived a great liking for me, and would gladly have accompanied me as a servant, if his occupation and reputation as a medicine-man would not have suffered thereby. Among other things, he initiated me into the secret ceremonies of the third circumcision, the so-called »men's circumcision». The revelation of the abominable customs connected with these rites is punished with death, if the offence is discovered.

Makıtı, »headman», a neighbour of the foregoing, for whom I had the opportunity of performing a service.

Mulı, a disreputable and half degenerate individual living near the mission station of Ikutha. His rapacity betrayed him into showing me, among other things, the place where a valuable *kıpıtu* (see p. 166) was kept.

Further I must express my gratitude and recognition to many other people, among whom are the following:

Professor C. V. Hartman, to whom I owe the opportunity of undertaking my journey to East Africa;

Professor J. A. Lundell, who by kindly accepting my work for publication in Archives d'études Orientales, has secured for it the possibility of greater circulation. He has also given me many good suggestions with regard to the printing of this work and has bestowed a great deal of disinterested work on reading proofs.

Mr S. Charleston M. A. and Mr H. Alexander M. A., lecturers at the University of Upsala, who have helped me with the English text;

The Hon. Mr C. V. Hobley, C. M. G., who drew my attention to the Akamba; The Hon. K. R. Dundas, D. C. in Machakos, who took an unfailing and kindly interest in my work, and rendered me great assistance. The same may be said of the three missionaries, Mr C. F. Johnston, of the African Inland Mission, Machakos, Mr G. Säuberlich and Mr J. Hofmann, of the Leipziger Mission, Mulango and Ikutha.

Finally, I will only point out that a work such as the present one should preferably be worked up on the spot, in the milieu which it deals with. When one gets home and begins to systematise the material, one finds that, in spite of every care, a great many things have been overlooked which, for the sake of completeness, it would have been desirable to include.

Chapter I. The Akamba — their country and neighbours.

1. Geographical extension.

The Akamba are one of the most north-easterly Bantu peoples in Africa, and one of the largest tribes in British East Africa. Speaking approximately, the Akamba inhabit the eastern slope of the East African highlands, between the upper course of the river Tana and Uganda Railway. More exactly, their country, *Ukamba*, forms approximately a right-angled triangle, one side of which is a line running from the summit of Mount Donyo Sabuk[1] in a north-easterly direction along the Tana's tributary Thika, and the upper course of the Tana, up to the Mumoni range, the extreme northern outpost of the Akamba. The second side practically falls along the stretch of railway between the stations of Kiu and Mtoto Andei[2], on the Uganda line; while the hypothenuse is formed by a chain of mountains which, running principally in a longitudinal direction from north to south, form the extreme eastern branch of the East African highlands, Ndau, Muutha, and Leopold chains, &c. The greatest length of the country from north to south (Mumoni — Mutitu wandei) is, as the crow flies, 225 km.; its breadth from east to west, about 130 km.

The stretch defined above is Ukamba proper, to which must be added the few villages which lie on the eastern slope of

---

[1] »Donyo Sabuk», under which name the mountain is generally known in East Africa, is Masai language. The Akamba call it *ƙıma ǰʒa nǰaϐı* = 'the nzavi mountain'; *nǰaϐı* is a sort of bean.

[2] This name is one of the many examples of how a native name can be distorted when adopted by Europeans. The word is *mutıʈu wa nðeı* in Kikamba, and means »the vulture forest».

the mountain ranges of Ngolea and Kyulu, south-west of the railway[1].

There are, further, a number of scattered Kamba colonies in both British and German East Africa. The settlement of these usually dates from earlier famines, and they are therefore principally composed of people whose ancestors, in such times of visitation (unfortunately not unusual in East Africa, at least in former times), left their native parts to seek their livelihood elsewhere, and who, when the famine was over, remained in their new homes. Thus, in the Kikuyu country, it seems there are to be found a large number of Kamba villages near the government station of Fort Hall, and in the eastern part of the Rabai district, in the hinterland of Mombasa, among the Wanyika, there live several thousands. Some of these lived there already when Krapf, the indefatigable missionary and explorer, came across them about 1850, and according to their own account they had lived there for about 15 years. They immigrated, says Krapf, during the great famine of 1836[2].

If we proceed to the Kilimandjaro territory, we come across a number of villages between Taveta and Lake Jipe, and a good distance south of this lake live a smaller number, in the most south-easterly parts of the Pare Mountains, on the boundary zone of the inhabited highland and the steppe. Still further south, also on German territory, there are found scattered villages in many places in Usambara, as for instance, north of the height commanding the Musi valley and the depression at Maramba, whose inhabitants, when Baumann came into touch with them at the beginning of the eighteen-nineties, said they had migrated there about two generations ago from Ukamba[3]. Very possibly they were driven from the soil of their fathers by the same great famine which drove to Rabai the Akamba now found there. Finally, Last[4] came across a great number of them still further south, in the province

---

[1] North of Ngolea there lies a small mountain, Noka, which is inhabited by the Anoka, a small tribe living largely by hunting. No European has yet visited them, but according to the account of the Akamba round Kibwezi, they speak a sort of Kamba dialect.

[2] J. L. Krapf, Reisen in Ostafrika, 1837—55.

[3] O. Baumann, Usambara und seine Nachbargebiete, pp. 165, 171, &c (see also maps).

[4] J. T. Last, Grammar of the Kamba Language (Polyglotta africana).

of Usagara, near Mamboia (about 80 kilometers south-west of the most easterly point of the Pangani River). These had emigrated from the north. The tendency to penetrate in small detachments further and further south is still found to-day among the Akamba, and in some decades they may, especially if any great famine again occurs, be found south of Usagara. Perhaps they are already there.

The Akamba living in strange parts not only preserve their language and customs fairly pure and are loath to marry into the tribes among which they live, but they also maintain communication with their kinsmen at home. In East Ukamba — whence the principal emigration seems to have taken place — I have often met with visitors from Rabai; and, on the other hand, I have at Lake Jipe met with people from Ukamba.

In spite of this feeling of affinity, it is however natural that they cannot live a long time in a foreign country without being, to some extent, influenced by its inhabitants; and this has caused many of the Akamba proper to look down upon their scattered countrymen. When talking of them, they may often be heard to say: »N. N. is no real Mukamba». Those living in Rabai have even got nicknames, and up-country are called *atumwa* (slaves) or *maɓıkılambua* ('those who have followed the rain'). They got the first name because, when they emigrated, it was said they went to be slaves to the people on the coast; the latter name, of course, was applied because they emigrated on account of a continued drought with its accompanying famine. To tell the truth, these »rain-followers» give the impression of being somewhat degenerate, and they have the reputation of being great cattle thieves — a suspicion which is not lessened by the fact that they prefer to build their villages as far in the bush as possible, where it is not easy to come upon them unawares.

According to the official calculations for the collection of the hut tax, the population of Ukamba proper is about 230,000.

*　*　*

If the great geographical extension of the Kamba people is taken into consideration, support is found for the reliability of my experience that it is one of the principal peoples, and that

Kikamba is one of the most widely spoken languages in that part
of East Africa. This statement I should like to emphasize even
to the extent of saying that, next to Kisuaheli, the »lingua franca»
of East Africa, Kikamba is the most useful language to know for
those travelling in the parts of East Africa mentioned above. It
is understood and spoken by a large number of Akikuyu, the
nearest neighbours of the Akamba to the west, more especially in
the eastern parts of the Kikuyu country, and also by many Masai
on the steppes in the south-west. My knowledge of the Kamba
language stood me in good stead also during my visit to the
Kilimandjaro district, among the Wataveta, Wadjagga, Wakahe,
&c. If to this is added the fact that in by-gone days the Akamba
were one of the leading trading peoples in the present British
East Africa, there is additional support for what has been previously said about the spread of the knowledge of their language.
They not only were, and still are, skilful hunters, and brought
quantities of ivory from elephants which they had killed themselves
down to the coast, or were met on the borders of their country
by Arab and Suaheli purchasers; but through their hands also
went quantities of ivory which was obtained from the tribes in the
tracts where elephants abound, round Mount Kenia and elsewhere.
Ukamba lay like a wall between the coast and the interior, and
it was too risky an undertaking for the inhabitants to venture to
transport their ivory through Ukamba themselves. Thus masses of
ivory from the interior also went through the hands of the Akamba.
What has just been said about ivory applies also to the slave
trade, though on a smaller scale. When there was a possibility of
cattle-stealing also, they were prepared to cover considerable distances. Krapf, the warm-hearted and enthusiastic missionary, was
for these reasons very anxious for the conversion of the Akamba,
as, on account of their roving propensities, they came into touch
with many different peoples, and were therefore, in his opinion,
more suitable than others to spread the message of the gospel.
In his time, he says, they used — in large caravans, numbering
from two to three hundred — to make trading and hunting trips
200 to 250 »leguas» into the interior (1 leg. = 3 English miles).
The elephant hunter A. Neumann states that he met Akamba
hunting by the Guaso Njiro[1], nay, even north of that river, among

---

[1] A. Neumann, Elephant hunting in Equatorial East Africa.

the Samburu; and according to Paulitschke, the »Mimidi am Guasso
Njiro [a Galla people] wurden von den Wa-kamba bedroht» [1]. At the
little harbour of Mkunumbi, north of the mouth of the Tana and
immediately west of the town of Lamu, the Galla residents told
the author that marauding bands of Akamba found their way even
thither [2]. As the crow flies, it is nearly 250 km. from there to the
eastern boundary of Ukamba. According to Baumann, they used
also to go — generally as traders — down to the harbour of Tanga on
German territory, and then came from Ukamba proper. During the
insecurity caused by the great Arab rebellion against the Germans
(1888), the above-mentioned traffic ceased.

2. Earlier dwelling=places and kinship.

Statements as to the **origin** of the tribe are contradictory,
and it seems impossible to come to a definite conclusion in the
matter. So much is, however, certain, that the stretch of country
east of the river Athi has been peopled from Ulu, the country
west of the same river, and this cannot have happened so very
long ago, since the differences in language and customs are almost negligible. All statements on this point agree, and on
matters of custom Ulu sets the standard for the whole country.
Often, when in East Ukamba I made enquiries as to some certain custom, I got the answer: »You ought to know that better
than we, you who have come from up there» [3]. From this point
of view, it was lucky that I chanced to begin my studies in West
Ukamba, where the ancient customs of the tribe have been best
preserved.

But if one wants to go further and find out where the people
of Ulu came from, one gets at once on uncertain ground. Many
Akamba declare that the tribe has never lived anywhere else, and
refer to the current myth about the first men, some of whom
are said to have been thrown from Heaven on a mountain in

---

[1] Paulitschke, Ethnographie Nordost-Afrikas, I, p. 67.

[2] G. Lindblom, Krigföring och därmed förbundna bruk bland
Kamba-negrerna i Brit. Ost-afrika, p. 136.

[3] *ulu* or *ųlu* simply means 'up there', and undoubtedly the
country has been so called because it lies higher than East Ukamba.

the Kilungu district in southern Ulu. Some place the ancient home
down towards the coast, in the neighbourhood of the Giriama
country, while others mention the country round about Kilimandjaro as the original settlement of the Akamba. This view is also
advanced by Kraft, according to whom the Akamba were originally nomads in the neighbourhood of Kilimandjaro, but afterwards, »probably under pressure from the Masai», emigrated
to the present Ukamba. In the new country they could not,
however, live solely as nomads, but were compelled to cultivate
the soil. This statement must be taken with reserve, but so much
seems certain, that in very early times Kamba colonies were found
on Kilimandjaro[1]. Professor J. W. Gregory believes that the tribe
came from the south, since east of Tanganyika there is a province Ukamba, which is mentioned already by Stanley[2]. Incidentally
the word is also found as a place-name in Unyamwezi, in German East Africa. Such a similarity of names may be a pure
coincidence, and on that alone nothing can be built. The question
of earlier dwelling-places and migrations is, moreover, nearly everywhere one of the most difficult to solve in the study of a people.
A glance at the map shows that the migrations of small groups
of Akamba during the last few centuries have been almost exclusively from north to south, never in the opposite direction,
and that these migrations have been determined by the occurrence of highlands, which have always been followed[3].

Difficult of solution is also the question of the meaning of
the name of the tribe. Of at least a hundred of the older
men questioned, none seem to have so much as thought of the
matter. Hildebrandt thinks the word may be translated by »travellers», from the verb *hamba* 'to travel, journey about'[4]. It is

---

[1] Cf. B. Gutmann, Dichten und Denken der Dschagganeger, p. 28.
Cf. also A. Widemann, Die Kilimandscharo-Bevölkerung, p. 2, and
M. Merker, Rechtsverhältnisse und Sitten der Wadschagga, p. 32.

[2] J. W. Gregory, Great Rift Valley, p. 347, 363.

[3] Without proving in any way his statement or indicating the
source from where he has drawn it, Deniker (Les races et les peuples
de la terre, p. 536) writes about the Akamba and Wataita: »Ces
Bantous d'immigration récente sont venus du nord-est, du pays des
Gallas».

[4] J. M. Hildebrandt, Die Wakamba und ihre Nachbarn, p. 348.

true that this verb does not occur in Kikamba, but it is found
in several other Bantu dialects. The name would also be sufficiently descriptive, and reflect one of the fundamental characteri-
stics· of the tribe. I have not, however, been able to discover any
support for this hypothesis about the original meaning of the name.

*   *   *

Division. From an ethnological, as well as from a linguistic,
point of view, various disparities are to be found among the Akamba,
but these are slight and immaterial, compared with those found
among other Bantu peoples. This is a remarkable fact, since the
tribe occupies an extended area, and is divided up geographically
into several centres of population, separated from each other by
inhabited country.

Geographically, as well as linguistically and ethnographically,
the country is divided into two parts, between which the river Athi
forms a boundary. Of these parts, Ulu or Yulu (i. e. »up there»)
lies west of the Athi; East Ukamba has no special name. Offi-
cially it is called Kitui district, after the government station of
the same name. Its inhabitants have, as already mentioned, emigrated from Ulu. Judging from the slight dialectical differences,
one is probably entitled to draw the conclusion that it cannot be so
very long since the Akamba passed over the river Athi — most
likely not more than 150 or 200 years. The Athi and the uninhabited table-land Yata, extending along its eastern bank, divide
the tribe into two chief parts, having each its own dialect. The
Akamba in the east are called *aᵽaɪsu* by the people in Ulu, and
their dialect *kɪᵽaɪsu*. Even this shows that they are conscious
of differences between the different groups. The ethnological differences are, firstly, differences in clothing, and secondly differences
in manners and customs. It often happens in East Ukamba that,
if they are uncertain what the ancient usage is in a certain case,
they go over to Ulu to get enlightenment. Again, in the matter
of language, when the people of Ulu hear a word that they do not
use themselves, they say, »that is no *kɪkamba kɪluŋgalu*» ('real
Kikamba'), and then they call it *kɪᵽaɪsu*. The meaning of this
word is uncertain; there is said to be a people *aᵽaɪsu*, north of
the Tana, but the Akamba have no communication with them. It

might be possible that the present East Ukamba was formerly inhabited by another people; but according to most statements, the
country was uninhabited when the earliest pioneers of the Akamba
began to occupy it (cf. p. 20)[1].

Brutzer, the German missionary, holds the contrary opinion[2].
I venture to quote the following from his »Vorwort«: »Dort in
Kitwi finden die Ngove [according to him, the real Akamba coming from Ulu] einen ihnen sprachlich verwandten volksstamm vor.
Diese Akamba betreiben ackerbau und bienenzucht. Sie werden
von den Ngove als Kamba anerkannt, erhalten aber den namen
Kikuli (hundspavian), weil sie wie affen auf die bäume klettern
um ihre bienenstöcke aufzuhängen. Die Kikuli geben auf die
frage der Ngove als ihren ursitz 'Mbee' an«. Mbee or Mbere
lies north of the Tana, and is inhabited by a tribe closely related
to the Akikuyu.

In spite of persistent enquiries, I have not obtained similar
information from a single old man, nor have I ever heard the
words *ŋgoβə* or *kɩkulɩ* used, unless I have introduced the subject
myself. In Ulu the words seem even to be unknown, at least to
many people. What I gathered about the two ideas in East
Ukamba agreed with Brutzer's statements in the following respects:
Both *ŋgoβə* and *ɩkulɩ* are Akamba, but the former consider themselves of greater distinction. They keep cattle for the most part,
while the *ɩkuli*, who live chiefly east of Kitui, have a great number of bee-hives, and have to climb into the trees a great deal
to look after them. Hence the name *ɩkulɩ* 'baboons', which
seems also to be the nickname for many poor people. On the
other hand, no one was able to tell me anything about those
ɩkulɩ as having alone inhabited the Kitui district in earlier times.
A point in favour of Brutzer's hypothesis is the statement made
to me by some natives that the *ŋgoβə* have certain peculiarities
of vocabulary. The investigations I made on this point were not
crowned with success.

In Ulu, the most south-westerly district, Kilungu, occupies a
unique position in many respects[3]. Its inhabitants were extra-

---

[1] Mr. Säuberlich, the missionary in Mulango, informs me that about
south-east of Ikanga (East Ukamba) there is a small district Nthaisu.

[2] E. Brutzer, Handbuch der Kamba-sprache, p. 1.

[3] Cf. *kɩluŋgu* 'part, portion', a name which, whether intentionally
or not, is very appropriate.

ordinarily wild and brutal, were notorious as great cattle-thieves, and had long been engaged in ruthless warfare with the other Akamba in Ulu, whom they called *æβaụ*[1]. According to Gregory, they were descended from some Akikuyu who, about two generations ago, had settled down in this district and succeeded in maintaining themselves there[2].

The most south-easterly corner of Ukamba, Kikumbuliu, which projects towards the Taita country, exhibits less striking peculiarities; the language seems to resemble *kɪβaɪsu* in certain cases. In East Ukamba again, the most northerly part, Mumoni, which extends to the upper course of the Tana, forms a separate whole. Both linguistically and ethnologically its inhabitants resemble the neighbouring tribe in the west, the Akikuyu.

On the whole, then, Ukamba can be divided into four centres of population: Ulu, in the west; the Kitui district, in the east; Mumoni, in the north; and Kikumbuliu, in the south-east. In the following account, attention will be paid to the differences they exhibit in the matter of customs, rites, &c, whilst the disparities in the matter of material culture must wait for consideration until the author has had an opportunity of working up his observations on the subject. The respective dialects have been treated in the introduction to the author's paper »Notes on the Kamba Language».

3. The neighbours of the Akamba.

If a glance is now taken at the tribe's neighbours, we notice in the west and north-west the large Akikuyu tribe, also one of the Bantu peoples, with whom the Akamba have carried on a feud since time immemorial. The Akikuyu are said to have a tradition that they once separated from the Akamba[3]. Among the latter I have found no corresponding tradition, unless it is to be traced in the legend of the man with three sons, Mukavi (Masai), Mukamba and Mukikuyu. On the other hand, some clans of the

---

[1] Cf. *mwɪβaụ* 'cousin'. Hofmann, the missionary, in the manuscript of his dictionary, translates this word by 'einer des gleichen stammes'.

[2] Gregory, Great Rift Valley, p. 84, 347

[3] Routledge, The Akikuyu of Brit. East Africa, p. 2.

Akamba claim to be identical with a couple of clans in Kikuyu. It is very possible that once upon a time some Akamba emigrated to Kikuyu, became acclimatised there, and formed new clans. In this way a small fraction, at least, of the Akikuyu would originate from Ukamba (cf. also p. 118). The last great famines have provided many examples of such migrations. That the two tribes, moreover, are closely connected is shown by the language, for a Kamba and a Kikuyu usually understand each other fairly well.

South of the Kikuyu country, the highlands of Ulu border immediately on the Masai steppes, the old Masai province of Kapotei. The Masai were the Akamba's most deadly enemies, but they understand — perhaps better than any other black race — how to defend themselves and their herds against the dreaded nomads; nay, they often successfully took the offensive against them. In several places in the east it is claimed that the cattle-stock originated from stolen Masai cattle. The Akamba call the Masai *akavi*, doubtless a corruption of the old tribal name *Wakuafi*.

In the south-east, Ukamba is connected by the lengthy Kikumbuliu with the Taita highland, whose inhabitants, Wataita, exhibit in many respects a likeness to their neighbours in the north. The Akamba seem to have been on a friendly footing with the Wataita, for they were obliged to travel through their country, when they went down to the coast loaded with ivory. In the east, there is no inhabited country until the river Tana is reached, and between that and the eastern border of Ukamba lies a belt of about 160 km. of desert, ill-supplied with water, which, as far as Europeans are concerned, is still a blank space on the map of Africa, and which the official maps are compelled to cover by printing the names Galla, Borana-Galla, &c, in all directions. Early in 1912, I went through this territory in the company of A. C. Champion, A. D. commissioner in Kitui, who was sent out by the Government to follow the river Nthua, as to the course of which information had been lacking up to that time[1]. We found the country round Nthua uninhabited, though the Galla undoubtedly make periodical hunting expeditions thither, as there are plenty of elephants there.

On the Tana live the Wapokomo, a Bantu people and an off-shoot of the more southerly Galla. Communication between

---

[1] Cf. A. C. Champion, The Thowa River.

these tribes and the Akamba was exclusively of a hostile character, consisting of cattle- and woman-stealing raids. Missionaries working among the Pokomo told me that the Akamba were a real scourge to that peaceable tribe, and also to the Galla living in that neighbourhood. The latter, however, sometimes went over to East Ukamba in their turn, on plundering expeditions. In earlier descriptions of travels in these and neighbouring districts are found cursory references to the Akamba's plundering expeditions. To take one example, Captain F. G. Dundas (1892) mentions that the Wapokomo and Galla on the river Tana were much troubled by the Akamba and Somali, and he himself encountered a considerable body — according to his account several thousand men — out on a plundering expedition along the upper reaches of the Tana [1].

There is no doubt that only half a century ago Galla extended in a more southerly and westerly direction, towards the middle course of Athi (Sabaki) and down towards Mombasa, than at the present time. Thus old Akamba men in the Ikutha region have told the author that the river Tiva, which flows practically through the centre of the present East Ukamba, was formerly the boundary between Ukamba and the Galla country. Even further south, at Kibwezi, Galla are said to have lived. However, after a succession of conflicts with varying fortune, the Akamba finally drove the enemy back, till the great desert east of the highland prevented any further advance. It is well known that the Galla were forced southwards by the Somali, and then a part of them went over the Tana. These in their turn undoubtedly tried to expel the Akamba, but were not successful. Instead, while the Somali beset them from the north, they were severely harassed by the Akamba and Masai from the south. Paulitschke probably summed up the position correctly twenty five years ago, when he wrote: »Die Oromò am Tana und Sabaki sind denn auch buchstäblich dem untergang preisgegeben — — — Das land zwischen dem Sabaki und der stadt Mombas ist auch bereits ganz frei von Oromò-elementen« [2]. At the present time there are practically no Galla found south of the valley of the river Tana.

---

[1] E. Gedge, A Recent Exploration, under Captain F. G. Dundas, up the River Tana to Mount Kenia, p. 514.

[2] Paulitschke I, p. 24.

In this connection, I will take the opportunity to criticize the location of the Galla's most southerly distribution on many maps. In spite of what is quoted above from Paulitschke, the latter nevertheless colours red (Galla) one continuous stretch from the upper Tana in a meridional direction to the inflow of the Tsavo in Sabaki, and thence in a narrowing wedge, down towards Mombasa. From this we naturally come to the incorrect conclusion that about 1890 the Galla occupied this territory south of the Tana. At most dots or some other slight indication would have been suitable to show the scattered colonies of Galla which were still found in this region. In the same way, Gerland represents the Galla as occupying a considerable region between the Tana and the Sabaki, larger than that he allots to the Akamba and the Akikuyu together [1]. Even on the big English Ordinance Map of 1905, a number of names of Galla tribes are set out just in this region [2].

Finally, if we turn from Ukamba towards the north, we find — north of Mumoni on the upper course of the Tana — the small but warlike tribe of Tharaka, or Athaka, as the Akamba call them. Very little is known of them as yet, but the view has been advanced that they are an offshoot of the Pokomo [3]. Unfortunately the author has had no opportunity of visiting them in their own country, but he has studied their language, which has, in many respects, been found to resemble Kikamba and Kikuyu, whilst Kipokomo shows closer relationship to the languages spoken on the coast, Kinjika and Kisuaheli [4]. According to some of the Akamba in the Kitui district, the Atharaka are descended from the Akamba [5].

---

[1] Gerland, Atlas der Völkerkunde, in Berghaus' Physikal. Atlas, Pt. VII.

[2] Sheet »Kilimandjaro» in Maps published by the Topographical Section, General Staff (Africa 1 : 1000000).

[3] C. V. Hobley, Akamba and other East African tribes, p. 2.

[4] Cf. G. Lindblom, Outlines of a Tharaka Grammar (Introduction).

[5] According to Champion, one of the few Europeans who have visited the Tharaka-country, the Atharaka say that »their forefathers came from south-east, and that they occupied the Kitui district before the Akamba crossed the Athi, but that they were gradually driven back by the Akamba till they sought refuge amongst the hills which they now occupy — — — No doubt many Kikamba customs have been absorbed, but I am strongly of the opinion that the Atharaka are not an off-shoot of the Akamba, but an entirely different race». A. C. Champion, The Atharaka, p. 69.

On the whole, the Akamba have natural boundaries on all sides, since nowhere do they live side by side with a neighbouring tribe, but are separated from their neighbours by stretches of uninhabited country, grass- or bush-steppes, which usually suffer more or less from lack of water.

Of the **Akamba's names for their neighbouring and other tribes,** I have made notes of the following, besides those already mentioned:

The Wasuaheli they call *asumba*, formerly *mapomba*, i. e. 'those who carry burdens' (*pomba* 'to bear a burden'), probably because the Wasuaheli formed the larger proportion of the bearers in the caravans which used to be fitted out at the coast and go up-country.

The Wagiriama are called *aswi*, their language *kiswi*, and their country *uswini*.

The Wataita are called *andi*, which is said to come from *ndi* 'strings'. When the Kamba merchants went to Kiswani (Mombasa) in former times, they used to meet people who carried ropes and strings of baobab fibre. Baobab, the bast of which is in great demand, grows in East Ukamba, but I have never seen it west of the Athi.

The Waduruma = *aluluma* (the Akamba cannot pronounce *r*).

The Wambee or Wambere, a tribe on Kenia = *ambele*.

The Galla (less frequently Somali) = *atwa*. The Galla country = *utwa*. According to Paulitschke, the Watwa (Wa-Tua) are a hunting tribe between the lower Tana and Sabaki[1]. I do not think it is improbable that the Akamba confused these with the Galla, all the more since they sometimes occupy a sort of vassal position to the latter.

The Somali = perhaps *aŋgoloŋgo*.

The Nubians = *anovi*. A considerable number of them are to be found in the larger places in East Africa, many of them serving with the English and German colonial troops.

---

[1] Paulitschke, Ethnographie Nord-ost Afrikas, I, p. 34.

According to Krapf, the Akamba were called *Waumanguo* by the Wasuaheli; according to Hollis, *el lungñu*, or »those with an evil smell» by the Masai. Hollis gives no explanation of this name[1].

The Akamba on the coast sometimes call their relations in Ulu *nžaɓı*.

An old, now almost obsolete, name for the Masai is *kıpoŋgo*, remarkable on account of the use of *kı-* (a prefix denoting a thing) in a personal name.

4. Ukamba. The chief features of its physical geography.

If one really wishes to understand a people and its development, one must have some knowledge of its milieu, the land it lives in, and especially the climatic conditions. As has already been mentioned, Ukamba comprises the eastern portion of the East African highland, which falls rather abruptly towards the east. Ulu seems to lie at an average height of about 1500 meters above the Indian Ocean, while about 50 or 60 km. east of the river Athi the altitude is less than 1000 meters. Numerous mountain chains, running principally from north to south, intersect the country, and have an elevation of as much as 1000 meters. Typical of the mountain chains and of the hills are the very narrow combs, which are sometimes only some 10 meters in breadth. One has hardly reached the summit before the opposite descent begins. The geological formation of these mountains is granite and gneiss, which often protrudes in the higher parts. The loose layer of earth consists, especially in the east, of the same red laterite as is found so abundantly up in the Kikuyu country.

Among the higher peaks may be mentioned Nzaui, in Kilungu, where, according to the legend, the first people lived. Between the chains of mountains, the country varies from undulating to level plains, often of the savanna type, but usually overgrown with a more or less dense bush, which, with its thorns of all shapes and sizes, is a plague to travellers. The boundaries between the different territories often consist of small rivers or streams,

---

[1] Hollis, The Masai.

with deeply worn channels. All such isolated little heights are called *utumo* by the natives.

In the matter of water-supply, Ukamba has been treated very scurvily by nature. There are no lakes, and the rivers, except the Tana and the Athi, are usually empty, except during and directly after the rainy periods. The Athi, under the name of Sabaki, empties into the Indian Ocean at Malindi. Conditions are best in Ulu, where numerous streams flow along the mountain slopes. Further east, the water question becomes a troublesome problem during the dry season. Large holes — sometimes several meters deep — must be cut in the dried-up river-beds, and the women will sometimes sit there for hours, before they can fill their calabashes with the water which slowly wells forth, and which is sometimes of such a colour that travellers hesitate to use it even to wash in. Down in the south-east (especially in Kyulu), there are villages which, during the dry season, are so far from their water-supply that if the women start out one morning they cannot get back again until the following day! However, time is nothing to the African native, and at the river they meet acquaintances and have plenty of time for talk and gossip, while waiting for the water.

Ukamba lies in the equatorial zone, between about $0°$ $30'$ and $3°$ south, and consequently has two rainy seasons: a lesser, in Nov. —Dec., and a greater, which begins in March and lasts until June. The rain is, however, often late in coming. The rainfall decreases from west to east. Thus in Kikuyu it is usually somewhat greater than in Ulu, which in its turn gets more than East Ukamba. According to Eliot, the average during 6 years for Kikuyu station was 36.14 inches annually; for Machakos in West Ulu 34.76 [1]. Hofmann, the missionary, during a long course of years, made observations of the rainfall at his station Ikutha, in East Ukamba. His observations are interesting, as they go as far back as the great drought at the end of the eighteen-nineties. They have never been published, and I therefore give them here, with Mr Hofmann's permission. The figures represent German »zoll».

---

[1] C. Eliot, The East Africa Protectorate, p. 153. Cf. also **Directory** of B. East Africa, Uganda, and Zanzibar, p. 38.

Month	1897	1899	1902	1903	1904	1908	1909
January	4.75	0	0	2.84	1.68	0	0.50
February	0.85	0	2.60	4.09	0	1.66	0
March	2.68	0.02	2.73	1.09	2.91	0.18	0
April	1.20	0.14	3.16	2.54	0.46	6.41	0
May	1.17	0.10	0.37	1.50	5.40	0.57	0
June	0.02	0	0	0.60	0	0	0
July	0.67	0.20	0	0	0	0.12	0.49
August	0.57	0	0	0.22	0	0	0.03
September	0.35	0	0	0	0	0	0
October	0.88	0.09	1.75	0	1.22	0.84	1.34
November	3.00	6.88	12.06	3.50	17.34	3.62	5.96
December	1.22	1.79	7.87	5.37	3.14	3.31	12.94
Total	17.36	9.22	29.74	21.75	32.15	16.71	21.26

Further, the annual rainfall in Ikutha amounted in 1905 to 24.57; in 1906 to 38.94; in 1907 to 26.34; and in 1910 to 20.49 »zoll».

A great source of trouble in these parts of East Africa are the periodically recurring droughts, when the rain fails completely during one or more »rainy seasons», and the horrors of famine are let loose in the land. The last famine, a minor one, was in 1908—9; the one before that, a very severe one, coupled with cattle-plague over large stretches of East Africa, was in 1898—99; a third was about twenty years ago, and so on. In 1898—99, in some places in Ukamba, 50 % of the population is said to have perished; in other places as much as 75 % [1], and the bleached bones of such of the victims as were not eaten by hyenas lie there still to-day, scattered over the country. I found many such remains in the Ikutha district, and, in the east especially, there were many over-grown fields to be seen, while all too often were found fragments of clay vessels and the three cooking stones of the hearth, signs which show that once upon a time a hut had stood there. The famines still live in the memories of the people and have acquired special names after some particular characteristic. Thus, that of

---

[1] According to the calculations of Mr. Säuberlich, Leipziger Mission.

898 is called »the carriage famine» (*ʒoa ʒa ŋgali*), because it raged while the Uganda railway was being built. It is certain that the risk of hundreds of natives dying of starvation is considerably diminished now, since grain can be quickly brought up-country from the coast by the railway.

The climate in the western regions can, on account of their elevation above sea-level, be compared to that of the countries round the Mediterranean, and one is really only reminded of the proximity of the equator by the fact that Europeans must protect their heads from the rays of the sun. The nights here are cool and refreshing. Even when the sun is directly overhead, the heat is seldom oppressive. During July and August, the sun is often hidden for several days in succession by heavy clouds and mists, and it is then often so chilly that one feels cold in the middle of the day. Mosquitoes and fever are seldom met with. Even a little further east it grows fairly hot, and in spite of the dry atmosphere, many places are considered dangerous for the health of Europeans. This applies especially to the most northerly district, Mumoni. Not only Europeans, but also the natives, suffer from fever. However, no extremes of temperature occur. During my visit to the region of Kibwezi, in Sept. 1911, the mean temperature at the middle of the day was 28—30° C. Besides, towards evening, there blows over the whole of East Ukamba a sometimes rather strong easterly wind — probably from the Indian Ocean — which lowers the temperature.

With regard to the **vegetation,** the bush-steppe previously mentioned is predominant among the hills and mountains. It is of the same type all over great parts of Africa. Large trees are seldom to be seen; only those of medium height and under. They do not grow close together, but scattered about; a coarse kind of grass grows between them, though not, as in Northern Europe, in continuous sward, but in patches, between which the soil is bare. Different species of acacia and mimosa are predominant among the trees. Typical of the drier bush are varieties of the genus Sanseviera. The several plants often grow close to each other, and they are easy to recognise from their long, fleshy, grey-green leaves. Further up on the hill-sides grow species of Euphorbia, resembling cactus. The Euphorbia candelabrum especially gives the landscape a characteristic appearance, where it is to be met with. In the east only, along the banks of the rivers, are found some palms, such as the dum palm (Hyphene) and the wild date palm (Phoenix reclinata). The baobab is only found east of the Athi — the climate of Ulu is far too temperate for it — but a couple of species of Ficus are found there. Around the villages, and as weeds on the fields, grow Rhicinus communis in abundance, often attaining the height of a smallish tree.

No forests are found in Ukamba, if by »forest» we mean what we understand by the word in Europe. Only on the tops of some of the higher mountains, such as Mutitu, north of Kitui, are to be found small remains of primeval forests. These undoubtedly had greater extension in earlier times than they have now, but the Akamba are an agricultural race, and require the slopes of the hills for their fields. One can often see that a forest has once grown on a place which now is bare. Solitary trees and immense stumps bear witness to the fact. A small, thickly populated district close to Machakos is called *mutitum* ('in the forest'), and the old people say that it was once entirely overgrown with forest and the haunt of elephants. Now the district is almost entirely devoid of even fuel, to procure which women have laboriously to dig up the remains of trees long since dead.

P. I

INDIVIDUAL LIFE

Chapter II. **Child-Birth.**

1. **General Customs.**

When a woman finds she is pregnant, she tells her husband (*navıtanetıe mıweı* 'I have passed the month'). They then sleep together once more only. During pregnancy the woman lives principally on milk and *kıteke*, a sort of porridge made of the flour of Sorghum or millet (Penicillaria). Fat, which the women are otherwise very fond of, is not eaten during the last three months, as it is considered to render the delivery more difficult; nor does the woman eat bananas or *ısʐo*, that is to say beans and maize boiled together, otherwise the most usual food among the Akamba. Honey is thought to be especially injurious, since the fœtus is said to derive much nourishment from it and so grows a great deal, which makes the delivery more difficult, and may even cost the woman her life [1]. Others think that honey has the effect of checking the growth of the fœtus. There are no other special regulations with respect to diet, but the person concerned decides for herself what she will or will not eat. I have only been able to discover one case of a certain food being »tabu» for a pregnant woman, and that is the meat of animals killed with poisoned arrows. If the mother eats of such meat, the child will die. It is not unusual to see them eat earth from white-ant heaps or the red laterite with which the ants cover the tree-trunks. They can usually give no reason for this, but declare that they have an irresistible longing for it. It seems as though this had something in common with the longings of pregnant women for certain kinds of foods, often quite extraordinary in character. In some cases the motive alleged was the belief that the birth is hastened by it, so that

---

[1] I have found this belief also among the Wataveta at Kilimandjaro. G. Lindblom, Anteckningar öfver Taveta-folkets etnologi, p. 167.

such earth is eaten by women in the more advanced stages of pregnancy, immediately before the beginning of the rainy season. The woman then has much to do in preparing the fields for the rains, digging, sowing, &c., and she is therefore quite naturally anxious to free herself from a burden which hinders her in her work.

As far as I could discover, the Kamba woman is not looked upon as »unclean» during pregnancy, and is not isolated in any way. It is very usual to see women, even in a fairly advanced stage of pregnancy, continuing their usual occupations[1].

The spirits of departed ancestors are supposed to create and shape the child in the woman; they also decide whether it shall be a boy or a girl, dispute about the matter, and try to forestall each other. While one spirit sleeps, his wife, perhaps, makes the child a girl, and when the husband wakes he finds himself fore-stalled[2]. Of course this does not imply that the Akamba are igno-rant of the connection between sexual intercourse and conception. They only think that the spirits, as well as the husband, play an indispensable part[3].

---

[1] If the above mentioned separation of husband and wife at the first sign of pregnancy, otherwise common among Bantu peoples, among the Akamba has anything to do with »uncleanness», I cannot tell.

[2] According to Hobley (p. 89), every married woman is at the same time wife to her husband and to one of his ancestors, and her fruitfulness depends largely on the latter. Personally I certainly never heard anything of such a »spiritual husband», but neither will I deny the existence of such a conception.

[3] The numerous legends about conception without sexual intercourse, found among the most widely separated peoples — examples of which are also found in the author's collection of Kamba folk-lore — can-not possibly be based upon ignorance of the effect of sexual inter-course upon conception, not even as a survival from a by-gone time, when such ignorance may have existed. Those who are not content to look upon such tales as the products of a lively imagination pure and simple, may instead regard them in the light of the belief of a primitive people in magic powers, through which anything soever can come of nothing. Thus, primitive man is not ignorant of the necessity of sexual intercourse for conception, but that does not prevent his belief that fertilisation can take place without it — namely by magic. See also A. Goldenweiser, in The American Anthropologist, 1911, p. 598 ff. (a criticism of E. S. Hartland, Primitive Paternity, the myth of supernatural birth, I, 1909; Hartland gives a selection of »myths of supernatural birth»). See also A. van Gennep, Religions, moeurs et legendes, p. 14 ff.

When the woman's time has come, some of the neighbouring women are called in to assist at the delivery. There are no special midwives, but any old woman with experience in such matters can help. The husband may not be present. The woman usually stands upright in front of the hearth in the hut. She holds on to two of the roof supports and stands in a straddling position. Some of the women take a firm grip on her legs, two hold on to her shoulders, and another receives the child. They talk and laugh if all goes well. The navel cord (*mukauti*) is cut with an ordinary knife. According to Hildebrandt, it has however first been tied with a piece of baobab bast, »die etwa 2—3 zoll vom nabel nahe bei einander umgeschnürt werden». The placenta (*nsuu* or *ŋgua ŋa kana* 'the child's dress')[1] is buried outside the hut. It seems as though no artificial means are employed, as a rule, to make its removal easier — a string of bast merely is bound round the woman's abdomen. But sometimes a sort of sea-snail, of which a part is powdered, is used. The powder is laid in the shell, which is filled with water, and this the patient drinks. The child is washed in warm water.

The length of time a mother rests after the birth depends upon circumstances. Sometimes she returns to her work the same day, fetches water, works in the fields, &c. If she has daughters who can work, she usually keeps to the hut for a few days.

To ease the birth, »medicine» can be obtained from the medicine-man. It is called *ŋðesŧo* (< *þesŧa* 'to help'), and usually consists of an antelope horn (for example, that of a Thomson gazelle) filled with various substances (a so-called *kɨþɨtu*). This is repeatedly stroked over the woman's abdomen and dipped in a calabash full of water, which she afterwards drinks. Whether any real, or supposedly real (that is to say, not magic), medicine is used in difficult cases, is unknown to the author. In his ethnobotanical collections, which contain some hundreds of plants, there are, however, none for such a purpose. Even when the birth is safely over, the child is sometimes subjected to special treatment, especially if the woman has previously lost many babies; for a desire is naturally felt to prevent the deaths of children. Hof-

---

[1] Called »the child's house» by the Ronga round Delagoa Bay. H. Junod, The Life of a South African tribe, p. 37. Cf. also Ploss, Das Weib in der Natur- und Völkerkunde II, p. 245.

mann describes such a case[1]. Among other things, according to him, a special entrance to the hut was made for the mother and child, and the child was carefully concealed from everyone, until it had undergone a certain magic treatment. The diversion of evil influences by changing the entrance to the hut ·is very common among primitive peoples.

A child which is born before term is carefully wrapped up and placed in a large clay vessel to keep it warm. Such a child is often called *muınde* (< *ında* 'to sink, tuck down')[2].

When the birth is over, the woman may not lie on her bed, but takes the sleeping skin from it and lies on the earth floor of the hut, in the place she usually occupies when the family are assembled round the hearth. Neither does the woman seem to have to keep to any special diet. The following ceremony must then be gone through: Two small children, a girl and a boy, have their heads smeared with fat, and are sent with small calabashes to the river to fetch water. On the way there they may talk to each other, but not to anyone they may meet. They break off a branch of the wild fig-tree (*kıumo*) and pick some blades ·of the grass *ıkoka*, and then go and fill their calabashes. If the new-born child is a girl, the girl covers the opening of her little vessel with the twigs they took with them, and the boy his with *ıkoka;* if it is a boy, they do the opposite. When they get back to the village, the mother again smears their heads with fat, beginning with the boy, if the new-born baby is a boy; in the contrary case, with the girl. Part of the water is used to wash the child and part for the porridge to be described below. The small quantity of water used shows clearly that this is entirely a matter of ritual[3].

Preparations for the feast which is to take place on the following day are now begun. A large cooking-pot is placed on the hearth and *ısżo* is prepared for the women who now come to pre-

---

[1] J. Hofmann, Geburt, Heirat und Tod unter den Wakamba, p. o.

[2] The verb is used specially for bananas, which are picked unripe. They are laid in a pot, which is buried in the earth, and so they are allowed to ripen.

[3] A custom which resembles that described here is mentioned by Routledge from the Akikuyu, a Bantu people west of Akamba. See Routledge, The Akikuyu of British East Africa.

pare dishes for the feast. This *isŗo* is called *utĭndĭtĭ*. The number of the women invited must not be odd, *mwa*, for odd numbers are generally considered to be unlucky among the Bantu
peoples. The women make porridge (*ŋgĭma*) of Eleusine flour.
When the porridge is ready, the mother with her child takes her
place at the entrance to the hut. A *ŋgoŗ* (the piece of skin in
which a baby is carried) is bound on the back of a little girl or
boy, as the case may be (cf. p. 32), who then carries the child
to the entrance of the village and back again. This rite ushers in
the important phase of a child's life during which it is carried on its
mother's back. The mother then takes a leaf and removes the
child's motions for the first time. The ceremonies are concluded
with an offering to the spirits of the ancestors of the child: an
old woman throws a big piece of *ŋgĭma* over the roof of the
hut, saying something to the following effect: »Ye who live out
there, take this, and know that a child has been born here». The
woman who makes this offering at once becomes barren, so it is
always done by an old woman who is past child-bearing. The
mother can then sleep in her bed again.

According to an unconfirmed statement the following ceremony
must take place before a confined woman can associate with the
rest of the women in the following day's *ŋgĭma*-eating. Her husband
goes into the field and cuts four pieces of sugar-cane, two with
dark and two with light bark. From one sugar-cane of each kind
he removes the top and the leaves, which must not be done with
a knife, but only with the hands. Then he goes home, carrying
two canes on each shoulder, and brings them in above the door
to his wife's hut.

The next day a feast takes place on the *nža*, the cleared
space in front of the hut, and friends and relations are invited.
A he-goat, or if they are well-to-do people, an ox, has been slaughtered. Early in the morning, the women begin to eat *ŋgĭma*
and fat, all the while discussing eagerly what the child shall be
called. Suggestions are made and rejected, till at last a certain
name is agreed upon [1]. No special ceremony occurs in connection with the naming of the child, nor need this necessarily take

---

[1] Hildebrandt states incorrectly that it is the mother that names
the child; see above-mentioned work, p. 397.

place on the third day [1]. The men's carousal takes place later in the day. In the evening, the women dance and sing songs, in which the child is called by the name chosen. The skin of the slaughtered animal ought not to be sold or given away to anyone else; very often the woman uses it to sleep on, or the husband makes clothes for her out of it. However, if the skin is disposed of, a strip of it is first cut off and fastened to the skin (ɲgoɩ) in which the mother carries her child on her back.

On the fourth day, the father usually hangs round the child's neck a necklace, ɩpa, consisting of one of the fine iron chains made by the Akamba. This chain may not be made of anything but iron, or it will bring bad luck to the child [2]. As soon as the ɩpa is hung round the child's neck, the child becomes a real human being; before that it is looked upon as being in more or less intimate connection with the spirit-world, from which it has come, and is called kɩɩmu (cf. ɩɩmu 'a deceased relation, spirit'). In order that the new-born child shall be recognised as a real member of the tribe, it is therefore not enough that it is born and receives a name, which is otherwise, among primitive communities, usually the ceremony by which the new individual is taken up as an integral part of the tribe.

The next night the parents must sleep together. The child is then placed between the mother's breasts, and afterwards always occupies this position at night, till the mother menstruates for the first time after her confinement. The parents then sleep together again. On this occasion the child must lie behind the mother's back. This is called olula kana 'turn the child' (nɩnonɩɔ nðakamɔ nɩnaoluɩlɔ kana 'I have seen the blood, I have turned the child', says the woman). If not placed as mentioned above, the child will die.

If one takes into consideration the aversion to iron which, according to popular belief, spirits always entertain, it is not too bold

---

[1] My investigations into the names and principles for naming among the Akamba are worked up and will be published in connection with my linguistic studies. I will only mention, in passing, that later several additional names are given — suggested by different events in the life of the individual.

[2] Perhaps one may conclude from this that the wearing of the ɩpa is a very old custom, dating from a time when copper and brass had not begun to be imported and iron was, consequently, the only metal found in the country.

to conclude that the object of *ipa* is to protect the child from the malicious spirits, *aimu*[1], to whose attacks a baby is considered to be more liable than other people, especially if it comes from the spirit world, as they believe here[2]. If this is so, we may wonder why several days are allowed to elapse before this prophylactic is applied. We might think that they ought to be anxious to procure protection for the child as soon as possible after its birth.

Hanging the *ipa* round the child's neck and the subsequent coition are important ceremonies, which may on no account be omitted. If a girl has an illegitimate child and her lover deserts her, another must act as husband and father. Her father then takes her to one of his friends, who places the *ipa* round the child's neck and performs the ritual coition, and then the girl goes home. The man receives a goat for his trouble. If he has the opportunity and can afford it, he gladly buys the girl, and she becomes his wife. It is very usual that children are born before marriage, but the lover generally makes the girl his wife.

If a child dies while it is still *kimu*, the mother may not touch another baby, unless its mother is pregnant or has just had sexual intercourse with her husband. Otherwise the other child will also die. Nor may the mother of a child who has just died while it is still *kimu* touch another woman — not even her belongings. Neither when they go out to fetch wood or water together may she help with the loads, &c. She is looked upon as unclean, but she is not isolated, and she is allowed to associate with the others, as long as she does not touch them. If this rule is violated, the woman who has been touched is subjected to an ordinary purification ceremonial (cf. p. 103) in order to prevent evil consequences. The goat necessary for the purifying process is then presented by the husband of the unclean woman. The latter remains in her exceptional position until she next menstruates. Before that she may not sleep with her husband, for it would be fatal to the next child.

If a woman who has been confined has relations with any other man than her husband before she menstruates for the first time after the birth of her child, the child will most probably die.

---

[1] Cf. Ch. XII, Religion.
[2] Cf. Frazer, The Golden Bough II, p. 235.

The Akamba attach great importance to birthmarks, especially if the same birthmark has been borne by a deceased member of the family. They have no doubt then that the latter has allowed himself to be reincarnated in the child, and that settles the question of what the child shall be called. To cite an example of this, a child in the neighbourhood of Machakos had a scar on its forehead. The father's grandmother had been killed by a stab in the forehead from the spear of a Masai, and, according to all accounts, a deceased brother of his had had the same mark. In this case I could get no satisfactory answer to my enquiry as to whose spirit had taken up its abode in the child. There seems, however, to be no fundamental obstacle to a woman being reincarnated in a male child. It is most usual for the spirit of a deceased relation to come in the night (most probably in a dream) to the pregnant woman, and tell her that it intends to be reincarnated in the child she shall bear [1].

The woman's experiences during pregnancy, and perhaps still more her mental life during that period, are not without influence on the child she is going to give birth to. If, for example, she is very fond of a man who is not the father of her child, and in consequence often thinks of him, the result will be that the child will resemble him when it has grown a little [2]. The father's sayings and doings, on the other hand, seem to have no effect on the child. A very wide-spread belief, found also among Europeans, is that a pregnant woman can be impressed by some particular thing. The author has not personally met with this belief in Ukamba, but there is no reason to doubt Hildebrandt's assertion that it is prevalent there. He also says: »Empfindet die frau rechtzeitig, dass sie sich versehen hat, so muss sie die arme nach hinten bewegen und dazu sprechen 'weggesagt', dann wird das versehen unschädlich».

---

[1] F r a z e r adduces a number of examples of the same or similar beliefs from, among other peoples, the Lapps. »Taboo and the Perils of the Soul», The Golden Bough II, p. 368.

[2] Writing of the Baganda, Roscoe says: »It was looked upon as unfortunate if a pregnant woman came in contact with, or even saw, any child that was not healthy and strong ... If a woman laughed at a lame person, it was thought that her child would be lame». J. R o s c o e, The Baganda, their Customs and Beliefs, p. 49. Cf. also Ploss I, p. 878.

The birth of a child is a great event in the lives of primitive people, and they can never have too many descendants. One might think that girls would be more welcome, since, when grown up, they are a source of great gain to their fathers. But this is not the case among the Akamba. In by-gone days especially, a son was more welcome, for it was hoped that he would, when grown up, take part in the men's raiding expeditions and bring home many cattle as booty. The days of plundering expeditions are now past, but they are not so far distant that this point of view has changed. Another important point is that every head of a family desires to have as many people around him as possible, as his influence and importance are thereby increased. Grown-up sons build their huts close to or in the near neighbourhood of that of their father, and as long as he lives, they are under his authority. On the other hand, daughters do not help to increase his authority, since they leave their homes and clans when they marry.

2. **Abnormal Parturition.**

Anyone born with the feet first (*mundu wa kṵu* or *mundu wa mḭṵo*) may not marry anyone born in the usual manner (*æ na mau* 'he has legs', it is said). This also applies to anyone born with *ŋgunḭkḭlḭa* [1], that is to say with the bladder-like covering (caul), in which the child lies, unbroken. The prohibition has, however, the nature of a ritual observance, and if such a man is rich, it may happen that a man will peremptorily order his daughter to marry him. But a girl born with a caul has no chance of getting a husband who has not had the same »defect». When such a person is circumcised, a special knife is used, so that the blood of others may not be mixed with his. If there is no other knife handy, the knife is smeared with mutton fat before being used. If a calf or other domestic animal is born with a caul, the owner may neither sell it nor give it away, but he may keep it for himself. The descendants of such an animal are held to be quite normal.

Those who cut their teeth in the upper jaw first, *mundu wa kṵu-mḭlo*, or in East Ukamba *kḭluḭlu* (*umḭla* 'to come out in a certain place'), also occupies a unique position. Such a person is consi-

---

[1] Probably from *kunḭka* 'to cover'.

dered to have an evil influence upon certain kinds of foods, and
also upon the plants or animals from which these foods are obtained. He may not drink milk until some other person has drunk
of it, or else it will »be like water», and the cow which gave it
could never give nourishing milk again. He may not eat bananas
from the oldest trees in a plantation, or their fruit will become
hard and uneatable. Of the fruit of more recently planted trees
he may, however, eat, without working evil. When meat is eaten,
also, he must wait until the others have eaten a little, otherwise
the meat will be affected like the bananas.

In the case of twins (*maɓapa*), in olden times one was killed.
The reason for this custom among the Akamba, as among some
other tribes, may have been that the birth of twins was looked upon
as something unnatural, which might bring bad luck[1]. Nowadays
both are allowed to live; but though the native, under normal circumstances, wishes to have as many children as possible, they are
not welcome. They are troublesome for the mother and hinder
her in her occupations, since she can only carry one of them on
her back and the other must be placed on her breast. If, on the
other hand, a cow has two calves, it is considered a great misfortune,
and to ward off evil consequences, both cow and calves are killed.

3. Abortion.

In connection with birth, a few words may be said on abortion, which is at times practised by young girls. Free intercourse
is permitted between unmarried youths and girls, but it is considered a disgrace for a young girl to be with child, and she will
have difficulty in getting a young lover, often being obliged to
content herself with an older man. When the dances of young people
are at their height, the desire to be able to take part in this recreation will by itself be sufficient to induce a pregnant girl to try to

---

[1] If it were known that the birth of twins was a rare occurrence
among a people, it would be easier to understand how this unusual
event would be regarded as something unlucky. Unfortunately I have
no information as to the frequency of the birth of twins among the
Akamba (as far as I can remember, I have never seen any). The
small amount of information which is to be found on this subject, from
other Bantu peoples, is contradictory. Cf. Ploss I, p. 778 ff. and
A. Post, Afrikanische Jurisprudenz I, p. 281 ff.

free herself of the unwelcome burden, which begins to weigh down her body. In the earlier stages of pregnancy, she consumes quantities of melted butter or soot from the roof of the hut (*mwae*). At the more advanced stages, a decoction is prepared from the roots, leaves, and fruit, of several well-known plants, which are considered to be highly poisonous, namely *kɪlɪa mbɪtɪ* (Jatropha species), *mutanda-mbo*, or *ɪua-mbumbu* (Phytolaccæ). The decoction is drunk. It is considered very poisonous, and if the desired result is not obtained, the woman seems in most cases to pay the penalty with her life.

Appendix.
Customs and rites connected with menstruation (*mwoŋgo*)[1].

It is a well-known fact that the first menstruation especially is regarded as an important moment in the life of the more primitive woman, and we must therefore not be surprised to find that the Kamba girl as well must, during her first menstruation, observe extreme care, as it is believed that otherwise she may become barren. If she is out of doors when the event occurs, she leaves everything she is doing and goes home immediately. If, for instance, she has gone to fetch water, she immediately puts the calabash down, for if she brought the water home to the village and the young men drank from it and afterwards had connection with other women, she might become barren. Similarly if she has gone to fetch fuel, she must not bring her load home; for if the youths, who are continually running after girls, were to warm themselves by means of this wood, she would run the same risk as in the case of the water.

As soon as possible the girl informs her mother about her condition and afterwards rests — without however being isolated — as long as the period lasts. Her mother informs her husband about the matter, and on the night of the following day the parents perform the ritual coitus. This is called *kuseubɪa mwɪtu* 'purify the daughter' and indicates that the girl is considered unclean to a certain extent, although she does not seem to be dangerous to

---

[1] Cf. Hobley, The Akamba, p. 65.

those around her, but she herself alone, in her capacity of a future mother, is exposed to danger. She is afterwards washed with water, and this washing takes place before her parents have had intercourse. If the washing takes place before this, it is thought that she will become barren. The water is poured out inside the hut at the entrance to the *we*, the partition where the parents have their sleeping-place. It is probably not incorrect to place these rites in the category of »imitative magic», designed to further the girl's task when later on she is confined.

A menstruating girl carefully avoids all sexual connections, and even the young men are very careful on such an occasion, for they are afraid lest they should have to pay the goat which is imposed as a fine if the girl should become pregnant (see further Chap. XI). A man who cohabits with a menstruating girl has, in addition, when the girl gets married later on, to pay a goat to her husband, and from this the means of purification (*gondu*; see further Chap. VII. 2) is prepared, with which the girl is purified. If, in spite of this, her first child should die immediately after birth, her former lover is obliged to pay an ox to her husband.

Married people on the other hand always cohabit when the wife is menstruating, since the Akamba believe that a woman can be impregnated only during the period of menstruation. On the other hand, however, many negro tribes regard even a married woman in this condition as unclean and she has to remain isolated [1].

If again a father during his daughter's menstruation has intercourse with a woman other than his wife, he may not, if his daughter afterwards gets married and has a child, see this grandchild of his before he has been purified with *gondu*. The goat needed for the preparation of this is brought to the daughter's home and there killed, after which a man skilled in *gondu* smears his eyes with the purifying substance. With his eyes shut he is then led forward to the child and told to open his eyes. Before he was purified these were »evil», and his glance might have had an injurious influence on the baby.

From the following definite case, which came to my knowledge, it seems to be clear that, with the exception of the parents,

---

[1] Se examples in Ploss I, p. 273.

— who on the contrary ought to do it — none of the menstruating girl's nearest relatives may have sexual intercourse, as long as she is in that condition. A man cohabited with his wife while his sister was having menses. When later the girl got married, her husband demanded that she should be purified, so that their children should not suffer.

As we shall see in Chap. VIII, burial and the ceremonies connected with death are performed by elders, *atumia*. An elder whose wife has catamenia can, however, take no part in these. If he is invited, he refuses, saying: »I have an accident at home». If he does attend a death and then cohabit with his wife — which always happens when a married woman menstruates —- the child she bears may die or be injured in some other way. This idea should perhaps be placed under the heading »contagious magic».

Menstruation may sometimes influence the time for the burial of a dead person, because if a married woman in the family has *mwoŋgo*, it can not take place before she has had connection with a man. At the most, the corpse may be laid in the grave, but it may not be covered with earth.

A man who takes a wife and wishes to bring her home to his village must not do this if there is a menstruating woman in his home. He waits until the menstruation is over.

The author has not found any instance of the use of the menstrual fluid as medicine or any purely magical use; nor has he noticed, either, the existence of any fear of this fluid as specially mysterious or potent, a belief which is otherwise widespread even outside primitive people. Judging by the author's observation — which probably only yielded a cursory glance at the rôle played by menstruation in the everyday life of the Akamba (cf. p. 34, 35) there is nothing for men to fear in it.

According to the statements of several of the Akamba, many of the customs connected with menstruation are probably founded on the ideas (mentioned on p. 30) of the rôle of the ancestral spirits at the impregnation of a woman. It is certain, however, that several different ideas have found expression in the customs here described. It may be added finally that these seem to have no connection with the rites of initiation discussed in the next chapter.

Chapter III. **Circumcision and initiation rites.**

In Kikamba circumcision is called *nžaɪko*, from *aɪka* 'to circumcise'. The Akamba, however, do not employ this word to denote circumcision only, but use it to designate two other kinds of initiation rites, which really have nothing to do with circumcision. They have therefore three *nžaɪko* festivals, namely:

1. *nžaɪko ɪla nɪnɪ* 'the small circumcision', also called *nžaɪko ɪa kabɪo* 'the circumcision with the knife', or *nžaɪko ɪekondɔ* 'the circumcision of the foreskin' (*ɪkondɔ* or *ɪkolɔ* 'foreskin');

2. *nžaɪko ɪla nænɔ* 'the great circumcision', also called *nžaɪko ɪa mbusɪa* 'the circumcision of the rhinoceros', or *nžaɪko ɪa mulelɪ*;

3. *nžaɪko ɪa aumɔ* 'the circumcision of the men', also called *mbæбanɪ* (in Kikumbuliu) or *mbabanɪ* (in Kitui and Mumoni). The German missionary Mr H. Pfitzinger told me that the word is derived from *kuбaбana* 'to surpass another in strength or power', also 'to be angry'. As the name implies, these ceremonies — in contrast to the foregoing — are undergone only by males.

All these feasts are held in *þano*, the longer dry season, from August to October. They always follow in the above order, and, moreover, the first two take place yearly over the whole country, while the third is held only every few years and only in eastern Ukamba.

There are no traditions about the origin of circumcision and initiation rites, nor does the former seem to be dictated by reasons of hygiene.

1. The real circumcision (*nžaɪko ɪla nɪnɪ*).

The least important of the three *nžaɪko* is the actual circumcision; yet all of both sexes must submit to it, if they wish to be regarded as members of the tribe. This is typical of nearly all peoples which practise circumcision. There is no fixed age for the operation, and puberty has nothing to do with the matter.

In passing, I will here call attention to the distinction which van Gennep has established between »physiological puberty» and »social puberty», two essentially different things, which but seldom fall together[1]. With this distinction clear before our minds, we shall more easily understand the significance of especially the second and third ṇžaɩko.

A father decides arbitrarily when he will have his child circumcised. The maximum age is the marriageable age, for the simple reason that no one who is not circumcised can get a wife. Children of from 4 to 5 years old may be circumcised together with almost full-grown boys, whose circumcision is delayed by special circumstances, such as the poverty of the father; for a certain fee must be paid to the performer of the rite, and if a man cannot afford this fee, he must postpone the circumcision of his children[2]. The performer, mɩwaɩkɩ, is an elderly man of consideration who is versed in such things. Hence it can be said that the officiator is a paid professional. The medicine-man, as such, has nothing to do with the matter.

In the circumcision of the males, the whole foreskin is removed. The foreskins are put among the refuse of the sugar canes, »so that the children may not see each other's»; for, as a rule, many children are circumcised at the same time, the parents clubbing together to engage an operator. When the ceremony is over, the foreskins are gathered up in a skin and thrown away. Curiously enough, they do not seem to fear lest the ablated prepuces should fall into strange hands and be used in black magic. The instrument is a sharp knife of the usual native make, but any knife will not do; a particular knife is always used, and may not be used for any other purpose. The operation is simple, but if the knife used is blunt, terrible torture is caused to the

---

[1] A. van Gennep, Les rites de passage, p. 93 ff.

[2] Routledge (p. 154), mentions the same circumstance in connection with the Akikuyu and among the Amwimbe, one of the minor tribes of Eastern Kenya, akin to the Akikuyu: »the age varies considerably and depends largely upon the wealth and position of the father of the boy or girl». G. Orde Browne, Circumcision ceremonies among the Amwimbe, p. 137.

patient. The wound is not treated in any particular way, but a little dry, fine earth is applied to it. According to Hobley, however, »the crushed roots of a reed are applied to the wound as a dressing». The wounds heal rapidly, usually in about 2 to 3 weeks; but the older boys sometimes have considerable trouble for several months, and cannot sleep at nights for the pain.

In the case of girls, the labia minora and preputium clitoridis are cut away. An old woman, usually the wife of the *mwaɪkɪ*, operates on them, and none but women are present.

On the second night after the circumcision, the children's parents have coitus, »in order that the wound may heal well». Without this act, which is an essential element in so many Kamba customs, the circumcision is not complete.

It is said that, after circumcision, the children develop rapidly, and soon reach maturity.

The ceremony of circumcision is accompanied by a sort of public festivity. The young people put on all their ornaments and perform dances, and of course much beer (*ukɪ*) is drunk. It must, however, be observed in this connection that a man who has not yet a child who is circumcised may not take part in these drinking bouts. Sacrifices are made to the ancestral spirits (*aɪmu*), but presumably only in order that the wounds may heal quickly. Circumcision is not to be regarded as a genuinely r e l i g i o u s act among the Akamba.

There still remain some details to mention:

A woman who wishes to have her child circumcised, but who has not yet got her own hut, must first build one.

On the evening before the operation, the children may not drink water or eat sugar cane, »so that there shall not be so much blood»; afterwards they may eat all sorts of food.

If a child should happen to urinate during the process of circumcision, it is regarded as a sort of pariah throughout its whole life, and cannot marry anyone else than one who has been guilty of a similar offence.

Unfortunately, the author has never had an opportunity of being present at an actual *nẓaɪko*. In 1911 these ceremonies commenced in the beginning of June in the district of Machakos, and I had been told that they were to be performed in a certain village at 4 o'clock in the morning. But when I arrived there

I found that the members of the council of elders had decided to postpone the operation for the time being, as the weather was considered to be too cold for the children (at 4 a. m. the thermometer indicated only 8.5° C.). The reason for choosing such an early hour was stated to be that they wished to avoid »the evil eye».

2. "The great circumcision".

The great *nžaɩko* also has the character of a popular celebration, but it is regarded as much more important than the abovementioned. Every Kamba man must have taken part in it, if he wishes to be regarded as a true member of the tribe and a properly educated person. When we know this, we can understand the meaning of the expression *ṇdaɩkwa nžaɩko ɩla nænǝ* 'he has not yet gone through the great *nžaɩko*', which is often heard when anyone behaves badly. The person who has not gone through this *nžaɩko* is looked upon as an inferior sort of person, and is put on a par with a *kɩɩmu* (see p. 34). If it is a young man, he has no chance of getting a wife; if it is a young woman, the young men will not have anything to do with her. The children born of such a union would die.

This is true of Ulu, and is therefore certainly the original custom, but in the Kitui district they are not so particular. Nevertheless, if a child is born, it must be smeared with a purifying medium, *ɣondui*, in order to avert all evil.

The chief idea underlying this initiation is no doubt connected with the emerging from childhood into manhood (womanhood), the assumption of responsibilities, sexual and social.

These rites are held annually during the longer dry season (Sept. to Oct.). Generally speaking, no *nžaɩko* may take place during the rainy season. In 1911, the first was held at the end of September, and the second towards the end of the next month, *mubᴣu* 'the hot'.

There is no age limit for participation in the second *nžaɩko*; most of the children are certainly of ages ranging from 8 to 12, but there are always a number of older ones. The reason is that the candidates must pay a fee, which they or their parents have not always ready at the appointed time, and they may then put it off from one year to another. It is very usual, too, that children do not undergo both the first and the second *nžaιko* during the same year. It happens, further, that a father punishes an obstreperous child by postponing the time for its undergoing the second *nžaιko*. In Ikutha I saw a candidate for the second *nžaιko* who looked about 40 years old. He had served for many years in distant parts as an *askarι* (soldier), and had only recently returned to his native parts, which he had left at a quite early age. At present many Kamba boys enter the service of Europeans in Nairobi or elsewhere. Mr Pfitzinger, of the Leipziger Mission (Kitui district), told me that on one occasion he saw a married man of from 30 to 40 years of age at such a *nžaιko*. Such examples show what importance the Akamba attach to the matter. A man such as the above-mentioned soldier may perhaps have been in contact with Europeans for many years, and may find the whole bissines somewhat unnecessary, but if he wishes to remain at home he must complete his education according to regular usage, however much he may have learned from contact with whites.

The conductor of the ceremonies and festivities in connection with this *nžaιko* is also called *mwaιkι*, and is probably the same man as the conductor of the first *nžaιko*. According to Mr Pfitzinger, the same man was always the conductor in his district. If there is no fixed *mwaιkι*, a reputable elder, who has himself children that are to undergo the ceremonies, applies to the council of elders, *nžama* (p. 135), for permission to conduct them. He invites them home to a beer-drinking bout, and puts forward his proposal; if the elders agree, the matter is settled, and they arrange the time, which is then announced.

On the conductor's plot (*ƀomɔ*) is built a hut with two entrances, one for the boys and one for the girls; the children have to sleep there on grass and leaves, on different sides of the hut. This is built by the elders under the direction of the conductor. Of course, the work proceeds to the accompaniment of appropriate beer-drinking, during which the *mwaιkι* pours out a little beer in the hut, as an offering to *Muluŋgu*, The Supreme Being, with prayers that the children may develop well. In East Ukamba such a hut is called *ιƀunu*. The one I saw near Ikutha, in 1911, was the usual bee-hive shaped type of hut that the Akamba use, but about three times as large as an ordinary hut. In Ulu only one such hut is used as a rule, namely that of the *mwaɪkɪ*, which, when used for such a purpose, is called *kɪeŋgo kɪa ŋžaɪko*[1]. If a special hut is built for the purpose, it is called *ɪluanda*.

The night after the *ŋžaɪko* hut is ready, the conductor must have sexual intercourse with his wife, before the candidates move into it. The novices are called *asɪŋgɪ*. As instructors are employed a number of mature married men called *aɓwɪkɪɪ* (presumably from *ɓwɪka* 'to cover'); in the same way, the girls are under the direction of elderly and experienced women. These *aɓwɪkɪɪ* are chosen by the parents of the *asɪŋgɪ*. When a really big *ŋžaɪko* takes place, one *muɓwɪkɪɪ* may have as many as twenty candidates in his charge. The *aɓwɪkɪɪ* meet in advance, and draw up the programme for the ceremonies and the dances, which usually continue for seven days. They then practise the songs which are to be sung, for many songs are included in these festivities. The duties of *aɓwɪkɪɪ* in instructing and taking charge of the candidates are called *kutǎ*[2].

The *asɪŋgɪ* take off their ornaments and are completely naked, with the exception of a piece of cloth or a piece of skin round their heads; for during the whole time they must take particular care not to touch each other's heads, or their hair will fall off. Their bodies they have rubbed with fat and ashes.

Early in the morning, after the *mwaɪkɪ* has had coition with his wife, the *asɪŋgɪ* are taken to the *ŋžaɪko* hut, where they pass a great part of the day singing. One of the songs runs thus:

mwasɪa, ɛ, lelɔ:	You say eeh, listen:
tata nɪwambaɪka, ɛ,	My father has me circumcised, eeh,
waŋgɪlɪa aɪmu kutɪndaa	He ? remains
nɪumba ta kana.	in the hut like a child.
mɪwaɪtu maendɪɔ ku?	Whither have our mothers gone?

---

[1] *kɪeŋgo* is the name of the hut in which the cowherds live when the cattle are tended at some distance from the village.

[2] The author has never heard this word used in any other connection. Hofmann, however, has it in his dictionary, and translates it with »teach, instruct». In every day speech, however, 'teach' is *manesɪa*, causative of *manɪa* 'to know'.

| *maendɩɔ kuua.* | They have gone to cook (food). |
| *twɩ na nẓḁ nænɔ.* | We are very hungry. |

During this first *nẓaɩko*-day, all the *asɩŋgɩ* must proceed to the female leader's hut, and that is done under the following circumstances:

On the ground, beginning at the entrance to the *nẓaɩko*-hut, are placed a row of objects, which extend to the woman's hut. On one occasion, objects were placed as follows: a lump of wood (*kɩtɩŋgɩ*), a leather strap (*mukwa*), a pile of ashes (*mṵ*), a large calabash vessel (*ua*), and a calabash (*kɩkṵ*). The *asɩŋgɩ* advance in an ordered troop, and when they reach the first object (the lump of wood), they stop and sing:

| *mabɩŋgo mwabɩŋga, ḁ!* | You have closed the way with obstacles, aah! |
| *twabɩŋgwa nɩ mukẓamo.* | The way is closed to us by something that lies across it. |

Then the lump of wood is thrown on one side, and they proceed to the next object, where they sing:

mwasẓa, ẹ, lelɔ:	You say, eeh, listen:
nẓamu nɩ nænɔ,	the animal is large,
ɩaɩŋga maɩŋga.	it coils into coils[1].
ɩkẓa nabṵ mukẓamo!	Throw the obstacle over there (to one side).

The strap is thrown aside, and they come to the ashes:

mwasẓa, ẹ, lelɔ:	You say, eeh, listen:
wakasabuku,	hare,
wakasabuku bulẓa mṵ!	hare scrape up ashes[2]!
ubɩtɔ nabṵ, mukẓamo!	Go to one side, obstacle!

Before the calabash vessel they proceed to sing:

| *mwasẓa, ẹ, lelɔ:* | You say, eeh, listen: |
| *wombombo.* | *wombombo* (a sort of refrain) |

---

[1] The strap is compared to a writhing snake.
[2] The boys compare themselves to a hare, raising up dust as it runs, and they take up ashes and throw them at each other.

nžwe sṭa mutwə nı	the hair on the head is burnt
sṭabeə kana nata?	is'nt it[1]?
ŋgwonıə unṭænžə, aa, aa	I have seen ? aah, aah!
nžua ıkumı nıßætwə,	ten calabash vessels may be moved
	away,
mukṭamo.	obstacle.

Now they reach the last obstacle, the calabash:

nımwasṭa, ẹ, lelə:	You say, eeh, listen:
mwaıtu, mwaßıŋga, ẹ.	Our mothers, you have closed the
	way, eeh.
mwaßıŋga ua nžua	You have closed with the vessels
na ıkụ sṭonðə.	and calabashes all.

The singers sing under the direction of a chief singer (*ŋguı*).
All the obstacles are now removed, and they have reached
the old woman's hut, where they are given beer to drink out of
spoons. They sing again:

asa, asọkı.	Father, father, beer.
undu tambəlıłṭa kwınža	Why should we begin to dig
na nðı ṭa mutandı?	with a grave stake of the *mutandı*
	tree?[2]

When all have got beer, the *asıŋgı* return to their hut. They
do not, however, sleep much during the two nights they spend
there, but while away the time by singing songs. Some songs are
sung alternately by boys and girls, and they are extremely obscene.
One of them runs as follows:

(the boys:)

haə, haə, lelə:	Hae, hae, listen:
kıno nı ndıa	the *kıno*[3] is a fool,
kıtundumelə ŋguanı	she dwells in the clothes,
haə, haə	hae, hae.

(the girls answer:)

mwasṭa, ẹ, lelə:	You say, eeh, listen:

---

[1] The calabash is compared with a bald head.
[2] A tree bearing red flowers, of which digging-sticks are made.
[3] The name of the female pudenda.

kea nı ndıa	the *kea*[1] is a fool,
kıtundumelə mæni,	it dwells among the testes,
na, nı ndıa	and is a fool
kıkundawa unou nı kıno.	to allow the *kino* to drink fat.

The meaning is that, by much sexual intercourse, the man grows lean, while the woman thrives on it.

Like the songs, the conversation also is of a very dubious nature, and, according to my informant, is directly intended to show that no feelings of shame exist under these circumstances, though in daily life considerable modesty is shown in connection with such matters. But now no consideration may be paid to such feelings, even if a *muponi* (chap. V) be present.

In spite of the erotic character of the whole performance, and although the young people are accustomed to fairly free sexual intercourse, nothing of that kind takes place during the *nžaıko* time, as it is considered to have a harmful influence on their future. The *aßwıku* have carefully instructed them on that point. Yet others who have nothing to do with the ceremonies come and try to persuade them to disobey the instructions.

During the second day, the ceremonies reach their height in the appearing of *mbusʒa* »the rhinoceros». This, which has been prepared beforehand, consists of a structure resembling a box, joined together with sticks and covered with branches, so that it is impossible to see the man who goes into it and produces the bellowing noise, which is supposed to be an imitation of the roar of a rhinoceros, intended to frighten the women and children. The *mbusʒa*, which has up to this point been concealed in the waste, is carried by four men. When it is brought near the village, it roars. It is put down close to one of the entrances of the *nžaıko* hut, so that the man can enter it unseen; the hut is divided into two parts by hanging skins, so that the *asıgı* shall not be able to see the *mbusʒa*, but only hear it. The animal bellows continuously, and to show his courage each of the male candidates must go one by one to the hanging with a stick in his hand, with which he beats the hanging, saying: *wıkou nı mwana wa ŋgaına* 'he who does this is N. N's son' (mentioning his

---

[1] The name of the male pudenda.

father's name). This is called *kwaþa mbusᶎa* 'shooting the rhinoceros'.

According to the description that was given me, the mysterious noise is produced in the following way: The man who is playing the rôle of *mbusᶎa* carries by a cord round his neck a small clay vessel, containing equal quantities of water and beer. By blowing into the liquid with a pipe (a twig of the *mwaeþa* tree) he produces a sound which resembles the bellow of the rhinoceros.

Only the boys take part in what has now been described. After the *mbusᶎa* has disappeared as mysteriously as it came, it is the turn of the girls to undergo a similar but less trying test. The sound which is to frighten them is produced by an old woman, who shakes a calabash containing seeds, probably *wᶎmbᶎ* (Eleusine).

In Ulu the *mbusᶎa* is not produced until darkness has fallen, presumably in order to make the whole performance more mysterious, and to frighten the *asᶎgᶎ* more. At the *ŋžaᶎko* at which I was present in Kitui, it was done at about five o'clock p. m.

During the night before the third day, the conductor of the ceremonies must again have intercourse with his wife, the girls' *mwaᶎkᶎ*. That night all the *asᶎgᶎ* sleep on the open space before the *ŋžaᶎko* hut, and they must not light a fire. On the following morning, the fee must be paid to the *mwaᶎkᶎ* and his wife, and the *aᵬwᶎkᶎ* are entitled to try to remove their charges in order to get them off paying. To prevent this, the relations and friends of the *aᵬwᶎkᶎ* stand on guard round the place. They make fires round it, and some of them do sentry-go in turns, and even patrol between the fires, meeting half-way. These assistants of the conductor must also have their remuneration, which they lose if any of the *asᶎgᶎ* get away. It sometimes happens, too, that they fence the place in, so that it shall be even harder for the *aᵬwᶎkᶎ* to steal off with the *asᶎgᶎ*.

The third day. On the next morning, the *asᶎgᶎ* pay the fee to the *mwaᶎkᶎ* and his wife. For a boy the father pays perhaps half a rupee, for a girl about 30 cents; but as a rule the parents club together, and 4 *asᶎgᶎ* pay one goat, 10 to 14 pay a young bull, 16 pay an ox, which is considered to be worth more than a bull. For twenty girls one bull is paid.

When the fees have been paid, the *aɓwɪkɪɪ* take back their charges. They are now given miniature bows, a few decimeters long, and small, fragile bird-arrows (*maŋgɪ*), which latter are made of the plants called *mukulwa* or *mulʋɪla-mbɪa*[1]. The boys are sent with these weapons to hunt lizards, grass-hoppers, etc. These little animals then represent wild beasts, enemies, &c. Although the present-day Akamba are principally farmers and cattle-raisers, yet they are also skilful hunters, and, according to their own traditions, they were originally a hunting people. This pretence of hunting on which the boys are sent is, therefore, certainly symbolic of the occupation which was once upon a time the most important of the Kamba man, and is perhaps supposed to make them good shots, both in the chase and in war. The girls, on the other hand, are sent to break small twigs, that is to say, gather fuel, which is a part of every woman's daily occupation.

After they have finished hunting, the *asɪɪgɪ* return singing to the open place before the *ŋ̌aɪko* hut. The two *mwaɪkɪ* each take a calabash vessel full of beer, which they drink and then spit out over the multitude as a blessing. The *mwaɪkɪ*'s task is now completed, and the *asɪɪgɪ* may return to their homes. On the way home, they sing songs, one over the first cow-droppings they see on their way, another over the first goat-droppings, and so on.

At home in the villages, the mothers have arranged *maɓɪɪgo* 'obstacles', to puzzle the *asɪɪgɪ*, and still more to discover whether the *aɓwɪkɪɪ* have given their children good instruction and thus earned the remuneration which, as we shall soon see, even they receive. From *muɓea* (the entrance to the kraal) right up to the door of the hut, the women have placed various objects, such as a bow, a quiver, a calabash, a grinding stone, and so on. Every conceivable object is made use of, and even a baby may be laid in the row. The *asɪɪgɪ* may not enter the hut until, with the help of *aɓwɪkɪɪ*, they have discovered the meaning of these obstacles, or have discovered what the women have done to the objects. Thus, for example, the giraffe- (or zebra-)hair binding

---

[1] With regard to the first-named, cf. Chap. XI. The latter is a plant with bright red flowers. The musical bow with which the medi cine-man gets into communication with the spirits is struck with a stick cut from this plant.

tied to the shaft in one or two places, has been removed from one arrow in one quiver; or the women have detached one end of the string of one bow and tied it in a different way; or one of them has concealed an object in her nostrils, or among the beads which they wear in a broad belt round the middle. The devices are even obscene sometimes. Thus, according to what I was once told, on one occasion the solution was that the novice had to insert his penis into the genital organ of the »hindering» woman.

When all the solutions have been discovered, the mother smears the *musɪ̦ŋgɪ* with fat, and then 'he may enter the hut. He receives a present from his father, and in the same way a girl receives a small gift from her mother.

While the *asɪ̦ŋgɪ* solve the »obstacles», they continue with their singing. The following is a specimen of such a song:

mwasɪ̦a, ę, lelə :	You say, eeh, listen:
ŋgabɪ̦ŋgɪwa na mbɪ̦u	I shall be shut out by sword
na matumo na sɪ̦au sɪ̦onðə	and spear and by every possible thing,
ę, nambɪ̦u na matumo, &c.	eeh. By sword and spear, &c.

That day the *asɪ̦ŋgɪ*, provided with their miniature bows, go round from hut to hut and collect small presents, such as chains (in the fashioning of which the Akamba are past-masters), bracelets, and other ornaments. These objects are hung on the points of the bow, and the boys continue to wander round until their bows will hold no more. The ornaments go to the *abwɪku* as remuneration for their work. Every father of a family, besides, gives his child's *mubwɪku* about one rupee's worth of beer, if he has had one pupil to take charge of; if he has had two or more children under his charge, he gets beer to the value of a goat.

Further, on the third day, each boy is given a little stick about one decimeter in length. On the evening the songs and dances are in progress, they are to approach the unsuspecting girls and insert the stick into their genital organs. My informant emphasized that this is only a pleasantry (*ŋguɪ̦*), but it is considered, nevertheless, that if any boy neglects to do this, the children which he may subsequently beget, will easily die. Here and there in our account we see traces of the great rôle which sexual matters

play in these initiation ceremonies. One of the most important
duties of the *aƀwɪku,* too, is to instruct the *asɪŋgɪ* in sexual matters, and this is undoubtedly a way of preparing the young people
for matrimony.

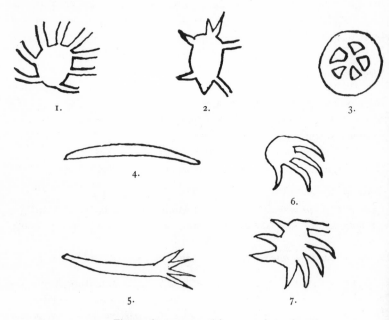

1. 2. 3.

4.

6.

5. 7.

1—7. Figures from *musaꞩ* sticks, somewhat enlarged.
1. Open space (yard, *ƀomꝛ*) with paths leading to it. 2. Tortoise. 3. Ornamented
seat of a stool (*mumbo*). 4. Python. 5. Cow's tail. 6. Star. 7. Star.

8. Piece of *musaꞩ* stick, natural size. Millipede, clan-mark on beehive, moon, star.

The fourth day. On the night before the fourth day, the
novices sleep on the ground in their mothers' huts, and their
parents must have ritual coition. On the fourth day are distributed
the *musaꞩ* sticks, called *ukaꞩ* in Kikumbuliu. The *musaꞩ* is a thin
stick of about 80 centimeters in length, made by the *aƀwɪku* from

branches of the *muɓɪwa* tree. In its bark are scratched figures winding round the stick, and as to the meaning of these figures they are examined by the *aɓwɪkɪɪ*, who explain to them what they do not understand. A father will often instruct his son beforehand as to the meaning of these »pictographic riddles», as Hobley calls them, so that the son shall not appear all too ignorant at the examination. When the *nžaɪko* festivities are over, the

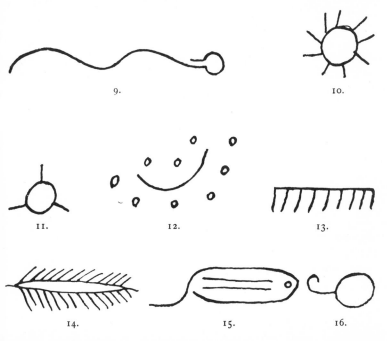

9. Snake. 10. The sun. The Akamba call the rays »legs». 11. Stool with three legs. 12. Moon and stars. 13. Chain with short side links. 14. Centipede. 15. Woman's belt with two rows of cowry shells. 16. Calabash with narrow neck.

boys' parents place the *musaɪ* sticks under the bed, and again have coition. After that the sticks are destroyed.

There are several *musaɪ* sticks in my ethnographical collection from the Akamba. A part of such a stick is shown in the figure 8; Hobley (p. 71) reproduces a whole stick. The most usual figures are of the sun, the moon, the stars, tortoises, lizards, millipedes, roads, dancing-places, clan-marks on bee-hives, &c.

I have collected such sticks with figures cut in them (though they are much longer and thicker than the *musaɩ* sticks of the Akamba) from the Wataveta near Kilimandjaro. They are given to the newly circumcised, who have to interpret the signs. Besides the sticks, they receive bows marked with similar signs. These are more conventional than the figures on the *musaɩ* sticks[1].

In addition to the figures just described, there are others which the *aɓwɩku* draw in the sand. Several of these are depicted in the figures 9—16.

Although it is an embarrassing matter for anyone to betray too great ignorance in these matters, yet the figures have no deep meaning, but seem mostly to be looked upon as a joke. In the third *nžaɩko* we shall meet with another sort of conventional signs with a far more serious practical significance.

Further, on this fourth day, the *asɩ̥gɩ* have to steal sugar cane, and prepare from it beer for the *aɓwɩku*. This beer is called *uki wa utulǎa wumbu* 'beer to push forward the milk juice with' (see the following section).

T h e f i f t h d a y. Early in the morning, the *aɓwɩku* go in search of a wild fig-tree (*mumbu*). It must be found in an easterly direction. All of them, commencing with the eldest, spit on the tree, praying: »Fig-tree, we have come to pray you to give us milk juice for the *asɩ̥gɩ*» (*kɩ̥umbu kɩ, nɩtukɩə ukuɓoɽa, utunæ̆ɡə wumbu wa unæ̆ɡa asɩ̥gɩ*). They make an offering of a little food and milk by the tree, and smear a little fat on its trunk, on the right side for the boys and on the left side for the girls. The juice is obtained by pricking the tree with a nail, after it has been smeared with fat in seven places. Each of the *aɓwɩku* catches juice in a little calabash for his *asɩ̥gɩ*. At nightfall they go and fetch the *asɩ̥gɩ* to the tree, where they take a little milk-juice on one finger and give it to the *asɩ̥gɩ*, who pretend to eat it[2]. During the preceding days, the *asɩ̥gɩ* have not been allowed to consume milk, meat, sweet potatoes, or certain kinds of beans (Phaseolus and Cajanus Indicus), but now they can have all sorts of food. Since the

---

[1] See, further, G. Lind blom, Anteckningar öfver Taveta-folkets etnologi, p. 178.

[2] The fig-tree plays a part also in the initiation rites of the Akikuyu. See F. Bugueau, La circoncision au Kikuyu, Anthropos 1911, p. 626. The fig-tree is a kind of sacred tree all over Africa.

beginning of the *ŋžaɩko*, they have lived on maize, Eleusine porridge, and gruel. We recognise here the well-known circumstance that certain kinds of food are tabu for novices, and they may only eat them when they are initiated.

At the fig-tree is performed another ceremony, which, in the second *ŋžaɩko,* is the only thing which has any connection with real circumcision. A slight cut is made at the base of the glans (*mu6wa*), and a little beer is poured on the wound.

If the selected fig-tree does not give any milk, the *a6wɩku* understand that some malicious person who is conversant with such matters, has, for sport, »closed» all the fig-trees in the district, in order to cause them difficulty and compel them to search around for another tree, in doing which they tire themselves out, prick themselves on thorns, and so on. Usually, however, there is someone among them that knows how to »open» a tree »closed» in this manner. To this person the others must pay a fee, consisting of ornaments, a few cents each, and so on.

The *asɩŋgɩ* pass the sixth day quietly at their homes, where beer is brewed, and the women prepare gruel (*usụ*) for the following day's festivities.

The seventh day. The *asɩŋgɩ* carry out a sham cattle raid, the »cattle» being represented by the round, yellow fruits of a sort of Solanum (*ŋdoŋgu*); they have cowherds to watch them. All the *asɩŋgɩ* are equipped as for a warlike expedition, carrying bows, arrows, and a calabash containing provisions for the journey. When the enemy approaches, the cowherds pelt him with the Solanum fruit, calling out: »The Masai (or the Galla) are coming!» This is the way in which the cattle stealing connected with the *ŋžaɩko* is carried on in Kikumbuliu. In Ulu the practice is that, when the cattle are being driven home in the evening, the *asɩŋgɩ* rush out and attack the cowherds with *ŋdoŋgu* fruits, clods of earth, &c, and pretend to steal the cattle. The women wail: »The Masai have come! The Masai are here to steal our cattle!»

After a real war-expedition, when a young Kamba warrior returns home with stolen cattle as booty, his parents must have ritual coition. By analogy with this, the *asɩŋgɩ*'s parents have intercourse when the above-described sham cattle-stealing takes place. This, however, does not take place until the evening of the following day. The seventh day is not considered a good day, for odd numbers (*mwa*) are looked upon as unlucky in many respects, and this applies especially to the number seven[1].

As has been mentioned, the festivities generally extend over seven days. During the whole time, the other young people who have already been circumcised, indulge in great dances, for which they put on as many ornaments as possible. These dances are called *n̆z̆uma*, and those who have not yet been circumcised may not take part in them.

The members of the great clan *anz̆auni* (chap. VII), who live i the neighbourhood of Machakos, extend the time for the second *n̆z̆aiko* to nearly a month, instead of the usual six or seven days; the reason for this is that so many young people of this clan are said to have died after the ceremonies.

———

Now our description of the second *n̆z̆aiko* is at an end. Naturally the procedure varies somewhat in different places, especially in the matter of the sequence of the different items. Thus Hobley's account differs in a good many particulars from mine, yet in the main our descriptions tally.

Other songs in connection with the »Great Circumcision».

On the whole, all these songs seem to be the same over the whole of Ukamba, with the exception perhaps of Kilungu, where they are said to be very old and interesting. We have already seen (in Chap. I) that that district differs in many particulars from the rest of the country. Unfortunately, I have not had an oppor-

———

[1] When the cattle are out at pasture, they are never watched by the same cowherd for more than six days at a time. And if the medicine-man shakes seven objects from his fortune-telling calabash, when he is consulted, this is looked upon as boding ill-luck. In his study over circumcision among the Kikuyu, Father Bugeau says: »Peu importe d'ailleurs le nombre, pourvu que ce ne soit pas sept: ce nombre est en effet de mauvaise augure. Aussi évite-t-on soigneusement d'être sept dans les repas et les réunions». E. Bugeau ibid. p. 623.

tunity of hearing any songs from Kilungu. The one which follows is from Machakos.

sɨua ɹaƀoa ukaɓɩ, ę,	The sun goes down in Masai-land
na kwɩtɩu ɹatɩa makæŋga aaa.	and leaves us its reflection, aah.
mwasɹa, ę, lelɔ:	You say, eeh, listen:
tukataɓa, lela,	We shall steal, lela,
aɔ, aɔ, tukataɓa ŋombɔ	ae, ae, we shall steal cattle
sɹa akaɓɩ,	from the Masai,
tukataɓa maweo onðɔ.	we shall steal over all the steppes.

What I saw of the second *ŋʒaɪko* in Kitui, in Oct. 1911.

On Oct. 31, 1911, I happened to learn that the second *ŋʒaɪko* was proceeding in a village in the neighbourhood of Kitui government station. I immediately betook myself thither, arriving about 4 o'clock in the afternoon. I found crowds of people of all ages and both sexes assembled on an open place in front of the hut of the conductor of the ceremonies; dancing and singing was at its height. The dancers were divided into several groups. One of these consisted of such as had gone through the third *ŋʒaɪko* — consequently only men — and no others were allowed to partake in this dance (*ŋʒuma*). Of the song that was being sung I could only catch the following words: *tuɩtula ætuɩ, nɩ ta ta utula maæŋgo* 'We do not dance with the girls, it is like dancing with bee-hives'. The fact of the matter is that the women do not know the dances that belong to the third *ŋʒaɪko*, and those that came to look on were chased away. I heard them say: »We do not like this dance». When I appeared on the scene, the dancing stopped, and I was politely but firmly requested to depart again. What I had the opportunity to see of the dance was not of an erotic character. All the *ŋʒaɪko* dances, however, seem to be different from the ordinary dances danced for amusement.

Another group of dancers was composed of those who had gone through the second *ŋʒaɪko*, that is to say, both males and females.

The principal personages in the third group were the *asɩɡɩ* for the year. They had their heads bound up, were without ornaments, and were covered with old blankets and pieces of cloth. Together with a crowd of girls and married women, they went ceaselessly round in a circle, clapping their hands and singing.

In the middle of the open space stood the * nẓaɩko* hut, from the interior of which proceeded intermittently the roars of the *mbusɩa*. Every now and again some of the *asɩŋgɩ* were taken into the hut »to beat the *mbusɩa*». The *asɩŋgɩ* carried thin switches, about 2 meters in length, and when the dance was ended, they went round pretending to beat people. Everything they did, however, gave the impression of being done in fun, and the whole performance resembled innocent amusement.

I was told that this day was the last *nẓaɩko* day for the year.

On the following morning, the *asɩŋgɩ*, carrying bows of some two meters in length, were seen going round from hut to hut, begging for beads, which they strung on their bow-strings. Generally they were given only two or four beads by the same person: it was considered that to give three, five, or seven beads would bring bad luck, and the *asɩŋgɩ* refused to accept such an odd number.

---

3. "The Circumcision of the Men".

The third *nẓaɩko,* which is only practised in Eastern Ukamba (the Kitui district and Kikumbuliu), is much more secret than the second, and the proceedings are only known to those that have taken part in it. These are all bound by oath to secrecy. The breach of this oath was punished by instant death in earlier times, and even nowadays such punishment is not out of the question. At best the delinquent escapes with the payment of a fine of ten cows. A Kamba may not refer to these rites even in general terms, and merely to ask about them costs two bulls. A man may not even talk about them to his wife. When I had become initiated into these matters, I used sometimes to amuse myself by putting questions to my bearers, during rests between marches, in order to see their amazed and scared faces. My first questions were generally ignored, but if I persisted, they answered: »Master, we know that nothing in Ukamba is unknown to you. But if you know these secrets, you ought also to know that they are not talked about. If you do not cease plaguing us with your questions, we will lay down our loads and leave you».

Under such circumstances it is not surprising that missionaries who have lived in the country for twenty years, are ignorant of these matters. As a matter of fact, up to a few years back, they were unknown both to missionaries and officials. Of the two existing accounts of the third *nžaiko*, besides my own (from Kikumbuliu), one is by Mr Hobley (from Kitui), and the other, which is not yet published, is by the above-mentioned missionary, Pfitzinger (from a district north of Kitui station)[1]. All the accounts show great similarity, especially my own and Pfitzinger's, which agree in all essentials. Pfitzinger got his information some years ago from a converted native. But although the latter had become a Christian, he only ventured to make his disclosures with great hesitation. My own information I obtained from a medicine-man in the district of Kibwezi, with whom I had got on intimate terms and who was my most frequent companion during a month's time[2].

On the other hand, it is doubtful whether any white man has ever been an eye-witness of these ceremonies. While I was still staying in the neighbourhood of Kibwezi in 1911, preparations had already been commenced for the »men's circumcision», but I only learnt this fact after I had left the place. It is celebrated only every third or fourth year, and not every year, as is the case with the other two *nžaiko* festivals. The natives say that it is so dangerous and harmful that, if it took place oftener, the rains for the year would fail, and a famine would ensue.

This *nžaiko* has no more to do with religious practice than have the other two. The object is simply and solely that the Kamba youth may reach the culmination of the education and knowledge that the tribe can bestow on the individual — to make him a *mundu wa ŋguma* 'a man of reputation'. He who has gone through these ceremonies is a real man and has a safe claim to the *mutumia* dignity (see p. 138). As in the case of the second *nžaiko*, the novices are called *asiŋgi*.

---

[1] By the courtesy of Mr K. Dundas, Machakos, I was enabled to study this manuscript, which had been handed over to the government.

[2] See the account of my travels in Afrikanska ströftåg, p. 195 ff.

The conductor of the third *nžaɪko* is one of the respected elders. He selects a remote spot in the wastes, away from the paths and near a river. Here he sends four men who have gone through these rites, and they have to build a hut. Round this hut they make a cleared space, which is strewn with sand or fine earth. The place is consecrated by killing a goat and mixing its *muꞩo* (the digested contents of one of the stomachs, see p. 103) with the sand. Then they go to prepare the *mbæɓanɪ*, which corresponds to the *mbusꞩa* of the second *nžaɪko*. A *kɪusꞩa* tree is found[1], and from it are made two pipe-shaped staves, into which a thinner stick is inserted. By means of fibres of the *mwapa* tree, which is a *ꞩondu* tree (chap. VI), the staves are bound together at an acute angle. Another goat is killed when the staves are ready, and they are smeared with its *muꞩo*. Then the *mbæɓanɪ* is concealed in the river.

While three of the men are making the *mbæɓanɪ*, the fourth remains at the place to see that nobody approaches, who has no business there. If anyone does come, he is seized and must pay a fine of a bull, the meat of which is eaten by those who take part in the festival. An unbidden guest even risks life and limb.

Now the three men return to the conductor's village, and inform him that everything is ready for the novices. In the evening they go out into the waste and fetch the *mbæɓanɪ,* which is taken to the village. It is carried point foremost, resting upon one man's shoulders, two other men carrying the legs of the angle. According to my informant, these legs have »a large opening behind, which is blown into, and a smaller one in front». When they approach the village, they blow into the pipes, which give forth a hollow, drawn-out sound. Anyone who gets in the way of the *mbæɓanɪ* is seized and fined a bull or ten goats. Generally, however, the *mbæɓanɪ* is heard far and wide, and· outsiders keep out of the way. Then the conductor's village is reached, where all the men have assembled; the women may not be present, but go to sleep in their huts. Deep silence prevails, and even so inconsiderable a noise as a cough or a hawk is punished by the imposition of a fine of several goats; only the *mbæɓanɪ* is heard. The conductor asks why they have come there, and adds that

---

[1] Leguminosæ sp. which blooms on the naked twig.

no children are left there. After the singing of some songs, the *mbæɓanı* is taken back to its hiding-place, without the *asıŋgı* having seen it. The *mbæɓanı* may be said to correspond to the »bull-roarer» of the mysteries of the Australians and other peoples.

The same night, the *asıŋgı* are led to the selected place; they are clothed, or rather unclothed, in the same way as the novices in the above-described *ņžaıko*. As in this *ņžaıko*, they have protectors, *aɓwıkıı*, one for every two *asıŋgı*. These *aɓwıkıı* are men who have already gone through these rites. They give them all sorts of instructions, warn them to do all that is demanded of them, and on no account to refuse to do anything, or they will pay for it with their lives.

Besides the *aɓwıkıı*, there is another category of functionaries, the so-called *ŋgala*, younger men, whose duties are to plague the *asıŋgı*. *ŋgala* means both 'spark' and 'flea'; thus they must annoy the novices with the same persistence as that shown by biting fleas. In social rank they are lower than the *aɓwıkıı*.

On the place where the performance takes place, several fires are lighted, one for the *asıŋgı*, one for the *ŋgala*, one for the *aɓwıkıı*, and one at which sit the elders, members of the *ņžama* (see chap. IX). The divisioninto groups is thus based on ranks, and no one may sit by the fire assigned to a group which is higher in rank than himself. The elders have good supplies of meat at their fire, for the *asıŋgı* have paid for the privilege of going through the ceremony, besides which the men take this opportunity of buying a higher rank in the community, and this costs a bull or a certain number of goats, which are eaten in common. The animals are cut up according to certain principles, since members of the lower ranks may not eat of all parts of an animal. This point will be considered in a later chapter dealing with age- and rank-classes. None of the meat set apart for consumption on this occasion may be taken home to the villages. Only the elders may crack the bones to get at the marrow, and all bones are collected at their fire. Anyone who breaks this rule is fined several goats.

When the feasting has proceeded for some time, the hour arrives for the *asıŋgı* to begin their proofs. Their eyes are bound, and they are led by their protectors to the sandy place, where they are ordered to throw themselves prostrate. They now begin to sing certain songs, some of which I have recorded, but I have not been able to translate them. As they sing, they throw up sand with their hands and feet. Soon the hollow, bellowing sound of the approaching *mbæɓanı* is heard. The *asıŋgı* are ordered to lie immovable, and not to look about them; they are also told to shout: *ulu, ulu, ulu*. Their protectors form a ring round them, and throw sand on them with their feet, as though to conceal them from the monster. The bringing up of the *mbæɓanı* is only intended to instil respect into the novices, and it is soon borne away again.

The *asıŋgı* are then given a few pieces of meat to eat. If any of them crack a bone while eating — and they are closely watched — it is looked upon as a grave offence, and the father must pay a fine of a goat. Then they are permitted a short sleep, and this they enjoy beside the *aɓwıkıı's* fire, as a protection against the *ŋgala*.

On the following day come the real tests, some of which give the impression of pleasantries. They must, for example, suck up sand through a tube, pretending that they are drinking beer. Then they pretend to be drunk and create a disturbance and fight with sticks.

The *ŋgala* make natural noises (break wind), upon which the *asıŋgı* must give vent to long-drawn aah's, an expression of reverence and respect which is used by a young person in answer to an older man's greeting. Further, the *ŋgala* take a lump of anything, often of human excrement, order the *musıŋgı* to open his mouth as wide as possible, and push the lump into his throat; the lump must be swallowed, however inclined the victimma y be to vomit.

There is much to be said in favour of the supposition that this method of procedure is not a fortuitous method of tormenting the novices, but that it is connected with a magic rite, as a great many facts indicate that human excrement is considered in many quarters to possess a magic power. In the myths of the Kwakiutl urine is used as a means of making the children grow up quicker, and in the Australian initiation rites the youths have to eat the excrement of old women[1].

---

[1] See K. Th. Preuss, Der Ursprung der religion und kunst Globus 1904, p. 326.

These burlesque games, however, are quite insignificant compared with the actual tests, some of which mean real torture to many of the victims. Each one must throw himself headlong on the ground, roll in every direction, and then walk with the help of his head and legs, without using his hands. If he does not walk fast enough, the *ŋgala* beat him. A pointed peg is driven into the ground, and each of the *asɪŋgɪ* must pull it out with his teeth. The feat is rendered very difficult by the position which the performer must adopt: he must squat (not sit) on the ground, and then, without help of his hands, bend his head and seize the peg. It often happens that he falls forward in doing so, and wounds his mouth on the peg. If he does not pull the peg out quickly enough, he is beaten until he does accomplish it. Sometimes, however, his protector intervenes and pulls the peg out for him.

Next the *asɪŋgɪ* must run between two lines of the *ŋgala*, who are armed with sticks from two to three meters in length, with which they beat the runners. It is said that, if a *musɪŋgɪ* is disliked or if he has enemies among the *ŋgala*, it often happens that he is crippled or even beaten to death.

Following these games come obscenities, which my informant described to me with obvious embarassment, repeatedly laying stress on the fact that the whole performance was nothing but fun (*ŋguɪ*). Each of the *asɪŋgɪ* must hold up his penis until erection ensues. A lump of wood is then bound to the member, and he must then march round in this plight, amid the continuous laughter of the audience. Next a hollow, some ten centimeters in length, is scooped out in the ground and filled with water. This represents a vagina, and in it all the *asɪŋgɪ* must perform the act of copulation. When the water is used up, the hollow is filled in.

These tests are mentioned also by Mr Pfitzinger, who adduces other similar ones. For instance, »each one must perform upon the other, to demonstrate how he has sexual intercourse with a woman».

For forty-eight hours they remain in the remote spot engaged in such performances, and during the whole time the *asɪŋgɪ* get nothing to eat beyond a scrap of meat. At the expiration of this period, they are led home amid singing. The songs are of an indescribably lewd content. When they arrive in the village, they are condescendingly greeted by the *ŋgala* with *wakʲa, kana ka* 'Good day, you child' (*wakʲa* is a greeting to children from their elders the respectful answer is *aah*). When the *asɪŋgɪ* open their mouths to reply, they get their ears boxed, or else get all sorts of things stuffed into their mouths. Or else the *ŋgala* relieve themselves, and when the excrement appears, the *asɪŋgɪ* must again say »aah». A multitude of such »pleasantries» are enacted. Among others, every *musɪŋgɪ* is told to call his father to him, and he must then place his penis in the latter's ear. Anyone who refuses to submit to this is fined a bull.

That night the *asɪŋgɪ* may sleep in their homes, and the parents must have sexual intercourse.

On the following morning begin the great dances, which continue for five or six days. During the first days, the *asɪŋgɪ* remain in the plantations, where they live on food which their mothers have put in a certain place for them, but without saying anything about it to them. The food may not contain any salt. They have been provided with long sticks by the *aɓwɪkʊ*, and with these they beat all the women and others who have not undergone the third *nžaɪko*, who cross their path. Mr Pfitzinger says: »The *asɪŋgɪ* are not afraid of striking our own boys, messengers, or herdsmen. Even an *askarɪ* (soldier) could only save himself by threatening to shoot them. Everybody is afraid of the sticks of the *asɪŋgɪ*». When the women go to the river to fetch water, they are fallen upon, their calabashes are smashed, and the girls are raped. My informant strongly emphasized that *asɪŋgɪ* under the third *nžaɪko* are not regarded as human beings, but as animals, *nʲamu*. Without any doubt all these ceremonies and performances are intended finally and definitely to raise them from the condition of children without tribal rights. In a similar way, the neophytes among certain Australian tribes are looked upon as dead. The same is the case also in West Africa.

In reply to my question as to whether they would dare to assault a European, they answered that they would probably refrain from doing that, but they attack a native of another tribe without hesitation.

If a stranger coming along the road is attacked by the *asɪŋgɪ* and kills one of them in self-defence, he cannot be made responsible for his act. It is as if he had shot a *ŋgulɪ*, a baboon, and the father of the victim may not even ask who is the perpetrator of the deed. Instead, the *mubwɪkʊ* of the murdered man is blamed, and then he gets no remuneration for his work. For he is considered responsible for the mishap, since he has not given his pupil sufficiently precise instructions.

Thus, that the neophytes may with impunity break the rules established for the peace and order of the community is typical of all initiation rites. I must subscribe to the following remark of van Gennep: »Pendant toute la durée du noviciat les liens ordinaires, tant économiques que juridiques, sont modifiés, parfois même nettement rompus. Les novices sont hors de la société, et la société ne peut rien sur eux . . .»[1].

In order to escape being attacked, those who have gone through the third *nžaɪko* have secret signs by which they can be recognised. Probably these signs differ in different districts, but for Kikumbuliu I have made a record of the following:

A figure resembling a trident is drawn in the sand, and the attacked are asked what it is. The answer is, *mbæбanɪ*. Or they take two small twigs, each in the form of a hook; they hang one on the other, and hand them to the one that is to be tested. If he is initiated, he seizes the lower one which is hanging freely and turns it round. If he takes hold of the upper one, he thereby shows his ignorance, and receives a beating. Another way is to lay a stick over a path: the initiated then move it to such a position that it lies along the path. In another district again, the stick must be moved so that it points towards the conductor's village. Or finally, a little sand-heap is scraped up, and a stick is stuck into its side. The stick must be moved over to the opposite side.

After the expiration of a day or two, the *abwɪkʊ* take home their pupils, who have not, in the meantime, been allowed even to speak to their mothers or brothers and sisters, but have been looked upon as animals. The first day they are home, they do not speak to their parents, but sleep for the most part, and their mothers bring them food[2]. Then they wash and put on their clothes and ornaments, and a little hair is shaved from their

---

[1] A. van Gennep, Les rites de passage, p. 161.
[2] Reintegration rites. In the Congo, for instance, the novice is fed like a new-born baby.

foreheads. *nɪtænᴣɪə asɪŋgɪ* 'we have shaved the *asɪŋgɪ*', they say[1]. The *asɪŋgɪ* are now born again (*kusᴣawa*) and have again become human beings. The sticks which they have carried up till now are broken up and burnt by the *aɓwɪkɪɪ*, so that the smaller children may not get hold of them. The ceremonies are now at an end, and the parents are happy over and proud of their sons, who have now advanced to the dignity of real men. Now dances (* nᴣuma*) are indulged in with zest and abandon. In these dances, however, no uninitiated may take part; for a breach of this rule the fine is a goat.

The third *nᴣaɪko* is held in great dread by the uninitiated, and the women are heard to express their apprehensions that their sons may return from the tests in the wastes as cripples, or even that they may be killed there. People from Ulu who come eastwards during the *nᴣaɪko* time, do not dare to remain in the vicinity of the place where the ceremonies are being celebrated, but prefer to wander forth into the night, braving lions and rhinoceroses. It is undeniable that these customs are a plague for a large proportion of the people.

As has already been indicated, this *nᴣaɪko* does not occur at all in Western Ukamba, the real home of the tribe, for which reason it is certain that it is not an original custom. Whence the people to the east have acquired it, is unknown to me; the Akamba themselves do not seem to possess any traditions about it. Possibly it is a local extension of the second *nᴣaɪko*.

4. The occurrence of secret initiation rites and secret societies in these parts of East Africa.

Like all ordinary initiation ceremonies in general, the rites of the three *nᴣaɪko* are very similar to the rites of initiation into secret societies. Examples of such initiations are frequent in Africa (The Congo, the Guinea Coast), and are, as regards their

---

[1] van Gennep says: »on rase la tête de l'enfant pour indiquer qu'il entre dans un autre stade de la vie . . . le traitement qu'on fait subir aux cheveux rentre très souvent dans la classe des rites de passage», loc. cit. p. 239.

origin, difficult to distinguish from ordinary initiation rites[1]. The Akamba have no secret societies, and even if those who have passed through the third *nžaɪko* experience a certain feeling of affinity, yet, when the ceremonies are once over, this feeling obtains no practical expression — that is to say that, unlike the secret societies, it plays no rôle in their economic and political life.

If we now pass to the neighbours of the Akamba, I cannot, in the literature on the subject, discover any definite indications of anything corresponding to the third *nžaɪko*. Accounts dealing with the Akikuyu and the Masai contain nothing of that nature. Among the Amwimbe of Eastern Kenya, who are kin to the Akikuyu, it seems that for some time previous to circumcision, the novices have to undergo a special course of instruction and initiation in a special hut in the forest[2]. As far as concerns the Wapokomo, on the Tana, it is known that among them »existieren organisierte geheimbünde, deren zweck ist, den einzelnen zum mann zu machen»[3]. If we proceed from Ukamba eastwards, we find that there exists a type of secret society among the Wagiriama[4], as also among the Wa-Rabai, both in the hinterland of Mombasa[5]. We have seen in chap. I that the old trading route of the Akamba to the coast passed through these tracts, and that there is a considerable Kamba colony near Rabai. There is therefore a conceivable possibility that the Eastern Akamba have been influenced by their eastern neighbours in the matter of their secret initiation rites. At all events, it is scarcely probable that they alone practise such rites as those belonging to the third *nžaɪko*. I have no knowledge of the state of things among the Wataita, south of the Uganda railway.

On the whole, very little is known of secret initiation rites

---

[1] See, inter alia, R. H. Nassau, Fetichism in West Africa, p. 247 ff., and L. Frobenius, Die Masken und Geheimbünde Afrikas, p. 117, 218. H. Webster's Primitive secret societies, N. York 1908, I have not had access to.

[2] Man 1913, p. 137.

[3] S. R. Steinmetz, Rechtsverhältnisse von eingeborenen Völkern in Afrika und Ozeanien, p. 291.

[4] Described by Rev. W. E. Taylor in his Vocabulary of the Giriama language, a work to which I have not had access.

[5] H. B. Johnstone, Notes on the customs of the tribes occupying Mombasa subdistrict, p. 265.

and secret societies in East Africa. From this point of view, the present chapter — as supplementing Hobley's account — would seem to possess considerable interest.

*　*　*

My account is now concluded, and further comments are superfluous. We have been able to show the existence of procedures which are typical of initiation rites all over the world. We have thus been able at least to distinguish: 1) a series of rites which loosen the ties binding the novice to his former environment; 2) other rites which cause the novice to return — as a new man — to his ordinary milieu.

In conclusion I recall one circumstance which may be worthy of mention. Teeth-chipping is practised among the Akamba, but I have not been able to discover the least corroboration for Mr Hobley's statement that »the teeth are chipped after the first *nžaιko* or circumcision, and by the man that operates on that occasion»[1]. The custom, which otherwise is certainly associated in some places with the rites of puberty, has nothing to do with it in Ukamba, but is exclusively intended to improve the appearance. It may certainly be considered a tribal mark, but is not even obligatory; it is simply a fashion, which however plays a great rôle as a means of making oneself attractive to the opposite sex. Hildebrandt is right when he says: »Diese operationen geschehen ohne begleitende ceremonien»[2]. The operation is not performed by any special person, the young men often assist each other. Here and there, however, is found someone who is specially skilful, and he is naturally relied upon for preference. In a chapter further on I will describe and illustrate the procedure.

———

Since chapter III was written, I have come across a detailed account of the initiation rites among a tribe in Eastern Equatorial Africa, namely »[Zauberglaube und] Manbarkeistfeste bei den Wa-pare, Deutsch-Ostafrika» (nach den aufzeichnungen des Herrn J.

---

[1] Akamba &c, p. 18.　　[2] loc. cit. p. 350.

Alberti bearbeitet von P. German) in Jahrbuch des städtischen, Museums für Völkerkunde zu Leipzig, pp. 72—88, Leipzig, 1913. The *Wapare* or *Wasu*, as they call themselves, inhabit the Pare mountain, between Kilimandjaro and the Usambara plateau. I visited North Pare in April 1912. The ceremonies are held in the woods about every tenth year, and are divided into two parts. They last from 2 to 3 months. Much in the account is reminiscent of the initiation rites of the Akamba, for which reason I venture to append some citations: »— — — Man hört eines nachts im walde ein lautes gebrüll. Nur eingeweihte wissen, das der alte [the leader of the feast is a respected elder] diese töne auf einem riesigen topf hervorbringt (p. 72). Der topf stellt den löwen dar, — zur hälfte mit wasser gefüllt. — — — Diese beiden [an old man and an old woman] machen das »löwenbrüllen», indem sie mit holzröhren in die töpfe blasen. Ueber sich haben sie ein schwarzes tuch gehängt, das auch den topf verhüllt (p. 75). Der knabe erhält als mentor einen erwachsenen, aber ihm nicht verwandten mann, der während des ganzen festes ihm als berater zur seite steht . . . . . (p. 73). Die burschen ziehen nackt in trupps im land umher . . . . . In der steppe müssen sie eine bunte, grosse eidechsenart fangen. Früchte und pflanzen stehlen die burschen, was ihnen niemand verwehren darf. Tags über tanzen die burschen oder werden von den alten gepeinigt — — — man bindet an den penis der burschen eine grosse, schwere bananenblüte, und so müssen sie viermal zu den entfernt sitzenden alten laufen, ange-treiben durch schläge — — — [The boys must promise not to disclose the rites]. — — — die alten zwingen den knaben den penis in das loch [made in a calabash] zu stecken und den coitus symbolisch auszuführen» (p. 77).

The rites have nothing to do with circumcision: »Es ist aber das eigentliche pubertätsfest, durch das der knabe als mannbar erklärt und in stammesgemeinschaft als vollwertigen mann auf-genommen wird» (p. 78). We have then social puberty, to speak with van Gennep.

From this detailed description and the above-mentioned indic-ations of similar customs among several other tribes, it would seem permissible to draw the conclusion that secret initiation rites are generally practised among the Bantu in Eastern Equatorial Africa, and that these customs resemble each other somewhat, even in details.

Chapter IV. **Marriage.**

1. **General Customs.**

It is a mistake to suppose that among primitive peoples women are usually given in marriage without any regard being paid to their own inclinations. The Kamba women have, on the whole, the right of choosing for themselves their companions through life, and the majority of marriages are founded on mutual attachment. The suitor, therefore, always makes sure of the girl's consent [1] before he finally approaches her father. He does not usually go himself, but sends his father to negociate the matter, or, if the latter is prevented from going, he sends his eldest brother. The eldest brother is in many respects a deputy for his father as regards his younger brothers and sisters. If a favourable answer is received, the first step towards paying for the bride is taken at once — *kwasʐa* or *kuƥoa mwɪtuɪ* ('to buy a girl'), as it is called — two goats being sent to the prospective father-in-law. They are called *mbuʐ sʐa nδeo* (< *ƥea* 'to seek'), since through them the suitor »seeks» knowledge of whether the girl and her father still hold to their word. If the goats are returned, he knows that it is not worth while to continue to *kwasʐa;* but if only the strap with which the animals were fastened is sent back, this is a token of consent. The despatch of these goats, then, corresponds to the proposal among more civilized peoples.

The night after the goats are received, the girl's father must sleep with his wife. The suitor then hastens to send a couple of calabashes of beer and from 2 to 4 goats (*kuβɪkɪla ukɪ waβɪkɪla mbuʐ* 'to follow the beer which followed the goats'). On the receipt of

---

[1] Examples of how the Kamba youth pays court to the lady of his choice, that is to say, of the first step on the road to matrimony, have been given by the author in a popular work, »Afrikanska ströftåg». p. 108.

these, the parents-in-law must again have ritual coition. Then are sent a further 5 or 10 goats and a buck (*nδæŋgɔ ʝa kwɪtea mbuʝ nδakamɔ nδɪ* 'a buck to pour out blood on the ground for the goats'). The latter must be slaughtered; if this is not done and the buck subsequently dies from natural causes, the father-in-law must send these goats back. More beer is now sent (*wa upambʝa nʒælɔ* 'to wash the calabash vessels with'). On this occasion the suitor is always eager to send plenty of beer, because his father now goes to the prospective father-in-law to arrange about the price to be paid for the girl in goats and cattle. Some time usually elapses before any agreement is reached, and while the negociations are in progress, the beer is drunk. If there is plenty of it, the father-in-law's humour is improved, and in consequence he becomes easier to deal with, when the suitor's father tries to beat down the price. The one praises the girl, the other finds her full of faults, and, among other things, calls her, perhaps, *kæletu ka* 'that little girl'[1]. Finally they come to an agreement.

The number of goats to be paid depends on the financial position of the suitor; on an average 40 to 50 are paid, besides cattle, and a rich man may pay 100 or more goats. In comparison with their neighbours, the Kamba women command unusually high prices, and it seems that prices were even higher in earlier days, when it was possible to steal cattle with impunity from the neighbouring tribes. They were also higher before the last great famine at the end of the nineties, when the tribe was undoubtedly richer than at the present time[2]. Among the Akikuyu, for example, the usual price is 40 goats and 5 sheep (no cattle).

Though the number of goats varies, the number of cattle is usually constant, viz. 2 cows and 2 bulls (or oxen), one of which is later on slaughtered to be eaten. If one of the cows repeatedly gives birth to bull-calves, the father-in-law has the right to send it back and demand another; if one of the cows dies, he has

---

[1] *kæletu* is the diminutive of *mwɪtu;* the diminutive is often used contemptuously. Cf. my »Notes on the Kamba Language», Uppsala 1917.

[2] According to Hofmann, the Akamba living on the coast formerly paid from 10 to 16 cows. Hofmann, Geburt &c., p. 11. With regard to the price of a bride in general in Africa, see A. H. Post, Afrikanische Jurisprudenz.

also the right to receive another in its place. In Kikumbuliu (South-East Ukamba), where cattle are not usually kept on account of the tsetse-fly, 60 to 100 goats are paid for a bride. Some of the Akamba living there, however, keep cattle in the higher-lying tracts, and sometimes pay 2 cows and a number of goats.

Since money (Indian rupees) is in general use in East Africa the prices of the different animals may be quoted, in order to give a better notion of the real value of the price of a bride. On an average in Ukamba, a goat or a sheep sells for 5—6 rupees; an ox or a bull for 20—25 rupees; and a cow for 60 rupees or more. Very fat animals command higher prices.

When the suitor may take home his bride depends more upon the father-in-law's pleasure than on the time when the purchase money is paid. However, the bargain is not concluded until all the cattle have been delivered, and the father can, in the mean time, take his daughter back when he likes. The time within which the cattle must be delivered depends upon the financial position of the suitor and also upon the father-in-law's greater or lesser indulgence in the matter of enforcing his claim. A poor man often spreads payment over two or three years, and I even know a middle-aged man who has not yet finished paying for his wife. When demanding the payment of such debts, it is by some considered »good form» to talk in metaphors, which the Akamba are apt to do on other occasions, too. For example, they may say: »Bring me the *kɪltu*» ('the pot splinter'), or 'the eyes of the black one' — both expressions referring to the eyes of the cattle pars pro toto. Another expression is: »Those who are tormented by the rain».

It is not enough that a part of the price has been paid for a man to be allowed to take his wife home. The members of her family, and the mother-in-law especially, must receive considerable preliminary gifts, which are not included in the actual purchase price. The latter receives perhaps a goat, bananas, gruel (*usu*), some pieces of meat, &c — in a word, a little of all sorts of food, which are brought to her by the suitor's mother and other women. This is called *kupoka*, and if a child happens to be born in the village at this time, it is often called *ŋðokɪ*. The girl's brothers and sisters receive presents, such as beads or wire to make ornaments of. Finally, the suitor, *muasẓa*, must work in his prospective father-in-law's fields, in which work his friends help him. On the whole, the opportunity is taken to fleece him and get as much out of him as possible.

If too long a time elapses before the father-in-law delivers up the girl, the suitor may lose patience and arrange with some of his friends to help him to abduct her. One day when she is working in the fields or going to the river to fetch water, she is surrounded and carried off. Those who come up on hearing her cries, are kept at a distance by the suitor's friends by means of long sticks, while others carry her off. Pretended (ceremonial) abductions, which are customary with the Akikuyu, the Akamba's neighbours to the west, are not usual among the Akamba.

The abduction described here is quite an exceptional occurrence; which takes place more or less with the woman's connivance, but it is probably this which has led Krapf and Hildebrandt to assert that the Akamba practise ceremonial bride-stealing. The latter writes: »In früheren zeiten war — so erzählt man — bei den Wakamba brautraub mit blutigen gefechten verbunden, gebräuchlich. Ein anklang daran findet sich noch in der sitte, das am hochzeitstage ein bruder oder freund des bräutigams die braut, wenn sie sich vom hause entfernt, um wasser am fluss zu holen, überfällt, ihr gesicht und schultern mit butter salbt und dem erwählten trotz scheinbaren sträubens zuführt» [1]. And Krapf says: »The bridegroom must then carry off the bride by force or stratagem» [2]. Neither the author nor missionaries living in Ukamba know anything of this custom. However, experience has shown that it is necessary to be on one's guard not to confuse the rare cases of real woman-stealing and the symbolic bride-stealing originating therefrom with running away with a girl [3]. The fundamental reasons for the ceremonies which are like the abduction of women, are, for the rest, the natural human feelings, such as feminine shyness and timidity, and also grief at leaving the paternal home, so that the accounts of ceremonial abduction

---

[1] Hildebrandt ibid., p. 401.

[2] Krapf ibid., p. 354. Cf. also the confused account in Hobley, Akamba &c, p. 62.

[3] See also Westermarck, The History of Human Marriage, p. 223.

which are found even in modern ethnographical works, must be taken with great reserve in most cases[1].

When a man at last gets permission to take his bride home, a certain day is agreed upon. The home-coming always takes place in the evening. When everybody is asleep, the girl slips out and goes with the man to his village, where the mother-in-law smears her neck with fat, as a token of welcome (chap. XII). This ceremony is certainly of religious-magic significance, and is intended as a protection against the possible dangers which the marriage just entered upon may entail[2]. No special ceremony takes place, nor has the language any special word or expression which could correspond to »wedding».

During the night the young wife sleeps in the man's bed, but they may not have any intercourse. Early next morning, while the others are still asleep, she gets up, sweeps out the hut, and makes up the fire for cooking, and then she goes to bed again, since she is shy — feels *ŋδonι*, as it is called, for her mother-in-law — and wants to show herself to her as little as possible. It would perhaps be too bold to describe this household work of the bride as ceremonial, symbolic of her duty. However this may be, it is a good expression of the most important work of a woman (next to child-bearing), namely, to work and keep house for her husband[3].

Later in the day, her friends and playmates among the unmarried girls come to give her presents (bananas and other foods), and they cry because they have lost her from their circle. The songs they then sing are called *mbaþɪ sɪa maŋo* 'the songs of the weeping' (from *ɪ̣a* 'to weep'). She is now of the married, and will never again join in the dancing or other merry games. In assumed anger they break up the supports of the bridal couple's bed, and take the husband's ornaments, which hang on the bed; this he has no right to prevent them from doing. At the same time they sing in shrill voices their songs of com-

---

[1] Cf. Crawley, The Mystic Rose, pp. 350, 367; and Starcke, Die Primitive Familie, p. 230 ff.

[2] Cf. Crawley on »The mutual dangers of contact» in The Mystic Rose, p. 325.

[3] On »das Symbol der zuzubereitenden Speisen», see Starcke, pp. 274, 280.

plaint, which are audible to a great distance. It sometimes happens that they return the next day and finish their work of destruction.

The conduct of these girls can hardly be an expression of their — or perhaps we may say an expression of the whole of their sex's — reluctance to relinquish one of their members to a man; nor can it be a sort of sympathy (directed against the man) for the friend who, from easily understandable psychological reasons, begins her new-married life only with a certain shyness and doubt. Analogous cases from other peoples render it more than probable that it is a matter of pure ceremonial custom, in a way intended to avert bad luck from the young couple [1].

*   *   *

The newly married man's liabilities towards the bride's family, however, are not yet ended. Even after he has got his wife home, he must send more presents to her family. The mother-in-law receives a goat »to see the child» (*mbuẓ ẓa kwona kana*), that is to say, in memory of the daughter who has left her home. The father-in-law, his other wives, and the girl's brothers and sisters, are also remembered with presents.

The newly married couple usually stay in the husband's mother's hut, at any rate until the first child is born, when they move out and build their own hut. There are no definite rules on this point, but it depends on the man's pleasure when he wishes to move. As previously mentioned, the young wife is shy of her mother-in-law at first, and some time usually elapses before she can, for example, bring herself to eat in her presence. I know one case where it took nearly a year for a girl to overcome her *ṇδoṇi* (see chap. V), to such an extent has the feeling become part and parcel of the national consciousness. However, it greatly depends upon the individual character.

As a rule, the girls are married between the ages of 12 and 18, the men considerably later. It sometimes happens, however, that a girl is promised to a certain man when she is quite young. Then she becomes so accustomed to look upon him as her prospective husband that it never occurs to her to raise any objec-

---

[1] See Crawley, p. 366.

tions to the match. We have seen that a young man follows his own inclinations in the selection of a wife; but since he is dependent on his father to pay the price, the latter has much to say in the matter, and if he does not approve of his son's choice, nothing comes of the match. This dependence of the son on the father continues in many matters, as long as the latter lives, and it is often said that a man's wife is not his but his father's. Cases of child-marriage occur, insofar that a rich man often buys a wife for his son without consulting him. However, no one can be married before he or she has been circumcised. If a man has several sons, a younger son must always wait until the eldest has a wife, since the father can never be certain that he can afford to buy another girl. As soon as all the sons have a wife each, a younger one can, however, take a second, even if the elder son has not yet done so.

If anyone has begun to pay for a girl and she should die while she is still under her father's roof, the suitor has the right to have her sister or to recover his property. If the father-in-law is not in a position to pay back what he has received, his nearest relations in the clan are bound to help. But if a man has taken his wife home, and she then dies, he has no claim to any compensation; nor has he any if she should be barren, a ŋguŋguu, as it is called in the Kamba language.

That marriage is founded on mutual liking and that the Kamba girl does not submit to her father's will without opposition, is proved by many examples. If, for the sake of a large purchase price, a father should marry his daughter to a rich old libertine who is repulsive to her, he not infrequently runs the risk of losing her altogether, since more than one girl in such a position has taken her own life, and has been found hanging by a strap round her neck to the roof of the hut, or to a tree out in the fields. At best, her lover abducts her and conceals her somewhere else, until a divorce is arranged.

2. Special Cases.

There are, of course, numbers of local variations of or additions to the above-described customs associated with matrimony. Formerly there seems to have been in force in the region of Mukaa a custom that, when a woman married, all those with whom she had had relations previously should give her husband a goat each. And in Kilungu, when a woman became pregnant, a man could give two goats as a present. If these were accepted, and the child was a girl, she was looked upon as the donor's prospective wife, and he took from 2 to 4 more goats and beer to the father; that is to say, he began to buy the girl. In the course of time, he paid the whole price, and, when the girl had been circumcised and thus become entitled to marry, he took her to wife. If, on the other hand, the child was a boy, he was looked upon as the man's special protégé when he grew up.

When one of twin sisters is married, the other unmarried sister is said to accompany her to the man's home and stay there some days, to bring luck to the couple. This custom is probably founded on the intimate bond which is thought to exist between twins, and it is probably of more recent origin, since, as we have seen, it was an old custom always to kill one of twins.

To this account it may only be added that marriage and sexual intercourse are, on the whole, strictly exogamous. See chap. VII.

3. Polygamy.

Every native desires to have many wives, since the number of wives he has is to a material degree a criterion of his importance and wealth. Then he also gets many children, so that the number of those he has authority over is increased, and thereby also his importance[1]. The fact that, at the beginning of pregnancy, all sexual intercourse between married couples ceases, undoubtedly promotes polygamy.

---

[1] Numerous proofs are found that the natives are inclined to look down on us Europeans for our monogamy, and because many of us are still unmarried even at an advanced age. Once when I was obliged to compel some oldish Kamba men to act as bearers for me, they expressed their displeasure at being treated so by a young man who had not yet been able to afford a wife. Barth tells that the Tuaregs in West Sahara had nothing to complain of in him except that he was unmarried. H. Barth, Reisen und Entdeckungen in Nord- und Central-Afrika, I, p. 489.

The first wife is always the chief one, and is called *kıɓetı kınænɔ* 'the big wife', or *kıku* 'the old one', without necessarily being old. The other wives call her *mwaıtu* 'mother'. They also have to obey her as children do their mother, and she superintends their work. The head of the house tells her what he wants done, and she then sets the »little» wives to work. The latter's respect for her is shown by the fact that they may not call her by her name; besides »mother», she is called *sɪoŋgama*, »N. N's mother», after her children. The latter are also called by the »little» wives by names other than their own. This is a sign of *ɲðonı* (see chap. V). A young wife who has not yet born a child may not eat porridge (*ŋgıma*) with one of her older fellow-wives who has ceased to bear, or she will become barren.

Relations between the wives are generally good; if they quarrel, the husband may castigate them. Much dissension is prevented by the superior position of the »big» wife, but especially by the fact that it is usual for every woman to have her own hut, prepare her own food, have her own cows to milk, and her own fields to till. Cases of jealousy do occur, but the »big» wife usually likes to see her husband take more wives, because they lighten her work. She can, on account of her superior position, leave to them all the heavier work, such as hewing wood, carrying water, shutting the cattle-kraals at night, opening them in the morning, &c. In this way a division of labour is often effected, so that turns are taken at the different sorts of work. If a man has only one wife and later, when he is old, buys a young girl, the latter usually stays in the elder wife's hut, and is treated as a daughter by her, but must do most of the work under her direction. The hut-tax introduced by the British Government [1] brought about a change in the old custom of giving every wife her own hut, since, in order to escape paying the tax, the natives put several women in the same hut. Some years ago, however, the tax began to be levied on the number of wives, instead of on the number of huts, and there is no longer any reason for the natives to reduce the number of their huts.

Since marriage is chiefly an economic question, it is not to be wondered at that, in spite of the prevalence of polygamy, a

---

[1] Three rupees per hut.

large number of Akamba cannot manage to get more than one
wife. »The poor man is a monogamist all the world over», says
Weule aptly. The most usual number of wives is one to three,
and, if statistical investigations were made, the percentage of those
who had more than three would be found to be very low [1]. We
should find the same state of things among most of the Bantu
peoples, so that the popular conception of polygamy, that every
man has a large number of wives, is far from being correct. Naturally, besides the economic question, one important factor is the
proportion between the different sexes; and therefore, as has often
been maintained, polygamy can never be the normal form of
marriage, since it would require twice as many women as men.
Seeing that warfare among the Akamba has ceased, it is probable that the proportion of men will increase, and that therefore monogamy will become more general. I append a list of 26
families (see p. 87) from Machakos district, but the number is,
of course, too small for any positive conclusions to be arrived at.

From economic reasons, some men must remain unmarried
a long time, and Hofmann says that, in the districts round his
mission-station, Ikutha, in East Ukamba, alone, he could count up
quite a respectable number of elderly bachelors [2]. However, there
seem to be none who die as bachelors. As we shall see presently,
in case of need, a poor man can always get a widow for his wife,
or he can simply elope with the lady of his choice. Old maids,
on the other hand, are not met with at all.

A married woman can quite lawfully have relations with other
men, her husband often placing her at the disposal of a man of
the same clan, or of a friend, who comes on a visit and stays
over night. The language has a special word for this, *kuβıta*.
The rich Kamba man is proud to be able to entertain a crowd
of guests in this way, each one having a separate hut at his disposal. The same custom is found among other East African
peoples, such as the Masai, where the guest thrusts his spear
into the ground outside the hut, which, with all its contents, is

---

[1] Kitilli (Kitui district), the richest man in Ukamba, was a great exception with his fifty wives, distributed in many places. Mbota, one of
the most important personages in the Machakos district, had seventeen
wives.

[2] Hofmann, Geburt &c, p. 10.

then at his disposal [1]. Although such relations are considered lawful by the Akamba, the man who indulges in them must be purified before he can enter his own hut again. The purifying medium, *ɣondu,* consists of certain roots, which are pounded and mixed with water. The man takes a little in each hand, and rubs them along both sides of his body. He may now enter his hut again. This ceremony must also be observed as regards one of his own wives, if the man, after coitus with one wife, goes to another who has a little baby; otherwise she refuses to receive him, saying: »I do not want my child to die».

A remarkable fact, for which I have not been able to find any explanation, is the following: If a man has several wives (A, B, and C), and they have sons who are married, every man has a right to have sexual intercourse with the wife of the half-brother corresponding to him in age; that is to say, A's eldest son can sleep with the wife of the eldest son of B or C; A's second son with the wife of the second son of B or C; and so on. A *kɩmwæmwɔ,* i. e. a man who has no true brothers or sisters, has the right to sleep with all his half-brothers' wives — presumably because he is, in a way, at the same time his mother's eldest, youngest, and middle son.

4. Divorce.

Although, on the whole, it may be said that among the Akamba a marriage is entered upon for life, yet divorce often occurs among them, as is usual among a people at a low stage of civilization. The reasons for this are many and various. The husband perhaps thinks that his wife is not industrious or is not a good cook, or he discovers that she is unfaithful [2]. If he can prove that his dissatisfaction is justified, he may send her home to her father and is entitled to repayment of the purchase money. For this purpose he keeps a notched stick (*kɩka kɩa kutala mbuɩ,*

---

[1] M. Weiss, Die Völkerstämme im Norden Deutsch-Ost-Afrikas, p. 386. As is well known, this custom is found over the whole world; cf. E. Westermarck, The History of Human Marriage, p. 74.

[2] Unfaithfulness seems, however, very seldom to lead to divorce; see chap. XI.1.

'a stick to count goats with'), or a bundle of pegs, one notch or peg for each animal he has paid. He can also change her for one of her sisters, an exchange which the father-in-law is very anxious to effect, as then he escapes repaying the price of the bride. It is not unusual for a woman to elope with a lover, and then if the husband wishes to be divorced from her, it is an essential condition that he takes her back to her father, if he wishes to claim repayment of the purchase money. In the Machakos district, Western Ukamba, many a married man has been put to great trouble to look for his wife in the Kikuyu region in the west, whither she has fled. The delicate question in divorce is that of the repayment of the purchase price of the bride, and everywhere where women are bought, this is a contributory factor to rendering marriages less dissoluble. If the husband is willing to forego repayment, or if, on the other hand, the father-in-law is ready to repay at any moment, there is usually nothing in the way of a divorce at any time. Thus, in a way, the wife is as free as the husband to dissolve the marriage.

A wife's unfruitfulness is a ground for divorce among many negro tribes; but among the Akamba it does not seem to be a sufficient reason for a man to dissolve a marriage, for the difficulty is got over by the man's taking another wife. On the other hand, a man's impotence is good ground for a divorce, since it is a woman's pride to have as many children as possible [1]. An impotent man is called a *ndæwa* ('an ox'). It sometimes happens that a young man who is suspected of being a *ndæwa*, is challenged by the unmarried girls to prove the rumour unfounded, or they will have nothing to do with him.

Among all less civilized peoples, I believe, the children are left in the charge of the mother after divorce, and this is the case also among the Akamba. The father can keep them if he wishes to, but then he forfeits the purchase money. This is quite just according to the native view, for a man takes a wife chiefly to get children, and if he keeps the children when he is divorced, he has got value for the purchase money, and has nothing more to expect.

[1] The unfruitfulness of the husband seems often to be good ground for divorce among Bantu peoples; cf. e. g. W e u l e, Wissenschaftl. Ergebnisse meiner Ethnograph. Forschungsreise in den Südosten Deutsch-Ost-Afrikas, p. 61, 97.

From the same point of view, the husband who has paid for his wife is the owner of a child which she gets by anyone else. Sir Charles Eliot relates that, during the great famine at the end of the eighteen-nineties, many Kamba women ran away from their homes, and, to obtain food, went and lived with Hindoo workmen on the Uganda railway, which was then in course of construction. When the famine was over, their husbands came and tried to claim the children that their wives had had by the Hindoos. The women themselves were a minor consideration. Eliot says aptly: »It is characteristic that the legal owner of a woman is regarded as the owner and father of her children, whoever the real progenitor may be»[1]. This conception of the right of ownership in children seems to be typical of the Bantu peoples among whom paternal right prevails[2].

5. Widows and the fatherless.

According to native law, when a man dies, the widow (*muka wa ndıwa < tıa* 'to leave over') goes to his eldest brother. The latter may, if he likes, make her over to another person, who then has to pay the owner for her. If she is old, so that he does not care to keep her himself and has no prospect of selling her, he may lend her to someone. Thus, in the Machakos region, elderly widows are given to men of the Kikuyu tribe, many of whom work there for the Akamba. A poor man who cannot afford to buy a wife is glad to take over a widow. Children which are the fruit of such an alliance, however, belong to the owner of the woman, which agrees with what has been mentioned above. If a man leaves many widows, it is usual to divide them among his brothers. If, again, he has no brothers, the nearest heir has the disposal of them.

Although all the father's wives are regarded by the children as their mothers, it is not unusual for a young widow to be given to one of the man's sons by an older wife, with which son

---

[1] C. Eliot, The East Africa Protectorate, p. 125.
[2] Some further examples are given by J. Kohler, Rechte der deutschen Schutzgebiete, IV. Das Banturecht in Ostafrika.

she is more of an age. This is, however, conditional upon her
never having had sexual intercourse with the deceased husband
(the father). If such is not the case, a man with many wives
can transfer one of the youngest to his son during his lifetime [1].

For reasons for the origin of the custom that a brother inherits
a deceased brother's wife, see »Law of Inheritance» (Chap. XI. 2).
With her owner's permission, a widow may also return to her father. However, she is only deposited with him, so to say, and
her owner has no right to demand her purchase money back
again. If he makes any such claim, the father-in-law says: »My
daughter is your wife; if you do not wish to keep her in your
own house, it is your own business». If, on the other hand, anyone else wishes to have her now, he must buy her from the father, who then hands over the purchase money to her husband.

In the event of a widow not going to her brother-in-law, but
to a stranger, she must first go through a ritual coitus with another
elderly man (*mutumıa*), otherwise her prospective husband's earlier
wives will become barren, or her children will die. The difference
between this coitus and that which is customary as an ordinary
purification after a death (Chap. VII. 2) is not clear to me.

I take the opportunity to point out, in passing, that such ritual coitus is particularly often practised by the Akamba, in practically all conditions of life. It can only be performed by a man
who has gone through all the phases of a Mukamba's life. He
must have had at least as many experiences as the woman he is
about to purify. If, for example, in the case just mentioned, the
widow has circumcised children, a man who has not yet taken
his own children to be circumcised cannot perform the ceremony
with her.

He who takes over his brother's widow, looks upon her children in every way as his own. If they are girls, he receives all the
purchase money when they are married [2]. However, the children
always call him *mwændwasa* 'uncle'. What is more interesting
is that, if he himself gets any children by the woman, they also

---

[1] It is quite usual in polygamous families for a son to inherit one
of his father's widows, who is not his own mother; cf. Westermarck
ibid. p. 512.

[2] As we shall see in Chap. XI, he cannot, however, to his own
advantage, dispose of the sons' inheritance from their father.

say *mwændwasa*, and not *nau* 'father'. We shall see below (Chap. XI)
that the property of a dead man who was childless does not
go to the brother, but to the son the latter may have by the widow. Thus it can be said that, in a way, the deceased is looked
upon as the child's father. The question then is whether the son
is really looked upon as actually begotten by the dead man — the
idea does not seem to be altogether unreasonable in the case of
a people that worships ancestral spirits — or whether the essential factor is the right of ownership, which may be supposed to
continue even after death. The last assumption is supported by,
and can be considered as an extreme consequence of, the natives'
conception of the right of ownership in children, which is clearly
and concisely defined by Eliot in the citation given above [1].

Thus, even if the boundaries seem vague, there is reason to
maintain that a form of levirate exists among the Akamba, side
by side with the custom for the brother to take over a dead man's
widow on purely practical and economic grounds. We shall revert
to the point in Chap. XI. 2.

6. Statistics of Families.

The table on the opposite page shows a surprising excess of
boys over girls, but the figures can only be considered as approxi-
mate, since I do not know the proportion between the sexes of the
dead children. Hobley gives the following statistics for 38 Kamba
families [2]: wives 117, male children born 195, female children born
197. Here the girls are slightly in excess, a state of things which
is more appropriate for a polygamous people. According to the
work of Hobley cited below, however, the number of boys among
the Bantu-Kavirondo (north and east of Lake Victoria) is in excess,
or 57,5 % of the total number of children. It would be interesting to study how polygamy can exist under such conditions.
As far as the Akamba are concerned, my material is too slight
to allow of reliable conclusions to be drawn from it. It must,
however, be borne in mind that, even if it is the case that
more boys than girls — or at least an equal number of each — are born,

---

[1] Cf. Starcke's treatment of the question of levirate in »Die
Primitive Familie», p. 150 ff.

[2] Hobley, A-Kamba, p. 12.

Name of Father	Number of wives	Number of children living ♂	Number of children living ♀	Number of children dead
Wa mbua wa ?	2	5	3	?
Mbithi wa ?	4	4	4	—
Matata wa Kiambi	1	2	4	6
Munge wa Kavala	2	3	4	2
Bwana wa ?	2	4	3	3
Katumo wa Mulomba	2	4	6	1
Muniambu wa ?	1	2	1	3
Kituku wa Mulomba	2	3	2	2
Ngotho wa Nguli	3 [1]	2	1	4
?	1	—	1	3
Mukula wa Kisangi	6	4	5	3
Ngao wa Kiambi	3	2	3	9(?)
Seke wa Niaa	1	4	1	2
Mbonge wa Kithome	1	—	3	2
Nthenge wa Nguio	2	4	1	—
Musuva wa Munene	2	6	3	3
Nsau wa ?	2	5	4	3
Kisoi wa Kiene	1	5	—	—
Munsu wa ?	1	7	2	2
Muniambu wa Wakenia	1	2	—	3
Nsau wa Kivati	2	5	5	1
Ndambuki wa Mbuo	2	6	2	4
Nginia wa Kaliu	2	5	3	—
Matuanga wa Nsau	3 [2]	10	6	2
Kitavi wa Ngavi	2 [2]	3	—	1
Muli wa Inguli	1	3	3	2
Total 26	52	100	70	61

[1] Of whom one, as I chanced to learn, was barren (ŋguŋguu). It is not improbable that several among all the wives are barren, since barren women are rather numerous among the Akamba.

[2] Besides one deceased.

another factor must, in bygone times, have contributed to levelling
the numbers of the sexes, namely, the incessant feuds waged both
with their neighbours and among themselves. One may also venture
to assume that a greater number of boys than girls die in infancy.

The number of children that die is striking — according to
my statistics, more than, 25 % of the whole number born. As a
matter of fact, the death-rate among children is always high among
primitive peoples, and in Ukamba there is rarely a family to be
met with which has not lost at least one child. Most of them
die in early infancy, as a result of injudicious treatment and espe
cially owing to unsuitable feeding. All too early the natives begin
to stuff the children with the same food as they eat themselves:
boiled beans, maize, and such things, which for them are altogether too indigestible. The children also suffer a great deal from
the cold. These factors are, however, hardly sufficient to account
for the high death-rate adduced above. The figures are, as a
matter of fact, misleading, insofar as a large number of these
children died during the great famine of 1897—99. All the fathers
of families are, it must be mentioned, middle-aged or elderly men [1].

Finally, I will here again point to the difficulty of collecting
statistics relating to polygamous families, whether the investigator
wishes to do it personally or contents himself with accepting the
statements of the natives. Just as the Akamba consider it is unlucky to count their cattle, so they think that the number of their
children should never be revealed to other people. If they do tell
the number of their children, or if the information is obtained from
other persons, it must always be remembered that a native in
most cases includes the children of a deceased brother among
his own, since by native law a deceased man's wife falls to his
brother, who then looks upon his brother's children in every
respect as his own.

---

[1] According to the material collected by Hobley from the nilotic
»ÿa-luo» (Kavirondo), on Lake Victoria, 44,5 % died out of 126. C. V.
Hobley, Anthropological Studies in Kavirondo and Nandi, Journ. Anthropol. Inst. 1903, p. 255.

Chapter V. Relations between persons connected by marriage.

1. The conception of *n̩ɗoni.*

As soon as a man marries, he assumes a certain position towards his parents-in-law and the members of their family, and has a number of rules of conduct to observe towards them. Since there is no corresponding custom with us, and it is difficult for that reason to formulate a short definition of it, it is undoubtedly best to retain the native word, *n̩ɗoni,* and later to give as complete an account of its significance as possible. *n̩ɗoni* really means »shyness, feeling of shame», and is, both in meaning and application, identical with what the Zulus and allied tribes call *hlonipa*[1]. Besides, as is well known, the phenomenon is not unusual within exogamous groups. The person with whom one stands in a relation of *n̩ɗoni,* is called *muponi* (pl. *aponi*)[2]. Men as well as women have their *aponi,* that is, really, persons towards whom they must appear »shy» — that is to say, they must carefully avoid them in every way. To neglect this brings misfortune, so that we are here in the presence of a sort of taboo.

The most important *n̩ɗoni*-person is the mother-in-law. A man and his mother-in-law must not mention each other by name; if they meet on a path, the man steps on one side, or even both do so. A woman covers her breast when she sees her son-in-law, and they avoid looking each other in the face. When visiting his father-in-law's village, he may not enter his mother-in-law's hut, as long as she is inside it, but must remain outside. He

---

[1] Cf. D. Kidd, The Essential Kafir, p. 236. Callaway, The Religious System of the Amazulu.

[2] *Muponi wakwa* or *muponwa,* 'my *muponi'.*

may talk to her from outside, but often he prefers to have an in-
termediary, if there is anyone present. If the mother-in-law
goes out or withdraws to the *we̯* (a part partitioned off in the
back part of the hut), he may go inside the door and sit
down, but may not go further in. If, on his arrival at his
father-in-law's village, he sees his mother-in-law outside it, he hides
himself in the bushes, and if she shows no signs of going away,
he goes off in another direction, to await a better opportunity. If
the father-in-law has several wives, all of them and their elder
daughters are his *aponı*.

ṇ̃oṇı relations naturally begin already when a man begins to
pay for a girl — thus before she has been taken to his home as his
wife. One day I heard a youth call one of my servants *muponwa*
('my *muponı*'), and I therefore asked the latter if they really
were *aponı*. »No», was the answer, »but the mother of the girl
he is buying is called Kavuva, just as myself». Although the
man in question was thus speaking to a person who was not
his prospective mother-in-law, and the latter was not present, he
could not mention the name they bore in common. It may be
added that it is principally the first name, that which is given at
birth, which must not be mentioned — with later ones it is not
necessary to be so particular.

Among some peoples this restraint ceases with the birth of the
first child, but I have not been able to discover that this is the
case also among the Akamba. On the other hand, the *ṇ̃oṇı* feeling
between mother-in-law and son-in-law is modified with time, so that
they can talk and associate with each other more freely. By making
certain payments to the mother-in-law, as for example a good
she-goat, the right can be acquired to sit by the fire in her hut,
when she is away or in the *we̯*. If the son-in-law comes on a visit,
she is ready to withdraw there, so that he can go to the hearth.
The acquisition of this right is called *poa mwakı* 'to buy fire'.
A modification such as this has certainly been brought about for
the sake of convenience. The distance to the parents-in-law's
village is often long, and the nights in the highlands of Ukamba
are often cold; perhaps it rains on the way, &c, and so the visitor
really needs to sit by the fire to warm himself.

Here may be cited an event by which the *ṇ̃oṇı* relations
between a certain mother-in-law and her son-in-law were dissolved,

or, as the natives say, »killed» (*uạ nǒoni*) — as far as I know a unique case.

Kisese, an elderly man living north of Machakos, took part in a drinking-bout close to his mother-in-law's village. When very drunk and incapable of recognising people, he went to her hut in the evening, where he crept into the *wẹ* and went to sleep, not waking until the following morning. The consternation of the people at this event was indescribable, and even Kisese must have felt sheepish at first. Having been a leader in the time of the wars, however, he was equal to the occasion. He at once sent a messenger home for a fat ox and some goats, which he presented to his mother-in-law, saying: »From this time forth all *nǒoni* is over between us two». If he had been a youth, it would probably have cost him dear, but as he was a rich and influential man, he got his own way.

Kisese's action was highly approved of by several younger married men, and I have heard them say that when they become *atumia* 'elderly men' (Chap. IX.1) they will do likewise. Perhaps they will. If the example were widely followed, it would be an interesting illustration of how an old custom is violated by chance, and how the new one thus introduced gradually gains ground. To make this possible, the originators of the new ideas must be influential persons; but the matter is undoubtedly facilitated if the old custom is irksome and oppressive, or felt to be so at least by reasoning individuals.

For further and more usual methods of »killing» other kinds of *nǒoni*, see below.

All the elder sisters of a man's wife are also his *aponi*, as is also the case with a woman and her father-in-law and her husband's elder brothers. Between a man and his wife's younger sisters there is no *nǒoni* — they may even lie in his bed, but naturally without any intercourse. This difference is indicated by the language — an elder sister-in-law is called *muponi*, but a younger one *mwamoa, mwamu, mwamwǝ* ('my, thy, his younger sister-in-law'). A woman calls her elder brother-in-law *ukulu* or *mukuǝ waitu* 'our old one', also *asa* 'father' (often with *munini* 'the little', added to distinguish him from the head of the family)[1].

---

[1] *ukulu* and *mukuǝ* are no doubt only different formations from the root *kulu*.

She calls his wife *inꝫa* or *mwaitui* 'mother'. A younger brother-in-law, though not *muponi,* she does not readily address by name if he is present, but employs some other expression instead. If two brothers are married, the elder is *muponi* to the wife of the other. They have their places on opposite sides of the fire-place, but the woman likes to take refuge in her bed when her elder brother-in-law is there — it often happens that two sons, who are both newly married, live together in the mother's hut.

A kind of *ŋðoni* exists also between women, namely, between a young wife and her mother-in-law, her husband's elder wife, or his elder sister. This *ŋðoni* feeling is, however, not mutual, but is only felt by the young wife, and finds expression in a sort of exaggerated timidity for the persons mentioned. Undoubtedly this is to a large extent due to a purely natural shyness. She dares not even eat in their presence. To banish this shyness it is usual for the older wives to take a bowl of fat each and smear their new »colleague» with it, after which it is considered that the timidity will soon vanish. She must not address her husband's elder sister by name, but must call her *ukulu* (cf. above). However, of all her *aponi,* a young wife shuns her mother-in-law most, and to be able to enjoy more intimate relations with her, she must pay some small tribute. As mentioned before, a young couple usually live in the husband's mother's hut, until the first child is born. For the right of sitting beside her mother-in-law on the hearth, the daughter-in-law gives her bananas, &c; previous to this, they sit on opposite sides of the fire-place. The daughter-in-law, however, may not yet go into the *we;* if she wants anything out of it, she must get it with a stick or hook. The right to enter the *we* is obtained by a further gift of bananas, in return for which, however, the mother-in-law makes her daughter-in-law a small present, such as beads or other articles of adornment. Some time usually elapses before this right is acquired. I have met women who have been married 2 or 3 years, but who have never set foot in the mother-in-law's *we.* In such cases, the reason is usually to be sought in the younger woman's temperament, for some can only with difficulty overcome their *ŋðoni* feeling, whereas the mother-in-law usually seems to have no objection to bringing about freer intercourse, for she can then with less difficulty avail herself of her daughter-in-law's services. Parents-in-law are not each other's *aponi.*

The man who does not observe his *ŋðonı* obligations, such as going to one side when he meets his *mupoŋı* &c, is looked upon as a *muŋændu*, an obstinate and incorrigible fellow, and no woman who knows about it will give him her daughter in marriage.

It is, however, obvious that the *ŋðonı* relations in regard to avoiding one another must often be irksome for the natives, and this is probably why they can be done away with in the less important degrees, as, for example, between a man and his younger brother's wife. This is called *uạ ŋgeanı* 'to kill the mutual refusal'[1]. The woman presents her male *mupoŋı* with a couple of bunches of bananas (*ŋðumba*), and receives perhaps a goat in return, and then they agree not to avoid each other any more. They can now converse freely together and sit beside each other. This relaxation, however, is not possible between a mother-in-law and her son-in-law, and the case cited above must be looked upon as exceptional.

2. **Taboo of Names.**

It has already been indicated that *apoŋı* may not mention each other's names. A synonymous word is employed instead. From an other side, if a *mupoŋı*'s name is the same as that of some object or such like, the object in question must, in conversation, be referred to by another name for it. As, for instance,

for *kıoko* 'to-morrow', is substituted *unı* 'to-morrow'
» *kılonžo* 'noise' » *ŋguaƀa*
» *ılondu* 'sheep' » *ŋondu* 'sheep' (same root)
» *nžukı* 'bee' » *ndoŋoŋı*
» *nžoka* 'snake' » *nıamu ıa nðı* 'the animal of the earth', or *mvılu* 'lizard'
» *wa mbua* 'of rain' » *ŋduƀu*
» *ŋgomo* 'chisel' » *kıƀoŋgoı* (< *ƀoŋgoa* 'to sharpen').

An example may illustrate this name-taboo and the ingenuity which is sometimes shown in surmounting the difficulty. In British East Africa small change, called *mbesa* (kisuaheli *pesa*) among the Akamba, is provided with a hole in the centre, so that it can

---

[1] *ŋgeano < leana* 'to refuse one another'.

be threaded on a string. Once when I had bought something from a woman, she said: »Give me one ear-ring (ɩ́ɓvulɩ)», instead of, »Give me one m̥besa», because her mupoɲɩ was called m̥besa.

If a man is called mwæu 'the white', his mupoɲɩ cannot, for example, say: ŋgua nɩ nžaṵ 'the stuff is white' (nžaṵ is the n-form of the root -æu), but must search for another word, such as ṇðeuɓu (< pɛuɓa 'to be clean'). On the other hand, I have not found the taboo carried as far as, for example, among the Zulus, where it sometimes applies to parts of names, namely their emphatic syllables [1].

It must also be due to a sort of ṇðoɲɩ that a woman may not mentión her husband's name, nor a younger wife that of an elder one, or even those of the latter's children. The observation of these things has, among certain peoples, given rise to a special language for women, but in the case of the Akamba, I have only found slight traces of this.

The Kamba wife's method of avoiding mentioning her husband's name is the same as that used among apoɲɩ, i. e. she uses an expression with a corresponding meaning, often made up by herself. For instance:

for poma 'plot'		she uses	ɩ́ɓuɓeoɲɩ 'place to make a fire on'.
»	mwatu 'beehive'	»	»	mwaŋgo 'beehive'
»	ɩtwɩku[2] 'gorge, ravine'	»	»	ɩomuka
»	mwɛ̣ 'moon'	»	»	musesɩ̣a nðɩ 'a person who looks at the ground from a protected place'.

If a woman is questioned about her husband's name, she lets other people answer for her, if they are present.

Even if the word poma 'plot' is not a personal name, many married women will not utter it, presumably because this place is so closely connected with their husbands, who spend a great deal of their time there, talking and drinking beer or making weapons and tools. Instead of it the ˙wives say muumaloɲɩ 'the place on which one comes out' or ɩ́ɓuɓeoɲɩ (cf. above).

For the method by which the co-wives and apoɲɩ mention a

---

[1] Kidd ibid. p. 237.   [2] Cf. twɩka 'to burst'.

young, newly-married wife and an elderly wife with children see
also the end of chap. VI. Her husband's younger brothers, on the
other hand, who are not her *aponi*, call her by her name.

To use such periphrastic appellations is called to *kwṇea*.

The taboo-ing of relations' names is found all over the world.
Frazer has made a collection of such phenomena[1], the reason for
which he, for his part, assumes to be in all essentials the same as
that which renders a person unwilling to mention his own name,
that is to say, »a superstitious fear of the ill use that might be
made by his foes, whether human or spiritual»[2].

From what has already been said, it is almost self-evident
that *aponi* may not touch each other's personal belongings, such
as clothes, &c. Nor may they sit on each other's chairs. It
sometimes happens that, when drunk, a man violates this regu-
lation in the case of one of his less important *aponi*. Then he
must pay a number of goats and an ox, which is killed and eaten.
The *ṇḍoni* is then considered to be at an end between them.

A certain degree of *ṇḍoni* also exists between cousins of
opposite sexes, although they are not *aponi* to each other. They
may not approach too near to each other or touch each other's
clothes, &c. However, an interesting exception is the relation
between a man and the daughters of his mother's brother (*mama*).
He can associate with them freely, sit on their chairs, &c. »They
are just like his own sisters» (Kioko). The cousins may also take
each other's belongings, and the owner may not object. A man
may take great liberties with his mother's brother's wife, and it
it is said he may even flog her without incurring any unpleasant
consequences. As far as I can discover, however, his privileges
do not extend to the point that he may treat her as his wife,
which is the case among the Baronga at Delagoa Bay[3]. Similar
curious relations between a sister's son and his mother's brother and
family are observed among so many Bantu tribes that they may,
perhaps, be looked upon as survivals from common customs of

---

[1] The Golden Bough II, p. 318.
[2] Ibid. p. 349.
[3] H. A. Junod, Les B-a-Ronga. Etude éthnographique sur les
indigènes de la Baie de Delagoa.

ancient times, when matriarchate seems to have been prevalent among the Bantu peoples[1].

Finally it may be mentioned that the word *muꝑonwa* (my *muꝑoni*) is used as a form of greeting between *aꝑoni;* the answer is *muꝑonwa.*

If we now take a final survey of what has been said about the *ṇðoni* feeling, we find that it may vary both in quality and intensity. Strictly speaking, *ṇðoni* comprises a number of mutual observances between certain individuals of opposite sexes who are in some way connected by marriage; the intensity depends upon who the individuals are. *ṇðoni* can be removed, and it is worthy of note that a breach of its rules gives rise to its removal. Another form of *ṇðoni* is that which a young wife feels in the presence of her mother-in-law and older sisters-in-law; this is not mutual, and its intensity depends upon the character and temperament of the person in question.

We now come to the reasons for this custom. For the son-in-law's avoidance of his mother-in-law and vice-versa, at least three different theories have been put forward (Howitt and, after him, Frazer, Lubbock, Tylor). Crawley has shown that these, even if probable to a certain degree, hardly give the prime and fundamental reason for this phenomenon. He himself bases it upon the relations between men and women, for which he introduces the name »sexual taboo», considering the custom in question to be of a religious-magic character, »a horror religiosus, rather than a horror naturalis». In woman's general »dangerousness» for man we ought, according to him, to find the fundamental factor[2]. The relations between a young wife and her father-in-law will, then, be of the same religious significance. Finally, a fifth theory has been advanced by Reinach, who criticises Crawley and earlier investigators[3].

None of these theories seems to solve the question satisfactorily, and, as regards, the Akamba, I must content myself with saying that they themselves regard at least some of the *ṇðoni* restrictions

---

[1] Cf. Frazer, Totemism and Exogamy; and Junod, The Life of a South-African Tribe, p. 253.

[2] E. Crawley, The Mystic Rose, p. 391 ff., and (in a concentrated form) K. Th. Preuss, Die geistige Kultur der Naturvölker, p. 72.

[3] S. Reinach, Le Gendre et la Belle-mère, p. 649.

as intended to put a check on undue sexual intercourse. However, this may be a secondary explanation, and hardly explains the matter in the cases when it is exclusively a question of women avoiding each other. For an explanation of such a case, I have searched in vain in the authors mentioned above.

3. Avoidance between a man and his daughter=in law or daughter.

In this connexion I will also mention the avoidance which exists between the father of the family and his daugther-in-law or his grown-up daughter. This avoidance is also a kind of *nðonı* and seems to be designed to prevent improper relations between the persons mentioned, when they are in daily contact with each other by living in the same hut. Thus the man avoids associating with them unnecessarily, and within the hut he has at the hearth his prescribed sittingplace, which is diametrically opposite the mentioned women. If possible he even avoids sitting at the fire in their presence, but retires into the *wę*. In cold weather he then warms himself with an apparatus consisting of embers laid on potsherds. He even likes to take his food for himself into the *wę* or, in fine weather, out on the plot (*þǫmə*). He may not approach the sleeping-place of his daughter or daughter-in-law, but if he wishes for some objects which is on or under this, some-one else must get it. If the father is not in, the women can sit where they like.

The other members of the family also have their fixed places at the hearth. The mother sits on the right of her husband, at the entrance to the *wę* and near the pan, which she watches. The sons may sit where they like, a grown-up son, however, not too near his grown-up sister. Usually he sits at the outside of the hearth, nearest to the door, so that he can rush out without any hindrance in case any wild beast should try to get into the cattle craal. During the times of the attacks of the Masai he occupied this place also on account of them. The son may sit beside his mother; he may even go into the *wę* to fetch something[1].

---

[1] A description of the different places for the members of the family is given farther on, in connexion with the account of life in the hut and the village.

If the father of a family should for once in a way go to the young people's dancing-place and take place in the dancing, and his daughter is present, he pretends not to see her. Under no circumstances may he dance with her, which is explained by the erotic excitation which is a result of the dance.

Chapter VI. **Terms of relationship.**[1]

It is now generally recognized that a knowledge of the natives' method of indicating the conditions of their relationship is
of great importance for obtaining a clearer conception of their
social organization. For this reason the author gives here the
terms of relationship which he came across in his daily intercourse with the Akamba. Unfortunately I must content myself
with noting them; the lack of access to literature prevents a
closer analysis. It may be mentioned, however, that several of
these terms occur also in the Kikuyu language (according to
McGregor's vocabulary). No resemblance to those used by the
Masai (given by Merker) is to be found.

Note the many terms with possessive suffixes in the following
list. They are never used without such a possessive.

Father: small children say *nau*, sometimes *tata*. The father
of another child is *au* 'your father'.

Elder children and grown-up persons say *aṣa* 'my father'. *ṛpɔ*
is the father of another person: *ṛpɔ wa kɪlonžo* 'Kilonzos father'.

Mother: a male calls the mother *mwaɪtu* 'our mother' (evidently a possessive), plur. *mwaɪtu*. A female says *ɪnṭa*, *ṭa*, which
also means the mother of another person. *mwænṭu* (possessive)
'Your mother'. Small children sometimes call the mother *nɑna*.
More seldom *nuḵwɔ* is used for 'mother'.

(My) brother: *mwɑnaaṭa* 'the child of my mother'; (my) half-
brother: *mwɑnaaṣa* 'the child of my father';
the brother of another person: *mwɑna·æp̄ɔ* 'the child of the
father'.

---

[1] Cf. B r u t z e r, Handbuch der Kamba-sprache, p. 74.

Sister: *mwɪtuaɹa* 'the girl (or daughter) of my mother'.

Half-sister: *mwɪtu-aṣa* 'the girl of my father'.

The sister of another person: *mwɪtu(wa)ɪnɹa* 'the girl of the mother'.

My elder brother or sister: *mukuwa* 〕

Your   »   »   »   »   *mukuu*   〉 only used as possessives

His   »   »   »   »   *mukuə*   〕 (from the root -*ku* 'old').

The eldest   one of the brothers and sisters *ɪkɪβaβɪ*,

The youngest » » »   »   »   » *ɪlumaɹta*.

My younger brother or sister: *mwɪnawa* 〕

Your   »   »   »   »   *mwɪnau*   〉 only used as possessives.

His   »   »   »   »   *mwɪnaə*   〕

The diminutive forms, *kalɪnawa, kalɪnau* etc., are also used.

mwana-nɹukwə 'child of the mother' (cf. above) is sometimes used for brother or sister.

mwana wa mwaɪtu, 'the child of our mother' is also used for 'my brother' or 'my sister'.

Husband: *mwɪmæwa* or *mutumɪa wakwa* (*mutumɪa* 'old man') 'my husband', *mwɪmæú* 'your husband'. The terms are only used in these possessive forms. As a woman is not allowed to pronounce the name of her husband she will often, if she has to refer to him, call him »the father of So-and-So»: *ɪβə wa mulɪ,* 'the father of Muli'.

Wife: *muka (w)akwa, mukakwa* 'my woman'; *kɪɓœtɪ kɹakwa, kɪwandu*[1] *kɹakwa* 'my wife'.

Grandfather: *uma, umau wakwa* 'my grandfather'; *umau, umaə* 'your, his grandfather' — possessive forms.

Grandmother: *susu, usu. usúə* 'his grandmother'.

Grandchild: *nɹ̌ukulu; musukua, musuku, musukuə* 'my, your, his grandchild' — possessives.

Uncle, paternal: *mwændwaṣa* 'my uncle'. *mwændwau* 'your uncle' (< *au* 'your father'), pl. *amwændwau.* — *mwændwɪβə* is the uncle of another person[2].

Uncle, maternal: *mama, mwɪɓaú, ɪnaemɪú.* The maternal uncle of another person: *ɪnaumə* (cf. *ɪnɹa* 'mother', -*umə* 'male').

----

[1] This word is heard rather seldom and is only used to address elder wives.

[2] Is this connected with the verb *ænda* 'to love'?

Aunt maternal: *mwænd̦a* (> *ṇa* 'mother'?), pl. *mwænd̦a, am-wænd̦a; mwændwa-n̦uk̦wə, mwændwa-ṇn̦a* (cf. mother)[1].

Aunt paternal: *mwændwaṇ?*

Cousin: *mwɪɓạwa* 'my cousin', pl. *æɓạwa.* — *mwɪɓaú* 'your cousin' etz. (possessive forms).

Nephew, niece: vide »cousin».

Father-in-law, mother-in-law, elder sister of the wife: *mu-poṇɪ, mupoṇwa, mupoṇu, mupoṇɪ* 'my, your, his father-in-law' etc. The father-in-law of my child: *sṇtawa. sṇtaú* is 'the father-in-law of your child' (possessives).

Younger sister of the wife: *mwạmwa, mwamṇ. mwạmwə* 'my, your, his sister-in-law' (possessives).

A married woman calls the elder brother of her husband *ukulu* or *mukuə waɪtu* 'our elder brother' (cf. »elder brother»). She also calls him *aṣa* or *aṣa munṇnɪ* 'my little father', in distinction from the head of the family. His wife as well as her mother-in-law she calls *mwaɪtu* or *ṇn̦a* 'mother' The elder sister of her husband she calls *ukulu*.

The prefix *g̦a-*: a young wife who has not yet a child is often called after her father *g̦a-g̦gan̦a* 'the child of So-and-So'. *g̦a-kɪọko* 'the child of K.' The prefix which occurs in several Bantu dialects[2] is no doubt a derivative of some older form of the verb *sʮa* 'to bear' (cf. the Tete-dialect at the Sambezi River *nya*).

The prefix *sʮo* (< *sʮạ* 'to bear'): a married woman is often called after her first child *sʮo-g̦gan̦a* 'the mother of So-and-So'. *sʮo-mṇlɪ* is 'the mother of Muli'. If the other wives of her husband may not mention her name they often address her in this way.

* * *

Almost all terms of relationship may be used as greetings: *mupoṇwa!* Answer: *mupoṇwa* (my *mupoṇɪ*).

Cousins greet each other with: *mwɪɓaú* or *ṇnaɪmɪú* or *ṇɪmɪu-ɓawa.* Answer: *ṇɪ mama* (cf. the maternal uncle). Cousins who are children of two sisters say: *wa mwænd̦a!* Answer: *wa mwæ-*

---

[1] Is this connected with the verb *ænda* 'to love'?

[2] See v. d. Mohl, Praktische Grammatik der Bantu-sprache von Tete, Mitteil. des Seminars für Afrikan. Sprachen, VII: 3, p. 56, and P. G. Adams, Die Sprache der Banôhô, ibidem X: 3, p. 39.

ndɨa! umau! — umau! is used as a greeting between grandchildren (cf. grandfather).

Parents-in-law greet each other with: *sɨtɑwa — sɨtɑwa.*

Chapter VII. **Death.**

1. **Burial.**

A burial and all the ritual connected with a death can only be carried out by old men, *atumìa*, who are quite conversant with all the customs of the tribe. When a man lies at the point of death, some *atumìa* are summoned to watch the dying man during his last hours, and especially to prevent the rats from touching him, in the event of his dying during the night. They take up their positions, one at his head, one at his feet, and one on each side of him. If the rats succeed in getting at him, even in touching him but slightly, another death will shortly occur in the village. If however, it does happen that the rats gnaw the corpse, a piece of mutton is damped with the juice of a certain tree, and laid on the place. The old watchers are not particularly awed by the vicinity of death; they wile away the time with noisy chatter, and help themselves to snuff from the dying man's snuff-box. The women, on the other hand, really mourn, and their lamentations are audible far and wide. For from two to five days they do no work in the fields, and on the day the death takes place they eat nothing. It is usually considered unbecoming for a man to show his feelings, but even a man may be seen to weep.

After death has supervened, the old men go to dig the grave, which is made in the neighbourhood of the hut. They often quarrel over it and try to get out of the work, especially if the ground is hard. Nor is the hole dug very deep, they content themselves with making it just deep enough to prevent the body being scraped up by hyenas. The minimum depth may perhaps be set at one meter. They first dig straight down and then out at the sides, so that a round hole is made. The corpse is then laid on a bier of sticks and carried out by two *atumìa*. One man steps down into the hole to receive the body and lay it in the round cavity. Immediately after death, and before the limbs have had time to stiffen, they are bent up towards the body, a custom which is very prevalent among Bantu peoples, and general among more primitive nations[1]. The dead man is laid upon his right side, with his head resting upon his hand, as though he were sleeping. A woman is laid in the same manner, but on the left side[2]. The face is turned to the east or the west. The body is naked, except for a piece of cloth or an old blanket over the head, to keep the earth from the face. None of the belongings of the deceased are placed in the grave. A low mound is raised over the grave. In former times especially, they often put an earthernware vessel on the mound, to mark out the place. If the village is afterwards removed, there is nothing to prevent the place being cleared for tillage, but the mound is not touched, and stones are laid on and around it, whereby the site is more distinctly indicated. A grave is avoided after dark, for there is said to be a risk of meeting its owner.

In Ulu it is customary, before the *atumɪa* begin to dig, for the grandson (son's son) of the deceased, if he has one (however young he may be), to turn the first sod with a grave stake. If the grandson is only a baby, a little stick is placed in his hand, and he scratches up a little earth. This is called *bululɪlẓa*. The

---

[1] Cf. R. Andree, Ethnologische Betrachtungen über Höckerbestattung. Andree here gives a survey of the spread of this method of burial among living as well as prehistoric peoples, and reviews the different hypotheses as to the origin of the custom.

[2] This method of burial, with the head on the hand, must be a very old custom, if any conclusion can be drawn from the language and the natives' own statements. For the Akamba assert that it is from this method of burial that the local expressions for »on the right hand»: *kwoko kwa aumə* = 'the men's hand', »on the left hand»: *kwoko kwa aka* = 'the women's hand', are derived. Probably this is a secondary interpretation, and the right hand is probably called »the men's hand» on account of its superiority over the left. I may mention in this connexion that Miss A. Werner, after investigations into 37 Bantu languages, discovered that the right hand is often called »the male hand», and sometimes »the strong hand», &c. The left is sometimes, though not so often, called »the female hand» and also »the inferior hand». See A. Werner, Notes on the Terms used for »right hand» and »left hand» in the Bantu Languages, p. 112. This paper has been supplemented, as far as the Congo languages are concerned, by Stapleton, Journ. Afr. Society 1904, p. 431.

mportance of the act is shown by the fact that the person concerned receives a cow, which is given by the father's (or grandfather's) married sister.

Only the *atumia* may be present at a burial, and only they
may touch a dead body. For others it is taboo, and to violate
this brings on the disease called *pabu;* but the old men who
have carried out the burial need not be purified[1]. They must
then perform a ritualistic sweeping of the hut where the man
died, a cleansing process which may not be performed by women.
In payment for their services they receive a goat, which is killed
and eaten on the spot.

The prohibition for persons, who are not entitled to do so, to
touch a corpse, also extends to parts of the skeleton. Originally
the prohibition seems only to have applied to deceased members
of the same clan, but since it was impossible to be certain of this,
the prohibition has been extended to embrace the whole people.
A concrete example of this dread of touching a corpse is afforded
by the following incident. During my visit to Ikutha, I had one
day collected some skulls in a sack, and ordered my servant Kioko,
a man of about thirty years of age, to carry the sack to the camp.
He dared not refuse, but immediately afterwards came and asked
permission to return to his home, about five days' march distant,
to be purified. And yet he had not come into direct contact with
a single skull, but had only carried the sack. I could not do
without him then, but later on, when he had an opportunity of
undergoing purification, I was obliged to present the necessary goat.
On the other hand, even a young person may touch a dead person of another tribe than his, or her, own. Another case which
was related to me in Machakos is the following. A youth who
was out hunting shot an arrow, which hit a corpse. For this his
father was fined five cows, and the boy had to be purified.

A married woman is buried in the cattle-craal, *nǯa,* if the husband has no other hut but hers. If he has, she is buried in her
hut. It does not matter if a man dies indoors, but when a woman
dies in her hut, it is shut up. All serviceable domestic implements
are first removed, and then the hut is allowed to fall into decay.
This takes place quickly enough, and in a few years nothing

---

[1] This is contrary to the custom in, for example, Tonga, Portuguese
East Africa. See H. Junod p. 143.

remains but a heap of sticks. Sometimes the hut is burnt, but
this is not necessary. A hut thus deserted on account of a
death is called *ṃbea*. The reason for this custom is that a
woman's soul or spirit, *kịu*, is thought to return to the scene
of her activities during life, and therefore there would be no peace
for the survivors in such a hut. The husband would never be
able to persuade another woman to move into it. According to
the natives' own account, the reason why a woman is so attached
to her hut is that the roofing of the hut is her own work. The
wife and not the husband is looked upon as the owner of the
hut. But if a wife has been in due order separated from her husband, and subsequently dies somewhere else, it is not necessary
for a hut built by her to be shut up. Her late husband has no
longer anything to do with her.

When a married woman dies, her children are given to another
wife, as well as her calves and goats. A woman is buried naked
too, but her ornaments are not taken off until she is lying in the
grave; the other women say that they could not bear to see her
deprived of these things.

Little children are not buried by *atumịa*, but by old women.
When a child dies so young that it has not had the two middle
front teeth in the lower jaw knocked out, the *atumịa* do it after
death [1], for it is considered that no one ought to have all his teeth
left when he dies. When a child dies, its parents must, according
to general rule, have ritual coition. But if a man has two wives,
and, for example, one of the »little» wife's children dies, then the
man may not personally perform the ceremony with her, if the
»big» wife has not yet lost a child. He must then employ another
man, or the »big» wife will contract *pabu*, a ceremonial disease
which I shall describe in another part of this monograph.

The above remarks apply chiefly to the region of Machakos,
Western Ukamba. In the eastern part of the country, the customs
are somewhat different, the dead are often not buried, but dragged
out into the bush and left to the hyenas. This applies especially to women, younger men, and children. The latter particularly,
I believe, are after death regarded as impotent for good or ill,
just as they have been during life, and consequently it is no use

---

[1] The Akamba sharpen from 2 to 6 teeth in the upper jaw and
knock out the two middle ones in the lower jaw.

roubling oneself with them. It seems as though the custom over he whole of Ukamba was originally to throw out all except a *nutumia* and his first wife (the »big» wife)[1]. This practice was also found formerly in the Machakos region, but nowadays even ittle children are buried there. The explanation may perhaps be ound in the fact that the population is so much denser and vegetation sparser in those tracts, so that there are not such suitable hickets to place the dead in as there are further to the east. Even around Kitui, practically everybody is buried, even little children, while in Ikutha, further to the south, throwing-out is extensively practised (Hofmann). According to Säuberlich, economic considerations also play a rôle in the method of burial, since some people are not in a position to pay the *atumia* for their work in digging the grave.

Finally, individual differences in funerals, burial, or laying out he body, occur all over the country. Thus, if several persons die at the same time in a village, the occurrence is readily ascribed to the method of burial then in vogue, and a change is made. If up to that time the bodies have been buried, they are subsequently thrown out, and vice versa.

According to Hofmann, the mortally sick are sometimes carried out into the thicket, where they are left to die. A fire is made, and the sick person is placed beside it with some food, and left. This practice seems, however, to be only exceptional; I, at least, have never heard of it in the region of Machakos, in spite of careful enquiry; but it occurs in the Kikuyu country. Another difference between the Machakos district and Eastern Ukamba is that, in the last-named country, they let the dead have some of their possessions with them in the grave; the man especially his beloved snuff-box, *kiangi*, and perhaps also his bow and arrows; the woman her grinding stones, the household implements she has used most, &c. In a *mbea* the owner's household chattels are not taken, but left as they were when she used them last. Her stool stands at the hearth, the pot over its three stones, the grinding stones lie in their places, &c.

I have a note of the following practice from Kikumbuliu, the

---

[1] The theory that throwing-out was the earliest practice seems to be supported by the custom of throwing out a stick, mentioned below.

south-eastern part of the country, more exactly the district o
Kibwezi.

All married people are buried in the cattle-craals, others are
thrown out. The dead are laid in their graves on their sleep
ing-skins, *ndawa* (on every bed there are two skins, one for the
husband, and one for the wife). Ornaments and personal house
hold appliances, but not a man's weapons, are thrown away, o
broken up and laid in the grave. Before this is filled in, the eldes
son and heir goes to the edge of the grave, and scrapes down a
little earth with his foot. As a protection against hyenas, large
pieces of wood are often laid on the grave, and goat-dropping
(*mbivi*) on these[1].

2. Purification after a death.

Before the *atumia* who have had charge of the burial have
completed their task, and before they go away, they prescribe fo
the inhabitants of the village their rules of conduct; no one may
have sexual intercourse until the village has been purified. All the
inhabitants have become unclean on account of the death, and anyone
who offends against the directions given, contracts *pabu*, a disease
which often overtakes just the person who has become ceremo
nially unclean. The purification is performed by an old man (*mu
tumia wa makwa*) who is specially versed in such matters, and it may
not be undertaken by anyone and everyone. As this ceremony o
purification is one of the most usual of its kind, and is also per
formed on other occasions when purification is necessary, we wil
describe it here. It is carried out in the following manner: The
old man who is performing the rite, slaughters a goat, which is
consecrated by being given some purifying medium (*ŋondu*) to
drink[2]. The idea is probably that the animal must be purified be
fore it can be used. The contents (*muɲo*) of the small stomach

---

[1] This agrees substantially with Brutzer's description of the Akamba
living in Rabai, in the hinterland of Mombasa. E. Brutzer, Der Geis
terglaube bei den Kamba, p. 4.

[2] A very common species of Solanum with yellow round fruit
found in East Africa, is called *ŋgondu*, and this is undoubtedly wha
led Hobley to state, incorrectly, that this fruit »plays an important part»
in purifying medicines. Hobley, A-Kamba, p. 67.

which is called *kɩpatɩa*, are taken out and mixed in a calabash
with *ɣondu* (certain sorts of plants)[1]. Those present all sit on
their hams in a circle, and the old man first sprinkles them with
the mixture, and then the walls and the bed in the hut where the
death took place. There is not any fixed day for this purification,
but people are naturally anxious to get it over as soon as possible.

An important essential in the process of purification still remains to be carried out, before life in the village can return to
normal conditions: the widow must sleep with the dead man's
brother or successor, as her husband; or, if he has no brother,
with a *mutumɩa* among the dead man's relations. This is called
kuseubɩa kɩbɩetɩ 'to purify the wife'. If there are several widows,
the »big» wife only need undergo this ceremony. When a woman
dies, the husband must purify himself with one of his other wives;
and if he has no other wives, he must find another woman whose
husband has recently died. When a child dies, the parents must
have coition.

There is no time specially fixed for the carrying out of these
purifications. As is evident from what has been said above, they
cannot be performed if the owner of the village is away. If some
other member of the family is not present when the death takes place,
a stick of the length of the dead man is taken and kept in the
hut where the death took place, until the absent one returns; then
it is given to him with words something to the following effect:
»This is N. N., who died while you were away». The stick is
then carried out of the village and thrown away — in a way a
second and fictitious burial. Although the new-comer was away
when the death took place, and the village has been purified since
then, he is also obliged to undergo the purification, before he can
enter it[2].

During the time which elapses between the death and the
purification, the village is naturally not visited by anyone. Even
inanimate objects are not taken into it. Formerly, when the natives

---

[1] Among many other East African peoples (e. g. among the Wataveta at Kilimandjaro) the contents of the stomach play an important
part in the rites of purification. The stomach is called *kitasra* in Taveta language.

[2] Cf. Hobley, Further researches into Kikuyu and Kamba Beliefs and Customs, p. 422.

went out on a plundering expedition, the stolen cattle were kept
in another place until the purification had been carried out, and
even then, for safety's sake, the cattle were often sprinkled with
ɡondu, before they were taken into the village.

When a man who has a married daughter dies, the son-in-law
is callad *mwɪtu* 'girl, daughter', for a time, because he has taken
the daughter of the deceased as his wife. The latter ought not, of
course, to visit her father's village before the purification has been
carried out, and she may on no account taste any food there;
she would then become unclean, and if she returned to her husband and had intercourse with him, it would be calamitous for
them. Thus a dead man's village ought not to be visited, and
to eat there is absolutely forbidden.

After the rites of purification following on the death of a
rich man have been performed, it is at times customary to kill
an ox, the blood of which, together with beer and the *muɟo* mentioned above, is poured out over the grave. This is an offering
which is thought to flow down to the dead man, and a prayer to
the following effect is directed to him: »We give you this, may
you bring luck to the village and our cattle!»

A widower may not shave his head till the consequences of
the death are removed by sprinkling with *ɡondu* and the subsequent coition[1]. In the same way a widow must let her hair grow
until the brother-in-law has had intercourse with her or with the
»big» wife, if there are several widows. No outward sign of mourn-
ing is borne — it may happen that the woman cease their
work in the fields for a day or two. In olden times in Machakos,
when the corpses were customarily thrown out, their heads were
shaved, »so that the hyenas could not so easily drag them away».
It was not, however, considered quite right to do this, and it was
not done in the village, but at the place where the corpse was
left. It ought not to be done before towards sundown.

---

[1] The Akamba's style of hair-dressing is very varied. Thus many
go periodically with their heads shaven, and then let the hair grow again.

P. II

SOCIOLOGY

Chapter VIII. **The Clan system and Totemism.**

By the term clan, we here mean a part of a tribe, the members of which are related or in some other way connected by means of a common bond. Apart from the belief in common descent from a real or mythical ancestor, the most common type of such a uniting bond is a common totem. As is well known, by a totem is meant some animal, or less often some plant or inanimate object, which is thought to stand in a certain relationship to a certain group of individuals. As to the relations between the individuals and their totem-animal, the following features may be considered to be of general occurrence:

1) The totem applies to a certain group of individuals (a clan), between whom marriage is forbidden.

2) These individuals believe that they are in some way akin to the totem, often that they are descended from it.

3) There exists a mystic bond between the individual and his totem-animal. He believes that in the hour of need his totem will protect and help him, and he always exhibits a certain reverence for it. This reverence is generally so shown that he will not injure his totem in any way, will not kill it, eat its flesh, and so on. We shall find from what follows that the general definition of the terms »clan» and »totem» given here is entirely appropriate in the case of the Kamba people[1].

---

[1] The strongly totemistic clans that are encountered among the Akamba are not a peculiarity of this people. On the contrary, totemism is met with in its characteristic form in many tribes wherever the Bantu peoples are found. For a comparative study of Bantu-totemism, see van Gennep's excellent bibliography in »Religions, Moeurs et Légendes» II, p. 62. Brief information about totemism in German East Africa may be found here and there in Zeitschrift f. Rechtswissenschaft, e. g. in vol. XXI, p. 358 (1908), vol. XXIII, p. 209 (1909).

1. The Kamba clans and their totems.

In Kikamba the word for clan is *mbaị*, which is also used for
»tribe, people, race, family», in extended meaning (see further below). I have been able to make a list of 25 chief clans, and it
is not unlikely that there are more. Many of these clans fall into
sub-clans [1]. I append the list of the clans I have found (see p.
136), most of which seem to be named after the ancestor, his
origin, or his employment. Thus, for example, the clan *mba-æpaŋga*
(from *mupaŋga* 'sand'), the founder of which is said to have been
a smith and to have collected iron from the sands of the rivers
(*mba* is a prefix indicating plurality, collectiveness; *mba-æpaŋga*
are 'all the members of the *æpaŋga* clan' collectively; *anakǝ* 'young
men', *mba-anakǝ* 'all the young men' collectively; *atumıa* 'elderly
men', *mba-atumıa* 'all the elderly men', and so on). On the other
hand, this prefix cannot be used with the name of a tribe; one
could not employ the combination *mba-akamba,* for example. The
same prefix with a collective force is met with in other Bantu languages. To mention a Swedish author in the same field, the missionary K. E. Laman records the same prefix with the same signification in his Congo grammar: *mindele* 'white men', *mba-mindele*
'the whites, Europeans' [2]. To return to the question of the meanings of clan-names in Kikamba, we have further, for example, the
clan of *atw* 'smiths', the founder of which clan is also said to have
been a smith. But the members of this clan are not still smiths,
nor is there any special smith-caste among the Kamba people. Another clan is that of the *amwıŋ* or *amwæị;* the founder is said to
have borne the name of *mwæị* ('moon') because he was born at
full moon. In one or two cases, I have found clans with two different names, but the names were synonymous.

The members of a clan do not live in the same place, but

The only connected and comparative work on African totemism is,
however, Ankermann's Verbreitung und Formen des Totemismus in
Afrika in Zeitschrift f. Ethnologie, 1915, in which A. has collected
information from the literature which appeared after Frazer's Totemism
and Exogamy (1910) and also offers views on the problem of totemism in General.

[1] Although the Akamba reckon descent through males, I employ
the term clan and not gens.

[2] K. E. Laman, Lärobok i Kongospråket, p. 36.

are spread over the whole area occupied by the tribe. Thus I
have met with several thousands of the clan *æombɔ;* but then this
clan is one of the largest. On the other hand, smaller clans will
be found limited to a less extended area. Those belonging to the
kana clan live in Mumomi, the most northerly part of Ukamba,
and in the region of Kitui, but when I asked about the clan in
other parts of the country, they did not even know it by name; which
is not surprising, when one considers how a clan is formed. For
the clan system does not seem to be by any means an antiquated
institution, but is still vigorous, and new clans often spring up.
When a man has many descendants, it is very common to employ
the prefix *mba-* in speaking of them: *mba-mbota* 'Mbota's clan'.
Thus the words *mbaɪ* and *mba* are also used in the sense of »family», and it is often difficult to understand, when a person speaks
of his *mbaɪ*, whether he means clan or large family (»grossfamilie»),
to which are often reckoned married sons with their wives and
children, or family in the ordinary sense. Thus a new clan arises
by degrees — in this case a sub-clan of Mbota's own clan. Quite
independent clans readily come into existence also. Marriage within
the same clan is, of course, forbidden, and if a man should take a
wife from the same clan, they are at once separated from the clan,
and so they become the founders of a new one.

Among twenty-five of the chief clans, I have found 19 totems,
but for several I have not been able to find the totems, though such
presumably exist. The may, however, also have been forgotten and
have then disappeared. As is to be expected in the case of a people
that is practically certain to have originated from a hunting tribe,
most of the totems of the Akamba originate from the animal kingdom. Of these totems there are two each possessed by two clans
in common: there are two lion clans and two hawk clans. On the
other hand, there is one clan, the clan *anðunžu,* which has two
totem-animals, the porcupine and the bat. Generally, however,
when a clan has two totems, one of them is of lesser importance,
for which reason it is called the sub-totem. Unfortunately I have
not been able to make out the connection between the porcupine
and the bat as totem-animals for the clan *anðunžu,* but it appears
that the bat is only the totem of certain families within the clan.
From the list on p. 136 it will further be seen that several clans
contain a number of sub-clans.

It may be mentioned, in passing, that I was in Ukamba for over eight months without finding the least traces of the totem system. These matters are so obvious and self-evident for the natives themselves that, even when they are talking about the clan system in other connections, it never occurs to them to mention the totem system, which is such an interesting field for the investigator. It was due to quite a chance circumstance that I discovered it, though I had long been fully convinced of its existence. I did not know how to set about making enquiries about it. There is no special word in the Kamba language for totem; Anckerman also shows, that such a word has not been found anywhere in Africa. The Akamba say *nîamu* 'animal', and when anyone wishes to know to which clan another belongs, he says, *nîamu îaku nî îau?* 'Which is your animal?' or else *mbaî îaku nî îau?* 'Which is your clan?'

Hobley incorrectly renders totem with *kîndu kîpuku* or *upuku* 'forbidden thing', more exactly and literally 'something bad, injurious'. Without doubt he has been led to this erroneous conclusion by the fact that, when one asks a native why he does not eat his totem, the invariable reply is *nî upuku* or *nî kîndu kîpuku* 'It is injurious', by which he refers to the results of such a violation of the totem.

Clan animals: the lion, the hyena, the bushbuck, the long-tailed monkey (Cercopithecus), the baboon, the jackal, the leopard, the bat, the crow, the hawk, the vulture, the green parrot, and a small black bird with a forked tail, called *kîndalî* [1]. Curiously enough, neither the elephant, the rhinoceros, the giraffe, nor the crocodile, appear as totem-animals. It is not surprising that the hippopotamus is not taken as a totem, since it is not found in the country at present inhabited by the tribe, viz. Ukamba. Yet it lives in the Tana river.

According to what the natives say, there is on the mountain Kivauni, west of Athi, a clan that does not kill a certain sort of snake, but I have never come across them. There is only one instance of a totem being taken from the vegetable kingdom, and that is the wild fig-tree, *mumo*, the totem of the *amumonî* clan. I have only discovered one totem chosen from inanimate ob-

---

[1] By the kindness of Prof. E. Lönnberg, I am able to identify this bird as probably being the drongo (Dicrurus).

jects, namely *kılea* 'sand containing iron', which is the totem of the above-mentioned clan *æpaŋga*, the founder of which was a smith.

I have no record of any totem for the *amwæ̧*, but it is clear that the moon (*mıwæ̧*) stands in some sort of connection with the clan (cf. p. 124)[1]. It is very rare to find heavenly bodies as totems. Frazer cites only two cases of the moon being taken as totem, both from India[2].

Besides its proper name, a clan is as often referred to by the name of its totem: the *ası̧* are also called *ɱba-muņ̣ambu* 'the clan of the lion'; the *awını* are called *ɱba-mbıtı* 'the clan of the hyena', and so on.

What Frazer calls »individual totems» are not found among the Akamba, nor totems for the different sexes.

2. The relations between a person and his totem.

(The religious side of the totem system.)

For lack of a better term, I here use (after Frazer and others) the expression »the religious side of totemism», though I shall endeavour to show that the totem system of the Akamba can scarcely be said to contain any religious elements. The question certainly depends very much upon how the conception »religion» is defined (for it is by no means clear what really belongs to religion), but it would seem that in general the religious rôle of totemism has been greatly exaggerated, a circumstance that has, indeed, been pointed out by many investigators. Frazer says that the religious side of totemism »consists of the relations of mutual respect and protection between a man and his totem». But »mutual respect and protection» may also be said to be characteristic of the relations between members of the same clan, though there is no temptation on this account to maintain that there is anything religious in such relations. And, furthermore, the most usual form of worship among primitive peoples is the offer of sacrifices, but the Akamba never

---

[1] Hobley (Akamba p. 4) states that their totem is »all dead animals» I never heard of this.
[2] Cf. Frazer, Totemism and Exogamy.

sacrifice to their totems. Indeed, it has not been possible to prove that any Bantu peoples offer sacrifices to their totems [1].

I shall now proceed to describe more in detail what I have ascertained as to the relations between a person and his totem among the Akamba. The members of a clan are considered to possess the characteristic qualities of the totem animal, and sometimes also other of its peculiarities. According to the natives' account, the lion does not eat livers, but leaves those organs untouched after a kill. Hence those belonging to the lion clan (*mbaasị*) do not eat livers, and will not even touch them, but use sticks to remove them, when animals are slaughtered. Otherwise, the result is an affection of the eyes. The prohibition against liver goes to such lengths that, for example, if anyone is roasting liver during a hunt, and the wind carries the smoke to the place where a man of the *asị* clan is roasting other meat, this meat thereby becomes unclean, and he can not eat it.

The members of the lion clan are as courageous and spirited as the lion itself in fight, when an attack is being made. The lion is looked upon as a particularly intelligent beast by the Akamba: »It is quite like a human being», they say. It is well-disposed towards its human kinsmen, and sometimes tries to help them. When men of this clan are out hunting and have met with no success, but have reconciled themselves to going to rest with empty stomachs, it sometimes happens that they hear the subdued roar of a lion. He has killed, and now wishes to share the prey with his relations. In full conviction of this, the men now proceed in the direction from which the roar was heard, and when the lion sees them he withdraws, »in order not to scare them». They take as much meat as they require and then go away, after which the lion returns to finish his meal.

The hyena clan (*awịmị*) is characterised by perpetual greed. If a man belonging to that clan is sitting in a company and happens to smell roasting meat, he involuntarily rises and proceeds in the direction of the meat.

Those belonging to the crow clan are very cowardly, and are always ready to take to flight, when there is a prospect of a

[1] Cf. E. Reuterskiöld, Sakramentala måltider med särskild hänsyn till totemismen, p. 62.

ight, just as a crow sitting in a tree flies away, when he sees a
hunter approaching with bow and arrows.

Members of the hawk clan are considered to be particularly
thievish, and, just as the hawk hovers in the air on the look-out
for something that he can swoop down upon — for exemple a piece
of meat outside a hut — so they sneak about prying after something
to steal. As has been mentioned, there are two hawk clans. One
is called *mba-mulela* (see list A, 8a), its members are specially
greedy for meat, and when they discover that meat is to be found
in their vicinity, they often try to steal it in the night. To this
end they have recourse to sorcery, for they can put the inhabitants
of the village from which they mean to steal into a deep sleep.
It is said that they formerly used to eat meat raw.

Normally a native may not kill his totem animal, nor eat of
its meat; nay, he may not even touch any part of it (taboo). On
one occasion I was able to turn this to good account, when I had
a new »boy» belonging to the bushbuck clan. The lock of one
of my cases had got broken, and in order to secure its contents
against any possible pilfering on the part of the youth, I laid a
piece of bushbuck's skin over the things. Every time he had to
fetch anything out of the case, he asked me to remove the skin
first. Similarly. if a man of the lion clan finds a dead lion, he
cannot take the skin. Exceptions from these general rules are,
however, to be met with, and there are individuals who kill their
totem animals without provocation — »respect for the totem lessened
or lost», as Frazer has it. Thus, one day I met a man of the
long-tailed monkey clan that had made himself a bag from the
skin of his totem animal. Those who offend in this manner,
however, are thought to bring misfortune down on themselves:
they themselves or their cattle fall sick and die, &c. Only in one
case is it permissible to kill the totem animal, namely when it is
an animal of prey and attacks a member of the clan, or his cattle.
There is, therefore, no objection to killing lions and leopards,
which steal round the villages at night, or long-tailed monkeys
and baboons, which commit damage in the fields. To the native
mind, this is exactly on a par with an offence committed by a
relative or a member of the same clan.

As an illustration of the close relations between a native and
his totem-animal, I will cite the following concrete example, which

is among my own experiences. It must not be looked upon a
an example of totemistic sacrifice.

One evening I had pitched camp on the River Athi. During
the afternoon, I had shot an antelope, and my bearers were enga
ged in stuffing themselves with great quantities of the meat. Then
we heard the repeated roars of a lion, a few hundred meters away
in the bushes. After a while, I saw that one of the bearers rose, took
a large piece of meat, and walked forth into the darkness. I was surpris
ed, and wondered what the fellow was at, for the natives are gene
rally afraid of the dark, especially when they know that there i
a lion in the vicinity. After a few minutes, the man came back
and I at once asked him what he had been doing. He answered
»You heard the lion roaring? I belong to the lion clan, and
heard a kinsman calling me. He is certainly hungry, perhaps old
and feeble, so that he can no longer kill, as of old. Is it, then
not my duty to share with him my superfluity, when I sit here
by the fire in comfort, and have more meat than I can manage
to eat?» And so, without fear of the darkness, the fellow had
wandered in the direction from which the roaring had been heard
convinced that his kinsman in the bushes would come and eat the
piece of meat he had placed out there for him.

One of the most important obligations which the members o
the same clan have towards each other is to help each other in
all straits, and this obligation holds not only between human mem
bers of a clan, but between a man and his totem-animal. I will
cite an example to the point. One afternoon I had started ou
with some Akamba to shoot guinea-fowls, when we suddenly came
across a long-tailed monkey, which had been caught in a trap. To
my surprise, one of my companions went and liberated the ani
mal, although the natives usually hate these monkeys, on account
of the damage that they do in their plantations. In reply to my
question why he had not killed such a mischievous animal, he
replied: »I belong to the clan of the long-tailed monkey, and i
was therefore my duty to help her when in distress. If I had
found her on my fields, I should certainly have killed her, but
out here in the woods she does no damage, and it is not her
fault that she got caught in the trap.»

The natives think that totem-animals help their human kins

men on occasion, as is clear from what is related above about the lion (p. 118).

The dances of the Akamba have no connection with their totem-animals. In the descriptions of the initiation ceremonies, we have seen that candidates during the ceremonies are looked upon as animals — baboons; yet I have not been able to discover that this conception has anything to do with totemism.

In this connection it may be pointed out that the totem system has nothing at all to do with the fact that several clans — or individual families within certain clans — do not eat the flesh of the bushbuck (*nðwaʐa*), although that animal is not their totem. Such a partial prohibition is, for example, laid on the *ṃba-atwi*. It is only that they are persuaded that, for some reason or other, the meat is injurious. For the same reason, certain families in the Machakos district do not eat the flesh of the hartebeeste (*ŋgondi*), and cannot be persuaded to touch the flesh of this antelope. On the other hand, the bushbuck is the totem of the *ṃba-kipumbɔ*.

3. Relations between persons of the same totem (clan).

(The social side of the totem system.)

Although, in the case of men in a primitive state of society, it is very difficult to distinguish between religious and social phenomena, yet such a division has its justification, and it must be admitted that in practical life totemism has a much greater social than religious importance. In the social sphere, the most important expressions of totemism are exogamy and the obligation of mutual help, the most pregnant expression of which is blood-vengeance.

Marriage between individuals of the same clan is strictly forbidden, even if the parties live in different parts of the country and have never heard of each other before [1]. If such a forbidden union between members of the same clan is entered into, it is a very grave crime, and the culprits must submit to a process of purification (by means of *ŋondu*), which is carried out by an old man who is specially versed in such matters. This marriage-pro-

---

[1] According to Hofmann, the Akitutu constitute an exception from the general rule, and marry within the same clan.

hibition is easily understandable, if it is remembered that a clan originally springs from one man, and consequently, from the natives' point of view, its members are near of kin. It is, however, to be observed that the usage is sometimes a little unsettled, and it may happen that a man without objection marries a girl of his own clan, if she belongs to a distant branch of the clan, with which he has nothing in common but the clan-name. In most cases, however, such marriages are contracted in ignorance of the existing kinship. If one ventured to enunciate a general rule for the case when marriage between members of the same clan might be considered permissible, it would (according to various statements obtained from natives) possibly run as follows: When parts of the same clan are so distantly related that they do not help each other in paying fines for manslaughter, marriage may take place between individual members[1].

At the dancing festivities celebrated by the young people, a young man may not dance with a girl of the same ṃbaị. This prohibition seems to be natural enough when it is remembered that the dances, which are generally celebrated at night and when the moon is full, usually end with sexual practices. Apart from this, dancing together often leads to mutual affection and marriage, which is out of the question between members of the same clan.

Exogamy is the negative aspect (the »Thou shalt not») of the social side of totemism: we now come to the positive aspect — »thou shalt». It is the absolute duty of the members of a clan to help each other in in all sorts of distress. Their most important duties are to bear their share in the raising of fines for manslaughter, and, in case of need, to revenge each other's deaths by blood-vengeance (cf. Chap. XI).

---

[1] About the relations between sub-clans and the chief clan, and between the sub-clans inter se, Hobley writes as follows (p. 64): »Now originally members of these sub-divisions were not allowed to marry, but curiously enough they could marry back into the original stock». Hobley does not give any explanation of this, and during my investigations I have not considered such a case, for which reason I shall not venture to offer any opinion. In the case of an insignificant sub-clan of ṃba-mulata-ịɓıa, however, I have recorded a statement of a single individual that members may take wives from the original stock, which seems to support Hobley's assertion.

I will cite an example of this feeling of solidarity, which is characteristic, although the cause was somewhat trivial. A man came on a visit to a place, where he happened to quarrel with another man. Some friends of the latter came up and were about to settle accounts with the stranger, but he was undismayed and shouted: »Come on then, enemies to . . . . — and here he mentioned the name of his clan — here you shall see one who is not afraid!» There was by chance among his assailants one of the same clan as the stranger, and when he heard that they were clan-kinsmen, he immediately went over to the stranger's side, and helped him against his own friends!

4. Further peculiarities of particular clans.

Among other characteristic peculiarities of particular clans, I have made a record of the following:

All the members of the *anžiu-* clan are considered to have the misfortune to possess the *kžæni*, that is to say »the evil eye». It is born with them, and they themselves have nothing to do with it. Yet it can be employed by an ill-disposed person in terrible ways. Those who belong to the clan cannot praise anything or anybody which they are looking at without its leading to misfortune for the person or thing praised. An expression of admiration of e. g. a herd of cattle is enough to bring sickness or death down upon the animals. In order to turn away ill-luck, a *mwanžiu* spits when he expresses admiration of anything. Generally speaking, spitting has a religious-magical significance among many peoples in Africa, even outside the Bantu groups.

Belief in the »evil eye» is met with, I think, all over the world, even among civilised peoples, and seems to be as old as humanity itself[1]. It is necessary, however, to distinguish between the intentional and the unintentional evil eye, with the latter of which we have to deal in our case here. In their effects both are identical.

---

[1] Cf. R. Andree, Ethnographische Parallelen und Vergleiche, p. 35. Inter alia, A. says (p. 44): »In Schotland kannte man das böse auge als The ill ee (The evil eye); man glaubte, dass es in bestimmten familien vorkomme und in diesen erblich sei. Der besitzer verwandte es gegen seine feinde, aber man konnte es auch gegen bezahlung zur rache an dritten personen verwenden».

One of the largest clans is *anžaunı*, which is specially known for its beautiful girls. There is, however, one drawback, and that is that a woman of this clan brings ill-luck on the man that makes her his wife. According to the natives' own account, it is very usual for a man who has taken a wife from this clan to die a few months later without any ostensible cause. This might lead one to think that these ill-starred girls would find it difficult to get married, but this is by no means the case; the temptation to marry them is too great, on account of the good looks they generally possess.

Further, we have *amwæι̯*, whose ancestor, as has been mentioned, is said to have been called *mwæι̯* ('moon'). They may not sweep out the hut on the last day of the month, insofar as the refuse may not be thrown out of the hut on that day, but only swept together in a heap.

Next we come to the *mba-kĭþumbə*. Their women may not make pottery, a task which otherwise falls to the lot of the women among the Akamba.

It is not seldom found that the peculiarities distinguishing certain clans are put to practical use. A task of the sun clan, among the Bechuana, is to produce sunshine on dull days. Of especial interest are the »intichiuma» ceremonies among the aborigines of Australia, by means of which the members of some animal clans think that they are able to increase the supplies of the animal which is their totem [1]. Traces of a similar utilitarian employment of a clan's members I have found in two cases among the Akamba. The above-mentioned *asι̯*, of the lion clan, can heal burns. A *musι̯* must, with an empty stomach, chew the leaves of Cajanus indicus (Kik. *musu̯*) and then smear his saliva on the burn. In this connection must be mentioned also *mba-mbua* (*mbua* = 'rain'). In times of severe drought in Ulu, it was formerly customary to sacrifice a child to the spirits (cf. Chap. XII). It is characteristic of the members of this clan that they are very fond of bathing, and are not afraid of the coldest water. When infants are washed by their mothers, they generally make grimaces, but the little *ambua* only laugh, and thoroughly enjoy themselves in the water.

---

[1] Cf. Spencer and Gillen, The Northern Tribes of Central Australia, p. 283 ff.

According to tradition, the oldest clan is *ɱba-kɪɪmu* or *ɱba-aɪmu* (*aɪmu* = 'spirits of the forefathers'), who trace their descent back to the earliest human beings. According to the myth, Mulungu, the Supreme Being, who has created all things, cast the man and woman from which the clan was descended down from heaven. They fell down on Nsaui, a rock south-east of the province of Kilungu, and the clan is called *ɱba-mulata-ɪ6ɪa* (*ɪ6ɪa* 'stone'). Another name is *ɱba-aœɪ*. Even in play, it is forbidden to take up a child of this clan in one's arms and swing it, otherwise it will immediately rise into the air and disappear.

In olden times, when a severe drought was experienced in East Ukamba, it was usual to sacrifice a child of the clan to the spirits of the forefathers [1].

Apart from the above-mentioned taboo and prohibitions, which are binding on the whole clan, there are innumerable other prohibitions, which affect perhaps only single families. Strictly speaking, these have nothing to do with the clan system, and are altogether distinct from the restrictions of totemism, but they deserve some mention in connection with a treatment of such phenomena, if only to show that, when we meet with such cases, we must not be misled into formulating from them general rules for the whole clan. I will only cite a single example. As we have seen, when a child is born in Ukamba, a great feast is held, an ox is killed, and beer-drinking is indulged in. In the Machakos district, however, there is a large family of the *ɱba-kɪpumbɔ* clan which does not observe this custom. The reason for this is simply that this family once lost three infants one after the other, which disaster was considered to be due to the observance of the custom, for which reason it was changed. As is well known, the native can extremely seldom find a natural explanation of the misfortunes which afflict him. The case is also of interest as showing how a custom can arise; for it is a fact that, in spite of the tenacity with which natives cling to tradition, changes are often made when circumstances seem to warrant it [2].

---

[1] Cf. »Religion», Chap. XII, for further particulars.

[2] According to my experience customs may be divided into three kinds: 1. those in force over the whole tribe, 2. those in force among single clans (mostly prohibitions), 3. those in force in single families (self-imposed prohibitions).

5. The admission of individuals to a clan.

A stranger can be admitted to a clan. He and the head-man
of the family to which he wishes to be admitted both strike the
so-called clan-*kɪpɪtu* (see Chap. XI: 3), promising to avenge each other's
deaths and in case of need to pay their shares of the cattle which
must be delivered by way of fine in the case of manslaughter; in
one word, to fulfill all the obligations of a member of the clan.
The new-comer now belongs as completely to the clan as if he
had been born in it, and consequently he cannot choose his wife
from among its members. In the most westerly part of Ukamba
live some Akikuyu; some of them work for wealthy Akamba,
and some have come there because they thought there were
too many white settlers in certain parts of the Kikuyu country.
Most of these strangers have gained admittance to Kamba clans.

On the other hand, it would seem that an individual cannot
be expelled from his clan; at least none of those whom I asked
about the matter knew of any case. They thought that such a
procedure would bring grave misfortunes down on the clan.

Sometimes the Akamba are heard to refer to a Kikuyu man as a
member of such and such a Kamba clan, without his having been
admitted to it. The reason for this is that some Kikuyu clans
are said to be identical with others in Ukamba. *Anɪɪru* is said to
be the same as *anẓɪu*, and to possess the same »evil eye». The
two words are, indeed, identical, but on the other hand, their
totems are different. According to Hobley, the former clan has
»the elephant and all birds», the latter a small black bird,
kɪndalɔ. The names of other Kikuyu clans given by Hobley present no resemblance to those of Kamba clans[1]. K. Dundas also
states that »many of the Kikuyu clans claim descent from certain particular tribes, thus . . . the Akkachiko and Achera from
the Kamba»[2].

---

[1] C. V. Hobley, Kikuyu medicines, p. 82.
[2] K. R. Dundas, Notes on the origin and history of the Kikuyu
and Dorobo, p. 136.

6. The taboo=ing and worship of animals of non=totemistic origin.

The confusion of totemism with animal-worship and other similar phenomena is often met with in literature dealing with such subjects [1]. »Le totemisme (sous son aspect religieux) est de la zoolâtrie; mais toute zoolâtrie n'est pas du totemisme», says van Gennep aptly.

As we shall see, animal-worship is not practised directly by the Akamba, but only indirectly. In order to avoid misunderstanding and to emphasize strongly the difference, however, it may be mentioned here, while dealing with totem animals, that there are a number of animals which, although they are not totems, may not be killed or eaten. Such animals may be divided into two groups:

1) individual animals, which are held to be reincarnations of ancestors' spirits; and

2) whole species, which, for different and often unknown reasons, have been taboo-ed.

A python (*ita*) which comes to a village is not killed, but milk is set out for it, since it is considered to bring good luck and increase to the cattle; this belief is shared by many Bantu tribes. Some Akamba do not seem to know any reason for the custom. According to others, again, the *aimu*, or spirits of departed kinsmen, sometimes take up their abode in a python or green *mamba* (*ndau*), and for this reason these snakes are not killed, when they are found in the neighbourhood of the villages. If we compare the attitude assumed towards pythons by other Bantu tribes, everything points to the fact that this is the correct explanation of the way in which they are treated. In passing, it may be pointed out that we have here an example of the fact that the origin of a custom may be forgotten, while the custom itself continues to exist. On the other hand, a python which is encountered in the woods is killed out of hand. All pythons are not inhabited

---

[1] Söderblom sums up briefly and succinctly the difference between totemism and animal-worship: »1) As a rule totemism embraces a whole species, while animal-worship is confined to a single animal. 2) The totem animal is sacred to its clan, the worshipped animal to any number of people.» N. Söderblom, Öfversikt af Allmänna religionshistorien, p. 11.

by spirits, but only those that, by going into a village, show that they indubitably take a special interest in it[1].

Tortoises (*ᶇgṵ*) are not eaten, and if a youth, for example, should eat one, his fellows sing lampoons about him, calling down curses upon him. A man who has eaten a tortoise finds it difficult to get a wife, and yet the tortoise does not seem to be regarded as an unclean animal.

What has been said about the tortoise, also applies to the porcupine (*nᶻę*), as regards some people. No doubt, this animal's peculiar covering places it in a unique position.

A general characteristic among Bantu tribes is that they do not eat fish; fish are looked upon as being akin to snakes.

The hammer-bird (Scopus umbretta) is not killed, and the natives do not even dare to climb up into the tree in which it builds its great nest. To do so would bring on the disease called *musalə*, a sort of eruption.

Various other animals are regarded in a similar light. Some are bearers of omens and are therefore not killed; chief of these is the woodpecker, *ᶇgomakomi*[2].

7. Rudiments of a matriarchal community.

Among Bantu peoples, even among tribes that reckon relationship exclusively through the male, isolated customs are met with, which suggest the matriarchal system. Probably we are here in the presence of survivals from olden times; at least there seem to be no signs of a development towards a system of mother-right, while on the other hand, there are no objections to looking upon descent through the male line as the younger system[3].

---

[1] Cf. further »Religion», Chap. XII: 1.

[2] Cf. further Chap. XIII: 6, XIV: 3 and G. Lindblom, Öfvertro och liknande föreställningar rörande djur bland Ost-Afrikas negrer, speciellt bland Kamba-stammen. In this paper, a considerable number of animals are considered. A considerable, though somewhat unsifted, mass of material for comparison is found in J. Weissenborn's Tierkult in Afrika. Although W. takes the term animal-worship in a wide meaning, yet he mentions nothing of totemism in Africa.

[3] On mother-right in Africa, see A. H. Post, Afrikanische Jurisprudenz, p. 13 ff.

Among the Akamba, I have found the following features indicative of matriarchate:

I. A man's position in respect to his mother's brother is peculiar in several respects:

a. About his relations to his mother's brother's wife and daughter see p. 95.

b. At the division of blood-money, the brother of the mother of the victim receives one cow (see Chap. XI: 1).

c. In the festivities which are celebrated in honour of a young and brave warrior, after his return from a successful expedition, the mother's brother plays an important part (see Chap. XII).

d. In Kikamba »uncle» (mother's brother) is *mama*, which word is also employed as the reply to a greeting between cousins (the children of the mother's brother).

II. If anyone happens to kill his own child, he pays damages to its mother (see Chap. XI: 1). It is unknown to me whether, in such a case, the child's uncle (mother's brother) interferes, as happens sometimes in other places.

III. If, as I think very probable, matriarchate has really once existed among the Akamba, we might, further, expect to find some traces of it in such an ancient and original institution as totemism. Indeed, I venture to believe that I have found· such traces, namely the following:

The prohibitions (taboo) which are imposed upon a certain clan, also become binding upon the man who takes his wife from that clan. Thus, if I marry a woman of *mba-asʲ*, I may no longer touch liver; if my wife is of the *amwæʲ* clan, I may not clean up the hut on the last day of the month; and so on. The prohibitions are not, however, binding on the children of the marriage; they belong to the father's clan in everything. For example, a woman of *mba-asʲ* may not eat liver, nor may her husband, but the children may do so.

8. The Clan Marks.

Clan marks are used on horned cattle, arrows, and bee-hives.

a. **Clan marks on cattle.** Such a mark is called *kʲo* (< *oa* 'to mark with the clan mark') and is branded on the animal's skin with a glowing iron. Originally these marks were certainly employed for practical purposes, to indicate ownership and prevent theft. In the old days, the Akamba were incorrigible cattle thieves, and even stole from each other. In more recent times,

Clan marks for cattle.

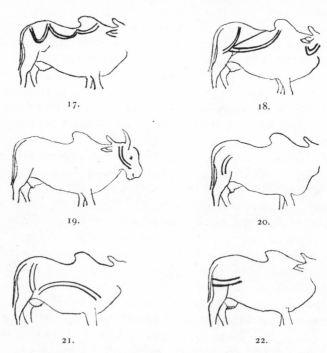

17. *œpaŋga* (1—2 sides).   18. *akıpumbə* (on both sides).
19. *anžaunı*[1].   20. *ambua*.   21. *œpaŋga* (on both sides).
22. *ataŋgwa ma mba katętı* (on both sides).

the practice seems to have improved considerably, and the natives themselves say that the reason is that times are safer. They no longer dare to steal cattle for fear of the English Government.

I employ the term »clan mark», although it would perhaps be better to say »family mark», since every head-man of a family seems to have his special mark. If the natives are asked anything

---

[1] Goats and sheep are said to be marked in the same manner. Hobley gives a great many clan marks for cattle (Akamba etc. p. 24)

about a certain mark, however, they always reply that it is a *kɪo*
for such and such a clan; so that from the mark it is possible
to see to which clan a family belongs[1]. Hence the expression
»clan mark» seems to be fully justified. Yet, great confusion
prevails concerning the use of these marks, partly because they
are no longer necessary, and partly for other reasons. For
instance, if a large number of a man's animals die without any
discoverable cause, he possibly comes to the conclusion that it is
his *kɪo* that has brought him his bad luck, for which reason he
chooses another. I have been told that he then often takes that
of his mother's family. Or he contents himself with simply making an alteration in the old one. The *ataŋgwa*, in the district of
Machakos, have two parallel curves on the animal's two sides (see
fig. 22). As, however, once upon a time many calves belonging to
one family died, their animals were marked only on one side thereaf-
ter. In many respects, these marks are becoming decorations pure
and simple, which appears from the fact that, if a man sees a *kɪo*
which appeals to him, he just imitates it. This contributes, of
course, further to increase the confusion.

Only horned cattle are marked with the *kɪo*. It is seldom
that all the animals are marked, but the proportion marked depends upon the whim of the owner[2]. As a rule, goats and sheep
are marked (cut) only on the ears, and only exceptionally in the
same way as the horned cattle.

The Masai, the Akikuyu, and the Atharaka, the Akamba's
neighbours, employ similar property-marks[3]. Probably they were

---

[1] Hobley says the same, ibid. p. 22.

[2] With regard to this point, Hobley (p. 22) makes a reservation, for
which I have found no confirmation: »Curiously enough, all the cattle
are not branded, but usually only those sent away to buy a wife with,
or those paid as blood-money for a death». On the other hand, it seems
to me quite probable that among the marked cattle are also those
used for the purposes mentioned by Hobley. In the event of their
having to be returned to the owner, the fact that they are marked
would prevent any confusion arising as to which they were.

[3] Merker, Die Massai (reproduction on plate I, p. 163): »Die
marken der rinder und esel zeigen an, zu welchem geschlecht bezw.
untergeschlecht der besitzer gehört». Routledge, The Akikuyu, p. 45:
»Each clan has its own cattle-brand». A. M. Champion, The Atharaka,
p. 88.

Clan marks on arrow heads.

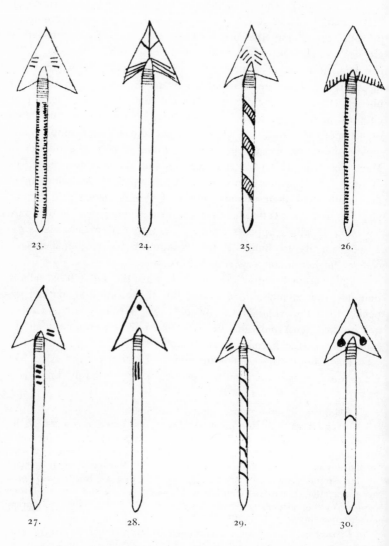

23. *ɣombə ma mba-mululu.*   24. *ɣombə ma mba-maɩ̯.*   25. Another
subclan of *ɣombə.*   26. *akɩ̯ɲumbə.*   27. *apaŋga.*   28. *anʒaum̯.*
29. *ɣ̂taŋgwa.*   30. *akɩ̯tutu.*

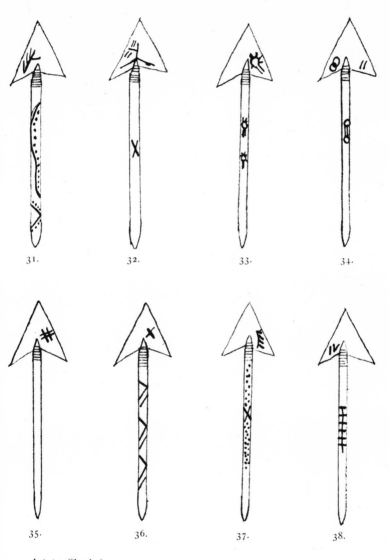

31. *akitutu* (Īkutha).   32. *amaŋlu* (see list B).   33. *asi̱*.   34. *akitondo*.
        35. *kanu̧*.   36. *amuto̧*.   37. *awini* (East Ukamba).

borrowed by the Akamba. Hobley says: »They say that the
practice of branding their cattle only dates back a generation or
two, and was copied from the Masai»[1]. I have not found anything

Clan marks on bee-hives.

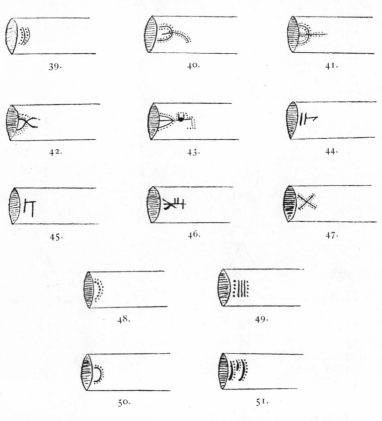

39. a(i)taŋgwa.   40. ambua.   41. anžaum.   42. amunda.
43. amutæᵢ (Kikumbuliu).   44. kana.   45. anžᵢu.
46. akᵢtondo.   47. akᵢpumbɔ.

to confirm this assertion, but I consider it very probable that the
Akamba have taken the idea of marking their cattle from the
Masai. Tradition and other circumstances point to the fact that they

[1] Hobley, Akamba, p. 22.

were originally a people of hunters, and further, according to many accounts, they got their cattle from the Masai. It is a fact, too, that, at least in the Machakos district, their cattle are for the greater part descended from cattle stolen from the Masai.

  b. **Clan marks on arrow-heads.** On arrow-heads (*ußanu*) the clan marks are scratched on the iron points themselves, besides which the small arrow-shafts have a special mark (cf. figs. 23—38). On the wooden-pointed bird arrows no marks appear. Every clan has its special mark, which, however, varies in different parts of the country. As is the case with other marks, this mark serves a practical purpose. Often they do not know each other's marks, to avoid possible imitation and consequent quarrels as to who has killed an animal. Since the natives are now forbidden to hunt the larger animals, they have no longer any reason for marking their arrows, and especially round the two government stations, the practice is rapidly disappearing. The same confusion reigns in the matter of arrow-marks as in the matter of property-marks on cattle, and here also they are nowadays often used purely as decorations. The loose little wooden shaft especially is marked largely according to taste.

  c. **The clan mark on bee-hives.** The oblong wooden cylinders which, with but slight variations in shape, are used as bee-hives over the whole of East Africa, are marked at one end with the owner's mark. Even within the same clan, each owner has his special mark (see figs. 39—51), for which reason these marks cannot exactly be called clan marks. These marks are sometimes scratched in with a knife and sometimes branded on with a glowing iron.

  Finally, I will add that **earthenware vessels** are also marked. These marks, however, have nothing to do with the property-marks; they are a sort of manufacturer's mark, and are put on by the women who make the vessels. All Kamba women are not experts at pottery-work.

  If we compare the three different sorts of marks — those on cattle, those on arrows, and those on bee-hives — we find that they do not seem to present any definite likeness to each other. According to the accounts of some, which I mention with reserve, cattle and bee-hives originally had the same

9 List of clans and their totems

A. Machakos

Clan	Totem
1. *aɪ̯eni*[1], sg. *muɪ̯eni*	
2. *anžauni*, sg. *munžauni*	The jackal (*mbɪ̯wa*)
3. *anžiu*, sg. *munžiu*	The *kɪndalɪ* bird (Dicrurus)
4. *awɪnɪ*	The hyena (*mbɪtɪ*)
5. *ʿombɔ*, sg. *mɪ̯ɪ̯ombɔ*	The long-tailed monkey (*ŋgɪma*)
a) *ʿombɔ ma mba-maɪ*	
b) » » » -*mululu*	
6. *akɪ̯pumbɔ* or *akɪmɪ̯*	The bushbuck (*nδwaɪ̯a*)
7. { *apaŋga* or { *ʿpaŋga*, sg. *muɪ̯paŋga*	Sand containing iron (*kɪlea*)
8. *ʿtaŋgwa*, sg. *muɪtaŋgwa*	The baboon (*ŋgulɪ* or *ɪ̯laɪ̯*)
a) *ataŋgwa ma mba mulela* eller *mba ŋguŋguu*	The hawk (*mbulusɪ̯a*)
b) *ataŋgwa ma mba katetɪ*	
c) » » » *mupæk)*	
d) » » » *mukuba*	
9. *asɪ̯*, sg. *musɪ̯*	The lion (*munɪ̯ambu*)
10. *amuɪ̯*	» »
11. *akɪtutu*	The hawk (*mbulusɪ̯a*)
12. *atwɪ*, sg. *mutwɪ*	
13. *amwɪ̯* or *amɪ̯wæɪ̯*	
14. *akɪtondo*	The crow (*ŋguŋguu*)
a) *akɪtondo ma mba mbulɪ*	
b) » » » *nδɪmba*	
15. *amumonɪ*	The wild fig-tree (*mu̯mo*)
16. *ambua*, sg. *mumbua*	
17. *akɪtuo*	
18. { *ʿwanɪ* or { *ʿwanɪ*, sg. *muɪwanɪ*	} The leopard (*ŋgo*)
19. *amunda*, sg. *mumunda*	
a) *mba-muŋeɪ̯a*	
b) *mba-nžalu*	
20. *amutɪ*	
21. *amutæɪ̯*	The secretary bird (*ndeɪ*)
22. *aæɪ̯* or *mba-mulata-ɪ̯bɪa* or *mba-kɪɪmu* or *mba-anžɪkwa*	
23. *anδunδu*	Porcupine (*nže*) and bat (*ubuɓu*)

---

[1] *aɪ̯eni* is the clan's name = *mba-aɪ̯eni; anžauni* or *mba-anžauni* &c.

collected by the author.
district.

Remarks

The founder of the tribe is said to have come from the steppe
in the west (*wʋ̣eni* 'on the steppe').
Very large clan.
Large clan; the name from adj.-root -*zu* ('black'), in the n-class *nɩu*.

Originally from Kilungu.   Large clan.

Founder of the clan called *kʋpumbə*.
Founder of the clan was a smith, he got iron from the sands of the
rivers (magnetite), cf. *mupaŋga* 'sand'.

From *lela* 'to hover in the air like a bird in search of prey'.

From *mukuɓa* 'nail'.
Do not eat liver.

Nearly related to the above.
mutwɩ 'smith'.   Founder a smith.
mwæ̣ 'moon'; name of the founder, who was born at full moon.

ɱbulɩ, more usually *ɱbuɩ* 'goat'.

< *muɱo* 'wild fig-tree'. Formerly the same family as nr. 6. Foun-
der born at the foot of such a tree, therefore called *muɱo*.
< *ɱbua* 'rain'.
< *kʋtuo* 'shoulder'.

< *mwɩwa* 'thorn'.
Cf. *munda* 'tilled field'.

amutæ̣ from *ɲdeʋ* (root -*teɩ*).
Cf. *aɩmu* 'forefather's spirits'; *ʋɓɩa* 'stone'; *ɲɩka* 'bury' (from
kisuaheli *zika?*).

muɩ̣eni 'a member of the clan of *aɩ̣eni*'.

marks. According to Merker, the hunting tribe of *wandorobo* had
the same mark on bee-hives and arrows[1].

Have these marks anything to do with the totem, or were
they really the original totem mark? Only one mark seems to
speak in favour of this, namely, the lion-paws which the *asʋ* (lion
clan) set on their arrow-heads (see fig. 33). A similar case is that
of the wolf clan among the Delawares, who painted a wolf-paw
on their huts[2].

B. **Kikumbuliu (district of Kibwezi).** Of the above-mentioned clans, I have, from this district, noted nos: 2, 4, 5, 8, 9,
10, 13, 14. 16, 19. Additions: *amuʋlu*, sub-clan of *ǫombɔ* (*aombɔ*)
which is said to come from Nsaui in Kilungu; *akʋtondo* (14) are
also called *mba-ŋguŋguu* (cf. above 8) here.

Further, *anɛ̣ʋ*, which clan Hobley includes in his list of the
Mumoni clans.

C. **Ikutha District.** Of A I have here found nos: 1, 2, 3,
4, 5, 6, 8, 9, 11, 14, 15, 18, 21, 22. The *aǣʋ* are also called *aeʋnʋ*, the
locative form; *anɛ̣ʋ* (see B) is here called *anðʋ*.

Of *ǫombɔ* is here found the sub-clan *awʋlu*, presumably = *amwʋlʋ*
(B). The *asʋ* (9) are here also called *mba-muले̣-ʋtema* (*lea* 'refuse'
and *ʋtema* 'liver').

D. **Kitui District.** Here are found, besides many of the
above-mentioned clans, *mba-kʋtuku* and the large clan of *mba-ŋgo-
kituku* (quiver decoration of ostrich feathers) is the name of the
founder of the clan, as is also the case with *ŋgo* 'leopard'. This
clan must not be confused with the *ǣwaʋ* (A 18), the totem of which
is the leopard. What the totem of the clan itself is, I do not
know.

E. **Mumoni.** In this part of the country, I have found two
clans which seem to be otherwise unknown: *aŋgokʋ* and *kanɑ*, or
aǣʋ. The latter, however, is found also in the district of Kitui.
Its totem is a small green parrot (*ŋgwǣʋ*). The *anðʋ* (B, C) are
here said to be a sub-clan of *amwǣʋ* (A 13).

---

[1] M. Merker, Die Massai, p. 226.

[2] Frazer, Totemism and Exogamy I, p. 30.

10. The origin of the totem system among the Akamba.

The difficult and much-discussed problem of the origin of the totem I will only briefly touch upon, and concerning the Akamba, I will in much subscribe to the following expression of opinion by M. P:n Nilsson[1]: »For my part, I am largely inclined to support the old view that the totem originated from the names by which the primitive tribes used to designate each other. These names were quite naturally taken from surrounding natural objects, and especially from the animal world, with which savages are so well acquainted. From the principle of the magical connexion between a name and its bearer — according to the primitive conception, a person not only has a name, but he *is* what he is called — the various phenomena of totemism can easily be explained, particularly the fundamental idea of mutual connexion between a group of persons and the species of animal or the class of objects or the natural phenomena which bear the same name». This name-theory, however, must not be confused with H. Spencer's rationalistic explanation, that totemism is founded upon a mistake: the memory of a forefather, »the wolf», fades in the course of time, so that in the end the belief emerges that a wolf really was the founder of the clan.

At the beginning of the chapter, I mentioned that a clan seems to originate from a single man, whose name (sometimes his occupation) was often afterwards associated with the name of the animal or object which is the totem of the clan. Thus the founder of the clan of *amwæɀ* was called *mwæɀ* ('moon'). The *amumoni* 'those at the fig-tree', are said to spring from a certain *mumo* (fig-tree), and so on.

The old assumption that the sacredness of the totem animal is due to the fact that it is believed to be the habitation of the spirits of the forefathers, seems now to have been generally abandoned in science. As far as the Akamba are concerned, I venture to think that I have shown with sufficient clearness that no such belief exists among them, even if there are circumstances which, on a superficial consideration, support the idea.

---

[1] Primitiv religion, p. 44.

11. **Fictitious Relationship.**

A. Among the Akamba themselves. Another class of re
lationship is that of sworn brotherhood. Just in the same way as
the bonds of natural relationship are very strong and the feeling
of affinity within the family (clan) stands out in violent contrast
to the old hostility and dissension between the different parts
and districts, so does sworn brotherhood unite men with strong
bonds. If two men wish to become blood-brothers, the prelimi
nary step is the mutual exchange of presents, consisting of beer
and goats, which latter they kill and consume together. The final and
conclusive ceremony consists in their meeting in the hut of one
of them: a calabash of beer is produced, out of which they alter
nately take mouthfuls of the liquid, which are then ejected back
into the vessel. Then each makes a slight incision in the back
of the right hand, and sucks the blood which wells forth from the
hand of the partner. The blood brotherhood is now sealed, and
if either of them afterwards breaks it, he will be overtaken by
misfortunes and certain death. Even if both should tire of the
friendship, they cannot sever the bond without incurring calamitous
consequences.

This relationship seems to be equally binding and to have
the same consequences as the natural relationship, of which it is
probably an imitation. The children of the parties look upon
each other, and are looked upon, as brothers and sisters, and may
not marry together. Two men united by such a bond are under
the obligation to render each other mutual help. If one of the
foster-brothers is a party in a law suit, or if he is charged
with some crime, the other appears at the trial, even if he has
important affairs of his own to see to. For example, if the son
of one of them receives a blow at the dancing place — during
the dancing, the youths engage in violent rivalry for the favour of
the girls, and hence blows are often exchanged — the sons of
the other family come to his assistance.

B. With individuals of another tribe. The above account
applies to sworn brotherhood between two Akamba, but if a Kamba
desires to become a blood-brother with a man of another tribe
the following is the method of procedure:

A goat is killed and cut into pieces. The two men make a little scratch on the inter-clavicular notch and on the chest. The blood which issues is caught on pieces of the goat's flesh, and each man eats a piece with the other's blood upon it. From the goat's skin are cut rings, which they place on each other's fingers. The ceremony has the same effect as an oath »sworn over a strong *kithitu*», and the breaking of such an oath brings with it death (see Chap. XI: 3).

They are now as brothers born of the same mother, show each other the greatest hospitality, and one of them cannot deny the other anything», said an old man to the author. Should one of them be killed while on a visit to his blood-brother, the latter claims the blood-fine from the culprit.

When the Akamba used to pass to and from the coast for trading purposes, the cunning Swahili and Arab traders used to profit by this custom, by entering into blood-brotherhood with them, and then the Akamba would sell their ivory cheap to their new kinsmen. Although they had reached a higher stage of civilisation, this was the only way in which the people of the coast could cheat the »washenzi» ('the savages'), for the latter possessed too much business capacity. But the otherwise greedy Akamba's conception of the significance of blood-brotherhood caused them to lose sight of their own advantage.

Another variant of sworn brotherhood, which probably exists both between two Akamba and between a Kamba and a man of another tribe, is the following:

A person who is sorely persecuted by an irreconcilable enemy, who aims at his life, can not only save his life but even turn his foe into a friend, if he can manage to get an opportunity of sucking the breast of his wife or daughter, even though the latter may be but a child[1]. The two then become more than friends: they regard one another as brothers[2]. Their children may not marry, but on the other hand, they may have sexual intercourse,

---

[1] Among several peoples women are regarded, in a way, as asylums, according to E. Westermarck »probably from fear of the magic power attributed to their sex». See W:s article Asylum in Encycl. of Religion and Ethics.

[2] We should rather expect, from this symbolic suckling, that the relation would be that of father to son.

which, of course, is out of the question between real sisters and
brothers, or between members of the same clan. It seems that no
other obligations, such as mutual help &c, are imposed on the
children.

Another method of entering upon a sort of sworn brotherhood
is mentioned by Hildebrandt, but it has not been met with by the
present author. It consists in the smashing of a small earthenware vessel, specially made for the purpose. By the performance
of a certain ceremony, the bond thus formed can subsequently be
dissolved by one of the parties, without the knowledge of the
other[1].

---

[1] See further Hildebrandt, Ethnographische Notizen, p. 386.

Chapter IX. **Social Organisation.**

1. **Age= and Rank=Classes.**

The terms for persons of the opposite sexes, of different ages and social grades within the community, are as follows: *kana* 'child', *kaɓɩsɩ* 'little boy', *kɩɓɩsɩ* 'boy', *kælætuɩ* 'little girl', *mwɩtuɩ* 'girl' (also a young wife who has not yet had a child), *mwanakɔ* 'young unmarried man, warrior', *ŋðælɔ* 'young married man', *kɩɓætɩ* 'wife with children', *mutumɩa* 'elderly man'. This classification is, however, very general, and more detailed explanations and additions are necessary.

No special test or ceremony is required for a *kɩɓɩsɩ* to become a *mwanakɔ*. The circumcision feasts have nothing to do with it. It is his general maturity, or, let us say, the beginning of puberty, which decides the question, and when his father thinks him old enough and intelligent enough, he gives him the ornaments which are distinctive of a *mwanakɔ*, and then he soon gains recognition as such. Hence the assumption of the ornaments is not enough in itself, and if a very young boy should appear decked out in them, he would not become a *mwanakɔ* on that account.

Even a married man remains a *mwanakɔ*, as long as he takes part in the dances of his unmarried contemporaries. When he grows tired of them, or ceases to take part in them for some other reason, he is looked upon as a *ŋðælɔ*. The birth of his first child might perhaps be looked upon as a determining factor. Mr Hobley says, incorrectly, that »a nthele can only have one wife»[1]. The number of wives plays no part in these distinctions, but is purely an economic question. It sometimes happens that a well-to-do man buys a wife for his son, while the latter is still

---

[1] C. V. Hobley, Akamba &c, p. 49.

a *kıbısı* (though he must have been circumcised). For the same reason, it is possible for a *mwanakɔ* to have two or more wives although it does not very often happen. A woman does not become a *kıbæti* immediately on her marriage, but is still called *mwıtu*, till her first child is born.

Age-classes and rank-classes above *ŋδælɔ* are composed of *atumıa* (sg. *mutumıa* [1]). The above classifications can, strictly speaking, only be considered as classifications of age-classes. Now, we meet besides with a social grade, since anyone who wants to be a *mutumıa* must make a payment to those who are already *mutumıa*. This dignity is usually reached at an age of 40 to 50. There are however, younger *atumıa*, and, on the other hand, there are middle-aged men who have not yet made their payments. Out of politeness, these are, however, called *mutumıa* in everyday speech, although they have not yet attained that dignity. The outward sign of a *mutumıa* is the little round stool (*mumbu*), which he carries everywhere with him, usually hanging by a chain over his shoulder. When he wants to sit down, he places the stool on the ground. Younger men have no right to use such stools [2]. However, all *atumıa* are not on the same level. The highest in rank are those who administer the government of the country and watch over the religion, *atumıa ma nšama* and *atumıa ma ıpæmbo*. They carry a pronged staff (*maka*) as a symbol of their dignity. If anyone else ventures to carry one, he runs the risk of being ridiculed.

According to their rank, the *atumıa* consume different parts of the animals which are killed at public feasts and on the places of sacrifice. The attainment of a higher grade among the *atumıa* is chiefly a financial question. The lowest grade is easily reached by the presentation of a goat to the members of the *ŋšama*. The person concerned has now the right to eat a goat's head, and is called *mutumıa wa mutwɔ* ('*mutumıa* of the head'). The next

---

[1] Among the Akikuyu, the neighbours of the Akamba to the west, *mutumıa* curiously enough means »a married woman who has at least one circumcised child».

[2] The stools are often prettily wrought; I shall revert to the subject more fully in the description of the material culture of the Akamba. Hobley has pictures of some fine specimens (p. 34). He does not, however, emphasize the fact that they may be used only by *atumıa*.

step is to bring a bull, which entitles him to the meat of the animal's lower leg. Another bull gives him the right to the upper parts of the leg. When he is in a position to present still one more, he advances a step further, to the loins and brisket. Some time usually elapses before he advances further than this. However, a fourth bull entitles him to eat from the hump of cattle (*k̠ao*), which is considered a great delicacy. A fifth and last step now remains: another bull must be paid, before he may eat of the tongue and head of cattle. Further he cannot advance, for a *mutumɩa* of the fifth grade has gained the right to eat all kinds of meat, that is to say there is no one of higher rank than his. To pass through the different grades in this manner is called *kukula*, and in East Ukamba *kukusa*. Of course, everyone cannot attain to the highest grade. It is not permissible for anyone to touch the meat which falls to the share of those of higher grades, even if the latter are not taking part in the feast. Their portion is, in that case, put away, and taken to their village by the *anakə*, who, on these occasions, slaughter the animals which are going to be eaten, and attend to the preparation of the meat.

Women and youths also may only eat of certain parts of an animal, whether they are at a big public feast or at a purely private meal in their own family circles. To the women's lot fall one of the legs, the stomach, the meat on the sides of the belly and on the ribs (*ɩtulo*), while the men take the neck, lungs, liver, kidneys, and heart. The last-mentioned portion and part of the brisket usually go to the *anakə*. The hams, the back, and the meat on the shoulder-blades (*n̠ama ɀa kɩtuo*, from *kɩtuo* 'shoulder') fall to the *atumɩa*. When the animals are slaughtered at home in the village, the father of a family eats from the hams, and the eldest son from the back. Once the latter becomes *mutumɩa*, the father may no longer touch the head or the hams, nor may he eat with the other *atumɩa* at public feasts any longer: it seems he is considered too old.

The eating regulations now described must only be taken as approximately correct, since I have received very different statements from different persons in the course of my enquiries. However, that they are considered to be very important questions, is shown by the fact that anyone who — without permission — eats what does not fall to his share, can be cursed; thus, for example, a youth who presumes to eat the head. Hence this is taboo for him.

To return to a consideration of the *mutumɪa*-dignity, we have seen that neither age nor the number of wives possessed is decisive for promotion to a higher rank, but a necessary condition is payment, the animals paid being then eaten by those entitled to them. Hildebrandt cites something similar from the Wanika, on this side of Mombasa, and Schurtz correctly regards this phenomenon as a step towards the formation of clubs[1]. In reality clubs do exist among the Akamba, though in a rather undeveloped form. I allude here to what the natives call *kɪsuka*. This signifies a gathering of *atumɪa* and *n̥ðælə*, who meet together for amusement, to eat meat and to drink beer, which is provided partly by the entrance payments of new members, and partly by purchase for the *kɪsuka*. Those who have not made their payments — 1 to 3 goats and some beer seems to be the minimum — may not be present at the meeting. There are also different grades within the *kɪsuka*, which are attained in the same manner, and carry the same privileges, as those described above. Hence those who have paid only a little may not eat all sorts of meat. Unfortunately, I have neglected to gather information as to whether these two payments for attaining a higher grade are made independently of each other, but I think that the grade which is already attained in *n̥ɟama* entitles a man to enter a corresponding grade in *kɪsuka*, without further payment. Most of the members seem to be at least »men of the head», that is to say they belong to the lowest grade among the *atumɪa*. In East Ukamba the *kɪsuka* seems to be exclusively a sort of club, while — as we shall see later — in Ulu the members have duties to perform in the public service[2]. Finally I must also mention that I have not discovered that the *kɪsuka* is in any way of the nature of a secret society, either as concerns the outside world or as concerns the different grades inter se. Age-classes and secret societies are

---

[1] J. M. Hildebrandt, Ethnogr. Notizen, p. 400. H. Schurtz, Altersklassen und Männerbünde, p. 133.

[2] According to C. Dundas, it is, in the Kitui district, members of the *kɪsuka* who carry out the burials. It seems to me that, at any rate in the Machakos district, this can be done by any of the older *atumɪa*, whether he belongs to the *kɪsuka* or not.

in no way so closely allied in East Africa as they are in West Africa, where the one implies the other [1]. That outsiders are not admitted to the *kɩsuka* is due entirely to the fact that no one may take part in the festivities who has not contributed towards them. Neither are women admitted, nor may they even prepare the meat which is eaten at the meeting.

There is no special hut (club-house) for these feasts, but they are held in different places out in the open air [2]. Nor is there any hut for the unmarried men (»männerhaus»), though they may not, as a rule, sleep in their parents' huts; they must sleep anywhere where they can find shelter. They often take refuge in the provision sheds (*ɩkumbɩ*). Among the Akamba, the nearest approach to a public hall is the dancing place (*kɩɓuʐo*), common to several villages, where the young people meet for dancing in the evenings. On the return home from these dancing meetings, free love is usually indulged in.

Just as different rank-classes are found among the *atumɩa*, so are found among the married women (*ɩɓæti*) such as take a higher position than the bulk of the women, namely *ɩɓæti sɩa ɩpæmbo* or *sɩa nžama*, who have obtained the right, together with the *atumɩa*, to administer the cult on the places of sacrifice consecrated to the spirits of their ancestors. For particulars as to the acquisition of this privilege, see Chap. XIII.

It has already been mentioned in passing that the division into age-classes implies differences in dress and personal adornment. However, since these differences are of very slight importance or interest, they may be passed over here. I shall, instead, deal with these matters in the following chapters on the material culture of the Kamba people.

In this chapter it may be appropriate to discuss also the conception of *ʉka*. The word is best rendered by »age-class», since

---

[1] Cf. W e u l e, Negerleben in Ost-Afrika, p. 370.
[2] The meeting huts which have begun to spring up during the last few years here and there in Ukamba, have come into existence entirely on the initiative of the English civil servants for use in legal proceedings and other public meetings. They are called *ɱbalasa* (from Kisuaheli *baraza*).

an *uka* includes approximately all persons of the same age, independent of sex. The word *nɗukɔ* is used side by side with *uka*. The division has no connection with circumcision, as, for example, is the case with the age-classes among the Masai, and seems to have no practical significance; at least I have never heard the word used except when ages were being compared, when two persons who were of the same age were said to be of the same *uka* or *nɗukɔ*. According to a statement which I have not checked, it seems, however, that in former times in the war expeditions, warriors of an *uka* formed a separate division, which, when pitching camp, had — among other things — its own fire, which is reminiscent of what Merker calls »corporalship» among the Masai [1]. The *uka*-division is to be met with among several tribes in British East Africa, as, for example, the Wataveta at Kilimandjaro, where the conception of *irika* is more exactly defined: is founded on circumcision, embraces a limited period of fifteen years, and is of practical significance [2].

---

[1] Merker, Die Massai, p. 49.

[2] Cf. Lindblom, Anteckningar öfver Taveta-folkets etnologi, p. 160. The Akikuyu have also the word *irika*, which Routledge incorrectly renders by »clan». In the Kikuyu language »clan» is called *muheriga*: Routledge, With a pre-historic people, p. 20. K. R. Dundas (Kikuyu Rika, Man 1908) gives for the Akikuyu of both sexes six *rika* or age-classes.

Chapter X. **Government and Administration.**

From early times, a patriarchal form of government has prevailed among the Akamba. Every *mutumɩa* exacts obedience from the members of his family, and he has absolute authority over his sons, even long after they are grown up and have families of their own. Questions which concern several villages or a certain stretch of country, that is to say, questions of more general interest, are dealt with and decided by a local assembly of elders, called *nžama*. There is no special leader or chairman of this assembly. Some descriptions of how the heads of families generally, though unofficially, intervene to maintain public discipline, as, for instance, when the frenzy of dancing threatens to demoralise the young people, are given in my »Afrikanska ströftåg» (p. 154 ff.). There have never been any chiefs, although occasionally a rich person with a commanding personality has succeeded in attaining to the leadership within an extensive territory, as did Kivui in Kitui[1]. Kivui lived in the time of Krapf, and was personally known to him. He was practically a kind of chief, a position which he had gained through his higher intelligence and his great physical strength. At the same time he was a great medicine-man, and possibly provides an illustration of Frazer's theory that kings and chiefs have their origin from medicine-men, whose social influence sometimes advances them to the position of chiefs[2]. He made his people victorious against their enemies, and many Akamba are said to have paid him taxes, and so even the Masai livɩng at Donyo Sabuk.

In times of war, however, experienced warriors were selected as leaders, the so-called *asɩlɩlɩ* and *apɩanɩ*, but their authority was only temporary, and in times of peace they occupied no public position in the tribe. On account of their great reputation, how-

---

[1] Krapf, Reisen in Ost-Afrika II, p. 264.
[2] Frazer, The Golden Bough I: 1, p. 332.

ever, they often represented it in transactions with the Arabian merchants and other trading caravans which came up to Ukamba from the coast. They usually decided whether the caravans should be allowed to pass unmolested, and the leaders of the caravans were anxious to enter into a sworn brotherhood with them, according to the usual Kamba custom, so that they might thereby obtain protection for themselves and their property.

The home government is in the hands of a council of the elders, *ṇžama*, of which only *atumɩa* are members. This corporation is of a purely local character, and there is no authority for the whole country. The *mutumɩa*-grade does not in itself carry with it the right to a seat in the *ṇžama*, for which a separate and special payment is exacted. The most important function of the *ṇžama* is to act as a court, in which all cases are tried and decided. It also decides on wars of aggression (plundering raids); *kɩɡolɔ*, lynching, which is practised by the Akamba, may also only be ordered by the *ṇžama*. Next to its duties as judging authority, its most important function, however, is the care and maintenance of the religion, the offering of sacrifices, &c. For an account of these matters and a description of how the *atumɩa* share this right with the old women, see Chap. XIII.

To the religious duties of the *ṇžama* pertains also that of carrying out the ceremony of purification, on the advent of all public misfortunes, such as the outbreak of epidemics, cattle-plagues, &c.

These old men and women of the *ṇžama* and the *ɩpæmbo* (place of sacrifice) are the custodians of the tribe's traditions, in the manners and customs pertaining to which they are well versed. They see that they are maintained, and they have, on the other hand, authority to prevent the rise of customs which they consider harmful, and can even abolish customs which are already in existence. Anyone who is in doubt as to how he ought to proceed in a certain case, according to the custom of the tribe, goes to a *mutumɩa wa ṇžama* for information, for which he pays a small fee, such as a goat, or, if he is a rich man, a bull.

This short description of the system of government, however, no longer tallies with the actual facts, since there is no sphere in which contact with Europeans so quickly makes itself felt on the old order of things as the political. Englishmen certainly follow in their colonies a principle of allowing the old order to remain as far as possible, and in consequence, among other things, the *nžama* still remains as the judging authority; but by the side of it, a system of chiefs has been established, the country being divided up into small districts, each having a »chief» (and under him »headmen»), who is responsible for the payment of the hut-tax within his district. At first the most influential man in a district was appointed chief on principle. However, since the older men seemed to have a difficulty in understanding and appreciating the reforms for which they are required to work among the people, during the last few years intelligent younger men, who showed a better understanding of the new order of things, have been appointed. A »government school» has been established in Kitui, and to it are sent the sons of these »chiefs», to learn to read and write, in order that they may succeed to their fathers' offices. Perhaps in time a hereditary chieftainship will be established in this way. The institution is still quite new, and most of these chiefs find it very difficult to assert their authority over the other *atumɩa*, who have never been accustomed to acknowledge any other authority than the *nžama*, of which, indeed, they were usually members themselves[1].

The following little episode may serve as a typical example of the feeling of independence among the Akamba: Pfitzinger, missionary of the Leipziger Mission, who began to work among the Akamba about 20 years ago, at first took it rather amiss that the older men addressed him simply by name, without using the Suaheli word *bwana* ('master'), which is, otherwise, the usual word of address for Europeans in East Africa. He tried to give the persons in question a slight hint through his servants, but got the reply: »Among the Akamba there is no master!» Nor has the language any word for »master».

---

[1] Hobley does not treat of the system of government in his work, but mentions that the Akamba have chiefs, and even hereditary chiefs. From his description one inevitably gets the incorrect idea that chieftainship is one of their original institutions, while in reality it is very characteristic of the political organisation of the Akamba that they have never had chiefs.

Chapter XI. The administration of the law and judicial customs[1].

One of the most strongly predominating features of the negro's intellectual endowment seems to be his legal mind. Thus the negroes have legal customs and prescriptions connected with the administration of the law, which testify to extreme penetration and a good power of judgement. The punishments inflicted are often surprisingly humane and just. Negro law has, accordingly, attracted the attention of investigators, and many of modern Europe's jurists have not found it beneath their dignity to spend time in studying it; nay, new ideas have even been obtained from this source, which it has been possible to incorporate into the law systems of Europe, and this is of especial interest for the history and philosophy of law. It is scarcely necessary to add that many of the Bantu peoples' legal customs are not specially typical for them, but are of a general nature.

To go to law (*ɪkwanɪ*) is one of the most exquisite enjoyments in existence for a Kamba negro, and in what a number of actions every old man has been a party! One of the most ingenious riddles of the Akamba — in their own opinion — runs thus: »Tell me a case which is disagreeable»; answer: »The case of him who has vermin in his hair». Such a riddle would, of course, have no meaning, unless it was generally considered rather enjoyable to take part in a law-suit. More than once during my wanderings, I have met an old man whose face was beaming with satisfaction, the reason for his good humour being that he was on his way to the law-court. For a case which is not decided, they use the expression *ɪkwanɪ ʌanʌwa manʌɪ* 'the case drank water'. »To judge» is

---

[1] For a comparative study of legal customs in Africa, see the account — which is purely descriptive, but comprehensive and systematic — given by Post in »Afrikanische Jurisprudenz».

sıla or *sılıla*, but there are, on the other hand, no words for »law», »prescription», &c.

Since there are no professional lawyers, every man pleading his own case, at least every elderly Kamba man is familiar with the law and legal customs of his tribe. Although unwritten and only carried down by oral tradition and by practical application, some of these laws are constant and of general application, so that they well deserve to be called laws. A knowledge of them is one of the most important items of a negro's education. It can thus with good reason be asserted that, relatively speaking, judicial education is infinitely wider spread among the negro tribes of Africa than among the civilised peoples of Europe.

The organisation of the judicial system of a people depends on a lower stage on its general political and social organisation. As has already been mentioned, the most important function of the *nžama* is to form a court which deals with and decides all kinds of cases. There is no superior court. The meetings usually take place in the open air, and a crowd of interested listeners flock to them. The word *nžama* means 'secret', and has possibly come to be used as the name of the court, because, after the disputing parties have been heard and the case debated, the oldest and most experienced *atumıa* withdraw to decide on a verdict. Little weight seems to be attached to the evidence of witnesses, but the verdict is pronounced on the evidence of the disputing parties. The latter do not hesitate to make wrong statements, so that it is a very difficult and lengthy business for the judges to arrive at a decision.

The executive authority in Ulu is discharged by the *kısuka* (cf. p. 146), who have thus, when necessary, to put into effect the decisions arrived at by the *nžama*. If, for example, the plaintiff refuses to be present at the trial, members of the *kısuka* go and fetch him. When anyone persists in disobeying, they (*kısuka*) may be ordered to impound a certain number of his goats, &c. The men of *kısuka* are present when cases are tried, and sit and listen, so that they may later on, in their turn, gain admission to the *nžama*, if, for example, one of its members should die. The *kısuka* is thus a preparatory institution for entry to the *nžama*. I have already shown that, in East Ukamba, the *kısuka* have no such official position, as in Ulu. However, a similar executive body is also found in the east, though under another name, viz. *mbalasa*. But the foreign ring of the word is suspicious; probably we here have an instance of the attempts of the English to re-organise the native law.

On the whole, the judicial and political life of the Akamba very much resembles that of their neighbours and kinsmen, the Akikuyu. Thus *nžama* corresponds very closely to *kẓama* (from the same root) among the latter. On the other hand, the Akikuyu seem to have, instead of *kɩsuka*, an institution called *nẓama*, »a practical executive police», according to Routledge[1]. Among the Wataweta also, the oldest men constitute an assembly called *nẓama*, which is headed, however, by the chiefs[2].

1. Criminal law.

Blood=money and blood=vengeance. The blood-money exacted for a man's life in Ulu is 11 cows and 1 bull, which latter goes to the *nžama*; in the east it is 13 cows and 1 bull. In Ulu, 10 of the cows comprise the fine for taking life and are paid to the man's relatives, and the eleventh cow is especially allotted to the widow as a sort of compensation. It is called *gombə ẓa ndulọta*, 'the cow of the broken bow', since it is given to the widow as compensation for her man's bow, which will never again, in its owner's hand, go out on plundering expeditions and bring home wealth to the village. »This cow is now your husband», the old people say to her, meaning that the animal will contribute towards her subsistence. She sells the milk, and so, if she wishes to, she can employ a Kikuyu man to work in the fields for her. If a man leaves several widows, however, only the »big» wife receives a *gombə ẓa ndulọta*. Of the blood-money proper — the 10 cows — one goes to each of the following: the murdered man's father, father's brother, and mother's brother. Other relations receive, perhaps, one between them, while the remainder go to the widow in trust for the children. If there are several wives, they divide the animals. They may not sell them, so that, when the sons are grown up, those may not make trouble and say that their

---

[1] Routledge, The Akikuyu, p. 198.

[2] Cf. C. Hollis, History and customs of the people of Taveta, in Journal of the African Society 1901.

property has been dissipated. They are very particular in the matter of cattle paid as blood-money. But if a young man who has as yet no children should receive part of the fine, he may with impunity sell the cow which may have fallen to his lot, for in this case there are no children to make trouble afterwards.

It is very seldom that a murderer is in a position to pay 10 cows himself. In by far the majority of cases he is helped by his relations; sometimes he only contributes a single cow himself[1]. If he is very poor and has a daughter, he can, as a last resource, sell his daughter to someone as a wife, and in that manner obtain the wherewithal to pay his fine. The first cow paid as blood-money must be paid by the murderer himself. Until he has done this, his relations will do nothing, since the payment of this animal shows the murderer's honest intention of settling the matter. The cow is called *gombɔ ɀa wumo* (<*umɀa* 'to take out, to pay down'). When the cow has been handed over, the widow sleeps with a *mutumɩa*.

About half as much is paid for a woman's life as for a man's — in Ulu 4 to 5 cows + one bull to the *atumɩa*; in the east, 7 cows + 1 bull. For children the same is paid as for adults of the same sex.

The man who is unfortunate enough to kill his own child, pays fines to the mother and his nearest relations, since through his act he is considered to have injured the whole family. If a man kills his wife, he pays blood-money to her father, who then repays the bride price. The relationship between the parties is then dissolved. This, however, seems to depend upon circumstances, and chiefly upon whether the wife has borne her husband children or not. In the latter case she has not, according to the opinion of many, fulfilled her chief duty as wife; her father has been paid for her once, and has no further claim.

It occasionally happens that a man refuses to pay blood-money, and it then becomes the duty of the murdered man's relations (or clan) to demand blood-vengeance on the murderer and his family. There is no obligation to take blood-money, and it seems to be rather usual for the dead man's relatives to refuse the fine, and to prefer to follow the principle of »a life for a life».

---

[1] Cf. Post, Afrikanische Jurisprudenz I, p. 71.

The younger men especially are glad to follow the old rule, while the older and more discreet and prudent *atumɩa* of both parties try to arrange an amicable settlement. They are by no means always successful in this, and a state of actual war arises between the two families. They always go about armed, try to attack and burn each other's villages, &c. The prevailing insecurity, however, is felt by both parties, and the »war» is usually neither lengthy nor bloody; the battles are fought at a respectful distance, so that the loss of life shall not be too great. As soon as the party aggrieved has succeeded in killing the murderer or one of his relatives — blood-vengeance is only exacted from men — all excuse for fighting is removed, theoretically at any rate. But if they have killed two men, they have committed an offence, which must, in its turn, be avenged by the relatives of the killed men. Thus blood-feuds have quite a different character from other feuds. It might perhaps be thought that the combatants ought to be able to cry quits, when one man has fallen on each side, but such is not the case — full blood-money must be paid for both those who have been killed. It must be admitted, on closer consideration, that this is quite just. The largest share of the blood-money goes to the murdered man's family, who ought in all fairness to have some compensation for the loss they have sustained [1].

Blood-vengeance is only exacted for crimes which result in death. The fines given in the following list are considered normal as compensation for bodily injuries caused by assault or other means. No amounts are absolutely fixed, but the defendant's economic position is taken into account; if he is a man in a good position, the fine is likely to be increased:

loss of one finger			1 goat to 1 bull
»	»	two fingers	1 bull
»	»	one eye	1 bull + 1 goat
»	»	one arm	1 cow + 1 bull
»	»	one leg	5 cows
»	»	both legs	about 8 cows.

---

[1] B r u t z e r gives a description of a family feud among the Akamba in Rabai, in his »Begegnungen mit Akamba» (p. 3). Since the Akamba have passed completely under British control, there are no longer any family feuds.

Anyone who is slightly injured, but recovers without suffering any subsequent ill-effects, receives no compensation. A somewhat remarkable method of procedure, which is sometimes practised to prove a right to blood-money, is the following:

Suppose that a person has been badly maltreated by another, but has recovered, without suffering any lasting ill-effects. When he dies, perhaps many years later, it is possible that the relations open the body to see whether the injury the dead man once suffered has possibly caused his death. If they really can prove that this is the case, they can claim full blood-money. The heir makes the first incision with his knife, at the post-mortem examination; this possibly makes the action legal.

*   *   *

Anyone sending a person on an errand or other commission is responsible for any accident he may suffer in the execution of it. A case which came within my personal experience is the following: An old man sent a neighbour's son home to the village with an axe. The boy tripped and cut his foot. They went to law over the matter, and the father of the boy claimed compensation, saying: »I did not tell my son to take your axe. If you had not sent him, he would not have injured himself». The other man had to pay a goat.

For r a p e the fine is a goat. If the woman dies as a result, or becomes pregnant and dies in child-birth, the full blood-money must be paid as for manslaughter.

If an unmarried woman gives birth to a child, and her lover cannot or will not marry her, he pays a goat. The matter is usually settled privately, and is not dragged before the *nžama*. If the culprit is a youth, the girl's guardian sends another *mutumїa* to his father to demand a goat. The youth is asked whether the child is his, he does not readily acknowledge the paternity, only recommending that the goat be paid. The mother keeps the child. The reason for the smallness of the fine is that the child is looked upon as considerable compensation. But if the woman dies while she is still pregnant, the lover must — at any rate in Ulu — pay 4 cows and 1 bull to her father; that is to say full blood-money.

Adultery. The lover usually gets off with the payment of a goat, even if the woman gets a child. This belongs to her husband (cf. p. 84), who soon comes to look upon it as his own. If the lover continues his guilty relations with the woman, he is said to »show contempt for» her husband, and then open hostilities are liable to break out between the relations of the two men. In the Kitui district, the lover has to pay a bull, not because the value of cattle is less there, but because the older people wish to prevent such irregularities. The unfaithful wife receives no punishment, except such as her husband himself thinks fit to administer to her.

Illicit relations between a young man and an old woman who is past child bearing, are thought to result in the youth's becoming impotent, probably from the belief generally prevalent among primitive peoples that »like begets like». Therefore both of them must undergo the usual ceremonial purification (with *ŋondu*). The two goats which are required for it are paid by the lover. As far as I know, such alliances are only exceptional and mostly take place by mistake. For at night a youth often steals to his lady-love's hut and to her bed, without making a sound, so as not to wake the other inmates of the hut. It seems really to have happened that a man out for that purpose has come upon an older woman, who was by chance spending the night in the girl's bed.

The fine for indulging in coition from behind is one goat; the parties concerned must be purified, or they will become sterile.

Sodomy seems to be unknown among the Akamba, but occurs among the Masai, where, according to my Kamba informants, small boys use sheep for the purpose.

Theft. Even a cursory glance at what has been written about the judicial system of the Bantu peoples, is sufficient to show that well-nigh everywhere the punishment for theft is surprisingly severe. It is not unusual for a thief to be condemned to death, though he usually gets off with the payment of heavy fines, often — and especially on a repetition of the offence — of many time the value of the stolen goods[1]. We shall find similar principles among the Akamba. The reason for this can hardly be an appre-

---

[1] Cf. Post, Afrik. Jurispr. II, p. 85 ff.

ciation of the fact that it is wrong to steal, but rather a strong feeling of the sacredness of the property of the individual or family.

The *nžama* can — or, strictly speaking, could, because nowadays it is forbidden by the government — condemn a thief to death, but it is most usual for him to be condemned to pay for the damage (usually double the value), and also to give the judges one goat or more, some beer, &c, in payment of costs (depending on the magnitude of the theft). Anyone who is not in a position to pay the fines, must here also have recourse to all sorts of expedients; he is often obliged to sell his daughter or sister cheaply, in this way to get together the necessary sum. Formerly capital punishment seems to have been inflicted more than at the present time, when it is scarcely ever resorted to, except in the case of an incorrigible thief. The thief was shot with poisoned arrows, or hung up in a tree, where he was allowed to remain »as a punishment and a warning to others». Parents used to take their children to the place and show them the end of a criminal, as a warning example to them.

To a certain extent, it may be said that the Akamba differentiate between theft and petty larceny in deciding on punishments. The punishment just mentioned is only inflicted when the theft is of such articles as are required for everyday use, and which are the result of work and industry: cattle, the products of the field and foods prepared from them, honey, &c. Less severe is the punishment inflicted for the theft of such articles as are only used occasionally, and thus are not essential for the maintenance of life, and which would in any case have ceased to be in a few days. In these are included beer and meat, for the Akamba live principally on vegetables. Although they are very fond of meat and have large herds, they can very seldom, except on festal occasions, bring themselves to kill one of their beloved oxen, and still less a cow. On the other hand, a goat or a sheep is slaughtered now and then. Anyone stealing, for example, some pieces of meat, is readily forgiven, in supposing that he had such a great longing for meat that he could not restrain himself (something which every Kamba man can sympathise with). Even if the thief is discovered, the owner will probably not insist on proceedings being taken, but will often rest content with recovering the stolen goods, when a slaughter takes place in the village where the thief lives; and the incident is closed. If the case should be taken before the *nžama* by someone else, the owner would very likely simply declare that the matter was already settled.

The theft of honey from the bee-hives is considered a very serious offence, and is very severely punished. I have recorded a case where a man was fined 1 bull and 5 goats for it. For a second offence the fine is doubled, for a third trebled, and so on. The reason why the fines are so high would seem to be that the bee-hives are usually hung out in the wilds at a long distance from the owner's village, so that it is impossible to watch them. Hence very heavy fines have been fixed to protect them. A honey thief is an extraordinarily despicable person, and this has penetrated so deeply into the national consciousness that, even if a man is nearly dying of starvation, he can only in extreme cases bring himself to take honey from the bee-hives without permission. Honey-stealing is punished very severely also among other East African tribes. Thus, I was told in Taveta, near Kilimandjaro, that it was formerly the custom there for the number of cells in the stolen honey to be counted, if it could be found, and the owner was entitled to demand a goat for each cell. And of the Akikuyu, Routledge says that »theft of honey is a recognised offence of a serious character»[1].

Other punishments. The African system of punishments seems to be based, on the whole, on the principle of compensation, and the accounts given above show that most crimes can, and usually are, made good by fines among the Akamba also. Capital punishment is only inflicted on persons who are dangerous to public safety and hence to the whole community, such as sorcerers and incorrigible thieves. Since the establishment of the English rule, however, the native court cannot condemn to death. Imprisonment is unknown among the Akamba, but the *nžama* used occasionally to banish people for sorcery and theft. Slavery has never been a native institution, and hence is not resorted to as a method of punishment. According to Krapf, there were many slaves in his time, but some were prisoners of war, and some were brought down from the coast. Most crimes are committed

---

[1] Ibid. p. 58. Among the Kimbunda in Central Africa, honey-stealing is considered to be one of the four worst kinds of theft. Cf. Post II, pp. 92, 188.

under the influence of drink; when sober, the Akamba have that respect for the law and the constitution which may be said to be general among the Bantu tribes.

Torture to extort confession is only resorted to in private within the family circle, as for example when a husband suspects his wife of unfaithfulness. He makes a loop in his bow-string and puts one of her fingers into it — a very usual method of extorting confession in many places in Africa. Or he may hang her up to the roof of the hut by a tendon tied round one of her little fingers.

mukoɔ is the name given to a person who, without committing any actual crime, for some reason or other makes himself so despised and hated by everybody that nobody will have anything to do with him. As the name implies, he is compared with saliva, spit (*makoa*), and is considered equally worthless. And still more, just as it would never occur to anyone to take up the saliva he had once spat out, so there could never be any question of allowing that man to regain the place he has lost in the community. Even if he should arrange a beer-drinking bout, something much appreciated by the older men, he could not expect to have a single guest. Completely isolated and boycotted, he usually cannot endure it very long, but moves to some distant locality, where he is unknown.

The fines are the same, even if a crime is committed by a madman, by a drunken man, or by accident. But accidental manslaughter does not give rise to a blood-feud. To kill anyone accidentally is called *aɸa mundu na mbaŋga*. It appears that among the Akamba extenuating circumstances can hardly be said to exist, at least where human life is concerned. This seems to be true of African law in general. No consideration is paid to the motive for a crime or to the way in which it was committed, but only to the result. The damage is just the same if a person has, for instance, been killed accidentally or murdered.

A man is responsible for the acts of his wife and children, and consequently he has to pay their fines, when they commit any offence. This is easily understood, since a woman has nothing to pay with; »her only possessions are her clothes and ornaments, her grave-stake and bast sacks», as a native aptly said to me. Although I have no records on the point, it is probable from

what has already been written, that the head of the family is also
liable for any debts contracted by any member of it.

2. Civil cases.

One of the commonest sources of dispute among cattle-raising
tribes is the cattle, and innumerable law suits occur in connection with them.   If a man buys an animal and it dies without any
ostensible cause, and therefore probably of a complaint it had
before it was bought, he has the right to demand another of the
seller.   The animal's skin must, however, be sent back, as well
as something else as compensation for the meat. If the purchaser
refuses to agree to this, the buyer proves his right by swearing on
kɩpɩtuu (see below).   In the same way, anyone who has had a cow for
many years, can demand another in her place, if she only gives
birth to bull-calves.   The owner then says that he has »not yet
begun to taste the milk» of the cow in question. It is not unusual
to see the skull of a cow or a bull placed in a tree in a Kamba
village.   It is then almost certain that it is from an animal which
is the object of a law suit still in progress.

I once attended a law suit over cattle near Machakos, and
the cause is so illustrative that I cannot refrain from mentioning it.
The plaintiff had exchanged a cow, which he believed to be sterile,
for some goats; but with her new owner the cow soon proved
herself extremely fruitful, so that the original owner repented the
exchange and wanted it cancelled!

Law of inheritance. As regards the law of inheritance,
nothing is found among the Akamba that is not also found among
many other Bantu tribes. When a man feels that his end is near,
he puts his house in order, tells his dependants what outstanding
claims he has, his debts, &c.   The eldest son of the »big» wife
is heir to the cattle and other property. If she has no son of
the »big» wife, the eldest son of the second wife takes the lion's
share of the inheritance. If the children are under age, the father's
brother becomes the head of the family for the time being, and,
as such, he is the guardian of it and its property.   Therefore he
takes charge of the children and their inheritance, which he manages; but he must hand it over to them as soon as they are
grown up, although the brother's widow falls to him by law,

Even if the deceased was childless, the brother still does not get the inheritance, but only has to manage it in trust for any children which he may get by the widow. But if she should die childless, then the inheritance is his. However, if he has any brothers, part of it goes to them.

The inheriting of a dead man's wife has already been mentioned (p. 84 ff.). Seen from a judicial-economic point of view, it is hardly surprising that, among a people that buy their wives, the widow should go to a deceased man's brother. She cannot simply return to her parents, since they have been paid for her, but she belongs in a way to her husband's family and family group, just as does a piece of property. Especially when her son (if she has one) is under age, she is in need of protection and support, and the nearest relative to afford these is her husband's brother, and marriage is the form under which this protection is given. The matter does not, however, seem so self-evident when the widow has a grown-up son who could take care of her. It would then seem more suitable for the son to look after his mother. But it is the woman's first duty to bear as many children as possible to the family to which she now belongs, and therefore it seems to the practical negro to be nonsensical that a woman, who is perhaps still in her prime, should cease to perform this duty, just because she happens to have become a widow. Her son, otherwise the heir to the father's property, must be excluded from consideration in this connection, and so she falls to the nearest prominent member of the family — that is to say her deceased husband's brother. This is only a conclusion founded on general Kamba conceptions, but I believe that a more thorough investigation on the spot would make it clear why this custom prevails among the Akamba. Unfortunately the question is but one of the many which present themselves only when one is at one's desk at home, working up the material collected[1]. My presumption that a man's inheritance of his brother's widow is founded, in the first place, on the conception that a woman is property — for which the family has made a large outlay and from which it wishes to derive as much benefit as possible — seems to be supported by the fact that

---

[1] Cf. Starcke's investigation about »The brother's inheritance» in Die primitive Familie, p. 164 ff.

a son can inherit one of his father's younger wives (p. 84). We have also seen that a father can present one of his younger wives to his son, during his own lifetime. In both cases a fresh outlay for the purchase of a wife is saved.

Weapons, especially the chief weapons — the bow and arrows — are important legacies, which a dying man usually presents personally to his son. When he hands them over, he spits on them, which act will bring good luck to the weapons. If the father cannot do this before he dies, the son ought not to use them before the *atumɩa* — probably to avert the consequences of the death — have purified them with *ɡondu*.

A woman only inherits her mother's ornaments and household articles, but not real property, such as cattle and fields, since she herself is nothing more than »property». In reality, if she were able to inherit anything, it would go to a strange family on her marriage.

The extensive authority which the head of a family has over it descends, when he dies, to his eldest son, if he is grown up. He then occupies the position of a father towards his brothers and sisters, and has control of the property belonging to the family, especially, of course, of the cattle. Even when they have been divided among the sons, they are still looked upon, in a way, as family property, in the disposal of which the brothers are dependent upon one another. Even if they are all married, have built their own huts, and provide for themselves, the consent of the others must be obtained before one of them can dispose of a piece of the herd he has inherited, or even kill it for his own use.

3. Land tenure.

On uncultivated and uncleared land between the villages everyone has the right of building huts and cultivating. In the Machakos district it was formerly the custom for those who wished to settle down in the neighbourhood of a village, to buy permission to do this by presenting the elders of the villages with a goat, called *mbuɩ ɩa mapanɛɩ* 'the goat of the fence'. By means of this he acquired the right to put up *mapanɛɩ*, i. e. the thorny branches which form the cattle kraal, or, in other words, to build a village for himself.

Each man owns the land he and his family cultivate. Those who have more fields then he thinks necessary at the moment usually hand over those that are superfluous temporarily to a friend or neighbour. On removing from the place one of the family is left behind to look after the fields, or they are left in the care of some relative or neighbour. Or else they are sold for one or two goats or two to six rupees each, according to their size. A serviceable hut is sold for two to five rupees, according to its age.

The boundaries between fields, which belong to different owners consist of a kind of ditch, a shallow trough-like excavation which usually comes to be used as a path. Sometimes there is no sign of a boundary at all, sometimes again the fields are separated by uncultivated ground (*ulıli*, pl. *mandılı*).

The same owner rarely has his acres together, but the are scattered, one part up on the slopes of the hills, others, again, down on the level ground, if possible on damp ground. This splitting-up is usually intentional. By it they hope, if there is a bad crop in one place, to get a better one in another where the nature of the ground is different.

Wells and waterplaces seems to be common property. There are, howewer, private wells. Thus, for instance, I saw in East Ukamba how during the dry season holes were dug in the dry bed of the R. Tiva for the cattle, and then fenced in so that other people's cattle should not come there.

This is all I know about the ownership of land. Other details are given by Hobley (Akamba, p. 82).

4. *Kıpıtu* and the taking of oaths over it.

The most interesting point in the legal life of the Akamba, and the most important for the natives themselves, is undoubtedly the use of *kıpıtu*, or as it is called in East Ukamba, *muma*[1]. In trials, the judges, when they cannot come to a decision in any other way, resort to *kıpıtu* as a last resource, and let both parties swear that they are right. The breaking of an oath sworn over *kıpıtu* is considered to be followed by death, and the consequence is that

---

[1] Probably from *pıta* 'to bind fast', 'strangle', and *uma* 'to bite, to curse'.

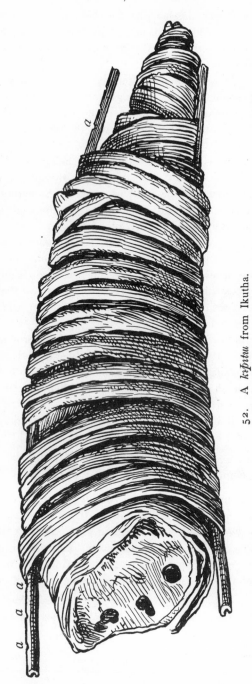

52. A *kɨfɨtu* from Ikutha.

Riksmuseum's Ethnogr. Coll. Inv. 12. 7. 311. *a* is a little incision, of which there are three on each end of one of the side-sticks.

the guilty party either confesses or refuses to swear, in which case
he is at once adjudged guilty. In this way *kɩpɩtuu* is used especially to discover thieves. At the end of a trial, both parties
often swear that they will perform exactly what has been imposed
upon them. They also used to swear to their honest intention,
in the case of internal feuds, to keep to any agreement entered into.
An oath over *kɩpɩtuu* can even be sworn apart from a law suit or
trial, i. e. in order to avoid one. With this object, on the return
from a plundering expedition and before the distribution of the
booty, an oath was always taken that every man should be content
with his share and not make trouble afterwards.

What, then, is the appearance of this object, for which the
native has more respect than for anything else in the world?
The *kɩpɩtuu* appears in many forms. A very usual form is the tusk
of a warthog (*ŋge*) or an antelope horn, filled with all sorts of
things, more often field-products and food prepared from them, a
little earth collected before the first rain of the year (*kɩmeu*), &c.
The *kɩpɩtuu* (fig. 52) that I had the good fortune to secure near Ikutha
(East Ukamba) was about 2 decimeters long, and consisted of a
dark, earthy mass, bound round with osiers[1]. According to all
accounts, it had been bought from the Atharaka, the small tribe up
on the Tana, which is considered very skilled in black magic.
In Ulu, the *kɩpɩtuu* are often obtained from the medicine-men
in Kikuyu. The price of a *kɩpɩtuu* is rather high, and consists of one or more oxen, or something of equal value. There
are also old *kɩpɩtuu*, which have descended from one generation
to another.

Of the ingredients used in the construction of a *kɩpɩtuu* occur,
besides foodstuffs such as beans and maize, Ricinus seed (*ṃbaʐkɩ*),
rust, slag and similar refuse from the smiths' workshops — called
by the way »the irons's excrement» (*maʐ ma kea*) — also fat from
dead people.

Besides these real *kɩpɩtuu*, which are possessed by private individuals, who procured them at great cost, there are others of less
potency, which almost anyone can construct for himself. They
are principally used for protection against theft, placed, for in-

---

[1] Now in the collections of the Ethnological department of the
Swedish State Museum (Riksmuseum).

stance, in the fields, thus a kind of amulet. We shall return to similar types in the chapter on magic.

The technical name for swearing over *kɨpɨtuɨ* is *kuna kɨpɨtuɨ* ('to strike *kɨpɨtuɨ*'), or still more generally *kuʒa kɨpɨtuɨ* ('to eat *kɨpɨtuɨ*')[1]. The ceremony is as follows: The *kɨpɨtuɨ* is laid on three small stones. It is important that it should not touch the ground, probably so that the ground may not be injured by the destructive magical power which dwells in the *kɨpɨtuɨ*. Round it are laid some twigs of *mwa*, a sort of acacia. Some stones are laid by the side, on which the person who is about to swear, stands while he takes the oath. These stones are indubitably used for the same reason as the three mentioned above, and perhaps also to give greater strength to the oath[2]. The number of stones seems to vary. On the only occasion I was present at the taking of an oath, seven were used; this number is also given in my notes, which are based on oral descriptions. C. Dundas mentions seven to eleven in Kitui, and Hobley only two. When two parties are going to take the oath, as at the conclusion of peace, they stand on opposite sides of the *kɨpɨtuɨ*, each on seven stones. Immediately beside them sit the *atumɨa ma nʒama*, to see that everything is done as it should be. The one that is going to take the oath, takes a twig and places himself on the stones, when the judges ask: »*nutonʒa kuʒa kɨpɨtuɨ?* 'Are you in a position to eat *kɨpɨtuɨ?*'. We will presume that he answers in the affirmative, and further (to take a definite case) that it is the case mentioned above, of which I was an eye-witness. It was about cattle; the plaintiff was awarded one cow and was made to swear afterwards that he would

---

[1] »To eat», in this sense, is also used by the Nilotic Nandi, in the highlands northeast of Lake Victoria. Hollis says: »The form of oath which is binding on all Nandi men is to strike a spear with a club and say: 'May the blade eat me!'» Hollis, The Nandi, p. 85. Among the Wasuaheli »to swear» is *kula amini* (i. e. 'to eat the oath'). This expression probably comes from some sort of eating by which, formerly, a man proved his innocence. Thus *kɨpɨtuɨ* was originally simply an ordeal. Oaths and ordeals seem often to have been identical in primitive practice. Other examples of »to eat» in this sense are given by Crawley in The Mystic Rose, p. 123.

[2] Frazer says: »The common custom of swearing upon a stone may be based partly on a belief that the strength and stability of the stones lend confirmation to the oath». The Golden Bough I, p. 16c.

not begin another suit to get more. He then took this oath: *mukanæŋga, ŋombɔ ɩmvɔ. nɩkɩsɩoka kwænda ɩŋgɩ ɩtɩna, ŋgaɩwa nɩ kɩu!* 'You shall give me a cow. If I come again and demand another afterwards, may I be eaten by this!' At the same time he struck the *kɩpɩtu* with the twig he held in his hand. This was repeated twice more in practically the same words. The twig must be from the *mukulwa* bush, otherwise the oath will be of no force. In a case of theft, the suspected person who wishes to prove his innocence says that, if he lies, he may be eaten by the *kɩpɩtu*. After that no further action can be taken against him.

Finally, a common example of swearing over *kɩpɩtu* to prevent further strife is the following: When blood-money has been paid for manslaughter, and the matter has been arranged, the relations of the deceased man swear that they intend to let the affair be forgotten, in something like the following words: *mundu wakwa utɩpæla 6ɩu, ŋgaɩwa nɩ kɩu, nɩsɩoka umwɩtɩa kɩndu kɩŋgɩ ɩtɩna, ŋgaɩwa nɩ kɩu!* 'If my man is not quite finished with, may I be eaten by this! (the *kɩpɩtu* is then struck with the twig). If I come back later and demand anything else from you, may I be eaten by this!' (the *kɩpɩtu* is then struck again with the twig.) The party who are paying also promise that they will not take the matter up again »when they have drunk beer». This is because experience has shown that, at drinking bouts, when the parties have become intoxicated, they are very disposed to take up old quarrels and law suits which have lain rankling in their minds; innumerable fights and deaths have come about in this way.

When the *kɩpɩtu* has been struck, a case is finished and the *nẓama* disperses. The judges receive from the contending parties a goat or an ox, which is killed and eaten. As has been mentioned, anyone refusing to swear is adjudged guilty. It is believed that if he perjures himself he will shortly die. If he does not die within a month or so, he is held to be innocent, even if the evidence against him was very strong. The culprit must then be sought elsewhere.

On account of the destructive power which is supposed to dwell in the *kɩpɩtu*, it is never kept in a village or near to cultivated land, but out in the wilds, where it is thought that no man can stumble on it. It is usually laid in a *ŋɛuŋga*, a hole or depression under some large stones. Anyone requiring a *kɩpɩtu* applies to the owner of one, from whom he can borrow it for some remuneration — as a rule, one goat. Different *kɩpɩtu* have varyingly great reputations for power and efficacy, and a man may go several days' march, as from Machakos to Kitui, to obtain a famous one. Some are said to be so powerful that the grass on the place where they are kept withers and never grows again. Again, rats and snakes that have got into the holes where *kɩpɩtu* are kept, die because of its proximity. The owner, always an old *mutmɩa*, loans out his *kɩpɩtu* with extremely minute instructions as to how it is to be treated, especially while being taken to and from the place where it is to be used. For this the following may be said to apply generally:

On no account may it be touched with the naked hands. The bearer smears his hands with mutton fat as a protective medium; then he binds the *kɩpɩtu* with bast from the *musænželɩ* tree, and carries it by the bast. He may not change hands; if he has, for example, begun to carry it in his right hand, he must continue to do so the whole way. If he gets tired, he may put it down on the ground [1], while he rests, but he must put it down on the same side of himself as he has carried it — in this case on the right. Anyone approaching is shouted to from a distance that *woʐ* (sorcery) is on the road, and then the new-comer turns off on the other side of the track, no matter how difficult it may be to get along. If he neglects this precautionary measure and then has coition with a woman, he will infallibly die. The bearer of a *kɩpɩtu* must also abstain from sexual intercourse during the journey. On the return journey, the same rules are observed as have just been described. In addition, every *kɩpɩtu* has its own special rules which must be observed. With one the bearer may not take snuff or eat with the hand which he uses to carry the *kɩpɩtu*; with another he may not take snuff at all; with a third he must, on crossing the first river on the way, sprinkle it with a little water, and at the second river, with a little sand, and so on [2].

During my visit to the district of Ikutha, I managed to bribe a broken-down old individual (the one mentioned in the in-

---

[1] That is to say, as long as he is in the wilds. Near villages and fields it is not readily put down without special precautionary measures being taken.

[2] Cf. Hobley, **Akamba** &c, p. 169.

troduction) to show me where a *kɪpɪtu* (the one just described) was kept. It lay in a crevice under a rock. The man laid goat's hair over it before he poked it out, and afterwards rubbed his hands with the milky juice of the *ɪluŋgu* plant. Even my servant, who had not touched the thing at all, purified his hands in the same way. The old man was very anxious for me to handle the *kɪpɪtu* according to his instructions, and was very alarmed when I took it up without further ado: he expressed the opinion that I should die at the end of a month.

When the *kɪpɪtu* has been struck, the litigating parties may not perform coition until the action has definitely been brought to an end, the outward sign of which is that the judges consume the ox which they have received. Before this, sexual intercourse is believed to be followed by death.

A woman may not own or carry a *kɪpɪtu*; neither may she take an oath over one; that is to say she may not have anything to do with one. As has been mentioned above, a man is responsible for the acts of his wife and daughters, and therefore, when necessary, he takes the oath over a *kɪpɪtu* on their behalf. If he refuses, the woman is naturally held to be guilty of what she is charged with.

As a result of the power which dwells in a *kɪpɪtu*, it can be used for magic purposes. Thus a man can strike a *kɪpɪtu* when he is alone, and at the same time curse an enemy. A person in Kitui was robbed of a cow, and so he struck a *kɪpɪtu*, saying: »Thief, when you drink of the milk of that cow, may you be eaten by this *kɪpɪtu!*« No secret is made of it when a *kɪpɪtu* is used in this way, and so the news of it soon reaches the thief, who, in most cases, is so terrified that he returns the stolen property. The man who has struck the *kɪpɪtu* may not have sexual intercourse until he knows that the other man has.

A *kɪpɪtu* may not be struck during the rains, while the crops are still growing in the fields. If an action is already proceeding, it is suspended until the next dry season. This seems to be due largely to the action of the women, who say that otherwise the rains will not come, and in addition grasshoppers and other plagues will descend upon the fields, and destroy the crops. In most cases the importunities of the women prevail. There are, however, those who are very loath to break off an action; but

then all the women go to such a man in a body and categori
cally command him to interrupt it. They generally get their own
way, for when they combine together and are roused, the women
are seldom opposed. Only in urgent cases is the *kɪpɪtu* struck
before the harvest is gathered in, and then it is done at a respectful
distance from the fields. These and the *kɪpɪtu* are then sprinkled
with a purifying medium, *ŋondu*, for which purpose a sheep or
goat is killed. The meat of the animal is eaten by the *atumɪa*.

**The use of *kɪpɪtu* in actions between persons who are
related to each other**. It has already been said that perjury
over a *kɪpɪtu* is believed to be followed by death. It must, however,
be noted that this consequence is not confined to the person who
commits the perjury, but may also — and this renders the *kɪpɪtu* so
much the more terrible — fall on other, perfectly innocent, members of his family or clan. Therefore a real *kɪpɪtu* is not used in
actions between persons who are related to each other. They
either rely on each other's word or have recourse to the existing
ordeals, which are only intended to discover the culprit, but have
otherwise no consequences which are disastrous for him or his
relatives (for ordeals, see p. 173). However, in such cases,
an oath is sometimes taken over an object called *ndundu*, which
is very like a *kɪpɪtu*, though it has not quite the same dangerous
properties, since only the guilty person loses his life, if he has
perjured himself; but no evil befalls his relatives. This *ndundu*
is made fresh every time it is to be used, and in the following way:

A bull is killed, and a small piece of practically every part
of the carcase is cut off. The points of the heart and tongue
and the neck-bone, *ŋgata*, are specially important ingredients of
ndundu. Everything is gathered together, mixed with blood in a
calabash, and packed into the gall-bladder; the *ndundu* is now ready.
Branches of about one meter in length are then cut from the long-
thorned species of acacia called *mwea* or *mwɑ*, and these branches are then stuck into the earth, and the *ndundu* placed upon
them. The branches correspond to the stones upon which the
kɪpɪtu is placed, and, like the latter, the *ndundu* ought not to
touch the earth, or it loses in strength. The man who is to
swear takes a long acacia thorn and, according to the usual form-
ula, says that, if he did so and so, he may be eaten by the *ndundu*.

At the same time he pierces the bladder with the thorn and licks its point. This act is probably symbolic — in the event of his perjuring himself he will burst like the bladder[1].

Just as we interpret the stones as a symbol of stability, giving enduring force to the oath, so can the use of the acacia be considered in the same way. Certain kinds of acacia are extremely hardy, almost the only tree which thrives in desert-like districts poor in water. Also because of the fact that the acacias, contrary to many other trees, do not lose their leaves even during the worst droughts, the native easily come to look upon them as something especially permanent and vigorous; as little likely is a stone or an acacia to perish entirely, as for the power of the oath to be annihilated.

* * *

The use of the *kɪpɪtuɪ* has been adopted by the English civil servants on the Government stations at Kitui and Machakos, in cases which are brought before them, and which they cannot clear up by hearing witnesses or in any other way. During my visit to Kitui at the end of 1911, all the suspected persons in such a case readily struck the *kɪpɪtuɪ*, although the Commissioner, Mr Scolefield, said that he was convinced that one of them was guilty. There is therefore some doubt whether, in spite of their obvious terror of the *kɪpɪtuɪ*, the natives do not sometimes perjure themselves over it. However, it is not impossible that Mr Scolefield's native assistants had, perhaps intentionally, made some mistake, so that the influence of the *kɪpɪtuɪ* was nullified.

4. Ordeals.

Even the use of *kɪpɪtuɪ* may, in a way, be looked upon as a sort of ordeal. But an essential difference is that perjury over the *kɪpɪtuɪ* entails immediate death, while the ordeal is only intended to disclose the culprit, the punishment being afterwards decided upon by the court. Another difference is that the medicine-man, *mundu muɔ*, generally conducts the ordeal; members of the *nẑama* are certainly present, but only in the capacity of controllers. The

---

[1] B r u t z e r describes something of the same sort in Der Geisterglaube bei den Kamba, p. 14.

Akamba themselves do not distinguish materially between their various methods of discovering a criminal, and the ordeals described below are often heard spoken of as *kɨpɨtuɩ* (for example the first is called *kɨpɨtuɩ kɩa kɨɓʑu* 'the *kɨpɨtuɩ* of the knife'). Otherwise they are called after the objects with which they are chiefly carried out; no general expression for the idea »ordeal» is to be found[1]. As has already been pointed out in passing, a primitive stage in a people scarcely differentiates between oaths and ordeals.

Among the Akamba, I have found the following five ordeals in use. The first of them at least is sometimes used by both parties, that is to say the complainant must also submit to the test.

A. *kɨpɨtuɩ kɩa kɨɓʑu* (the '*kɨpɨtuɩ* of the knife'), an ordeal widely spread in Africa, in which the suspected person has to touch a red-hot iron. Among the Akamba it is carried out in the following way: Suppose that a person has been robbed of a goat. A knife, which he or the medicine-man has treated with magic medicine, *mupæa*, is put in the fire. When it is red-hot, it is taken out, and the suspected persons have in turn to touch the iron with their tongues, saying: *æpwa nɨnosetɔ mbuʑ ʑa ŋganʑa, kɨɓʑu mbɨɓʑe* ('If I have taken N. N's goat, may the knife burn me!'). The natives believe that only the guilty one is burnt. The fact of the matter probably is that the guilty man betrays himself by obvious signs of fear, or prefers to confess at once, when he sees that he cannot escape; while the innocent, believing implicitly that they cannot be hurt, go forward calmly to lick the knife. It is thus that the medicine-man, in most cases a fairly good psychologist, soon sees clearly who is guilty.

B. Another ordeal which is also used very much in the dark continent, and which may be looked upon as a variant of the preceding one, is to make a needle red-hot and stick it through the under lip of the suspected person, near the corner of the mouth. »If he is innocent, he feels nothing, and the wound does not bleed; if he is guilty, the needle does not get far in before he confesses».

C. *kʑuma* (the bead) is an ordeal which is said to originate from the Kikuyu district. The suspected persons sit in a circle.

---

[1] In the Kikuyu language, the word for ordeal is *muma*, that is to say the same word as is used in East Ukamba for *kɨpɨtuɩ*.

The officiating functionary, the plaintiff or the medicine-man, rubs his hands with magic medicine (*muрæa*) and white earth (*ea*), and smears some under the eyes of the suspects. Then he takes two china beads, of the kind which are ordinarily used in the manufacture of ornaments, and goes from one to the other, saying: *kɩuma, andu a onδə, umbonɩə mundu wɩ na mbuɩ ɩakwa* ('bead, show me who has stolen my goat among all those who are here') — the words are taken from a special case, when a goat had been stolen. When he has said this, he blows on the beads. In front of an innocent person, the beads lie still in his out-stretched hand; but in front of the culprit, they are said to fly violently towards his eyes, where they stick, and can only be removed by the medicine-man. The principle for discovering the guilty man is, of course, the same in this case as in the previous one: the medicine-man knows pretty well, or soon discovers, who is guilty. Besides, the result of this test naturally depends chiefly upon his good pleasure.

D. *ŋgunɩko* is used specially for discovering thieves. The word signifies 'plug, lid'. A small calabash, about the size of a snuffbox, is filled with water, in which the medicine-man has mixed »medicine», after which the opening is smeared over with bees' wax. A narrow tube or a hollow straw is passed through it. The medicine-man goes from one to another of the suspects, and when he comes to the thief, the water spurts forcibly out over him through the tube. Brutzer also describes this ordeal from what was told him by another missionary, but in this case the calabash was fitted with a stopper without a tube, and there was a hole in the bottom, over which the medicine-man put his finger[1]. When he comes to the guilty person, the stopper is forced out, and the water flies over him. In this case also, the medicine-man has no doubt discovered in some way or other which the guilty man is, and then lets the water spurt out over him.

E. The poison test is very widely employed in Africa. We will merely recall the generally prevalent *muavɩ*-drinking in Central Africa. The Akamba use the bark of a tree, *mboŋgolo*, which is pulverised and mixed with water; the suspect must drink the mixture. The drink has a strongly intoxicating effect, but I

---

[1] E. Brutzer, Der Geisterglaube bei den Kamba, p. 14.

do not believe that it is fatal. If there are several suspects, they must all drink and then sit down and wait for the poison to take effect. The one who is the first to be affected is thereby proved guilty of the crime in question. He sometimes behaves just like one possessed, imagines that someone wants to murder him, calls out »Let me go!» and so on.

F. Finally, according to Brutzer, o r d e a l b y f i r e is employed also among the Akamba[1]. The suspect has to run through a fire. I have not met with this ordeal, but it is mentioned in an animal fable of which I have made a record: a hyena and a hare are suspected of having stolen a ram, and must prove their innocence by jumping over a big basket which is on fire. From this story we may be entitled to draw the conclusion that the fire-test was employed among the Akamba formerly at least.

Hildebrandt cites some ordeals, which he asserts originate in Ukamba. They come, however, from the people on the coast, as is indicated by their Suaheli names[2].

5. The administration of justice by lynch=law (*kɪɣola*).

Among the Akamba, there exists a custom which unconsciously reminds one of the so-called lynch-law in the United States of North America, although, as we shall see, the comparison is not exact in several particulars. Persons who are suspected of causing the death of other people by means of *woɪ* (that is, witchcraft) and are thus dangerous to the public safety, can be killed with impunity by the united intervention of all the adult male inhabitants of the district. The same is also true of incorrigible thieves. Yet, action is not taken simply on the accusation of a single individual. They go to work quite soberly and, according to the native conception, quite legally, since the *nžama* must first give its consent to the execution. To ascertain whether the person suspected is really guilty, members of the *kɪsuka* are sent to several medicine-men in different districts, who, with the help of their divination apparatus, discover who the guilty person is, and tell the several messengers. When they get back, they must go singly, without holding

---

[1] Brutzer, Der Geisterglaube, p. 14.
[2] J. M. Hildebrandt, Die Wakamba, p. 388.

any communication with one another, to report before the *nžama*, and to swear over *kɨpɨtu* that they have truthfully reported the words of the witch doctor. If all the medicine-men have indicated the same person as guilty of the many deaths which have occurred in the district lately, then all is clear, and the elders consent to his death[1]. Without these, the *kɨgolə* — so the lynching mass is called — can do nothing. Under the leadership of a *mutumɨa* of the *nžama*, the *kɨsuka* and the young men betake themselves to a remote spot in the wilds. None of them may stay at home, all must take part. They tell the women and children that they are going on a warlike expedition, for example to steal cattle from the Masai; they take weapons and provisions with them. Sometimes, in order that their departure may be the more secret, they seize the opportunity while the women are away working in the fields. When the latter return, they find that their husbands and sons have disappeared, and with them all the food that was ready prepared. The *atumɨa*, with the exception of the leader of the *kɨgolə* mentioned above, remain at home. They constitute the judicial authority, while the young men constitute the executive authority.

The young men are now all gathered in the wilds. They still do not all know who the guilty man is, till the leading elder says to one of his near relations: »Give us an arrow out of your quiver». No more is necessary for all to understand. The handing over of the arrow is an acknowledgement of the lawfulness of the deed on the part of the family of the doomed man, and strictly speaking the man may not be put to death until the arrow has been delivered. This arrow must be one of the first to pierce him. They stay from four to five days in this remote spot, an ox which has been brought with them is eaten, and each man binds himself by oath over *kɨpɨtu* to obey the leader implicitly.

They then go to kill the victim in his village, in the fields, or wherever he may be. With wild cries of »*ɲɲa, ɲɲa!*» the throng rush forward, and arrows are let fly at the unhappy man. When he sinks to the ground dying, large branches of trees and stones, if such are handy, are thrown at him. Afterwards, as if pursued by furies, all rush back to their hiding-place, sprinkling their heads with ashes on the way. The use of ashes in purifying rites is known in many different quarters.

---

[1] The same procedure is described from Loango. Post II, p. 153.

In civilised countries, at military executions, it is the custom for some of the rifles to be loaded with blank cartridge, and the marksmen themselves do not know who fired the fatal shot, so that none may have pangs of conscience. Something similar happens sometimes when the *kɩŋolɔ* is carried out, especially if they can approach close to the doomed man unobserved. No one may then shoot first, but on a given signal — for example the holding up of the leader's staff — a shower of arrows is let fly.

But we return to the *kɩŋolɔ*, which has gone back to its hidden refuge. All the members of it are now »unclean», as is indicated by the ashes, and they cannot return home until they have been sprinkled with *ŋondu*, that is to say, undergone a purifying process. As has already been mentioned in another connection, such a process is always carried out by a *mutumɩa* specially versed in such things. A deputation consisting of members of the *kɩsuka* is sent to the elders to ask for *ŋondu*. When they get near to the village, they call loudly to the elders, say that they have completed their work, and now wish to be purified, so that they can return to their homes. They must sit at a long distance from the elders, and if there is a river or stream in the neighbourhood, they place themselves on the opposite side of it. The nearest relatives of the executed man have to provide the goat or the goats necessary for the purification. No lamenting may be indulged in; if the victim's women-folk cry, the family must pay another goat. An old man versed in matters connected with *ŋondu* takes the goat to the *kɩŋolɔ* hiding-place, and purifies the members. They may now return home, though not all at once. In separate groups of two or three, they go towards the village by different tracks. The act is over, unclean blood has been let out of the body of the community.

No blood-money is paid to the relatives of a person killed by *kɩŋolɔ*. It is usually old women who are the victims, less often old men; we are thus in the presence of veritable witch-processes. Young people are not usually considered to be versed in the black art. It is certain that many innocent old people have met with a tragic fate at the hands of a *kɩŋolɔ*, but many poisoners, have also met with well-deserved punishment. Occasionally the doomed man gets wind of his danger in time, and saves himself by flight; but it has also happened that a member of the *kɩŋolɔ* has been disagreeably surprised to find himself the one pointed out by the medicine-men. It has also happened that a reckless dare-devil has fortified his village, provided himself with food and water, and simply threatened to shoot down anyone who dared to approach. To endanger their lives unnecessarily in open battle is foreign to the nature of the Akamba, and fire is absolutely powerless against the green thorn hedge round the village. So the *kɩgolɔ* perhaps thinks it as well to give way, and to pardon the person concerned, on a promise of amendment, especially if he offers to pay fines.

This is, in the main, the course of the method of punishment which may be called »African lynching». If one is critical, the expression is faulty. When we talk about lynching, we usually mean the proceedings of an incensed crowd, generally a mob, who, in unbridled fury and generally with great cruelty, administer justice on their own account. As we have seen, this is not at all the case with the *kɩgolɔ*, which, on the contrary, acts by order of the leading men of the community, the elders, and can thus be looked upon as the reaction of the protective instinct of the community against a threatening danger.

As is well-known, witchcraft is considered a particularly grave offence in Africa. That so many innocent persons fall victims is another matter, and may be traced to the superstition of the people. Other motives, such as jealousy and a desire for vengeance, often have something to do with it. The reason why the *kɩgolɔ* is, in most cases, only resorted to in self-defence is that it cannot kill a single victim, but waits until there are two or more suspects. If there is only one, he is either driven from the place or must promise improvement. Thus it has happened in a place where the *kɩgolɔ* was ordered out, that the condemned man has saved himself by flight, but after a time, when the storm has blown over, has returned home, since a *kɩgolɔ* could not be sent out against him alone.

Immediately outside Machakos lives an old female »medicine-man» called *kabuɓa*, with whom I am acquainted personally. Several years ago, she was accused of having killed two of her neighbours by witchcraft, and was condemned to death by *kɩgolɔ*. She got wind of it in time, and fled with her husband to the fort, where she lived some years, until the affair was forgotten. About twenty years ago, a woman was killed who was

said to have taken the life of her brother-in-law. She was in an
advanced stage of pregnancy, and when she fell to the ground
pierced with arrows, she gave birth to a child, which, however,
did not survive. Mr Kanig, of the Leipziger Mission, mentions a
case at Ikutha in 1900 when an old woman was killed[1].

Mr Säuberlich told the author of a man who for some reason
was condemned to death, but got to know of this in good time, and
instead of flying resolutely supplied himself with food, water and
arrows for a good time and strengthened the hedge round his hut.
A large number of men came to seize him, but stopped at a respectful distance when he threatened to shoot the first who approached. No one would risk his skin, and after reflecting for a
time they thought it best to leave him in peace, especially as he
made overtures and offered to pay heavy fines.

Nowadays, when the whole of Ukamba is under British
rule, *kĩgolo* is forbidden. However, some of the officials think
that it is still practised in the more remote places.

6. The intervention of the women in the administration of justice.

On the whole, the Kamba woman goes through life calmly
and quietly, doing her duty and suitably subservient to her husband. Her most important work is looking after the fields, for
the weal or woe of the people depends principally on the result
of the harvest. Therefore, when something happens which, seen
from the women's superstitious point of view, threatens the growing crops or the village itself, they may be worked up into a
fury, and if they consider that the men take the matter too calmly,
they conspire together to enforce their views by their own efforts
— and they generally succeed. As an illustration of this, I
will cite a particular case.

As often happens, a man had lent a field, which he did not
at the time need himself, to another man. When he wanted it
back later, the wife of the other man refused to agree to his

---

[1] G. Kanig, Dornige Pfade eines jungen Missionars in Ukamba,
p. 20.

having it. In the meantime, however, the owner sent his wife
to set the field in order, but the other woman went there also.
In vain she was exhorted to give in. According to the women's
ideas, the controversy would bring bad luck to the crops on
all the neighbouring fields, since it might cause the rains to
fail. Therefore they decided to take the matter into their own
hands, so as to get it settled as soon as possible. They urged
the husband of the obstinate woman to present a goat, so that
the fields might be sprinkled with *ɡondu*, but he refused. Then
the women beat their big drums (*kɩpæmbɔ*) and met in council.
A deputation of two old women was sent to the refractory man
to demand the immediate presentation of a goat. He still refused,
and the women became furious, and went in a body to let him
hear — in none too mild language — their opinion of his behaviour. He did not dare to refuse any longer; and indeed it
is seldom that a man dares to oppose the women when they
come in that way. The goat they demanded was delivered and
carried off in triumph, to be slaughtered on the field in dispute.

If anyone persists in his defiance, the women strew leaves
in front of the entrance to his hut, and then the owner cannot
enter until he has submitted.

When the women come thus in a body, beating their drums
and carrying boughs in their hands, the men try to keep out
of the way as much as possible. Anyone coming across their
path is showered with derisive and insulting epithets; and in
the district of Kitui it is even said to have happened that the
men have been assaulted and maltreated. Only the oldest *atumɩa*
escape unmolested, but even they hide their faces in their blankets
while the crowd of women is passing.

It may be maintained that, by such behaviour, the women
interfere in a way in the administration of justice, desiring to get
a dispute which is injurious to the community settled more quickly
than it would be if the law took its normal course. Seen from another
point of view, their conduct bears a religious stamp, since the
spirits (*aɩmu*) are thought to be incensed at such disputes. After
the contents of the goat's stomach have been used for the preparation of *ɡondu*, therefore, the rest of the animal is offered
up in the usual way on the place of sacrifice (*ɩpæmbo*) to con-
ciliate the spirits (see Chap. XIII).

It is interesting to observe the submissive attitude of the
men, when such proceedings take place. The reason is perhaps
a tacit recognition of the justice of the women's demands. The
women are more conservative and superstitious than the men, and
in many things have their own rules to observe, which are respected by the men, even though they often do not attach much
mportance to them.

7. Curses.

As far as I know, the use of curses is really confined to the
family circle, within which they are used by a father or mother
against a refractory son. Though my observations on family life
are to be included in a subsequent chapter, I have, however,
found it suitable to append here some remarks on the use of
curses (*kɩumo*) to the section on criminal jurisdiction proper.

The head of a family in Ukamba has patriarchal authority
over his children. For example, he has control over his son's
earnings. It is not unusual, nevertheless, for some to be disobedient, and when the parents can in no other way — either by
gentle means or chastisement — master an insubordinate son, they
fall back on the last and most terrible resource — a curse.

A. **A father's curse.** An occasional reason for cursing is
that, without his father's consent, a young man begins to drink
beer (*ukı*), and continues to do so,.in spite of the express prohibition of his father. For, according to an old custom, youths
(*anakə*) may not drink beer before they have purchased their
father's permission, by making him certain presents. It also happens that, in order to take away from his son all desire for un-
lawful beer-drinking, a father utters a curse in advance, which is
to come into operation if the son ignores the prohibition. A
common way of cursing is the following:

The father takes the iron (*kɩo*) with which the cattle are
branded, and places it in the fire. When it is hot, he takes it
out, and, holding it over a calabash, he urinates[1] on it, saying:
»I who have begot you do not wish you to drink beer, since you
have not yet begun to pay me. May you be destroyed thus»

---

[1] As is well known, the human excrements play an important
part in the superstition and magic of all peoples. For a closer study,
see J. G. Bourke, Scatalogic rites of all nations.

(as the iron hisses from contact with the fluid)[1]. Then he takes the calabash and flings the urine from it to the west (»towards the setting sun»), uttering another curse: »I have begotten you with this my *kea* (penis), may you go down like this sun!»[2] Anyone who does not improve, or who is not released from this curse, is said not to live long — at the most a few months[3].

B. **A mother's curse.** A mother can also curse her son, if he takes no notice of her directions or does not perform the tasks she sets him, but instead blindly devotes himself to the favourite amusements of the young men, lounging about and dancing. She cannot, however, curse in the same way as the father, but proceeds as follows:

She takes a small quantity of different sorts of vegetable foods, some grains of maize, a little millet, Eleusine seeds &c, puts them in a calabash vessel, and sets this in the fire. When the vessel crackles and is consumed, she says: »I, N. N., gave birth to you; I have suckled you and washed you and carried you and removed your motions, when you were a child. But now, when you have eaten and grown strong, it is I who curse you: may you be destroyed thus (like the food in the fire), you and your children!»[4]

In my collection of Kamba folk-lore, there is a tale of two brothers, the sun and the moon, the latter being originally the chief, because he was the elder. He misbehaved himself, however, and drew down on himself his mother's curse. She laid it on him in the manner just described.

For a more serious transgression on the son's part — such

---

[1] The words are taken from a special case in the neighbourhood of Machakos; they run thus: *œpwa ninɀɔ nukusɀaiɀɔ, na ndɪkwœnda ukɪnɀwa ukɪ, na ndunamba undaɀa wokianɀ(a)ou.*

[2] Kikamba: *œpwa ninɀɔ nuusɀaiɀɔ na kea kɪ kɀakwa wopoa na sɀua ɀɪu.*

[3] Among the Wadjagga, curses by members of the family and relations are considered specially dangerous, those of the father and mother always entailing death. B. G u t m a n n, Fluchen und Segnen im Munde der Wadschagga p. 302. A. E. Crawley shows (article on Cursing and Blessing in Encycl. of Religion and Ethics) by examples from different times and peoples how generally the curse of the parents, especially of the father, is particularly strong.

[4] Kikamba: *ninɀɔ, ŋganɀa, nakusɀaiɀɔ na ŋgɪkwoŋga na ŋgɪupambɀa na ŋgɪtua, ŋgukuœtɔ na ŋgɪtua mbɀaɀaa maɀ maku, wɪ kana, na ɀeu, waɀa 6inɀa ninɀɔ ukuuma, watolekaŋgou na sɀana sɀaku!*

as, for example, stealing his mother's milk or one of her cows — the mother can lay a more serious curse on him. She washes her *ṇdamı* (the small rectangular loin-cloth worn by the Kamba women) and throwing out the water violently, so that it splashes in all directions, she says: »May you splash thus, as I have given you birth with this my *kıno!*» (the name of the female pudenda)[1].

The missionary Kanig tells of a mother who, in anger at her daughters disobedience, took a brand from the fire and stuck it in a vessel of water, so that the hissing wood was extinguished. At the same time she ejaculated this curse: »May your life be extinguished like this wood!»[2]

C. **How a father revokes his curse on his son.** The youth who has been cursed by his father, seldom dares to continue in his refractoriness, but tries to get the curse removed as soon as possible, and endeavours to obtain his father's blessing (*kẓaɸımo*) instead. His method of procedure is as follows:

He buys beer and takes it to his father as a present, asking for his blessing. If necessary he repeats this, until the old man is propitiated and yields. Then the father mixes milk and Eleusine seed together in a calabash bowl — without these accessories the blessing is ineffective — and orders his son to stretch out his hands. Taking a sip of the milk, he spirts his son's hands and chest with it, saying (the words were addressed to a son who was cursed for drinking beer without permission): »I give thee my blessing! Drink beer, but not too much; do not pick quarrels with people either, when you have drunk beer!» The son rubs his hands dry on his face, and the father spits a blessing into the calabash. The curse is now removed, and the young man has gained the right to drink beer.

D. **Curses used by young people.** The youths and young girls among themselves can also employ a sort of curse, which they lay on an unpopular person. If a girl gives evidence of *ŋgulu* 'self-will' — for example if she refuses to take part in the dancing of the young people or the excesses connected with it — the young men assemble and strike their *kıɸıtu*, consisting of a

---

[1] Kikamba: *womınẑukou, œɸwa nınẓə nausẓaıẓə na kıno kı kẓakwa.*
[2] G. Kanig, Kambakinder, p. 6.

red china bead (*kɨtǫ*). They all strike once with a stone, saying:
»N. N's girl gives evidence of *ŋgulu*. If, after this, I dance with
her, accompany her on the track, or even speak to her, may I
be eaten by this *kɨpɨtu!*» The girls treat their comrade in the
same way, and then the poor thing is absolutely isolated from
the other young people. She cannot go to other people of the
same age elsewhere, for as soon as they hear what has happened
to her, they also shun her. Her position soon becomes unbearable
— her parents also suffer — and sooner or later she gives way.
Then her father goes to their dancing-place (*kɨtuto*), and arranges
a day with the young men for his daughter to be allowed to come
and be received into the young people's circle again.

On the appointed day, the girl goes to the dancing-place,
taking with her two bunches of bananas (*nðumba*) and two large
calabashes full of porridge, mixed with a lot of fat. The former
are presents to the men, the latter to the girls. She stands apart
from the others, and a youth asks her if she is willing to abandon
her defiant attitude. The answer is in the affirmative, and she
may now choose out four youths and four girls, who bless her by
spitting on her. The curse is thereby removed.

What makes this curse so dreadful is the belief that a woman
who is under such a curse, can never, even if she manages to get
a husband, be certain of being able to have children. And this
implies something infinitely terrible to every Kamba girl.

Chapter XII. **Warfare and customs connected with it**[1].

In the greatest part of Africa the continual feuds and plundering expeditions between the tribes belong already to the past. It is now too late almost everywhere to carry out any practical studies of the natives' methods of war, and concerning these things ethnology has, for the most part, to rely on the statements of older people. In the abundant ethnographical African literature one finds, as a rule, this side of the native life treated in a surprisingly cursory manner, except in the case of tribes with real military talent, such as the Zulus in South- and the Masai in East-Africa, among whom there exists a real military organization, capable of attracting interest. One is therefore compelled to make use of the only way left out of the difficulty, namely to collect accurate information from older men who have themselves at one time taken part as warriors in the feuds of their tribe. But these sources should be used as soon as possible, as when the old men of the present generation have died it will be too late, the younger men having already grown up under the new conditions.

In Ukamba a »pax brittannica» has already prevailed undisturbed for a decade. My description is, on account of this, exclusively based on oral information from former leaders of the Akamba's predatory expeditions against their neighbours, the Kikuyu and the Masai tribes. Careful comparison and verification of the different statements made should give the description a certain correctness. The Kamba negroes have certainly never been a warring people of note, but yet we shall find that they were not quite strangers to the idea of tactics. We shall

---

[1] The chapter is translated, with alteration and additions, from Ymer 1914.

see that for attacks a force was divided into several parts, each with its definite task, that the various divisions were arranged according to certain principles, that there existed a rudimentary form of searching and guarding, etc. Although the description is that of a period that is past, we may be allowed in our account to use the present tense.

I. **Preparations for an expedition.**

Most of the native campaigns are from our point of view pure plundering expeditions, as they are undertaken almost exclusively to steal cattle. They serve partly to satisfy the desire for meat, partly to increase the herds. Another important reason for them is that many are too poor to buy wives for themselves and so they wish by means of a campaign to procure in a rapid and congenial way the cattle necessary for this purpose. As is to be expected from the character of these expeditions, no formal declaration of war is made, the successful issue of the enterprise depending to a great extent on its being a surprise. For an offensive war is needed the consent of the assembly of the elders, the *nžama*; the leaders are some old and experienced warriors, called *asılılı*. As soon as the *nžama* have given their assent to a campaign, the *asılılı* get an almost dictatorial power, while in peace time they do not exercise any special function in the community. They are, however, prominent members of the *nžama*[1] Liability to serve as soldiers falls first on the unmarried men (*anakə*), then also on the younger married men (*nɗælə*). In a manner it may be considered that universal compulsory service prevails, inasmuch as no one can refuse to accompany the army, as soon as the *asılılı* have obtained the *nžama*'s assent to the war. Those who for some reason are away from their village, are informed and have to come home as soon as possible. If anyone stays at home without a good excuse (sickness, etc.), he is at best insulted and may not come out with the other people to meet the returning conquerors, but must hide in his hut. It has even happened that such a man has been killed. Usually, however, it was the younger element who were eager to be off plundering and stormed the

---

[1] Cf. Chap. X, p. 149.

members of the *nɀama* with requests to go. The latter then in-
quire of the *asɩlɩlɩ* about the prospects of success for the suggested enterprise, and if they consider the occasion unsuitable,
usually nothing is done.

Once the decision for a campaign has really been made, the
asɩlɩlɩ go to the medicine man (*mundu muə*) to ascertain if it is
undertaken under favourable auspices. If this is not the case, it
may happen that the carrying out of the plan is put off. For
our description here, however, we shall assume that the answer
is favourable. Then they get protective war medicine from the
medicine man, and other »medicine» to rub on the cattle they
hope to steal, so that it will follow them »like dogs». If they
are pursued and have to run, the cattle do the same; in a word,
they will have no trouble at all in driving them away. On the
instruction of the medicine man the *asɩlɩlɩ* then offer sacrifices to
the spirits of their dead forefathers, especially to the eminent
warriors of former times, at the sacrificial places that are dedi-
cated to them.

2. **Armament and equipment.**

Before going further a few words on the warriors' armament
and other outfit may be given here. The Akamba's arms are
the bow and arrow and the sword; they do not use spears, clubs
and shields, which are the principal weapons of their neighbours
in the west and south-west, the Akikuyu and Masai[1]. On their
heads they wear a kind of cap made of skin or imported blue
calico, *mbækə* (*kaniki* in the Suaheli language), which is obtained
by Arabian or Suaheli traders from the coast, and in earlier times,
when cattle were plentiful, was paid for by a goat for a little piece.
Round the brow there was also a strap, and to this were fastened
pieces of leather, from which some long white ostrich feathers proudly
streamed[2]. Resting on one shoulder and running diagonally over
the chest was worn a kind of oval frame (*wea*), made out of the

---

[1] For more about the weapons see the chapter »Weapons».

[2] On the other hand they do not, as Hildebrandt states, use the
frame for the face with short black or white ostrich feathers which is
well-known among the Masai. J. M. Hildebrandt, Ethnographische
Notizen über Wakamba und ihre Nachbarn p. 358.

mane of the giraffe or zebra. Round the waist they liked to fix
a bit of red cloth (*mukumba*), reminiscent of the belts worn by the
native military police (*askari*) in the service of the government.
Their insteps were adorned with the strips of the colobus monkey's
black and white skin, so well-known in many East African tribes.
Probably we have in this a borrowing from the Masai's war
costume. A difference lies in the fact that the latter wear the
points turned backwards, but the Akamba have them pointing
forward. They also used to fix bells on their knees, to increase
the noise as they rushed forward to attack[1]. On longer campaigns the warriors did not wear their ornaments on the march,
but kept them in a bag of leather (*nguso*) which was carried in
a strap over the shoulder. Only when they came into the proximity of the enemy did they take them out. Their usual everyday ornaments, armlets of metal, etc. they prefer to leave at
home, as they lessen their activity, make it more difficult to run,
etc. Provisions, such as batatas (sweet potatoes), flour and gruel
(*usu*), are taken with them on the road. When the warriors' food
is got ready at home in the village, on no conditions are unmarried
girls allowed to take part in the preparation. This would cause
injury to the warriors, a belief which must doubtlessly be considered
as a kind of sexual taboo, as the girls would certainly have intercourse with the youths at home, and then the food prepared
by them would »get into the legs» of the warriors and make
them heavy.

3. **The attack.**

Let us accompany a pillaging expedition against the Masai
kraals, which were formerly situated on the steppe south-west of
Machakos. My imformants are chiefly two old men in the Machakos district, who in the days of their strength had been capable *asilili*. As objects are seen a long way round on the steppe,
a halt is made at a long distance from the kraal which is to be

---

[1] I do not know if these bells were worn on any definite principle. Among the Masai those who took part in the fights wore large
bells on their legs, so that the sound might help to call the troop together.
Merker, Die Masai, p. 87.

attacked, e. g. 5—8 kilometres, according to the nature of the ground. Protected by the darkness of the night spies are sent out (*apɩanɩ*), preferably older warriors, often some of the *asɩlɩlɩ* themselves, as they do not believe that the young warriors are capable of displaying the necessary calm and caution. The most important task of the spies is to find out the place of the warriors' kraal, the situation of the other kraals and how the cattle is kept[1].

On their return the spies do not inform the warriors of the result of their search, as if they did it might easily happen that the younger and more eager men would, if the prospects for the attack were very good, immediately rush forth and so perhaps spoil everything. Among the »medicine» that the *asɩlɩlɩ* have obtained before they set out there is usually a magic soporific, which causes the enemy to fall into a deep sleep, if it is placed in his fire. The medicine is fixed to a long stick, and, on the night when the attack is to take place, a *musɩlɩlɩ* steals forward to the warriors' kraal, breaks through the wall or door of a hut and with the help of the stick lays the medicine in the fire.

Before the attack every man has to take an oath on the *kɩpɩtuɩ* that he will not fly, but will obey the leaders' orders (»If I fly, may I be eaten by this *kɩpɩtuɩ!*»). Then they vie with each other in making bold promises: »If I do not kill a Masai to-day, may this *kɩpɩtuɩ* eat me» (*ŋgalɩwa nɩ kɩpɩtuɩ kɩú*), says one. Another makes the bold promise to force his way into a hut and compel a Masai woman to give him milk, etc. The doubtful and faint-hearted ones are encouraged by the *asɩlɩlɩ*, who hold out prospects of a rich booty: »Are you afraid? Be men! We can't get cattle for nothing. If you only go forward bravely and obey our commands, each one of you will bring home fine, fat oxen and pregnant cows, which your mothers and wives will milk in the cattle kraals. But if you are cowards, so that we must turn back again with our errand unaccomplished, the women will laugh at you, when you come back again to the village.» The *asɩlɩlɩ* do not take part in the actual fighting, but when every-

---

[1] We must remember that among the Masai there are special kraals for the married people and others for the warriors. The cattle are kept at night in an enclosure, situated in the middle of the closed circle which is formed by the huts.

thing is arranged and the advance begins they remain behind. Their work is to make plans and to organise, they are usually too old and heavy to fight. The command is taken over instead by some younger experienced and capable warriors, who will some-time succeed the *asɪlɪlɪ* in their office.

The attack itself is usually started at daybreak, as soon as it is sufficiently light to seize the cattle. The hostile force is now divided into different parts, each with its name and special task. If we suppose that the objective of the attack consists of a kraal for the married and at some distance off another for the warriors, the Akamba's grouping will be as follows:

The point of greatest danger is of course the warriors' kraal, and so they direct against it a section called *muena*, consisting of picked warriors, the best shots, half of them young men, *anakə*, half younger married men, *ŋðælə*. The reason for this intermix-ture is that the young men, left to themselves, are altogether too impetuous and thoughtless. For the task of this group is not to engage in hand-to-hand fighting, but, on the contrary, to try to keep the Masai warriors at a distance with their arrows and in this way prevent them from coming to the help of the others.

Against the other kraal is sent a section called *ŋgɪla*. Its task is to seize the cattle and bring them to a third section, *ɪta*, which is waiting behind and takes no part in the fighting. It will then take the booty away in safety. The grouping has been carried out and the advance begins. To give the signal for this it is said that light-signals were sometimes used, i. e. the reflection of sunlight by means of mirrors. It is clear that the people of East Africa have used mirrors for a very long time; these were for-merly obtained from the Arab and Suaheli traders, and still earl-ier they bought them themselves in Mombasa. Absolute silence is enjoined; it is important to get as far forward as possible un-perceived. But as soon as they are discovered, a mighty shout is raised and they let the piercing notes of the war-flute (*ŋgulɪ*) ring out[2]. The war-flutes are carried by a number of men in each

---

[1] Similar principles are followed by the Masai. Cf. M. Merker, Die Masai, 2 aufl. p. 87.

[2] The *ŋgulɪ* consists of a decimetre long piece of horn of a smaller antelope species. It is blown at the wider end, while the thumb is held against the turned-down mouthpiece. I have got the same in-

section; the Akamba o not like to fight without this music, it has an inciting effect on their senses. The flutes have been

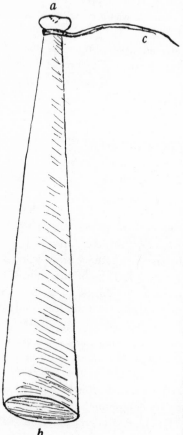

smeared with medicine by the medicine man before the departure from home. A number of signals, such as »Halt!» are blown with them. There are attempts at the construction of a code of signals, as a number of old men can with the *ŋgulɪ* reproduce certain words and expressions, which are understood by others. When a Masai troop approached the villages, they blew, for instance, *aka-61, aka-61, mæ-kuka, mæ-kuka,* 'The Masai, the Masai, are coming!' The flute is also blown in case of an attack by enemies so as to call the men to arms, as well as at the ceremonial entry of a hunting-party into the villages on their return from a successful elephant hunt.

The battle-flute is blown at the wider end (b, see fig.), and at the same time a finger is allowed to oscillate against the end that is like a mouthpiece (a). It is carried by means of a strap fixed round the waist or to the quiver.

Fig. 53. Warflute (*ŋgulɪ*) made of the horn of the Thomson gazelle.

Nat. size.

Riksmus. Ethnogr. Coll. Inv. 12. 7. 106.

As has been stated, the warriors' kraals (Kikamba *mbɪlɪ*) are surrounded by a section, the *muena*. Without bows and arrows the *el-moran* are, in spite of their formidable spears, pretty harmless, if they can only be kep at a distance. The boldest of them

---

strument from the Waduruma, a sub-tribe of the Wanyika, in the coast-land within Mombasa.

try, with shields in front of them, to break out, and if the watching Akamba are not powerful men with good bows, they succeed in their purpose, and after that it is very difficult for the attackers to get clear. They are thus quite aware of the danger and in front of the warriors' kraal are placed the best shooters, who are able to pierce the shields with their arrows. As soon as any of *el-moran* try to break out, they get an arrow through the body. It is, of course, still more favourable for the agressors if the attack can be effected so completely that the Masai have no time to come out of their huts, which is the case if the Akamba succeed in getting into the warriors' kraal unperceived and dividing themselves before the entrances to the huts.

During this time the second section, the *ŋgɪla*, is busy driving the cattle away. Everyone tries to mark as many animals as possible by giving them a slight sword-cut in a certain place or by hanging their leather bags (*ŋgusu*) round the animal's neck, etc. By this means they consider that they obtain a right to the animal at the coming distribution of the spoil. Sometimes it falls to the one who first strikes it with his bow. Men and married women, especially pregnant women, are killed without mercy, »so that they may not be able to give birth to more enemies». The girls who live in the kraals of *el-moran* as their paramours are also killed, if an opportunity offers itself. The men's ornaments are taken home as trophies. On the other hand a woman's ornaments are never taken; they bring no honour: »It is like taking things from a corpse, for women cannot fight», said an old warrior to me. For the same reason women are not shot, but their heads are crushed with a sword or the first suitable weapon, such as their own axes, a bit of wood or a stone. To waste an arrow on a woman is almost equivalent to throwing it away; arrows are needed for more important work. Quite young girls and children are collected together and driven away by the third section, the *ɪta*, at the same time as the cattle. The *muena* and *ŋgɪla* have to stay behind and keep the enemy in check, if the latter is strong enough to pursue, until the *ɪta* have had time to get a good bit of the way home with their plunder[1]. There is also another reason for not making the force which has to watch the cattle

---

[1] *ɪta* also means 'expedition, plundering expedition'.

Arch. Or. L i n d b l o m

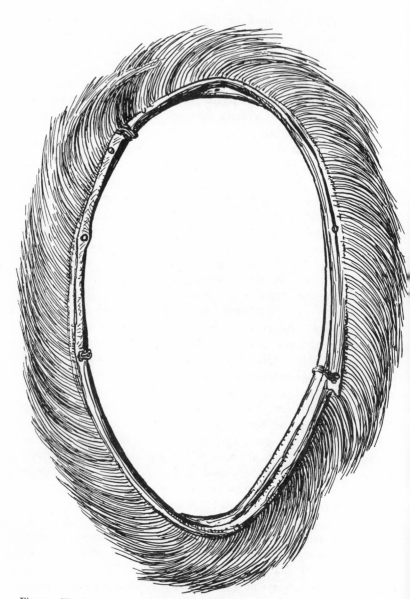

Fig. 54. Warrior's breast ornament (*wea*) made from the mane of a zebra. Riksmus. Ethnogr. collect. Inv. 12. 7. 109. $^1/_3$ nat. size.

too strong, namely the wish to avoid disputes as to the distribution of the booty. Such disputes have occasionally led to a battle between the conquerors themselves. Even the admirably disciplined Masai often find it difficult to abstain from them.

When the *ita* with the cattle and prisoners have got an adequate start, the other sections also retire. If the Masai are numerous and pursue, the attacking party run an obvious risk of being outflanked by them, the *ita* being caught up and the cattle being recaptured. During the retreat they usually have, on this account, a rough form of escort which is arranged in this way: on both sides of the line of retreat patrols are sent out on a rather broad front; they warn the others if the enemy attempts a flanking movement.

If the attack is unsuccessful they do not wait for the enemy, but try as quickly as possible to get back. On such occasions their tactics are to spread like chaff before the wind and afterwards perhaps to collect again at some definite place, often chosen beforehand. By means of this the pursuit is obviously made more difficult. A certain signal on the war-flute can make the fugitives stop. During the flight fine and self-sacrificing features may be observed, based on the strong feeling of interdependence and of the duty of helping their kinsfolk, which is so characteristic of the Akamba. Thus, for instance, a man runs to his brother-in-law, who is wounded and quite exhausted and can only with difficulty drag himself forward. Although the former is in good condition, he stops all the same, takes his relative's quiver as well as his own and tries to keep back the pursuers, thereby perhaps saving the other man's life at the cost of his own.

Even if there is an opportunity, the Akamba do not bury those who have fallen in battle, not even those who come back wounded to the village and die there. For they believe that for each fallen man that is buried another warrior must die.

Dead enemies are not mutilated, at the most an arm may be chopped off in a hurry, when there is no other way of taking its ornaments off. Of the following statement of Hildebrandt, I have been unable to find any confirmation at all, as far as the Akamba are concerned: »Als siegestrophäe emasculieren die Gala und mehrere Somalistämme die erschlagenen feinde. Dieses thun auch die Wakamba und Wanika, schneiden auch andere gliedmassen, hände und füsse, ab, die sie, siegreich nach hause zurückgekehrt,

in die dorfbäume hängen»[1]. The customs in this case could not
have altered since H:s time, as his statement is disputed by many
old men, who remembered very well *Bwana Ndege* (Kisuaheli
'Mr. Bird'), as H. was called by the natives, the chief object of
his journey being to collect birds.

But to return to our raiding expedition. When the Akamba
have arrived so far on the way home that the danger of pursuit
is no longer present, a halt is usually made and the booty divided.
In the Machakos district this was done by some men out of each
uka or age class being appointed to divide up the cattle, while
the great mass waited at some distance. Before the distribution
was carried out, an oath was taken on the *kipitu* to the effect
that no one would begin to quarrel afterwards. The *asilili* obtained more than the others, as the result of the enterprise had
been due to a great extent to their plans for it. Among the
»common men» those who had specially distinguished themselves
obtain more than the others. If, for instance, the booty is so
small that there is only one animal between five warriors, two
asilili get one between them, etc. Thus the *asilili*, despite their
important position, have no further great advantages over the rest,
a manifestation of the feeling of equality which characterizes the
whole of the Akamba's social life. Little attention is paid during
the division to the above described method of denoting possession that is employed during the attack itself. Only leaders
and spies might, if they urged their claim vigorously, be allowed
as a result of their merits to keep the animals they had succeeded
in marking. A distribution of booty rarely passed off to the
satisfaction of all, and in spite of the oath on the *kipitu* numerous actions were brought about cattle that had been marked by
one person and afterwards fell to another. As late as 1911 during my stay in the Machakos district I heard of an action by
which an old bull was given back to a man who several years
ago during a raiding expedition had struck it with his bow but
who had afterwards lost it at the division of the spoil.

Prisoners are treated well on the whole. The girls become
the conquerors' wives, the captured children are soon looked upon

---

[1] J. M. Hildebrandt, Ethnographische Notizen über Wakamba
und ihre Nachbarn, p. 386.

as their own. »These are my children, which I produced with my bow», they used to say jokingly. Often, however, the prisoners were sold as slaves to the trade caravans from the coast.

4. The homecoming of the warriors after a successful plundering expedition.

We have seen that the warriors who most distinguish themselves get a somewhat greater portion of the booty than the others. The man who brings home as a sign of victory a Masai spear, i. e. who has killed a Masai warrior, is esteemed above all others. He is then called *mutiætumo*, an title of honour which is used instead of his ordinary name for the rest of his life. A man who has taken a sword, an *ol-morani's* leather dress, etc. also gets a title of honour for these tings; his reputation is, however, not so great as the *mutiætumo's* [1].

As trophies from a successful expedition the warriors bring back weapons and clothes from the enemies they have killed. These things, now called *matuso*, may not be immediately taken into the villages, but must first be treated in the following way:

Weapons and other captured objects are hidden in the wildness, and an expert old man is sought out to *tula mbaŋga* 'break the peril', as it is called. He gets beer as a gift and gives the warriors instructions to build an enclosure at a certain place and there take all the plunder. The old man takes his place there, and each of the warriors who has taken a Masai spear bends the point of one of his arrows and then shots a wooden arrow, an imitation, constructed for the occasion, of the real arrows, against it or the spears he has brought back, saying: »These spears belong to X's son» (mentioning his fathers' name). The old man who has conducted the ceremony must afterwards have connec-

---

[1] The etymology of this word is uncertain. It is clear that it is a contraction of *mutia* (= ?) + *ıtumo* (= spear). The missionary E. Brutzer, Handbuch der Kamba-Sprache, arbitrarily translates the word with »speerträger». Speaking of a warrior coming home with a trophy they used for instance to say: »ŋganịa nutwıı (~ nutusıı) uta 'X. has taken possession of (?) a bow' (< kutwa 'tear off' ?). Of other appellations of the same kind I have found *mutiọta* (uta 'bow'), *mutiọbịu* (uvbịu 'sword'), *mutiaŋgua* (ŋgua 'dress'), *mutiapıaka* (pıaka 'quiver'), *mutiandọ* (ndọ 'scabbard').

tion with a woman and finally obtains a big, pregnant cow and an ox for his trouble. As far as the warriors themselves are concerned, I have not obtained any information to the effect that they undergo any special purification ceremony, which otherwise is often the case among African tribes [1] (cf. however just below).

After this treatment of the booty comes the principal feature in the festivities which follow every sucessful campaign. The warriors go in a procession with their trophies round the villages to be admired and to receive presents from their relations and friends. This custom is called to *kwaŋga* [2]. In this triumphal procession a *mutɪœtumo* takes the place of honour. Let us follow one of these after his arrival home to see the reception he meets with.

The homecomer is smeared with fat by his mother. This is certainly considered to purify him after contact with inimical, and therefore injurious, persons and weapons. The father slaughters an ox in honour of his son. From the skin of the animal he cuts a long strip, in one end of which a hole is made, while the rest is split into several flaps. A strip of this sort, which is called *ukualo* (pl. *ŋgwalo*), is placed on one of the *mutɪœtumo*'s index fingers, another on the shaft of the spear. After getting this outward token of his dignity he is ready to begin to *kwaŋga*, followed by his friends and comrades. Amongst those who are visited his maternal uncle, *ɪnaumɔ*, seems to be the most important. He gives him a bull and places a leather thong on another of his fingers. A man who has captured more than one spear seems to have been allowed to hand one over to his maternal uncle. From his paternal uncle, *mwændwɪþɔ*, he gets a bull in the same way. It has happened that when one of these near relations has had no cattle, he has given his daughter in marriage to one of his friends and as an advance of the price of the bride has demanded a bull to present to the *mutɪœtumo*. From other relations he gets some goats, from one two, from another four, all according to the resources of the giver. Some give nothing at all. His father also gives him goats, if he has no horned cattle, perhaps about ten. In this way the *mutɪœtumo* can get together a whole little flock, a part of which he slaughters for a feast to his friends.

---

[1] Cf. Frazer, The Golden Bough 2, p. 172 ff.

[2] Presumably the same word as *kwaŋga* 'stroll around'.

When the *mutiœtumo* and his band, going round *kwaŋga*-ing, approach a village, they strike up songs of victory, which extol the exploits that have been achieved. A song of this sort, which has probably been in more general use, runs as follows when translated literally: »You wonder: he who sings the song of victory, who is he? He is *mutiœtumo* X. (here follows his real name), who has fought with the men of cattle, but if we had not helped each other, he should not have come out of it successfully. *aaaaah!*»[1] The women of the village greet those who are coming with shrill cries: *lili, lili, lili, lili!*, the women's usual way of expressing their joy and delight about something[2].

The other conquerors, the *mutiota* and the rest, march round in about the same way but with more modest forms.

Each successful raiding expedition is followed by intense feasting, for which a part of the captured cattle is slaughtered. The older men are assembled for great drinking-bouts, and when the beer begins to go to their heads, they outbid each other in boasting about their sons' exploits. It was hard then for a man without sons, who perhaps did not even have any relatives at all to show off, to sit silent listening to the bragging of the other old men. Many a time, said one of my informants, such a man killed a young *mutiœtumo* by magic, merely to escape hearing the others' jubilation.

By showing courage and recklessness in battle a disreputable man may win back his good name and reputation. Ngila, an old man near Machakos, is said to have been in his young days such an incorrigible thief, that it was decided to put him to death as an individual who was a peril to the community, but he saved himself by paying heavy fines. During an expedition against the

---

[1] By »the cattlemen» are meant the Masai, who are nomads and live principally by their flocks, while the Akamba, on the other hand, practise agriculture. The song is as follows in Kikamba: *muikulịa: usu wina ŋgakali n'u? kotœ mutiœtumo ŋganịa waukịtiə na mundu wa ŋombə, na kœka kutœpiwa, ndaбita, eaaaah!*

[2] The same thing is true about the Djagga women in Kilmandjaro: »— — — jubelruf der weiber [at a successful birth], den sie auch sonst bei anderen freudigen ereignissen ausstossen: bei rückkehr der männer aus dem kriege, bei erlegung eines wilden tieres u. s. w. Es ist ein helles jubilieren und trillern auf dem vokale i = lilililili». B. Gutmann, Dichten und Denken der Dschagga-Neger, p. 83.

Masai which was carried out shortly afterwards he was so reckless
that he came back with two spears. From that moment his fame
in the district was great and is so to this day. On the other hand,
a man who is cowardly in battle, has for a long time to put up
with many an insulting epithet. He also finds it difficult to get a
wife, for few girls will bear to hear such things about their future
husband.

Finally one more detail: a young man who has fought his
first battle may not have coitus on his arrival home before his
parents have had it. If he does so the cattle he has brought
home die, or he is unsuccessful next time: *ntuseuɓʑə uta wa mwana*,
»we shall purify our son's bow», says the father.

5. Defensive fighting.

According to the accounts of older travellers the Akamba formerly guarded their boundaries against their old enemies, the
Masai and the Akikuyu; this was done by means of look-out
sentries. Whether these sentries were permanent and relieved
according to certain principles, the accounts do not show, but
according to M. Schoeller, who saw such sentries on the boundary
of the Kikuyu country, the were »hoch organisiert» [1]. S. came
across similar sentries among the Wasotik, up towards Lake
Victoria and south of the Uganda railway, and Dr. G. Kolb
saw at the south boundary of »the Kitu country», on the southern
slope of Kenia, permanent frontier guards in clothes made of grass,
with shield, spear, bow and arrow [2]. Now the tribes mentioned
are more or less hillfolk, and Schoeller assumes that their custom
of having frontier guards is due to the fact that people in a
mountainous country have greater difficulty in observing the approach of an enemy than in open ground. One might equally well
think that the people who observe such precautions feel inferior
to their neighbours; besides, the mountain heights with their good
views invite such arrangements. The Akikuyu, who might also
be correctly called a hilltribe, seem, however, not to have used
frontier sentries.

---

[1] M. Schoeller, Mitteilungen über meine Reise nach Equatorial-
Afrika und Uganda 1896—7, II, p. 181.

[2] Petermann's Mitteilungen 1896, p. 227.

In spite of this vigilance it often happened, of course, that the Kamba villages were surprised at night time by the enemy or that pastured flocks were taken away. The hedges of thorn and the barricades which surround the villages and which we shall describe in detail later on, did not always form an effective protection. The agile Masai made their way over these, among other ways by spreading skins over the thorns. As the huts are kept closed during the night, the Masai used sometimes, when they were not discovered, to wait silently till the inhabitants woke up, and when they, suspecting nothing, emerged, they were struck down with the long spears.

But even in broad daylight the Masai attacked succesfully in open combat. They crept forward to the barricades, protected by their shields, which they pushed in front of them and which the Akamba's arrows could not as a rule penetrate.

When the Masai troops were reported to be in the neighbourhood, the alarm was sounded on the big drums and the women set up cries. The cattle were driven near the villages so that in case of need they could be taken within the barricades. From the hills they carefully watched the enemy's movements, and the younger men went to meet him, while the *atumɩa*, who were no longer capable of fighting, stayed at home in the village to defend it.

6. Civil feuds.

When it was a question of an attack or defence against other tribes, the Akamba were always united. But when no external danger threatened or prospects of booty did not bring about a union, perpetual internal quarrels and feuds prevailed. One little *kɩɓalo* or district was in more or less open feud with the other, and there was usually a certain risk attached to going beyond the brook or hollow which divided two adjacent districts. When cattle were put out to grass, the risk was run of having them carried off by their own countrymen. The young men of a district risked being attacked, if they went to other dancing places and danced with the girls there. Only the women could go unhindered wherever they liked. Finally, as we already know, the different families and clans, although their members are spread in different quarters, composed, and still compose, independent groups, within which blood-vengeance prevails. An offence against one member is an offence against the whole family.

The civil fights were concluded with real treaties. The leading men from both sides then often met at the boundary between the inimical territories, a stream or the like, unarmed yet rather afraid of each other. Peace was sworn on the *kɪ́pɪtu*. The negotiators from the one side then accompanied the opposite party's representatives home and a feast was partaken of. For the killed the full mulct for manslaughter was levied on both sides, prisoners were liberated on the payment of the same blood money as for those killed, which in Ukamba is eleven cows and a bull. These fights became in reality, perhaps chiefly on account of the mulct for manslaughter, pretty harmless, and were fought out preferably with arrows at a respectful distance. After a fight with other tribes no blood-money was paid nor was peace confirmed by any definitive act.

A peculiar position is taken in these internal combats by the Kilun'gu district in the south-eastern part of the country[1]. The dwellers there were of old known for their wildness and rapacity and continually had feuds with the rests of the tribe. They are considered almost as strangers, inasmuch as no compensation for men killed in battle was considered necessary. With regard to their speech as well and partly in their manners and customs the people in Kilun'gu are somewhat separate from the other Akamba. The characteristic of the Kilun'gu men's warfare is the extraordinary cruelty with which they behave. The prisoners, for whom they can hope for no ransom, are tortured by them in a way that calls to mind Indian torture. Of this I have been informed as follows

The victim is laid on his back on the ground with arms and legs stretched out. Through his hands are struck pointed wedges his feet are fastened firm by piles driven in. Over the head of the unfortunate man was fastened a branch so that he could not raise it. He was then left to his fate.

Another popular method was to cut the prisoner's noses off or to skin them. This was done by taking off small strips of skin from the forehead right down to the feet of the poor wretches

---

[1] On the special position of Kilun'gu see p. 16.

who were then driven out into the desert with scornful ejaculations: »Go back home and tell your people that here in Kilun'gu all is well. Here there is no one ill or weak». Most of those tortured in this way died on the road.

Sometimes, it is said, they used to tell a prisoner to imitate the bellowing of cattle. If he did this, his life was spared for a ransom. To extort this more quickly they had finally, among other customs, that of fastening the prisoners close to a fire.

* * *

This description is now almost ended. I shall only add an attempt at a brief analysis of the Akamba's skill in war, compared with their neighbours, the Masai. The latter have in East Africa played the same military rôle as the Zulus in South Africa and have been at all times a scourge to the resident negro tribes. It is consequently very interesting to observe how the Akamba seem to have been able to keep them pretty well within bounds. And they did not always content themselves with a succesful defensive in their own land, from the heights of which they had certain hopes of defending themselves with their arrows from the Masai armed with spears. We have just seen how they ventured — a thing that probably no other tribe would have dared — to go out on the steppes and attack the Masai kraals, often with great success. The names *mutiœtumo*, *mutiota* are not infrequent, and many a stolen Masai woman lives as a wife in the Akamba's huts. In the Machakos district there are various half-blood Masai, the product of such marriages. On the plain just west of the present government station of Machakos there were formerly some Masai kraals, but the Akamba were troublesome and the Masai had to move farther out. Presumably, however, these Masai were numerically inferior.

I have had the opportunity of discussing this subject with a man who already in the beginning of the nineties lived among the Akamba and who has witnessed many of their expeditions, namely Säuberlich, the missionary in Ikutha. He confirms what I have just said about the Akamba's ability to defend themselves against the Masai, but declared that this was only the case with the peoples in West Ukamba. He remembers vividly how one day about 20

years ago the Masai, while the Kamba warriors were away in
another direction, hurried and took their cattle. But the Akamba
came back, caught the plunderers up, took their animals back
and killed a great number of the Masai. At that time, however
the Masai's might was already greatly broken by severe plagues
among the cattle.

In East Ukamba, on the other hand, the ravages of the Masai
had more results. The population here showed the usual terror
of them and fled merely at the rumour of their approach. At the
last Masai attack in the district of Ikutha mission station they all
fled to a steep cliff, where they used to take refuge in such cases,
and Herr Säuberlich relates how one man was so afraid that he
could not walk, and so his wife had to carry him away on her
back. I think that the cause of the Machakos people's brave conduct was their proximity to their hereditary enemy. In numerous
fights they had learnt that the latter was not invincible, whereas
those who lived farther east, where the Masai did not come so
often, did not even dare to make an attempt to test the worth of
the halo which shone round their name.

In hand-to-hand fighting with the Masai, according to Herr
Säuberlich's statement, two Akamba usually tried to attack one
Masai. One, with sword in hand, engaged in a feigned skirmish
with the Masai and tried to capture his attention, while the other
waited for the occasion when the warrior, who was protected by
his big buffalo-hide shield, should expose himself, when he immediately placed a poisoned arrow in his body.

East Ukamba is separated from the Tana river by a territory, 160 kilometres broad, uninhabited and poorly watered. The
Akamba went over this very often to the glen of the Tana to
plunder the Galla and Wapokomo, two tribes rich in cattle, the
latter a small peaceable Bantu tribe[1]. They were a terror to
these people and extended their incursions very far. In Mkunumbi
a little port north of the mouth of the Tana and just west of the
town of Lamu, some Galla told me how plundering bands of the
Akamba had found their way even as far as there. Yet it is
nearly 150 kilometres as the crow flies from there to the Akamba's
eastern boundary.

---

[1] Cf. above p. 19.

The Kamba warriors never employ in battle artificial means
to raise their courage and desire for battle, as was the custom,
on the other hand, among many of the Masai. The latter drank a
decoction of the leaves of the *ol umigumi* (Pappea capensis?) and by
means of this were able to get into a veritable Berserker rage. The
Akamba told me how solitary Masai warriors were seized by such lust
for battle that they sprang madly from their section and rushed
on beforehand so as to get to blows as quickly as possible, upon
which they were shot down by the Akamba. Although the latter
know of the *ol umigumi* tree — it is called *muƃa* in the Kamba
language — they do not use it, however, in the same way as
the Masai warriors. On the steppes west of Machakos there are
some of these trees, whose bark is here and there cut away on
the stem, which the Masai are said to have done when they went
forth to fight against the Akamba.

* * *

Now the grass grows on the Akamba war-paths, the battle-
cry is no longer sounded from savage throats and the swords have
almost in the real meaning of the word been transformed to
ploughshares; for they are often used for clearing work in the fields.
The native pastures his humped cattle in safety at the foot of the
hillocks of his homeland. Do not think, however, that they fully
realise the value of the new order of things; many heartily wish
the white men to leave the country so that the old plundering
life may begin again. The young men listen with longing looks
to their fathers' tales of ancient plundering expeditions. My own
cook and retainer, the most intelligent and the finest native I
know, who has for several years been an *askari* (soldier) in the
government service and in many things showed an astonishingly
intelligent apprehension, often used all the same to lament the
fact that he was nearly thirty years old and had not yet killed
a Masai. He almost despised himself.

BELIEF AND SCIENCE

Chapter XIII. **Religion.**

In the foregoing chapters we have seen that religion and morals are intimately connected with individual and social life; now we come to the religious conceptions of the Akamba, in the strict sense of the expression. These tally on the whole with those found among most of the Bantu peoples in the east and south. Thus they consist of:

1. a developed worship of the spirits of their ancestors (*aĩmu*);
2. a vague belief in a Higher Being (*muluŋgu*, *ŋgaĩ*).

1. **Spirit=worship.**

Spirit-worship is based on the conception of the continued life of the soul after death. The word for »soul» is *kĩu*, which is often used in the sense of »spirit», that is to say the soul of a departed ancestor (cf. *aĩmu* below); *þaĩu* only means »life» in a purely physical sense, synonymous with *mbœ6a* 'breath'. *þaĩu* has been adopted by the missionaires, who, in translations of the Prayer Book, render »eternal life» by *þaĩu utakaþœla* (lit. 'the life that will never end'). *kĩu* also means »shadow», and in reality there is a certain connection between a man's soul and his shadow[1]. After death the body is buried or thrown out, and is then torn to pieces by the hyenas (»everyone can convince himself of this with his own eyes»), but the soul immediately goes down to the nether regions, where most of the departed spirits (which are called *aĩmu* in their new state) live after death. Their existence there is an immediate continuation of what they experienced during life. He who

---

[1] This is one of the reasons for the well-known dread of the natives for being photographed. They believe that they then lose their shadows, and anyone doing so must die. No other superstitious conceptions seem to be connected with the shadow by the Akamba; it is not, for example, considered dangerous to tread on it.

was rich in this life continues to be so in the spirit world; he who died unmarried gets married there; the women perform their usual tasks, &c. For amusement they dance the special dance of the spirits, *kɪlumɪ*. There is no separation of the bad from the good. The female *aɪmu* are not inferior to the male. Animals are also considered to possess souls, which is quite natural if we take into consideration how near to themselves the natives consider animals to be. However, their souls are thought to die with them, and are thus quite different from the souls of human beings.

The conceptions just described are general throughout the whole of Ukamba, though in the southern and eastern districts (Kikumbuliu and the southern parts of the Kitui district) the spirit-world is not located under the earth, but on the unpeopled mountain Kyumbe, situated in a north-easterly direction from Kilimandjaro, between that mountain and the Uganda railway. Kyumbe is thought to be a meeting-place for all spirits from many parts of the country. The mountain is shunned, and no one will go there without good cause, because the *aɪmu* do not like to be disturbed by human beings[1].

Anyone passing the mountain must on no account speak of it as Kyumbe; if they must mention it, it must be by the name of *muluŋgu* or *ŋgaɪ*, the name of the Supreme Being, of whom more below. The bold man who dares to approach the home of the spirits is often stopped by voices, which ask: »Whither goest thou? What brings thee here?» &c. This conception of Kyumbe as the favourite mountain of the spirits seems to be unknown in Ulu.

Many tales about the mountain are current among the inhabitants of East Ukamba. To illustrate the conception, a note that I have made may be inserted here:

A man was once going there from the Kibwezi district to look for wild honey. Then he heard a voice: »Who goes there?» He stated his errand, and the voice told him to go to such and

---

[1] The word *aɪmu* is found in many East African dialects (muzimu, mulimu, &c). *aɪmu* in Kikamba, sg. *ʊmu* (which is, however, not so often used) is possibly derived from *ɪma* 'to dig'; the corresponding expression in Kisuaheli is *mzimu*, cf. *kuzima* 'to extinguish, to put out'. A. Le Roy derives all these from the root *-ima* 'être droit, être vivant'. Cf. Le Roy, La Religion des primitifs, p. 138.

such a place and cut into a certain tree, where he would find
much honey. On the following day he was to go home without
turning round to look behind him. He was also to tell the people
that it was the mountain of the spirits, and that they did not wish
to be visited. Concerning Kyumbe and *aimu*, a former missionary
in Ukamba says: »Dort leben sie. Dort sieht man von ferne wohl
auch ihre feuer und hört ihre unterhaltung. Von da werfen sie
nach dem vorübergehenden mit steinen. Geht man aber nä-
her, so verschwindet der spuk, und man sieht weder kohle noch
asche. Von diesem hügel aus ziehen die geister im ganzen lande
umher, um krankheit und seuche zu bringen» [1].

Apart from Kyumbe, there are found all over Ukamba solitary places, especially mountains, which are believed to be the
abodes of the *aimu*. Such are Kivauni, immediately to the west of
the river Athi; and Muutha, on the eastern border of the settled
country [2]. At the foot of the mountains and on the slopes are
villages, but the heights are inhabited by *aimu*, and people are
very loath to ascend them. They believe that they often see the
lights of fires on the top of Kivauni.

The *aimu* always show a great interest in the living race, and
are thought to keep themselves informed of everything that happens among them. The native feels a close bond between himself and his dead, and the latter often come at night to visit
their old village. They can be talked with, though they are not
usually visible. The strongest proof of such an intimate bond
is the belief that the *aimu* decide as to the reproduction of the
race, since they form the foetus in the woman. There are many
barren women among the natives, and, as has been seen, sexual
connection between a man and a woman is not always enough
to produce children [3]. However, every birth does not seem to
be regarded as a re-incarnation, as is the case, for example,
among the Central Australian natives, among whom the theory of
birth is simply the theory of the re-incarnation of an ancestral
spirit [4].

---

[1] G. Kanig, Dornige Pfade eines jungen Missionars in Ukamba, p. 17.
[2] Hobley, Akamba p. 86, mentions several.
[3] Cf. Hobley, Akamba p. 20, about spiritual husbands.
[4] Spencer and Gillen, The native tribes of Central Australia.
Spencer and Gillen, The Northern tribes of Central Australia, p. 174.

Occasionally a spirit appears to a barren woman, and announces to her that she is going to give birth to a child, and some time afterwards she actually does give birth to one. A barren wife in the Machakos district one night heard a voice which said to her: »Thou shalt give birth to a child!». She got up to see what it was, but saw no one. When she had lain down again, she again heard the voice, and once more got up, but to no purpose. The next morning she told her husband, but he said: »Nonsense! Dreams have no meaning» (*ndoto nɩ sɩa mana*). However, a year later the woman gave birth to a child. It has already been mentioned that, before it has received a name, a baby is called *kɩɩmu*.

A word may be inserted here about the natives' conception of dreams. The appearance of *aɩmu* just described, of course takes place in dreams, which are considered actual events. It is also thought that dreams come from the spirits. On waking up, anyone who has had a bad dream takes a firebrand, puts it out, and throws it away, saying: »May my bad dream go out like this fire-brand!».

Among the Bantu peoples is found an undeveloped belief in the transmigration of souls, and this is also the case among the Akamba. In the chapter »Child-birth» (p. 30) it has already been said that the *aɩmu* readily allow themselves to be born again in a child, and here we have the common notion that ancestors are re-incarnated in children. Sometimes this is apparent at once from a birth-mark or someting else that was characteristic of the deceased. However, a spirit which will allow itself to be born again, usually appears to a pregnant woman in the family circle, and tells her who it is and that it intends to take up its abode in the child to which she shall give birth, and that therefore the child shall receive the name of the spirit. Further, the *aɩmu* very often take up a temporary abode in human beings, especially women, who then become liable to hysterical attacks, and do not regain their peace of mind again until the spirit has been driven out. We shall revert to this point later.

The worship of animals. It also happens that *aɩmu* take up their abode in animals, frequently in snakes, such as pythons (see p. 127). It does not seem that the natives think the spirits dwell permanently in these animals; they only occasionally avail themselves of this method of visiting their living relatives.

A wild cat sometimes used to come in the evenings to a village near the mission station of Mulango, and a little food used to be thrown to it. The people said that it was a deceased relation and even mentioned the name. Many similar cases could be cited. The explanation is the same as in the case of the pythons: when a wild animal so far departs from its usual habits that it approaches human beings fearlessly, it is thought that a special reason must exist. It cannot be an ordinary animal. These animals must not be confused with the totem animals; very few of them are among the totem animals (neither the python nor the wild cat are), which, moreover, are not considered to be re-incarnated *aimu*. Totemism and animal worship are two different ideas.

Thus we come to the important conclusion that among the Akamba there exists a belief in the transmigration of souls side by side with totemism, and independent of it. Frazer cites something similar from the Bahima, east of Uganda, and with reason indicates that the conception is strong evidence against the theories that would trace the totemism of the Bantu peoples to the belief that the souls of the dead take up their abode in animals.

With the conception of *aimu* is also combined that of various animals who are looked upon as the domestic animals of the spirits or even as their household property. Thus the elephant is sometimes called the »spirits' cattle», and the medicine man, as he more than any other is in communication with the spirit world and is the connecting link between it and mankind, may not kill an elephant. The common little land tortoise is said to be used by the spirits' wives as a grindstone when they grind their seed into flour. It is believed that this, like the elephant, cannot die a natural death. The praying grasshopper (Mantis religiosa) is used by the male spirits as a snuff-box(!) and a smaller species by their women[1]. This is thus called in East Ukamba simply *mwaŋgi wa aimu* 'the spirit's snuffbox', to which the etymology of *muŋgaimu*, the term in use in the west (Machakos), may also be referred. That in this word as well we are dealing with *aimu*, the spirits, is obvious at once. Further, the spider's net is called the

---

[1] I remember in passing that Mantis plays a certain part in the religions conceptions of the Bushmen and also of the South African Bantu peoples. See, for instance, Junod, The Life of a South African Tribe II, p. 312.

sack (*kɟondo*) of the woman spirits. These small insects are not
killed without reason. A good many of the conceptions associated with them seem nowadays to be partly regarded as jokes.
They also seem to be dying out and are probably relics of older
superstition, now almost forgotten.

From what has been said, it is seen that the *aımu* can show
a certain friendly interest in their descendants. For instance, they
sometimes give information, through a medium, of an impending
attack by the Masai, and in the next chapter we shall read how
they play an important part in the Akamba's treatment of the
sick, as all knowledge about healing plants is thought to come
from them and to be communicated by them to certain persons.

The most characteristic feature of the conception of *aımu* is,
however, that they are considered to expect constant attention
from their living relations, in the form of sacrifices. The sacrifice
is a gift which the *aımu* need; by it also the connection with
them is maintained and strengthened. The least inattention in
this respect is avenged by the sending of all sorts of misfortunes
down upon the negligent one, such as diseases of both men and
domestic animals, and even death. Therefore, when an accident
happens, it is feared that it is caused by the *aımu*. A case that
came under my own notice may be cited. Once, on paying a
visit to a hut, I found that a little child that had been running
about and playing, had chanced to fall into the fire. The child's
father then went to the medicine-man to find out whether, for
some reason or other, the spirits were angry.

The result of these beliefs is that the natives never know whether
they have sacrificed enough, and so they live in a constant state
of anxiety lest they shall incur the displeasure of the jealous
and capricious spirits. Judging from this fear and from experience
of many primitive peoples in other parts of the world, one might
be led to suppose that the Akamba avoid naming deceased persons, so that their attention may not be unnecessarily attracted.
I have not, however, found anything to support such a supposition [1].

----

[1] According to Frazer, The Golden Bough II, p. 353, J. M.
Hildebrandt points out a similar fear among the Akamba of mentioning the dead by name. On the page quoted (Ethnogr. Notizen &c, p.
405), however, Hildebrandt speaks of the Masai, not of the Akamba.

In spite of the native's respect for the *aımu* and their power to do practically anything, he also believes that he can deceive them when necessary, and often by very simple means. This is undoubtedly on account of the everyday human traits ascribed to the spirits. To quote an example, I once asked a woman why she called her little boy *mbıtı* 'hyena', for hyenas are loathed above all other animals by most African peoples, since they eat corpses. She then said that she had already had three children who had died in infancy. In her opinion — and every other native would reason in the same way — so many deaths could not be natural occurrences, and for some reason or other the *aımu* must grudge her her happiness. So when her fourth child was born, she called it »hyena», in order to give the spirits the idea that she cared no more about the child than about a hyena. The idea was that the *aımu* would, as a consequence, not consider it worth while to take that child from her also.

It may be indicated as still another feature of the conception of *aımu* that they are considered to be subject to the laws of mortality. Those who have existed for a time are believed to disappear and to be replaced by new ones, which vanish in their turn. The reason is probably that when one generation of natives has died out, the spirits that they believed in and feared are soon forgotten, since the succeeding generation have others[1].

Hobley says that the *aımu* »never are seen in human form». However, one very often meets with natives who assert that they have met spirits at night-time. They most often appear in human shape, and the forms in which they like best to present themselves are those of unusually tall, one-legged beings. On the mountain Kaani, on the road to Kitui, it is said that two one-legged spirits often appear, one a youth and the other a girl.

---

[1] »Their life after death is vaguely dependent on the memory of the living. When people forget an ancestor, he practically ceases to exist». Kidd, The Essential Kafir, p. 88. The Wadjagga in Kilimandjaro even designate the spirits of the present and past times with different names. »Das sind die jüngeren vorfahren, zu welcher die kenntnis der lebenden noch hinabreicht. Man nennt noch ihre namen oder wenigstens ihre würden. Ältere geschlechter der toten, die dem gedächtnis der lebenden entschwunden sind ... zeigen sich auch den menschen nicht mehr»: Gutmann, Dichten und denken der Dschagganeger, pp. 144, 145.

They stop travellers and ask them where they are going. Many places, especially of worship, the places of sacrifice, the special haunts of spirits, they cannot pass at night; though the Akamba themselves say that the spirits do not appear nearly so often since the arrival of Europeans in the country. The American mission station at Machakos is built on an old place of sacrifice, and the *aimu* are said to have been specially troublesome just there before the arrival of the missionaries, while they have now completely vanished. The popular conception of *aimu* much resembles that of our ghosts, and 'like the latter, the *aimu* preferably appear before midnight. The information that is to be obtained on these matters from other sources supports the assertion that the idea that the dead occasionally reappear is generally spread among the Bantu peoples[1].

2. The cult of sacrifice.

What has just been written with regard to the fear of the *aimu* and the necessity of constantly propitiating them, is an essential point in the manism of the Akamba, and one upon which their cult of sacrifice is founded. The sacrifices consist entirely of food, and stress must be laid on the fact that the spirits are thought really to need material nourishment. They feel hunger, thirst and cold, just as human beings do. Further, to show what a general human conception the Akamba associate with *aimu*, the following interesting account may be quoted from Brutzer. A medicine-man is giving instructions to the *atumia*: »Geht auf den opferplatz des N. N., baut die hütte des N. N., welche eingefallen ist. Er schläft draussen, und weil er draussen schlafen muss, wird kein regen fallen, damit er nicht vom regen beregnet werde. Bringt ihm auch speise, er hat grossen hunger. Bringt ihm auch samen zum säen»[2]. The signification of part of the above is explained by the account given below.

In addition to these sacrifices, made with the more general purpose of keeping the spirits good-tempered — if the expression may be used — sacrifices are also made with a definite pur-

---

[1] Cf. Gutmann ibid. p. 144. A. Werner, British Central Africa, p. 66. H. H. Johnston, British Central Africa, p. 449.

[2] E. Brutzer, Der Geisterglaube bei den Kamba, p. 7.

pose, in difficulty or stress, or when something particular is desired, which can be obtained with the help of *aimu*. In a poorly watered country, such as Ukamba, with its oft-recurring droughts, which, as we have seen, bring famine to thousands and thousands of people, they have, unfortunately, all too often great reason for offering sacrifices for rain, of which more later on. On the whole, the Akamba are diligent in offering sacrifices, and it would be

Fig. 55. Sacrificial hut, situated in a grove. It contains a sacrifice in the form of corn and at the entrance is placed some sugarcane.
(The white object is the author's hat.)

difficult to give an exhaustive account of all the occasions on which sacrifices ought to be made. We content ourselves with appending a summary of the most important and typical cases. For the sake of surveyability and clearness, we divide the sacrifices into such as are offered by private individuals or families, and such as are offered by all the inhabitants within a certain radius. This principle of division cannot always be said to apply, and sometimes it is difficult to differentiate.

A. **Sacrifices by individuals.** Among the Bantu peoples in general, the cult is intimately bound up with family life, and

is exercised by the fathers. In every Kamba family offerings
are made regularly at every meal. They consist of a little food
and drink placed on the floor of the hut. This is done by the
father; a son cannot offer sacrifices as long as his father lives, nor
can a woman, except in special cases, and then only when the
medicine-man so directs. When meat is eaten, fourteen small
pieces are offered; if a male relative is there on a visit, he offers
seven pieces and the host seven. At drinking-bouts, beer-brewing,
snuff-making, &c., a little is also offered. The beer that is offered
is called *kɪpaŋgona kɪa ukɪ*. The medicine-man in particular, when
he is drinking beer, always pours out a little as a gift to the *aɪmu*.
We have already seen that family sacrifices are made on other
occasions — births, deaths, &c.

When passing a place of sacrifice they usually throw a little
food there, such as a pinch of tobacco or some other trifle, especially if they are out for some real purpose, such as seeing to
their beehives out in the desert. It is also very usual for them
to throw a stone there, a custom that is, of course, known among
various races. To this ritual use of stones we shall return at the
end of the next chapter.

Anyone undertaking a long journey offers several sacrifices
on the way. He offers the first at home in the village, and the
next at the exit to the village, just as he is leaving it. When
crossing the first river he comes to, he offers a little of the food
he has with him for the journey on both banks. The quantity of
the offering is always insignificant: a few grains of maize, a pinch
of flour, a few drops of gruel from the travelling calabash, etc.
This is not, as Hobley suggests [1], an act of worship of the spirits
of the river; as far as I can discover, the Akamba have no conception of such spirits, nor indeed of nature spirits in general.
Instead the sacrifice is, as is usually the case, offered to the *aɪmu*
or *ŋgaɪ*, which here means some well-known deceased caravan-
leader, to obtain protection during the journey. In olden times
especially, when they used to take ivory and cattle down to the
coast, often in large caravans, they used to offer sacrifices at many
places on the way. The great caravan-route to Mombasa led (in
East Ukamba) over the mountain Mwathe, south-east of Ikutha,

---

[1] Hobley, Akamba, p. 57.

and there travellers used to smear a rock with fat, as an offering
to the departed caravan-leaders who in old times successfully led
their following to the journey's end, in spite of lurking Galla and
Masai. The old highway fell into disuse when the Uganda railway was built, but the cave on Mwathe is still smeared with fat
by those who journey by.

B. **Public sacrifices.** In addition to the private cult of sacrifice
practised within the family circle, is found another, more public, cult,
which is common to all the inhabitants within a certain area. Prominent
among these sacrifices are such as are occasioned by special conditions, such as a threatened epidemic, a delay in the rains, &c.
Offerings are then made to a deceased medicine-man or some
other prominent person, who, during his life-time, played a part
outside his immediate family circle. To these *aımu*, sacrifices are
offered at certain places of sacrifice, called *ıþæmbo* (< *þæmba* 'to
sacrifice'). Sometimes these places are situated on or beside the
grave of the person in question, sometimes on some other spot
which is supposed to be a haunt of *aımu*, and which is usually
a thick copse with one or more large trees, preferably wild fig-
trees (*mųmbo* or *mųmo*, different species)[1]. In East Ukamba,
where these trees are not so common, sacrifices are offered among
the rocks, or at the foot of baobab trees, where the dead are
often laid. The places of sacrifice have names. Thus one at
Machakos is called simply *mųmbonı*, 'at the fig-tree'; another
is called *kasumbanı*, 'by the little hut' (diminutive of *nɀumba*
'hut'), in reference to the little hut which is often built over
graves. There are an abundance of *ıþæmbo*, and near Machakos
there are several with only a few minutes' walk between them.
Families living close together (those who have a common open
place or *þomə*) not infrequently use one and the same place of
sacrifice.

Even cellars seem to be used as places of sacrifice. As least
the author knows one near Ngelani, north of Machakos, in which
they were said to place offerings.

One searches through the whole Bantu world in vain to find
any fixed or periodically recurring religious festivals that are

---

[1] The fig-tree is sacred in many parts of Africa, and also beyond
the bounds of this continent. Cf. A. Werner, The natives of British
Central Africa; and Frazer, The Golden Bough I: 2 (see Index).

celebrated by the whole tribe. The Kamba medicine-man usually
decides when it is time to offer sacrifices within a certain district.
He may not, however, officiate at the sacrifice himself; this is managed by certain old men and old women called *atumɪa ma
ɪβæmbo* and *ɪ6ætɪ sɪa ɪβæmbo*, or *ɪ6ætɪ sɪa ṇžama*[1]. Only older men
and women can attain to this dignity. Besides, the leading men in
the *ṇžama* ought also to be the most prominent at the *ɪβæmbo*, so that

Fig. 56. Place of sacrifice at the foot of a figtree.
Note a skull and bones of sacrificed animals.

the *atumɪa* of the *ṇžama* and the *atumɪa* of the *ɪβæmbo* can hardly
be looked upon as two separate groups. On the contrary, I have
shown in Chap. X that the management and exercise of religion
are among the duties of the *ṇžama*. Consequently those who, by
paying large fees, have become prominent in the *ṇžama*, also play
a rôle at the places of sacrifice. The fees paid fall partly to the
ɪβæmbo and its members; if the animals are not all sacrificed at

---

[1] The expression *ɪ6ætɪ sɪa ṇžama* is somewhat misleading, and
must not be taken to mean that these women are attached to the court,
which is not at all the case.

once, they are kept till another time. A father and son cannot belong to the *ɪpæmbo* at the same time; the son can only become a member when the father has retired on account of natural infirmities.

If a woman wishes to be *kɪɓætɪ kɪa ŋžama*, her husband must present the male members of the *ɪpæmbo* with goats and beer, and the female members with bananas, beans, and other field products. When the new member of the *ŋžama* goes to the *ɪpæmbo* for the first time, her husband gives her a goat to take with her. The people then see her new dignity and say: »Look! N. N's mother has become *kɪɓætɪ kɪa ŋžama*». An old woman described to me the occasion when her mother and the women of the same generation obtained entrance to the *ŋžama*. A festival called *mboka* was celebrated. The woman procured beforehand a great number of bananas, »to the value of from three to four goats», which were put into calabashes and, in the usual way, put down into the earth to ripen. On the day appointed, the old women who already belonged to the *ŋžama*, came to the village, danced *kɪlumɪ*, and slept there overnight. The next day the *atumɪa* of the *ŋžama* came to drink beer, large quantities of which had been brewed, and the youths and girls also gathered in the village for dancing. The owner of the village slaughtered an ox, of which the men ate one side and the women the other, sitting by their respective fires. The members of the *ŋžama* slept in the village. The next morning the young people returned to the village to dance, and then the bananas, *mboka* (i. e. vegetables), from which the festival with its accompanying dances has got its name, were eaten. Nowadays bananas are not so extensively used as formerly, because, it is said, they are too expensive, nor are they so plentiful as they were[1].

A sort of novice grade for *atumɪa* of the *ɪpæmbo* is *anakɔ* of the *ɪpæmbo*, also called *atumɪa anɪnɪ* 'the little atumia'. Their function is to help the older ones. They buy up beer on their account and take it to the place of sacrifice. There they flay the sacrificial animal, roast the meat, and wait on the *atumɪa* while they are eating. It costs only one goat to obtain this dignity.

---

[1] As a memory of this custom the word *mboka* is still used by the older women with the signification of dancing in general (instead of the otherwise usual *wapɪ*), an expression which one cannot understand unless one knows of the old custom just described.

What is the method of procedure, then, when offering at the *ɩþœmbo*? The sacrificial animal, whether goat[1], bull-calf, or ox (they grudge killing a cow-calf even for the spirits, cows being their most precious possession, which they can give up only in case of absolute need) is killed by a *mutumɩa* in the usual way, by suffocating it, after which it is flayed and cut up. The skin is given to a member of high standing, but he often has to pay a goat for it. The meat may only be cut by a *mutumɩa*. Part of it is laid at the foot of the tree as the sacrifice, and blood and beer are poured on the trunk. The greater part and, as I think I have shown, the best pieces, are eaten by those present, for a sacrificial meal is part of all primitive sacrifices. For the persons offering sacrifices to appropriate the best pieces themselves is nothing new; on the other hand, religious historians do not agree as to the reason for this, and I do not venture to put forward any hypothesis in the case of the Akamba[2]. After the *atumɩa* have sacrificed, the old women offer various products of their work, in the field (maize, sorghum, beans, flour, &c), after which they march in procession round the tree. Not infrequently a little hut, about a meter in height, is built on or near the grave to which the sacrifice is being made, and then the offering is laid there. Such huts are simplified models of the ordinary dwelling huts, but they are quite bare.

During the sacrificial meal which now follows, the members of the *nžama* sit nearest the tree, men and women separate. A little further away sit the other married persons, and finally, behind them, the young people. Those who do not belong to the *ɩþœmbo* may not approach the tree, even if they are *atumɩa*. The violation of this rule is punished by a fine, usually a goat.

The medicine-man occupies a unique position at sacrificial feasts. As has already been mentioned, he decides when they shall take place, since the spirits speak through him, but otherwise he plays an unimportant part in them; and even if he is an old *mutumɩa* of high standing, he may not present the sacrifice or cut the meat. In many ways he is in the position of a minor; »he is like a child» (*nɩ ta kana*), as the natives say.

---

[1] As is well known the goat especially is in Africa used to a great extent as a sacrificial animal.

[2] Cf. P:n Nilsson, Primitiv religion, p. 124.

On the whole, all sacrificial ceremonies are carried out in the same way, but no fixed rites or formulas exist.

The Akamba are diligent sacrificers, and round the *ıþæmbo* there lie many skulls and bones of sacrificed animals, and the ground is covered with a thick layer of mouldered grain &c, especially at an ancient place of sacrifice that has been used for generations. However, the sacrifices are not excessively costly; from ten to twelve *atumıa*, perhaps, have a share in the sacrificial animal, and besides that, most of them take part in the meal. Formerly the herds seem to have been bigger and then it was not unusual for one man alone to offer a goat, which does not happen so often nowadays at the public sacrifices. Sometimes animals other than goats and cattle are sacrificed, such as sheep and fowls; though in such cases it is always the medicine-man that gives express instructions to this effect. Milk is offered on behalf of the cattle, so that they may not be mauled by wild animals.

An *ıþæmbo* may be moved from one place to another, which is done by the *atumıa* who officiate at it. At Machakos, where the African Inland Mission Station is built on a place of sacrifice, the latter was moved, so that they might be less disturbed. At many *ıþæmbo*'s a clay vessel is found buried in the ground, containing a goat that had been buried alive in it, or killed by suffocation. This vessel is moved when the place of sacrifice is changed.

Brutzer describes how a private place of sacrifice, built by a man in memory of his dead wife, was moved from the mission station of Jimba, situated at the coastland within Mombasa [1]. The man had moved and now wanted to transfer the sacrificial place, which was situated under a shady tree, to his new dwelling-place. He made his appearance, accompanied by his three wives, began to dig the ground up and after some searching found the objects he wished to take with him, which turned out to be three small stones and three sticks. »The stones were pieces of the three big stones on which the deceased had prepared food. These are the essential things. They are a symbol to show that the woman is still present at the place. The three sticks either belonged to her hut or were the remains of the little place of sacrifice that the survivors had erected over· the three small stones and in which

---

[1] Brutzer, Begegnungen mit Akamba, p. 16.

they have been accustomed to place sacrifices to the spirit.» The women took possession of the relics, and then the four went off to build up the sacrificial place again in the neighbourhood of their new village.

The sacrifice of children was formerly practised in times of severe visitations, when it was necessary to propitiate the spirits in an exceptional manner, especially in cases of continued drought. The child required for the purpose was kidnapped, often from the Kikuyu country. Round Machakos, a child was taken from the rain clan (*ṃba-mbua*), and the mother received goats in compensation for her loss. The child was smeared with fat and buried alive with the goat, also alive, at the *ɩpæmbo*[1]. In East Ukamba a child seems always to have been taken from the *aeɀ*-clan, also called *mulata ɩbɩa* (see p. 125), which has on this account been given a third name, *ṃba-nžɩkwa* (< *pɩka* 'to bury')[2].

It is¹ an acknowledged fact that everything new and strange inspires fear in primitive peoples. At the sight of or on meeting anything new and unusual, the Akamba generally offer sacrifices, so that the new thing may not excite the wrath of the spirits. Such an event was the building of the Uganda railway, since it was thought that »that rope of iron» laid across the country would prevent the rain from coming. Säuberlich, the missionary in Mulango, told me that some years ago a lame native with an unusually small, dwarfed foot passed through the country. He was stopped and not allowed to proceed until he had paid a goat as an offering to the *aɩmu*. And when the flag-staff at the Government station at Kitui was raised, sacrifices were diligently offered in the whole country round about. This long thing that pointed straight up into the air would certainly keep the rains away, it was believed. Krapf tells how the Akamba said that,

---

[1] Rubbing with fat, which, as we have already seen, is practised on many occasions by the Akamba, is also found in other places, and has undoubtedly a magic-religious significance. Cf. Meinhof, Afrikanische Religionen, p. 32.

[2] I have not heard the word used in Ulu, but both J. Hofmann and S. Watt include it in their vocabularies (Wörterbuch der Kamba-sprache, 1901 — in M. S. — and Vocabulary of the Kikamba language). Loan word from Kisuaheli?

on account of his arrival, the rains would not come, for which reason they killed a sheep and sprinkled the path with its blood.

*   *   *

For the sake of clearness, I will make an addition to the above description of *aımu*. In the Akamba's rich treasury of folk-lore there is a characteristic type of story, in which the leading rôle is played by a monster called *ımu*, who usually appears in human or some similar form. This monster also appears in other East African peoples' folk-lore; in spite of the similarity of name, it seems to have nothing to do with *aımu*, spirits. This is confirmed by the Kikuyu language, in which the word for spirit is *ŋgoma*, while the fabulous figure is called *ilimu*[1]. The Akamba's fables about *ımu* seem most nearly to resemble our own about giants and ogres. The heroes in the former are usually of supernatural strength, but at the same time stupid, just like the giants in our fairy tales. They are also often man-eaters. Human beings get into difficulties through them, but nearly always extricate themselves by their ready wit.

3. Tales about *aımu*-spirits.

In order to illustrate further the conception of *aımu*, I may be allowed to insert some tales about spirits, which are considered by the natives to be really true and not legendary. These tales may lack scientific value and tend to give the treatise the character of a mere assemblage of material, but since no one seems to have discovered them before me, their insertion here may be to some extent justified.

I. Near the railway station of Kibwezi there is a rubber plantation belonging to a German company. Some time ago the manager decided to enlarge the area planted with rubber trees, and therefore began to clear a piece of forest. One day when the work was in full swing, the native workmen heard a voice, and

---

[1] Cf. Routledge ibid. p. 315 ff., which contains a couple of tales about *ilimu*. For *irimu* among the Wadjagga, cf. Gutman, Dichten und Denken der Dschagga-Neger, p. 59.

saw a little man sitting in a tree (a rather usual form of apparition for the *aɩmu* in these tales). He asked why they were
clearing the ground, and sternly forbade them to touch certain
trees, among them the one in which he was sitting. They reported
the matter to their master, but he gave them strict orders to
proceed, and they dared not refuse to do so. The result was
that all the workmen died at their work, and the remains of their
bones lie there to this day. Some time afterwards, the European
fell ill — the climate in Kibwezi is very unhealthy — went to
Mombasa to be nursed, but died there.

2. One evening a woman in the neighbourhood of Machakos
heard the dull sound of the women's spirit-drums, and decided
to proceed to the village from which the sound seemed to come.
When she arrived there, everything was quiet and still, but she
clearly heard the drums a little further away. She continued to
follow them, but the same thing happened again, and then she
realised that it was the spirits.

3. One evening a youth was sitting alone at home in his
hut. Then someone outside called him by name, and said: »Let
us go to N. N's village, where the others have gone!» Believing
it to be one of his friends, he went out to see, but no one was
there.

4. Mbota, an old man of repute in the neighbourhood of Machakos, and one of the Government »headmen», woke one night
and saw a form sitting by the nearly extinct fire with its back to him.
Thinking it was his wife sitting up late and working at plaiting a bast
sack, he took his bow and struck her. When the supposed wife
turned round, he saw a wonderful creature, half human, half
animal. »Why do you strike me?» it asked. Mbota asked
pardon for his mistake, and the spirit disappeared. The next day
Mbota slaughtered a bull and began a feast of atonement, which
lasted several days; but before the end of the year one of his
sons died.

5. The following is a story that shows how the spirits can
sometimes help their relations who are still living:

Quite near the mission station of Mulango at Kitui there is
the little hill Nengia, surrounded by cultivated fields. From olden
times the hill has been a place of sacrifice and *aɩmu* are believed
to haunt it in great numbers. One evening shrill cries of help

were heard to come from there, and when people rushed there, they saw that the ripe crop in the field at the foot of the hill was in flames. There were, however, a whole lot of people already there trying to put out the fire, which had started because the proprietress of the field had lit a heap of dry leaves and other rubbish. Of the people who were putting it out a number were recognised as recently deceased relations, all the rest were unknown. But it was understood that they were spirits who had gathered togheter to stop the destruction that threatened their dwelling-place. The unknown people were thus spirits of earlier generations, persons who had died so long before that no one then living remembered them. The woman who had caused the fire was sentenced by the elders to pay a goat, which, to propitiate the spirits, was killed on the hill, and this was sprinkled with *ŋondiu*.

The following stories are more avowed fables.

6. Into the River Tiva, a little north of Ikutha, falls the stream Witu. The word is the collective form of the word *ætui* 'girls', a name which the stream, previously nameless, is said to have received from the following circumstance: A number of girls were once working in the adjoining fields, when they were surprised by a violent thunderstorm, from which they sought shelter in a cave by the stream. Then an ant-lion (*kakwọ6uŋgu* [1]) came creeping towards the entrance, but was driven back by some of the girls. The animal again tried to enter, but was again driven out. When this was repeated, someone said: »Oh, this is the owner of the cave. Let us go away, it must be a spirit». In spite of the bad weather, several of the girls went out again, but those who had driven out the ant-lion did not trouble to move. The girls had scarcely got out, before the walls of the cave collapsed, so that of the entrance only a narrow crack remained. The other girls ran home at once and related what had happened. The *atumia* at once set out for the place, but nothing could be done. For a time the imprisoned girls were kept alive by having food passed to them with long spoons, but at last they all died. Thus was their unkindness punished by the ant-lion.

---

[1] < *kukwa* 'to die' and *u6uŋgu* 'lie'. So called because it pretends to be dead when one touches it.

7. A couple of hours' journey east of Kitui lies a solitary high and steep rock, Nsambani ('among the males'). It is shunned by the Akamba, because it is considered to be a haunt of *aɩmu*. Anyone offering sacrifices to them and then walking round the rock changes sex; thus a man becomes a woman and vice versa.

8. In the neighbourhood of the above-mentioned rubber plantation at Kibwezi there is a round pond, which is regarded with superstitious fear, and considered to be the haunt of departed spirits. The legend of this pond is as follows: In by-gond times a village stood here, whereas now there is only a muddy sheet of water, at times disturbed by a crocodile or two that lurk in the depths. One dark and rainy evening, a frog came hopping into one of the huts. Among the Akamba this is an evil omen, and the frog was driven out by the children; it came back and was again driven out. It tried another hut, but with the same result. In a third it was driven out once, but when it came again, the mother told her children to leave it in peace and let it warm itself quietly by the fire. The frog warmed itself by the fire and then began to talk to the woman: »Take as many of your household goods as you can carry, and leave this place with your children without delay, I shall destroy the others for their unkindness; I am a spirit». The woman obeyed, and when they reached the *ƀoma* (the open place outside the village where the men usually sit), they heard a rush as of an enormous volume of water. They saw the village sink into the depths and all the inhabitants drowned. However, they still live down there, for in the morning is often heard the crowing of the cock or the bleating of the goats, and in the evenings the light of the fire on the *ƀoma* sometimes shines up. The owner is called Kilui, and the place Kilui's pond. It is shunned, and no one will clear a field at its edge, although water is so scarce in these parts. In times of severe drought, the elders take a goat to the spot and bury it alive there, as a sacrifice to the spirits.

Hobley has recorded several »legends connected with *aɩmu* beliefs»[1].

---

[1] Hobley, Akamba p. 86 ff

4. **Spirits other than** *aimu*.

A sharp distinction should be made between *aimu*, the spirits of ancestors, and *mbæбo*, though many Akamba do not trouble to make any distinction in everyday speech. The latter are spirits from the neighbouring tribes, Akikuyu, Masai, Galla, Wanjika, &c[1]. Spirits of Europeans are even met with. The Akamba do not worship any of these spirits, but the latter often plague their women, and must then be driven off with great trouble. To these foreign spirits belong the *aimu ma kitingo*, which were specially troublesome some years ago, and caught people during the *kiesu* dance, of which more below. These spirits came to the country with the Europeans, and it is not known where they have their haunts.

Hobley tells of another sort of spirit: »It appears that, quite apart from the ordinary *aimu* . . . . . . there is another class of spirits called *aimu ya kitombo* . . . . . . they are evil spirits, and are supposed to be the disembodied relics of people who have killed their neighbours by the help of black magic»[2]. In spite of assiduous search, I have not found a native or a missionary who knew anything about this sort of spirit. The only result of my inquiries was the information that *kitombo* is a sort of dance, which went out of fashion about 1908[3]. Since, however, spirits of different kinds make their appearance every now and again in Ukamba, as, for example, the *aimu ma kitingo* just mentioned, and their presence is expressed in dances, it is not unlikely that we are here in the presence of such a temporary plague of spirits, which, in all its varying forms, one may very well look upon as a sort of psychical disturbance. In any case, the sort of spirits mentioned by Hobley is not generally typical of the Akamba's belief in *aimu*.

In Kikumbuliu they also knew of another kind of possession, called *kisuka*, which was also caused by foreign spirits, though I

---

[1] Spirits from the last two tribes only seem to appear in the most easterly part of the country. The Akamba in Ulu live too far away to be able to have any communication with them.

[2] Hobley, Akamba p. 85.

[3] According to Hofmann's dictionary, *tomba* means 'to bow'.

could never find out which. This annoyance was particularly feared, as it was considered that the woman possessed could be made barren. The spirit was exorcised in the usual manner by drumming, and in addition a goat was killed, with the blood of which the possessed person was smeared. When she fell on the ground with convulsive spasms, she was given some light blows with a stick that had been rubbed with *maɓuo*, a kind of *ɣondu*, prepared from several different plants and specially potent in its effect. Only a few get to know its ingredients and the method of preparing it, so that it commands a comparatively high price (about 5 rupees). According to another description in a certain case the *maɓuo* was placed in a vessel of water, a hen was killed, and its blood, together, with three small feathers from the bird's belly, was added to the *ɣondu*. The vessel was raised three times to the mouth of the sick person, but she was allowed to drink only at the fourth time. During three days they then danced to the accompaniment of the spirit drum, and on the fourth the patient was washed with *maɓuo* over the whole body. As a protection against a renewal of the attack she got three small amulet bags (*mɓɪɳgu*), filled with *maɓuo*.

Finally, for the sake of completeness, it should be pointed out in this connection that, irrespective of manism and the belief in *mɓæɓo*, the Akamba do not seem to believe in other sorts of spirits. Conceptions of demons and nature spirits, spirits in forests and water-courses, among rocks and on mountains, &c, seem to be unknown, unless one reckons the fabulous figure *ɪmu* dealt with above.

5. Exorcism of spirits and religious dances.

A. **Exorcism of *aɪmu*.** In the Akamba's worship of spirits, dancing is an important feature, whether it is a question of healing a person possessed — that is to say, of driving away a troublesome spirit — or, on the other hand, of getting into communication with the spirit-world voluntarily, to question the spirits about something one wants to know. This is done mostly by medicine-men. Thus in dancing one gets into that ecstatic condition in which one comes into communication with the spirits more easily The ecstacy is certainly brought about principally by the music which accompanies the dancing — the dull, monotonous sound of the great spirit-drum, *kɪpæmbɔ*. The use of the drum at spirit séances is, as is well known, widely spread, and reaches its climax in the shaman-ism of Northern Asia[1].

The dance connected with the worship of the *aɪmu* is called *kɪlumɪ*, and we have already seen that they believe that the spirits themselves enjoy passing their time in dancing it. In con-

Fig. 57.   Women assisting an exorcism of spirits.

sequence people often dance without any special object, just to please the spirits, wherefore *kɪlumɪ* should be considered a part of the cult, especially as it is customarily danced when the sacri-fice is produced on the place of sacrifice. *kɪlumɪ* is danced by the medicine-men and the older women, and a few *atumɪa* usually take part also.   But if a young girl is seen dancing *kɪlumɪ* by day, she is certainly possessed of an *aɪmu*. This is shown by hysterical epileptic fits of very varying degrees of intensity. The

[1] Cf., for example, J. Stadling, Shamanismen i Norra Asien, p. 68 ff.

most usual symptoms are spasmodic twitchings of the body and
the uttering of shrill cries of »iii, iii!».   The spirit does not settle
in any particular part of the body, but the head is considered to
be attacked most, »since the possessed person behaves like one
deranged».

I will now describe a couple of cases:

On July 5, 1911, a great *kilumi* was held near Machakos.

Fig. 58.   Women dancing the *kilumi*.

A very old woman had become possessed by *aimu*, who, using
her as a medium, conveyed to the people the intelligence that
they should stay at home for the next ten evenings and nights,
if they did not wish to risk meeting spirits in the tracks.   The
medium was so feeble that she could not take part in the dancing,
in which the person possessed is usually the central figure, but
she was placed apart, surrounded by a few women, who carefully
listened to her disconnected talk — that is to say, what the spirits
were supposed to speak through her.   In the *kilumi*, which was
held near the village of the person possessed, only a small

number of women took part, though a large crowd stood and looked on, or sat on the ground occupied with their handiwork (sack plaiting), or looking after their babies. A little way off sat the members of the *nžama*, drinking beer, while at another place the young people were engaged in dancing. The whole thing gave the impression of a sort of popular festival, and was only intended to please the spirits, and not to gain anything in particular from them.

Machakos, August, 1911. A woman became possessed of *aimu*, and word was at once sent to the *atumia* of the *nžama*, who arranged a *kilumi* and dancing for the young people. Dancing went on for five days, the women even dancing *kilumi* at night. On the fifth day, when the spirit was considered to be driven out, the women put Eleusine seed and millet flour in their calabashes as an offering to the *aimu*. The person possessed then went in a circle round the whole assembly, accompanied by two *atumia*, who poured beer on the ground, and two old women of the *ipæmbo*, who sprinkled flour. Thus a protecting line was drawn round the crowd, and the spirit was called upon to go elsewhere. It did not matter whether it went to trouble others! The *atumia* killed a bull, and the meat was divided among the members of the *nžama* who where present. The hide was cut into strips, which were given to their wives to make into carrying straps &c, while the contents of the stomach were offered to the *aimu*.

At another exorcism of spirits, of which I was a witness, *gondu* (the usual ceremonial purifying medium) was put on all the paths that led to the village to which the spirit had come, in order to prevent its returning there.

It also happens that, to be still more certain that the spirit shall not return, the medicine-man sends it into an animal, such as a goat or a sheep. One of the animal's ears is cut off and hung round the neck of the person possessed, food is offered in the hut, and then the medicine-man says words to the following effect: »This goat is yours. Stop troubling N. N. further, and go into the goat!» This method of procedure is said to have a speedy result; whether the medicine-man uses any incantation, I do not know. The animal is then killed and the meat offered as a sacrifice. Before the spirit is driven away a sacrifice is also made. It consists of food and blood of the goat mixed together in a gourd and then poured out on the ground.

B. **Exorcism of spirits of the** *ṃbæɓo*-**type.** A few of the essential differences between *aimu* and *ṃbæɓo* in the beliefs of the Akamba are as follows: The latter only plague women, while men, even if less frequently, can also have *aimu*. Further, the *ṃbæɓo*-spirit usually expresses, through the woman possessed, its desire for a certain object, while *aimu* more seldom make such demands. It is also characteristic of women who are possessed of *ṃɓæɓo* that, when they come into an ecstacy, they »speak with tongues». Usually only inarticulate sounds are uttered, but sometimes the medium is said to utter sentences in the language of the people to which the spirit is thought to belong. In the Kibwezi district I really did hear Kisuaheli spoken by a woman who was said to have a Suaheli spirit in her body, and who could not speak Suaheli in a normal state, though she had of course often heard it spoken. Pfitzinger, the missionary of the Leipzig Mission, said that he once saw a woman that was said to be possessed of an Arab-*ṃbæɓo*. Certainly she did not utter any real words, but only sounds; yet among them was also *r*, which is not found in the Kamba language, and which it is almost impossible for a Mukamba to pronounce. I have not met with this myself, but many natives have told me exactly the same thing.

We have just said that women possessed of a *ṃbæɓo* have strange desires. Thus, in Kikumbuliu I saw a woman who bore on her person objects from the Wasuaheli, Galla, and Masai, which objects had all been demanded by different spirits. A Suaheli spirit had demanded an embroidered cap of the kind usually worn by Wasuaheli and Arabs; the woman wore it on her head. The Masai spirits often wish for a piece of red cloth or a knife. Sometimes they ask for the most ridiculous things, such as a European shoe or knife. One day a native came running breathless to Säuberlich, the missionary in Mulango: his wife was possessed and must have a European plate! Sometimes a spirit will be satisfied if the woman can only see a certain object. In one case of which I was a witness, a Masai spear was demanded. Since the woman's hysterical fits do not cease until the object demanded is procured, and it is believed that she would otherwise die, her husband does everything in his power to fulfill the

spirit's desire. This is often a costly matter, and down in Kikumbuliu, the district in Ulu which seems to be most afflicted with
these spiritual disturbances, I know some who have paid from
twenty-five to thirty rupees to satisfy the spirit's caprices — rather
a large sum for the majority of the natives.

Although the women are more superstitious than the men, it
does happen that an intelligent and artful woman may make use
of the spirits to get her own desires satisfied. For instance, she
may for a long time have longed for a piece of many-coloured
cloth, but her lord and master has not been pleased to grant her
desire. She pretends to be possessed, makes a terrible noise, and
says that the spirit can only be appeased with a piece of cloth.
To recover his lost domestic peace the otherwise dignified Kamba
husband gives himself no rest till he has found the desired object,
then the spirit disappears. Thus it may justly be said that, even
in East Africa, woman's artfulness is more than a match for man's
wisdom.

I will quote an example of such deceitful feminine tactics
from my stay in the district of Kibwezi.

A married woman developed a great desire to eat meat —
they live principally on a vegetarian diet — and therefore asked
her husband to kill a fat buck, for which she had a special fancy.
The husband refused, saying that he had destined that particular
animal as an offering to the *aimu*, the next time that one was needed.
Persuasion was of no avail, but the woman did not abandon her
plans. Some days later she was attacked by epileptic twitchings
and uttered shrill cries of »iii», the usual symptoms shown by one
possessed. The husband asked what was the matter. »It is a spirit»,
said the woman. — »Do you know what he wants?» — »Yes, he
wants that buck we were talking about». — »So be it then! Now
that the owner has appeared, I can no longer refuse». Then he
slaughtered the buck. When this was done, he went to a neighbouring village on some errand. As soon as he had gone, the
woman ceased pretending to be possessed. Beside herself with
joy at the success of her cunning, however, she could not keep
silent, but while she hushed her child, she sang a lullaby about
how easily she could deceive her husband and how she had only
pretended to be possessed. As ill-luck would have it, her husband
had forgotten an axe which he ought to have taken with him,

and came back to fetch it. The wife did not notice him, and he heard her song. Enraged at her deceit, he at once sent her back to her father.

Exorcism of the *mbæбo* is usually carried out in the following manner: The person possessed sits on the ground with her head wrapped in a dark cloth (at least such a cloth was used at all the many ceremonies that I saw, but I have unfortunately neglected to find out why). Those present beat their drums and sing. The songs seem to have very little meaning, and often consist of only a few words, which are repeated again and again. At the exorcism of a Suaheli spirit near Kibwezi, the following was sung: »Suaheli, you are rich, you are Kamba's brother. Give me bracelets!» Under the influence of the songs and the sound of the drums, life gradually returns to the woman; she tries to get up, but is often so weak that she cannot stand. When it is considered that the drums have been beaten sufficiently, the spirit is questioned as to who it is and what it wants.

The methods of exorcism naturally vary in details. One man who had gone to the medicine-man to get help for his wife, who was possessed, was told to lay three glowing coals in a little water, and at the same time to say to the spirit: »Go away now and cease to torment my wife. I will give you what you want as soon as I can afford to procure it».

I will conclude by describing the exorcism of a Masai-spirit at Machakos, in May 1911, at the house of the medicine-woman Kavuva. The proceedings were typical.

One evening I proceeded to Kavuva's hut, as several hours' intense beating on the spirit-drums had indicated that something was afoot. On my arrival I found the hut full of people of both sexes, though principally old women, those of the *ipæmbo*. A young woman — Kavuva's daughter-in-law — had become possessed by a spirit. She sits dumb and motionless in the middle of the floor, with her head wrapped in a dark cloth. Some men are beating with all their might on the drums and singing a song, and all those present join in the chorus. The noise has an intoxicating effect on the company; wildly and more wildly are the drums beaten, and louder and louder rise the songs. The one possessed, who up till now has sat absolutely motionless, now begins to move. She tries to get up, staggers, and nearly falls; but she receives support till she can stand. Her eyes are shut, her face absolutely expressionless; she resembles one intoxicated. They bind iron bells (*kɪamba*) round her arms and legs, and she begins the usual dance by moving her body in time with the music, slowly at first, and then more and more spasmodically. Several times she almost falls again. This continues for a time, and when the drummers, exhausted, cease drumming for a few seconds, she utters weird inarticulate sounds. Now she kneels and dances on the ground on her knees. She says that the spirit desires red-hot coals (*makɑ*), and therefore some are taken from the hearth and thrown in front of her. She dances on them and takes them in her hands, without seeming to feel any pain. They tell me that she is not injured by them; and that she does not seem to be affected by them in the least is explained by her exalted condition; besides, the skin on the soles of the feet and the insides of the hands is thickened by work.

Hysterical and other abnormal mental states easily work on others. This seems to be the case especially with women. Suddenly another woman, a young girl, springs to her feet with piercing shrieks and begins to dance wildly; she snatches up a knife and swings it about during the dance. She also has her eyes shut, and moves hither and thither like a sleep-walker, swinging her knife, which several times comes dangerously near my face. At last both dancers sink exhausted to the ground, and water is poured on their heads, to bring them back to consciousness.

When the one possessed has recovered a little, the questioning begins. She is asked what spirit she has in her body and what it desires. To compel the possessing spirit to tell its name is always the first condition for success in driving it away. The questions have to be repeated many times before she answers. At last she says it is a Masai spirit, who desires a piece of black cloth and a club. And, although she is quite exhausted, she says that the spirit wants more dancing, which seems to surprise everybody.

Now Kavuva, the medicine-woman, gets up. Neither she nor any of the other old women have taken part in the dancing up till now. She throws a little maize and some beans on the ground as an offering to the spirits, and smears the throats and necks of

those present with fat[1]. Then the dancing re-commences, wildly
as before. The old women have bound cow- and zebra-tails round
their wrists (fig. 58). These are nearly always used in such dances
by the old women, and are undoubtedly of magic-religious significance. Tails are also used by most medicine-men as plugs for
their divinatory calabashes.

The drums are beaten furiously, and the violent movements
of the arms cause the bells to rattle with a hissing sound. The
dance goes on again until the afflicted person again sinks to the
ground. The spirit is now driven out, and the patient is smeared
with fat and *kɨutu*, a sort of woodflour taken from the hole of a
certain sort of woodpecker (*ŋgomakomi*), the smell of which is
considered refreshing. Then the woman goes away to sleep, and
the next day she works in the fields as usual, as though nothing
had happened.

H. Junod in his excellent and exceptionally complete monograph on the Batonga describes a kind of possession that shows
essentially the same symptoms and is treated in the same way as
the psychical phenomenon we come across among the Akamba[2]. The
possessing spirits in this case are, however, less often ancestral,
but are usually those of the Zulu and Ba-Ndjao tribes. With
song, music and noise they try to make the spirit reveal his
name, »after which it will be duly overcome». — »The patient was
covered with a large piece of calico during the drum performances»
(p. 443). — »In the crisis of madness the patient sometimes throws
himself into the fire and feels no hurt.» — »The spirit will claim
some satisfaction: a piece of calico of such and such a colour.»
Finally the possessed one sings »generally in Zulu, and it is asserted
that, even if the patient does not know this language, he will
be able to use it in his conversation, by a kind of miracle of
tongues!» (p. 445).

C. **Kɨesu.** Time after time remarkable psychical disturbances of a religious character pass like epidemics over the Kamba
country, only to disappear as suddenly as they came. Such a disturbance was the *kɨesu*, which raged some years ago — according to

---

[1] The religious significance of smearing with fat has already been
emphasized.

[2] The life of a South African tribe, vol. II, p. 435 ff., and
Bulletin de la Société Neuchâteloise de Géographie X, p. 388.

Hobley in 1906[1]. It is said to have originated in Mukaa (Ulu), where a medicine-man said that he had been commanded by the spirits to teach the people a new (religious) dance. It spread from there like wild-fire over the whole of Ulu, and even east of the river Athi. The symptoms consisted in going into convulsions at the sight of a European or even a pith helmet or a red fez, such as is usually worn by the native Mohammedan. The afflicted one fell to the ground, writhing as if suffering from violent cramp, moaning and groaning. The natives in the neighbourhood of Machakos tried to avoid the attacks — when they saw a European in the distance — by wrapping their blankets over their faces till he had gone by. The person attacked was also said to have an irresistible desire to shake hands with anyone he met, a form of greeting not natural to the Akamba. Many natives assert that greeting by shaking hands, which is now fairly general, originated to a large extent from this period, although the example of Europeans has of course helped a great deal. These were the most striking features of *kịesu*, which word, however, really means a dance. The dancers carried knives in their hands, and when the fits came upon them, they cut themselves with the knives, »without bleeding». Similarly they are said to have carried firebrands in their hands without being injured.

C. W. Neligan describes a case of what he calls »*kijesu* ceremony», which he witnessed in East Ukamba in 1908[2]. The person in question was a woman, and the fit, which lasted from three to five hours, was caused by the sight of his pith helmet. The following day the woman had entirely recovered and took no notice at all of the helmet.

The meaning of the word *kịesu* is not quite clear. Säuberlich[3] connects it with *kisu* 'knife' (Kisuaheli), and the dancers certainly do carry knives. Others think it is derived from the word »Jesus», a theory which I find rather probable. I have been able to write down a record of part of a song which is sung during these dances, and in it they mention *vwana jesu* ('The Lord Jesus') and also *ŋgaị* ('God') »who comes to earth to purify mankind». It seems very possible to me, therefore, that the *kịesu*

---

[1] Hobley, Akamba p. 10.
[2] Man 1911 (with three photographs).
[3] Mentioned to the author orally.

arose in connection with the teaching of the missionaries. The Akamba themselves say that the spirits which, according to them, gave rise to *kĩesu*, came from Ulaya (Europe). It seems that only those who believe in them are attacked. The missionaries say that the natives who attended services at the missionary station escaped.

At the end of 1911, a certain mental unrest arose in Kilungu (the district south of Machakos), and the Commissioner in Machakos, who believed that the movement was directed against the Government, had the leaders — some medicine-men and older women — arrested and taken to the Government station. I have forgotten what the affair was all about, but it is certain that it was only a case of one of these periodical psychical anomalies. However, the over-excited minds soon calmed down in prison, and when the leaders were removed, the whole thing died away.

* * *

Madmen (cf. next chap.). In all times and among all races, mental maladies, even epileptic and convulsive attacks, have been ascribed to spirits or demons, who have entered into the person affected[1]. Mental disease, madness, is called *ndoka*, and is considered to be caused by spirits, so that, on the whole, madmen are treated in the same way as those temporarily possessed. A young man called Kitalu, at Machakos, who was at times deranged, was said to have his uncle's spirit in his body. Once when I saw him in a fit, the upper part of his body twitched spasmodically, and he wanted to start up incessantly. His speech was very confused. One day he paid a visit to the mission station, where he had previously worked in the garden, and said he was the owner of the whole property. I have seen several mad people in Ukamba; some have been so violent at times that they have had to be tied down. No form of worship of mad persons exists.

Prayers and sacrifices to trees. It is not unusual for prayers and sacrifices to be offered to a tree, but it always seems to be done at the command of a medicine-man, and according to his directions. Before we consider the significance of these proceedings, I will first give the material collected.

---

[1] Cf. R. Andree, Ethnographische Parallelen und Vergleiche, Neue Folge, p. 1 ff.

Some one goes, for instance, to the medicine-man, to ask for advice about a disease. He is directed to dig up some sort of roots with certain ceremonial observances. A man in the neighbourhood of Kibwezi, who wanted a cure for his sick son, was told to draw four lines on the ground with his fingers, in front of the tree indicated, and then to say: »Tree! I have a sick person at home. *mundu muə* (the medicine-man) has told me to come to you to get medicine. I pray you for *kɩpaŋgona*» [1]. After that he was to dig up the roots and boil them in the gruel (*usu̯*) the invalid was to drink. Another person had to smear ashes with three fingers on the trunk of a tree, that was pointed out to him. Another rather usual method is, before digging, to throw *wɩmbɩ*-seed (Eleusine) against the tree, three times from one side and four times from the other. Once I had the opportunity of observing a man who, standing with his back to the indicated tree, drove an awl into its trunk, at the same time directing his prayer to the tree [2]. He then goes home, to return next morning, when he smears the trunk with fat. Then he digs up the roots. In this case they are only used as a sort of amulet, pieces of them being bound to the sufferer's arms and legs; thus their use is purely magical.

We have already seen how, during the great *ṇzaɩko*, prayers are directed to a wild fig-tree (p. 56).

Brutzer cites some very similar examples of sacrifices and prayers being offered to trees. Since his work is rather difficult of access and no one else seems to have made any observations as to these remarkable and interesting customs, I take the liberty of quoting him, thus assembling all the material in one place: »Den *mundu muwe* [= *muə*] fragt man um rat, und dieser giebt das betreffende heilkräftige oder schützende kraut oder baum an.

---

[1] *kɩpaŋgona* means sometimes »sacrifice», sometimes »magic medicine».

[2] What the object of driving in the awl is, I do not know, but it seems to me that here we have a certain resemblance to the West African negro who knocks a nail into his fetish. I will therefore, for the present, suggest the following explanation: the supplicant attracts the attention of the tree (the spirit of the tree) by driving in the nail. That the tree may not, however, be angry at the pain he causes it, he stands with his back to it, to give it the idea that he has nothing to do with the proceeding.

Arch.Or. Lindblom

Man begiebt sich zu demselben mit getreidekörnern [cf. above Eleusine]. Sechsmal hintereinander bewirft man den baum mit einzelnen körnern. Beim siebenten mal wirft man den ganzen vorrat auf den baum, gräbt dann die pflanze aus und bereitet das pulver. Also ein opfer an den baum. — Oder man begiebt sich zum baum mit einem feuerbrand und wasser. Dass wasser stellt man zu boden. Geht sechsmal mit geschlossenen augen um den baum. Beim siebenten mal stellt man sich unter den baum, schaut nach osten und spricht mit geschlossenen augen: Baum, ich komme, dich um eine gnade zu bitten. Ich habe einen kranken und weiss nicht, was ihn krank gemacht hat. Er hat mit keinem menschen etwas vorgehabt. Ich komme, dich um eine gabe zu bitten. Ich komme hierher zu dir, baum, dass ich ihn damit behandle, auf dass er genese» [1].

Thus we find that sacrifices and prayers may be offered to trees just as to individual beings. I have not, however, managed to obtain any clear explanation of the circumstance. The natives only emphatically deny that the tree is thought to be inhabited by the spirits of the departed. It is very possible that here we have a manifestation of animism to deal with — an instance of the worship of trees resembling that which Krapf has already observed among the neighbours of the Akamba in the south-east, the Wanyika, who, according to him, believe that every tree has its »spirit», and in particular offer sacrifices to the cocoa-nut tree [2]. The question then arises whether the tree is thought of as the body of the tree-spirit, or rather as its dwelling, a thing about which the native himself perhaps has no clear ideas [3]. My previous assertion that the Akamba do not believe in nature-spirits of any kind, hardly conflicts with this conception, since it does not seem to be a question of such spirits here, but rather of the vegetative vitality of the tree — it is tempting to say its »soul», in accordance with primitive animism, but I avoid this word, since the natives with whom I discussed the point, denied that plants have souls.

On the other hand, what is evident from the above quotation is that there is a strong magical feature in this worship of trees,

---

[1] Brutzer, Der Geisterglaube, p. 12.
[2] Krapf, Travels, Researches, p. 198.
[3] Cf. Frazer, The Golden Bough 1: 2, p. 44 ff.

which is not surprising, since religion and magic go hand in hand during the early stages, and no sharp boundary line can be drawn between them. We find thus that the roots are not curative in themselves, but only become so when the tree is treated in the method prescribed by the medicine-man[1].

6. The conception of Mulungu (Ngai).

The most puzzling question that the study of the religion of the Bantu presents, is whether they have any belief in a Supreme God.

The expression *mulu*ŋ*gu* appears in forms which do not vary very much (*muu*ŋ*gu, muru*ŋ*gu*, &c), more especially in the eastern Bantu dialects. According to Le Roy, the name is to be found in at least some 40 dialects, and this figure is certainly a minimum. From the most northerly Bantu peoples, such as the Akamba, it is met with in most places down as far as the tracts south of Mozambique, and further in the southerly parts of the west coast. Even in the heart of the continent it is found, as for example among the Warundi, north of Tanganyika. I am uncertain as to the meaning of the word. Le Roy, without producing proofs for his assertion, translates it as, »Celui d'en haut, Celui du ciel»[2] (cf. below p. 246).

Among the Akamba, Mulungu is a conception which, both as regards meaning and name, corresponds to what is known from so many other Bantu peoples, viz. a divinity that seems almost impersonal, since there are no conceptions — or very vague ones — of its being and characteristics[3]. In spite of this,

---

[1] It would perhaps have been more suitable to include the whole of this description in the following chapter on the magic of the Akamba.

[2] Le Roy, La Religion des primitifs, p. 176 ff.

[3] The lack of concreteness in the Akamba's conception of *mulu*ŋ*gu* as a person, appears also from the fact that, in certain contexts, the word appears in the plural, but then it is formed according to the second class of substantives (prefix *mi*-), which embraces objects without independent individual life, such as trees and parts of the body. Then it generally means 'luck, good fortune, chance': *mulu*ŋ*gu musœo* 'good luck', *m. mupuku* 'bad luck'. There is, besides, another word *mulu*ŋ*gu* in Kikamba, which means 'pipe, tube', thus primarily

it cannot be maintained that the Akamba, any more than any other Bantu peoples, conceive Mulungu as a sort of impersonal power; that would be to ascribe to them too great a power of abstract conception. They look upon him as the creator of all things, and therefore call him also *mumbı* 'the one who fashions, the creator' (from *umba* 'to fashion', most usually employed in the meaning of »to fashion earthenware vessels»)[1]. More seldom is found *mwatwaŋgı*, 'the cleaver' (from *atwaŋga* 'to cleave into pieces'), since he originally formed all living beings, »as one hews out a stool or some other object with an axe». He is above both *aımu* and all the powers of nature.

Mulungu is not worshipped at all (or at least extremely seldom) by offering of sacrifices, nor in any other way. He dwells in the skies at an indefinite distance, is held to be well-disposed towards human beings, but beyond that has nothing to do with them. »Mulungu does us no evil; so wherefore should we sacrifice to him?» say the Akamba characteristically. This motive for not worshipping is found among many of the Bantu peoples, who, from the religious point of view, are undeniably somewhat cold and practical[2].

At most it is only occasionally, and then on some special occasion, that they pray to Mulungu. Thus at the birth of a child, I once heard the following prayer: »*mumbı*, thou who hast created

---

a piece of bamboo or some other hollow stalk. It is not, however, altogether impossible that originally, in »Primitive Bantu», the two words denoted the same idea. For in the Zulu stories we are told that Umkulunkulu, whom we probably have to conceive as identical with *muluŋgu*, came out of *uthlanga*, which seems sometimes to mean 'origin, primitive race', sometimes, which is interesting to us in this connection, 'reed'. The word is thought to have meant originally a stem with numerous shoots. See further Kidd, The Essential Kafir, p. 100 and W. Schneider, Die Religion der Afrikanischen Naturvölker, p. 64.

[1] Le Roy p. 174 cites identical examples from elsewhere.

[2] Cf. Gutmann, Die Gottesidee der Wadschagga am Kilimandjaro, p. 128: »Trotz aller ihren äusserungen über Gott ist es aber nun tatsache, dass die verehrung Gottes nur eine geringe oder gar keine rolle spielt. Nicht nur weil er trotz aller einzelzüge ihnen ein fremdes fernes wesen bleibt, während die ahnen ihnen vertraut und nahe sind, sondern auch weil für gewöhnlich von Gott ihnen keinerlei not und trübsal droht».

all human beings, thou hast conferred a great benefit on us by
bringing us this child!»[1]

This prayer is remarkable, inasmuch as it is not a request,
but a thanksgiving, something which hardly occurs among prayers
to the spirits. Above all, when the life-giving rains do not come,
prayers are offered up all over the world, especially in Africa.
It is obvious that it is upon the rains that the welfare of the
agricultural negroes entirely depends. Yet these prayers are really
addressed to the *aımu*, even though they sometimes seem to be
addressed to the Mulungu-Ngai. They are generally offered by the old
men and women when sacrifices are made at the *ıpæmbo*, the places
where offerings are made to the *aımu*. Such a prayer for rain, which
I heard, was offered to Ngai[2]. In our description of the second
nžaıko, we saw that the leader of the ceremonies poured out a
little oil as an offering to Mulungu, at the same time sending up
prayers that the novices might turn out well. For the rest, no
prayers are offered unless there is a special reason. »One does
not pray *mana*» (i. e. for nothing, without reason), said an old man to
the author[3].

A very interesting question, but one which it is scarcely possible to answer, is that concerned with the o r i g i n   o f   t h e   c o n-
c e p t i o n   o f   a   G o d among the Akamba. The view has often
been advanced that the conception of Mulungu, among the Bantu
peoples in general, has developed from the worship of ancestral
spirits, the original ancestor of a whole people having been finally
exalted to a divinity. All the champions of this idea employ the
same method of proof; one may be cited here:

»Dass nun diese gottesidee der Bantu, die jetzt allerdings be-
ziehungslos neben dem seelenkult steht, dies einst nicht tat, sondern dass sie aus demselben entsprungen ist und also aus ihm zu
erklären sein wird, lässt sich zur höchsten wahrscheinlichkeit er-
heben. Es sprechen dafür zunächst sprachliche momente. Die
genuine bezeichnung gottes im Bantu scheint in dem kafferischen

---

[1] Kikamba: *mumbı, ula wumbaa andu onðə, nutwıkıə næsa atue-
teə kana.*

[2] *ŋgaı, ıla ıetaə mbua nækaete andu, nıŋo toka kuvoŋa mbua:* »Ngai,
thou who . . ? . . the rain and bringest it to men, we have come to
thee to pray for rain».

[3] For examples of Bantu prayers, see Le Roy p. 297 ff.

Unkulunkulu erhalten zu sein. Es ist dies wort das mit dem präfix *un-* versehene und dadurch substantivierte adjektiv *kulu*, 'gross, alt'. Die verdoppelung ist steigerung des begriffs. Unkulunkulu ist also wohl soviel wie der 'uralte', der 'urahn'. Dies adjektiv hat sich nebst dem dazu gehörigen verbum in fast allen Bantuidiomen erhalten. Dasselbe wort Unkulunkulu ist in der gottesbezeichnung z. b. der Suahili, Wakamba und Wapokomo erhalten: Muungu, Mulungu und Muungo. Demnach wird es nicht zu kühn sein, den gott der Bantu als den geist des urahnen zu bezeichnen, so zwar dass der zusammenhang desselben mit den von ihm abstammenden anderen geistern dem bewusstsein verloren gegangen ist, und er dadurch eine singuläre stellung erlangt hat. So erklärt sich auch der durchaus schattenhafte charakter des Bantugottesgedankens. Das ist die gottesidee der Bantu. Eine veranlassung, ihn durch opfer zu verehren, besteht für den einzelnen nicht, er steht zu fern, um ihm schaden zu wollen; er denkt sich ihn als gut»[1].

The same idea is championed by Keane, who relies on such authorities as Bleek, Duff MacDonald, and Bentley[2].

I will not, from my own experience, give any expression of opinion as to the correctness of this idea, as far as the Bantu tribes in general are concerned. Several circumstances, however, seem to indicate the incorrectness of tracing the *muluŋgu* conception back to the spirit cult:

I.   Generally, though not always, a sharp distinction is drawn between *muluŋgu* and *aimu*. »Wenn die geister so gut wären wie Mulungu, dann stände es gut mit uns», said one man to a missionary[3].

II.   According to tradition, *muluŋgu* created the first men, thus also the original ancestor, for which reason, as we have seen, he can be given such a powerful »nomen agens» as »Creator».

---

[1] Raum, Über angebliche Götzen am Kilimandjaro, Globus 1904, p. 102.

[2] Keane, Ancestor worship, in Encyclopedia of Religion and Ethics, vol. I, p. 194.

[3] Kanig, Dornige Pfade eines jungen Missionars in Ukamba, p. 17. — It is hardly likely that the assertions of missionaries and Mohammedan natives could have given rise to this distinction. At most, contact with them may have helped, in individual cases, to render more distinct and personified the conception of *muluŋgu*.

III. Mulungu, »The Maker», existed before death came into the world (cf. below, myth II, p. 253).

IV. Mulungu is thought to dwell in the sky »among the clouds» (*matunı*), while the *aımu* dwell in the earth or upon it.

This difference between Mulungu and the spirits, which I have here tried to indicate, is also made — and on similar grounds — by B. Gutmann in the case of the Wadjagga, a people much resembling the Akamba in many respects[1]. Gutmann suggests that, at least to some degree, the Wadjagga have taken their conception of God from the Masai, although they have not adopted the Masai name for God, *ŋgaı̯*, or as Hollis writes, *Eng-aï*. On the contrary, the Akamba have done this in some parts, chiefly in the west, that is to say just in the parts bordering on the Masai steppes. It seems to me, therefore, that here they make a sharper distinction between *muluŋgu-ŋgaı̯* and *aımu* than in East Ukamba. Since, however, in spite of Merker's assertion, the Ngai of the Masai (see also below) seems to be almost as indefinite a divinity as the Mulungu of the Bantu peoples, the loan cannot in any appreciable degree have affected the Akamba's old conception of Mulungu. Even the Akikuyu, who have in many respects been considerably more influenced by the Masai than have the Akamba, have adopted the word *ŋgaı̯*. I scarcely think that they make any general use of the word Mulungu[2].

In spite of the fact, then, that (as I think I have shown) there really exists a difference between *muluŋgu* and *aımu*, the expressions are very often used indiscriminately: *muluŋgu-ŋgaı̯* is used in the same sense as *aımu*, and the locative form *muluŋgunı* in the sense of »of the spirit-world, among the spirits»[3]. The Akikuyu say *makaı̯* (the collective form of *ŋgaı̯*), which must be un-

---

[1] Gutmann, Die Gottesidee der Wadschagga, p. 131.
    »   Dichten und Denken der Dschagga-neger, p. 183.

[2] Routledge has only Ngai. Cayzac, La religion des Kikuyu, p. 311, writes as a heading: »Dieu (Ngai et Molungu, indistinctement)», but in his presentation employs only »dieu». It is to be observed that Routledge and Cayzac both say that the Akikuyu usually offer sacrifices (and pray) to God.

[3] It is probably this that has misled S. Watt, in his vocabulary, into translating *muluggu* by »spirit of evil». On the whole, Watt's work betrays a certain ignorance of Kikamba.

derstood as synonymous with *ŋgoma*, their usual word for the spirits
The same indifference with regard to the differentiation of ideas
is met with among other Bantu peoples[2]. It would seem, however,
that the native is conscious that he has committed a lapsus. Many
a time I have heard them speak of *muluŋgu*, meaning *aimu*; but
when they have seen my astonishment, they have corrected themselves and employed the latter expression.

A connection in which, in West Ukamba, Ngai (not Mulungu)
seems exclusively to be used, is in speaking of rain, which is
said to be sent by Ngai (but also by *mumbi* 'the creator'). And
when, sometimes, for certain reasons the rain may not be mentioned by its ordinary name, *mbua*, they call it Ngai, if they have
to speak of it (cf. Chap. XIV. 5). In this case it is clear that the
Akamba's Ngai is very closely connected with the Ngai of the
Masai, as this divinity is conceived by most investigators (who
do not adopt Merker's well-known theory), namely as a vague
sky-god or as heaven itself.

It is true that in this study we have nothing to do directly
with the Masai's Ngai, but since the word at least, and with it
also part of its signification, has been borrowed by the Akamba,
I will recall the fact that some investigators have compared Ngai
with the Melanesians' mana, the Dacotah Indians' wakan, &c, and
with conceptions of »power» and »the powers» in nature[3]. This
comparison of *ŋgai* with mana seems to be traceable to the oft-cited
assertion made by J. Thompson: »Their conception of the Deity
seems marvellously vague. I was Ngai. My lamp was Ngai»[4].
In a word, everything new and inexplicable to the Masai, was
ŋgai. It is more than probable that Thompson misunderstood
them[5]. The present author has not been sufficiently in con-

---

[1] McGregor, English-Kikuyu Vocabulary.

[2] »The word mulungu is also used to denote the spirit world in
general, or more properly speaking, the aggregate of the spirits of all
the dead»: Hetherwick, Some animistic beliefs among the Yaos of
Brit. Centr. Africa, p. 94.

[3] See, for example, Crawley, The tree of life, pp. 51, 234.

[4] Thompson, Through Masailand, p. 445.

[5] This is the opinion of Mr Hollis, the well-known expert on the
Masai language and on the Masai living on English territory, whom I
met in Nairobi in 1910. See also Marret, The Threshold of Religion,
p. XVIII.

tact with the Masai, nor has he a sufficient acquaintance with their language, to be able to form a reliable appreciation of the conception of Ngai; but as far as the Akamba's *ŋgaι* is concerned, I have never heard the word used with a similar meaning, expressing a property, either alone or preceded by a particle. My observations lead me to the conclusion that, in spite of all its unclearness, Mulungu-Ngai is at most »a relatively Supreme Being», to use Andrew Lang's expression. How, further, the natives represent this Being to their own minds is another question, which it would certainly be difficult to answer. To analyse the idea philosophically and make distinctions is beyond their capacity. At most, a few realise that Mulungu is the Absolute (as we use the word), who is superior to all natural and supernatural powers. What we must remember is only that we must not base a comparison between their idea of a God and our own on our own conceptions.

We now come to those who entertain great doubts about the Bantu peoples' belief in a Supreme Being, and instead attach to Mulungu and similar conceptions the idea of a nature-religion, animism, and so forth. For a refutation of these ideas I refer the reader to the above-mentioned work of Le Roy, whose general presentation in the main tallies with my own observations within my limited sphere of investigation. The facts set forth by this author, of which the most important are statements of natives belonging to different tribes, seem to afford clear proof of the natives' belief in a personal God[1].

And yet Le Roy seems to have taken rather a one-sided view of his task and to have attached most importance to the material which supported his theory. But just as we can bring together sufficient facts to afford a conception of a personal being — as he has done — so can we assemble other facts which suggest a vague and somewhat impersonal Mulungu. His significance varies even within the same tribe[2]. This contradiction, which is

---

[1] Le Roy ibid. p. 170 ff.

[2] The Jao of Brit. Central Africa seem to provide a strikingly good example of this: »The untaught Jao refuses to assign to the word Mulungu any idea of being or personality. It is to him more a quality or faculty of the human nature, whose signification he has extended so as to include the whole spirit world. Yet the Jao approaches closely to the idea of personality and a personal being when he speaks of

so inexplicable for us, assuredly does not exist for the negro; he does not make the same distinction as we do between the personal and the impersonal. The investigator who has best understood the inner essence of the Mulungu-type and paid due attention to all the variations and changes in the conception, is without doubt N. Söderblom. After having passed under consideration original monotheism, the nature-hypothesis, and the ancestor-hypothesis, he sets up his own theory of »the producer» (Swed. 'frambringaren'):

»The connection between the power-matter and the creator lies in the fact that, in both cases, a cause is sought for what otherwise cannot be explained. For us the distinction is as clear as possible between a sort of impersonal power, material, electricity, and a personal fashioner, producer, a supernatural creator or father. — — Mulungu, wakanda, manitu, orenda, is now a mysterious something in beings and things, now certain objects, now spirits, now a creative being. If the primitive conception vacillates between conceptions that (for us but not for them) appear as mutually excluding alternatives, and if that which is common to and constant in the expressions employed, is that these expressions designate the cause of that which is to be explained — then no very intimate contact with Christianity or Islam is necessary for the »power» to become a personal creator»[1].

»The more I have occupied myself with these beings belonging to primitive faith that resemble animals or men, the stronger has my conviction become that these beings which formerly, and even to-day, are advanced as a proof of an original monotheism, and which have later been arrayed among nature-gods or ancestors, could not be squeezed into any of our existing categories. They form a category by themselves. Their peculiarity must be respected — to keep them distinct from other conceptions the are concerned with and at the same time to express their essence, I would suggest the name »producers» (urheber)»[2].

The natives' dim conception of Mulungu and Ngai is appar-

---

what Mulungu is doing and has done. It is M. who made the world and man and animals». See further S Hartland's article »Bantu» in Encycl. of Religion and Ethics.

[1] N. Söderblom, Gudstrons uppkomst, p. 89.

[2] Söderblom loc. cit. p. 175.

ently insufficient to enable them to form any idea of the appearance of this being. This may be the reason why no representation of Mulungu has, as far as I know, ever been found. On the whole, ornaments or sculptures in human shape, such as, for instance, the West African fetish images, are, as a matter of fact, very rare among East African tribes. I found, however, in Ukamba a figure that a medicine man had cut out on his calabash and which he claimed to represent Ngai. He would not give up his calabash, so I had to be satisfied with drawing the figure. In fig. 59 *a* is Ngai's eye, *b* is his penis, »the source of all life», *c* is his three legs. Around the neck of the calabash another figure was cut out, a circle with strokes on the inside. It represented

Fig. 59. A medicine man's representation of Ngai and Mulungu.

Mulungu, »who lives in the sea». The man thus seemed to conceive Ngai and Mulungu as two different persons. My attempt to get a clear idea of his conception was, however, in vain.

I communicate this with the utmost reservation. I look upon the case as an isolated incident, a manifestation of a productive brain. I also learned that the man had lived for a time at the coast, where he had occasion to come into contact with different races and tribes.

*   *   *

Finally, a considerable number of customs connected with religion have been described in different places in the chapters of this work, but I have not considered it expedient to take them out of their natural contexts. The influence of religious conceptions upon social life in all its spheres is, of course, very strong among all peoples living in a state of nature.

7. Myths as to the origin of the world.

If one passes in review the numerous collections of folklore of the different Bantu peoples, one cannot but be astonished at their great lack of any feeling that causes and motives must be found, at their great lack of any feeling that the origin of the most important phenomena of existence needs explanation. Thus the Akamba and many other tribes are without any myths about the origin of Heaven and earth. Only about the creation of men and about death have they any original myths. The cause of this must be ascribed to the overwhelming predominance of manism in the religious sphere.

I here append, in all briefness, the two existing myths as to the origin of things.

I. **The Creation.** Of the first men, one pair, a man and his wife, came out of a termite hole (*muþumbini*). Another pair, likewise a man and his wife (the ancestors of *mba-aimu*), were thrown down by Mulungu from the clouds (*matuni*), bringing with them a cow, a goat, and a sheep. They fell down on the rock Nsaue, south-east of Kilungu, and there built a village. Both pairs had children, who married among themselves and formed new families. From some of their descendants came the Kamba clans; others gave origin to the Masai, the Akikuyu, &c.

On Nsaue are seen some marks in the rock, which are said to be the foot-prints of the first men and their cattle; there are also the marks of the stool of the head of the family.

The assumption that there were originally two pairs has probably arisen from the institution of exogamy.

The Jao tribe round Nyassa has a similar origin-myth: »Mankind is said to have originated at Kapirimtiya, a hill or, as some say, an island in a lake, far to the west of Nyassa. Here it is believed that there is a rock covered with marks like the footprints of men and animals, and that, when men were first created, the island was a piece of soft mud, and Mulungu sent them across it, so as to leave their footmarks there, before they were dispersed over the world. One native account says that 'they came from Heaven and fell down upon the earth': another that they came out of a hole in the rock, which was afterwards closed by 'the people of Mulungu', and is now in a desert place towards the north»[1].

II. **The coming of death to mankind.** Death as something inexplicable is by different peoples attributed to the Creator.

When Mulungu created man, he resolved to endow him with immortality. The chameleon was known to him as a certainly slow but very reliable being, for which reason he chose him to convey the important message to the children of men. The chameleon set off, took the matter lightly, and stopped now and then to catch flies. At length, however, he came to the human beings, and began: »I have been commissioned to, I have been commissioned to ...». He could get no further. For some reason or other, Mulungu however had changed his mind and decided that man should die, »like the roots of the aloe». The swift-flying weaver bird was sent out with the new message, and he arrived just as the chameleon stood stammering. The bird conveyed his message quickly and concisely, and since that day mankind has been mortal.

This myth is wide-spread in Africa, even outside the Bantu group. Generally the chameleon is the messenger, as in the above myth, while the second messenger is not always the same; sometimes it is the lizard, sometimes the goat, and so on. There are, furthermore, a great number of variations of the myth; even in the same place the tale is told differently by different narrators[2].

Fresh and smooth wounds are treated by pressing the edges of the wounds against each other and then on both sides narrow acacia thorns are stuck through the edges. The thorns are placed in pairs, crossing each other. Then the whole thing is fastened with cords. This method of procedure, which, as a matter of fact, has, of course, a resemblance to the newest methods of the modern treatment of wounds, is probably the same as is practised by the Akamba's neighboors, the Masai[3].

---

[1] Werner, The Natives of British Central Africa, p. 70.

[2] Cf. B. Struck, Das Chamäleon in der afrikanischen Mythologie, p. 174, and T. v. Held, Märchen und Sagen der Afrikanischen Neger.

[3] Given in detail by M. Merker, Die Masai, p. 190.

Chapter XIV. Medicine men and magicians.

1. General characteristics of the medicine man.

The medicine man is called *mundu muə* (plu. *aŋə*), which means »wise man», if *muə* is identical with the root *-uʒ* 'wise, shrewd' (*-ugı* in the Kikuyu language), from which we have the noun *wuʒ* 'shrewdness'. We must not confuse *mundu muə* with *mundu mwoʒ* 'bewitcher, dealer in black magic' (*woʒ* 'witchcraft'), which is discussed below.

It is not everyone that can be a medicine man, as a rule only those who have shown themselves predestined to this position from birth are eligible. The proof of this is that the child should be born with what one might call appendages, which constitute an indication from the ancestral spirits that he is to be a medicine man. Thus some have been born with a little peg in their hands and in the case of another new-born child there were found in the afterbirth five small stones, such as the medicine man uses in his calabashes for divination. These objects are taken care of by the child's mother, who buries them or carefully hides them in some other way till her son is grown up, when they are handed over to him.

Even while he is growing up the boy begins to appear different from other children. He gets on well by himself and very soon has dreams and revelations, by means of which he gets into communication with the supernatural world. Thus, to a great extent, his development is the well-known one that is general for the shaman in different parts of the world. It may also happen, however, that a child who is born without any remarkable concomitants begins later on to develop visions and a desire for solitude, and in this way gradually to show tendencies to develop into a medicine man. As far as one can see, the development seems to take place without any guidance from older medicine men, not infrequently concealed from outsiders, simply and solely by communication with the *aimu*. It is chiefly from them that all knowledge comes. In dreams they give the would-be-shaman, as well as the finished medicine man, instructions about healing herbs and other objects which he needs for his work. In the middle of the night he feels compelled to get up from his bed and, like a sleepwalker, neither fearing nor thinking of the wild animals, to rush out into the woods to look for a certain plant, about which he has received instructions in his dream. One evening the author came across a case of this kind, an elderly man, who came running along and whom it was impossible to persuade to stop. He had just recevied instructions from the spirits about a certain object — I could never get to know what — and he had to fetch it at once.

Brutzer describes the development of the medicine man in a similar way. According to him the young adept is consecrated for his work by his father with a special ceremony. As his paper is rather difficult to get at, I quote from him.

»Solche persönlichkeiten sind von geburt an zu diesem amt gekennzeichnet. Sie sagen: wer mit roten beeren[1], mbuu genannt, in der hand geboren wird, ist zum mundu muwe bestimmt. Auf das geschlecht kommt es nicht an. Die mutter nimmt die beeren und hebt sie in einer länglichen kürbisflasche auf. Das kind wächst heran. Vom 14. jahr an[2] findet das kind beim erwachen in den geschlossenen händen wiederum die mbubeeren. Die mutter bewahrt die beeren in jener kürbisflasche auf. Diese hat ihren platz in einem bastkorb. Ist der sohn etwa 20 jahre alt, so erscheint ihm im traume ein mensch, der ihm eine pflanze in die hand giebt, indem er sagt: 'Nimm, das ist eine pflanze, menschen zu heilen. Diese pflanze heilt diese krankheit, jene andere heilt eine solche krankheit'. Er hört die worte, fasst die pflanze fest, und beim erwachen findet er sie in seinen händen. Er giebt sie der mutter, und diese tut sie in den bastsack. So geht es einige zeit weiter. Darauf wird ihm von den aimu ein eregnis, das eintreffen soll, mitgeteilt. Am morgen sagt er es den leuten, die dann durch das eintreffen das vorhergesagten darauf aufmerksam werden,

---

[1] Probably the red seeds of Aberis precatorius (Kik. *kιϐutι*).
[2] It is certain that the time cannot be determined so exactly.

dass dieser mensch etwas besonderes sein muss. Sie fragen den
vater, ob sein sohn etwa ein mundu muwe wäre. Der vater be-
stätigt es und sagt, er wolle den sohn nun in sein amt einführen,
indem er den geist anbetet. Nun wird met gebraut. Man tut
Loofafrucht in das gebraute, um den met berauschend zu machen[1].
Man schlachtet eine ziege, die gross und fett ist. Blut und met
werden zu boden gegossen zur verehrung des Ngai. Darauf bereitet man viel speise. Die leute des geschlechtes versammeln sich
zum mahl. Man isst und ist fröhlich. Der vater betet zum Ngai
und segnet die medizinen und sagt zum sohn: 'Jetzt ist es genug.
Heile und wahrsage'. Damit übergiebt er dem sohn die kürbisflasche mit den roten mbubeeren, aus denen wahrsagend er den
leuten rat erteilt, und den bastkorb mit den medikamenten.» . . .

From this alone we see that the two most important functions of the *mundu muə* are to cure illnesses and to tell fortunes.
When he has acquired a knowledge of these things, he is ready
to appear in public. Sometimes, however, the new medicine man
seems to have difficulty in obtaining recognition. He is received
with suspicion, sometimes with scorn, and is declared by many to
be an impostor pure and simple. It is related of more than one
eminent old *mundu muə* that in the beginning of his career he
had to overcome difficulties such as these.

The position of a medicine man is not generally hereditary,
but it appears to be easy for several members of the same family
to become medicine men. Thus I know of several cases in which
a son succeeded his father in this office, if we can call it so when
these people are not really officials and have no official position.
In Kikumbuliu I met a *mundu muə* whose deceased father had
been a famous medicine man; his brother, also deceased, had
held the same position, and his son, quite a young boy, had been
born with a peg in his hand (cf. above) and had already begun
to have visions.

The hereditary character of the position of medicine man,
instances of which are found among many tribes (among others
the Shamans of the tribes in Siberia) may to some extent be due to
the fact that the stimulation of the nervous system, to which a

---

[1] This fruit (of the Kigelia africana) is always used by the Akamba
for fermenting beer. See Beermaking.

medicine man is continually exposed, is inherited by one of his children and so makes him disposed to the profession[1].

There are also female medicine »men», but they are more rare. Near Muutha in the most easterly part of Ukamba I became acquainted with one of these, Lunda by name, a stalwart person, with a greater reputation than most of the men in the district.

Externally the Akamba medicine men have no special mark of identification, and so it is impossible without some trouble to see if one is dealing with one of them. In everday life as well as on special occasions they occupy, however, in many respects a special position, and I collect here some cases to illustrate this which have come within my own experience:

1) If one is in the company of a *mundu muə,* it is considered disrespectful to go in front of him on a path.

2) When the medicine man wants to build a hut for himself, everyone in the district helps him. Before the work is started, the *kĭlumĭ* is danced by the female members of the *ŋžama,* and the young people perform their dances, though, on the other hand, dancing does not take place at the building of an ordinary hut. Further details will be given in connection with the description of »Housebuilding».

3) When a *mundu muə* is buried, the old men dance (at least in Eastern Ukamba) alone at the place, the only occasion, as far as I know, on which they dance by themselves and in corpore. They then hold a carousal. As is the custom at the death of important people, a big goat and some food is sacrificed at the grave, and in a prayer to Mulungu (the *aĭmu*) they wish the deceased happiness in the place »whither he has gone».

4) The position of the medicine man in relation to the ancestral cult is of special interest. As is evident from the preceding chapter, he is, together with the old men and the old women, the guardian of this cult, and he tells the *atumĭa* when it is time to sacrifice to the spirits and gives directions for the carrying out of the rites. Curiously enough, he may not take any active part himself in the sacrifice, but has, with regard to it, the same subordinate position as the younger people and children (cf. pp. 220, 222). This fact, of which I can give no satisfactory ex-

---

[1] Cf. further M. Barth, Die Medizin der Naturvölker, p. 59.

planation, is contrary to his great prestige in other things. As an illustration of this I quote a statement of an old man, with whom I was arguing about the chiefs of the Djagga tribe. He said: »We Akamba have no chiefs and are not used to them. But if any of us may be compared with them, it would be the *mundu muə.*»

5) Finally a medicine man may not touch a corpse. In this respect as well he is placed on the same footing as women and children.

*   .*   *

The medicine man is consulted on all the more or less perplexing occasions of life. Here we shall describe the different important branches of his activity. The two most important of these, divination and the curing of illnesses, have already been referred to in the account of his development.

2. Divination.

The main part of each medicine man's practice consists of *kuausɂa*-ing, i. e., with the help of the *aımu* to predict things, to state also whether a project will succeed ot not, find out the cause of a thing, etc.[1] He gives, for instance, a remedy for unrequited love, and is consulted in love-affairs especially, for illness or death among men and cattle, before entering upon a long journey; pregnant women wish to know if the foetus is getting on well, whether it is a boy or a girl; he gives remedies for sterility. To put it briefly he is consulted on all life's perplexing circumstances and all its questions.

Kuausɂa-ing usually proceeds in the following way. The medicine man spreads a leopard- or a goatskin on the ground. He then takes the musical instrument, by means of which he gets into communication with the spirits. It consists of an ordinary bow which has, however, a string of wire. Between this and the bow there is placed a sounding-board consisting of a calabash-shell with its outside edge against the string. The instrument may be said to be regulated, inasmuch as a notch on

---

[1] The verb *kuausɂa* is also used about a person who consults a medicine man and then it signifies »cause to predict, tell fortunes». The form (ending in -ɂa) is clearly a causative.

the calabash shows the point against which the string must be placed so as to give the desired note, when it is struck with a little peg. The medicine man then strikes alternately on the two parts of the string with the stick. This is always made out of the wood of the little bush called *muluɨla-mbɨa* (Malvaceæ, cf. p. 52). The instrument (fig. 61), which gives a not unpleasant sound, is used exclusively by the medicine men.

After the medicine man has played in this way for a little while, he takes the divinatory calabash (*kɨtɨtɨ*), containing seeds, small stones and other odd things (*mbu*). After shaking the calabash he pours out a part of its contents on this skin, saying something like: »Calabash, tell me carefully». From the number of the objects which have fallen out he draws his conclusions, at the same time questioning the applicant for help. Unfortunately I could never understand his method, but as a rule an even number is a good omen, an odd one bad. At least one individual gathered the objects into small heaps, five in each, and then drew his conclusions. According to Brutzer the *mundu muə* among the Akamba in the hinterland of Mombasa collects the *mbu* into heaps of three and five and gives his opinion from what are over[1]. It is probable that at least a portion of the *mbu* have a certain significance, just as, for instance, certain divinatory bones among the Akikuyu and the Batonga, of which H. Junod has succeeded in obtaining an admirably accurate interpretation[2]. A statement of Hobley (Akamba, p. 99) points to this. The music and the shaking of the calabash go on until certainty is arrived at. As a conclusion the medicine man likes to spit on his calabash, so as to give support and success to his statements. When handing over medicine to a patient he also usually spits, so as to give greater power to the medicine. A certain *mundu muə* spat three times in his calabash, explaining to me that by that means he »could see things more clearly»[3]. Another man, before he

---

[1] Brutzer, Begegnungen mit Akamba, p. 10.

[2] Routledge p. 268; Junod II, p. 495 ff.

[3] Circumcision shows an additional example — which, by an oversight, has not been given in its proper place in Chap. III — of the beneficial effect that is ascribed to spitting. When the circumcision is accomplished and the children are about to return again to their homes, the circumcisor (*mwaɨkɨ*) spits over the crowd as a blessing so that the pain of the wound shall be less severe.

began to *kuausɩa*, poured out a little beer on the four corners of the skin as an offering to the *aɩmu*.

The method of *kuausɩa*-ing here described is the most usual, but the details vary, so that it is safe to say that each medicine man has his own particular method.

A divinatory calabash of this kind must never be entirely emptied, or it will have an evil influence on its owner's powers of divination. The seeds that are usually found in the cala-bashes, are the big black ones of the wild banana and the beauti-

Fig. 60. *Kuausɩa*-ing. The medicineman is pouring out his pebbles on a piece of leopard skin.

ful red ones (with a black spot) of the *kɩbutɩ* tree (Aberis preca-torius), and others[1]. In the case of a man near Machakos I also saw some pieces of glass and porcelain. All these objects are collected by their owner according to the instructions of the spirits; but in each calabash there are some *mbu* of special pot-ency which the spirits themselves have brought to the medicine man during the night while he is asleep.

---

[1] The Aberis seeds are not infrequently used in African magic. In South Africa they are well known as »lucky beans». Junod says that they are very much used in Thonga magic. Junod, The Life of a South African Tribe II, p. 292.

The fact that a leopard skin is used to pour these *mbu* on is explained by the impression of strength which the leopard gives. Claws and also whiskers of leopards are generally used in the practice of magic. When buying leopard skins from natives I often found those parts of the skins removed. Sometimes they are made into powder and eaten in order to transfer something of the courage and strength of the leopard to the eating person (sympathetic magic). The use of the goatskin can scarcely be explained in the same way, but we know that the goat is closely connected with the spirits. It is the most usual sacrifice to them.

The remuneration for a consultation is usually only 4 *pesa* (6 cents), formerly two arrows, or it was given in natura. But then comes the fee for »the medicine» which the *mundu muə* pre-scribes and as a rule makes and sells himself. This may cost a goat or even more, and it is by means of this that the medicine man makes his living.

It sometimes happens that the client does not tell the medicine man what he wants to know, but thinks that it is the duty of the latter, and a proof of his competency, to say himself what the visit is about. The doctor then soon gets his bearings by a few questions, which are usually reasonably simple, but at the same time can give a proof of a skill in cross-examination of which an astute judge need not be ashamed. If he is wide of the mark, he is scarcely disconcerted, nor does it seem to shake the client's faith in his skill.

The Akamba state that the power of the *mundu muə* to predict future events has more than once protected them from surprise attacks of the Masai. As we shall see from what follows he also uses this power of his to take measures against impending outbreaks of infectious diseases. Knowledge of this sort he seems to gain, however, less by the use of his divinatory calabash than by intercourse with the spirits in his sleep (in dreams).

Of the origin of the practice of *kuausʒa*-ing the Akamba tell a story, rather an unimportant one, but possibly with some details of interest:

»A man who had gone out into the desert to hunt heard a sound: *kasa, kasa* (an onomatopoetic reproduction of the rattling of a divinatory calabash). He went to look what it was and no-ticed a little man (in the stories the spirits appear as very small people), shaking out small stones and seeds from a calabash on a leopard skin. He asked him: 'What are you doing?' The little man answered: 'I am just *kuausʒa*-ing'. — 'What is that?' — 'Well, I am able to say fine words to you as to how you can become rich.' — 'Then I should like to *kuausʒa*.' — 'Then give me two arrows' (the fee). He gave him two arrows. And the little man shook his stones out and said: 'You will be rich from hunting'. And he hunted, killed elephants, and sold the tusks for many cattle. When he came home he was asked what had happened, and he told them. 'Let us go and *kuausʒa*', said the others. And they went, found the little man, and said to him: 'We want to *kuausʒa*'. — 'Give me two arrows!' They did so. He said: 'You shall become rich by walking'. And when they went to hunt they found dead elephants.»

The first man had such a good proof of the little man's power that others became eager to seek him out. It is exactly the same, of course, in real life. The medicine man whose divination appears to come true gets a big practice.

To *mana,* i. e. without any reason to touch a medicine man's divinatory apparatus or the other objects which are connected with his magic power, is dangerous, naturally because of the great powers that are supposed to dwell in the objects. One may become ill or die altogether. I remember a young man who happened to touch a medicine man's medicine bag. When, in the evening of the same day, he went to a dance, none of the girls danced with him. The cause of this misfortune was, as he immediately realised, that he had touched the medicine bag.

A medicine man will never sell his apparatus or dispose of it in any other way. I have tried in vain to procure a medicine bag with its accessories, the owner usually states as a reason for his refusal that he himself or his family would incur some misfortune if he gave it up.

When a *mundu muə* dies, the medicine bag and similar articles are left undisturbed till the next new moon; then they are taken out and each object smeared with cow-fat, after which they are again put in their places. They remain there until the deceased reveals himself to someone in a dream and makes known his wishes as to what they shall do with these, the most important of his effects. He often gives directions for a certain person to take charge of his apparatus.

*

As an appendix to illustrate and complete this sketch of the medicine man among the Akamba I will describe certain medicine men, partly those with whom I myself have come into contact, partly others, whom the natives have told me about.

1. To the author's camp at Machakos there came a *mundu muə* from the Kitui district, who was just on a tour through Ulu. His method of *kuausŋa*-ing was very simple, inasmuch as he only asked questions and did not use the usual divinatory calabash. When I wondered what was the cause of this, he answered that that method was »bad» for him and that his »Ngai» (i. e. a spirit) had taught him another. I let him tell my fortune and his statements included, among other things: »You own two villages at home in *Ulaya*[1]. You have a wife there, she is well and you will soon get letters with good news. In your body there dwells the spirit of a deceased relation». In the man's medicine bag, made of the skin of the hunting leopard, there were only six to eight small medicine calabashes, 1—1.5 dm. long. The small quantity which one of these can hold is, however, sufficient for a great number of patients, when one considers that each one gets only quite a small pinch. In the bag there was, among other things:

a) a calabash containing *ŋžœɓu*, a kind of black powder resembling soot, very commonly used and prepared from certain plants. Protects against lions amongst other things. In case of need a pinch is taken in the hand and blown out in the direction of the beast, who then goes off.

b) a calabash with powder resembling pepper. A pinch of this, laid on the tongue, protects one against infidelity on the part of one's wife or wives.

c) a calabash with powder from the roots of the *mwaŋ*-tree. The forehead, cheeks and chin are rubbed with this powder, which procures friendship among men and favour among women.

d) a calabash with white powder, which gives great fertility to women.

As is obvious, only magic remedies. On the other hand, there was nothing against real illnesses. With a good knowledge of human nature the medicine man takes care, in the first place, to be provided with remedies that are thought capable of procuring what is most desirable in the life of the native. It is thus with

---

[1] The Suaheli name for Europe.

these things that he earns most. The man in question, for instance, gained in one week six goats and twelve rupees in ready money, an income which was not considered specially big of its kind, though representing several months of work for a native labourer. And yet most medicine men seem not to be particularly wealthy [1].

2.   When I was once stopping at a village a few hours north of Kibwezi, I was just in time to see a medicine man working. A woman in the district had for a long time been ill, and as she did not get better her husband brought her to this *mundu muə*. After a brief examination he explained that the woman was possessed by a spirit and undertook to try to expel it, of course for a reasonable fee. He told her to lie down on the ground, covered her with bags of bast, and ordered her to sleep. After having struck on his musical bow by way of introduction and so got into communication with the *aımu*, he blew hard into her ears, armpits and back part of the knee-joints [2]. He also placed a row of the prickly branches of an acacia on the sacks which covered her body, and round this some of the spherical yellow fruit of the Solanum (fig. 61). He then took a stick with a long lash — the Akamba do not use whips (*munaɓu*), except as toys for children — and ran several times round the village cracking the whip the whole time [3]. The spectators seemed to consider this specially remarkable. When he came back he trod all the Solanum fruits to pieces, one after the other. He then took the whip again and went several times round the woman cracking it, then changed it for the musical bow and,

---

[1] Among the Zulus clever medicine men, often real phycisians, are in the habit of travelling through the country from place to place, often staying away from home for months. As rich people, owners to large herds of cattle, they then return to their villages. M. Barth, Die Medizin der Naturvölker, p. 59.

[2] I cannot remember anything which supports the view that the Akamba regard the breath as possessing magic power, but this method of procedure makes one think of a statement of K. Th. Preuss, who speaks of »die direkte abwehr von krankheit und tod durch den leben gebenden, gewissermassen desinfizierenden hauch». Der Ursprung der Religion und Kunst, Globus 86, p. 375.

[3] Hobley, however, describes an old elephant-hunter named Sulu — I know the man — who had a sort of whip. »Before going hunting it is customary to crack the whip seven times, and it is believed to bring good luck.» Hobley, Kamba protective magic, Man 1912, p. 4. Cf. also below p. 274.

striking on this, continued his circular motion. He now placed at
the woman's head a clay pitcher turned upside down and, laying
a rope around her, fastened it to the pitcher (to isolate her from
all evil influences?). Sitting on the pitcher he again struck on his
bow for a little while. He then brought a little calabash with
magic powder (*muþæa*), which he laid in small heaps on the patient's body and immediately afterwards blew away, one heap after
the other, which happened in such a way that he kept running

Fig. 61. Medicine man curing a possessed women
(mentionéd p. 264).

and began alternately at the woman's head and feet. He now sat
once more on the pitcher, struck a few blows on his bow, and
then bent down and sucked on the patient's forehead (pretending
to suck something out?). Another careful sucking took place
at the little toes of the sick woman.

The treatment described above lasted for quite a long time,
but the patient kept perfectly still the whole time. Her husband
seemed to think, however, that it was lasting rather long, for
he came up to me and asked in a whisper my opinion of the
effectiveness of the medicine man's method. As I was in a hurry

I asked the latter, who was working very hard, if it would soon be finished. But he explained that it was a specially difficult case and that there was still a great deal to do, and so I went off.

3. During my stay near Kibwezi I had as an inseparable companion a young *mundu muɔ* named Mbindya. He was an intelligent and sympathetic man, but in the beginning our mutual acquaintance was due to sheer calculation. Mbindya was my neighbour and I gladly took the opportunity of observing a medicine man at all times of the day for a long period, so as to see to what extent his work could be put down to conscious deception. On his side he regarded my company as propitious, as at our first meeting he had happened to find a rare plant (*muɓʑa wanɗı*)[1], which he had wanted for a long time but had sought for in vain. Besides, the fact that he was intimate with a white man helped to increase his reputation. Their position as medicine men and their power to control secret powers were characteristics of Mbindya's family, and he himself had developed into a medicine man in the way which is described in the beginning of this chapter.

During the time we were together I studied my friend carefully, and was present when people came to ask him for advice, etc. As far as he is concerned, I must answer the question as to whether medicine men themselves believe in their vocation and their power by saying that he gave one the impression of being firmly convinced on these points. But he was, of course, still young, 30 at the most. The only deceptions that he was consciously guilty of, were such small conjuring tricks as are instanced below, and these he frankly confessed to me to be of this character, adding that they were performed only to strengthen the people's faith in his power. Besides, prophecies sometimes, of course, come true, and also a sick person often recovers after being treated according to a more or less magical prescription, and such things help to strengthen the faith both of the medicine man himself and of others. On the other hand, there are always single individuals who certainly look with scepticism on the medicine man's operations — there have of course been doubters at all times and among all people — but in most cases these people

---

[1] A short red plant without leaves, with a long tap-root. It gives one the impression of a round mass like a mushroom.

are anxious to keep their opinions to themselves, for it might be unpleasant to incur a medicine man's odium. Hildebrandt tells of a »chief» Milu in Kitui, who said to H. that »er hielte nichts von ihren hokuspokus, könne aber nicht offen gegen sie auftreten»[1].

As evidence of how easily the natives believe in their medicine men's statements and find valid explanations when they do not come true, the following incident may be inserted. In January 1912, when Mr. A. Champion, A. D. C. of Kitui, and myself were on an expedition to investigate the course of the River Nthua on behalf of the government, and were about to leave the eastern frontier of Ukamba at Muutha and proceed farther eastward out into the desert, we had a visit from the above-mentioned medicine-woman Lunda. She asked to *kuausʒa* for us and our journey, and stated that the day after we found »remains of animals» we should kill »something big». Lunda's prophecy was hailed with joy by our people and had at least the useful effect of making them enter on the march out into the unknown with glad confidence. All »remains of animals» which we passed during the next few days, they looked upon as those to which Lunda had referred. Thus some hours after we left Muutha our native hunters found a heap of excrement with a long intestinal worm in it. They immediately thought that this had to do with the prophecy, and the two hunters each eat half the worm and offered a little snuff beneath the tree, where they found it. The fact that we shot nothing on the following day could not disturb their confidence; the medicine man had only meant something else. They argued in the same way about another object which we came across. The fact that we Europeans joked a little about this had no effect. And when we found the thigh-bone of a giraffe and the same evening shot one, the hunters were immediately sure that it was this to which Lunda referred to from the first. It is not difficult to be a prophet when one is supported by such faith.

Many medicine men are accustomed to perform many small tricks, pure conjuring tricks, which — as the above-mentioned Mbindya explicitly declared — are designed to awe their clients

---

[1] Hildebrand, Die Wakamba, p. 388.

as evidence of their power and thus to satisfy the demand of the populace for »signs and wonders». Thus I saw M. practise, among other tricks, the following: Appearing naked, he placed a little bean on his head and stuck others behind his ears and in the corners of his mouth, his armpits and the angles of his elbows. He then shook himself so that all the beans fell to the ground, counted them and showed that the number was the same as before. Then, in addition, he took a bean from each eye.

Another innocent trick consisted in M. taking a peg, laying it with one end on a level with the top of his little finger and the other end reaching to the forearm, where a mark was made. He then took the peg away, waved it in the air for the sake of appearance, and put it back again in the same place, when it was found to be a little shorter than the measured length. This was repeated and the pin appeared to be still shorter. The secret consists in a power to contract and expand the hand.

Some examples to illustrate the Akamba's idea of the power of their medicine men to perform wonderful things are given here:

Old Ngunu near Machakos — a man of great reputation, who was consulted by people from a long distance from the Kitui district — was especially noted for his love-powders, by means of which he was said to be able even to allure wild birds to himself and to make them perch on his knee when he sat outside his hut.

Nthenge (the buck), a medicine man at Kibwezi who died before my time, is said to have been able to »stretch his blanket out in the air and then sit on it, floating in the air». He is also said to have roasted meat by hanging a crock with meat in it on the ceiling of his hut. He then put »medicine» in the fire on the hearth, after which the flames, without injuring the walls, climbed up them and enveloped the jar till the meat was roasted.

Another person near Kibwezi whom I came across was said to be able to transform a stick into a snake, and yet another asserted that he could cut a goat's head off and make it come to life again. When I promised them a high reward for a proof of their powers, they could only produce foolish evasions.

Tricks as the above-mentioned are called in Kikamba $k\underset{\circ}{i}ama$, which is best translated as »miracles» performed by magic means.

3. The medicine man as a healer (of illnesses).

Illnesses are sent by the spirits, when they for any reason are angry with the living, or they are caused by black magic on they part of some evil-disposed person, or finally they may be real illnesses, contracted in a natural way. This last cause, however, seems to be regarded as the least usual. To get to know which of these three is the cause of the illness one goes to the medicine man, who ascertains the cause by divination. If the illness has been sent by the spirits because they are displeased with their surviving relations and consider themselves neglected by them, the medicine man often prescribes no other remedy except ordering that an offering should be brought and *kilumi*, the spirit-dance, should be danced.

To cure an illness is called *kwota* in Kikamba. It does not, by any means, form part of every medicine man's practice. Just as there are some medicine men who are exclusively occupied with *kuausia*-ing, so there are others who do nothing but cure illnesses. A *mundu mua* who gives himself exclusively to this and does not use divinatory calabashes is called an *itima*. The individual medicine man does not seem to be able to treat many different kinds of illness; he appears rather to be what one might call a specialist. This may perhaps explain the great number of medicine men. For different illnesses one must consult different people. It is said that the *mundu mua* cannot cure his own children nor can a man skilled in *yondu* do this.

The well-known method of a medicine man pretending to take from a patient's body the objects which have caused the illness, I have never seen practised, in Ukamba (cf. however the sucking of the sick woman's forehead and toes described above). Yet it seems to be practised, according to the statement of the missionary Säuberlich, who informed me that, among other cases, he once saw a *mundu mua* take out a tooth, after which the patient immediately declared that he was better[1].

Madness in discussed on p. 240. I wish to add here that a

---

[1] The Kikuyu medicine man sucks different objects out of the sick person's stomach, e. g. glass beads, grass, leaves and other rubbish, put there by some enemy. J. Cayzac, Witchcraft in Kikuyu, Man 1912, p. 127.

medicine man declared that he could cure madness in this way:
He dug a hole in the ground, in which the afflicted person was
placed, and then covered the hole up and lit a fire above it. The
next morning the patient would be well. The author saw a man
treated in this manner and he seemed normal after the treatment.
To cure madness the medicine men also use a decoction of the
leaves of the creeper *muɓolo* (Sapindaceæ), which is given to the
sick person to drink and with which he is washed.

Quite a usual way to cure an illness is for the sick person
to sit on the ground and the *mundu muə* then sticks pegs in the
ground all round him and fastens them with a cord. In this way
all evil influences are shut out.

The terms *mutɩ* and *muþœa*. We have already often
mentioned »medicine», and it is necessary to explain a little
more clearly what the natives mean by this. In Kikamba there are
two expressions for it, *mutɩ* and *muþœa,* which seem to imply
a real distinction. The first expression is more our sense of the
word 'medicine, physic', and is certainly identical with *mutɩ* 'tree,
bush, herb'. Most of the native remedies are, of course, prepared
from vegetable substances. These remedies, real or imaginary, will
be discussed separately later on, as they are not known merely
to the medicine men, nor are they — at least to any extent — used
in magic. They may thus be used by anyone. The *muþœa*, on the
other hand, is a medicine of a more or less magic character. Now
there are certainly a great many laymen who know that a certain
plant may be used as *muþœa* for a certain purpose, and one is
therefore tempted to ask why they go to the medicine man, when
they themselves possess this knowledge. It is true that they know
for what purpose a certain *muþœa* is used, but they do not know
how to use it. The result is that only those wo know »the key»,
so to speak, to a *muþœa*, its *kɩþɩao*, as the Akamba call it[1], can
use it. An instance may be given to illustrate this. The *muɓɩa wa
nðɩ*, a plant of somewhat rare occurence in the Kibwezi district, is
muþœa for sterility in women. The patient is washed for some
days with a decoction of this, which is also rubbed on her head.
When next she menstruates, she has coitus with her husband and
can then have children. This medicine, however, has no certain

---

[1] < *þɩaa* 'perform the rites which give power to a *muþœa*'.

effect before its *kɪpɪao* is used, and this is only known to the medicine man. It consists of the latter placing a portion of food round the plant as a sacrifice to the *aɪmu*, and at the same time expressing a wish that the medicine should have the desired effect. On p. 241 we have described the process of digging roots for medicine and this is just a case of a *kɪpɪao*. The roots alone have not sufficient efficacy.

4. The medicine man as a practiser of public magic (for the good of the whole community).

The removing of epidemics. When severe epidemics attack people or cattle (e. g. rinderpest) the Akamba go to the *mundu mua* with their difficulty. In Machakos it has been the practice on such occasions for the medicine men to order the *atumɪa* to pretend to drive the young people out to the steppe, where they then performed dances (their usual ones, but in this case with a religious-magic purpose). Towards the evening a goat was taken there and killed, and the young people were smeared with *ɡondu*, in the usual manner. Then they have to run home to the villages, thus returning in the same way as they came out. The idea is that the illness has been driven out from them and left behind on the steppe. The goat has possibly been regarded as a sort of scapegoat, for if it were only to be used in and for the preparation of *ɡondu*, it would have been more convenient to kill it at home. There are several examples of the goat being used as a scapegoat among the Bantu tribes, e. g. in South Africa (according to D. Kidd) and in Uganda[1].

It often happens that the medicine man can prevent infectious, epidemic diseases, as in his dreams he gets information from the *aɪmu* that such diseases are coming, diseases such as *mwɪmu* (rinderpest, or, when it affects human beings, a tumour-like disease) or *kɪapɪ*. I was told of a medicine man in Machakos, called Mbiti, who dreamed that he saw a crowd of people coming carrying sacks of bast, filled with the blood of cattle infected with *kɪapɪ*, a sign that this disease was approaching. The dream came from the *aɪmu*, who at the same time gave the man instructions as to how the disease might be prevented, and because of this

---

[1] Ashe, Two Kings of Uganda, p. 320.

they proceeded to act in the following way, when he had informed the elders of the danger which threatened:

In the evening the members of the *nẑama* gathered together at the medicine man's hut, and the young people came and danced there. In a crock a *ɣondu* was mixed, consisting of water, sugar-cane, flour from the Penicillaria (*mwę*) as well as *muɂo*, the contents of the stomach, from a goat and also »plants, brought from the wilderness». The mixture was distributed by an old man and woman and given to those present to drink. Next morning came the others, who did not belong to the *nẑama*, and the children. They were made to drink of a similar mixture, but with other ingredients. The former of these two drinks was considered the more potent, as the *atumɂa* possess greater magic power than ordinary people. Besides, the medicine man is in closer relation to the old people, with whom he often co-operates, and who give him assistance on several occasions, such as the building of his hut. On the other hand it is remarkable that the youths and girls on this occasion, as well as in the foregoing purification ceremony, are almost placed on a level with the oldest and most experienced people in the community. This may depend on a kind of influence of opposites: just because the young do not possess any magic power, it is sometimes convenient to put them on a level with those who possess this power in the highest degree.

The actual distribution af the *ɣondu* beverage proceeds as follows. The pitcher is placed right in front of two adjacent banana trees which are connected by a garland fastened round them at about a man's height. This garland, which is made of the plant *musoḳa* (Ipomoea), is also bound round the neck of the pitcher. Those who are present are made to take their places one by one between the two trees, turn towards the pitcher, and, after drinking, they have to move off to the right, between the pitcher and the banana tree on the right. Sometimes three banana plants are used, in which case those who are to drink stand between two and turn their back to the third.

Next day, the third, a goat of the colour that the *aɂmu* has indicated is brought to an out-of-the-way place, as out on the steppe, where all the people have assembled and where the young people perform dances. Some *ɣondu*, in which *mutɑ* — one of the most frequently used *ɡondu* plants — is the chief ingredient, is prepared from the goat, and the assembled people are sprinkled with it. The flesh of the animal is eaten as at an ordinary sacrificial meal. A part of it is probably also sacrificed to the spirits. Then they all return home running. The disease — or in this case the danger of the epidemic falling upon them — has been left behind on the steppe.

The above-described method of driving away an epidemic (*kwɪndukɪa uwau̯*) is called *ɪsɪuka*[1], a word which is certainly derived from the same root as *ɪsɪuko* 'ford over a stream'[2]. The banana plants fastened together form quite obviously a passage, a door, thus giving us a new example of the well-known conception of the entrance or the door as a boundary between the outer world with its many dangers and a region free from these dangers, and then as a means of changing from one condition to another. In the special case we have described the people were both purified with *ɡondu* and then went through the door, leaving all the evil influence behind them. This should of itself be sufficiently effective, and the third day's procedure is probably an addition from an originally independent purification ceremony. Its resemblance to the above-described method is in favour of this. In 1911 near Engelani (Ngilani), north of Machakos, I saw a door of this sort consisting of two banana trees. About a dozen people, I was told, had been suddenly attacked by *mwɪmu* (a tumour-like disease), and the population of the district were in great distress. Then one evening a man met an one-legged spirit on a path, who said to him: »Go to Mbiti (the medicine man) and tell him to take *muɪo* from a black goat and purify the people».

I have noted from East Ukamba two purification ceremonies of this type, one of which is in the main identical with the foregoing. The door is composed in this case of two trees or posts driven into the ground, between which the plant *musoḳa* (Ipomoea) is fastened. A goat is killed and *ɡondu* prepared from it. Each

---

[1] The word is translated by Hofman (Wörterbuch) as «der bogen durch den der *mundu mua* die leute schlüpfen lässt, wenn er sie gegen krankheiten feit».

[2] The only verb *sɪuka* that I know means 'to waken from an apparently dead condition, waken from death'. Cf. also *sɪoka* 'to return'.

person drinks and then goes through the door and then, by means of branches of *muta*, is sprinkled with *ɲondu* on the forehead, breast and back. The medicine man then cracks with a whip, (*munaɓu*), upon which all present, without looking back, have to run a good part of the way from the villages. On their return they get a little bit of the skin of the dead goat, which they fasten round the right instep with fibres of *kɪoŋgwa* (Sanseviera sp.). The seventh day afterwards they go away from the villages and throw the piece of skin away, saying: »Possessor of *mwɪmu*, take it (the disease), here it is» (*mwæn* *mwɪmu*, *osa n'usu*). The procedure is called *mwɪtano* < *kwɪtana* 'to cure each other'.

In Kitui I heard an account of another kind of *mwɪtano* that was in vogue there. The medicine man ordered everyone of both sexes and all ages to deposit on a path some red glass beads (*sɪuma ndun*) and a little red earth (*mbu*) as an offering to Mwi-tualali, an one-legged spirit who dwells on the mountain of Mutitu, about 30 kilometres north-east of the Kitui government station. This spirit, say the Akamba, was an old man, who lived very long ago. On the mountain there is to be found a pond in which he lives, but which I could not find when I climbed up there. In the pond there is also said to be a gigantic serpent, which sometimes sets the water in motion and rises up in it. I could never find out what was the relation of the spirit and the serpent to each other. As far as the latter is concerned, however, it is of the type that is called *mukuŋga-mbua*, one of the monsters of the popular imagination, a serpent of supernatural proportions, which devours human beings and cattle. It is said to appear in the Tana River, the lakes Naiwasha and Nakuru and some other places. Some years ago an Englishman is said to have seriously sought for this mysterious serpent, which is said to be so long that it »stretches over mountains and valleys». I immediately suspected that this was a case of some old conception of the rainbow, and this is suggested by the word *mbua* 'rain'. The Akamba, however, call the rainbow *utaɓɪ*. My surmise was confirmed when later on, during my study of the Tharaka language, I learnt that the rainbow there is called just *mukuŋga-mbura*. The Akikuyu call it by the same name and also believe that it is a big serpent, a conception which, in addition, is met with among different peoples here and there in the world. Another kind of gigantic serpent, which in the same way devours people, is said to dwell in a big grass basket in a hole on the bottom of the little river Manza just west of Machakos. The natives tell of a Suaheli who passed by there at nighttime and was drawn down into the depths, but succeeded in escaping with the loss of his tongue and an eye.

5. The connection of the medicine man with agriculture. Rainmaking.

The principal industry of the Akamba is agriculture, and the women, who have the management of this as their lot, like to consult the *mundu muə* concerning the time for sowing, reaping, etc. Sowing depends of course on the arrival of the rainy season, and as the rain is often late and sometimes fails entirely to arrive, the women are naturally very anxious to get to know through the medicine man when the fertilizing rain may be expected and how they must act so as not to hinder or retard its arrival. His instructions with regard to this have to be carefully followed, a breach of them might cause the complete non-appearance of the rain. Sometimes, on his own initiative, he interferes in the women's cultivation of the fields. Thus, during my stay in Machakos, a *mundu muə* forbade the women to drive the birds away from the fields, saying that he would do it himself by a special means. The medicine man appears also, with regard to agriculture, as a practiser of public magic for the benefit of the whole community, just as we have seen him doing the same thing, when it was a question of preventing impending epidemics.

At the occurence of a drought which threatens the harvest the women gather together, as we have already seen in chap. XI. 6, when they thought the crop in danger. Beating their drums (*kɩpæmbə*) they march from village to village, and each woman, who has land, must join them. No one dares to stay away, and those who do not come out quickly enough are loaded with insulting epithets. *ɩɓætɩ sɪɪ na ŋgolano*, 'the wives have a meeting', the Akamba say[1]. When the band has grown to an imposing number, they direct their course to the medicine man to hear his opinion about the drought. All the young people and also the

---

[1] *ŋgolano*: cf. *kolanɪa* 'to heap up, assemble'.

atumɪa prefer to keep away when the women come forward. In 1911 I chanced to meet a band of women who were on their way in this fashion to the above mentioned Ngunu. They were uttering shrill cries (*ɪɪ, ɪɪ, uɪ, uɪ*) and singing songs the subject matter of which was sexual. A part of these which I succeeded afterwards in taking down, is as follows:

ea, ę!	*ea, eeh!*
tauma kwasa	we come from afar
kumanðea kɪno munᶎo	to find salt for the *kɪno*[1],
kana kɪa kɪukɪa.	penis erigetur.
u, u	*uh, uh!*

The meaning of this is: we come to get rain, so that we can get food for our husbands, who cannot accomplish their sexual duties, if they are weak from hunger.

Having arrived at Ngunu's village the women danced the *kɪlumɪ* and spent the night there. No sexual intercourse with the medicine man, however, enters into the programme; on the contrary, it is clearly considered injurious to the purpose in view, for it is said that on a previous occasion of the same kind Ngunu could not master his passions and that this is the reason why only two out of about 20 children that he had are still living. During the night the medicine man placed himself in communication with the spirits and received instructions from them as to what should be done against the drought.

The dances were continued the next day, and then they young people as well collected at Ngunu's village and performed their dances.

As a matter of fact the rôle of the medicine man as a rainmaker is in no way prominent among the Akamba, and one can scarcely say he exists in comparison, for instance, with the rainmakers in South Africa. The author has neither seen or heard any mention of a medicine man using sympathetic magic to produce rain. His task in this case seems principally to be that of finding a way to propitiate the spirits, as it is they who, from malevolence or dissatisfaction with those who have survived them, prevent the rain from coming.

A certain amount of rain magic of a more private kind is,

---

[1] The female pudenda.

however, carried on. Some at least of the inverted jars, which are seen here and there in the fields, are thus meant to cause rain, while on the other hand others are merely to frighten the porcupines, which are to be reckoned among the most dangerous enemies of the crops. Otherwise rain magic, both general and private, is of a purely negative character and consists in the avoidance of certain acts during the time of rain or when the rain is expected. It is thus forbidden of old to boil in a crock in the fields, and the boys who protect the ripening crop from birds and other parasites bake their sweet potatoes, or whatever they have with them for food, in moulds of clay or other similar things. If anyone offends against this injunction and it comes to the *atumɪa's* knowledge, *ŋondu* is prepared and the field sprinkled with it. Its owner has to supply the goat necessary for the purification. This old custom is still observed in Ulu, but has fallen into disuse in East Ukamba, at least in the Ikutha district, where the very frequent droughts were explained to me as being a punishment from Mulungu (viz. the *aɪmu*), because the fathers of the Akamba living there had neglected the old precepts. This is an attempt to explain the difference between the more abundant irrigation and the more even rainfall of the western tract of land and East Ukamba's paucity of running water and its more fitfully occurring rainy seasons.

In Kikumbuliu during the rainy season they do not boil saltpetre, from which salt is prepared and which is used in the manufacture of snuff. We have seen in Chap. XI that an oath with *kɪpɪtu* may not be taken during this season. A further somewhat curious observation is that, because of the rain, a man may never beat his wife in the fields, when they are sown. Finally on p. 223 examples have been given to show how the natives consider that all unusual events have an injurious influence on the rain. Thus the great famine of 1898—99 was generally considered by the natives of East Africa to be due to the building of the Uganda railway, and, when the work on the railway approached Kisumu on Lake Victoria and the rain happened not to come even there, they were still further strengthened in their belief. This idea, however, was perhaps due less to the unusual incident per se than to the rails, the »rope of iron» laid over the land. As Hildebrandt has already pointed out[1], no instruments of iron have, from olden times, been used in the cultivation of the earth, and although already by his time a few iron picks had come into use, even to-day one can see Kamba women, even in the villages just outside the two government stations, using the primitive stake for digging. When, some years ago, in Kitui, a supply of iron picks were ordered so that they might be given out gratis among the natives, they remained for the most part it the station. The native would not accept them. That in many cases iron is surrounded by a taboo is a fact that has been known for a long time and is wide-spread and presumably due to the fact that the metal in question is considered as an object that has a special power, which may have a strong, and often fatal, influence on the things or persons that come into contact with it. For talismans to produce or prevent rain see p. 288.

6. Magicians.

It is clearly unnecessary to recall the vital rôle which magic plays in the life of primitive people. That this is the case also among the Akamba may be concluded already from what has preceded. It has been shown how, even in the simplest accident which may happen to him the native may suspect the influence the an enemy or a rival, trying to injure him by means of *woɨ*. The word may be conveniently rendered by »witchcraft, magic», this conception being then taken in both good and bad, protective and injurious senses (white and black magic). The concrete means is also called *woɨ*. When young persons suddenly die, this is usually ascribed to the *woɨ* of some enemy. In such an unimportant case as that of the goats going astray and running off when they are grazing, one may go to the medicine man to *kuausɨa*, to find out if it was an accident or brought about by some enemy; and if, for instance, some one happens to fall from the tree and hurt himself when occupied in hanging up beehives, it is certainly due to *woɨ*. We can easily understand that this is thought to be the case when something more unusual happens. It is thus considered very suspicious and due to *woɨ* on the part of some enemy, if one

---

[1] Die Wakamba, p. 372.

happens to be hit by excrement from a flying hawk or crow. The author heard of a person to whom an accident of this kind happened and who at once destroyed everything he was wearing at the time and was also purified with *ɉondu*. How afraid they are of coming upon *woʒ* everywhere is shown, among other things, by the fact that when guests are entertained, the host first tastes what is offered so as to show that it does not contain poison or any magic power. This is the case especially with beer.

Destructive *woʒ*, black magic, is punished with death — we have often seen it done by lynching, *kɨɉolə* — if it is dangerous to the community. The *mundu muə* never meddles with this, he is only a »white» magician; those who practise it are called *mwoʒ* (the same root as in *woʒ*)[1]. We have seen that, in general, one can only become a medicine man by being born with a disposition towards it, while it is enough to be apprenticed to a *mwoʒ* to become one oneself[2].

The Akamba in Ulu look upon the people in the Kitui district as more powerful in magic than themselves, and those in Kitui who want to become really proficient in black magic go up to the Athaka (Atharaka) and the Ambele (Ambere) in the north. It was my intention to visit the former people, but my carriers refused to accompany me. »We are not afraid of the Athakas' spear and sword», they said, »but they will destroy us with their magic». It is recognized as a characteristic feature of primitive people to mistrust strangers and to ascribe magic power to them. The

---

[1] Research into the literature would certainly enable us to discover this word with the same meaning in a great number of Bantu dialects, at least among the East and South dialects. I have noted *mrogi* in the Kikuyu language and in Kisukuma (south of Lake Victoria), *moloi* among the Bechuana and Bavenda, *mwabi* in Kimatumbi (Kilwa district, German East Africa), *nyawi* in Kimakonde (Lindi distr., G. E. A.) and *noyi* (pl. *baloyi*) among the Batonga in Portuguese East Africa. The verb *loga* in Kisuaheli and other dialects means 'to bewitch'. Meinhof, Grundriss einer Lautlehre der Bantusprachen, p. 173, gives a similar verbal root for »Primitive Bantu».

[2] Hobley expresses the difference between a *mundu muə* and a *mundu mwoʒ* in a somewhat obscure way (Akamba p. 53): »A medicine man is called Muoiin [in Kikamba no word ends in a consonant] or Muoii ... The Muoiin is a person who deals in black art ... A *mundu mue* is a more harmless person, he deals in what we may call white magic ...»

Akamba also go westwards, to the Akikuyu, and when formerly the trade caravans came to Mombasa, they took the opportunity of consulting the magicians at the coast. All this is done, however, chiefly to obtain protection and advantages for themselves; those who wish to practise black magic themselves are in the minority.

We shall now give some examples of how this black magic is practised.

A thief can obtain from a *mwoị* a magic substance which will make the dwellers in the village, in which he intends to steal at night, sleep so deeply that they do not waken after he has stretched out his magic *kıpıtuı* towards the village. This method has also been employed by the Akamba in nocturnal plundering expeditions against the Masai and Akikuyu, and thus as a general magic recognized and practised by the community. Further Krapf relates how the Akamba with whom in 1849 he journeyed up from the coast put *mupæa* in the camp-fires to make themselves invisible to their enemies. And a young man who visits his sweetheart at night-time in her mother's hut, before he dares to steal in, usually also produces deep sleep among those inside by means of magic medicine. This is done by opening the door a little and pushing the medicine into the fire with a long stick.

Those whose cattle are sick and who wish to damage their enemies' flocks take the blood of a diseased animal and with it smear the entrance to the others' cattle-kraals or pour the blood on the path leading to them. This method may be called a kind of contagious magic, though the effect, if there is any, is very likely due to pure infection.

To get rid of a real or supposed enemy, when one visits a beer party in his company at some other person's hut, it is necessary, when a suitable occasion presents itself, to put the magic medicine rapidly into his beer and stir it once, uttering silent curses. A thing that I have not myself heard of, but which Hoffman[1] relates, is that one can injure a person by undertaking some manipulations with his footsteps, which is, as is known, a widespread belief, not only among so-called primitive peoples. They smear a thorn with *woị* and put it in the man's tracks.

---

[1] J. Hoffmann, Geburt, Heirat und Tod, p. 20.

It has been mentioned that the word *kɪpaŋgona* means, first 'sacrifice' (see p. 218) secondly 'magic medicine'[1] (see p. 241). *kuɓandea mundu kɪpaŋgona*, lit. 'to plant *kɪpaŋgona* for someone', is the standing phrase for the prevalent method of depositing magic medicine for an enemy, for instance on the path to his hut or at its entrance. When he treads on the »medicine», he will soon die or at least become ill.

A *kɪpaŋgona* must be used exactly as the medicine man or magician prescibes. A depature from these instructions, even if involuntary, makes the *kɪpaŋgona* ineffectual, it is then »broken», as it is said (*kutula kɪpaŋgona < kutula* 'to break'). I remember a case when two persons were ordered by a medicine man to proceed in a certain way. While they were doing their best to carry out his instructions, a third person came to the place, and so the *kɪpaŋgona* »was broken». It is obvious that, under such circumstances, the witch doctor can easily find an excuse if his instructions do not bring about any result. His client could not have followed them sufficiently carefully.

But *kɪpaŋgona* is not always assigned to »black magic». *kuɓandea mwɪtu kɪpaŋgona,* for instance, means to make use of love medicine for a girl, for whom a man has an unrequited affection, so as to arouse her love in return but not to injure her.

There are people who, merely by stretching out their index finger towards an objectionable person, can cause his death. This power may even be possessed involuntarily (from birth?) by people who never use black magic; and to avoid mishaps, they keep their hands closed, when they want to point something out (*kwolota*), and point with the knuckle of the index finger.

In former times, it is said, there were men skilled in *wok,* who could kill an enemy merely by a look. A simple means of causing an injury, which can be used by anyone, is to place magic medicine in the open hand and blow it in the direction of an enemy, who is injured by it, even if he is a long distance away.

Some persons skilled in black magic have also the power of transforming themselves into wild animals — an idea that we

---

[1] These two different meanings of *kɪpaŋgona* are really not so unlike each other. A closer study of the sacrifice shows us numerous cases of a magical character and that, on the other hand, magic rites may pass over into sacrificial actions.

find among many African peoples — and in this form are able
to carry out their ghastly intentions with impunity. In Kikumbuliu
I heard of a man who was dragged away from his village during
the night by a lion, which was nothing but one of his enemies.
The expert in magic turns himself into a lion by daubing his face
with a certain kind of *muþœa* and by eating a small portion of the
powdered skin and claws of a lion. The people in Kikumbuliu
seem to occupy themselves a good deal with black magic, a part
of which is said to come from the Giriama tribe. It is said, for
instance, that an expert in *woṭ* can take the life of an enemy he
fears by giving certain instructions to one of his cocks. The cock
flies to the hut of the man indicated, perches on the roof and
crows. When the man comes out to see what is the matter, the
cock moves, by means of the *woṭ*-power of his master, into his
body (!). The man dies, unless they can discover what is the
matter with him.

In Kikumbuliu I was also told of a little mystic figure like a
man which »the whites make out of clay». By means of *woṭ* this
can be set in motion and sent into the body of an enemy's wife
when she is pregnant, thus causing a miscarriage. The thing is
called *kṭumwa* (i. e. miscarriage). It is possible that this idea
originates from natives who have seen European children playing
with dolls.

The well-known belief that hair and nails are an essential
part of a human being and therefore can be used in black magic
is also found among the Akamba. They are consequently very
careful not to leave hair or nails that have been cut lying about
but bury them or hide them in some other way. And even if the
hair is not picked up by a human being directly, it may be taken
by a bird, and then one does not know where it will finish up.
Swallows especially and the little red-hooded bird called *mbilimbili*
are said to look for human hair etc. to help build their nests with.
This is probably why the swallow and her nest are sometimes
used in black magic. For a similar reason practisers of this magic
make use of the hyena's excrement, which may contain something
that proceeds from a human being, because the hyena »devours
everything that comes in his way».

One seldom or never sees human excrement in Ukamba, at
least in the neighbourhood of the villages. It was only afterwards

that I remembered this, and so I must content myself with throwing out a suggestion that such cleanliness, which is also found among a great number of other primitive peoples, has the same basis as the careful removal of hair and pieces of nails, namely the fear of black magic.

We have now given an idea, though a slight one, of the number and nature of all the dangers which are threatened by the practiser of black magic. To protect himself the native must, on the other hand, use other magic. Thus one can get from the *mundu muɔ,* and even from a *mwoʐ,* a kind of universal remedy, a powder which protects one against almost all kinds of evils, against the designs of enemies, against wild animals during journeys, etc. Small cuts are made in the patient's skin and the powder is inserted in these. The author happened to see a *mwoʐ* treat a person in the following way: he made a cut at the ends of his nails (the outermost parts of the body) and then a scratch along his arms, over the shoulders, and up to the forehead, sprinkling *muþæa* in the cuts. Now and then one sees a man with a cut in his forehead, treated with *muþæa.* They generally inspire respect, and people will not willingly fall out with one who is protected in this way. This instilled magic power does not only passively protect its owner, but the protection may extend even as far as to injure a person who wishes to injure him. Another and more usual active effect of such medicine is for it to obtain favour with women.

At Nzaui in the Kilungu district there was (in 1911) a man called Mutune wa Taula, who was, at least in Ulu, widely known for his *makɩo,* a drink which protected the person who drank it against the magic described above under the name of pointing out (*kwolota*) and *kuɓanda kɩþaŋgɔna.* But, on the other hand, the person who has drunk *makɩo* may not, without danger to himself, use these two kinds of *woʐ* against others. People of all ages and of both sexes came to Mutune to buy *makɩo,* and for a rupee they got a little to drink. M. is said to have learnt this art from a Mukamba from Kilimandjaro.

When the *mundu muɔ* is treating a person upon whom a spell has been cast by means of *woɩ* he keeps his arms folded during the process; this is called *kuɓelanʒa moko* in the professional language.

Those who go to law to get an action decided are anxious to try to further their cause by means of magic. I remember an old man who, on such an occasion, had medicine beneath his nails and stuffed into the ends of his forked staff[1]. In addition, when he thought he was unobserved, he blew *muþæa* in the direction of his adversary.

Just as thieves facilitate their work by means of magic, so magic is used as a protection against robbery. Over the door of the hut is »planted» a *kɪþaŋgona*, which has the effect of preven-ting the thief from finding the way out again or, if he escapes successfully, of making his fingers stick fast, as it were, to the stolen object, and so he is easily detected. This *kɪþaŋgona* con-sists usually of a horn filled with *muþæa* and is thus of the type of *kɪþɪtu*. One often sees in addition protective objects of all kinds above the door of a hut. A goat-bell, which I once saw, was said to protect the people of the house from dying of illness. I have repeatedly seen eggshells, fixed on a peg, stuck in above the door. They are the shells after newly-hatched chickens. The poultry has its sleeping-place within the huts. If these pegs were thrown away, the chickens might die. The mental process of the native here is unknown to me, but he might possibly reason as follows: The egg has hitherto been a safe dwelling-place for the chicken. Now when he leaves it this security may be retained by putting the remains of the old dwelling-place above the en-trance to the new one.

Cattle, the Akamba's most precious possession, are of course also protected in various way by magic means, and, as one would expect, this is applied by preference to the entrance of the cattle kraals. Beasts of prey, lions and leopards, are specially feared. The protection against these often consists of an inverted jar con-taining *muþæa*.

I saw a *mundu muɔ* make the following arrangement to keep out disease from a cattle kraal. On each side of the entrance he

---

[1] The Masai put magic medicine beneath the nail of the index finger and point to an enemy, muttering curses. Merker, Die Masai (ed. 1904), p. 152.

fixed a pole down and into holes in the poles he stuffed medicine. In the ground between the poles were buried certain roots.

We can also easily understand that they try to protect the crops in the field by means of magic. In a jar which stood in a field I found the following objects: the horn of an antelope, filled with pieces of wood and soot; another horn, containing bits of an old bast sack (*kɀondo*); the bone of a bird, presumably a hen's; seeds of *mwę* (Penicillaria spicata); a sea-shell and two small bamboo tubes.

As a protection against stealing on a field of sugar-cane, its proprietor takes seven spikes of a porcupine (*muŋgu,* pl. *mɀuŋgu*) and bores a hole in the trunk of a sugar-cane with each of them, saying something like: »May he who eats this have his teeth destroyed!» Then each spike is thrown in the direction of the place where the sun sets (no doubt a symbolic action)[1]. It is said that if a person eats sugar-cane from a field protected in this way his teeth soon fall out. One might call this contagious magic of the second degree. For the Akamba, like the Akikuyu[2], believe that it is dangerous to pick the teeth or touch them in any other way with the spikes of the porcupine.

On journeys, especially when formerly the trade caravans went down to they coast, they obtained protection against the attacks of lurking Masai and Galla by blowing magic powder (*nžœ6u*) in the direction of the enemy's country and by placing the powder in the camp-fires so as to make them invisible. In the same way there was a remedy to protect oneself against rain during the journey.

7. Amulets (*kɪpɪtu, mbɪŋgu*).

We have already touched upon purely personal protective and lucky objects, real amulets, but we shall now examine this group a little more closely. They are called *kɪpɪtu* or *mbɪŋgu*[3], and the difference between these two varieties seems to be very vague. One might possibly say that a *kɪpɪtu* has a greater magic

---

[1] Cf. a mother's curse upon her son, p. 183.

[2] Routledge, The Akikuyu, p. 33.

[3] Probably derived from *6ɪŋga* 'to shut, shut out', here with the meaning of shutting out evil influences. *Mpingu* is also the name for amulet among the Wapare at Kilimandjaro.

power and might be called a talisman, while a *mbɨggu* acts rather more passively [1]. This *kɨpɨtu*, the purely individual means of protection, which is not dangerous to others, must on no account be confused with the formidable *kɨpɨtu* used at trials, peace ceremonies, etc. (p. 165 ff.). The amulets are made and sold by the medicine man [2].

These amulets differ very much in appearance. Many of them, however, like the *kɨpɨtu* with which an oath is taken, consist of a little horn (of the Thomson gazelle, the dwarf antelope or other smaller species of antelope). The shape of the horn in also imitated in wood, mostly ebony. Another type is made out of small square pads of imported cotton cloth, containing powder, and these seem to be always called *mbɨggu*.

I might mention the following amulets from my ethnographical collection from the Kamba tribe, now in the ethnographical department of the Swedish State Museum:

1) Three *mbɨggu* fastened with an iron chain. The little bamboo tube contains a powder which arouses love in women. The top of a horn bound with copper wire contains medicine for protection against enemies and wild animals during journeys. Kitui (Swed. State Museum, Ethnogr. coll. inventory 12. 7. 289).

2) *kɨpɨtu*, bound with copper wire and adorned with chains at the top. It is filled with love medicine and has been worn by a young man at a dance. It is at the same time an ornament. Machakos (Inv. 12. 7. 290).

3) *kɨpɨtu*, bound with iron wire. A protection against illness. Is, like the foregoing, also an ornament. Kitui (Inv. 12. 7. 291).

4) *mbɨggu*, made out of the tusk of a wild boar. The valley of the Nthua river (Inv. 72. 7. 292).

5) *mbɨggu* of ebony, carved in the form of the top of a horn. Makes the owner rich in cattle. The Nthua valley (Inv. 12. 7. 294).

6) *mbɨggu* of wood, carved in the form of the top of a horn. Kitui (Inv. 12. 7. 295).

---

[1] It is customary to make a distinction between talismans worn for good luck, and amulets which are preventive. The difference is, however, often hard to maintain. See A. G. Haddon, Magic and Fetichism, p. 29.

[2] Some prices are given by Hobley, Kamba Protective Magic, Man 1912, p. 5.

7) *mbɩŋgu.* »The medicine» is simply tightly wound round and fastened with twine made of bast. Ikutha (Inv. 12. 7. 296).

8) *mbɩŋgu.* A cloven tooth (crocodile?) in which the medicine is stuffed. Kitui (Inv. 12. 7. 297).

9) Two amulets, a large *kɩpɩtu* of antelope horn and a *mbɩŋgu,* which also consists of the top of a horn. The latter protects against poisoning. Kitui (Inv. 12. 7. 306).

The fangs of the lion and leopard are also found as amulets, a usage which is well-known in many African tribes.

An amulet is often quite a decorative article, wound round with its metal wire and adorned with china beads or red Aberis-seeds, which, in the case of a horn, are fixed in the dark sticky mass (beeswax, gum, etc), with which the horns are filled. In this way the amulet serves at the same time as an object of adornment. It is usually worn hanging round the neck or is fixed on the upper arm or round the wrist.

Amulets can be obtained for every possible object, for instance for success in love and hunting, for protection against magic (*woɩ*) and illness, against enemies and wild animals, etc. An old man who is wooing a young girl, who he suspects does not want to have anything to do with him, tries to improve his position by means of an amulet. A man who has a bad arm fastens a *mbɩŋgu* around it, so that it shall be better again more quickly. Several different qualities are often united in one and the same amulet. The chiefs and headmen appointed by the government frequently incur the ill-will of the other natives, especially if they are zealous in their work, and so they use amulets as a protection against poisoning, and against the placing of *kɩpaŋgona* in their way, etc.

A *kɩpɩtu* for protection against lions consists not infrequently of a round stone; the reason for this is unknown to me. It is stretched out towards an approaching lion and one says: »Go your way!» These methods of protection against lions are considered to be specially effective, which is not surprising, as it it very seldom happens that a lion attacks human beings without first being attacked by them. As has been already indicated, those who travel through the desert also take with them amulets as a protection against enemies, especially against the roving plundering Masai. So the traveller stretches out his *kɩpɩtu* »in the

direction of the country of the Masai». There are also *kɩ̄pɩtu* to
point with against a threatening rain cloud, so that one should not
get wetthrough on the journey and conversely to produce rain
(*kulatẓa mbua*). Stretching out a *kɩ̄pɩtu* in this way in a certain
direction for a certain purpose is called *kuɓuta na kɩ̄pɩtu*.

Amulets are sometimes even placed on cattle as a protection
against wild animals. I have on a few occasions seen these, in
the form of a horn or a medicine bag, hanging round the neck
of cattle.

One can rarely see in Ukamba proper on one and the same
individual as many amulets as there are on a Kamba from Yimba within
Mombasa, described by Brutzer who adds that the Akamba are
accustomed to hang a great number of amulets on themselves[1]:
»My informant, who certainly belonged to those who were enlight-
ened, wore on the brass spiral round his neck a talisman wound
round with metal wire. This was to protect him against sorcery
in general. Round his wrist there was a bracelet in which similarly a talisman was wrapped. This allowed him to see if there
happened to be any poison in the beer which was offered to him.
If the hand trembles while raising the cup to the mouth, it is
a sign that there is poison in it. On the bracelet also hung
two small pieces of wood on a short cord. These were to protect
himself against snakebites. Beneath the cloth round his loins hung
a talisman wrapped in pieces of cloth and tightly fastened with
string. This was to bring its wearer riches».

Amulets and other objects with magic power are not inherited,
but, on the death of their owner, go out of use, as no one else
can really understand their use. Sometimes they are allowed to
accompany the dead man to the grave, sometimes they are left
behind in his hut or are thrown right away.

8. Conceptions about the magic power in names.

A trait common to all primitive people seems to be an un-
willingness to give their names to strangers, because they are
afraid of sorcery. To them a name is an essential part of the
one who bears it or even quite identical with him, and if an ill-

---

[1] Brutzer, Die Geisterglaube, p. 11.

disposed person knows my name and mentions it he can get power over me and so injure me, by black magic among other ways. Among the Akamba a non-magic motive is also present. For it is — or at least it was in earlier times, when the blood-feud was stringently carried out — often a very wise precaution not to mention one's name, in this case the family name, i. e. the father's name, and still less the clan name, when one was staying in a strange place.

An enemy who is to be attacked should not be mentioned by his tribal name when one comes in proximity to him, no doubt to avoid the risk of arousing his attention. On such occasions the Masai are called *alaḳı* 'those who look for wild honey' (from the verb *kulaḳa* 'to look for wild honey'). A non-magic motive for avoiding the mention of enemies by their names seems, however, to be present here as well, for the spies, when they come in with an account of the enemy, refer to them by some peri-phrasis, lest the young and inexperienced warriors should, in their desire for battle, commit some rash acts, which they might possibly do, if they got to know of the proximity of the enemy.

The influence which, according to the opinion of primitive people, can be gained over the bearer of a name by uttering that name, is also effective not only in the case of people, but with animals too, nay, even for non-personal things (according to primitive ideas animals are often persons), objects of practically all kinds. We may be allowed to quote an illustrative example from the Gajos in Sumatra described by K. Th. Preuss: »So dürfen die blattern in der wohnung des daran erkrankten bei den Gajo nicht mit namen genannt und keine wörter gebraucht werden, die hässlich, faulend, stinkend bedeuten, augenscheinlich in dem sinne unseres ebenfalls hier als beispiel anzuziehenden sprichwortes: Wenn man vom wolf spricht, ist er da«[1].

To return to the Akamba, I have come across the following illustrations of their fear of uttering on certain occasions the name of an animal or an inanimate object.

The most profitable game is the elephant, and so hunters are, quite naturally, very much afraid of disturbing this animal

---

[1] K. Th. Preuss, Der Ursprung der Religion und Kunst. Globus 1905, p. 395.

needlessly and are on their guard, especially as the elephant is considered to be an extraordinarily wise creature. When they catch sight of the great pachydermata, they thus mention them in many different ways: *nde ŋgu* 'old poles' (referring to the tusks); or, as I heard in Kikumbuliu, *mbonda malia* or *wata* — the meaning of both these expressions is unknown to me. They are also fond of calling them stones (*mabia*), so that for instance the one of the hunting party who first catches sight of an elephant, says: »Yonder is a stone». This is to be interpreted as magic based on likeness: a stone does not move from its place and the native wishes that the elephant, like a stone, would remain motionless in his place, so that he might have on opportunity to shoot him.

Of the same reason the hippopotamus (*ŋgu*) is by hunters called *ŋgwælə*.

If it begins to rain when they are out on a martial expedition or hunting, they avoid speaking of rain, saying for instance, instead of »it rains»: »Ngai has come» (cf. p. 248). Otherwise the cessation of the rain would be postponed. The natives are very sensitive to rain and, in addition, a lengthy downpour is deleterious to the bowstrings.

Those who go to look for honey in the desert or to cut the honeycombs from the beehives hanging there do not mention the word *uki* (honey), but call their honey jar (*kiþæmbə*), for instance, *kinaþi* to get more honey.

And an additional example. The incessant circling of a vulture in the air is a pretty sure sign of the proximity of some carcass or dying animal. The native hunters, on catching sight of the bird, are inspired with sure hopes of an easily-caught prey, at best an elephant or at least a welcome addition to their food supplies (the Akamba do not mind eating animals that have died from natural causes, if this has only recently happened). For this reason they must not say that »there is meat somewhere in the neighbourhood» or anything like that, but they use some periphrasis instead, such as *maþaŋgo* 'dry leaves', here probably in the sense of »rubbish», something worthless. In this one might see a kind of effect of contrast: by giving a trivial name to an object which has not been seen, one tries to raise the value of the object.

The method depicted here of giving a person or thing another name is called *kwiŋea* in Kikamba.

9. Omens.

Primitive people readily find a special import in practically every accidental circumstance which occurs, and at the same time they have a mass of omens of constant and universally recognized signification. An omen, presage is called in the Kamba language *mupana*, with the addition *musæo*, if it is considered good, and *mupuku*, if it is bad. The Akamba get their most important omens from the animal world.

a. Omens taken from bodily action.

By *kŗoŗo* they seem to mean (nervous) twitchings of the joints in different parts of the body[1]. If one feels an itching in the lower eyelid (*kŗoŗo kŗa mæpo*), it means that one is going to »cry or see blood». This may just as well be a good omen, meaning that one is going to get good booty during an approaching hunt or that one is to be invited to eat meat at a friend's. *kŗoŗo kŗa moko*, twitching in both arms, means that one shall get a present. Twitching in the left arm (*kŗoŗo kŗa kwoko kwa aka* 'in the women's arm', i. e. the left) means that one is going to be compelled to give something away. A similar sensation in the head, *kŗoŗo kŗa ukunwa* (lit. 'to be beaten') signifies that one is to be beaten or to be tired out by carrying a heavy burden.

To sneeze (*kwapŗmwa*[2]) is also considered as an omen, although usually of slight import. When a sick person sneezes repeatedly it is a sign that he will soon be well. To many medicine men a boy's sneezing early in the morning is a good omen, meaning that he will have many consultations that day. To another medicine man, on the other hand, this may be a bad augury, while a girls sneezing is, on the contrary, a welcome sign to him.

My additional information about their ideas concerning sneezing may conveniently be mentioned here. A person who sneezes

---

[1] According to K. Th. Preuss ethnological literature contains, or at least contained before 1909, only the very scantiest material about this kind of presage. Because of this P. requests investigators who are going out to pay attention to this lacuna. The data he found himself are collected in his article »Die Vorbedeutung des Zuckens der Gliedmassen in der Völkerkunde», Globus 1909, p. 245.

[2] = to be blessed? (cf. *kwapŗma* 'to bless').

says *kula,* often with the addition: *kula mwana wa ŋganʒa* —
»*kula,* son of so-and-so», mentioning his father's name. I do not
know what *kula* really means, but the expression is said to indicate happiness or well-being. Presumably it has a meaning similar
to our »Prosit!» One of my acquaintainces of the *kɪpumbɔ* clan
used always to say, when be sneezed: *maɪpa ma mba-kɪpumbɔ* 'the
enemies of the clan *kɪpumbɔ'.*

A person who gives a baby an ornament or other small object to play with will not take this back, if the child happens to
sneeze while he is holding the object. If one took it, the action
would be highly disapproved of by those present.

b.   People whom one meets looked upon as omens.

When one is out on important business or has started a journey, it is a bad omen to meet a solitary man or woman, and also
three or more in company, if their number is odd[1]. Many people
turn back again and postpone their project after such a encounter.
On the other hand, if those one meets are an even number, two,
four etc., it is of no significance. These rules vary, however, in
different parts of the country.

c.   Animals as bearers of omens.

A great many animals play an important part in the Akamba's life as tokens of coming events, usually misfortunes. Thus
if the jackal's yell is heard several nights in succession, a misfortune is considered to be at hand: similarly if a cock crows in
the evening. If a frog jumps up towards you, you will, according
tho the saying of the old people, soon get ill or die. On the other
hand, it does not matter if the frog goes into a hut, which among
the Zulus means a death[2]. But if the black biting ants come
several times into a hut, the Akamba say that one of the dwellers
in the hut will die. The hedgehog (*kɪpaŋgaɪtɪ*), on the other hand,
brings good fortune with it, if it enters a hut. The *nžaɪ* is a very
common, non-stinging, brown night-insect, the size of a wasp,

---

[1] The Masai also believe that if, on a journey, one meets a solitary person on the road, the journey will be fruitless. Hollis, The
Masai, p. 324.

[2] Kidd, The essential Kafir, p. 273.

which is often a nuisance to the traveller, because it continually circles round the lamp, falls into the food as one is eating, etc. If it falls into the camp-fire of a hunting party, it is a sign that one of the company will be killed by some animal; this is also the case if one hears them up among the tops of the trees round the camp. In such a case the hunters usually turn back home as soon as day dawns.

If the domestic animals do something unusual, it is taken as a bad omen. Thus, for instance, if a sheep or cow, etc. rises up on its hind-legs to bite off the leaves of a tree, the animal is immediately killed. Goats, on the other hand, often do this, and so their behaviour is not taken as an omen, as it is natural to them, or, as the natives say; »This is their work»[1]. It is also looked upon as an evil omen if, when the cattle are grazing, a bull horns and runs home to the village without any obvious reason. The animal may then be killed by anyone without the owner's permission being asked.

As might be expected, various other kinds of birds are though to be the bearers of omens. The owl is a bird of ill-omen in Africa as well as in Europe, and if it is heard several nights in succession it denotes death. Now and then one sees old crocks hanging in the trees at the villages: they are put there to frighten the owls away. The most important and best known of all prophecying animals is also a bird, the *ŋgomakoma*[2], a red-headed species of woodpecker, to which the natives listened, especially in former times, before marching out on plundering expeditions.[3] It is considered to be a good or a bad omen according to the side on which one hears his pecking. The interpretation varies to some extent in different parts of Ukamba; the following detailed account is from Kikumbuliu, the south-east part of the country.

---

[1] The above undeniably logical argument does not seem, however, to be used by all Bantu peoples. It is said of the Bechuana: »If a goat climbs the roof of a hut, it is speared at once, because it would bewitch the owner if it were not put to death.» J. Mackenzie, Ten years North of the Orange River, p. 392.

[2] < *komakoma* 'to rap, knock'.

[3] It is difficult to say whether the birrd's cry and rappng alone have caused it to be considered a bird of omen, or whether the red feathers of the head have also contributed to this. For the significance of red feathers see N. Hammarstedt in Fatburen 1909, p. 201.

If the bird is heard straight in front, one will »see blood», i. e. get scratched in the thickets, be gored by a rhinoceros or wounded in fighting, etc.; which of these tings is most probable depends on the object of the expedition or the environment one is in or is going to be in. To hear the bird in front in an oblique direction and high up is also a bad sign, whereas if it is low in the same direction it only means that the listener will return without having effected his object. The left side is, on the other hand, the good side (in other districts the bad one), and if the bird is heard on that side, one has prospects of accuring women, cattle and other wealth. Finally, if it is heard from behind, it denotes that the listener will carry a burden, so that if he is going out hunting he will brobably shoot something, if he is about to cut the honeycombs from the beehives, he may be pretty sure of a good result, and similarly with those who are going to steal cattle, etc.

This woodpecker is looked upon as a messenger from the ancestral spirits; it is not killed, and its flesh may not be eaten by men. This prohibition does not apply to women, probably because as a rule they do not know of this bird, as they seldom have cause to go out into the desert, where the bird principally stays. In the immediate neighbourhood of Machakos, where trees are very rare and the bird is concequently not found, only a very few people seem to know of it. The Akamba who live there also carried out most of their campaigns on the steppe, where they probably had no opportunity of observing it.[1]

The natives state that even certain animals, such as the giraffe, wild boar, etc. are so shrewd that they listen to and understand the ŋgomakoṃi's call.

The different directions in which the woodpecker is heard have their special appellations:

from in front is called *tusẹa*, from behind *ŋguŋguo;*
high up on the right is called *ẹna*, low down on the right *ɓwaɓẹ wa aumɔ* 'the men's *ɓwaɓẹ*';
high up on the left is called *waṃu*, low down on the left *ɓwaɓẹ wa aka* 'the women's *ɓwaɓẹ*'.

---

[1] The Masai, however, have the species of woodpecker they call *tilo* (Mesopicus spodocephalus) as a bird of omen. If heard on the right or behind, it is good, if on the left, bad. Hollis, The Masai, pp. 323 ff.

As an instance of how much importance they sometimes attach to this bird of ·omen Brutzer relates how a party who had entered upon a long journey returned after four days because on the second day they heard the birds call[1].

10. Different substances *(ɣondu)* used at ceremonial purifications.

At different places in the foregoing work we have come across the word *ɣondu*, and we have seen that it means, in the first place, a purifier, used for religious or magic purposes to clean people, cattle, fields, huts, articles of clothing, in a word, objects of every conceivable kind. Its principal ingredients consist of parts of plants and certain intestines of animals, usually of the goat. Sometimes, as in the case of death (p. 108), such a ceremonial purification is obligatory, sometimes it is a more occasional precaution.

In its restricted meaning the conception of *ɣondu* contains nothing religious, nor is it used for purification, but is a more or less purely magic aid. For instance, there is *ɣondu* which, if eaten by a cow, causes her to breed only female calves and so increase considerably in value. Different kinds of *ɣondu* are used principally in connection with cattle. We shall return to this in describing the domestic animals of the Akamba.

The ordinary medicine man seldom meddles with *ɣondu*, contrary to the practice of the *ɪtuma* (p. 269). Generally the *ɣondu* expert is an experienced elderly man, who has got his knowledge and power from the spirits. Old Malata wa Kyambi in the Machakos district was a real specialist in *ɣondu*. He knew of a great number of purifying plants and had planted them at his hut, others in his field and others in the surrounding thickets. Thus the plants were specially cultivated for medical or at least ritual use. In addition he had collected a large supply of dried roots, which he stored up in different places here and there in the neighbourhood of the hut, for instance in a heap of leaves, a hole in the earth, etc. He gave as a reason for this that it was not »good» to keep them at home. The fact of the matter was probably that the objects were supposed to have more power if a

---

[1] Brutzer, Der Geisterglaube, p. 11.

little mysticism was attached to them. Malaba was an *itima*, but not a medicine man.

Of the many different kinds of *ɣondu* we shall, first of all, mention a common one which is used to purify both human beings and cattle. The parts of plants which are contained in it are the roots of *mulindıtı* or *kɨoɲgwa* (Sanseviera sp.) and those of *mukunda mbuɟ*[1] or *múlalɔ*. This kind of *ɣondu* is, among other purposes, used to sprinkle one who, after a rather long absence, returns home, as it is considered injurious to him if any of those who have stayed at home have had sexual intercourse during his absence. All those who took part in the trade caravans which used to go down to the coast and those who went on campaigns out into the Masai steppes were treated in this way on their arrival at home. The purification ceremony was carried out as follows (cf. p. 108): The roots of the plants mentioned were crushed and put in a calabash shell with water[2], a part of which is given to a goat to drink. The goat is killed and certain of its intestines (*kıpılıko*) are placed in the mixture, with which afterwards the person who has come home is sprinkled, and in which he has to tread with his feet. In a similar way they sprinkle his bed and all the inside of the hut, the entrance to it and the open places outside. Before this is done he may not eat any food in his house; he even likes to purify the food before he begins to eat.

According to information which unfortunately I have been unable to confirm, those who are at home must also be purified in this way, so that they may be exempt from the danger which they believe surrounds them on account of the sexual intercourse they have had during his absence.

A similar *ɣondu* is used to sprinkle on the crop which is springing up in the field (cf. below and the chapter on »Agriculture«). By some it is also used in house-building, when it is poured in the holes in which the rods, which form the frame of the hut, are set down.

Some other *gondu* plants are *ɣondu ɟa akaɓı* ('of the Masai'), *mululwɔ, koɟa, ndata kıɓumbu, wæa* and *ıtæta*. The last is especially used to purify women and cattle.

---

[1] < *kunda* 'to drink' and *mbuɟ* 'goat'.

[2] In the Kitui district no calabash shell or other household article is used, but the mixture is placed on leaves of the *kıuɲgu* plant.

An animal which has very many and different uses in the preparation of *ɣondu* is the rock Hyrax, *kɩɣouɔ* or *kɩkɩla*, as it is called when young. The contents of its stomach are considered as a specially powerful means of purification. The regulations for the capture and treatment of this animal are very detailed and must be carefully followed if the *ɣondu* is to have any effect. First a little food of different kinds (maize, beans, seed of Eleusine, etc.), the products of the field, must be placed, as an offering to Mulungu, among the rocks which the animal frequents. A Hyrax may not be shot with arrows but must be taken in a snare. At Kibwezi instructions were in force to the effect that to catch the animal it should on no account be called *kɩɣouɔ*, but only *kɩkɩla* or *ɩlondu* 'sheep' (cf. p. 290). The animal is then brought to a sacrificial place (*ɩβæmbo*), where the elders kill it by cutting off its head. The contents of its stomach are mixed with blood from the animal in a calabash shell, and the *ɣondu* is ready. For the sprinkling — and usually also at the sprinkling of other kinds of *ɣondu* — branches of *muta* (Verticillatæ-sp., with a strong aromatic odour) are used.

This *ɣondu* has its most important use in connection with agriculture. If the crop is bad, they turn to the medicine man as usual in their difficulty, and he readily indicates to them that the fields should be sprinkled with it. It should preferably be mixed in water from the first rain, thus a sort of homeopathic magic. It is easy then to see that it also happens that this *ɣondu* is used to produce rain.

Besides crops the cattle are also sprinkled, if they do not seem to be prospering, with *ɣondu* of the Hyrax. It is also used for human beings: barren women and those who are suffering from the illness called *βaβu* (see below) are smeared with it and it is given to drink to those suffering from general weakness and excessive thinness (*umoṣu*).

It should be noticed that this means of purification is different from those described before inasmuch as everything connected with it is managed and prescribed by the medicine man, while *ɣondu* in general, as has been already said, is administered by special people. Although the latter do not occupy themselves with black magic, they inspire respect and are as a rule paid punctually for their trouble, as it is believed that they have the power to be avenged on the patient by letting an illness loose on them, for instance to make them gradually waste away (*umoṣu*). This is said to happen by a certain treatment of the material used for the *ṇondu*, some part of which is always left in their bags.

The skin of the rock Hyrax is considered very good to use for pouring out the pebbles on in divination. Some of the Akamba will under no circumstances eat the flesh of the animal, while others on the other hand have no scruples against this[1]. Hilde-brand[2], who in addition mentions that the Akamba do not kill the Hyrax, says that the droppings of the animal are used as an astringent in circumcision.

The intestines of poultry and the excrement of the python are also occasionally used in the preparation of *ṇondu*.

11. The illnesses *paƃu* and *makwa*.

As has been mentioned in Chap. VII *paƃu* is a kind of illness which may attack a person who does not observe certain instructions about purification, especially those which must be carried out after a death (p. 108). The symptoms of the illness are general weakness, a gradual wasting away and especially a very rapid loss of flesh, which is not seldom in glaring contrast to the sick person's voracious appetite. If he is not purified in time, the illness causes his death. All the people who I was told had *paƃu* had a worn appearance and looked apathic and depressed[3]. To pine away slowly in this way is called *kupumua*[4].

The two most usual cases of *paƃu* in connection with deaths, before a village is purified after a death, are:

1. A relation who is away and comes on a visit to a village where a death takes place and eats food there contracts the illness (cf. p. 109).

----

[1] The Hyrax belongs to the animals which, according to the Mosaic law, the Jews could not eat. The prohibition of the Abysinians and Mohammedans from eating the animal perhaps originates from this. Brehm's Tierleben III, p. 592. A. E. Brehm, Vierzehn Tage in Mensa, Globus 1863, p. 297.

[2] Die Wakamba, p. 382.

[3] *paƃu* seems, in some respects, to be equivalent with the Suaheli word *thambi* 'sin'.

[4] Not to be confused with *kupamua* 'to rest, repose'.

2. If a girl from such a village has sexual relations she gets *paɓu*. If she has a child it will be very thin and miserable and »often have something like goat's hair on its back». If after that she has a wooer, her former lover has to pay a goat for the preparation of the purificatory *ɣondu* for her.

There are several other forms of *paɓu*:

On p. 105 we have seen that only the *atumɩa* may touch a corpse, while contact with a dead body brings *paɓu* to other people. By eating his totem animal or marrying a girl of his own clan a man can also catch this illness.

From *paɓu*, as from all other kinds of »ceremonial uncleanliness», one is purified by *ɣondu*. Every expert in *ɣondu* cannot, however, cure *paɓu*, but for this purpose specialists are required. Such a specialist is called *mutumɩa wa ukṵ*, and is the same person who in cases of death says what must be done to prevent further deaths and to avoid *paɓu*. It is said that to be successful in his work, he himself ought to have lost some near relative by death. A woman may also be a *mutumɩa wa ukṵ*.

I shall now describe in detail a purification ceremony of this kind that I witnessed near Kibwezi.

The headman Makiti had two wives and one of them gave birth to a child which died. Through not troubling about the instructions concerning ritual coitus on the death of a child (see p. 106) he caused his other wife, with whom he was living at variance, to have *paɓu*. At length, however, he decided to have her purified, and the ceremony was carried out by an elder who was expert in *ɣondu* outside M:s village on the path which led to it. The sick woman was placed on the path — to stand separate from the man — not in actual contact with it, but on a few large leaves on which were also placed a couple of branches of a *ɣondu* tree. Opposite her, on the other side of the path, M. took up his position, and behind him the other wife who was also regarded as being guilty of causing the illness. Another man brought forward a goat, which he ripped up alive, and took out the little stomach, *kɩpɩlɩko*, the contents of which he placed in a calabash vessel, containing pieces of various kinds of trees, which the *ɣondu* man had previously arranged. The poor goat lived several minutes. Generally the goat is killed first, but in this case if it had been first killed, it would not have given enough

power (*ßïnẓa*), explained the *mutumïa*. During this time the latter
had picked out a small piece of wood and, after laying the sick
wife's hands on M:s shoulders, he told him to address her somewhat as follows: »I am sorry to have done wrong to you, and just
as this piece of wood is now thrown away, so I throw away all my
ill-will towards you». Then the piece was given to the woman and
she, on her side, declared that she threw away all ill-will towards
her husband, whereupon she threw the piece of wood away. In
the same way some further special causes of contention were
treated, and for each matter which was settled a bit of wood was
thrown away. Now the old man took some of the prepared
ŋondu and stuffed it in the mouth of the sick woman and even
succeeded with some difficulty in getting some into the mouth of
her child, which she carried on her back. She had to spit it out
immediately, but the old man was very careful to see that she
spat it out between her feet. Makiti and his other wife had their
faces smeared with *ŋondu*. The ceremony was over, and the sick
woman ought now to get better soon.

In the Kikuyu language *ßaßu* is called *ßahu*[1], and Routledge
gives no less than 29 examples of this »ceremonial uncleanness».
He gives no information, however, about the symptoms and effect
of *ßahu*. The purification ceremonies he describes resemble very
much those of the Akamba; the purificatory substance is also
called *n'gondu*. Hobley[2] has collected no less than 62 different
cases of *thahu* from the Akikuyu, several of which I recognize from
the Akamba. No doubt a closer investigation among the latter
would give a considerable number from them too. The two tribes,
being in many ways so nearly related, seem especially to have
almost quite the same conception about this kind of sickness.

ßaßu plays an immense rôle in the life of these people. Every
day, almost every moment, the native runs the risk of getting into
conflict with some rule, the breaking of which will attract him *ßaßu*.

Omission of the above-mentioned purification rites after a
death may also sometimes bring about a ceremonial uncleanness
and with it an illness which is more severe than *ßaßu*, namely

---

[1] *ß* does not exist in Kikuyu, but *h* corresponds here to Kikamba *ß*.

[2] Kikuyu Customs and Belief. Thahu and its connection with
Circumcision Rites. Journ. Anthr. Inst. 1910, p. 428 ff.

makwa. The author cannot with any certainty say that he has seen anyone suffering from this, but the first symptoms are said to consist of pains in the extremities, especially in the joints of the knees and elbows (rheumatism of the joints?); the person who is attacked by it has in addition »hoarse hawkings». The limbs soon begin to swell and sores gradually break out on the body. The German missionaries in Mulango, East Akamba, who knew of this illness, considered it a kind of syphilis, but the natives themselves, who also know of syphilis, but only under its Suaheli name, deny this[1]. They say that *makwa* has not, like syphilis, come from the coast, but existed in the country since olden times and also appears among the neighbouring tribes.

makwa is a much more rare complaint than *pabu*, so that those who know how to cure it are also few in number. These people are called *mutumıa wa makwa*. The first qualifications necessary for this position is that one should have lost several of one's nearest relations by illness (no matter of what kind? or under circumstances that may cause *pabu*?). There is no age limit. Even a young man, provided he is intelligent, possesses the qualification to be a *mutumıa wa makwa*, if he has lost his parents and brothers and sister. Similarly in the case of a woman. According to Mr. K. Dundas, D. C. of Machakos, who was good enough to write and inform me of his enquiries about *makwa*, »an ordinary woman cannot become *makwa*, only a medicine woman».

A man visited by death in this way wanders long distances seeking eminent *gondu* experts to learn from. He has to learn about the different plants, where they grow, what parts of them are to be used and in what way they are used. He thus develops slowly into a connoisseur of a mass of plants and their uses. An almost necessary condition for obtaining real success seems to be, in addition, that he observes great or almost complete sexual continence.

I shall quote the following from Mr. Dundas's paper which agrees completely with my own results:

»There are no special initiation ceremonies, neither are there any special fees. There is no connection whatever with the »atu-

---

[1] Hofmann (with a reservation) renders *makwa* by leprosy (»aussatz?»). For my own part I have not heard of any cases of leprosy in these districts.

mia ma nzama» or the »atumia ma ithembo», and it is not necessary for a person to belong to either of these grades in order to
become an »ukuu» or a »makwa».

It is to be noted too that so far as concerns the natives of
this district [Machakos] at any rate there is no mystery or secrecy
attached to these things. In short the »makwa» and »ukuu» are
not grades, but positions attained to gradually by successful practice, in much the same way as a successful medical practioner
may finally develop into a Harley street specialist. The »atumia
ma makwa» and the »atumia ma ukuu» are not in any way to
be confused with the medicine men, who are supposed to be in
direct touch and communication with the »aimu». A person may
be a »makwa» or an »ukuu» only, or he may be both; of the
two the »ukuu» is considered the more important; on the other
hand it is said to be much more difficult to become a successful
»makwa». Kesungu, the great Kilungu »ukuu», combines both
functions and is also now on the way to becoming a medicine
man; but this is due to the fact that he is now credited with
becoming possessed with an »aimu». He was taught both »makwa»
and »ukuu» by a woman called Siomuteti».

To this statement of Mr. Dundas I will only add that the
medicine man does not know how to cure *paɓu* or *makwa*, and
further that in actual practice the *mutumıa wa ukụ* is a more
important person than the *mutumıa wa makwa,* because the cases
of *makwa* are more rare.

While *paɓu* is due to a psychical disturbance in the patient
the illness called *makwa* appears to be somewhat mystical[1]. The
consequences of his crime against the ritual prescriptions leave
him no peace, but are continually present in his consciousness, and

---

[1] The symptoms scarcely point to it, or else one would be very
much inclined to suggest consumption as an explanation. Junod (The
Life of a South African tribe II, p. 433) shows how this sickness
has been known for a long time among the Thonga and has been of
great importance in their ritual. It would be interesting to know how
widespread it is in Africa and the ideas that the natives have about it.
It is certain that it existed there before the arrival of the Europeans.
I do not know what consumption is called in Kikamba, but if Watt's
Vocabulary, which is usually very unreliable, is correct about this, the
Akamba have a name for consumption, namely *ulolomı*. This substan-
tive is not known to Hofmann (Wörterbuch), who has, however, the

the psychical depression which results brings with it a physical one also, which may end with the complete extinction of life. This great influence of suggestion is well known by numerous examples from primitive peo   , whose physical equilibrium, while it cannot be called nervous, is very unstable. It is enough to mention the Australian native who after discovering that his sick wife had lain on his rug died within a fortnight[1].

12. Snake=charmers.

Some medicine men may be called real snake-tamers, inasmuch as they capture and work with snakes. The taming of snakes in itself seems to have no other practical importance than to give people greater respect for the skill and magic power of the person concerned, although we shall soon see that these snake-tamers are also occupied in curing snake-bites, and as they themselves are immune from snake poisoning, it is thought that they can give others immunity against it. The knowledge of this comes ultimately from the *aimu*, who may, however, bestow it upon a person, no matter whether he is a medicine man or not.

The most famous of all the snake-charmers was the now deceased magic doctor Kimia in Ikutha, who was said to have learnt the art among the Wagiriama. He had many snakes which he kept in calabashes in his hut. Before he released the animals, he eat a kind of powder. He called them to him by whistling, took them with his hands and let them coil round his body. To show his power over them he used, among other things, to put the snake's head into his mouth. When on such an occasion he was bitten, he naturally thought that it was due to some enemy's witchcraft and went to a medicine man to be treated. The latter buried Kimia in the earth, took him up again, and buried a living sheep instead. Then he gave him instructions not to go on the roads on his way home but to travel cross-country, and on his

---

verb *kuloloma*, which he translates only with 'to be ill'. It probably, however, refers to some special sort of sickness, for the usual expression for »to be ill» is *kua*.

[1] W. E. A r m i t, Customs of the Australian Aborigines. Journ. Anthr. Inst. 1880, p. 459.

arrival he must enter by a specially arranged opening, not by the ordinary entrance. Not to use this on certain occasions is, as a matter of fact, a very common direction of the magicians.

According to information given to me by Hofmann, the missionary in Ikutha, Kimia once let a few snakes loose in the mission station so as to show his power. They took refuge in a hole in the wall and no one could get hold of them or drive them away till K. himself was pleased to do so.

A snake doctor can give another person his power to handle snakes and his immunity against their poison. On the body of the person who wants to receive this *βɩnɩa* ('power') he makes small incisions here and there, even on the tip of the tongue, and into these incisions he rubs a powder which is prepared from a poisonous tree[1], but also contains fat and parts of snakes. It must be poison, because the snakes have poison. Apart from this fact, its preparation is a secret. A bamboo tube with powder of this kind is in my collection. How this poison — if it really is poison — can be mixed with the blood without injury, is also the snake-doctor's secret. The patients whole body is now filled with *βɩnɩa*, which is concentrated in the blood and saliva. He has now become a snake-tamer and can kill a reptile simply by spitting on him. The snake is then said to have convulsive twitches and to die soon with wild twistings. It is thought that even ordinary saliva will hurt a snake — similarly with a mole — and arrows smeared with it kill these animals, while the usual poison used for arrows is said to have no effect on them.

These snake doctors treat snake-bite as well. Besides carefully sucking the poison out, they use as medicine their own blood and saliva, which is of course considered to contain poison. It is done by cutting themselves on the wrist and letting the person who has been bitten suck up the oozing drops of blood, besides which they rub their saliva on the bitten place and finally spit in the mouth of the patient, who has to swallow the saliva.

By means of the procedure here described one is protected against snake-bites and can without danger catch a snake, but real power over reptiles is not acquired before one has eaten some of the powder or been smeared with it.

---

[1] This is not Acocanthera Schimperi (Kikamba *muβaɩ*), which in these districts is used for making poison for arrows.

There are no professional snake-tamers in Ukamba, but during the latter period of my stay in the country (1912) I came across several young men who had small snakes and took them with them when they strolled about (fig. 62). One of these young men came to me one day with two *ŋguluku*, a common small snake, which the Akamba say is poisonous, though as a matter of fact they say this about most snakes. He put their heads in his mouth,

Fig. 62. Young man playing with a snake.

let them coil round his neck, etc. They showed the usual inertness of tame snakes, but one of them tried continually to get away, when their owner put them down on the ground. He said that he had given them »medicine» and showed me two kinds of powder, one black and one white.

My tentboy Kivuvu was also one of these snakemen. During one of our expeditions we came across a little black snake, according to the boy's statement a young cobra, which darted into the thick grass. Kivuvu wanted to show off by catching it, and started by going round the tussock three times »to prevent the

snake escaping». He then went into the thick grass looking for
the reptile, and when he caught sight of it, grasped it swiftly by
the neck. Then he asked me to make a little cut in his wrist,
he himself cut the snake a little on the neck and dropped a
little of his own blood into the snake's twisted »so that the
animal should know him and not go away». In addition
he put a white powder on the wound and then twisted the snake
round his neck where it lay quite still. One might possibly imagine, though it is not at all probable, that by means of mixing
the blood Kivuvu considered that he had entered into a sort of
bloodbrotherhood with the snake. He did not, however, trouble
himself much about the reptile, for he gave it to me when we
came home.

13. The magic significance of numbers.

Before we leave the question of magic, I wish, both as a
survey and for the use of special investigators of the subject, to
collect briefly the scattered information contained in this work
about the part certain numbers seem to play for the Akamba. By
numbers are meant partly the concrete number of persons or things,
partly the number of times certain rites and similar actions are
carried out.

There are number of good, quite indifferent, and bad import,
especially the latter. As we have already seen, odd numbers are
generally considered disastrous or at least unlucky, and the language has a special expression for them (*mwq*). Odd numbers are
of course considered as inauspicious omens, while even numbers
do not play any part at all as omens. Another thing that helps to
illustrate the conception of odd numbers is the meat meals during
the third *nžaɪko* (p. 63) and the feasts of the *nžama* and *kɪsuka*
(p. 144 ff.). When paying the fees for these and in order to attain
a higher rank in them the natives are usually careful to see that
the goats that are given in payment do not make an odd number;
this is especially the case for the *nžaɪko* meals. The malignant
cattle disease *ndalu* is believed always to carry off an odd number
of animals.

On the other hand we have quite a contrary state of affairs
at a medicine man's divination, as the pebbles that fall out of his
calabash are a good omen if they are odd and vice versa (cf.

however the number 7 immediately below). To our more logical minds this is an inconsistency, but it is easy to forget that inconsistencies are not so rare in primitive ways of thinking.

The idea that the number 7 has a special importance is, of course, very widespread, practically over the whole world[1]. Among the Akamba also it is the most prominent of all the numbers. This seems to be the case over large parts of East Africa as well, and one may with great probability account for this from semitic and mohammedan influence (the Arabs and through them the Wasuahelis, who have gone as traders from the East coast into the interior for a couple of thousand years). Among the Akamba seven is found both as a good and evil number; in most cases, however, it seems to be bad.

The following are some cases in which the number is quite clearly considered to be inauspicious:

When a native consults the medicine man on some matter to have his fortune told, and the latter shakes seven pebbles out of his divination gourd. Similarly in the method of procedure described on p. 285 of protecting one's sugarcanes against thieves by putting seven porcupine quills in the stalks; also in not allowing cattle to be watched longer than six days in succession by the same shepherd. We also remember that, in taking an oath on the *kiⁱⁱⁱu*, 7 stones are placed by the side of it; on these stands the man who swears and they probably help to a certain extent to make the breaking of the oath baneful.

The number 7 is thus an important factor in the Akamba's oaths and also in incantations and magic in general. Brutzer describes a »muma» or »kisitu» that stood at the edge of a field to protect it against thieves. In its complicated composition there was, among other things seven fruits of a Solanum species (no doubt the *ṇgondu* fruits) and a white shell with seven small spots. And he adds something that is not clear: »The effect of such a *muma* depends on the number of its parts, according as it consists of 7×3, 7×5 or 7×7 parts»[2].

According to Brutzer the Akamba call seven »the bad luck number», which agrees with the Akikuyu's conception of it (cf.

---

[1] F. V. Andrian, Die Siebenzahl im Geistesleben der Völker. Mitteil. der Anthrop. Ges. in Wien 1901, p. 225.

[2] E. Brutzer, Der Geisterglaube bei den Kamba, p. 13.

p. 58). Yet it is often used by the Akamba in cases when it is difficult to find anything inauspicious about it, but rather the other way about. The rites and dances during the second *nzaiko* feast, during which it can scarcely be the idea to harm those who take part, last seven days (p. 47). And during the same initiation a fig-tree is stabbed with a nail that has been smeared with fat in seven places (p. 56). At prayers and sacrifices, i. e. when the natives wish something good for themselves, the number also appears, as when they throw seed against a tree seven times (or, as in another case, 3+4) during prayers for a sick person (pp. 241 ff.), or when at mealtimes they offer 14 (7+7) bits of meat to the spirits (p. 218). Hobley gives an instance of the use of this number which he expressly says is meant to bring »good luck, namely a whip, used for magic purpose, that was cracked seven times to bring good luck to elephant hunters (cf. p. 264).

One might expect that the numbers 3 and 4 should be closely connected with 7, and that is certainly the case. When an oath is taken on the *kɪþɪtu* this is placed on three stones (p. 168) and the one who swears usually strikes it three times with the *mukulwa* twig. The number here seems thus to help in bringing about a baneful effect on one who breaks the oath. Sometimes, on the other hand, it is entirely opposite. When the medicine man — other persons do this as well — spits over someone or something with the intention of blessing or bringing luck, they usually do so three times.

The number 3, and also 4, occurs remarkably often in driving out the foreign spirits we read of under the name *kɪsuka* p. 229). The *ɣondu* then used, in which there were three hen feathers, was brought three times to and from the mouth of the possessed woman, before it was given her to drink. During three days they danced and on the fourth the woman was washed with *ɣondu*. Finally, as a protection for the future, three amulets were hung on each side of her body.

Among the rites connected with the building of a hut there is included the cooking of some food when the work is done. If the food cooked is porridge, four small pieces are thrown on the floor for the spirits.

The number 4 is also met with on other occasions. Four men carry the *mbusɪa* in the second initiation (p. 50); four men build the hut in the third one (p. 62), and four elders watch at a man's deathbed.

I cannot remember anything special about the number 2, but there is no doubt that it also has a certain importance. The stones placed at the side of the *kıpıtu* are sometimes, according to Hobley, only two in number. Sometimes, on the other hand, they are eleven (7 + 4).

Whether any symbolism of numbers is found in the Akamba's decorations, I do not know, inquiries about this having given no result. G. Backman M. D., in his review of the three first part of this work [1] (which are much more complete in the present monograph, calls attention, however, to the figures reproduced by me from the *musaı* sticks in the second *nǯaıko*: »the sun has 9 beams, the moon (new) is surrounded by 9 stars, the chain has 9 side-links, the millipede has 27 (= 3 × 9) feet, the chair has 3 legs. And in the picture on p. 54, which is also taken from one and the same musai stick, the open place (fig. 1) has 2 × 4 roads, the tortoise (fig. 2) has 4 legs, the star (fig. 6) has 4 beams, the star (fig. 7) has 2 × 4 beams, the thail of the cow has 4 tufts of hair. This repetition of definite number or multiples of them, in the one case 3, in the other 4, shows with pretty great probability that there are real and serious intentions behind the pictographic riddles of the musai sticks...» [2]

This indication of Dr. Backman has led me to investigate 25 of these figures, which give respectively the following numbers of carvings (the numbers divided by a + sign give the distribution on two sides of the object: 12 + 13, for instance, means the legs on each side of a millipede's body):

3, 4, 4 + 4, 4 + 5, 5 (twice), 5 + 3, 5 + 5, 5 + 6, 5 + 7 (twice), 5 + 9, 6 (three times), 6 + 6, 7, 7 + 3, 7 + 7, 7 + 8, 8, 9, 12 + 13.

As will be seen both 2 and 3 are found in their multiples and also 5 alone, but no conclusion can be drawn from this about the symbolism of the numbers, as all possible combinations oı numbers are present.

As a conclusion to this resumé of the significance of numbers among the Akamba I may add that they will never count their

---

[1] Printed as an Inaugural Dissertation, Uppsala 1916.

[2] G. Backman, review of G. Lindblom, The Akamba in British East Africa (Parts I—III), Ymer 1916, p. 361.

cattle. When they are driven into the craal of an evening, the
natives certainly look carefully to see that no animal is missing,
but they do not count them. Similarly they do not like to state
the number of their children (p. 88). The reason for this is
probably that they are afraid of attracting the attention of the
spirits, who are always envious. The same fear of counting people
and valuable possessions is found among other Bantu peoples and
is perhaps common to great numbers of people at a low level of
culture, but it seems to be specially prevalent among the Hamitic and Semitic peoples (not at least those in Africa, such as the
Masai), and from these probably has, with so many other things,
spread to the negroes [1].

_____

[1] See M. Schmidt, Zahl and Zählen in Afrika, Mitteil. d. Anthrop.
Ges. in Wien 1915, p. 196.

Chapter XV. **Medicine.**

To every people, no matter how low their stage of culture is, we must ascribe a certain knowledge of remedies and medicines for illnesses, a knowledge gained empirically and based on the experience of generations. But it is usually very difficult to say where this actual knowledge begins or ends, for the real remedies in question are usually accompanied, as we know, by ceremonies or rites, which give the whole procedure a more or less magic character. And in many cases the magic element seems to be considered as the essential thing. We have, however, discussed the magic weft in the Akamba's medicine in the preceding chapter, and in this one we shall, as far as possible, confine ourselves to concrete things.

As the author does not possess special medical knowledge and the principal portions of what follows have to be based on the natives' own inexact descriptions, it is certain that the account will contain various incorrect expressions. To a professional man, however, it ought to be a good starting-point for further and more scientific investigations into the knowledge of medicine possessed by the Akamba and their neighbours. The material I have collected is as follows.

1. **Illnesses (operations, wounds).**

A broken bone can be quite effectively treated. The injured limb is bound with a splint made of 4 to 6 pieces of wood fastened together with leather bands, the broken parts having first been twisted into their proper position. To keep the patient absolutely still, they use the radical method of placing him on the floor of the hut and then placing pegs round his outstretched leg. This is then fastened to these pegs and the patient, who cannot move now, is not released till the fracture is cured.

An interesting operation is the removal of the uvula (*ka-lɪmə*)[1] when this is swollen. A pair of long giraffe-hairs are placed round the uvula, which by means of these is drawn forward and then cut off with a knife. A cloth is then bound in front of the mouth »to hinder the cold». For about five days the patient has to be on a special diet and may then only eat hard and dry food, such as roasted maize and other baked food, especially hard-baked bananas. Ginger (called *tangawizi*, its Suaheli name), which is bought from the Indian traders, is also eaten. This complaint is said to have come from the coast. A similar operation is very often carried out by the Galla, who in cases of inflammation of the larynx and of the respiratory organs tear of the uvula with a with thread[2].

A usage about which I have very incomplete notes and which is therefore recorded with great reserve is as follows: when a child is from one to two years old, in the case of stronger children perhaps earlier, some of his teeth are taken out, the motive being to prevent by this means the pain which accompanies the cutting of teeth. The operation is performed with a needle and is carried out by an old man with special experience of such things. Of course these teeth are afterwards replaced by the growth of the layer of teeth below them. According to the Akamba the Akikuyu do the same thing, but I have not found any mention of it in the accounts which have been written about this tribe.

An arrow, especially one with barbs, which is fixed in a fleshy part of the body, is, when it is possibly to do so, taken out by knocking it through to the other side.

Fresh and smooth wounds are treated as follows: The edges of the wounds are pressed against each other, after which thin acacia thorns are stuck through the edges on both sides. The thorns are placed in pairs, across each other. Then the whole thing is tied round with cord. The method of procedure, which as a matter of fact shows a close resemblance to the newest methods of treating wounds, is probably the same as is practised by the Akambas' neighbours, the Masai[3].

A remedy for wounds made with poisoned arrows is in many

---

[1] Diminutive of *wɪmə* 'tongue'.

[2] Paulitschke, Ethnographie Nordost-Afrikas I, p. 184.

[3] Given in detail by M. Merker, Die Masai, p. 190.

cases a powerful sucking-out, which is preceded by binding tightly above and below the wounded place, if it is so situated that a binding of this sort is possible. In addition they also usually rub the blood of a newly-killed sheep on the wound and place parts of the intestines of the sheep on it. The wounded man is given urine of women to drink. We shall say something more about the Akamba's poison for arrows later.

An account of the treatment of snake-bite has already been given in the preceding chapter. It may be added here that for a python bite the dried excrement of the animal is eaten; it is said to be like a greyish kind of stone.

The occasional practice of opening a corpse, to try to establish the cause of death (see p. 157), might possibly be considered as a primitive stage of pathological anatomy.

*

The most usual remedy for headache is to fasten a cord or a wire tightly round the head[1]. Primitive people are very well aware of the power of a circular pressure to alleviate pain. For plants as remedies for headache see below (p. 314).

One often sees a native, wrapped in his blanket, lying on the ground exposed to the rays of the sun and thereby inducing perspiration. This is a prevalent method in Africa of curing fever (ndetæma). Malaria is common in certain parts of Ukamba, especially in the lower and hotter districts in the east, from Mumoni to Kibwezi, although the attacks of fever seem to be of a very mild character. The thin and somewhat worn appearance which so many of the natives have is no doubt due, to a great extent, to malaria. The medicine for fever will be discussed p. 319.

It is considered bad for sick people to drink cold water. As, however, they are often very thirsty, they are given a sort of gruel made of fresh milk or water and millet flour. It is drunk warm, considered very refreshing, and can be taken during any illness.

---

[1] A wire around the head is sometimes used as a pure ornament. I have seen no evidence to support the statement of a German traveller who says that the wire used in this way severely deforms the skull and causes an elevation of the vertex. A. Kaiser, Die wirtschaftl. Entwickelung der Ugandabahn-länder, Globus 1907, p. 53.

2. Medicines.

a. External injuries.

By far the greatest number of medicines are taken from the plant world, as the reader has already seen, and the word for 'plant, tree', *muti*, also means 'medicine'. I give here, beneath the different illnesses for which they are used, the medicinal plants I got to know among the Akamba[1]. The collection, which, when nothing is said to the contrary, comes from Machakos and the places closest to it, should be pretty complete for this district.

For fresh wounds: The milky sap of the plant *ilumbu* (Calotropis procera) is rubbed on the wound (Ikutha). A yellow lichen (*wæmea wa itula*) is crushed and placed on the wound, which is then covered with leaves and bandaged. Or the wound is washed with the juice of the roots and leaves of *kịo*, crushed together with sweet potatoes.

For burns: The brown »floss» from the spadices on the *ikaŋga* (Typha sp.) is placed on the wound. The leaves of *musu* (Cajanus indicus) are chewed and the saliva is placed on the wound (cf. further p. 124). Small children especially often get burned, as they easily fall in the fire when running around in the hut.

For a sore in the mouth the leaves of the *mutata* (Spilanthus) are chewed.

For tumours (*mwimbu*): In boils and tumours a hole is cut and the powdered leaves or roots of *mutula wa aumɔ* (Jasminum) are sprinkled in the wound (Muutha, East Ukamba).

For other swellings roots of *kabila wimbu* (cf. *mwimbu* 'tumour') are chewed and placed as a poultice on the swollen place. Or else leaves of the tree *mutanda-mbọ* are taken

---

[1] My ethno-botanical material from Ukamba, some hundreds of pressed plants, have been handed over to the botanical department of the Swedish State Museum. They are not yet defined, so that I cannot give the scientific names of the plants here. The names inserted have been kindly given by Prof. N. G. Lagerheim and Dr. H. Dahlstedt. Of about 40 medicinal plants I have also gathered and dried a sufficient quantity or a chemical analysis, which has, however, not yet taken place.

and put in a cloth bag which is placed near the fire. When it is well warmed, the bag is placed on the swelling (cf. our treatment with poultice). The long lianlike roots of *mukaẓaṳ*, a small tree, are crushed into a powder, which, mixed with fat or water, is rubbed on the swollen place. For swellings on the arms or legs they also use the sap found in the bark and inside the little tree *ɩlawa* or *mulawa* (Corchoras). The bark is crushed and the sap (*ɩlænda*) rubbed on the swelling.

For wounds and tumours they often use, at least in Kitui, certain powdered minerals and also excrement of poultry.

For hip-disease (*ɩkɩkɩ*) an incision is made in the hip and in the wound is strewn a powder made of an ostrich-leg[1] and roots of *mukawa* and leaves of *mutula*. The same powder is also mixed in water, which is given to the patient to drink. They also use leaves and roots of the little tree *mukæŋgaka* (Leguminosae sp.).

Women who have pain in their nipples (*nondo*) drink a decoction of the base of the leaves of the wild banana (Musa Livingstonia).

For itching they use *kẓuɓɩ*, a tall Rumex, which grows on the banks of rivers. The sap in its thick roots is placed in water, which is rubbed on the itching place.

For »pain in the ear» (in most cases probably due to inflammation in the outer acoustic duct) they use the sap in the stalk of the *kɩwa kɩa nduə*, an epiphytic orchid (Kibwezi).

For eye-affections (without closer analysis) they use several plants. The leaves of the bush *munaþa* are crushed and put on the affected eye.

In the same way are used the leaves of the fern *uþiu* and the leaves of the plant *luta* (with big lipshaped flowers), the sap of which is dropped into the eye. Finally the little tree *kɩɓasẓuŋgu* is said to have a great power in stopping pain in the eyes. Its branches are put in water overnight and the following day they are used as tubes to blow their sap into the affected eye.

To stopp pain in the eye they use the sap in the big potato-like tubers of the roots of the plant.

---

[1] Perhaps sympathetic magic? The ostrich has particularly strong legs.

b. Internal diseases.

For headache: From the leaves of the bush *muƃea* (Combretum) a powder is prepared with which the forehead is rubbed. The Wasuaheli, who call the bush *mkomango*, rub the same powder on wounds.

For heart-disease I have obtained only one remedy: a decoction of the roots of the spiny *mutumbu* bush is drunk by the invalid.

For illness in the liver (*ɪtæma*) the juice of the aloe is drunk. It is said to cause vomiting. Another method is to lick the arrow poison.

For illness in the »spleen» (*wasɪunŋgu*) they drink a decoction of the herb *kɪa mata*, in Kibwezi a decoction of the leaves of the bush *kɪtuŋgu*. They also use the roots of the herb *muƥəkæpə*. It also appears that they make an incision in the spleen, and then strew powder of the first-named plant in the wound.

The remedies for stomach affections seem most numerous of all, but in many cases I have been unable to get the character of the illness precisely described. For diarrhœa (*wɪtao*), however, they use: *kɪo* (Verticillatæ), the sap of the fleshy leaf of which is mixed with water and drunk; *musoka*, the sap of the leaf of which is used in the same way (Kitui); and *mwɪanžoṵ*, the roots of which are made into a decoction and drunk. Bananas are also eaten for diarrhœa.

For constipation: the bark of the *ɪtula* is crushed and added to water, which is then drunk; a decoction of the herb *kalaḵu* is drunk (when its leaves are chewed the saliva is coloured red).

A person who has eaten too much chews the leaves of the spiny *muƥunžɪ* bush.

Stomach-ache: The natives often have peculiar expressions for stomach-ache and other ailments of the stomach, such as »something is eating me inside» or »I have a snake in my stomach». This way of speaking seems to have nothing to do with black magic, nor do the Akamba believe, contrary to numerous other tribes, in any sort of spirit, which is incarnated in the form of an animal and enters human bodies[1]. But according to an old belief each person is created with a snake in his stomach, and

---

[1] Various proofs of this conception are given by M. Bartels in Die Medizin der Naturvölker, p. 21.

when one belches it is that which gives the sound within one.
It is possible that tape-worms have given rise to this idea. The
statement that I also had from the natives to the effect that when
drinking water they sometimes get a sort of worm in the stomach,
which can grow considerably afterwards, seems improbable. A
decoction of the roots of *ɪp*æa *utuka* (Amaranthaceæ) is drunk
for »snake in the stomach», so that it should die. In Muutha
(East Ukamba) they chew the leaves of the bush *kasɪbu* (*ɪsɪbu*),
which have a bitter taste, something like horse-radish.

For »a sore in the stomach» they drink a decoction of the
leaves of *mutata* (Spilanthus — cf. »mouth-sore», above).

Finally the following plants are used for »pain in the stomach» without more precise definition:

a decoction of the leaves of the bush *mutula wa aumɔ* (Jasminum) is drunk and also rubbed outside the abdomen; a decoction
of the leaves of *kɪluma mata mamu*, of the herb *mulaɓutɪa* or of
the little bush *mwạma* is also drunk. The last-mentioned is also
mixed with leaves of *kɪ̣ulu* and *muɓaɓa* (Compositæ).

For fever (*ndetæmạ*) I have found comparatively few remedies: a decoction of the leaves of the little tree *mukɪnɪ̣æɪ̣* is kept
in a cool place and drunk early in the morning; it is said to
produce vomiting.

The clusters of flowers of the tall plant *muŋgaɪmu* (Hyptis)
are treated and used in the same way; likewise a decoction of
the roots of the *muɓaŋganɪ̣a* bush. In Muutha they also used
the roots of the *mukumutɔ*. This medicine, which is said to cause
vomiting, is too strong for children. Finally they are also accustomed in cases of fever to rub the body with a decoction of the
leaves of the little tree *muɓạ* (Leguminosæ).

For a cough (*ukoa*)[1] many plants are used: they smell the
flowers of *mumetu* or *mulama*, chew the bark of the little *muɓwɪ̣a*
bush, the vanilla-scented roots of *muɓukulwa* or roots of the herb
mukænɪ̣a (Leguminosæ).

---

[1] Hofmann has in his dictionary *ukoa wa mbua*, which he translates by 'asthma'. I do not try to explain the etymology of the Kamba
names of sicknesses, but very probably they express something characteristic for an illness, the symptoms which are most striking to the
natives.

Whooping-cough, according to the statement of Herr Säuberlich, missionary in Mulango, is a not infrequent illness among children. In Ikutha it is said that as a remedy for it they shave the crown of the child's head, whereas in other cases, as we have seen, they prefer to let the hair grow during illness.

For a cold the leaves of *mukandu* (Verticillatæ) are stuffed in the nostrils.

For hoarseness they chew the roots of the creeper *muб̣olo* (Sapindaceæ) or those of *kaб̣ıla wımbu*.

For shortness of breath (asthma?) a decoction of the leaves of *mutanda-mbọ* is drunk.

For catarrh of the throat the roots of *ıwa ḷaka* (Clematis sp.) are chewed. A remedy obtained from the animal world is *mbweṗ̣a*, the nest (chrysalis?) of a certain insect (built of slime). These are powdered and mixed in water and the patient has to drink this.

For obstruction in the nose the root of the *mutı mukụ* tree is burnt. The patient, whose head is covered with a blanket, inhales the smoke through his nose.

Finally there are a large number of plants, of which I have found no more precise indication of their use than that it was for »pain in the chest». The roots of *kılıa mbıtı* (Jatropha sp.), which is considered so poisonous that many people will not even touch the plant with their hands, are powdered and mixed in the gruel which the patients drinks; it is also mixed with the powdered roots of *mwokḷa* (Plumbago), or these are chewed by themselves. The roots of *kḷua* (Hypericum sp.) are also chewed (Kitui), similarly those of the little *mukaḷaụ* tree. The bark of the *kısemæḷ* tree is chewed. Of the bark of the *ıtuası* tree is made a decoction which is drunk, similarly with the leaves of *mutula* (*ηdulu*) and a hot decoction of the leaves (with a burning taste) of *ıб̣oб̣otwə* (Capparis); a decoction of the seeds of the wild pepperplant (*muṗulụ*); a decoction of the berries of *wusua*, a low, spiny Asparagus. In Muutha they eat the powdered roots of the *mwalandaṗə* tree, added to water or food.

I do not know of any Kamba remedies for sexual diseases. They seem ·happily to be rare, and as far as I know the Kamba language has no expression for them (cf. the preceding chapter on *makwa*). Syphilis occurs, however, in East Ukamba, and during my stay at the mission station at Mulango the natives often came there to seek a cure for it.

For methods of abortion, which is now and then practised by young girls, see p. 38.

To remedy a s c a r c i t y o f m i l k in women who are suckling their children they use especially plants with a milky sap, some at least of which are certainly of an exclusively magic application, an instance of the old saying »like cures like». Thus they use the milky sap of the plants *kınosȥa nɗæŋgɔ*, *kıŋændıa nɗæŋgɔ* (Asclepias) and *muɓwa ıȥa* (*ıȥa* 'milk'). A decoction of *kamwelȥa* (Croton?) is drunk hot. In addition they use the long root-stock, similar to horse-radish, of the plant *mwilıa* (Asclepias). As we shall see later, the same or similar plants are used for scarcity of milk in cows and goats.

An illness, the character of which I could not understand, but which is said to be very severe and contagious and often causes rapid death, is *kȥaȥı*. It is said that the blood rushes out of the nose, mouth and even the ears of the patient. According to the statement of some people the illness is due to the heart (*ŋgo*) and the kidneys (*mbıo*), according to others it feels like a »fire in the stomach». It is stated that it can be cured. For it they drink a decoction of the leaves of *kıɓȥu* or of roots of *muɓındaɓındı* or *kıluma* (Aloe sp.). They also drink for this illness the blood of poultry and sheep or sheep's urine.

*

So far we have abstained from putting the question: who are the doctors among the Akamba? To a great extent, of course, it is the medicine men, who besides their magic remedies also use real cures. But the art of healing is not a monopoly of the medicine men, for besides them there is another class more worthy of the name of doctors, although even their knowledge is, of course, mixed with magic and superstition. To this class belong those persons who have no kind of official position, but who have learnt to know and to use a quantity of medicinal plants. Just as in the preceding chapter we learnt of specialists in methods of purification so these men are easily specialists in one or other of some few illnesses. Such a person was, to take an example, Mbonge at Machakos, a middle-aged man. His special ne was stomach ailments, for which he used partly powdered parts of plants, partly whole roots, which the sick people had to chew. One of his medicines consisted of powder made of the plants *mwimesіa muꝑіetі* and *muɓuaɓuį.*

＊   ＊
＊

About plants in magic and medicine see Chap. XVI: 1 (botany). An account of the remedies and medicines for diseases among cattle will be given in the chapter on the Akamba's domestic animals.

Chap. XVI. **Natural history.**

1. **Botany.**

If we consider what has already been said about the use of plants in magic and medicine, we have to acknowledge that the Akamba have names for and use a great number of plants, and consequently we can say with justice that they possess a certain botanical knowledge, based on the observation of surrounding nature possessed by a primitive people, which, even though sometimes led astray by superstition, is on the whole extraordinarily quick. We shall deal later with the numerous plants that are used in practical life.

Although the Akamba thus know a great quantity of plants, yet they are not infrequently uncertain about their names and they dispute between each other about these. To some extent this uncertainty is due to the fact that a certain plant sometimes has more than one name or is called differently in different parts of the country.

In my linguistic material I shall discuss the meanings of the plant-names. They usually indicate some characteristic of the plant, or are based on its use, e. g.

ɪ̨pæa utuḳu 'that which shines at night', a plant belonging to the Amarantaceæ family; its white flowers are visible in the dark.

kaɓɪla wɪmbu (*ɓɪla* 'to shut', *wɪmbu* 'swelling'). The roots, when chewed and laid on a swelling, stop it.

The natives distinguish to a certain extent families and species, so that plants that even botanically ignorant Europeans would perhaps not recognize as species of the same family are given the same (family) name, e. g.:

kɪ̨æɓa, Loranthus sp. with yellow flowers.

kɪ̨æɓa kɪla mutun̩ɔ 'the red *kɪ̨æɓa*', Loranthus with red flower.

kɪluma, Aloe. *kɪluma kɪla kɪ̨a wæo* 'the aloe of the plain' is a smaller species, growing out on the steppe.

The part played by plants in magic.

We have seen at various places in the preceding work that the vegetable kingdom plays an important part in the Kamba people's rites and magic. In many cases the explanation of this seems fairly obvious and is to be sought in, among other things, the striking appearance of a certain plant. This is the case, for instance, with the wild fig-tree with its imposing size and its magnificent green foliage; in addition it also contains milky sap. Other plants with a copious milky sap are favourite remedies for scarcity of milk in women and cattle (homeopathic magic). Occasionally the thing that determines the use of a plant is some small, quite unimportant detail, such as the black pupil-like spot on the Euphrasia, which has given rise to the well-known belief that these plants are good for the eyes. Or else the explanation is to be found in the appearance ef the plant, as, for instance, in the case of the Loranthus species mentioned below, which cannot fail to attract attention when they grow on a tree quite different in appearence from themselves.

For these or similar reasons, which are, as a matter of fact, universal, the Akamba have chosen the plants they use in their magic. Unfortunately I have to content myself with giving the following plants without any explanation of the reasons why they are used.

muɓolo (Sapindaceæ). The medicine men prepare from its leaves a decoction which they give to possessed people as a drink or with which they wash them.

mutæɓɔ (Sapindaceæ). A person who has caught an illness through black magic on the part of an enemy takes a handful of Eleusine seeds and throws them three times against this tree (cf. p. 241). The roots of the same plant are made into a powder with which the sick person's hands and head are smeared. If a man loves a girl who prefers another, he takes a little bit of *mutæɓɔ*-wood and carries it to a worker in magic, who treats the piece of wood with medicine. It is then placed at the entrance of the favoured rival's hut, who will then soon cease to care for the girl.

wanẓa seems to be a Cactus species, 0.5—1 dm. long, with star-shaped, brown, malodorous flowers. Together with other plants it is used in black magic to bewitch people.

muluɪlambɪa or *muluambɪla* (Malvaceæ). As we have already seen, this plant is used to make the stick with which the medicine man's music-bow is struck, and also for the miniature arrows used by the novices during the second circumcision. When the cattle will not eat, »but stand with their heads in the air» (are constipated?), the animals' bellies are struck with *muluɪlambɪa*-twigs.

mukulwa (Acalypha). Twigs of this little tree or bush are used, as we have already seen, to strike the *kɪpɪtu* with when an oath is taken on this, and also in the construction of the above-mentioned miniature arrows.

mu6ʒa wa nǒɪ (mentioned on p. 266). If several babies die in a family, the parents naturally go to the medicine man to find out the reason. He perhaps says that it is due to the father of the child and gives him a decoction of this plant to drink. In the case of one person who was pointed out to me the medicine man shaved off all the hair round the private parts and then washed his penis with this decoction, declaring that »now the child would not die». If cattle have miscarriages (*ku6una*), they too are given this »medicine» to drink.

kɪ6o6otwə (Capparis). During protracted rain twigs of this bush are put in the fire to make the rain stop.

kɪpaŋga mwæo, a creeper (Leguminosæ). The red seeds with black spots are often used by the medicine men for making amulets, etc.

kɪ6ɪlu. A species of the same genus as the preceding plant, and used in the same way.

upuko is a plant with a little, light-blue corona. A man who wishes to gain a girl's love smears the plant with magic medicine (*mupæa*) and then stretches it out in the direction of the girl's village, probably uttering some sort of incantation.

ŋguŋgu, the large, button-shaped, darkly veined seeds of the *mukuŋgu* tree, are worn as a sort of amulet, or rather medicine, for pain in the back. It is enough if a single seed is threaded on a string, which is fastened round the waist.

kɪæ6a (Loranthus) is used by the medicine men in the preparation of love-medicine, especially in the magic remedies they prepare for the young men when they are about to ask for a girl in marriage. Parasites and such things, plants growing on other trees, are very much sought after by the medicine men.

mwaį̈ is a tree from the roots of which is prepared a powder which procures favour from women.

munᶻu (Umbelliferæ). One ought to avoid using this bush for fuel, as its smoke is considered injurious to the eyes. »The woman who comes home with *munᶻu* wood gets beaten by her husband», I was told. The smoke is also said to make mens' testes swell and to cause abortion in pregnant goats (small cattle are kept in the hut during the night).

mukaų. A tree with pinnate leaves, two-lobed folioles. Its wood may not be used for fires, for if the smoke gets into people's eyes, they quarrel. Hunting parties, especially, avoid using this wood for their camp-fires. Muutha, Eastern Ukamba.

kıбáᶻ, a small thorny tree with very small white flowers. If it is used as fuel and the smoke gets into the eyes, they become diseased. Muutha.

A considerable number of plants are used in **purification ceremonies**, and we add the following *ɣondu*-plants to the list already given (p. 296):

muþıtu (Leguminosæ). A bush from which in Kikumbuliu *ɣondu* is made for sprinkling a newly-married wife, when she enters her husband's home for the first time.

mukæɣgæsᶻa (Commelynaceæ), a plant which puts out its yellow flowers at the beginning of the rainy season. A person who has eaten »bad food», for instance in a village before it has been purified after a death, rinses his or her mouth with *ɣondu* made from this plant.

muþumba, a low bush with white flowers.

kınosᶻa, »the plant that makes (people) fat»[1]. A person suffering from excessive thinness (*umosu*) and general debility is smeared with *ɣondu* made from the roots of this plant.

ıua mbumbu (Phytolaceæ). Is considered exceedingly poisonous and is used by girls to procure abortion (p. 38). Sometimes a native secretly gives twigs of it to his enemy's cattle. According to the natives it is only necessary for an animal to eat a single leaf of it to die. Perhaps this is a case of pure poisoning, but it is usually combined with magic elements as well, so that it may be more certain in its effect.

---

[1] *kunosᶻ*, causat. form < *kunoa* 'to become fat'.

2. **Zoology.**

As is to be expected of a people who, even if they cannot be called a hunting people in the real sense of the term, are yet occupied a great deal in hunting, the Akamba show that they have a quick sense of observation for animal life and a good acquaintance with the habits of animals, especially in the case of such as can be hunted. But even quite insignificant animals, such as small insects, from which, at least as far as one can see, they get neither good nor harm, come within the scope of their observation, and they have pondered.over and tried to explain this and that, a distinguishing feature of a certain insect, often a little detail only perceived with difficulty. Their stories and riddles show this especially. It is true that these explanations of causes are really most often only humorous, but this does not, of course, take away from their character of being the result of a good power of observation.

I shall publish my collection of animal names, like that of plant names, in connection with the result of my linguistic investigations. I may just briefly mention here that many names of wild animals denote some characteristic, at least according to the natives' opinion, of the animal. Examples of this are given below; thus we have the names of the gerenuk (Lithocranius), the little rat *kaɪlwa nɪ nɪ̈ɪa* and the snake *kɪ̈ændɑ ndæto*. Other names are purely onomatopoetic, as *ɪɣoɪ* 'donkey', *kamaɪ̈* 'kind of wild cat', *ɪmɑ* 'sheep' (a word sometimes used by women; otherwise 'sheep' is *ɪlondʉ*), *kɪkwaə* 'francolin' (its cry is *kwarre, kwarre*).

Some indications may be given of the way in which families and species are distinguished.

All fishes, as far as I know, have the same name (*ɪkuɪ̈u*), which is perhaps due to the fact that the Akamba do not catch fish, as they do not eat it. The country is also poor in rivers with fish in them.

Butterflies are all called *kɪmbalutwa*, whatever kind they may be. On the other hand, the natives distinguish between hairy and smooth caterpillars (*ɪamu* and *kɪnɪ̈u* respectively).

A great many beetles are all called *kɪɣolondo*, but there are also some with special names.

On the other hand one may also say that to a certain extent

there are names for different species. A dove is called *ɩɓuɨ̯*. *ɩɓuɨ̯ ɨ̯a kɨŋgulu* is a small turtledove. *ɩɓuɨ̯ ɨ̯a mbaɨ̯kɩ* is a larger species of turtledove ('the *ɩɓuɨ̯* of the Rhicinus seeds'), which is also called *ɨ̯a ŋguku* (black biting ants) or *ɩɓuɨ̯ ɨ̯a ŋgomoa* (the *ɩɓuɨ̯* of the fruits of the *mukumoa* tree). These names are clearly from the principal food of the bird. Other doves, on the other hand, are distinguished by their cry, such as the little *ɳdumbu* (its cry is *tu, tu*).

I have noted seven different kinds of lizards with different names, five kinds of locusts and in addition a special name (*ɱbandi*) for locusts in the hopper stage, and five kinds of ants.

We now proceed to describe the Akambas' ideas about various kinds of animals, in which, however, it has been very difficult to separate that which deserves the name of »zoology», and so I have included a certain number of superstitious conceptions in this description.

The lion, the Akamba think, does not eat liver, but always leaves it untouched, when it has killed an animal. Most old debilitated lions end their life by being killed and eaten by hyenas, who do not hesitate to attack a decrepit lion, when they are in a party of several.

The hyena is a hermaphrodite, an idea that Hollis found among the Nilotic Nandi east of Lake Victoria[1]. The great famine in East Africa at the end of the decade of 1890, when the natives died in great numbers, was a golden age for the hyenas, and they were at that time especially numerous and bold. Thus by means of throwing a corpse they were able to bring down a person who had tried to save himself by climbing up a tree several metres above the ground (!). The Akamba detest the hyena more than other animals, probably· because it eats their dead bodies, and many cannot be made to touch a dead hyena, so that it is exceedingly difficult, not to say impossible, to get them to skin one. Other East African tribes, such as the Nandi, on the other hand, show a certain respect for the hyena, and among the Masai it is considered as a sign from the Ngai that a dead person has been good, if his body, when placed out, is eaten the very first night by the hyenas[2]. The Wanyika even

---

[1] A. E. Hollis, The Nandi, their Language and Folklore, p. 7.
[2] Merker, Die Masai, p. 201.

have a veritable hyena worship. In the Akambas' folklore the hyena plays an important part, appearing in it as the personification of foolishness. Its voracity is also ridiculed and often caricatured.

The *kɪɡala-ɡala* or *kɪkoɔo* is a large beast of prey, »something between a lion and a leopard». No one I have met seems to have any more exact idea about the animal.

A more mysterious animal is *ɲgɪkwa*, which is said to be »spotted like a leopard» and to have »a tail and a head like a jackal, although it is somewhat larger than the latter». It lives among reeds and thickets along the rivers and is only dangerous to women, as it sometimes steals into the villages and kills some of them in order to have coitus with them and to suck the victim's blood. After this is done its strews sand in the women's mouth and genitals. Goats are also said to be treated in the same way.

The two last-named animals give me an opportunity to add that there is much to indicate that there are mammals still unknown, and even considerably large ones, in East Africa. Mr Hobley has collected a number of statements of trustworthy persons concerning such animals, and some of these stories are exceedingly interesting, as, among other things, they include such sensational possibilities as the existence of a new anthropoid ape in the bush along the Tana River and a kind of great lake animal in Lake Victoria and the rivers flowing into it[1].

It is thought that the elephant cannot die a natural death, a belief that has quite certainly arisen from the length of its life as shown by practical experience. It is also one of the wisest of all animals. When an elephant has been stung by bees, it returns at night to be avenged, pulls down the beehive and buries it in the earth. Many native elephant hunters, who have had to seek refuge in a porcupine hole or some other cavity in the ground, are said to have been killed by the pursuing elephant having seized with his trunk a long stick and tried to kill the hunter by thrusting it into the hole, then filling the latter with earth.

The elephant often appears in stories, but here, curiously enough, it does not maintain its reputation for wisdom but is often beaten by small and weak opponents. This is perhaps due

---

[1] C. V. Hobley, On some unidentified beasts. The Journal of the East Africa and Uganda Natural History Society, vol. III, p. 48.

to the tendency of the natives to let the weaker parties in the story generally come off with the victory, usually by means of trickery and shrewdness.

The *gerenuk* (Lithocranius) is called *kawıla mıą* by the Akamba, which means 'the little giraffe that eats the fruit of the *mwą* tree' (the *mwą* is a species of acacia[1]). When it is followed by beasts of prey it is said to climb up into a bush or a tree to escape its pursuers, a belief that is naturally derived from the fact that the gerenuk sometimes sets up on its hind legs in order to get at high berries or leaves.

Baboons are cordially hated by the natives because of the harm they do in the fields. These monkeys are so alert and cunning that it is not so easy to surprise them, and the killing of a baboon is therefore a happy event for the negro. In one case they have to be careful not to shoot them, however favourable an opportunity may present itself, and that is when they are out hunting. For a person who shoots a baboon may be pretty sure that he will not succeed in shooting any other animal that day. Elephants hunters like the Akamba especially are naturally disposed not to spoil their luck in hunting, when it is a question of big game. Professor E. Lönnberg made the same observations during his East African expedition.[2]

The natives state that on occasion the baboons carry of babies. When the women work in the fields, they usually put their babies aside under a shady tree so as to be more free. Various children are said to have been stolen by baboons under such circumstances and have disappeared for ever. Some of them are said to grow up among the monkeys, live their lives and propagate among them. I have not come across among the Akamba the rather obvious and frequently encountered idea (found, for instance, among the Wadjagga) that the baboons are human beings that have grown wild and degenerated.

There are several sorts of hares in these parts, but the nat-

---

[1] I have had occasion to see gerenuks in »the bush» west of Tana, which involuntarily made one think of giraffes. Cf. E. Lönnberg, Mammals collected by the Swedish Zoological Expedition to British East Africa 1911. Sv. Vet.-Akad. Handl. 48: 5, Stockholm 1912, p. 172.

[2] E. Lönnberg, Några exempel från Ost-Afrika på övertro rörande djur. Fataburen 1911, p. 245.

ives call them all by a common name. The Akamba say that when
the cattle are out grazing the hares often come up quietly and
steal the cows' milk away; i. e. suck them, an idea that is found
among various other African tribes. All over the world the hare
is an important animal in belief and practice and the negroes consider him to be the most cunning of all animals. In the animal
fables of the Bantu peoples he is most frequently the principal
character, corresponding to the jackal among the Hottentots, or,
to take an example nearer home, Reineke Fuchs in the German
animal stories, Reynard the Fox with the English. As has already
been mentioned, the hyena is opposed to the hare in the animal
stories as the representative of folly, and it is outrageously cheated
by the hare into committing a multitude of follies. Why the hare
should be considered as so specially intelligent, seems inexplicable
to me. The well-known and now deceased Bishop Steere of Zanzibar questioned his Wasuaheli friends about this, and obtained
the answer: »Just look at the hare: his mouth is continually
moving, as if he had something to say about everything»[1].

When walking along the paths in the Kamba country, one
cannot avoid seeing every now and then a little rat dart a good
bit in front of one on the road. The rat is called by the natives
kailwa ni nźia, literally 'the little one that is sent back by the
road'. For it is said that this creature never crosses a road; if
it were to do so, it would certainly die.

Certain birds of prey — I have forgotten which — are said
to be very keen on ostrich eggs. But as they are often unable
to peck a hole in them with their bills, they take stones in their
claws and let them drop down on the eggs, thus cracking them.

Some more birds that are the subjects of superstition may be
mentioned here. Many of the Akamba will not kill the *ilumi*, a
big hornbill, black with white on the wings and a red hanging
piece of flesh beneath its beak. In Taveta at the foot of Kilimandjaro I have seen this bird walking fearlessly on the ground
in the immediate neighbourhood of human beings, as the Wataweta
universally consider it disastrous to kill it. There is no doubt
that this security is due to the birds peculiar cry, a soft, hollow
hm, hm. The Akamba call him *ilumi* 'he who yells'.

---

[1] E. Steere, Suaheli Tales, London 1891 (Preface).

ŋguŋə, the shadow stork (Scopus umbretta) is a brown bird of medium size, which builds an enormous nest in trees. It is not killed, they will not even dare to climb up the tree where it has built. If one does so, one gets the illness called *musalə*, which consists of sores breaking out on the body, round the mouth, on the feet, etc. Another bird that is not killed is the *ŋδιǣ*, the ox-pecker (Buphaga), which takes ticks from the cattle and is considered to be very useful. When the cattle go astray, one hears its cry, *tjwi, tjwi,* and then it is only necessary to follow this. The Akamba often put milk and fat out for these birds, and if they succeed in catching any in their nests, they give them food, and fasten a ˈred ribbon round their legs and then let them go. The bird is said to bring wealth, if it is well treated; on the other hand anyone who kills it becomes a poor man.

Many of the Akamba believe that the python (*ιtʠ*) breeds all reptiles. When they are very small all the young ones look the same, and their mother keeps them in the same place. When they have grown a little, she steals away and then creeps along un-perceived and starts buzzing. Most of the young ones are then afraid and run away, a few, perhaps only one or two, are braver and remain. These few then grew up into pythons, while the rest have to be content to be smaller snakes, lizards, etc.

The *sιomelulιa* is a snake that is often met with near Kamba villages. It is also called *kιǣndǫ ndǣto* 'he who likes words', because it is said to creep along to the huts to listen to what people are saying, a belief that has presumably arisen from the fact that this snake is usually found in the proximity of the huts. It is said to be harmless; if it bites anyone, it is due to magic.

A very big snake, said to be bigger than the python, is the *ιaιpa*. I have not obtained any description of its appearance; it is possibly quite a mythical animal. But it is not improbable that it is only a case of an unusually big python, especially as the estimate of a snake's length is, of course, always exaggerated.

Another common smaller species of snake is the *ŋguluku*, 0.5 metre long, with dark and grey stripes running along the back, a narrow rusty brown stripe on one side and a yellowish-white belly. It is said to gather together small stones or the yellow globular fruit (*ŋgondu*) of a previously-mentioned Solanum species (*kιkondu*) and then watch over these treasure suspiciously. He who finds them and succeeds in getting possession of them will be a rich man. This is, however, a risky undertaking, as the snake-owner will untiringly pursue the thief to kill him, »though he go as far as Mombasa» [1].

This refers, presumably, to the snake's eggs, although it seems improbable that such a small species of snake should have such large eggs. The eminent authority on the Wadjagga, the missionary Gutmann, relates exactly the same conception among them, but in this case it is the python that is referred to, which seems a good deal more probable. B. says: Wie ein spielendes kind sammelt sie (the python) die gelben pflaumengrossen früchte eines nachtschattengewächses. Das sind ihre kühe, die sie eifersüchtig bewacht. Gelingt es aber in einem unbewachten augenblick eine der früchte zu stehlen, so wird man ein besitzer grosser herden werden». B. then adds very rightly that this is a false conception of the correctly observed fact that the python hatches its eggs by means of the warmth of its own body and at the approach of a human being is terrified for the safety of its progeny [2].

The *kıpı* is a dark grey blindworm, 25—30 cm. long, in which, as in all Typhlops species, it is exceedingly difficult to distinguish between head and tail. The Akamba think that the snake has two heads. Gutmann states the same about the Wadjagga, adding that this belief appears to be spread over the whole of East Africa [3]. According to Brehm the natives of the west coast of Africa and of India, and also many European colonists in these places, believe that the snake really has two heads [4].

The chameleon is believed to creep on to guinea-hens and other birds and thrust its long tongue round the bird's neck. No matter how it runs or flies, the chameleon holds fast, until the bird dies of hunger. He then waits near by until flies come and worms are formed. These are what he wants and so he kills the bird. The chameleon is shunned and hated among most of the Bantu peoples, and they kill him by putting snuff in his mouth.

---

[1] Paulitschke (Ethnographie Nordostafrikas II, p. 27) mentions a similar belief from the Somalis.

[2] B. Gutmann, Dichten und Denken der Dschagga-neger, p. 39.

[3] B. Gutmann, Die Fabelwesen in den Märchen der Wadschagga. Globus 1907, p. 243.

[4] Brehm, Tierleben (1913) 5, p. 263.

The reason for this cruel treatment is the previously described, well-known and widespread myth about the origin of death among the children of men (p. 253).

As fish are considered to be closely related to snakes, the Akamba, like so many other Bantu peoples, do not eat fish. I remember very vividly a day when for once in a way I had succeeded in catching some small fish. I and one of my servants, who had for a long time worked for Europeans and in this way become accustomed to eat fish, were just about to have a proper meal, when the man's wife came to see him. She had a good hour's walk to my camp, and had not seen her husband for over a week. When she saw what he had in front of him she was so indignant that she at once turned back without as much as a word to him.

It has already been shown that the Akamba do not eat fish, because fish »are related to snakes». They do not care to eat porcupines or tortoises either. As is to be expected of a hunting people, the Akamba eat, apart from these, almost all wild animals, contrary to their neighbours in the west and south-west, the Akikuyu and Masai, who only in extreme need can be made to eat game. A person who does so is considered inferior. I remember a march out in »the bush», miles from the nearest native village. The provisions we had taken with us were nearly finished, and we had to maintain ourselves principally by hunting. Among the bearers there was also a Kikuyu, who for as long as possible avoided eating the game that was shot and consequently went half hungry for several days. At last he could hold out no longer, but, excusing himself on the ground that he was far away from his own country, away from all honour and honesty, he eat heartily of an Oryx antelope that had been shot.

Various animals, according to the Akambas' opinion, have the effect on arrow poison that if one shoots one of them, the poison loses all effect on other kinds of animals. As animals in this category I have noted Coke's hartebeest, the duiker (Cephalophus), the mole and the barn-door fowl.

Hunters have in addition a great many things to observe, especially regarding big game, elephants, rhinoceroses, etc.[1]

---

[1] See the account of »the magic power of names» on p. 258.

As soon as an elephant is killed the oldest and most experienced hunter runs forward and with his knife cuts off the end of the trunk, which he runs off with and hides in the bushes, so that the youngest members of the hunting party, who are on their first elephant hunt, shall not se it. I have myself had an opportunity of verifying this. A similar practice seems to be common — or has been common — among many Bantu tribes, such as the Wakami and the Amaxosa, both of which bury the trunk of the elephant when they are out hunting[1]. The real motive of this is not known to me, but it is quite clearly connected with the remarkable qualities of the trunk — the elephant's hand, as the Wadjagga call it — as a prehensile organ. When a female elephant was shot it was an old custom to cut off its dugs and hide them. It is said that they resemble the breasts of a woman; this is said to be specially the case if the female elephants has suckling young ones. Many people had such an aversion to the sight of the dugs that they would not partake of the animal if they had seen them.

Finally I may remind the reader of the ideas about animals that have been described earlier on in the chapter on totemism, religion and magic.

---

[1] Kay, Travels and Researches in Caffraria, p. 138.

Chap. XVII. Cosmology.

1. Meteorology.

Hail (*maßía* 'stones') is considered to be a favourable sign, denoting a good harvest. According to Hobley (Akamba, p. 54), on the other hand, »it is said to be a sign of shortness of rainfall».

Clouds (*matu*) and fog (*mumbɩ*) are smoke from the fire of the Creator (*mumbɩ*, p. 244). According to another view it is the smoke from the huts of mankind. »Cannot everyone see how the smoke rises up in the air in still weather?» To what extent the natives themselves believe in this and other explanations I must leave unsaid. In many cases one might compare them with, for instance, our talk of »the man in the moon». At the sight of a cloudless sky they are sometimes accustomed to say jokingly that »the newly-married wife had swept well», a way of speaking that is based on the custom (see p. 76) of a newly-married young wife getting up early on the first morning in her new home and sweeping the hut.

The rainbow (*utaßɩ*), lightning (*utɩsɩ*)[1] and thunder (*kɩtandalɩkɩ* or, when distant, *kɩtundumu*) are considered to have no special meaning. *n'undu wa mbua*, »these phenomena are connected with rain», they say. When the thunder rumbles at a distance they sometimes say: »X:s father is beating a skin», a humorous comparison with a man preparing a goatskin so as to make it into a dress for his wife. The rain is sent by Ngai (*mumbɩ*), who leads it out through a *mutau*, a dug-out channel such as the Akamba use for the irrigation of the fields. When Ngai stops this up, the dry season (*ßanu*) comes. In joking speech I have heard the rain called *mwana ɩnɩa wa mumbɩ* 'the sister of the fog'[2].

---

[1] < *tɩsa* = 1. to become visible (of the moon), 2. to lighten.
[2] The conception of the rainbow is given in chap. XIV, p. 274.

Those persons I asked did not know of any case, or were
not aware how people would act if anyone were struck by lightning. They were sceptical with regard to Hobley's statement
(Akamba, p. 55) that »if anyone is killed by lightning no one will
touch or move the body; the people say the person is killed by
God. If anyone does touch a person killed by lightning he or
she will also be struck».

2. **Astronomy.**

The stars are called *ndata*, which also (if it is really the
same word) means a stave, stick, often of the club-like type that
the young men are accustomed to carry in their hands when they
stroll about. Rev. W. E. Taylor in his Giryama Vocabulary gives
ndata 'a walking stick' as a Giriama name for the evening and
morning star, while »star» in general is called *nyenyezi*[1].

The Akamba call the evening star *ŋgæṇaṇḓi* (probably a
causative of *kæṇa* 'to become visible' and *ṇḓi* 'earth'). I have
not been able to ascertain the name of the morning star, but,
according to Hobley, it is called *kithioi*. It is thus certain that
the Akamba, like other Bantu peoples, do not know that these
two are one and the same planet.

Comets are also called *ndata*. They are omens of misfortunes, war, famine, rinderpest and other diseases. An expression I
have noted, *ndata ja kisipo* 'the star with the tail', doubtlessly
refers to some comet[2]. The natives tell of a comet, *ndata ja joa*
the star of famine', that appeared about 25 years ago (1888?).
This is probably identical with the one Merker talks of, namely
a clearly shining comet in the eighties which was soon followed
by severe epidemics among the cattle, rinderpest and lung diseases[3].

Falls of aerolites (also shooting stars?) are omens of disease
and epidemics. A place in which it is supposed that parts of a
meteor have fallen down is sprinkled by the *atumia* with *ŋondu*
from a goat that is taken to the place and killed there. In the

---

[1] See A. Werner, Note on Bantu Star-Names, Man 1912, p. 195.
W. gives and discusses the names of the stars among some tribes in
South and East Africa.

[2] The Bathonga call a comet »the star with the tail» (*nyeleti ya
nkila*). Junod, The Life of a South African Tribe II, p. 287.

[3] M. Merker, Die Masai, p. 206.

northern part of Ulu the purifying fluid is also sprinkled in rivers, so that people should not be affected injuriously when they drink the water.

Earthquakes appear to be rare in these parts, and I have not heard any mention of such things in Ukamba or got any name for them. Hobley calls them Engai (Ngai) and S. Watt in his Vocabulary of the Kikamba Language — apparently a constructed vocabulary to a great extent — »the trembling of the earth» (*utetæmo wa nði*)[1].

I may be allowed here to mention in parenthesis the only information I gathered about the Akamba's »geology», namely about the mountain crystal that is sometimes found among the quartz. They call it *maɓɪa ma ndata* 'stones from the stars', and believe that it has fallen down from heaven. The Akamba told the German missionary Gerhold that mica, which is fond in abundance here and there, is »pieces of God's clothing and falls down with the thunder»[2].

Sun (*sɪua*) and moon (*mwæɪ*). According to legends the sun and the moon were originally brothers, and the moon was the more important of the two and shone more brightly. But because of disobedience and a consequent curse of its parents it had to give up its position and with it its more brilliant light to its younger brother. The detailed account of how this took place will be given by me in a special work on the Akambas' folklore. The same story is found as far west as among the Pangwe people in the Cameroons[3].

When the sun goes down (*sɪua ɪaɓoa*) they say jokingly that it is going home to the village to eat supper.

Eclipse (*sɪua ɪaɓoɪɔ muɓænɪa*)[4]. They remember an eclipse, apparently from the end of the nineties, when a voice was heard

---

[1] According to Mr Hofmann, however, earthquakes are not uncommon in conjunction with subterranean noise. He experienced one of these (Evangelisch-Lutherisches Missionsblatt, p. 195) on Boxing Day, 1897, when the natives said: »It is Chumbe» (a spirit hill south-west of Kibwezi). In »Geburt, Heirat und Tod» (p. 24) he also says that when such subterranean rumbling took place the Akamba used to say: »Now the dead are allowed to go in to God».

[2] H. Gerhold, Wandertage in Nordost-Ukamba, p. 11.

[3] L. Frobenius, Der Ursprung der Afrikanischen Kulturen.

[4] Owing to some misunderstanding Hobley (p. 55) calls an eclipse Mumbi. Probably he had been told by the natives that it was the work of *mumbɪ* (the Creator).

to call from the sky: »Leave your huts and gather together with all the cattle at the *ɓomɔ!*» Every father of a family then killed a goat and sprinkled his household and his cattle with *ɣondu*. After this eclipse came smallpox (*nduɠu*), rinderpest, the formerly mentioned tumour-like epidemic *mwɪmu* (= rinderpest?), which attacked wild animals such as buffaloes and hartebeests, and a disease not known to me called *loaɣa*.

While the moon is »in the desert», i. e. during the two (three) days the moon is invisible, it is no use going out hunting, as one cannot then succeed in killing any game. A man called Kasong'a at Machakos was born during this period and some people say that because of this he is successful in hunting during this time, while others, on the other hand, deny this exception to the usual rule.

At the first glimpse of the new moon's fine sickle in the west they say that the moon is »visible to the horns of the cattle». This expression is somewhat obscure, but it is perhaps not incorrect to connect it with the old worship of the moon. In Western Asia and Europe people sacrificed cattle to the moon in former times. Cattle were thought to be a representation of the moon because of their horns [1].

A lunar halo is called *kɪɓuɣo*, which really means »threshing place», the hard, dry ground where the women thresh millet (< *ɓua* 'to beat, thresh').

At Kibwezi they spoke of the moon's sex and apparently of various moons, namely a male one (called *nðamba* 'male') and a female one (*muka* 'woman'), but I did not succeed in getting a more detailed explanation of this way of speaking. A male moon was said, however, not to give rain [2]. On a calabash shell that I

---

[1] E. Hahn, Von der Hacke zum Pflug, p. 61. E. Hahn, Demeter und Baubo, p. 23 ff.

[2] This distinction between a male and female moon reminds one rather naturally of the moon-goddess of Babylonian mythology, Istar, who had by her side the male moon-god Sin. Just as Istar alone was the symbol of fertility, so, according to the Akamba's belief, the male moon cannot bring the life-giving rain. The connection of the moon with cattle by the Akamba also makes us think of the Babylonians. It is too risky to draw any conclusions from these interesting analogies, but they are worth pointing out in case anyone should feel disposed to investigate the matter further.

obtained from a medicine man, who used it for beer-drinking, these two moons are carved (fig. 63). According to the medicine man's statement the straight stroke (a) represents the path of the moon, the three points along it (b) are stars; c is the moon in an earlier phase, d is the full moon and e a big star (the evening star?).

Fig. 63.   Natural size.

3. **Determination of time.**

By day the time is determined with great care and accuracy from the position of the sun.   During the night they listen especially to the cry of the cricket (*ŋgɩlɩ*), and when it grows silent they know that the morning is near.   Those who are going on a journey then get up.

ɩta mwaka is a Crinum sp. with splendid red flowers.   The name, which means »he who calls on the year (the rainy season)», has been given to the plant because, when its flowers develop, they know that the dry season is coming to its end and that the longed-for rain is near.

There is a method of using the direction of the sun at different periods of the year to calculate the arrival of the rainy season and the seasons in general.   By drawing directing lines over isolated trees or some similar objects from a place with a somewhat open view, for instance a level piece of ground on a farm, one finds roughly the place for the sun's farthest advance in the north, and similarly the point to which it goes in the south. A number of intermediate points are also fixed, especially the place where the sun is when the rainy season normally begins. Such a place of observation is called *kɩsɩæsɩo kɩa sɩua* 'the place where one often looks at the sun'[1].

When it is necessary to determine a point of time for something that happened in rather distant past time, remarkable events serve as a help to the memory and as a point of departure for

---

[1] < *kusɩæsɩa*, an iterative form of *kusɩsɩa* 'to look'.

calculating time. Such events are, above all, the famines that time and again have visited East Africa on account of continual drought. In Ikutha I have noted from native tradition a number of such famines, each of which has its special name, and I have attempted to fix the times when they occurred.

ɀoa ɀa *malakwə* (Kisuaheli *maharagwe*, beans of Phaseolus vulgaris, which is otherwise called by the Akamba *mbọso*): a famine in East Ukamba 1908—09, during which the chief food consisted of these beans, which were got from the better watered Ulu and also from the Kikuyu country.

ɀoa ɀa *muɓuɳga* 'the famine of the rice', the great and long famine of 1898—99, which visited a large part of East Africa. There was little to eat except the rice which was distributed by the missionaries and the government. It is also called ɀoɪa ɀa *ɳgalɪ* 'the famine of the waggon', because of the building of the Uganda railway, which was considered to be the cause of the absence of rain.

ɀoa ɀa *ndaṭa* 'the famine of the star': this famine, which has been mentioned before, probably occurred in 1888 at the same time as a comet appeared.

ɀoa ɀa *ɳgætælə* (< *kæta* or *kætæla* 'to bleed cattle'): the year is unknown. In order to supply the deficiency of food the cattle were bled.

ɀoa ɀa *ɳgoɓo* (< *ọɓa* 'to bind'): year uncertain. Many people went to remote districts to look for food, but when they returned with their burdens, it is said that they were attacked and bound in their weak state, and then the food was taken away from them.

ɀoa ɀa *kɪasa*: year uncertain. An exceptionally long period of drought during which rain clouds repeatedly accumulated only to disappear again.

ɀoa ɀæluɳgɪ (< *luɳgɪla* 'to increase'): year uncertain. First there was a smaller famine, during which they eat up all accessible supplies in the expectation of having the next harvest. Instead of this there came a still more severe and lasting famine.

ɀoa ɀa *ɪtɑ* 'the famine of the python', probably about the year 1850, as several men of between 40 and 50 said that their fathers were children at the time. Pythons were said to be un-usually numerous and came up to the villages, so that the people said that they were the cause of the famine.

ꭓoa ꭓa kuꞶ̣ɩkɩla mbua (see p. 11), the great famine in the thirties.

4. Seasons and months.

The year is called *mwaka*, which really, however, means only »raintime», of which there are as a matter of fact two in the year. The great rains (March—June), usually expected at the end of March but often delayed, are called *mbua ꭓa uwa*. The smaller rainy season (Nov.—Dec.) is called *mbua ꭓanꝺoa*. July—August is a dry season, not hot but cool and cloudy. Thick, heavy fogs cover the valleys in the mornings or hover round the heights; the sun is hidden by clouds. This time is called *nundu*. The really hot time, *ꝑano*, begins later, in September.

The days of the week have no name among the Akamba nor among the Akikuyu, though they have, on the other hand, among the Wadjagga. »Month» and »moon» have the same appellation, *mwæꭓ*. So also among the Akikuyu and the Wadjagga (*mweri* and *mweri* respectively). Of the different names for the months and their sequence — I have taken notes about them from Machakos in the west and from Muutha in the east — I have not succeeded in getting a quite clear idea. It looks as if the use of the names of the months was dying out. As far as their significance is concerned a great many of them are merely numbers.

The names of the months in Muutha are:

1) *ꝑándatu* (6), said to be the first month of the year.
2) *mwonža* (7)
3) *nꭓanꭓa* (8)
4) *kænda* (9)
5) *ɩkumɩ* (10)
6) *muꞶ̣u* 'the hot one' (October). The rain begins at the end of the month.
7) *kala* (= *mwa*). The fields are dug and sown.
8) *wɩma* (< *ɩma* 'to dig'). The fields are cleared from weeds.
9) *mwanža*
10) No special name (= *oꬼgonono* in Machakos?).
11) »   »   »   (= *wa katano* »   »   ?).

The names of the months in Machakos are the same as in Muutha, though the order is different. Here they apparently begin the year with *mwa̧*, the month when work on the fields begins, so that they shall have time to get them ready before the arrival of the rainy season. The year is thus made to begin with the moment that introduces the agricultural period which is so important for the people's existence. At least in Ulu they always begin to reckon the months with *mwa̧*:

1) *mwa̧*. During *mwa̧* the fields are dug.
2) *wıma̧* (< *ıma* ('to dig'). During *wıma̧* the fields are got definitely ready and sown before the arrival of the rain.
3) *umau̧* or *mwanža*
4) *wa kata̧no* (the 5th)
5) » *pandato* (the 6th)
6) » *mwonža* (the 7th)
7) » *n̠a̧nža* (the 8th)
8) *wa kænda* (the 9th)
9) » *ıkumı* (the 10th)
10) » *mu6ı̠u* ('the hot one'). During *mu6ı̠u* they begin to clear the fields (*kukupa*). All dry remains of growth are collected in heaps and burned. Fires are seen everywhere, a fine sight after dark. The women are busily employed and go to work early in the morning. Men also take part in the work.
11) *ou̠gonono*, which I do not know where to place. It is said to be a »bad month». Without being actually ill, one never feels quite well during it.

In this way the month which is called the fifth (*wa kata̧no*) is the fourth in order. This inconsistency disappears if one thinks of the year beginning with *mu6ı̠u*, during which commences the work on the fields, of which the work during *mwa̧* is only a continuation. The primitive starting-point for reckoning the months has perhaps been continually pushed forward, as B. Gutmann has shown was the case among the Wadjagga[1], the character of whose year he holds to be a pure lunar year, the beginning of which is continually getting later. In this way, just as in the Arabic reckoning of time, the same month gradually comes to fall in different seasons.

Finally a third version gives the following names of the

---

[1] B. Gutmann, Die Zeitrechnung bei den Wadschagga, Globus 1908, p. 238.

months: *mwa* or *kala, wıma, mwıu, tulża, wıŋgonoŋo, p̣anu wa mbą*
'the first dry reason'), *wa muonža, wa nżanża, wa ıkumı, muḅıu.*

We have only got eleven months. The Akikuyu have 12
and the Wadjagga 12 (or 13). The names of the months in Kidjagga are also to a great extent ordinal numbers, while the Kikuyu names, given by Dundas, show no similarity to the Kamba
names[1].

---

[1] K. R. Dundas, Kikuyu Calendar, Man 1909, p. 37.

Chapter XVIII. Geographical ideas and conceptions of other peoples.

We have already seen in Chapter I that the Akamba, through their trade and hunting expeditions, have obtained a by no means inconsiderable knowledge of large parts of English and German East Africa and the peoples that live there. To the details already given about the extent of these excursions we may add here that in 1895, up at Kenia, Dr. G. Kolb came across a band of Akamba with slaves, and the latter told him that they had been taken away by the Akamba from their homes in Marsabit, on the east side of Lake Rudolph[1]. But even if, theoretically, such knowledge was disseminated by the accounts of those who returned home, these could, of course, only reach a small number of the people, and women and children especially, who always stayed at home, must formerly have had the same slight knowledge of geography that they now show, while the men, on the other hand, in many cases had a wider knowledge at the time when the »pax Brittanica» did not hinder their expeditions. Nowadays, on the other hand, many young Kamba men, who work in the service of Europeans, go to districts far from their homes, to Lake Victoria and other places.

Of the Europeans (*asuŋgu*) they know that they come »over the sea» to Mombasa and then farther. Many people in remote districts, especially women, believe, however, that the coast-land is the Europeans' country and Kisuaheli their language. Many even think that the white men have come from their land by a kind of tunnel through the earth. As a matter of fact the natives do not say »white» people, but »red», and they compare the colour of our skins, which they think unbeautiful, to that of raw meat. Many tribes (Akamba, Akikuyu, Masai, etc.) say that

---

[1] S. Kolb, Von Mombasa durch Ukambani zum Kenia, p. 225.

they have old prophecies about the coming of the Europeans, that they should come with »a giant snake over the country» (the railway).

The Akamba˙ are fairly proficient at languages, and a great many of them are tolerably at home in Kisuaheli as well as in Kikuyu and the Masai language (*kɪkaɓɪ*), and in the neighbouring languages in general.

Most peoples, and not only primitive ones, have probably once believed in the existence of more or less monstrous beings inhabiting the parts of the world that lie outside the boundaries of their own geographical knowledge. In this way some of the Akamba believe that people with tails live far to the north and north-east, beyond the countries of the Galla peoples and the Somali. Accounts of people with tails, who usually appear as cannibals, are found in my collection of Kamba folklore. Formerly, when, in spite of often extensive trade expeditions, their knowledge of geographical regions was in certain respects more limited than now, such beings were supposed to live considerably nearer, but as their geographical knowledge increased, the boundaries were removed farther and farther away. As far as this special belief in people with tails is concerned, it rests, at least to a certain extent, on a real basis, as it has its origin in the tail-like flap that is worn by many African tribes. To mention a single example, the married Kavirondo women wear behind them a tuft consisting of black cord.

Points of the compass.

With regard to the points of the compass east and west are given according to the sun, as is to be expected. The east is thus called (*m*)*umɪlo wa sɪua* 'the sun's exit' (< *umɪla* 'to come into'). The west is called *uɓwɪlo* (or *nǝwɪlo*) *wa sɪua* (*ɓwɪa* = ?). North and south have no special names but are given by geographical names or names of tribes dwelling in these directions, e. g. *kɪlɪnɟa* (Mount Kenia).

The Akamba believe that the sky (*ɪtu*, plur. *matu* 'cloud') touches the earth somewhere; this place is called *kɪtulu kɪa ɪtu* and corresponds no doubt to our »horizon». *kɪtulu* means 'end, finish' (in the concrete signification) and appears, for instance, in the expression *kɪtulu kɪa ɪma* 'the bottom of the pit'. Formerly, when the Masai still occupied and ruled the steppe at Machakos up to the foot of the Ibetini range of hills, the Akamba did not know the country west of this so well, and it is said that people at that time sometimes went over to Mua, a range of hills a few English miles to the west, because they believed that from there they could see »the end of the heaven». But when they came there, they saw that it was always farther away. »You *asuŋgu* (Europeans), who know so much more than we Akamba, have you found it?» they asked me. I tried to explain to them that the sky has no end and that it nowhere touches the earth, but they would not believe this.

They think that complete darkness prevails high up in the air.

Travelling.

We have already seen that the Akamba, perhaps more than any other of the tribes in the interior of East Africa, have roamed far and wide, partly as hunters, partly as traders, principally in ivory. Because of their knowledge of the countries and peoples in the interior many of them were in former times guides or practically leaders of the trade caravans coming up from the coast. C. Pickering, to quote an example, mentions a trading party to the Djagga country, »commanded by a Makamba man, who had often conducted similar expeditions, and who knew all the languages on the route» [1].

On their journeys (*kŋalo*) they take with them weapons, in their quivers they put the apparatus for making fire, and hanging on their belts they have sandals, which they do not use at home on ordinary occasions. They are taken with them not only to protect the feet against thorns and the roughnesses of the road, but just as much — and especially during the hot season — as a protection against the heat, which is sometimes so strong that it can be felt through the soles of thick marching boots. Food, such as gruel, maize and beans, is taken in calabashes, which are hung over the shoulders with leather straps. They are often beautifully polished with fat and the straps are adorned with beads.

Obstacles on the way in the form of deep rivers are sur-mounted by a good swimmer going over first with a long rope,

---

[1] The Races of Man, p. 200.

which he fastens to a tree. Then the others manage to get across by holding to the rope. When it is necessary to drive cattle over a river, they stretch a rope out in the same way and some men take up their positions along it. The cattle are driven into the water a little way above the rope. If the animals are driven towards it by the stream, they are forced to seek the shore by the blows of the men at the rope. If the stream is shallow and narrow and not rapid, those who cannot swim get across simply by walking on the bottom. When it is necessary they come up to the surface and take a breath of air[1].

The art of swimming, I may take the opportunity of adding, is very widespread among the Akamba, a fact which inspires respect, when one considers that great parts of their country are poor in water. They usually, like the Akikuyu, swim on their sides and tread water when they wish to rest.

Long journeys were dangerous undertakings, especially in older times, and so they tried in all conceivable ways to protect themselves against dangers, disasters and fatigue. First of all they had, of course, to consult the medicine man so as to find out if the journey was being undertaken under favourable auspices. In addition there were during the whole journey a great many observances of a more or less ritual character. Similar measures or precautions are practised practically over the whole globe during journeys.

When decamping to continue their march each morning during a journey, the leader takes a firebrand from the hearth, goes a few steps forward in the direction in which they intend to continue the journey and throws the brand out on the path, expressing a hope that no evil might happen during the day's march: »May we not meet lions, rhinoceros or Masai nor any other evil beasts!» This does not seem to be any prayer to the spirits, but it is possibly some sort of incantation. Another prominent person then takes grass and throws it in the campfire, uttering a similar wish. The signification of the grass and the fire in this connection is unknown to me.

---

[1] The natives of the southern slopes of Kenia can even pass rapid streams in this way when they on the head carry a load which makes them able to resist the pressure of the water. A. Arckell-Hardwick, An Ivory Trader in North Kenia, p. 356.

I have already described (p. 218) how during journeys they offer sacrifices to the spirits of deceased eminent caravan leaders.

Beginners at big game hunting and indeed those who take part for the first time in a military campaign have to submit to certain observances. Something similar applies to those who are out on their first long journey. The Akamba seem even to have a special word (*mupǫ*) for those who are making their first long journey. Before such a person may drink from a stream on the way, someone first dips the point of his bow in the water and lets the novice suck it. Otherwise some mishap might befall him during the journey. Hobley says further that on journeys in former times, before they could drink from a river, they had to cross to the other side and there »drop a stone». »This practice» he adds, »is evidently the survival of a ceremony connected with the propitiation of the river spirits» (for »river spirits» cf. p. 218). I have not obtained any confirmation of this statement about the stone. Certainly it is not unusual for people to take stones with them when wading over a stream, but this is probably only so that they may use them against crocodiles that may possibly be present.

Observances of a sexual nature are also connected with the undertaking of long journeys. Thus it is forbidden for any man to have connection even with his own wife, if she is with him on the journey. By doing this he might cause disasters, and the object of the journey may be endangered. Hildebrandt tells how Kamba travellers in his time resisted most strictly the temptations offered them in the coast towns, a thing that had practical utility, too, as to a certain extent it protected them from catching venereal diseases and carrying them home. The sexual taboo was carried to such an extent that the food for the journey was not to be prepared by unmarried girls, on account of their connections with the young men. A long journey is comparable in this respect with another important enterprise, namely a military expedition (see p. 189). Further, if anybody from a village is travelling and a death occurs there during his absence, nobody may have sexual intercourse until the absent one returns.

Just as the rites connected with war have disappeared at the same time as the warfare and will soon be quite forgotten, so those just mentioned in connection with journeys are scarcely practised

any longer. Even the conservatism of the African has its limits
and his practical view of things gets the upper hand of his fear of
offending against hereditary customs. I shall quote an utterance
of a man with whom I discussed the rites connected with journeys: »We no longer have need for them. If we go to Nairobi
and anything happens on the way, there are white doctors there.
And if we go to Kitui, there is a doctor (an Indian compounder
at the boma). And if we wish to go to Kiswani, we travel without danger by »the fire-carriage» (the railway), etc. Even if this
explanation of the disappearance of the old customs is not quite
satisfactory, it undeniably contains a great deal of truth.

Chapter XIX. **History and historical traditions.**

It is quite futile to try to get any insight into the history of the tribe through the Akamba themselves. There is an almost entire lack of any kind of tradition, both historical and legendary. The explanation of this is, to a great extent, to be sought in their state of society with its stamp of democracy and equality, which has prevented the rise of chieftainship and made it difficult for individuals of strong character to attain to any important position, so that their names are preserved for posterity. Nor do any important events in connection with their neighbours seem to have taken place; the fights with the Masai and the Akikuya have certainly been endless, but have consisted principally of plundering expeditions without any importance worth mentioning. The only man from a bygone time whose name is generally known in Ukamba is Kivui in Kitui, whom we know from Dr. Krapf's descriptions in 1851 and who had a great influence and reputation as a magician (cf. p. 149). It is interesting to see how Kivui, during the short time that has passed since his death, has become partly a legendary figure. Legends, especially about his strength, are prevalent among the people: no other man could carry his weapons, which were of enormous size and weight; his arrows, for instance, were almost as thick as a man's arm.

If we turn to the oldest historical sources, we find in them no information about the Akamba. Before the arrival of the Portuguese in East Africa we are confined to some Arabic writers, who have a fairly good knowledge of the coast and give us quite important information about it — thus we have Edrisi in the 12th and Ibn Batuta in the 14th century — but say very little about the interior. A number of statements in the old Arabic sources make it fairly probable, however, that the Arabian travellers had a certain knowledge of the peoples in the interior. It is not at all impossible that the term »moon people», which some of them speak of, refers, among other peoples, to the Akamba.[1]

The Portuguese too seem never to have penetrated into the interior. Consequently one looks in vain for any information about the Akamba in the writers that have dealt with the Portuguese period in East Africa[2]. Certainly about 1523 two Portuguese left Melindi with the intention of reaching the great lakes that were reported to exist in the interior, but after eleven days they came back in an exhausted condition.

There are, however, events that have made a great impression in the history, not only of the Akamba, but of the whole of East Africa. These are the great famines. As we have already seen, the people have retained a whole series of these in their memory, given each of them its special name and remember pretty exactly the times when they occurred as far back as the 'thirties. The worst of them, since Europeans came to the country, was probably at the end of the 'nineties. In 1899 there had been no rain for five rainy seasons, i. e. they had no harvest for five times in succession. The people tried to appease their hunger with what they could find, roots and wild fruit of slight or no nutritive value, such as the fruit of the baobab, which is common in the east. Yet most of them could not manage to slaughter their horned cattle, but had to die themselves before their cattle. In Ikutha Hofmann, the missionary, fed on an average 500 adults a day, and every two or three days 300 children on an average. This feeding could not be stopped until 1900. During this time the big mission house in Mulango was built, and Herr Säuberlich used to say jokingly that it was built of rice, because the natives had to work at the building of the station in return for the food that was given out.

During this great famine there arose a severe epidemic of small-pox, which in East Akamba came from the south, from the Kib-

---

[1] Cf. F. Storbeck, Die Berichte der arabischen Geographen des Mittelalters über Ostafrika. Westasiatische Studien (Mitteil. des Seminars f. oriental. Sprachen) 1914, p. 130.

[2] J. Strandes, Die Portugiesenzeit in Deutsch und Englisch Ost-afrika, p. 317. Guillain, Documents sur l'Histoire, la Géographie et le Commerce de l'Afrique orientale. O. Kersten, C. v. d. Deckens Reisen in Ostafrika, vol. III.

wezi district. The missionary Kanig describes how in Ikutha
120 people smitten with smallpox sat at one side at the distribution of rice. »Those whom hunger spared were taken by the
smallpox. The sick people often went mad. We noticed that
young and tolerably strong people were overcome by the disease
more easily than the old ones who were quite exhausted from
hunger»[1]. 50 % of the tribe are estimated to have died 1898—99.

In Chap. I. I have shown how the famines broke up families
and drove the people in big crowds to seek food in other places.
The natives told the author how, at the end of the 'nineties, bands
of them went to the better watered Kikuyu country but never
came back. Weakened as they were, they could not defend themselves, but were killed in great masses by the Akikuyu. On one
occasion several hundred of them were drowned in a small stream.
This cruelty on the part of the Akikuyu was certainly due to a
great extent to their fear of being infected by smallpox, of which
the starved wretches were full. A. Arckell-Hardwick, a trader,
describes how at the Thika River he met a big band of these
hungry wretches, who were driven off by his bearers[2]. There are
not many families in Ukamba that have not lost some member
during the last great famines.

Many of the Akamba who emigrated to the Kikuyu country
stayed there until 1900, »selling their cattle and leaving their
children in payment of food, to be afterwards redeemed, when
better days came round»[3].

The relations of the Akamba with their neighbours and their
trade expeditions have also been touched upon in Chaps. I and
XVIII. Those of the Arab and Suaheli traders who were allowed
to go through Ukamba, being dependent on the natives, tried to
be on good terms with them so that they could get their slaves
and ivory safely to the coast. This did not, however, prevent them
from luring the Akamba into transactions, in which the business
capacity of the latter, which was ordinarily high, was blinded by their
desire for the seller's finery. The latter consequently did splendid business. For instance, for the variegated cotton cloths that now cost

---

[1] G. Kanig, Dornige Pfade, p. 12.

[2] A. Arckell-Hardwick, An Ivory Trader in North Kenia, p. 354.

[3] H. R. Tate, Notes of the Kikuyu and Kamba Tribes of British
East Africa. J. Anthr. Inst. 1904, p. 137.

a rupee each, they got three goats. The article most sought after was the red cloth *mukumbu* and, of course, copper or brass wire. The merchant made a little heap of different articles and put on the top as a bait a cheap mirror, which they threw in for nothing. For bigger purchases they even got slaves, cattle and stolen Masai asses in payment and drove whole bands of these down to the coast.

Curiously enough it seems, however, to have been only in very recent times that the traders from the coast were allowed to enter Ukamba more freely. Burton goes so far as to fix the time by saying — I do not know on what grounds he has come to this conclusion — that before 1857 no Arab trader had visited the country [1]. The method of trading in his time he describes in the following manner: »Trading parties from Ukambani sold ivory to the Wanyika for four times round the tusks in beads, and these middlemen, often fleecing those more savage than themselves, retailed the goods at high profit to the citizens [of Mombasa]. The Wakamba of the coast are, of course, anxious to promote intercourse between Mombasa and their kinsmen of the interior» [2].

The trading also went on without middlemen, the Kamba traders meeting the Arab and Suaheli caravans in the Duruma country. Hildebrandt tells how the unity of value was cattle, which was valued in a certain quantity of cloth, beads, metal wire etz. Only seldom were the caravans allowed to enter Ukamba [3].

The slave trade carried on by the Akamba was probably, however, comparatively insignificant. An author who visited Zanzibar in the middle of the last century writes after hearing the opinions of the natives there: »They [the Akamba] do not bring slaves, except a few, but trade in ivory» [4]. A German traveller of a recent date says, on the other hand, that right up to the end of the 'eighties they were »pretty dangerous slave traders and were even suspected of cannibalism», the latter certainly a quite

---

[1] R. F. Burton, Zanzibar, City, Island and Coast, II, p. 67.

[2] The main caravan routes from Mombasa to the interior, especially the one to Lake Victoria, did not cross Ukamba but went over Taveta and the Masai steppe. Vide T. Wakefield, Routes of Native Caravans from the coast to the interior of Eastern Africa, Journ. R. Geogr. Soc. 1870, p. 303 ff.

[3] Hildebrandt, Die Wakamba, p. 385.

[4] Ch. Pickering, The Races of man, p. 200.

unfounded accusation[1]. During my stay in East Ukamba in 1911 one could, however, still say that slave trading took place to a certain extent, as I knew at least one man, in a good position, who secretly sold women to harems at the coast.

The war with the Masai was occasionally interrupted by peacable intercourse, during which the sons of the steppe bought vegetables and salt from the Akamba. The Akamba have apparently always been on good terms with the Wanika and combined with them in order to fight against the Galla, *atwa*[2], who seem to have had a firm footing in East Ukamba even in Krapf's time. The battles with them were waged with varying success, until at last the Akamba drove them back to the Tana. I shall take the opportunity of adding here to what has already been said on these battles in Chap. I that Mr. Säuberlich told me how, in spite of his earnest dissuasion, over 400 Akamba once went over the Tana to plunder but were so thoroughly beaten that only about ten came back.

In the 'eighties the English began to settle in earnest in Ukamba and then met with armed resistance. They had, however, scarcely any serious difficulties to overcome.

To this very brief glimpse into the Akamba's history I shall add the myth that the Akamba have about their common origin with the Akikuyu and the Masai. It tries to give an explanation to the old enmity between these tribes and is as follows[3]:

A very long time ago a woman gave birth to three boys, who were called Mukavi (Masai), Mukikuyu and Mukamba. The boys grew up, took wives and each man built his village. And they

---

[1] A. Kaiser, Die Wirtschaftliche Entwickelung der Ugandabahn-länder, Globus 1907, p. 56.

[2] The words *atwa*, *watwa*, *batwa*, with other forms from apparently the same root in primitive Bantu, appear, as is known, as the names of several peoples, as far as one can see of different origin, in South and Central Africa. A comparison of them, together with a very interesting and plausible analysis of the meaning of the name, has been given by Eric von Rosen in his large and excellent monograph on the Batwa that live at Lake Bangveolo, Träskfolket [the Swamp people], p. 88 ff. Cf. also above p. 21.

[3] A version of this story is given by R. F. Burton, Zanzibar, II, p. 64, who was told about a keeper of cattle with three sons: Mkuafi [Masai], the senior, Mgalla and Mkamba.

had children, who had different words (i. e. the three different sets of children each spoke its own language). Mukavi got milk and blood (kept cattle), while Mukikuyu and Mukamba got beans, maize, sweet potatoes and other food from the fields. But they also wanted cattle and went to Mukavi and asked for a cow for each of their children. Mukavi refused to give them any, saying: »You have got other food, which I have not got. I have my cattle and nothing else. If you wish to fight, I don't mind».

Mukikuyu and Mukamba went away and sat down to take counsel. Mukamba said: »Let us take our young men and seize the cattle by force». And they gathered together their children, went to the Masai's village and after a fight took a great many cattle, which they drove away. But in the night, while the warriors were asleep, the Masai come and took back most of the animals. In the morning the Akamba and the Akikuyu came to blows about the remainder, and then each went off in enmity to his own district.

And nowadays, when an old *mutumıa* (old man) in Ukamba feels his end approaching, he says to his sons: »A very long time ago the ancestor of the Akamba, Akikuyu and Masai was one and the same man. But our relationship and friendship died because of cattle. When I die now, take care not to come to blows because of cattle».

In those parts of East Ukamba where the Akamba come more into contact with the Galla than the Masai one brother in the myth is called Mutwa (Galla) or Mukala instead of Mukavi.

P. IV.

ART AND GAMES

Chap. XX. Decorative art.

Apart from the southern parts and the coast, which is influenced by a foreign culture, decorative art is very poor and undeveloped, in the whole of East Africa a state of affairs that is probably due less to psychological conditions than to the fact that among the East African tribes the men have always been fully occupied with feuds and looking after cattle. The same thing applies to the Akamba, whose time and interest has also been very largely claimed by hunting. For the sake of completeness, however, we shall give a brief account of the small amount of decorative art they really possess.

The Akamba apply their ornamental art — this term, like »ornament», is taken in a wide sense — chiefly to carving and painting. The calabash, owing to the ease with which it is worked, its appearance and its smooth and even surface, is, of course, the most promising material for attempts at decoration. On calabashes one thus finds most of the decorations as well as the greatest variety in motifs. Painted decorations, with black, red or white clay, which are put chiefly on the dance drums, are, of course, still easier to produce, but in spite of this they do not seem to be so well-liked as the carvings on the calabashes. We shall therefore begin with the calabashes, and, if necessary, one could limit oneself to these to obtain an idea of the motifs in the Akamba's decorative art.

The calabash decorations are carried out partly by carving with knives, partly by stippling with nails (awls), the latter process being slower. Specimens of both methods are given here. They are afterwards rubbed with ashes. The representations are, for the most part, reproductions from nature, and are thus in the style of free imitative art.

The most important contribution to ornamental art is made, as one might expect, by the animal world, and by the animals in it that are most used as ornamental figures over practically the whole of the dark continent, namely serpents, lizards and tortoises. This is especially the case, as we know, with the lizard, and among the Akamba as well this or the serpent is found in some shape or form on most calabashes. The varying forms are, at least as far as the lizards are concerned, not arbitrary; an attempt is made to reproduce a certain species, and they often succeed in bringing out something that is characteristic of the animal in question. The large and powerful lizard in fig. 66 (g), for instance, represents a Varanus. The big snake, on the other hand, in fig. 71, a python, is not very successful, while the flexibility of the tree-snake's narrow, slender body (fig. 64 k) is well reproduced. The black cobra »that has swallowed a rat» (fig. 66, h) is freely and realistically represented.

Chameleons are also found on two of my Kamba calabashes, in both cases, curiously enough, without heads. They are, however, not recognizable, but resemble lizards. The crocodile occurs sometimes (fig. 64, b), and it is worthy of mention, because according to K. Weule it is rare in African decorations. M. Heydrich does not discuss it at all in his work[1]. When one considers that the lizard is perhaps the most popular animal for ornamental purposes in Africa, it seems inexplicable that the crocodile, which is, of course, as easily drawn as a lizard, is used so little.

Mammals are reproduced less frequently, and when they occur, they are always wild animals: the elephant, the rhinoceros, the giraffe, the zebra and the antelope. There are very few reproductions of the latter from East Africa, and so I give here a Thomson gazelle (fig. 65, a) and a couple of hartebeests. The calabash decorated with the latter (fig. 68) gives a whole hunting scene from the steppe, which in its realism reminds one of the Bushmen's paintings. We see a hunter on the steppe overgrown with acacias hunting two hartebeests, one of which has the sloping back that is peculiar to this species of antelope. Beneath an acacia is lying a giraffe, which. is not badly drawn either.

Domestic animals are almost completely absent from African ornamentation, and the only things of this sort I have seen in Ukamba is the sheep in fig. 66 a.

---

[1] Afrikanische Ornamentik, Intern. Arch. f. Ethnographie 1914.

Fig. 64. Calabash bowl, Ikutha, East Ukamba. Riksmus. Ethn. Coll. Inv. 12. 7. 52. ¹/₃ nat. size.

The circle in the middle is Kilimandjaro. The concentric circles remind one of the lines showing elevation on a map.

On the left half: *a* zebra (note the hoofs); *b* crocodile; *c* frog; *d* a woman's stool; *i* the *ŋguluḵu* snake; *j* ¹/₂ rupee; *k* a snake (*ḭkua*) that lives in trees and is said to be very poisonous; *l* arrowhead.

On the right half: *e* rhinoceroses, the bigger one male, the smaller one female (notice the horns); *f* the plaited dividing wall of the *we*, the back part of the hut; *g* axe-head; *h* blindsnake (Typhlops sp.); *m* a human being?

Fig. 65.   Calabash bowl, East Ukamba.   Riksmus. Ethn. Coll.
Inv. 12. 7. 55.   ⅓ nat. size.
a Thomson gazelle; *b* the woman's tail (*mupiͅta*), studded with cowries.
This last ornament has obviously also given the material for the border
decoration; *c* frog; *d* human being.

Fig. 66. Calabash Decorations, Eastern Ukamba. $^{1}/_{2}$ nat. size.

a sheep, with a fat tail. This was obviously too small to begin with; *b* womans chair (shown by the tall legs); *c* part of a hill; *d* star (seven points); *e* comet, probably seen in the 'eighties and connected with a famine which then prevailed (cf. pp. 335, 339); *f* axe-head; *g* lizard *nɗanu* (Varanus sp.); *h* black spitting cobra (*kɨko*) »that has devoured a rat»; *i* railway train.

Nor do birds and fish play any part worth mentioning as ornamental figures among the Akamba, as is also the case among most negro peoples. They occur, however, as we see, occasionally (fig. 69, f—g; 71, e, g).

Among the lower animals we need only mention the millipede (fig. 69, a) and the centipede, both of which have already been reproduced from the *musaʼ* sticks (p. 54, 55).

Before we leave the pictures of animals I wish to draw attention to some small details of interest, although they are not peculiar to the Akamba nor even to African ornamental art in general,

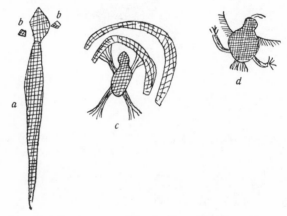

Fig. 67. Details from a calabash, East Ukamba. $^1/_2$ nat. size.
a snake; *b* its eyes; *c* frog; *d* tortoise.

but, on the other hand, are found wherever animal pictures are produced by an undeveloped art, the most familiar examples for us being children's pictures. I refer to the tendency to place the mouth, the two nostrils, ears and eyes on an animal that is reproduced entirely in profile. Our material shows several examples of this. The eyes are specially important, and so one is not surprised to come across such a case as the snake in fig. 67, where an eye is placed on each side of the head, as there is not room for them on the head itself[1].

Phytomorphic motifs are rare in Africa and among the Akamba.

---

[1] Other examples are given by K. W e u l e in Die Eidechse als Ornament in Afrika (Festschrift an A. Bastian), fig. 23, 27—28.

I have only seen them of once, in the case the acacias just
referred to (fig. 68).

Anthropomorphic decorations occur rather infrequently in East
Africa and on all my calabashes there is — apart from the hunter
in fig. 68 — only one human figure, namely 65, d. Fig. 64, m may
also be a human being, although it is executed in the same way
as the frog on the same calabash.

Fig. 68. Hunting scene on the steppe. Details from a calabash, East
Ukamba. ¹/₃ nat. size.

The most common motifs after certain animals are arrow-
heads, the sun and the moon (half-moon). The former consists of
only one circle and never has a human face. Comets are also
reproduced, sometimes in triangular shape (fig. 66, e). As is shown
by the examples, the natives take, in addition, as motifs practically all possible objects from daily life, tools, household articles
etc. The portion of a hill in fig. 66, c seems to be rather a unique
motif; note also the representation of Kilimandjaro on fig. 64.

The Akamba's ornamentation of their calabashes — and similarly their art in general — does not seem to have attained to any real conventionalization — and is therefore no ornamental art in the real sense of the word. One might, however, say that

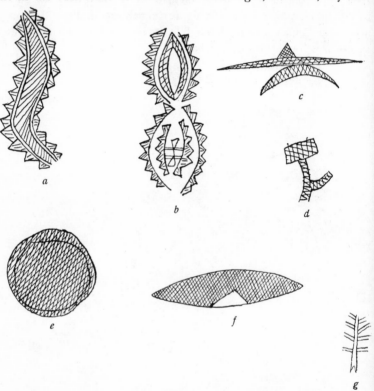

Fig. 69. Decorations from calabashes, East Ukamba. ²/₃ nat. size.

a millipede; *b* crab-like animal (*sɩo-manðala*); *c* the sky, beneath it the moon, above it an arrowhead; *d* branch of tree with a bee-hive; *e* rupee; *f* fish. Cf. *g* fish »with arms» from a *musaɩ*-stick.

such decorations as the millipede and the fish in fig. 69, and still more the one that is said to represent some sort of crab-like animal are on the way to being artistic. Other examples are shown in fig. 70, both motifs of which are unknown to me, but of which *a* seems to be derived from a lizard decoration and *b* from a human being.

On the other hand, as a specimen of real and thoroughly
worked out conventionalization — though of the simplest kind —
we may take the series of triangles and segments of circles that
are in common use over the whole of Ukamba as borders or to
distinguish different fields on the calabashes. The triangles are
said to be arrow heads. Both kinds of borders from Kamba calabashes are reproduced by M. Heydrich[1], who, from a source unknown to me[2], identifies the segment of the circle with the small
iron dancing bells (*kɨamba*).

The figures carved with knives in the bark of the *musaɨ* sticks
occupy a special position and their peculiarity is due partly to

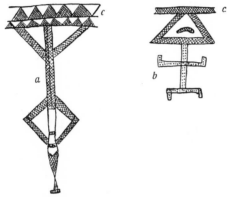

Fig. 70.   Conventionalized (?) motifs on a narrow calabash from East
Ukamba. $1/2$ nat. size.
a lizard; *b* human being? *c* are borders.

their material and technique, partly also to their function as a
sort of hieroglyphic, in the interpretation of which the novices in
the initiation rites have to undergo a sort of examination Whether the motifs are fixed by tradition or not, is unknown to me.

The paintings of the Akamba can be dealt with in a few
words. With the exception of the figures of animals, which I
have never seen used in painting, the motifs are the same as on

---

[1] M. Heydrich, Afrikanische Ornamentik, Taf. II, 64.

[2] Probably from the collections in the Leipzig Museum, brought
home by the German missionaries in Ukamba, or from Hildebrandts
collections in the Berlin Museum.

the calabashes. See also fig. 72—73 and the dance drums
fig. 109—110.

No sculpture in wood or any other kind of ornamental wood-
carving is found. Stools, spoons, snuff-bottles, etc. may show pure
and pleasing shapes but are without any embellishment. Only

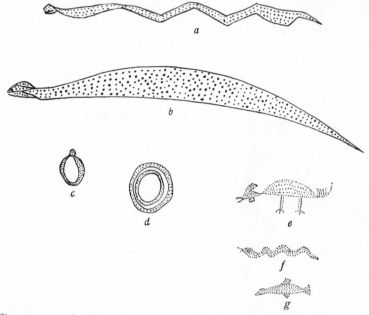

Fig. 71. *a—b* decorations on a medicine man's calabash, Machakos:
a snake, *b* python; *c—g* from East Ukamba: *c* tortoise; *d* rolled-up
leather-strap; *e* guinea-fowl; *f* snake; *g* fish. ¹/₂ nat. size.

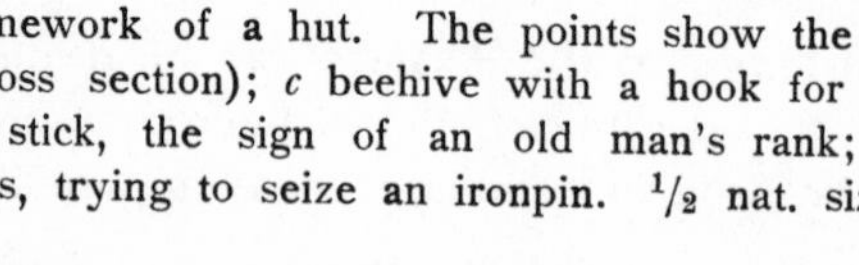

Fig. 72. Figures painted with red ochre on a long dance drum (*kuụ*).
a bed; *b* framework of a hut. The points show the poles stuck in
the ground (cross section); *c* beehive with a hook for hanging it up;
d fork-shaped stick, the sign of an old man's rank; *e* blacksmith's
tongs, trying to seize an ironpin. ¹/₂ nat. size.

among the accessories of the dance does one find any attempt at
the simplest kind of ornamentation such as carved or burnt lines.
Specimens of the most adorned dancing accessories I have seen

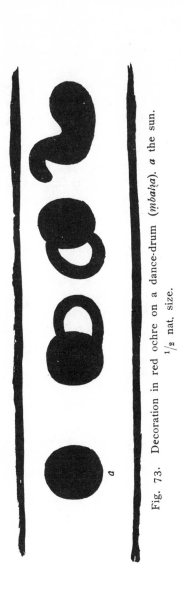

Fig. 73. Decoration in red ochre on a dance-drum (ɳbalɑ). *a* the sun. ½ nat. size.

Fig. 74. Dance accessory made of wood, bound with wire. Machakos. Represents a young man. ¼ nat. size. Riksmus. Ethn. Coll. Inv. 12. 7. 225.

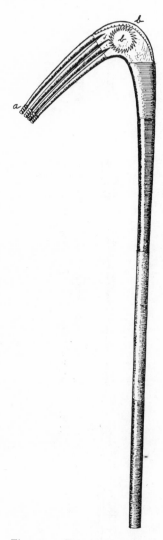

in Ukamba — both types are, however, rare — are reproduced here (figs. 74, 75). The first of these is of interest if we remember that anthropomorphical figures, especially wooden ones, are in general rare in East Africa. Thus I have not come across anything else of this kind in these districts. The figure is a youth, wearing on his head — in the shape of a metal bead, *a* — the white conus shell that the young men are fond of adorning themselves with. At the end of his fingers there are small metal beads, possibly representing rings. The fingers are four in number; primitive art usually shows a supreme contempt for the real number of fingers and toes. But the number of the latter is correct in this case.

I do not know what the other dancing accessory represents, and I have nothing to say about it except that it suggests a sort of dancing accessory or medicine man's stave that is used in certain quarters in the East Indian archipelago.

Fig. 75. Dancing accessory from Machakos, bound with copper and brass wire. *a* metal beads; *b* tin mountings. $^1/_4$ nat. size. Riksmus. Ethn. Coll. Inv. 12. 7. 224.

In the department of metalwork we find very little decorative art, and this really consists of the simple engravings, in conventional designs (straight and curved lines, ovals, dots, zigzag decorations, etc.) that are found on armlets and bracelets (fig. 84—86). Yet in certain respects the Akamba's decorative art reaches its highest point with the help of metal material, namely by means of wire. I refer to the symmetrical decorations that are sometimes put on the old men's stools with wire, which is drawn through the wood with great skill and patience (fig. 76). Hobley reproduces a number of such chairs, and also details of the decorations on them [1]. But he does not inform us that unfortunately this art is practised by only extremely few individuals. As a matter of fact I know for certain of only one man, and he is the very one that made the stools that are reproduced by Hobley. During the whole

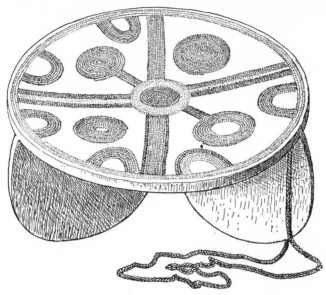

Fig. 76. Old man's chair with wire decorations. The circle in the centre is the owners village with four paths running from it. The four other circles are moons. $1/3$ nat. size. Riksmus. Ethn. Coll. Inv. 12. 7. 73.

of my stay in Ukamba I only succeeded, in spite of many attempts, in coming across a single stool of this kind, the one in fig. 76. M. Heydrich states [2] — the source of his information is unknown to me — that the Akamba have learned to use wire in this way from the coastal tribes, especially the Wagiriama.

The china beads that are used for »loin clothes», ornaments for the arm, etc., are made in simple patterns: triangles, rectangles and zigzag designs.

---

[1] C. V. Hobley, The Akamba, p. 34 ff.
[2] Afrikanische Ornamentik, p. 62.

In passing I wish to remind the reader that the clan and ownership marks placed on arrow-heads, cattle and beehives for practical reasons seem to be in a fair way of becoming purely decorations (pp. 130 ff.). This is also the case with the »trade marks» on the pots, which have as yet no decorative purpose, but might probably very easily give rise to ornamentation.

Finally we must stop a moment to discuss the motives for the Akamba's decorative art. There scarcely seem to be any others but purely æsthetic ones and sometimes, as in the em bellishment of the calabashes, the pleasure of the work for its own sake. Possibly some medicine man puts magic signs on his apparatus. But on the whole it is all pure ornament. The figures of animals have no connection with totemism; the production of the sun and the moon have no magic or religious import. Whether it was otherwise at an earlier time, we cannot decide.

Chap. XXI. Clothing and Personal ornaments.

1. Clothing.

Everything goes to indicate that a few decades ago the Akamba wore few or no garments. In Krapf's time »many of the men were perfectly naked, whilst others wore a mere rag in imitation of the fig-leaf of a sculptor, and even the women had a very scanty covering below the waist, being otherwise completely naked from head to foot» [1]. At most a strip of cloth or something of the sort wound round the hips seems thus to have been the usual dress about 1850. Krapf adds however that »they have clothes, but do not usually dress themselves». He is probably referring here to the imported cloths, American sheeting (*americano*) and blue calico (*ɓæk*ɔ, Kisuaheli *kaniki*), which they got at the coast in exchange for ivory and cattle for slaughtering and which in Hildebrandt's time — when of course the communications with the coast were less risky and therefore more brisk — seem to have been in fairly common use in East Ukamba [2]. They were worn in the form of a plaid, 2—3 metre long, which was thrown over the shoulders and falling over the chest was fastened at the side. They were made waterproof by being rubbed with fat and red ochre. Many young girls still wear a piece of white cotton cloth rubbed with ochre, but as a rule this garment is replaced nowadays by the considerably warmer blankets, imported principally from

---

[1] The skin garments for men referred to by Hobley (Akamba, p. 40), of different sizes for the different age classes *(atumɩa, anðælɔ* and *anɑkɔ)*, which he says have been in use a long time ago, seem to be unknown to Krapf as they are to the writer of this book.

[2] In the Machakos district, on the other hand, according to v. Höhnel (Zum Rudolph-See und Stephanie-See, p. 800) even at the end of the 'eighties most of the men went completely naked, wearing only ornaments.

India, which are used by both sexes and are carried with a certain·
easy charm. When an old man comes striding solemnly along,
draped in his blanket, he reminds one of a dignified Roman in
his toga. These blankets protect them against both rain and cold,
and are used as a covering at night.

The married Kamba woman's proper dress, which is in general
use in Ulu, is, however, the *ua*, a calf- or goat-skin, which has
been stripped of its hairs and rubbed with the usual ochre salve,
and which is fastened over one shoulder. The *ua* is made for the
wife by her husband and is a gift of his. It does not completely
cover the breasts, as the Akamba feel no shame at having them
uncovered. The method of making it is to stretch the skin out
to dry in an apparatus (*kıbaɔo* < *kuɓa* 'to scrape the hair of a skin')
consisting of a frame made of osier switches, to which it is fastened, so as not to touch the ground, by three pegs fixed in the
ground on the long side of the skin and two on each of the short
sides. The hair is scraped off· with an axe. The skin is then
placed against a stone and rubbed with the hands and feet until
it becomes soft. It is finally rubbed with fat and red ochre (*mɓu*),
the primitive method of shamoying used in Africa. It is almost
impossible for a collector to obtain one of these skin, as the women partly will not, partly dare not give them up.· If they did,
their husbands would be so angry that they would even leave
their wives.

Neither Krapf nor Hildebrandt mentions 'these female dresses,
but they visited only East Ukamba, where even at the present
day they are not used. Two possible explanations of its origin
may be given. If we remember that the skin garment in Africa
belongs to an older stage of civilisation and is widespread in the
southern and eastern parts of the continent — used, among other
.tribes, by the Akambas' nearest neighbours, the cattle-keeping
Masai and Akikuyu — it is not too bold to assume that it is an
old primitive garment that was discarded by the people in the
east when they, better off than their relations west of Athi,
were able to obtain cloth from the coast. The climatic conditions, which have, of course, a great influence on dress, may also
have contributed to this, East Ukamba being lower and therefore
considerably warmer than Ulu. Further, in almost all things Ulu
is looked upon as setting the fashion for the other parts of the

country, as here the old customs have been kept
most unaltered. On the other hand it may, however, be thought that the people of Ulu have
borrowed the skin garment from their neighbours because of the colder climate and because
the communications with the coast were poorer.
It is, however, not long since this skin dress
was worn by men as well in certain places[1], as,
for instance, the Kilungu district. The Akamba
in Machakos say that this was due, among other
things, to the fact that the Kilungu men, notorious
cattle-thieves, were better protected by this garment against the thorny thickets, when they went
out at night to steal cattle.

Another leather garment is the woman's tail
mupita), a narrow bifurcated strip of leather,
which is fastened beneath the belt of beads that
all women wear. It is too narrow to be of real use
to sit on and is intended principally to cover the
anus, and is thus a manifestation of the ideas of
the tribe concerning the proprieties. A married
woman's tail is usually so long that the ends trail
on the ground. It is usually unornamented, while
the young girls' is trimmed quite coquettishly
with beads or small chains (fig. 77). In old times
all the tails were without ornaments and the girls
wore instead, at the base of the tail, a sort of
flap of metal beads (called *isæso*) resembling the
kimæṇgo mentioned below.

This tail is not found in the whole of East
Ukamba either. In this case we may assert with
greater certainty that here an original custom has
been abandoned, presumably on account of the
increasing use of cotton cloth. In Krapf's time
the tail must still have been in use, as he says
that the Kamba women at Rabai in the hinter-

Fig. 77. Young
girl's tail, decorat-
ed with beads and
fine iron chains.
Riksmus. Ethn.
coll. $^1/_6$ nat. size.
Inv. 12. 7. 116.

---

[1] This was the case in the 'nineties, according to M. Schoeller,
Mitteil. über meine Reise nach Equatorial-Afrika und Uganda II, p. 304.

land of Mombasa wore it, and these Akamba had emigrated from
the present Kitui district.   One may also see them still worn by
young girls as dancing ornaments.

Finally in Ulu a rectangular loin-cloth (*katuŋgə*) that is worn
by girls is also made out of skin.   This is decorated with beads,
sometimes arranged in geometrical patterns on the piece of skin,
sometimes forming hanging strings.   Sometimes the whole rect-
angle consists of beads, with a fringe of hanging metal chains at
the bottom.   It is thus an ornament at the same time.

Before we leave these garments of skin, it may be added that
leather straps, such as are used
for carrying loads, etc. are made
soft by being drawn through a
hole in a piece of wood.

A loin cloth or apron for
girls, which owing to its appearance, weight and clumsiness must
also be classed among ornaments,
is the *kɪmæŋgo*, which is fastened
round the waist with leather straps.
It is made of imported thick brass
wire, which is flattened out and
made into small cylinders (*nžalə*)
that are threaded on to leather
straps. The one reproduced here
(fig. 78), one of the larger ones,

Fig. 78.   Girl's apron, made of
brass cylinders. $^1/_3$ nat. size.
Riksmus. Ethn. coll. Inv. 12. 7. 119.

consists of over 700 of these and weighs about 4 $^1/_2$ pounds. The
top rows are not made of brass but of iron.

To make an »apron» of this sort is a laborious task; about
ten cylinders a day appears to be the maximum rate of production. It accordingly commands a rather high price or about three
goats. Because of this it is only the better situated natives who
procure the garment. Nowadays, however, it is rarely seen except
on some small girl and then of course in a small size. It is probably
scarcely made any more, and will perhaps soon quite disappear.

The usual loin-cloth (*ndǫmɪ*) that all women wear is a small
rectangular double piece of cotton cloth, rubbed with fat and red
clay. The men do not wear any garment of this sort.

I will here mention an observation made by M. Schoeller which is unknown to me and all other authors. As I do not understand him clearly, I will quote. He says that »männer und knaben das männliche glied unter dem lendengürtel, in diesem fall unter einer schnur oder einem metalldraht hindurchziehen und auf diese weise gewissermassen die beschneidung ersetzen»[1].

No headgear is worn. A number of old men, however, wear during the hottest part of the year as a protection against the sun a round scull-cap of black goat- or calf-skin, which fits so tightly on the head that it is difficult to distinguish at a distance.

Sandals (*kɩatu*) are used only on journeys and even then not by everyone. They are of the usual type: a leather sole, coarsely cut to the shape of the foot and fastened with straps. Before the small stools came into use the natives took a piece of leather called *kɩ6ɩƥ*ə with them on their travels to sit on when they rested.

2. **Ornaments.**

The Akamba wear a great number of ornaments (*maƥ*ǫ) of various kinds, especially metal ones, but they never overload their bodies with them on ordinary occasions. On account of the composition and chⲟice of colours these ornaments are attractive even to European ideas of beauty, and the fine execution of the work must arouse admiration. »These metal objects», says v. Höhnel in his previously mentioned description of his travels, »show with regard to work and taste a skill that puts everything of this sort we have formerly seen in Africa completely into the shade». Generally speaking everyone makes his own ornaments for himself, but the young men, who also use the greatest number, are specialists in this department and devote a great part of their time to this occupation. A married woman gets her ornaments from her husband, a girl from her father, his friends or her admirers among the young men.

The metal ornaments of various kinds are characteristic, but it is especially trade wire that is used in an ingenious and skilful way. Besides ornaments for the different sexes there are also

---

[1] M. Schoeller, Mitteil. über meine Reise nach Equatorial-Afrika und Uganda 1896—1897, II, p. 314.

those for different ages, and they also vary in the different parts
of the country.

The women wear round the waist a belt of beads (*kɩ̯ɑma*),
which in the case of young girls may be 2 dm. broad and resembles a sort of corset. The older women, however, only wear
a few strings of big blue ring-shaped glass beads of the older
type, while the girls' broad belts consist of white and red china
beads, which show up beautifully against their dark skins. Blue
and white beads are also used together. Originally all married
women wore blue beads (*kɩtæ̯tɩ*) and the girls red and white ones,
but nowadays many of the younger wives retain the belts of beads
they wore as girls.

Men do not wear these belts. It is only at the dances that
the youths decorate themselves with wire spirals (*mulɩa*) round
their waists and chests. These spirals are twisted round a thick
iron wire. They are closed by one end being put into the other
and twisted half a turn, so that the two ends interlock. When
they are placed on the upper part of the body they are fixed
sparsely at a few fingers' breadths interval. They are also used
as neck-rings (called *ndɩ̯ɡa*), either alone or several one above the
other, forming a sort of collar. They are also worn round the
neck by women, who only wear them round the body in exceptional cases.

A number of women also wear round the waist a strip of
leather trimmed with cowry shells (*ɡgutu*). This seems to be an
older decoration which is dying out. Cowry shells are not much
used in Ukamba nowadays as ornaments; they have been super-
seded by china beads and trade wire.

There are a great number of neck ornaments of different kinds.
Besides the above-mentioned metal spirals the old ringshaped blue
glass beads are also used as necklets, which are worn exclusively
by old women. A characteristic decoration of the young men
and of girls too is the *ɩmɩlɩ*, a neck-ring of bast, tightly bound
with links of small white china beads. This ornament, very tasteful in its simplicity, is worn by youths around the head as well.
In East Ukamba, where it is called *ɩɓatɩ*, it usually consists of
beads of different colours. As a rule variegated bead ornaments are
preferred in the east, while those of one colour are liked best in
Ulu. Thus we find in general use in the east and characteristic

for the Kitui district a broad flat neck-ring (*ŋgalıa*, called *ısoa* in the west) composed of many rows of green and blue china beads threaded on steel wire, fastened close to each other in the same plane.

On these neck-rings there often hangs a round flat piece of the shell of a Conus mollusc (*kıɓuc*), which is much in favour as an ornament in East Africa. The Kamba youths make them themselves from the top piece of a Conus species about 0,5 dm long, which is sold by the Indian traders but was formerly brought

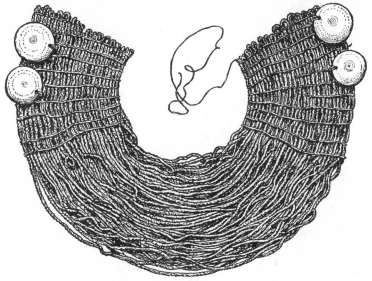

Fig. 79. Girl's collar, East Ukamba. Iron chains with Conus shells attached. ¹/₄ nat. size. Riksmus. Ethn. coll. Inv. 12. 7. 125.

from the coast. It is also common for the young dandies to wear them at the top of the forehead fastened to the hair.

The *kıɓuo* is used with a successful effect as an appendage to the *ŋguʃı*, a decoration for the neck or collar for young girls consisting of thick iron chains which partly cover the shoulders and fall down over the breast. At the back they are bordered by these shells, which stand out beautifully against the dark skin Fig. 79 shows a rather modest example of this type. The East African Company's old copper *pesas* sometimes are fastened together into tasteful chains, which are worn over the shoulders.

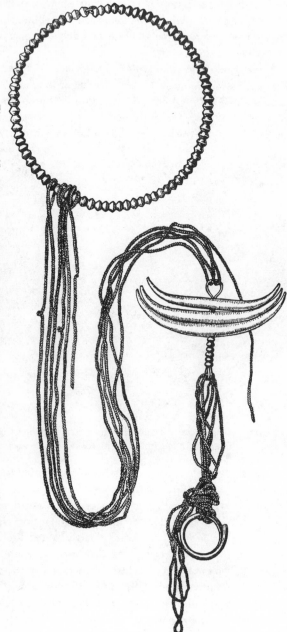

Fig. 80. Necklet of metal beads. Brass chain with ornaments of tin attached. ½ nat. size. Riksmus. Ethn. coll. Inv. 12. 7. 167.

Chains of different metals and fineness are much used as necklets. Those made of iron are especially worn by married women.

Necklets are also made of metal beads (*ndeka*), which the young men make themselves. They are threaded on wire. The neck-ring in fig. 80 consists of these.

The older men, who do not use many ornaments, do not always wear necklets. One sees on them, however, one or more chains or rings (*ukumu*) of thick metal wire, twisted round another piece of metal wire

Fig. 81. Neck-ring of copper wire $^1/_4$ nat. size. Riksmus. Ethn. coll. Inv. 12. 7. 165.

(fig. 81). Fig. 82 shows a breast ornament for older men, a very thick, spirally twisted copper wire, hanging on a neck-chain of the same metal. As a rule hanging objects of one kind or another are fixed on the neck ornaments, especially chains. In fig. 80 we thus see a brass chain with an ornament of tin, representing the utensil used to whisk blood in order to separate the fibrin. Flat copper rings made of thick wire or the old copper pesa are commonly used as hanging ornaments.

A special group of necklets consists of those that are made by twisting the narrow roots of the *kyulu* grass. These — a number of other roots are used as well — have, espe-

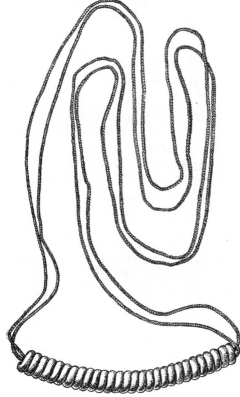

Fig. 82. Breast ornament of copper. $^1/_2$ nat. size. Riksmus. Ethn. coll. Inv. 12. 7. 168.

cially when in a fresh condition, a peculiar, somewhat suffocating smell, which the natives like and which stimulates their sexual desires. This necklet is consequently worn specially by the young men and girls, but also by married women when they sleep with their husbands. Several of them are usually worn fastened together and they are also worn on the head. The older men seem never to use them. The aromatic lilac buds of *musonzonƺa* (Spæranthus,

Lippia?) are used for necklets for children. Similarly in Kitui they wind the strongly-smelling *muta* plant (Verticillatæ), which is also a *ƺondu* plant, round the neck, and when the girls go to dance they sometimes put *ko*, a strongly aromatic Mentha-like species of Verticillatæ, in the chains they wear on their ears.

Kɩpua is a necklet made of the roots of a rather large grass, small round pieces of which are cut and threaded on cords (fig. 83). It is worn by women and sometimes by young men.

Fig. 83. Necklet, made of grass roots. ¹/₄ nat. size. Riksmus. Ethn. coll. Inv. 12. 7. 131.

In the places where Coix lacrymae Jobi grows, such as at the River Nthua (*nɗua*), necklets are occasionally made of its seeds (*ƺgalə*), the well-known Job's tears. In former times, while trade beads were still rare, these seeds were said to have been used as ornaments. The Akamba thus use seeds, pieces of wood and other vegetable substances as ornaments only to a very slight extent, while the Akikuyu, on the other hand, do so very much. The necklets coming from Kikuyu, made of small sticks of hard dark wood, are called by the Akamba *nɗaƺga* and are occasionally met with.

Round the wrists both men and women wear metal armlets, which have the common name of *kɩtaƺga* (or *kɩtaƺa*). They are made of trade wire, which is either kept unaltered in thickness or is melted into broader armlets as shown in fig. 84—86. As we

see, simple ornaments are often engraved[1]. Especially in the case of
the narrower kinds several are worn together, so that a part of
the forearm is covered. The *anakɔ*
wear a special *kɪtɔŋga*, a kind of
cuff of alternate copper and brass
rings, often covering the whole
forearm. This ornament, which is
at most about ten years old, is
very beautiful.

Fig. 84. Armlet of copper. Nat. size.

We find on the Kamba women the arm spirals of thick wire
that are common in Central Africa, and men too sometimes wear

Fig. 85. Armlet of brass. Nat size.   Fig. 86. Armlet of brass. Nat. size.

a spiral round the upper or lower part of the arm. In the Machakos
district many women wear an ornament of this sort below the
knee as well, a custom that is not found in the east, and is cer-

---

[1] A great number of these decorations are oval in shape, with
pointed ends, as shown in fig. 84. This type of decoration is also
found among the Masai, the Somalis and the Galla, but, in spite of its
simplicity, does not seem to occur among negro tribes. It is therefore
possible to assume that the Akamba borrowed this ornamentation from
their Hamitic neighbours mentioned above. Among the objects —
about 260 in number — from Ukamba and adjacent districts that were
brought home by Dr. G. Kolb in the 'nineties and handed over by
him to the Natural Historical Court Museum in Vienna there are also
some armlets of quite the same type as shown in fig. 84. Dr. W.
Hein points out that the ornamentation on these is quite ike the ovals
on the armlets from the bronze age in Europe, which is interesting to
note, even though one cannot immediately draw any conclusions from
this as to the origin of these pointed ovals of North-East Africa. See
W. Hein, Armringe von Eibesthal in Niederösterreich und von Ukamba
in Afrika. Sitzungsber. d. Anthrop. Ges. in Wien 1898, p. 53.

tainly borrowed from the Masai or the Akikuyu. They are said
to have been fashionable in former times on men as well, and
one may still, although rarely, come across some old man wearing
this leg ornament. Apart from it not many ornaments are worn
on legs or ankles. A chain or cord with blue or white beads is,
however, usually worn, and at dances the young men twist fine
chains round the lower part of the leg.

As the thick wire is bound tightly round the extremities and
is seldom taken off, it easily causes troublesome abrasions. The
natives try to alleviate the pain arising from these by putting soft
leaves, etc. between the metal and the wound. The author has
seen girls who have endured sores caused in this way for weeks,
which would have been healed in a few days if they had left off
the spirals. This they will not do
on any condition, saying that the
young men would not care for
them or would not want to dance
with them without their ornaments, and so they prefer to suffer
for their appearance.

Fig. 87. Armlet of tin with copper
insertions. $^1/_2$ nat. size. Riks-mus.
Ethn. coll. Inv. 12. 7. 176.

Some additional ornaments for
the arms may be mentioned here:
samba is a rectangular piece
of embroidery with white, blue
or red beads, which is worn by women, sometimes by the *anakɔ*,
on the upper part of each arm. The beads form geometrical
patterns, usually triangular. The patterns seem to have no special
signification. Used most in East Ukamba.

Fig 87 shows a tin armlet with insertions of copper wire. It
is worn on the upper arm by older men and also by women. This
type, like the above described armlets of copper and brass, is
made by persons specially skilled in this work, who melt the metal
and pour it into a mould that is either cut out in wood or formed
in sand. Armlets of this type are also cut out of ebony (*mubɪggo*),
which is mounted with small metal pins.

Armlets of ivory (*ukopo* or *ŋgopo*), which are worn only by
men, are comparatively rare in Ukamba nowadays. They have,
however, never been in common use, but have only been worn
by elephant hunters or rather eminent persons. Even in Hilde-

brandt's time they were only worn »by a few nobles». Fig. 88
shows the form typical for Ukamba; the thickness varies, however. The elephant also provides
the material for another sort of
armlet, namely those that the hunters, when they kill one of these
animals, usually cut out of its hind
feet. They are very proud of this
ornament. The natives say that
they cannot cut these out of the
pachyderm's forefeet, as the horny
material from which the ring is
cut is there present to a less

Fig. 88. Armlet of ivory. ½ nat.
size. Riksmus. Ethn. coll. Inv.
12. 7. 182.

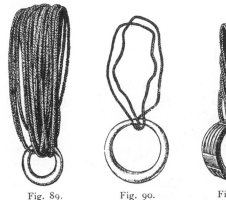

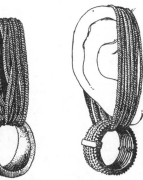

Fig. 89. Fig. 90. Fig. 91. Fig. 92.

89—90. Ear-rings of tin with metal chains, typical. ½ nat. size.
91. Earring of tin. 92. Ear-ring, consisting of 7 copper rings,
held together by cross-pieces of tin.

extent. As, of course, the natives are no longer allowed to hunt
elephants, these ornaments have become rather rare.

We now pass to ornaments for the ears.

The Akamba never deform their ears like the Masai, Akikuyu
and other tribes influenced by the Masai, but only make a small
round hole in the lower lobe of the ear. The hole is made with
an acacia thorn and is kept open by inserting some object in it
until it is healed. Only metal ornaments for the ears are worn,
no wooden ones as in the case of the Masai and their imitators.
Here and there in the east there are certainly seen boys with

short wooden peg (*kıkulu*) in the lower lobe of the ear; these, however, are not ornaments, but are used to stretch the hole, which
in certain places in East Ukamba is made somewhat larger than
the ordinary size.

Ear decorations are used mostly by the young people, who
to a great extent make them for themselves, as they do almost
all ornaments, when they begin to go to dances (cf. p. 143).
Characteristic for the tribe are round tin rings, *ıbulı* (figs. 89 and
90), which are placed either in the hole in the ear or hung with
chains over it, as shown in fig. 92. Another very common variant of the *ıbulı* is cylindrical, adorned with grooves running along
it, as shown in fig. 91. Of these the one that is placed in the
hole in the ear-lobe is the older. From these two basic forms
local variants have then arisen, such as when in the Machakos
district they began in 1912 to wear instead of *one* ear-ring a
number of thin ones attaining altogether about the same thickness
as the single one. An example of these ear-rings of the latest
fashion, which are also made of copper, is given in fig. 92, which
shows seven jagged copper rings, held together by cross-pieces
of tin. But it is unnecessary to discuss these unimportant things
any further; it would only burden the account with details of
very little value.

Finger-rings (*ŋgomə*) are used and worn on any finger, usually several of them on the same finger. They are made of metal
which is either kept smooth or engraved with the same decorations as the armlets. There are also rings made of fine, spirally
rolled wire or else of hollowed-out one-cent pieces (small money
for British East Africa), which were at first made of aluminium.

A finger-ring that deserves special mention is the one called
by Hildebrandt the Akambas' »war-ring», which »in the shape of
an extended shield protects the index finger and the back of the
hand against sword-cuts». It is only seldom met with nowadays
and seems to have been borrowed from the Galla» (H., p. 356). This
type of ring is found in the collections in the Berlin Museum
brought home by H. As I have not seen it, I dare not give a
positive utterance on the question, but I must state that for my
own part I have never heard of such war-rings among the Akamba,
nor do I know them from the southern Galla I visited. The latter
use, however, another sort of »war-ring», not as a protection but

as a weapon, namely a ring with two sharp edges, which is worn
on the little finger and with which they strike, for preference, at
the face, cutting from the top downwards. Om the other hand I
have seen a few older Kamba men wearing rings of the type described by H., but these seemed to be only worn as trophies
taken from the Masai or Akikuyu [1]. The fact that the owners
would on no conditions dispose of them to me supports this.
Among the Masai at least they are only ornaments, as they are
worn only by women. Merker definitely states that the Masai
do not make them themselves, but say that they come from the
Kikuyu country.

Hildebrandt's expression »war-ring» has caused misunder-
standings in books. Thus Frobenius [2] has classified them among
the few battle rings found in Africa, probably overlooking H's
statement th it they were used as a protection and only noticing
his supposition that they were borrowed from the Galla.

In this chapter I shall also mention certain finger-rings and
armlets in the form of a narrow strip of leather, which is worn
by the older men. I am not certain as to their purpose, but they
do not seem to be pure ornaments, but a sort of souvenir, sometimes cut out of the skin of sacrificial animals, sometimes of such
as have been consumed at some festive meal. As is the case
among the Akikuyu a number of the older men also wear a goat's
beard with the strip of skin belonging to it fastened round the leg
below the knee.

Finally we must add a few words concerning the variations
and alterations within this group of ornaments. Although, of
course, the primitive peoples, generally speaking, keep to their traditional customs, there is one department especially in which they,
like all human beings, give freeer play to the caprices of fashion,
and that is just in this department of ornaments. We understand
from what has been already said that during late years these
have shown some small changes. Unfortunately the oldest source
we have, Krapf's work, gives no information as to ornaments in
older times. Hildebrandt, on the other hand, gives (p. 352 ff.) a
good description of the ornaments in his time. In many things

---

[1] Reproduced by Merker (Die Masai, fig. 61) and Hollis (The
Masai, pl. XIV).

[2] L. Frobenius, Der Ursprung der Afrikan. Kulturen, p. 117.

the variations between then and now are of secondary importance, but some details may be given. Thus the round pieces of the shells of ostrich-eggs (resembling the white Conus shell), that were worn fastened to the belt of beads, seem now to have quite disappeared, just as the pieces of German pfennigs and brass counters with holes at the edges, which H. introduced and which, according to him, became very popular. The present typical ear-rings do not seem to have existed either, but there were simpler forms instead, made of wire. It is of greater interest to observe that at that time some persons had 4—6 holes at the edge of the muscle of the ear, but the small hole in the lobe was the most usual fashion even then.

A number of other ornaments, dating from the end of the 'eighties, are described by L. v. Höhnel[1].

If all these ornaments are to have the best possible effect they must be kept bright and shining. So they are polished continually and washed with sand and water. For this purpose they also use the leaves of certain plants, especially of *kɪubɪ*, a Rumex species, the seed of the baobab and the pulp of the tamarind fruit, which contains a strong acid.

3. Hairdressing, treatment of the beard and of hair on other parts of the body.

There is no head-dress that can be called typical for the tribe; one may say instead that there are great number of fashions. Especially among the men everyone seems to wear his hair as he thinks best. The same person also alters his coiffure; he will, for instance, have his head clean-shaved for a time and then later on let the hair grow again. One sees clean shaven heads in both sexes and at all ages. Sometimes, on the other hand, a little hair is left at some spot, for instance in the shape of a round spot on the neck or forehead, or a piece like a comb along the head. Another way is not to shave the head, but to keep it cut short except above the forehead, where it is allowed to grow. A rather popular fashion among the young people — perhaps influenced by the inhabitants at the coast — is to shave thin lines on the head,

---

[1] Zum Rudolph-See and Stephanie-See, p. 800. See also M. Schoeller's work mentioned above, vol. I, pl. XXVII ff.

between which the hair, rubbed with fat, is left growing in similar thin lines. The married women often plait their hair into tufts and rub the whole head with fat and red ochre. This coiffure, which may really be called characteristic for the married women, is called *mutundu*; it is less often seen on men. The *anakɔ* usually let a small tuft of hair — called *kɨpuku* — grow out in order to be able to fasten the white Conus shell more easily on the head.

According to information that I received the present genera-tion of old men in the Machakos district wore as *anakɔ* their hair plaited in a pigtail in the Masai and Kikuyu fashion; the latter tribe, like so many others, also imitated the Masai in this respect.

It is more uncommon to see people with long and freely grow-ing hair. Those who suffer from illness for a time, however, let the hair grow and when one sees long hair it is pretty certain that the wearer is ill. Similarly a child's hair is allowed to grow if its mother was ill at the accouchment. In only one case do I know of long hair being worn for another reason, namely by a medi-cine man on account of special orders from the *aimu*, the spirits.

The hair is shaved with a razor (*wænzi*) of the usual knife type; as a matter of fact any kind of knife is used. It is made wet with water; no kind of soap is used. The men shave each other; the women are, however, always shaved by the men. A person who shaves a medicine man must, on account of the magic powers he possesses, take care not to move round him while shaving. From our point of view it is, strictly speaking, incorrect to translate *wænzi* by 'razor', as the beard, as we shall see, is never shaved, but is pulled out. The razor is sharpened on a rather large stone (*inɔ* 'whetstone'), which usually lies at the *pomɔ*. How the hair that is removed is hidden has already been mentioned in connection with magic.

The eyebrows are also shaved with knives. The hair beneath the armholes and on the private parts is either shaved or pulled out with tweezers.

Both sexes pull out the eyelashes with tweezers. These are made of iron and are of a type widespread in East Africa (fig. 93). The young people adorn theirs by twisting metal wire or giraffe-hair round them, so that the neat little articles serve at the same time as ornaments. The natives always carry them with them, usually fixed on a chain round the neck, on which the snuff-bottle is worn. They usually have several at the same time (I have seen as many as five), which clearly indicates the ornamental character of the object (fig. 94).

The tweezers reproduced here, which are called *ŋgoṣə*, are typical of those used by the young people. The old men use either similar ones, although about twice as big, or else such as are shown in fig. 95. They are called *ŋgǫla*.

Every adult native removes the different kinds of hair we have spoken about. The young people begin to do this as soon

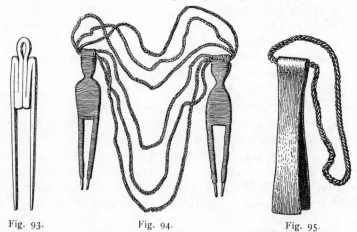

Fig. 93.   Fig. 94.   Fig. 95.

93. Tweezers for removing hair. 94. Tweezers for removing hair, twisted with copper wire. 95. Tweezers used by older men. $^1/_2$ nat. size.

as they are big enough to be interested in the opposite sex, which happens about the same time as they begin to take part in the public dances. It is thus done with the view of embellishing their appearance and making themselves as attractive as possible to the other sex. But it is also a rule of the toilet that applies to everyone and a fashion that anyone who cares about his appearance is very careful to follow. They also try to appear as »clean-shaven» as possible on the different parts of the body, and it is exceedingly common to see men squatting at the *þǫmə* pulling out especially the hairs of their beards, which of course grow most quickly. The process is sometimes a trifle painful. With their alert sense of humour the Akamba have made this troublesome but necess-

ary occupation give rise to a riddle, which, translated freely, is
as follows: »What is the contest at the *pɔmə* which must be settled
as quickly as possible?». Answer: »The contest between the
mutumɩa and the *ŋgɔla* (tweezers)».

According to Hildebrandt (p. 350) the Akamba think that the
removal of the eyelashes produces keenness of vision, a reason for
this practice that is unknown to me.

4. Perfuming and painting of the body.

I shall take the opportunity of mentioning two additional
matters in this connection, namely the custom of using certain
aromatically smelling plants as a sort of perfume for the body
and garments, and the use of pigments for beautifying the body.

The perfume, if we may call it so, consists of powdered parts
of plants mixed with fat and is called *kɩutu*. They use especially
woodmeal from certain trees, in which woodpeckers have pecked
holes. Material for *kɩutu* is also obtained from: *kɔ*, a species of
Verticillatæ mentioned above; the small greenish-black, pleasantly
aromatic fruit of the *ŋgænea*, a little tree with strong thorns; the
vanilla-smelling roots of *mubukulwa* (Apocynaceæ? Asclepiadeæ?)
and the flowers of a Gnaphalium species, the native name for
which I do not know.

kɩutu is much used at dances, not only those of the young
people, but also in the religious spirit dances. I cannot decide
whether in this case it merely has a refreshing effect or if it also
has some religious import, but a certain importance seems to be
attached to it, as the *kɩutu* that is used at these dances is sought
for by the medicine men.

Pigments on the body are used especially by the young
people at the dances. Many women, however, even at ordinary
times, use the red ochre (*mbu*) which they rub in their hair to
paint their cheeks with as well. With it the young people paint
spots on their cheeks and draw rings round their eyes when they
go to a dance. Another red species of earth, which is lighter
than *mbu* but is used in the same way, is *nɗa*. A lump of ochre
is often seen lying in the larder. A white colouring-matter, probably a kind of chalk (*ɩa*), is also used. The *anakɔ* paint, among
other things, fine zigzag lines on the legs with it. With the deep

yellow pollen of a Typha species (*ikaŋga*) they paint rings round
the eyes and smear the edges of the eyelids, for which ochre is
also used. Finally they are accustomed to stick some white or
deep red or yellow petals on the face, which form an effective
contrast to the skin.

5. Cicatrization and tattooing.

Cicatrization is employed to embellish the body by both sexes,
but mostly by women. Raised scars (*ndǫ*) of a lighter colour than
the skin are produced. They are situated on
the breast, back and abdomen, and are made sometimes with a knife (*ndǫ ịa kabịo*), sometimes with
needles (*ndǫ ịa mukuba*). They sometimes form simple lines, as for instance a circle of points round the
nipples, sometimes decorations, such as zigzag
lines, half moons; arrow heads, etc. (fig. 98—102).
That the wounds may heal more quickly they are
rubbed with fat. To make the scars raised they
use a rather painful means, namely the milky juice
of the *kịaþa* (Euphorbiaceæ), a small tree with
whole leaves. On women the scars on the front
of the body are made by women, those on the
back part by men.

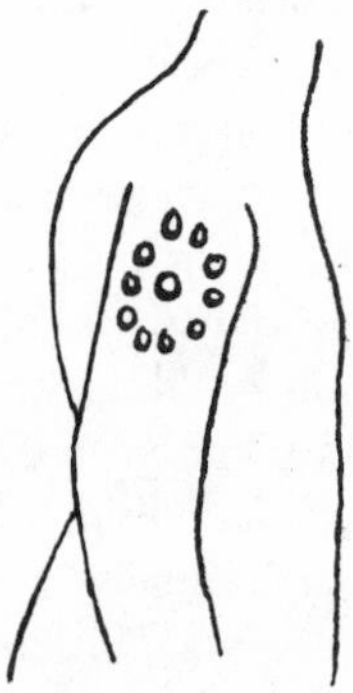

Fig. 96. Cicatrice
on a man's upper
arm. ²/₃ nat. size.

There is no tradition about the origin of the
cicatrization. It seems to be looked upon exclusively as a means of embellishing the natives' exterior. A fact, however, that indicates a deeper,
perhaps primitive conception that has now fallen
into oblivion, is that this cicatrization is carried
out preferably when the crop is ripe, according
to a statement made to me »when the *mwǫ* (Penicillaria spicata) is ripe».

Fig. 97. Cicatriz-
ation on a man's
arm. ¹/₂ nat. size

Many men put a number of small swellings, a little bigger
than a pea, on the deltoid muscles of the arm (fig. 96). On many
one also sees a larger swelling *ndǫkæþo* that reminds one of a four-
pointed star (fig. 97). This usage, which is found among the
Akikuyu as well, is perhaps borrowed from the Masai.

Tattooing is found less frequently among the Akamba, and then

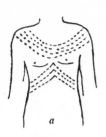 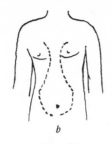 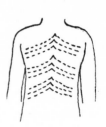

Fig. 98 a. Fig. 98 b. Fig. 99.

98 *a, b.* Cicatrices on man. Front. *a* rather common form; *b* lyre-shaped. Among the Masai this form with different variations is the most common. 99. Man's back.

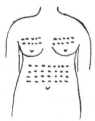 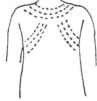 

Fig. 100. Fig. 101 a. Fig. 101 b.

100. Cicatrices on a woman. 101 *a, b.* Women's backs.

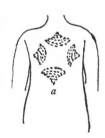 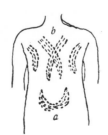 

Fig. 102 a. Fig. 102 b. Fig. 102 c.

102 *a, b, c.* Women's backs. *a* half-moon, a common pattern; *b* cross-roads (*makwatana ma nžɪa*).

practically always on the face, the cheeks. Figures representing the sun and the moon are the most common (fig. 103). They are black, darker than the colour of the skin, and are produced in the following way:

The skin is scratched with the rough stalks of the plant *kaẓwla* (Rubiaceæ, Galium?) used like files. Then the powdered root of the plant *mwoḵẓa* (Plumbago)[1], called by the old people *wala*, is taken, dipped in milk or the juice of sugarcane and placed on the wound. The compress is left on the wound for a night and is then removed. When the wounds are healed, black marks are left. The method is said to be very painful; the wound swells, »burns like fire and one cannot sleep at night».

Fig. 103.   Black tattooings on the face, usually one on each cheek. The first one represents the sun, the two next ones the moon.

6. Teeth-chipping and extraction.

Both sexes deform a number of the front teeth of the upper jaw by chipping (*kuseuḇẓa*[2] *maẓo*). This custom is found over the whole of the tribe, but differs in different districts, partly in regard to the number of teeth so deformed, partly in regard to the shape. Each district, however, keeps pretty regularly to its custom, and so one can decide fairly accurately by his teeth from what part of the country a native is. Thus in Ulu six, less often 7—8 teeth are cut and drawn out into narrow, sometimes awl-shaped points, but in the Kitui district only four with triangular, shorter and broader points (fig. 104). In the whole of East Ukamba, from Mumoni to Kikumbuliu (and in Kibwezi) only two teeth are cut, and these are shaped in the same way as in Kitui. In Ikutha, however, I saw teeth with curved points (as in fig. 105), sometimes suggesting half-moons, and there are possibly local variations in several places.

---

[1] Presumably Plumbago ceylonica, which the Masai use for the same purpose. Merker, Die Masai, p. 151.

[2] = to cut, pare? Or is it identical with *kuseuḇẓa* 'to make beautiful?'

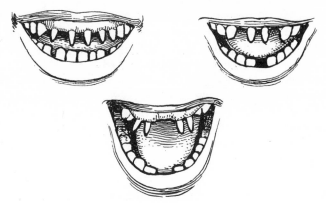

Fig. 104. Teeth of three young Kamba men, Machakos. From a
photograph by C. F. Johnston, missionary.

The most primitive custom seems to have been to cut only
two teeth. It was then a fairly obvious development to embellish
the appearance still more by increasing the number.
Hildebrandt gives the number as four in his description,
but this only applies to East Ukamba. What the case
was in Krapf's time is not clear from his work; he only
says that »the teeth are artificially pointed». According
to the natives themselves the fashion prevalent in Ulu,
especially in the Machakos district, of pointing six
teeth or more is a recent one, which in 1910 had not
been carried out for many years. The latter statement

Fig. 105.
Pointed
teeth from
Ikutha,
East
Ukamba.

Fig. 106. Teeth-chipping, as describel on p. 394.

could easily be tested by investigation; I neglected, however, to
do so. When one comes to work out one's material at home
there is a great deal that one finds has been overlooked.

The pointing of the teeth is carried out in the way shown
in fig. 106. I may say in passing that I am rather pleased with
this photo, as during my year's stay in Ukamba and daily contact with the natives I only saw the
operation performed this one time.

A person who is going to have
his teeth pointed lays his head on the
operator's knee. He has a bit of wood
placed between his teeth, so that his
mouth is kept open and his jaws kept
steady. The instrument (*ŋgǣsa*) consists
nowadays of a European knife, on which
only a short piece of the blade has
been left, ground like a chisel (fig. 107).
The primitive instrument, which is now
seldom seen in use, is more clumsy
and is made of native iron in the same
shape as the Akamba's broad-axe (fig.
108).

Fig. 107.
Tool for
teeth-chip-
ping. Knife
of European
manufac-
ture. ²/₃ nat.
size

Fig. 108.
Tool for
teeth-chip-
ping, the old
original type.
¹/₂ nat. size.
Riksmus.
Ethn. Coll.
Inv. 12.7.256.

The operator places the instrument
against a tooth and strikes it carefully
with a stone or a piece of wood. In
this way he cuts away piece after piece,
in somewhat the same way as a sculptor
uses his chisel. The work takes about
5—8 hours, and is not carried out by
any special man, but by anyone who understands the art. The
young men often do it to each other. Of course they prefer to
trust someone who has a reputation for skill and can produce
really elegant points. Women cannot chip teeth, so the men perform the operation on them as well. When the work is done,
the beautified individual goes proudly to be admired by the girls
(the girls similarly to the young men) and to be envied by those
of his friends who have not yet had this improvement in their
appearance.

The consequence of this ill-usage of the teeth is that they

can no longer be effectively used for the purpose they are intended for and, what is still more serious, they are usually quite destroyed after a short time. They then level what are left, if it is necessary, bore holes in the roots with a pointed iron pin, an awl (*mukuɓa*), and fix in »false teeth». These are made of bone, preferably of the goat or hartebeest, which is said not to grow yellow so quickly. The fatter the hartebeest is, the better its bone is said to be. It is usually very difficult to distinguish these artificial teeth from the natural pointed ones. They are often whiter and finer than the latter, so that many natives actually prefer them to their own. The false teeth hold quite firmly and can only be taken out after being shaken for a while. They cannot be used for chewing.

They seem to prefer to carry out this operation at a certain time of the year, namely the period that shows no extremes of temperature or, as the natives themselves express it, »when the *mwę* (Penicillaria spicata) is ripe». For they say that »the teeth do not like too strong sun nor too cold weather either». We remember that the same expression, »when the *mwę* is ripe», is used to denote the most suitable time for carrying out cicatrization. For this too they choose perhaps the time of the year when the part of the body that is being treated, in this case the skin, is least exposed to strong heat or cold.

Teeth-chipping is widely spread in Africa, but in these districts the Akamba is the only tribe that practises it[1]. Nor is the custom found north of them in East Africa. They have no traditions at all about its origin. The motive for the usage has already been touched upon on p. 70, to which I refer the reader. Whatever it may have been originally, it is at the present moment — and has certainly been for many decades and longer — exclusively a thing of fashion, merely a refined manifestation of the desire on the part of the natives to embellish their external appearance. Just as for this reason, for instance, they bore the lobes of their ears, so they deform their teeth. »A person without pointed teeth looks like an animal», say the Akamba, a statement that is reported from several other peoples, although it is of no importance for the

---

[1] According to Hildebrandt (p. 304) some of the Wanyika file a deep notch in one of the front teeth of the upper jaw. The edges of the tooth then remains in the form of two points.

question of the origin of the custom, as this view of the matter, as v. Ihering observes, is, of course, a secondary one in relation to the origin of the custom [1]. The fact that the deformation is only carried out after the young people have reached the age of puberty does not prove any connection with the rites associated with puberty. For it is only at the arrival at this age that the sexual impulses awaken and with them the desire to please the opposite sex and to associate with them, the latter desire finding expression especially in the wish to dance. To make themselves as attractive as possible for the dance they put on a great many ornaments. But they are not content with these, and try even to beautify the body itself, sometimes by painting, sometimes by direct injury to some of its parts. Thus teeth-chipping, like cicatrization, is comparable to the use of ornaments [2].

If one cares to do so, one may call teeth-chipping a tribal mark of the Akamba. It is, however, not obligatory to undergo this, although, for reasons easily understood, they do so all the same. Many realise the foolishness of it, but consider that the gain is greater than the loss.

In addition the Akamba take out two teeth in the lower jaw. This is done with a wooden peg, at the point of which a metal bead is fixed, and on which the operator strikes with an axe or other weapon. It is impossible to decide which of the two kinds of deformation is the older. The last-mentioned kind has its special name in Kikamba (*kwıɓa*), while the Ovaherero, for instance, have the same term (*okuha*) for both methods of procedure [3].

If one asks the young men why they have their teeth deformed, one always gets some of the following answers:

(1) Because it is a custom (the power of custom).

---

[1] H. v. Ihering, Die künstliche Deformiering der Zähne. Zeitschr. f. Ethnologie 1882, p. 218.

[2] I agree in other repects with the view of teeth-chipping in Africa that R. Lasch has put forward in Die Verstümmelung der Zähne in Amerika und Bemerkungen zur Zahndeformation im allgemeinen. Vide also W. Joests great monograph, Tatowieren, Narbenzeichnen und Körperbemahlen. Ein Beitrag zur vergleichenden Ethnologie. Joest considers all these things to be cosmetic, ornaments only.

[3] Dennert, Über die Sitte der Zahnverstümmelung bei den Ovaherero, Zeitschr. f. Ethn. 1907, p. 930.

(2) Because the girls think it is beautiful (the most important motive).

(3) Because one can spit nicely (the person who can spit farthest through the gap in the teeth of the lower jaw is admired).

A short story may be added, which illustrates in its way something of the importance attached to the deformation of teeth. It is certainly only a story, but at the same time a realistic picture, though an exaggerated one:

Some girls went to have their teeth pointed and removed. They were all improved in appearance, but one of them got much finer points than the others. On the way home one of them said: »Let us see who can spit the best and so find out which of us has got the most beautiful teeth». And they spat eagerly, the girl in question, however, farthest of all. Then her friends were seized with such envy that they threw her in the river and she was drowned.

A couple of the Akamba's many riddles have teeth-chipping as their subject. One, which tries in a humorous way to explain the origin of the custom, is as follows: »Who has taught us to point our teeth?» Answer: »*kıluma*», an Agave species with serrated leaves. Another is: »Tell me the man who lives amidst swords and spears?» Answer: »The tongue».

Chap. XXII. Music and dancing.

1. Musical instruments.

The Akambas' musical instruments are few and simple. Those commonly found are used in dancing, especially at the young people's dances, which are their favourite recreation. The most important instrument is, just as everywhere in Africa, the drum, of which there are the following kinds:

1) The ordinary dance instrument (*mbalıa*, in Eastern Ukamba *ŋguþa*). It is a cylinder of thin wood, narrowing somewhat towards the bottom, which has at the top a membrane (germ. »anpflöckung») fixed with pointed wooden wedges hammered hrough the walls of the drum. It is open at the bottom and thus belongs to the tube type (the german »röhrentrommeln»). The skin, from a goat, ox or other mammal (never from the snake or lizard), is soaked before being put on and then tightens when it dries. The player stands with the drum fixed between his knees and beats it with both hands. A cord of bast or sinews fixed in a hole serves to carry the drum to and from the dancing place. Most of the drums are unpainted, without any ornamentation. Fig. 109 shows one painted with red earth.

2) A drum of almost the same type as the preceding, but considerably larger (diameter about 0.5 cm.) and not growing narrow at the bottom is the *kıþæmbɔ*. It is used only by old people, especially by the old women and preferably at religious festivals and exorcisms as music to the dance *kılumı*, the spirit dance of the old women. Formerly it was also used as a signal drum at hostile attacks. The drummer sits astride the instrument, which rests on the ground, or else he (she) sits on the ground himself and leans the drum against the inner part of one of the thighs.

The *kıþæmbɔ* drum has, etymologically, certainly nothing to do with *kuþæmba* 'to sacrifice' or its derivative *ıþæmbɔ* 'place of

Fig. 109.
Dance drum (*mbaḷẓa*).
¹/₄ nat. size.

Fig. 110.
Dance drum (*kẓa*).
¹/₈ nat. size.

sacrifice', although, as a matter of fact, it is closely connected with spirit worship. The word is, instead, probably identical with the term for the vessel of the same name, i. e. a cylindrical wooden vessel with a lid of skin.

3) A cylindrical drum with skin at both ends is called *ŋgoma*. The way in which the skin is put on is unknown to me; if the drum is indigenous, it ought to be by means of pegs being driven in. The *ŋgoma* was formerly used in one of the women's dances of the same name, which was afterwards succeeded by the *kɪlumɪ* and the *kɪpæmbɔ* drum. The drummer sat on the ground with the drum horizontally over his knees and beat it with one hand against each end.

At Kibwezi I have seen *ŋgoma*'s with two skins fastened with cords, but these are certainly, through the medium of the coast tribes, of Suaheli (Arabic) origin, which is borne out both by the method of fastening the skins and by the name (Kisuaheli *goma* 'drum'). Besides being used by the Suaheli and Arabs these drums are, as a matter of fact, also used by the Wanyika and the Waduruma and other tribes in the hinterland of Mombasa that have been influenced by the Suaheli and with which the Akamba in the south-east are in contact.

4) A dance drum for youths of quite another type is *kɪa* (formerly called *muɓuŋgu*). It consists of a spool-shaped wooden cylinder (fig. 110) with a bottom of skin (a) and a handle at the top (b). Inside the tube a stretched metal wire goes from the bottom up to the peg (c) fixed above the mouth. The specimen reproduced here is the biggest I came across.

The instrument is used by being held by the handle and rhythmically knocked against the ground, giving out a soft sound (the german »stosstrommel, stampftrommel»). The metal wire, which is, however, not obligatory, is intended to strengthen the sound. There are tubes of different thickness, which give different tones (intentionally?). Otherwise the sound is more softly monotonous than that of the *mbalʑa*, the present drum of the young people. The *kɪa* is now out-of-date, though it is found lying in many a hut.

This drum for knocking with seems to be fairly unique. Its prototype is probably, however, a bit of bamboo tube closed at the bottom, and, as a matter of fact, Hildebrandt (and, after H.

perhaps, R. Hartmann[1]) says that in his time such bamboo tubes were exclusively used by the Akamba, who got them from Kenia. No bamboos grow in Ukamba. As there was probably not always access to bamboo, they tried to make these drums of wood. It also appears as if the wooden *kʑa* drum arose after Hartmann's time and has now also disappeared. Percussion drums of bamboo, usually hung with small metal bells, are still found, however, among the Wapare, where I have collected them myself, and according to Frobenius also among the Waseguyu, i. e. generally speaking in some scattered places in East Africa[2].

There is no need to enter into the occurrence of this type of drum in Indonesia and Polynesia; I refer the reader to Frobenius. To draw conclusions from this occurrence as to remains of Malay-nigritic culture in these parts of East Africa appears rather inappropriate. The discovery that a sound can be produced by knocking a piece of bamboo against the ground is a very obvious one, but bamboo is so rare in Africa that the instrument could not attain any general dissemination there. It is not improbable, however, that this type of drum had formerly a greater distribution, but from the time when real drums came into use in Central Africa, they were preferred on account of their better sound and because they had the additional advantage that the material for them was everywhere easily accessible. Hildebrandt, who is a careful observer, does not, curiously enough, mention any real drums from Ukamba. May one draw the conclusion from this that these had not yet come into use in his time? (The Akikuyu, who in many respects are closely related to the Akamba, do not use drums.) If this is the case, it is quite easy to understand that after real drums came into use, they soon gave up the more difficult work of hollowing out a narrow wooden tube.

For reasons unknown to me Ankermann does not discuss percussion drums in his monograph on African musical instruments. Perhaps he looks upon them more as dance staves, under which appellation, for instance, Koch-Grünberg groups his knocking drum from North West Brazil, which, we may mention

---

[1] Abyssinien und die übrigen Gebiete der Ostkuste Afrikas, p. 233.

[2] L. Frobenius, Der Ursprung der Afrikanischen Kulturen, p. 187. F:s description of these bamboo tubes as open at one side does not apply to those I saw among the Wapare.

in passing, offers an interesting resemblance to that of the Akamba, with regard to decoration as well[1]. The term »dance stave» is, at least for the East African knocking drums, unsuitable, for the purpose of the tube is to produce sounds, even if possibly they are sometimes by chance swung in the hand.

For the decorations of the dance drums referred to here we have to turn to the chapter on the art of decoration.

* *

String instruments. The drum in its various forms is the only instrument that can be said to be in general use. There are two kinds of string instruments, but both are used only by specialists, if one may use the term.

An instrument that is used exclusively for a certain purpose and by a certain class of men, is the music-bow (*uta* 'bow'), with a wire string, which the medicine man uses when he gets into communication with the spirit world (fig. 111), as has been already described (p. 258). This music-bow is the only one in Africa that I know of which has the sounding body fixed between the string and the bow. Of the Akambas' musical instruments it is the only one that has no independent name. From a geographical point of view its occurrence in Ukamba is not remarkable, as Ankermann has shown the distribution of the music-bow over all that part of Africa that is inhabited by negroes. We may perhaps explain its occurrence in Ukamba only among the medicine men as a relic from an earlier and lower stage of culture[2]. For it is, of course, scarcely likely that this music-bow is a new instrument that has not yet attained any wider dissemination than among the medicine men. E. von Rosen, on the other hand, takes the few musical instruments fitted with calabashes that he found among the Batwa in the Bangveolo swamps to be an article of luxury that has not yet become widespread[3].

---

[1] Th. Koch-Grünberg, Zwei Jahre unter den Indianern (see Index under »Tanzstab»).

[2] The metal string is, although rare, not unique. Frobenius, Der Ursprung der Afrik. Kulturen, p. 122, mentions it from Angola.

[3] E. von Rosen, Träskfolket, p. 265.

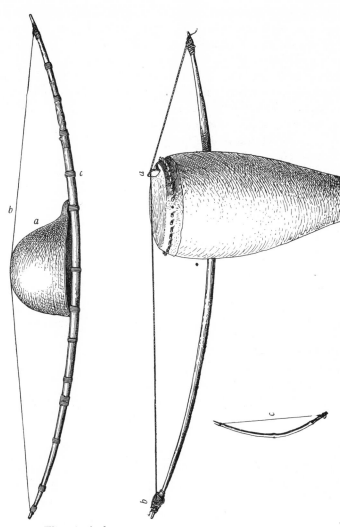

Fig. 111. The musical bow of the medicine man. *a* calabash as a sound-box, *b* wire, *c* wire as ornament. ¹/₈ nat. size. Riksmus. Ethn. Coll. Inv. 12. 7. 100.

Fig. 112. The *mbœ6ə* — fiddle with its bow, *c*. ¹/₆ nat. size. Riksmus. Ethn. Coll. Inv. 12. 7. 98.

The other string instrument is the *mbæɓə* (fig. 112). The sounding body is a calabash, the string a cord that is still more stretched by means of a little piece of calabash used as a bridge (a). The string-holder in our figure is bow-shaped, but in my collection there are also instruments with a straight stick and a piece of a side-branch still left at the end for fixing and tightening the string. This form is reproduced by Ankermann[1]. His specimen from the Berlin museum has no string, so he has reconstructed this without the bridge belonging to it. Similarly it is without the little bow of bast string (*c* in my fig.) with which the *mbæɓə* is played, and this causes A. to make an incorrect assumption about the method of playing it and consequently an incorrect classification of the instrument. The interesting thing about the *mbæɓə* is just the bow, the only example of the use of this that I know from East Africa south of Abyssinia.

The instrument is not common; I have seen it only in Kibwezi and Ikutha. It gives only a weak sound, and so it is never used at dances, but exclusively as a pastime, for the pleasure of the player himself and his audience. It is really the only one of the Akambas' instruments in which musical talent has any opportunity to show itself; its occurrence thus proves that there is such talent among the Akamba. One can come across real virtuosos, whose playing approaches actual melodies. It is said of these that they »can speak» with their instruments.

The *mbæɓə* is clearly not an indigenous instrument among the Bantu negroes, but we must look upon it as a form of the Arabs' *rebāb* (the Persians' *revave*)[2], variants of which, also with one string, are found spread over Northern Africa, north of the Bantu territory. Even the name *mbæɓə* must be identical with *rebāb* or some form of this word. A further question is that of finding out how the Akamba got the instrument, as it does not seem to be found among the neighbouring peoples towards the coast, whence the Arabic influence in East Africa has, however,

---

[1] Die Afrikanischen Musikinstrumente, fig. 7. It is also depicted without any string by M. Schoeller, Mitteil. über meine Reise nach Äquatorial-Ost-Afrika und Uganda, 1896—97, vol. II, fig. C. II. S. does not, however, say exactly what the object represents.

[2] C. Sachs, Real-Lexikon der Musikinstrumente, Berlin 1913.

come. The *mbæƀə* I came across were found, however, only in East Ukamba[1].

Among the string instruments may also be counted a toy that the boys make from pieces of Sorghum stalks. When the Sorghum is reaped, they take 6—10 stalks of equal length, about 2 dm., and fix them together with a bast fastening. Along each one is a string split and the strings are stretched by means of a stick fixed across each end of the instrument. The strings are struck with a little peg. This toy is also called *mbæƀə*. The type appears in a larger and more complete form among several East African tribes, amongst others the Kavirondo, where I have also seen them used as toys.

Wind instruments. Of these there are in my collection horns of the greater Kudu and the Oryx. The former has the hole one blows through on the concave side, which according to Ankermann is most usual. I have, however, never seen them in use, but they are said to have been used on festive occasions, such as the solemn entry of a hunting party returning from a successful hunt.

The little war-flute (*ŋguli*), which is also made of horn, has been discussed and depicted on p. 192. Hildebrandt (p. 391), on the other hand, describes the war-flute as a »tubular flute of the thickness of a finger and with three holes», while Hobley's account agrees with mine. We shall soon find that the name *ŋguli* is also used for a tubular flute, but, on the other hand, there are no such flutes, at least at present, in Ukamba with three holes, but only with four, the most common number for African flutes.

The ordinary bamboo flute (*mutulælə*) is never used at dances but only as a pastime for young men and boys. The Kamba flute always has four holes, which are burnt out and which lie on the same side as the notch for the mouthpiece. The two first fingers of each hand are used and are held alternately over the holes.

A composite wind-instrument, which the young men use similarly for their amusement is the *sǫ* (plural *masǫ*). It consists of a bamboo tube about a metre long, fixed into a funnel of calabash

---

[1] To judge from a picture in J. G. Wood's Natural History of Man, Africa, p. 444, the Wahuma in Karagwe have a kind of *rebab*, played with a long bow.

as a resonance chamber (fig. 113). The upper end of the tube is stopped up. It is blown at a rectangular incision, 3 cm. long. I

Fig. 113. Wind-instrument (*sǫ*). Reed shaft with burnt ornaments. ¹/₈ nat. size. Riksmus. Ethn. Coll. Inv. 12. 7. 105.

have tried in vain to produce sounds in this trumpet, a task which demands practice and good lungs.

Fig. 114. Flute (*nžumąli*), toy for boys, ¹/₄ nat. size. Riksmus. Ethn. Coll. Inv. 12. 7. 277.

From a linguistic point of view the name *sǫ*, with the absence of a class prefix, gives the impression of a loan-word. Ankermann (fig. 97) reproduces quite the same instrument from the Ussukuma, south of Lake Victoria.

Among the small boys' toys there are also some little objects that come under the heading of musical instruments:

nžumąli is a complicated flute, consisting of a piece of tube with four holes burnt out and a rolled-up maize leaf as a funnel for the sound (fig. 114). The mouth aperture is made at a joint of the tube. This little flute is the only one that has a reed, a piece cut out on the tube (*a* in the figure). Bast is fastened round the tube over the base of the reed (*b*), and a straw (*c*) is placed in front of it to keep it open. The lower end of the maize leaf is kept together by an acacia thorn or a little peg (*f*)[1].

Flutes with vibrating reeds seem to be rare among the negroes[2]. Because of this and still more because of its name, I assume that this little

[1] I do not know any instrument with a similar funnel for the sound from Africa, but I take the opportunity of mentioning that in the Ethnogr. Museum of Stockholm there is, coming from India (Inv. 81. 204) a horn of rolled-up strips of palmleaf, rolled in the same way as our maize leaf above (»Borikna poukni»).

[2] Hildebrandt (p. 391) mentions one from the Wataita.

toy flute has arisen under Suaheli-Arabic influence. *Nzomari* or *zomari* is, according to Steere, »a kind of clarionet, a pipe». I do not know what it looks like, but as far as the Suaheli word is concerned, it is clearly identical with the Arabic *zumāra*, which is certainly, however, a double flute.

The boys also make a sort of double flute or pipe of two short pieces of stalk (0.5 to 1 dm.) of Rhicinus communis, fastened alongside each other with bast. A bast fastening between the openings gives additional firmness. The pipe is called *ŋgulı*, just like the war-flute. It gives a strong, shrill sound, which it needs, however, a certain amount of practice to produce.

This type of flute seems to me to be fairly isolated. If we leave out of account the divergent Arabic-Egyptian double flutes, I know only one similar instrument, namely the flute from the Jaunde in the Cameroons reproduced by Ankermann (fig. 74) after Frobenius (fig. 114). This is said to be blown from the top, whereas the Akamba pipe is blown, in the regular African way, from the side.

This investigation of the Akambas' musical instruments shows that although few in number, they offer a good deal of interest. We have found, on the one hand, instruments of a primitive type that are undoubtedly indigenous, such as the drum for knocking with and the music-bow of the medicine man, on the other hand several others with foreign, Suaheli-Arabic, characteristics. For a complete understanding of the latter it would be desirable to know more about the instruments among the tribes between Ukamba and the coast, but for this the author lacks the necessary material.

2. Dancing.

It is not necessary to be an ethnologist to know that dancing, if not actually the dearest of all the pleasures of primitive peoples, is one of the dearest of them. Similarly it plays an important part in religion.

Dancing in general is called *wapı* in Kikamba and to dance *kwına wapı*, really to 'sing the dance'. Song and dancing are really inseparably connected (more closely connected than dance

and music) and the dance is alway accompanied with singing. In
the young peoples' dances the singing is conducted by a chief
singer (ŋguɨ), who is at the same time the leader of the dance. As a
sign of his dignity he sometimes carries a long stave in his hand,
which in some ways may be compared to the baton of the leader
of an orchestra. He leads the various figures in the dances and
with some word, for instance *basɨ* (enough), he shows when it is
time to pass to a new one. The ŋguɨ is also the author of the
songs that are sung during the dances. When one of these has
been sung so long that it is known, or when for some other
reason they have grown tired of it, it is he that makes up a new
one. One may say that almost at every full moon they take up
a new dancing song. The dances take place, of course, preferably on moonlight evenings and nights.

There is great rivalry and envy between different chief singers,
and they try to eclipse each other. It has also happened that
they have tried to bewitch one another by magic (*woɨ*).

A ŋguɨ must never eat the lungs of animals; this is thought
to be injurious to his own lungs and may spoil his good voice.
The most important thing about a good leading singer is, of
course, the strength of his voice; he has to be able to sing louder
than all the others.

»To dance» is also called *kutula*, which, however, always means
dancing with girls. Another expression is *kusuŋga*, which originally
had no special significance.

Each little district has its dancing place (*kɨtuto*)[1], where the
young people gather together in the evenings. Especially when
the girls have been together helping each other in the work in
the fields, they are wont to gather for a dance after its finish. The
different dances take place periodically, and seem to be arranged
according to the seasons, inasmuch as during a certain time only
a certain dance is danced and then disappears altogether for a
time, during which they go in just as eagerly for another dance.

The most common of the young peoples' dances is *mbalɨa*,
so called after the drum of the same name, which is the only

---

[1] < *kututa* 'to sweep'; the dancing place is always swept before
being used. It serves also as a meeting-place, a sort of club room for
the young people, who meet together here occasionally and discuss
their common concerns. (Cf. p. 185.)

instrument used in this dance, in which it serves to mark the time. As this dance is danced in the Machakos district, one can distinguish three parts. First a general dance in couples, i. e. the young men and girls arrange themselves in two ranks so that the partner stands opposite his lady and turns towards her. The ranks are sometimes quite military in their straightness, sometimes more curved. They bend a little forward and the young man puts his right cheek against the girl's right (fig. 115). The forearm is bent upwards, the upper arm rests against the side of the body. The upper part of the body is swayed in time with the music, the drums, and at the same time they rub their cheeks against each other. This rubbing is the most important part of the whole dance, as it produces pleasant

Fig. 115. Detail from a *moalʐa*-dance, Machakos. The man puts his right cheek aganist the girls right.

feelings. They like to stand so near each other that the girl's breast touches the man during the movements. As a matter of fact one can hardly call it a dance in our meaning of the word, as the feet do not move from their place, only the upper part of the body sways to and fro (fig. 115).

This goes on for about ten minutes, after which the girls retire and collect together in a cluster in a corner of the dancing place. There they remain standing with their arms round each others' waists, a characteristic position for Kamba girls. During this time the young men form a semicircle and stand thus for a little while singing. Then the girls, still in a cluster, begin to move forward, until they are standing in the semicircle of the men, with their arms all the while round each others' waists. They now have to choose partners to begin the dance again — for it is the girls that »ask for a dance» — and they make their choice known by moving a few metres towards the chosen man or simply by stretching out a hand. The young men are standing in tense expectation as to whether they shall be asked to dance by those

they like best. Besides, the girls are always in the minority, so that some of the boys are usually left without a partner. That the former are smaller in number is due to the fact that many of them are married when they are yet quite young and little. As soon as they are married they do not go to the dance of the young people, which, on the other hand, a married man may do. When the girls have made their choice, the dance begins again.

Fig. 116. The »band» at a *ṃbaḷa*-dance.

During the dance the men are practically naked, as they roll up their blanket into a sort of belt round their waist. On the dancing place there is always a small fire burning, at which the musicians now and then warm their drumskins so as to bring back their tension. The »band» consists of four to five drummers, who cluster together in a corner of the dancing place (fig. 116). At the fire those who are not so keen on dancing also squat so as to warm themselves and talk. Over the whole dancing place there are also darting about half-grown, still uncircumsized boys, who watch the dance with envious glances and try to practise the art for themselves until they have the right to take part. The more advanced among them make attempts at flirtation, but are dismissed by the girls, often pretty forcibly.

The custom of the girls' asking for the dance gives the Kamba girl an opportunity of showing which young man she likes best, and in this way the foundation of many marriages is laid during these nights of dancing. This is thus an advantage, but, on the other hand, the young men are easily made by this means into ridiculous fools unable to act for themselves, hunting for the girl's favour, while the latter are often as haughty and arrogant in their conduct as a spoilt and celebrated belle of the ball. If there are any young men present who are displeasing to them, it often happens that they declare they will not dance as long as these men are there, and actually leave the place if their request is not granted. The young men submit, drive the displeasing individuals away and run after the fair ones to implore them to stay.

Quarrels and disputes easily arise at the dancing place on account of jealousy, especially when »foreigners», i. e. youths from villages situated farther off, come there and »spoil» the dance. The whole thing may then very easily end up in a general fight. In ancient times the boys did not dare to go to dances outside their own little district, and where outsiders were bold enough to make their appearance in order to compete for the favour of the girls, there was always a fight. There were, however, populous districts, in which the *anakɔ*, gathered into bands, out of pure love of contention, used to go from one dancing place to another, and, if the natives at these places dared to utter the slightest murmur, they were driven away from their own dancing place. Such disputes show a resemblance to the fights of cock birds at a place of copulation.

To understand a dance properly and to get to know the feeling it produces the investigator ought to dance it himself. Even without such experience it is easy to understand that the *mbalȥa* dance has a strong erotic stamp, although it cannot be called mimetic; the Akamba do not seem to have such dances. The flirtation is very undisguised and every now and then a young man whose feelings have become too strong tries to entice a girl aside into the thicket surrounding the dancing place. As a rule these nocturnal dances end up with general sexual intercourse on the way home.

The young people thus have the most unrestricted freedom during these dances. No elder people go there, as it is generally considered wrong to concern oneself about who is making love to one's daughter.

On moonlight nights the dances go on till long after midnight, and any one who is not accustomed to the monotonous drumming and singing and noise finds it difficult to get to sleep. When the nights are dark, they dance in the afternoon. About 3 o'clock the drumming begins, calling them to the dance, just like the accordion in the country districts of Sweden. On the paths appear flocks of youths, singing and striking their drums. They are splendidly attired with all their ornaments, on the polishing and fixing of which they have spent much time and trouble. In the neighbourhood of the government stations they even carry small mirrors, purchased in the Indian bazaar, in which they look at themselves now and then to see that everything is in its place.

These afternoon dances, which end early and from which they all go home at the same time, are more innocent than the ones held at night.

The most popular pleasure dance after the *mbalṭa* is the *musṭa*. In this no drums or other musical instruments are used, but the time is indicated by rattles, small bells (3—4 cm.) of iron or copper, containing stones or pieces of metal. The bells are fixed on a leather cord, that the young men wind round the right leg, which is often quite covered with bells. They thus stamp the time with the right foot. This dance also consists of different figures, which are carried out partly by the youths alone. In these latter intermezzos the dancers move about, and they stamp round, now in a long, twisting line, now in a sort of round dance, but without holding each others' hands[1]. During these they carry instead various dancing accessories, such as bows, staves and clubs of different types. The girls take part in certain parts of the dance, but as I unfortunately forgot to make careful

---

[1] Reproduced in my popular work Afrikanska ströftåg, p. 157. A picture of the *mbalṭa* is found there on p. 153; *mbœbə*-playing men on pp. 196, 211.

notes about this dance and dare not rely on my memory, I must omit the details.

Contrary to the *mbalʉa*, the *musʉa* always takes place in the afternoons, before darkness comes on, and is attended by a great hort of spectators. The number of those who take part in it is also greater than in the former dance, and so a considerably larger dancing place is needed for the *musʉa*. The young people from the different small districts (*kʉɓalo*) come in a close crowd marching in procession to the common dancing place. The young men usually carry their bells in their hands and put them on when they have gone a bit of the way, after which they come on in procession, the men in single file and after them the girls from the same district. It is quite a fine sight to see them; they do not go direct to the dancing place, where the spectators are waiting, but go in procession, now zigzag, now in a curved line towards their goal, and then suddenly, when they reach the place, they turn aside once more and make another big swing.

The *mbalʉa* and the *musʉa* are the two great pleasure dances. I shall add some dances, the nature of which I am not quite certain about, as I only know them from descriptions. One of these is the *kʉlamu*, which is danced by the young people in certain places »when the maize is ripe» (originally a ritual harvest dance?) [1]. During this dance clapping of hands sometimes takes place; further details are unknown to me. The dance is only performed in certain places (not in Machakos), because the elders forbid it as they say it is »wicked» and may bring about famine.

In the Kitui district in former times a dance is said to have existed, in which a kind of stilts were used, with the dancer's feet about half a metre above the ground. This dance does not seem to have existed in West Ukamba.

The *ʉɓwʉlu* is danced by the married women and the younger married men (*nɗælə*) together and in pairs, a man and a woman turned towards each other. This is the least aesthetic of the dances I have seen in Ukamba. It is true that they stand on

---

[1] It is not improbable that ritual dances in connection with the harvest are found in certain places. Hildebrandt says (p. 390): »Obscene movements of the body are peculiar to dances at sowing and harvest time». Further research on this point would be of great interest.

the same spot, as in the *mbalṇa*, but body and legs are bent in all conceivable ways, such as in hip-movements, and similarly a great many arm movements are carried out. Now the dancers are crouched and bent towards the ground, now they stretch themselves as high as possible, with their arms swinging over their head. I have only observed this dance in connection with exorcism, etc., and so it is perhaps exclusively of a religious nature. As music they use the *kṇpæmbɔ*, the big spirit drum.

Religious dancing. The general ritual dances in connection with the cult of ancestors is the *kṇlumṇ*, which has already been discussed on pp. 230 ff. It is danced, generally speaking, in the same way as the *mbalṇa* (the couples lean their cheeks against each other), when men take part in it. When women dance with each other there is a little interval. The movements are, however, more violent and spasmodic than in the young peoples' dance. The time is given by the *kṇpæmbɔ* drum. The drummer strikes once with one hand and then three short strokes in succession, of which the last is strongest, with the other. This monotonous music goes on without interruption, only with an increase of rapidity when they go into ecstacies. In addition the women wear iron bells round their arms, of the same type as those used in the *muṣṇa*, but considerably larger. From the upper arm hangs down a cow or zebra tail called *mwiŋgu* ('tail' is otherwise *kṇsṇpɔ*), which swings to and fro during the violent motions (vide fig. 58). These tails must have a certain significance from a magic-religious point of view; tails are also used by the medicine men as stoppers for their medicine calabashes.

kṇlumṇ does not seem to be an old dance, for the older people say that it was preceded by *ŋgɔma*, which was accompanied by drums of the same name. In the *ŋgɔma* the women are said to have carried swords, arrows and spears, the latter being war-trophies, as the Akamba themselves do not use spears.

Mr Säuberlich told the author how there was formerly in Kitui a dance called *mbæɓo*. I connect this dance with the spirits of foreign tribes (see pp. 234 ff.). It is forbidden, however, by the elders under a penalty of two cows, because during its performance there arose so much trouble and immorality between the men and the younger women.

Of the religious dances I have also already mentioned *kɨœsu* (p. 238) and those connected with the circumcision rites, of which at least a certain number have special names (see *nžuma*, p. 59).

*

We thus undoubtedly find different dances for different occasions, and even the pure pleasure dances seem to change with the seasons, as has already been shown. At one time they devote themselves entirely to the *mbalɨa*, and then finish with it altogether and go in for the *musɨa*, from which later on they go back to the first, and so on. Yet the Akamba do not seem to have any old dances, national dances so to speak. These dances emerge and disappear just like our fashionable dances. When a novelty of this sort begins, all the young people, especially the girls, are very eager and restless until they have learned the new art, and then they give themselves up to it passionately, only to let it quite suddenly go out of fashion for some other.

When the natives really get into the grip of dancing, they — especially the young men — are seized by a regular passion for this amusement, which is beyond all description. Dancing is then their whole life, the sole thing they are interested in. This leads to unpleasant consequences both for those around them and for themselves. Under such circumstances it is practically impossible for the travellers to get bearers and this is difficult even for the government service. When there is no other remedy one has to take bearers forcibly — a thing of which I have had experience — and when the young men can keep away, it is their fathers or elder married brothers who have to go with the burdens on their backs. The older people have to suffer in other ways as well while the youngsters rush from one dance to another, sometimes on regular dancing tours, as during the present peaceful times there is little risk in visiting even distant dancing places. Many of them neglect their task of watching cattle, which the exasperated father has to do himself; others ought perhaps to have crushed sugarcane for beer for the old men, who have now to go without their precious beer.

If nothing else is of any avail, the old people have recourse to the most effective remedy within their reach, that is prohibition of all dancing. And if they are really annoyed, they do not stop at this, but forbid all intercourse betwen boys and girls, so that they are not allowed even to speak to each other, when they meet out on a path. The refractory youths cannot stand this for long, as without dancing and girls life has lost its greatest pleasures for them. So they submit and keep quiet, as long as they can.

3. Song.

We said that singing is inseparably united with dancing. The dancing songs are sung for the most part in chorus, but certain parts are preferred by the chief singer — the leader of the dance — alone. Further there are songs sung in unison by young girls on various occasions, such as when they work together. Solo songs are also sung by women, for instance when they are crushing maize, lulling their children to sleep, etc. Men also like to sing alone during their work. Thus I have often heard solitary young men singing as they were digging up a field. And they are not content with humming softly, but sing with the whole power of their lungs. These songs of labour, as one might call them, usually consist of some few words, repeated ad infinitum, as for instance, when I heard a man uninterruptedly sing the following, only interspersed now and then with some vocalization: *nɨŋgukwɨnža ɟeú* 'I am now digging'.

All these songs of various kinds are songs for the occasions, sometimes improvised for the moment by the singer himself, sometimes such as a recognized singer has improvised and which have then become popular. Old songs handed down by tradition are certainly entirely lacking, with the exception of the songs connected with the initiation rites, which are reproduced in Chap. III.

There are no wandering singers. An apparently unique exception was a man known over almost the whole of Ukamba, Kieti by name, a blind singer from the Ikutha district, who sang to the *mbæɓǝ* songs composed by himself. His wife, who guided him on his wanderings, he is said to have won by his singing. He was a very uglylooking man, his face being altogether disfigured, as in his childhood he was bitten by a hyena.

I discuss the subject of the Akambas' songs quite briefly here, because the songs I noted have been worked out as a separate work and are to be published in connection with other examples of the art of composition and intellectual life of the tribe, their stories, proverbs and riddles. To take down a song is rather difficult, as a person who can sing a song is unable, in most cases, to reproduce it in any other way, and thus cannot recite it, which is necessary if one is to take down the words. I have also recorded a number of songs with the phonograph, but in this there was another difficulty, namely to make the natives speak into the phonograph. The men were pretty willing, but the women were impossible, although I asked those that I had been in daily contact with for months and whose confidence I enjoyed. My phonographic records are incorporated with the phonographic archives of the Ethnographical museum in Stockholm.

To describe the musical character of the Akambas' songs in a few words, we may mention that they always begin very high up in the scale of notes, with a series of vowel sounds, before the real words begin. A kind of refrain, usually consisting of a longdrawn i (see the initiation songs), is often heard. Melody in our meaning of the term appears just as little in their songs as in their music, but their manner of uttering the words may be described as a sort of singing speech.

_____

Chapter XXIII. **Toys and games.**

To begin with I take the opportunity of observing that, in the case of many peoples who are otherwise well known, little or nothing is known about their games and similar amusements. Even clever investigators, who have carried out admirable researches, often pass by this subject silently or content themselves with saying that the natives have no real games, a statement that has more than once proved to be rather rash. To a great extent this is, of course, due to the fact that the authorities in question have only stayed a short time among a certain people, during which they have not had an opportunity of making such observations, especially as certain pastimes are only indulged in during certain times in the year.

If we examine the Akamba's games and pastimes, we find that the grown-up people concern themselves very slightly with such things; they are the children's business. To a great extent these children, like others, try to imitate the occupations and work of their elders. We know that the child's desire for activity finds expression in games, and like all healthy children, no matter what race they belong to, the Kamba children are seldom idle. Thus the boys, for instance, make small bows with bast strings and arrows of pipes or twigs, by means of which they engage in shooting small birds. They even construct small bee-hives of calabash and hang them up in the trees. It sometimes actually happens that the wild bees take possession of such a »hive». The boys like to imitate the young men's dances, and then make dance drums of calabash, the ends of which they cut off and then fix a bit of skin on one end.

The girls, for their part, soon begin to practise preparing cords of bast and with them plait small sacks, a work which they see their mothers doing on every conceivable occasion. In the sacks they put small calabashes, filled with earth, which represents porridge or other food. Similarly they make vessels of clay, and they lay out small fields on which they plant. Of course they also cook food, with earth and water, etc.

The boys and girls play »father, mother and children» together. They build small huts of grass and imitate the grown-ups, an imitation which is sometimes so carefully done that not even

Fig. 117. Doll (woman) made of pipe-shaped stalks. *a* arms.
$^1/_2$ nat. size. Riksmus. Ethn. Coll. Inv. 12. 7. 284.

the sexual part of a marriage is omitted. As is well known, such things cease to be a mystery to children of primitive people at a very early age.

The Kamba children have few toys in the real meaning of the word. Rattles are used by small children, although I have seen them only in the simple and primitive form of a dry fruit with hard seeds inside. Thus the fruits of *musili* (Crotælaria) are tied to pegs and then used as rattles.

I have seen the girls playing with dolls, though this is rare. These have names and are also called by their little owners *mwa-*

nakwa 'my child'. On the other hand no word for »doll» seems
to exist. The dolls I have seen are made out of pipe-shaped stalks
in the most simple manner and are adorned with ornaments (fig.
117). The picture shows a woman with her loin-cloth, which is
taken from a real one. Round her »neck» she wears chains and
round her waist a pearl belt, just as women are clad. This type
of doll always seems to lack a head. If the doll represents a
baby, the mother owner makes a baby-carrier out of a cloth and
carries the doll on her back in a cord over her forehead.

Fig. 118. Clay doll (woman). The strokes on the breast represent
the tattooing of scars. The ear is bored through but there are no
ornaments. $1/2$ nat. size. Riksmus. Ethn. Coll. Inv. 12. 7. 287.

A type of doll which sustains the illusion better are the
figures of clay which I saw at Mulango (fig. 118). They are certainly coarsely made, but in part very realistic, with sexual organs
and scar-tattooing. As I have not seen these at any other places
but Mulango, I must suggest the possibility that they may be imi-
tations of the missionary children's dolls there.

Among toys for boys I have found the peg-top (*ndælæli*)
which is roughly cut out of wood, without notches, and is struck

with a whip of bast (fig. 119). It is spun with the whip in exactly
the same way as is done by European boys. Whether this top is
indigenous is at least open to doubt. On the other hand the tops
which smaller boys make by sticking a peg through the globular
fruits of the *mukomoa* tree are certainly native. This top is spun
by the hands alone[1].

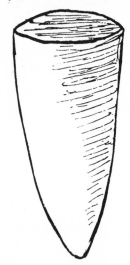

Fig. 119.   Wooden top.
Nat. size. Riksmus. Ethn.
Coll. Inv. 12. 7. 273.

The boys also trundle hoops (*ndʲa*
'wheel') made of flexible branches.

kʲsæŋgæla kʲa kʲkʲ 'calabash sherd'
is a little wheel, cut out of a bit of calabash-shell, and threaded on a little peg,
which is placed crosswise in the fork of
a stick.   The wheel, which is driven along
the ground, is probably originally an imitation of a real cart.

Like our children the boys also make
air-guns out of hollow branches of plants
and fix a peg as a butt at one end and
in the other a clod, which is sent out by
the force of the air. This toy appears in
several places both in West and East
Africa[2].

The sling (*kʲkupa*), of the well-known
type, is also used by boys. The bigger
boys, plait it carefully with strings (fig.
120), the smaller ones make it out of a
piece of banana skin. With a good sling they can throw at least
a hundred meters. These toys have also a practical use, as they
are used for chasing the birds out of the cornfields.

Of the bullroarer I have only seen a single example in Ukamba,
used by quite a small boy. In consisted of a pointed oval slice of
wood, coarsely cut out, with a cord fixed in a hole at one end.

To the domain of toys belong finally the small musical instruments of several different types which the boys construct. Their

---

[1] Hobley, Akamba, p. 56, says incorrectly that »they do not
make tops».

[2] Karutz, Über Kinderspielzeug. Zeitschr. f. Ethnologie, 1911,
p. 239.

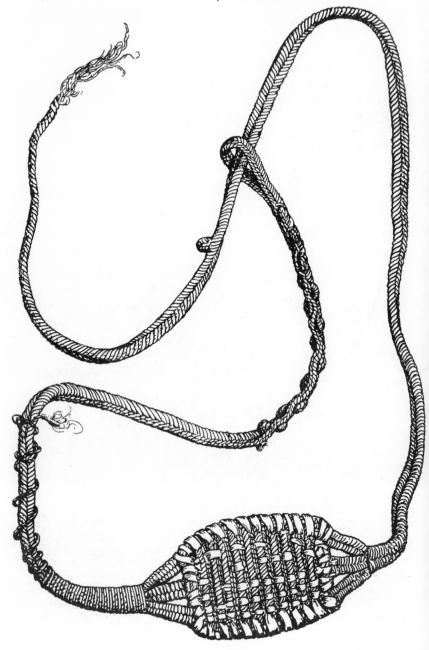

description is already given in connection with that of the real
musical instruments (p. 406).

✳   ✳   ✳

We now pass to real games. The word for 'game' in the
general sense in the Kamba language is *ɩpau̯* and 'to play' *ku-
pauka*. I have observed only the following boys' games.

kuɑpa ndɩa 'shoot the wheel'. Those who are playing
form two sides, and each player is provided with two maize spadices, which are joined in the middle by a cord about 1 dm. long.
The two groups stand at some distance from each other, and from
the one is rolled a »hoop» of osier switches past the other. The
members of this try to throw their spadices through the hoop.
If this is accomplished one of them goes over to the opposing
side and from there tries to throw his spadices through the wheel,
when it is sent back by his own side. If this fails, he becomes
the enemie's 'slave'. Thus the game goes on until as many as
possible of the one group have become slaves [1].

In the following game the sole player has a secret accomplice
among the lookers-on, who usually sit in a circle. A row of pegs
or the like are laid on the ground, and the one who is skilled in
the game goes away and asks one of those present to touch a
peg. He then says which peg it was and asserts that he is able
to find this out by means of the smell, as he first pretends to
smell all the pegs. The explanation lies in the fact that beforehand he had agreed on a certain sign with his secret accomplice.
For instance the latter may imperceptibly raise the toes on one
foot, when the other comes to the peg in question.

A similar pastime, almost identical with one of the Swedish
children's Christmas games, is for a boy, at the request of his
secret accessory, to cover his head with his blanket and then guess
to whom among those present the accessory hands a knife. The
latter takes two knives and sharpens the blades against each other,
pretending in that way to talk to the finder. According to a
previous agreement with the latter, he then hands the knife to

---

[1] This game is also found in West Africa. J. H. W e e k s, Anthropological Notes on the Bangala of the Upper Congo River. Journ.
Anthr. Inst. 1910, p. 405.

the one who last said something before he told the other to hide his eyes.

Another game of the same character as the two preceding is the following. One of the lookers-on puts an object in a bamboo tube, and the expert in the game then says what the tube contains. This is done by his stating that he needs leaves of a certain tree in order to be able to guess correctly, and he disappears a minute to fetch these. He returns with a small bough, swings it closely over the bamboo tube and then says that he needs another sort of leaf. On returning with this he swings it as well over the tube and then says what it contains.

I have seen this game carried out in a very skilful and effective manner. The simple explanation is that the person who performs the trick has another bamboo tube quite like the real one, and changes the two without being noticed. The first bough is used to hide this. Then when he goes off to fetch new leaves, he looks to see what the tube contains and on his return places the right tube in its place again, a manipulation which is concealed by the second bough.

Such small tricks puzzle the uninitiated greatly and they exercise their brains to find an explanation. To get to know the secret they make payments consisting of ornaments, such as neck- or ear-rings, and then in their turn teach the trick to others for a similar fee.

These games are to a certain extent thought-reading games. There are, however, also games which deserve to be called real »jeux d'esprit», and which even grown-up people enjoy. The nature of one of these is as follows:

A man and his wife and son are out walking and have to pass a number of rivers, which are represented by pegs or grooves made in the ground. Between the streams lie ranges of hills, thus representing the ground such as it appears in the greater part of the highlands of Ukamba. The question is now, with head turned away, to let the wanderers pass as many rivers and hills as possible, during which it is to be observed that never more than one at a time may be in the same place and that of course there should be no gaps between them. The moves ought, besides, to be made very quickly. The game begins by the leader saying *twændə* ('let us go'), upon which the one who wishes to try his hand at the game says: »The old man goes down in the river (*mutumɩa aɓota*), the old man climbs up (i. e. on the hill), (*mutumɩa alɩsa*). The wife goes down in the river (*kɩɓætɩ kɩaɓota*), the wife climbs up, the son goes down», etc. If he makes a mistake he must give up. The number of the rivers seldom exceed four, but I once saw a man, who for a rupee in payment cleared ten rivers, without doubt a very good mental performance.

The same game exists among the Wadjagga. B. Gutmann says that usually a collision occurs in the fourth valley (= »river» in our case). He holds that the game has been imported from the coast[1].

The boys go in for games especially when they are minding cattle. One of these games consists of making two rows of holes in the sand, five or six holes in each row. One of them hides a stone or a bit of a maize spadix in one of the holes and then fills them with sand, upon which the others guess where the stone is. This is called *kulɩmaṇa*, really 'to outdo each other'.

*

No real sport exists. The boys compete in walking on their hands as far as possible (*kutambuka*, really 'to walk'). Similarly they try to stand on their heads.

A competitive game described by Brutzer, the missionary, is as follows. An old pot or something of that sort is set up as a goal in an open place. This is guarded by a boy with a stick, by means of which he has to prevent the goal being reached by a peg which another boy strikes with the help of a stick. When the goalkeeper knocks the projectile back, the distance to the point where it falls is paced and for every ten full paces he obtains a point. When the goal is hit, he has to change places with his opponent[2].

A pastime popular among smaller boys reminds one of the well-known old Swedish game of »hoppa kråka», »hop the crow» (curvetting). The players stand in a row, crouch down and begin to sing:

---

[1] B. Gutmann, Kinderspiele bei den Wadschagga, Globus 1909, p. 301.

[2] E. Brutzer, Was Kamba-jungen treiben, Leipzig 1904, p. 13.

kɨoa wamanda-manda,	The frog jumped,
ukuʝɨ kulɨka ndɨanɨ,	she is going to enter the pool,
ɨla ʒalɨkɨlɔ mukuŋga	in which went the *mukuŋga* snake[1]
na sɨana sɨakɔ.	with its children.
ɨndɨʝɨ!	Now go!

They then jump along saying *mba, mba* (this is an onomatopoetic rendering of the sound a frog produces when it jumps on ground soaked with water.)

Of special games for girls I have only observed »hide and seek» (*kuɨbɨʝulanɨla*). Some of them have to find out the whereabouts of the rest, who hide in all conceivable places, such as the bushes, round the village, in the storehouses, inside the huts, etc. When they have hidden, they shout *kulu*; then the search may begin.

Exactly like European children the Kamba children sometimes count to find out who shall begin a game and this is done by using a rigmarole of words, apparently without any meaning. There has of course been a meaning at one time, but through continual mechanical repetition the forms have been so mutilated and twisted that they are almost impossible to identify. Brutzer gives from the coast Akamba one of these rigmaroles for counting out: *tali, talita, mundjinga, mungelele, kwatambea, mayembe, kandzili, kavelendzeli, kaunekadzuu, mwitango*[2]. B. adds: »The one who gets the tenth word, *mwitango,* has to begin. They have heard these words from the grown-up people. They do not know any meaning for them. If one asks: »What does it mean?» the parents answer: »I don't know, I heard it from my father.»

Only occasionally and in exceptional cases does one see gambling. Games of chance do not exist at all.

A game is played with Solanum fruits. An unlimited number of people can take part in the game. They sit on the ground, each with his little heap of the Solanum fruits mentioned several times before, which serve excellently as marbles. The one who begins takes two marbles from another player, places one in front of him and throws the other up in the air. He now has to

---

[1] See p. 274.

[2] Brutzer, Begegnungen mit Akamba, p. 32.

take up the one which is on the ground and then catch the falling one with the same hand. He can go on till he fails, and in this way he tries to win all the others' marbles. There is no stake.

Another game with the same fruit is *kuapa ndoŋgu* 'to shoot Solanum fruits'. An even groove about 1—2 dm. broad is made in the sand and a player takes his place at each end. Both have a heap of these fruits and place a similar heap in front of them in the groove. The one who begins knocks his ball with his fingers and tries to hit his opponent's, which then becomes his.

kuapa ŋgu 'to shoot pegs of wood' is the name of a similar game. A heap of soft stalks of plants, a little longer than a lead-pencil, is placed in front of the players, who sit on the ground. The one who is playing takes a peg pointed at the end which he holds with the point upwards between the middle finger and the ring-finger, supported against the innerside of the thumb, while the index finger is free, point straight forward. When the fingers are released, the peg is jerked violently downwards. The point ought then to stick in one of the stalks, which then goes to the thrower. This is continued till he fails[1]. The game demands a great deal of training to become skilful at it.

A game needing calculation and reflection is *kŋusı*, a form of the well-known and widespread *mancala* game. As in the latter they sometimes use a board with indentations in it, but as a rule holes are made in the ground, two rows with 10—20 holes in each row. In each hole are placed four small stones or large seeds, preferably *ŋgau*, the fruit of the *mukau* tree. The two players sit with »the board» placed lengthways between them. The stones are moved according to certain rules; I have forgotten what they are, but remember that they are the same as among the Masai[2]. The one who can place a stone in a hole which has become empty may take the contents of a hole oppo-

---

[1] This game is described by C. V. Hobley, Kamba Games, Man 1912, p. 179 in which a drawing shows two different ways of holding the peg. H. says correctly that the game is called *kwatha ngu*, but he calls the missile *muku* (more correctly *mukṇ*), which means simply 'peg' (singular of *ŋgṇ*).

[2] Merker, Die Masai, p. 36.

site. In this way they continue till the stones are finished. The one who has got the most has won.

It is supposed that this game is of Asiatic origin and has come over from Asia to Africa, where its extension is thought to coincide with the boundaries of the influence of Arabic culture. Its Kamba name, however, *kɲusɿ*, seems to be native and does not show any relationship to other appellations of the game which I have seen.[1]

---

[1] See S. Culin, Mancala, the National game of Africa, Rep. of the U. S. A. Nat. Museum 1894, p. 595. Reprinted Washington, 1896.

ECONOMY

Chapter XXIV. **The village and the hut.**

1. **The village.**

The Akamba build their villages on the slopes of hills, never right up at the highest parts, where they are exposed to the winds. One finds them only exceptionally on level ground, and then in the densest thickets, where the huts are difficult to discover. The cause of this method of building is an attempt to protect themselves as far as possible from hostile attacks, as up on the slopes they have a good view over the sparsely wooded country. During the daytime it is thus impossible for an enemy desirous of plunder to approach unperceived. As numerous streams have their sources on the slopes of the hills, the conditions with regard to water are also usually better here than down in the plains. There are villages situated as high as 500 metres and even more above the ground, but in spite of this the natives run up and down the steep paths several times a day, the women frequently with heavy loads of field produce. They have a peculiar way of making the ascent easier, namely singing or whistling with all their might, which would entirely take the breath away of a European.

When we Europeans speak of a »village» we usually imagine a greater or smaller collection of homes situated quite near one another. This is, of course, the case in West Africa, where the huts are often arranged in rows with a path through the village. In Ukamba the huts owned by one man alone form one village (*musɔ̃*), and so a village may consist of a single hut. At most two or three families live close to each other, but otherwise the different homes are scattered over the hill-slopes without any arrangement. I saw the biggest collections of huts in East Ukamba, where six or seven families sometimes build the thorn hedges that surround the huts so near each other that they form a single wall, sometimes over a hundred metres long. This was down on the flat ground, where the risk of hostile attacks is greater, and in such cases one may observe a clear tendency to draw towards each other for mutual protection.

Let us examine more closely the appearance of one of these Kamba villages. Around it runs a sort of barricade of prickly branches (*mapanžu*) fixed in the ground, and outside and over

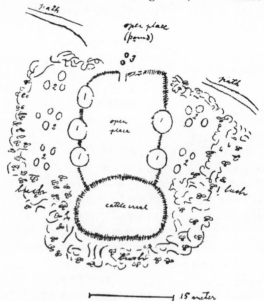

Fig. 121.　Kamba village, Kitui, owned by one man.
Surrounded by dense bush.
1. Huts (5 in number, consequently the man has 5 wives).
2. Storehouse (3—4 to each hut).　3. Big shady trees under which the old men are accustomed to sit.

these are placed other branches. Those of the prickly acacia are specially suitable, as the thorns hook on to each other so that the whole forms a connected wall. In the spaces and outside bushes soon shoot up and make the barricade still denser. There is an entrance to the interior through an opening in the hedge, which is often so arranged that one has first to go through a narrow passage (*mubɩa*), enclosed on both sides by the barricade, before one gets in to the huts. The cutting of the material for this fortification is done by the men, while the women carry it to its place.

In former times, when the natives were never safe from the enemy, the villages were much more fortified than now. The hedge was then often as much as 5 metres or more broad, and on the inside there was also a row of piles driven in the ground. Even double hedges were found. In spite of this it happened, as we have seen in the chapter on war, that the Masai warriors, at dead of night, stole over them. During the dry season there was

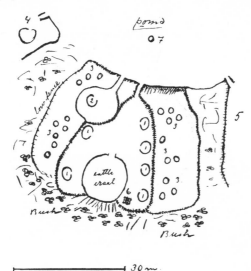

Fig. 122. Kamba village, Kitui. Man with 6 wives. The mother's hut
in an enclosure by itself on the left.
1. Huts. 2. Hut of the man's mother (a widow). 3. Storehouses.
4 and 5. Villages situated at a little distance from the one
in the middle. 6. Dust-heap. 7. Big shady tree.

also the possibility of the enemy succeeding in setting fire to the defences. Nowadays the hedges serve only as a protection against wild beasts, and they are allowed to fall into decay in districts where these are not found.

During the night the opening of the hedge is shut by means of thorny branches, which are drawn in with the thick ends forward so that the branches point outwards. It is impossible to remove them from outside. A higher stage of development is a sort of gate that I saw in East Ukamba, consisting of four wooden rails. On the top rail are threaded 6—10 thick poles, in which holes have been bored. The holes are burned out with glowing iron.

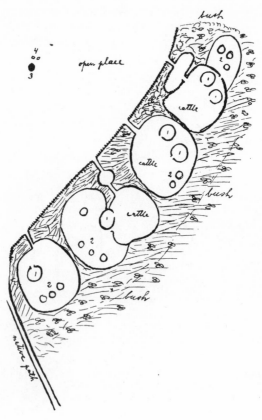

Fig. 123.   A village, Kitui.   4 families.   On the side connected with
the bush the enclosures are weaker.
1. Huts.   2. Storehouse.   3. Big shady tree.   4. Whetstones.

In the evening these are lowered towards the threshold, and then a rail is pushed to inside [1]. See fig. 124.

---

[1] According to A. Schachtzabel, Die Siedelungsverhältnisse der Bantu-Neger (Int. Archiv. f. Ethnographie, Leyden 1911), p. 27 this type of gate is general in Central Africa.

Inside the enclosure is the cattle craal, a circular open place of 12—20 metres in diameter on an average. A man who is the fortunate possessor of many cattle naturally needs a greater space. The animals sleep here during the night and are milked morning and evening. At this place the droppings of the cattle accumulate, so that during the rainy period the whole forms a bottomless mass, in which the women sink up to their knees when they

Fig. 124.   Entrance to a village in East Ukamba.

go to milk the cows. It even happens that the milking cannot be accomplished at all here, as the cows are up to their bellies in the mud.

Quite outside the village and common to all the huts lies the open place, ꝑoma, always with a shady tree, beneath which the old men spend a good deal of the day, talking and taking snuff. They also like to take their meals there and then the food is carried out to them by the children. Similarly they often hold their beer-parties at the ꝑoma, and the fathers of the families carry on their domestic industry, make chairs, spoons, arrows sheaths for swords, digging sticks, etc. When several men squat at a common ꝑɔmɔ, they appoint a sort of leader for this, who is called *mutumĩa wa ꝑɔmɔ*[1]. The women are never allowed to sit there, but they may use the place for domestic purposes, such as threshing. During the cold season it is the duty of the boys to make a fire each morning and also in the evening at the ꝑɔmɔ, so that their fathers can warm themselves. It is also usual to fix up a screen as a protection against the wind.

The old men set great store by their chats at the ꝑɔmɔ. They revive their old memories, talk about their youth, about the fights with the Masai and the stealing of cattle and women. They like specially to talk about women, and their stories are often so indecent that they used to say themselves that they cannot be told in the presence of women. But the women are often, however, not a bit better in their conversation together.

2. **The hut.**

Along the enclosure — sometimes inside it, sometimes forming a part of it — are the huts, one, two or more, according to the number of wives. They are of the usual beehive shape that is met with in so many places in Africa[2]. The framework consists of pliant young trees stuck in the ground and narrow rafters (called *ŋgeti*), which are joined by means of withies placed crosswise above them and forming concentric circles. At the points of intersection the material is fastened together with cords, and then the whole structure is covered with long grass. To keep this more securely fastened, bands of withy are also placed round the hut on the outside. The section of a hut is usually from 3 to 4 metres, its height at the centre about 3 metres. Near the centre stands the thick post (*kĩtuɔ*), consisting of a cut tree-trunk, that supports the hut[3].

---

[1] See Ch. Dundas, History of Kitui, p. 422 ff., which gives a good description of villages in East Ukamba.

[2] In Mumoni, where in several respects the Kikuyu influence is prevalent, there are huts of the Kikuyu type, i. e. with special walls and roofs (»kegelhütte» type).

[3] Suitable material for hutbuilding is supplied by the following, among other, trees: for the framework (*ŋgeti*) the flexible branches of the

In erecting a hut the owner gets the help of relations, neighbours and friends. If anyone tries to avoid taking part in the work, he incurs great displeasure. The men cut down trees and build the framework, while the women cut grasses. The preparatory tasks, collecting the building material, take the longest time, a week or more, the actual erection of the hut is often done in a day. At a place that has been made level a circle is first drawn with the foot. This, like all the principal work on the hut, is done among the Masai by a woman, but among the Akamba always by a man, as they say that women would draw a little circle so as not to have a big hut to cover.

The door to the hut usually consists of a screen put together with sticks or (as in East Ukamba) stalks of palm leaves. To the east I have also seen a large flat piece of wood, hewn laboriously out of a thick trunk of a tree. Formerly, when it was necessary to have a protection against enemies, this more massive door was probably used more extensively than is the case now. Such a precaution is rather unnecessary nowadays, and the negro does not work strenuously when there is no need. There are no peepholes in the doors, nor are they placed on vertical pins, as I have seen in use among the Wapare. The door is kept shut simply by some piled-up bits of wood or a pole drawn across. The opening itself is very narrow and often so low that one must creep on one's hands to get in. In huts situated on slopes the door is always placed at the lower side so that the rain cannot run into the hut through the opening.

Let us enter and look at the interior. The floor consists of earth that has been trodden smooth. In former times it is said that, at least in certain districts, the floor was covered with the droppings of cows. This custom still survives in the Kamba people's folklore [1].

---

musụsu bush (Leguminosae), which is also used for the framework of the big storehouse for corn (kuɲga); mupakwɔ, one of the larger plants (Compositae), mutambụ, a thorny bush; for the covering of the roof the grasses mbẹlu (Andropogon), kıkıɲ (Andropogon), mbwœa (Panicum sp.) and ụlɑ (Tricholæna rosea), from the latter of which the kuɲga is also made. The elastic underpart of the bed is made of muɓapɑ (Vernonia), among other things.

[1] The author took down a story in Kikumbuliu (published in Hela Världen, 1917) in which this custom appears and is mentioned as a matter of course.

In the Kavirondo country north-east of Kisumu I saw walls
and floors covered with a mixture of cow manure and clay, which
forms a hard, flat and easily cleaned surface. Even at the mission station there they have let the natives cover the floor with
this mixture, which serves fairly well as a substitute for cement.
In Kikumbuliu, where the ground is more sandy and consequently
less firm, they still cover the threshing place with cow manure.

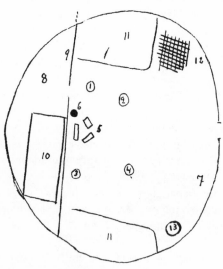

Fig. 125. Sketch of a Kamba hut (cf. p. 97). 1. The place where the wife
sits at the hearth. 2. The place where the husband sits at the hearth.
3. The place where grown-up daughter (or son's wife) sits. 4. The
place where grown-up son sits. 5. The fireplace. 6. The support
for the roof (in this hut unusually far from the centre). 7. Place for
aponi, when they pay a visit. 8. *we*, the sleeping-compartment of
the husband and wife. 9. *ututu*, wall separating the *we* and the exterior
part of the hut. 10. The husband's and wife's bed. 11. Sleeping-place
for the children. 12. Wood store (*kɩɓœta*). 13. Hen-coop.

Across the farther part of the hut there is a partition made
of basket-work or sticks standing close to each other (*ututu*), with
an entrance, and inside it is the *we*, the wife's (and the husband's) sleeping-place. If several wives live in the same hut,
which may happen in exceptional cases with a young man, the
»greater» wife lives in the *we*, the others outside this compart-

ment. In the more roomy outer part of the hut, there are, one on each side of the fireplace, sleeping-places for the sons and the daughters. The bed consists of a bunk made of narrow, elastic sticks (*mwau̯*, pl. *mi̯au̯*), from which the bark has been peeled off. These bunks are placed on four posts and slope gently towards the foot of the bed. The bunk is covered with a skin. When a native wishes to sleep he wraps himself up in his blanket and always pulls it over his head. In certain places curtains made of plaited palm leaves or of imported cloth are used round the bed. Beneath it during the night calves and goats are tethered to pegs fixed in the ground. In a corner there is a big broken jar or a little nest of sticks from which a sitting hen peeps out.

The usual central point of the hut is, however, the fireplace, consisting of three stones, on which a pot is bubbling a good part of the day and night. There is no opening for the smoke to go out, and so the ceiling is always full of soot. The numerous riddles of the Akamba generally deal with the pan on its three stones, the symbol of the home in the Kamba country. »Tell me the rich man who has three entrances to his village», runs a well-known riddle, and another with the same meaning is: »What sort of a little woman is it that sits on three chairs?»[1]

Almost every hut in Ukamba looks like the one we have described, as the wealth or poverty of the owner is of little or no importance with regard to the size and furnishing of the separate huts.

The fire burns on the hearth practically all day and night, especially during the cold season. In the evening, when they go to bed, a big piece of wood is always placed on the fire, and it burns slowly and lasts all night. Even at other times the fire seldom goes completely out, although it may appear to do so, but beneath the ashes there are always embers, which one can easily blow into life again. And if it does go out, they go to the next hut or to their neighbour and get new. This is why in

---

[1] The state of affairs described by Hobley, Akamba p. 30, is entirely unknown to me. He says that »there are two fireplaces in a hut, the children cook at the one near the door and their parents at the inner one; the children cannot go and sit at the inner fireplace». On the contrary it sometimes happens on cold evenings that the parents make a little fire within the *we̯*.

a village one never sees fire being drilled [1], which is the usual
method of firemaking for the Akamba, as for most Africans. The
firesticks are meant for journeys, and the longer one, which is
rotated between the hands, is kept in the quiver, the shorter one,
which is placed underneath, in the travelling bag. The former
one is called *wɪndɪ*, the latter *kɪka*, probably the same root as in
muka 'woman' and *ŋga* 'hen'. In jocular speech this is also called
»woman» and the stick for drilling with »man» [2]. The stalks
of Cajanus indicus (*musɔ*) are very suitable for drilling sticks

Fig. 126.   Fire-making.   The man to the right has a flute of
Oryx horn.

and the wood of the wild fig-tree for the underneath piece.
The drilling stick need not be made of harder wood than the *kɪka*.
To increase the friction some grains of sand are placed in the
hole in the lower stick. In front of it are placed some dry leaves
or dry grass, on which the pulverized wood falls and begins to
glow. I have seen clever natives drill fire in 20 seconds. As a
rule, however, it takes longer, and several men relieve each other
until the result is attained. Women cannot make fire in this way,
nor have they any use for it, as they never go out alone on

[1] Professor Weule made the same observation during his journey
in the southern part of German East Africa. K. Weule, Kultur der
Kulturlosen, p. 66.
[2] Frazer, The Golden Bough, I: 2, p. 208 ff., shows that these
terms are found among different peoples of different races.

long journeys[1]. Even among the men it is by no means all who know the art.

If the fire on the hearth goes out during the night, it is considered a bad omen, especially if it had been decided to undertake something rather important during the day. If, for instance, beer has been brewed for a present to a future father-in-law of the son of the house, it should not be used for this purpose. But they may drink it themselves without any risk.

Rites and customs in connection with hutbuilding. Such important undertakings in the life of a family as deciding upon a dwelling place and building a hut are, of course, bound up with ceremonial observances. The natives wish to have the best possible guarantee that they shall not settle down at a place that may be injurious to the growing children and the cattle. The man and the wife go in the first place to the medicine man to get him to choose a suitable place by divination, or else they do it for themselves by going out to try to find a good omen (*mupana museo*), e. g. to listen to the cry of a bird. If they do not come across one on one road, they try in another direction. When an apparently suitable place is found, the man breaks two small branches, and the wife takes a handful of grass, which they hide in a bush near the place. When later on the hut is built, a branch is twined in on each side of the door and the grass is put above it. This is to bring domestic happiness in the new home.

Similar methods of procedure are found among different peoples, and these may certainly be included in the category of rites that are called »bauopfer» by German investigators. This does not mean only real sacrificial actions, but practically any action of a ritual kind by which something is placed in a hut, with the intention of warding off misfortunes and bringing good luck and permanence to the new dwelling[2].

When setting up the important post that supports the whole hut some cow droppings are first placed in the hole in the ground.

---

[1] I do not think, however, that the Kamba women are forbidden to drill fire, as is the case among the Nandi, where firemaking is »an exclusive privilege of the men». Hollis, The Nandi, p. 85.

[2] See P. Sartori, Über das Bauopfer, Zeitschr. f. Ethn. 1898. p. 1 ff.

This is similarly intended to bring good luck to the owner, especially to increase his flocks.

When the men have finished their work on the framework
of the hut and before the women may begin covering the roof,
the owner's bow is hung up on the wall and also »the wife's bow»,
i. e. the bast sack in which she carries the products of the field.
This is a rather interesting detail, probably a very old custom,
which confirms to some extent the idea that the Akamba are
originally a hunting people, during which stage of their history
the bow was of course the man's most important possession, but
during which the woman certainly began to be occupied with
some primitive agriculture or at least contributed to a considerable
extent to procuring the necessaries of life by collecting edible
wild plants.

Before the hut is covered, a fire is also made in it for the
first time. Similarly all iron tools, such as axes, knives, etc. must
be left outside the hut before this is done. It is believed that
the hut will be cold and draughty if there are iron objects in it
before it has been covered.

Hobley tells how, when a new village is founded, the owner
walks around it with an amulet in his hand, »and it is believed
that wild animals, leopards, lions etc. will not enter it»[1].

The first food that is eaten in the new home, if the latter is to be
good in the future, should be Eleusine porridge (ụgịma). The
husband eats first, then the wife, and then the children. Some is
also thrown on the floor as an offering to the *aimu*. This is thus
another example of the great part that Eleusine plays in rites and
also an additional fact showing the antiquity of this kind of grain
as a cultivated plant in East Africa.

Finally, when the hut is ready and the inhabitants have
moved in, the man and his wife must have ritual coitus during
the second night. Before this, however, the previously mentioned
eating of ụgịma must have taken place. If the husband tries to
have connection with his wife before this, she always refuses, and
if in spite of this he succeeds in getting his way, she throws away
all the cords she has got ready for the work with the hut, and
makes new ones. Before they have eaten the ụgịma porridge the

---

[1] C. V. Hobley, Kamba protective magic, Man 1912, p. 5.

husband must not have connection with any other woman either, but must observe complete sexual continence.

In connection with these ceremonies it may be mentioned finally that when a stranger comes on a visit to a village, they are careful to see that he goes out the same way as he came in. It has happened to the author more than once that when, after paying a visit to a hut, he has tried to take a short cut over some broken-down part of the fence, he has been called back and asked to go back by the proper entrance through which he came.

Hutbuilding for the medicine man. The building of a medicine man's hut offers a number of variations from that of an ordinary hut. We have already touched on this on p. 257. Everyone who lives in the district takes part in the work. Before the work is begun the old women (of the *nǯama*) dance the *kɪlumi* on the place where the hut is to be built, and the young people perform their dances. The old men and women who have a long way to go home sleep at the place during the night so as to be able to begin the building work early the next morning. The youths bring up the materials and the *atumɪa* erect the framework of the hut, after which the women cover it. Only the old ones, those of the *nǯama*, may cover the highest part and the part nearest the ground, the middle part is done by the »small» women (*ɪla nɪnɪ*), i. e. those who occupy a subordinate position at the bringing of sacrifices up to the sacrificial places. These women are not allowed to enter the hut during the work. The posts on which the medicine man's apparatus, his divinatory bag, medicines, etc. are to hang are made of a special kind of wood (*mupɪŋgɪ*). They must be put in their places by the *atumɪa* of the *nǯama*. The work must be completed in one day.

*   *   *

Although the Akamba are a settled people they have a great deal of the impulsiveness of the nomad with regard to oft-recurring changes of habitation. It is very common for them to live only a few years at the same place and then move. The causes for this vary, but the most important and most common are of a superstitious nature. When misfortunes occur again and again

and nothing else seems to be of any use, they try, on the advice
of the medicine man or on their own initiative, to escape from
these by changing their dwelling-place. In this way a family may
move incessantly from place to place. It is in particular repeated
deaths or infectious disease among human beings or cattle that
they try to escape from, or if the cattle do not seem to get on
well generally or the children to grow up well, etc. If the wife
turns out to be barren, the medicine man may prescribe a removal to another place as a remedy.

If a man has several wives, he first builds, at the removal,
the »great» wife's hut. If the »small» wife's hut were built first,
it might hurt the »great» one, who has then to get her hut within
a special enclosure.

When a wife becomes a widow and then perhaps wishes to
move to her married son, she must not live in his hut, for that
might injure her on account of the sexual relations between the
son and his wife. But after a specialist in ceremonial purification,
a *mutumıa wa ŋonduı*, has been called in and has drawn a groove
in the ground and sprinkled it with *ŋonduı*, she may build a hut
for herself on the other side of the groove. Although she thus
may not live in the son's hut, she can, however, visit it as much
as she likes.

✳   ✳   ✳

Generally there is rather good order and cleanliness in a Kamba
hut. The wife sweeps every morning with a besom (*uбıaıo*) made
of pliant twigs. Sweepings, remains of the previous day's meals,
such as the spadices of maize, and droppings of goats and sheep
are swept up in a goatskin and thrown out over the hedge around
the cattle craal. For this refuse there is a special place called
utunda (pl. *ŋdunda*). If one comes across a hut that is untidy it
is in most cases because the wife is ill and has no daughters big
enough to help her with the work.

Under certain circumstances, however, the hut may never be
swept, namely when the man is away on important tasks, such
as hunting big game, or when he is on a campaign for stealing
cattle (for the observances about sweeping the hut for a certain
clan see p. 124).

Although they try in this way to keep the hut tidy, there is, as we have already seen, often much to be desired in the way of cleanliness in the cattle craal. Outside the village, on the other hand, it is fairly clean, and one seldom sees, for instance, human excrement, provided there are no small children in the place.

A few metres from the hut are situated the storehouses (*ikumbi*), of which there are 2—4 to each hut, thus one for each wife. They are about the height of a man, of the same type as the dwelling huts, although more lightly and airily constructed than these. Underneath them there is a low pile-work, so that the floor, which is made of sticks, shall be a few decimetres above the ground. Here food is kept in calabashes and in the big wicker baskets (*kiŋga*). In big families the young unmarried men (*anakə*) also use the provision-sheds as sleeping-places. To protect the storehouses against white ants and other injurious insects ashes are sometimes strewn round them. The big wicker baskets are plastered with cow-dung for the same purpose.

In Kikumbuliu the storehouses, which are there called *kiʈsumba*, are situated in the fields, and when the crops are about to ripen, they are inhabited, usually by young girls, who keep watch against baboons, wild boars and porcupines. The girls live here entirely during this time and do their own cooking.

3. Home life.

Life in the village begins at daybreak, when the cocks begin to crow and solitary dogs to bark. The huts remain closed for a little while, but soon the first of their inmates are seen, the women going to milk the cows. Those who get up last are the young people, especially if they have danced a good part of the night, in which case they are very out of sorts and sleepy. When the milking is finished, the cattle are driven out to graze by the boys, who take turns in watching them.

In the evening the natives go to bed between 9 and 10 o'clock, pretty soon after the evening meal. They like to talk for a little while, and perhaps some begin to dance. At this time the girls often imitate some of their friends who dance in some strange way. They are good imitators and their performances produce a good laugh.

We know already that the *mutumıa*, the paterfamilias, is the head of his family. He is possessor of everything, and if a married son is living at home, he is considered to own even the latter's wife. It is thus not uncommon to hear a man say: »My wife is not mine, she belongs to my father». If the young man cannot make his wife obey — it happens sometimes that she refuses to do the work he gets her — he complains to his father, and respect for him is then sufficient to produce obedience. If, on the other hand, the young woman persists in her defiance, she gets a thrashing from the old man, and then she soon gives in.

Family life is on the whole very calm, but it sometimes happens that a man chastises his wife corporally if she has deserved this. He does not, however, like to do this out of doors, as this would furnish amusement for his neighbours at his expense. He waits instead until she comes home from the fields in the evening. Then it may happen that she gets a good thrashing. Then man takes the nearest weapon, for instance a firebrand from the hearth, and is not too careful with his blows.

Such intermezzos are not, however, common, and one must not conclude from them that the Kamba woman has a very subordinate and oppressed position, at least she does not consider it so herself. I have had occasion to hear well-meaning missionaries eagerly depicting to the women their hard lot, and they were completely at a loss to understand them. To cut this matter short, I must content myself with referring the reader to Chap. XIV. 5 and adding that the elderly women and usually the mothers have a great deal to say, not only within the family but also in general affairs. I know for instance several cases from Machakos where the husband gave the rupees he earned by selling skins to the merchants in the Indian bazaar to his wife for safe keeping and then went to her each time he needed money. And examples have been given on p. 235 of how the woman can often make her husband do much by trickery and can rule over him[1].

The Kamba wife is seldom lazy but is always seen busy. Even on the way to and from the fields she finds time to do something useful, plaiting a bast sack or chewing fibre for mak-

---

[1] Cf. B. Gutmann, Die Frau bei den Wadschagga, Globus 1907, a treatise that also applies in many respects to the Akamba and certainly to several East African tribes.

ing cords. If she has a young child, she carries it with her everywhere on her back, and when it has grown a little, one can see it sitting at the top of a bundle of wood that the mother has collected and is carrying home on her back. It is remarkable how these small mites know how to hold fast and how they can sleep undisturbed during the mother's work. When there are daughters, they help to carry their young brothers and sisters, and one often sees little girls, not yet ten years old, struggling around with the smallest of the family on their backs.

Babies are carried in a *ŋgoṭ*, a rectangular piece of skin, fitted with straps. It is made by the father of the family himself out of a calfskin and is usually adorned with a row of cowrie shells. The calf must not have died a natural death — that would obviously have an injurious influence on the child — although apart from this the Akamba make use of both the flesh and skin or animals that have died from natural causes. The women do not allow anyone to step over a *ŋgoṭ*. The child might then get diarrhœa.

The *ŋgoṭ* is evil-smelling and dirty, but nevertheless a very precious and important possession, on which the future welfare of the child depends to a great extent. There are some that descend from one generation to another. It is impossible for an ethnographical collector to buy the garment; the women will not part from it on any conditions, not even for the highest conceivable prices, such as a cow, and the suggestions I made with regard to this were always received with exclamations of astonishment and indignation. If it were sold the child would surely die. Nor will a mother lend her *ŋgoṭ* to any other woman, not even to any of her co-wives.

As is often to be seen among Negro tribes, the Kamba children are suckled by their mothers for an unusually long time, and it is not uncommon for children who have long since learned to walk, even those who are certainly 6—7 years old, to run every now and then to their mother and suck her breast. To wean children they rub the breasts with the bitter juice of the leaves of the aloes growing on the steppes.

Suckling with cow's milk and with a teat occurs. A piece of skin is stretched over the opening of a calabash bottle and a hole made in the skin with a nail.

Small children are kept very clean and washed every day all over the body with cold water. When they grow up, they have to look after themselves with regard to this, and as they crawl about a good deal on the ground playing, they are often exceedingly dirty. When there is a chance, as, for instance, when there is a stream in the neighbourhood, they like, however, to bathe. The girls rarely neglect to do this when they go to the river to fetch water.

The boys sometimes quarrel and fight with each other, as is the custom of boys all over the world. The games can easily pass into fights, which are sometimes carried on according to certain rules and are preceded by a sort of challenge. When two boys quarrel, one says to the other: »Spit, and I shall do away with your expectoration (*twila mata, n̄balanʒə*)!» If the other accepts this challenge and spits in front of his opponent, the latter obliterates the saliva with his foot. The gauntlet is then thrown down and taken up and they begin to belabour each other with their fists or with sticks. The quarrel is often accompanied by insulting words such as ant-eater (*luma*), dog (*sulu*), hyena (*m̄bɨtɨ*), wart-hog (*ŋgę*) or snake (*n̄ʒokạ*). Stronger expressions are: »Your mother is a witch» (*mwænʒu nɨ mwoɨ*), »Your father is a thief» (*nau nɨ kɨɡæɨ*) or »Your whole family consists of thieves» (*m̄baʐ ʐakɯ ʐonðə nɨ ɨɡæɨ*). A common term of abuse is to call someone a Kikuyu, which is interesting as showing that the Akamba have a considerably higher opinion of themselves than of this allied tribe. When a Kikuyu comes to a Kamba village, it may even happen that small boys put on an air of superiority towards him. Such expressions as »Your mother has run away from her husband!» or »You are a sheep, accumbens matri!» (*we ɨlondu, wɨtɨndaa na mwænʒu*)[1] are still more offensive.

---

[1] M. Merker, Die Masai, p. 110, tells how the Masai youths use similar offensive terms of abuse: accumbens matri, accumbens sorori, acc. patri (used by young girls to each other), etc. Similar insulting expressions are especially met with among Orientals or peoples standing under Arab-Mohammedan influence. Vide O. Stoll, Das Geschlechtsleben in der Volkerpsychologie, p. 767 ff.

Chapter XXV. **Weapons.**

As in the case of the Wataita and the Wanyika tribes, so in the case of the Akamba the bow is the principal weapon. In hand-to-hand fighting they use swords. They have never used spears and shields; the latter are found only in exceptional cases among African tribes that use bows.

The bow (*uta*) is the usual East African type[1], the Ethiopian bow according to Frobenius[2], or the straight-staved bow, as Eric von Rosen, from another point of view, graphically calls this form, because the stave, before the string is fixed on, is straight[3]. The stave of the Kamba bow is round, thickest in the middle and narrowing uniformly at both ends, which end in points (*mbıa*). It is relatively short, about 1.20—1.30 metres. The largest bow I have seen, 1.56 metres long and with a diameter at the middle of 2.3 cm., is in my collection and has belonged to an elephant hunter. The string (*ua*) is made of sinews (*ılaŋgu*), two rather narrow cords of sinew twined together into one. It is fixed about five centimetres from the points and is sometimes supported by a piece of leather placed above or below it; this piece of leather is put on the stave in a fresh condition, so that when it has dried and contracted, it is immoveably attached like a ring round it. At one place where the string is fastened a piece of superfluous string is usually bound round the bow; this is, however, so short that it cannot be used as a reserve string in case the bow-string breaks. They usually have instead an extra string or some sinews in the quiver.

---

[1] F. Ratzel, Die Afrikanischen Bögen. Abhandl. d. Sächs. Ges. der Wissenschaften 1891, p. 304.

[2] L. Frobenius, Skizze der Bogenforschung in Kulturtypen aus Westsudan, Petermanns Mitteil. 1910, p. 166.

[3] E. von Rosen, Träskfolket, p. 176.

The bows used for elephant hunting seem often to be larger than the bows for fighting, but for the most part the same bow is used for both hunting and fighting. The bows used by half-grown boys for shooting birds are smaller, and smallest of all, of course, are the toy bows of the small boys. In the dance *musᶓa* bows of medium size are also used, which the youths carry in their hands and which are tightly bound with wire and have their ends adorned with metal beads. It is to be noticed that these bows are not used to shoot with.

The bows are made of several different species of trees, such as *kᵢƀaṵ* (Dombeya), *mutuƀa* (Turneraceæ) or *mwaṵ*. They are made from the thicker branches as well as from bigger pieces of wood. The latter variety is, however, considered the best, because they do not contain pith (*nᵤunᵢ̣ə*). This of course, makes the bow weaker, and especially on military expeditions, when the natives sometimes go very far from home and have little prospect of getting hold of another bow, it is important that the one they have taken with them should be strong and reliable. For without their bows the Akamba are pretty helpless in battle.

The tools used in making the bows are the axe and knife. To make them pliable they are rubbed many times with fat and held over fire. No special bow-frame is used, but the operation is carried out slowly by hand. When it is ready, it is polished with rough leaves, among others those of the plants *kᵢtæᶓ* (Cordia), *muƀᵢtu* or *mukṵ* (also called *ᵢkṵ*). In the neighbourhood of the government stations they also use for this purpose sandpaper, which is obtained in the Indian bazaar.

When a branch is taken as the material for a bow, they make the lower part of the branch also form the lower point of the bow, i. e. it is always held downward when shooting. I have not seen this fact mentioned in the literature of the subject, but it is probably in practice in other parts although it has escaped attention. It also appears as if even investigators who give detailed descriptions of bows often neglect to observe the method of their manufacture, a point that is by no means unimportant. E. von Rosen, on the other hand, gives an excellent picture of the making of bows in his previously mentioned work on the Batwa in the papyrus swamps of Lake Bangveolo.

The Akamba even distinguish the two ends of the bow by

different names, as they call the upper end *mbıa ẓa muꝑẓa* (*muꝑẓa* 'end, top'), and the lower one *mbıa ẓa ıtına* (*ıtına* 'bottom, base').

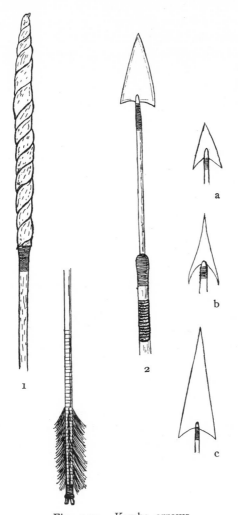

Fig. 127. Kamba arrows.
1. Arrow rubbed with poison, bound with skin. 2. Arrow without poison a—c. Variations in the shape of the arrow heads. 1/2 nat. size.

The bow is in some ways the Akamba's most important possession, for with it they can, as they express it themselves, procure cattle and wives, either by plundering expeditions or hunting, in the latter case especially by elephant hunting, for the sake of the ivory. For this reason the bow is submitted to ritual treatment, so as to bestow strength upon it, and then certain rules of taboo are connected with it, so that it shall not lose its strength. Thus to give good luck to a new bow a bird is shot — the species does not matter — and its blood is smeared on the ends, middle and string of the bow. In the hut the bow has its place by one of the posts of the bed. If on any occasion it has been left behind outside the village, its owner may not indulge in sexual intercourse as long as it is away. The same thing applies in such a case to the Akamba's second most important possession, their cattle: when they are away, as for instance when they are grazing on an outlying farm, intercourse is also forbidden. And just as in the case of a transgression of this custom the cattle must be sprinkled with *ɡondu* before they can come in to the village again, so the bow has to be purified in the same way. It is curious that the *ɡondu* that is used for this is prepared by a child that is not yet circumsized, the only occasion I have heard of when the purificatory substance is prepared by a child. One of the herbs used is *ndata-kɪɓumbu*.

The Akamba arrows are rather small, on the average 0.60 —0.65 centimetres long. Those used for hunting and fighting (*musɪa*) have shafts of wood, exceedingly even and finely constructed (fig. 127). To make certain that they are quite straight the maker holds them in front of him, shuts one eye and glances along the shaft. Like the bows they are finally polished by being rubbed with rough leaves. Trees and bushes suitable for making arrows are *mukwœo, mukaka* (Croton sp.?), *mualɪka, mukutu* and *muɓwɪɪa* (Verbenaceæ?). At the somewhat widened back end of the shaft there is the notch for the bow-string (*mbako*) and above this there is a narrow ring of leather or thick sinew, to prevent splitting. For the same reason the upper end of the shaft is somewhat widened. For greater safety the shaft is also bound round its upper end with sinews, which are chewed until they are quite soft. The arrows have three guiding feathers, and great importance is attached to having stiff feathers. They use preferably feathers of birds of prey, such as those of the *ndeɪ*, the secretary bird (Falco serpentarius). They are stuck on the

arrow-shaft by means of the gum of certain trees or the sap of
the root of *ıkuası ʐa ndu* (Gloriosa sp.?), and for greater security
they are also bound fast with fine bast threads. To give the
arrows an ornamental appearance the lower part is painted with
a beautiful bright red colour. This is now often bought in the
Indian shops, but is originally a natural product, being made of
ılıtu, which is crushed and mixed with roots of *kaʋolạ*, the same
plant as is used in tattooing. The colouring matter is mixed together on a banana leaf or some such article and is spread on with a
stick. To strengthen and ornament the shaft still more they like
to bind the shaft above the notch as well and also up towards the
upper end with hair from the tail of the zebra (*nʐaʐ*) or hartebeest
(*ʋgatatạ*).

In a hole at the end of the arrow-shaft there is fixed the decimetre long wooden foreshaft (*uʄunʐı*), which in its cloven end holds
the head itself (*ıʋmu*). To prevent splitting and to keep it fast
the foreshaft is also bound at the front with sinews. The arrow
heads, which are cut out of a thin hammered-out piece of iron and
then ground sharp, are triangular, all of the same type, although
the indentations at the base vary somewhat in size. As has already been described in connection with the clan system, they
are accustomed to cut the owner's clan mark on the foreshaft. The
foreshaft is intended to stick in the object aimed at, while the
shaft falls to the ground and can be taken up again. In this way
the arrow is prevented from coming out of the wound on the
game during its flight through the weight of the shaft or by the
shaft fastening in the thicket.

In the Ikutha district I found arrows with heads and foreshafts
of iron, in one piece, just as, for instance, among the Wapare.
This type is said to have quite recently come into use among
the Akamba.

The Akamba make the most ornamental and perhaps also the
best balanced arrows I have seen among the sixteen East African
tribes I have come into contact with. They are little masterpieces
of their kind, even in respect of their careful execution. In descriptions of travels one reads many expressions of admiration
about these arrows. »The most substantial we have even seen in
Africa», says von Höhnel, for instance. Weule in his monograph
on the arrows of Africa points out how the arrows of the Akamba,

like those of their neighbours, the Wataita and the Wanyika, are
among the foremost in Africa for exact workmanship[1]. The five
Akamba arrows he weighed gave an average weight of 22 gr.
with a difference of only 0.4 gr. These figures are taken from a
very small material, but have caused me to weigh some of my own
arrows — all of them were not accessible to me — and I have
found that 21.8 gr. was the average weight of four arrows with
their points bound and 19 gr. that of 22 others without leather
and partly with, partly without, poison. The absolute difference
is, however, rather large for my arrows, the maximum weight is
25 and the minimum 15 gr. It should, however, be added, that
the arrows come from different makers.

That the degree of careful work on the arrows that is shown
in their weight is by no means accidental and meaningless is
shown by Weule. Both the Akamba and the Wataita have of old
a reputation as good archers, and because of this they enjoy
the respect of their neighbours.

I have nothing of interest to communicate about the power
of penetration of the arrows, but the natives themselves state that
many of them could shoot through the Masai shields and kill the
men behind them. They also say that the war arrows were formerly larger and more powerful than they are now, with points
stiff and sharp as knife blades.

Arrows of the kind described here are mostly poisonous. The
arrow poison used over wide stretches of East Africa — from
Somaliland and Abyssinia right down to German East Africa and
still farther south — is everywhere the same and is made out of
an Acocanthera species, especially A. abyssinica, which in Ukamba
grows sparsely in the Machakos district as well as here and there
elsewhere in Ulu. I have also seen it a few miles south of Nairobi, and it is found, in addition, in many other places which are
situated high[2]. It is not found in East Ukamba, but there the
natives get the poison by barter from Ulu or from the Taita or
Giriama country. The tree is called by the Akamba *muɓaʒ* and
the poison *ɩɓaʒ*, names which strongly remind one of the Somalis'

---

[1] K. Weule, Der Afrikanische Pfeil, Leipzig 1899, p. 7.
[2] Of the distribution of the Acocanthera species see F. Stuhlmann, Beitr. zur Kulturgeschichte von Ostafrika, p. 425.

wabei or *wabayo* — which is made partly of the same, partly of a closely-related species — and one is tempted to conjecture some sort of connection.

To prepare the poison the wood of the Acocanthera is split into small bits, which are boiled for 8 to 10 hours in a covered jar of water. During the boiling the mixture is stirred from time to time. When it is thought that all the goodness has been boiled out of the wood, it is taken out and the poison is boiled still more. When the water has evaporated, the poison lies in a pitch-like, dark and sticky mass at the bottom of the vessel. To make it more easy to manipulate it is mixed with ashes and formed into a dough, after which it is ready for use. It must not be kept in a cold and damp place.

Those who work with the poison are careful to see that they have no wounds on their hands. With a wooden spatula, *kɩɓakɩ*[1] (fig. 128), it is smeared copiously on the arrow-head and all the foreshaft. So that it shall keep soft it is bound with a fine strip of skin from kids or small antelopes (fig. 127. 1). The skin is made thin by scraping it with knives and is softened by being drawn repeatedly over the back of the knife and being worked with a stone.

The quality of the poison varies in different places, as sometimes other ingredients are also added
to the pure vegetable poison. A man who was considered to prepare unusually strong poison added
the head of a snake species. Another eminent specialist in the preparation of poison gave me the following list of extra ingredients for his poison:

Fig. 128.
Wooden spa-
tula to rub
poison on the
arrows with.
$1/2$ nat. size.

Snake heads and certain poisonous spiders (*mbua-mbuɩ*) and roots of the plants *kɩlɩa mbɩtɩ, kalamba ɩuta* and *kɩpuɩ*. The first of these, a Yatropha species, and one of the most important plants the Akamba know of, we have already made the acquaintance of, and we perhaps remember that, among other things, it is used for removing the embryo (abortion). *kalamba* is a little tree, 1—2 metres high (Apocyneæ — thus of the same family as the Aco-canthera), with a milky sap, bluish green, smooth leaves and beau-

---

[1] < *kuɓaka* 'to paint, smear'.

tiful purple-coloured flowers. The two others are quite unknown to me.

The making of poison is of such great importance that it is easy to understand that certain magic observances of a prohibitive nature are connected with it. The sexual taboo especially is stringently observed, inasmuch as a woman may not even be present during the manufacture, or else the power of the poison would be destroyed[1]. The boiling is therefore carried out preferably at a place apart, and when the women bring food to the men during the work, it is put down at a respectful distance. Further the arrow-poison may be made only by the *nzœlɔ* or the *atumɪa*, young men are not permitted to make it. When I asked my boy Kioko, a man of about 30 years of age, to show me the process, which he knew, he refused, saying that he was too young.

I have not been succesful in finding out anything about the effect of the Acocanthera poison — it is known that it affects the heart. The only attempt I made was to make a slight cut on the leg of a hen and smear poison on the wound. The hen refused, however, to die and continued to look for food quite calmly. The natives are, however, very much afraid of the poison and state that big game, such as a lion or a leopard, cannot get far after a well-aimed shot. Elephants, on the other hand, run for miles before the poison takes effect. These statements appear to be correct, as according to other authors middle-sized antelopes die after a few minutes[2]. The poison thus has a very strong effect.

According to the natives the poison is also most powerful when it is warm, i. e. just after it is made, while it gets weak with time. According to M. Krause's investigation[3], this appears to be incorrect. The fact of the matter probably is that when

---

[1] The Wandorobo are also very careful about this, as I know from my own experience. See further M. Weiss, Die Völkerstämme im Norden Deutsch-Ost-Afrikas, p. 396 and M. Merker, Die Masai, p. 246.

[2] M. Weiss op. cit. p. 397, M. Merker op. cit. p. 247.

[3] See further M. Weiss op. cit. p. 396. In addition there have, of course, been various descriptions of this and other African arrow poisons.

the poison is old and consequently dry and hard, it dissolves more slowly in the wound, and so the natives quite naturally conclude that its strength has decreased.

The treatment of wounds caused by poisoned arrows has been touched upon in connection with medicinal methods (p. 312).

From the arrows used for hunting big game we pass to the bird arrows (*taŋgi*, pl. *maŋgi*), which are mostly used by boys and young men. Their shafts are cut from reeds, etc. (among others from *uᵽuŋga ula munæŋɔ*, a rather large Sonchus species). They are not so careful about the feathering, but content themselves with softer feathers, such as those of guinea-fowls[1]. A notch for the bowstring is made in the reed and above this it is bound with thin sinews just like round the upper end, where the arrow-head of hard wood is fixed in. Good material for the heads of bird arrows is furnished by the *mutuᵬa* (Turneraceæ), the straight, hard branches of which contain but little pith. There are several different kinds of arrowheads, most of which are not specially characteristic for the Akamba, but are met with over great parts of East Africa. The simplest kind consists of a straight, pricker-like head, which the boys sometimes adorn with carvings, probably an imitation of the clan marks on the heads of the real arrows. Simple developments of this basic form are shown in b and c in fig. 129. The four short sticks fastened with bast in c (*ndati*) are to prevent the arrow from going too far in and disappearing in the thick grass in the case of a miss. E. von Rosen has described and reproduced an iron-headed arrow with a similar arrangement, a little cross-piece of wood, from the Batwa and several tribes round Lake Bangveolo[2]. He is the first to describe the type, which, however, is certainly found as a bird arrow with a wooden point here and there, at least in East Africa. That it has escaped attention is probably due to the fact that bird arrows, which are mostly used by boys, often seem to have been overlooked by the investigator. On the other hand the iron-headed arrows from Bangveolo are probably unique of their kind and have the cross-piece evolved, owing to the loose nature of the ground. The

---

[1] An arrow on which guiding feathers have not yet been fixed is called *muluᶄa*. This word thus does not denote a special kind of arrow, as Hobley, Akamba, p. 43 imagines.

[2] E. von Rosen, Träskfolket, p. 186.

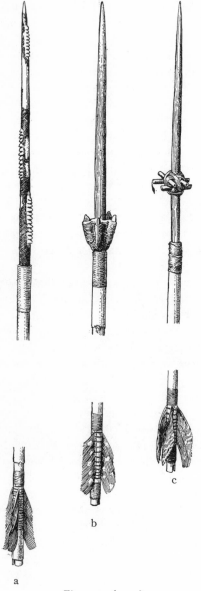

type may very well have developed from a bird arrow, a supposition that is supported by its awl-like head, the other Batwa arrows having heads of a more developed shape. In *b* there is fixed at the base of the head something that is called *nžœpo*, consisting of four small pegs held together by cords or gum and designed to give the arrow a greater possibility of hitting the mark. Another well-known arrangement, which in East Africa has probably been carried farthest by the Wapare, who use clumsy heads, is to have a pointed piece of trunk with thick, cut-off side-branches.

From the flat head of equal thickness it is very easy to pass to one with simple barbs cut out here and there (*e*, *f*) and then to arrange these in a certain way (*a*, *g*). When perfectly arranged we have the barbs in three rows (*d*). This form, however, is more unusual. Sometimes the bird arrows are smeared with a little poison, as seen in the streaks on *a* and *d*.

As is seen we thus easily get a pretty good typical series of our bird arrows.

Fig 129 (a—c).
Kamba bird arrows.
$^1/_2$ nat. size.

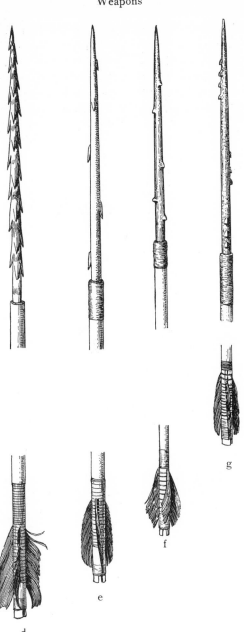

Fig. 129 (d—g).
Kamba bird arrows. ¹/₂ nat. size. Riksmus. Ethn. Coll. Inv. 12. 7. 14—19.

I do not, however, by any means maintain that the line of developement must necessarily have been the one indicated, even though one must admit that the primitive peoples generally go slowly and gradually, if they have to look after themselves. But such a thing as putting some simple barbs on an arrowhead may, it seems to me, be the result of a direct and primary thought, especially in districts where there are as models

Fig. 130.   Quiver decoration of ostrich feathers. $^1/_4$ nat. size.
Riksmus. Ethn. Coll. Inv. 12. 7. 7.

numerous plants (Acacia species and others) with thorns of various shapes, which catch on to the walker. It does not, however, necessarily follow from this that these barbed wooden arrow-heads must have come from thorns of plants and succeeded these, although this is, of course, possible. C. V. Hobley thus shows[1] how in some of the arrows of the Congo pygmies »a long tough thorn,

---

[1] C. V. Hobley, The Evolution of the arrow. The Journ. of the East Africa and Uganda Nat. Hist. Society, vol. III, 1913, p. 33.

probably from one of the Acacia family, is grafted on to the shaft»,
and of a certain type of Kavirondo arrows he says that »it is believed to mimic an acacia thorn, which is frequently of the same shape».

The arrows are kept in a cylindrical quiver (*piaka*) made of
skin, with a detachable lid, the universal type in these parts. It
is carried in a leather strap over the shoulder. From the lid there
often hang down a couple of short straps fitted with cowry shells.
Just as among other tribes they like to adorn the quiver with
black ostrich feathers, fixed with a bit of leather (fig. 130), over-
which a solitary long white plume often rises. In the hut the
quiver has its place on a bedpost.

While shooting arrows both eyes are kept open. The arrow
is held between the index and the long finger. When shooting
at long distances the arrow is not aimed directly at the object,
but a little higher up, or else it would hit the ground in front of
the object. This implies that the shooter understands his weapon
well and gives an opportunity to note that it is by no means a
matter of indifference with what bow one is shooting. As Weule
shows[1], a man who shoots with his bow must know his weapon
as well as a soldier knows his rifle and must have got used to
his bow.

In our days it is difficult to get a correct idea of the Akamba's power of wielding their weapon, as they have too little occasion to exercise it, being forbidden to hunt by the government.
My experience in this respect does not agree with their old reputation as good shots. I have, however, seen boys shoot pigeons,
and at ten metres' distance repeatedly hit a fruit the size of a
ball. In Hildebrandt's time the bow was still essential for the
struggle for existence and he says »that at a distance of 30 steps
a good shot hits a fruit of the size of one's fist almost every
time[2].» It is not clear, however, if he is referring to the Akamba here.

* *

Finally we come to the **sword** (*ubju*). This is of the usual
East African type, which has been described so often that it is
unnecessary to do it here[3]. I merely wish to state that it is typ-

---

[1] Der Afrikanische Pfeil, p. 6.
[2] Die Wakamba, p. 361.
[3] Vide Hildebrandt, Die Wakamba, p. 363.

Fig. 131. Kamba sword. Small
and not so typical; worn by a
young man. $^1/_5$ nat. size.
Riksmus. Ethn. Coll. Inv. 12. 7. 3.

Fig. 132. Club-shaped
stick to carry in the
hand. $^1/_8$ nat. size.
Riksmus. Ethn. Coll.
Inv. 12. 7. 250.

Fig 133.
Club with
head of stone,
wrapped in a
piece of skin.
$^1/_4$ nat. size.
Riks. Ethn.
Coll. Inv.
12. 7. 230.

ical of the Kamba sword that the blade is longer than the sheath
(*ndọ*). It is carried for preference hanging in a strap over one
shoulder, but also, as among other tribes, in a belt round the
waist or in the hand. The short sword reproduced here (fig. 131) is
not a really typical shape, but serves more as an ornament and
has been worn by a young man. The sheath is painted with
bright red ornamentation, the same colour as is used for the arrows. A similar colour is obtained from several plants, among
others from the bark of the *mwæa* (Mimosa species), which is put
in water.

* *

Before leaving the weapons, a few words remain to be said
about **clubs**. As is well-known, the club is a common weapon
in East Africa; it is made for the most part of wood and is
used for hitting and throwing. The Akamba, however, do not
use them, and I have not had any confirmation of Hildebrandt's
statement about them. On the other hand it is a fact that there
are many objects which resemble clubs, but they are to be considered as dancing accessories or as a kind of stick, which the natives
like to carry in their hands when out walking. That many of these
objects, which we might take to be clubs, are not so considered
by the natives themselves, is shown by their language, as they
are certainly often called *nžuma* 'clubs', but just as often *ndata*
'stick'. So much is certain, that they are not used in fighting,
and at most they may be used for an occasional throw at a bird.
The type of these dance-clubs and sticks varies, but they generally have the shape of a pole gracefully cut out (fig. 132) and
are often adorned with artistically twisted metal wire. So that the
wood shall get a fine polish it is rubbed with fat.

A real club of an interesting type is, however, found, although
rather sparsely among the Akamba. Even this, however, they use
only for carrying in their hands and do not make themselves,
but get it from the districts on the south slope of Kenia. On a
very narrow wooden shaft is placed a stone head, a quartz ball,
surrounded with some wooden splints, and then the whole is sewn
over with a piece of leather (fig. 133).

This type of club has already been described and reproduced
by L. Rütimeyer from three specimens in the ethnographical

collections at Basle University [1]. To judge from the reproductions these are quite like those brought by me from Ukamba. They are said, however, to come from the Ja-Luo tribe in Kavirondo, a statement that I cannot of course dispute, but of which I am doubtful, as during my stay in the Kavirondo country I never saw or heard of such clubs [2]. Rütimeyer is, in addition, of the opinion that we are here concerned with a pre-historic relic, a hammer, but, as far as my own specimens are concerned, I can see no reason at all to believe this. It is true that I have only troubled to remove the casing of skin on one of my stone balls, but it seems to have been knocked together recently and shows no sign of wear, which it ought of course to do if it had once been used as a tool. If, on the other hand, Rütimeyer's assumption as to their age is correct, it is clear from my specimens that a new production of these stone balls has continually taken place or has at least taken place down to a recent time. But even if one has to deny that these clubs are pre-historic — I am only speaking for my own specimens — they are still exceedingly interesting and even rare. As far as I know they are not known from other parts of Africa, and as far as the museums are concerned, even the great Berlin museum appears to have no such club.

---

[1] L. Rütimeyer, Über einige altertümliche afrikanische Waffe und Geräte und deren Beziehungen zur Præhistorie. Zeitschr. f. Ethn. 1911, p. 240 ff.

[2] After the proofsheet of the above was even ready Prof. Rütimeyer kindly wrote to me saying that he bought his clubs at Oldham's in London, the well-known dealer in ethnographical objects. As mistakes about the origin of objects sold in this way occur not infrequently my doubts about Kavirondo as the locality of these clubs have been further strengthened.

Chap. XXVI. **Hunting.**

According to their traditions the Akamba were originally a hunting people, and there is a great deal to support the truth of this tradition. Thus even at the present day they enjoy a very good reputation as hunters and compete with the professional hunting peoples, especially the Wandorobo, for the honour of being considered as the most skilful nimrods in these parts of East Africa. They have from time immemorial devoted themselves to elephant hunting because of the profit attached to it, and these hunts of theirs extended not infrequently beyond the boundaries of Ukamba, for instance as far as the poorly watered and largely un-inhabited deserts north of Kenia. Nowadays, however, as might be expected, hunting is of subordinate importance compared with agriculture and cattle-rearing.

Elephant hunting. The preparations for a hunt for elephants or other big and dangerous game and the rites connected with entering upon such a hunt show great resemblances to the pre-cautions taken on entering upon military and plundering exped-itions. »Is it not war to hunt such animals as the elephant, the rhinoceros, the buffalo and the lion?» said an old warrior to the author. A skilful elephant hunter has a great reputation, and he is compared to a victorious leader in war. For both bring wealth home with them. The leaders of a hunting expedition are also usually the same as those of a military campaign (*apɩanɩ*). We may note in passing that this agreement between the ideas and the arrangements of hunting and military expeditions seems to exist among most primitive tribes that follow these pursuits to any considerable extent. The magic rites connected with hunting and war are also often identical [1].

---

[1] This view is propounded and developed in Hubert and Mauss' excellent work on magic in the Année Sociologique, vol. VII, p. 132 ff.

Elephant hunting is usually carried on by a number of men together. The hunting party (*nžɨɨma* or *nɨma < kusɨɨma* 'to hunt') is composed of an equal number of representatives from each *þomə*, the open place in front of a village. Several neighbouring families have a *þomə* in common.

Before the expedition is begun, as before a military campaign, the natives go to the medicine man to find out under what auspices they are entering upon the campaign. A beer-party is also held with its accompanying sacrifices[1] to Mulungu, i. e. the *aɨmu*, the ancestral spirits, amid prayers for a successful result. On such occasions they sacrifice especially to some deceased famous hunter. Such a man is usually buried, like other eminent men, at the foot of a wild figtree where sacrifices are made. If any unfavourable omen is met on the way home from the place of sacrifice, they go back there and sacrifice again. After a successfully concluded hunt thankofferings were similarly presented to Mulungu.

When a hunting party marched out it consisted to some extent of young men who were about to make their first attempt at hunting. These inexperienced beginners had, the day before the beginning of the march, to present the old experienced hunters and leaders with beer and an ox as a treat.

From the medicine men the hunters procured abundance of things to bring good luck in hunting, such as powder to rub on the bow and bowstring, to increase their certainty of aim, and medicine to rub on their eyes, to sharpen their vision. Once when I went out elephant hunting with the Akamba they poured a sort of powder in the barrel of my rifle. The leader on that occasion brought with him a talisman consisting of sticks fastened together, which was said to have the power of enticing the elephants out. Just as on military expeditions the leaders also had magic medicine, which prevented the animals from running away, even so that if they are shot on one side, they shall then kindly turn the other! Hobley describes[2] how the old elephant hunter Sulu carried about his person charms and medicines of various kinds: to ensure game being seen, to make the hunter shoot straight, to let him get the beast he wishes and, if he approaches a fierce animal, not to be attacked by it.

---

[1] *kuumɨa kɨþaŋgona* 'to deliver sacrifices'.
[2] C. V. Hobley, Kamba protective magic, Man 1912, p. 4.

This idea that religion and magic are part of the necessary preparations for hunting or military expeditions in order to ensure success is a fact that applies to all mankind.

As has been mentioned, during such hunting expeditions the natives often travel very far from their native district or the nearest cultivated place. If there is a good supply of game, they construct a sort of headquarters, consisting of simple huts. This work is carried out by the novices, who are treating in rather a bullying way. They have to do all the menial work, chop the wood and cook the food. They are not allowed to live in the huts, but sleep outside. There is a good deal to support the idea that this sleeping on the ground is of a ritual character, as in the case of the novices during the initiation rites. When the hunt is taking place in the neighbourhood of the headquarters, one of them stays at home and cooks the food.

As a rule novices are not allowed to go alone to shoot at an elephant, even if the opportunity seems to be a very favourable one, but if they discover an animal, they have to report it to the leaders. The intention of this is presumably to prevent them, in their inexperience, from disturbing or frightening the animals away. On the other hand many of the recruits are so frightened at the sight of the huge pachyderms, which they see perhaps for the first time, that they tremble and feel anything but inclined to attack them.

A person who has not been present before when an elephant or rhinoceros has been killed may not go up and look at one of these animals before its tail has been cut off and removed. The prohibition does not seem to apply to any other kind of big game. If this rule is not observed, the beginner is supposed to have but a slight prospect of being able to kill an elephant and would thus miss what is perhaps the best chance of procuring cattle and wives for himself. We have already described (p. 333) how the end of the elephant's trunk is cut off and buried in the sand before the novices have caught sight of it, and in the case of a she-elephant, although for different reasons, the same thing is often done with her dugs. We have also spoken already about the fear of mentioning an elephant by name during the hunt (p. 289).

The novice is not allowed to partake of all the parts of an elephant that has been killed; thus he may not eat the *ubuko* (a

part near the heart) or *kɪƀə* (part of the back). These restrictions
are probable comparable to similar ones with regard to the eating
of meat in general, which we have mentioned on p. 144 ff.

The beginner who has himself killed or helped to kill an
elephant is on his return home at the end of the hunt initiated
into the secrets of hunting by one of the leaders as a reward.
He pays for this instruction with a goat.

Elephant hunting is carried on or was carried on — the natives are, of course, forbidden nowadays to hunt elephants — in
several different ways. They sometimes used the well-known dis-
guised pitfalls, although I never saw any of these in Ukamba.
They used to a greater extent the equally well-known snare —
widespread in Africa — in the shape of a poisoned spear falling
from above. This apparatus (Kik. *kɪambu*) is described below
under »Traps».

A method of hunting which is much in vogue but which, however, imposes a hard test on the hunter's patience, is to build platforms
of branches up in the tree at the elephants' watering-place and
from these to send a shower of poisoned arrows on the animals,
often at some metres' distance[1]. In most cases, however, they
prefer to follow their tracks and steal upon them while they are
feeding or resting. It is a rule that the one who first catches
sight of an elephant is not to attack him alone, but the whole
party or as many as possible shoot their arrows at the same time
so as to increase the chances of success. When the game is
distributed attention is paid to the effect of the arrow-shots. We
remember that the arrows are marked with their owner's clan
mark.

If any one is killed during an elephant hunt, two tusks are
handed over to his wife and children.

A successful elephant hunter usually braids a ring made of
the sinews of the elephant's feet round his bow for each elephant
he kills. In my ethnographical collection there is a bow with numerous rings of this kind.

There is no doubt that the natives still have a quantity of
ivory concealed in the grass-covered roofs of their huts or buried

---

[1] An account of the preparation of arrow-poison is given in connection with the description of weapons p. 455.

in the ground. The government buy up their old ivory at 4 rupees a pound, but they are no longer disposed to sell it at this price. Many of them still think that the Europeans will once leave the country for ever, and then they will sell their ivory to the Arabs and Suaheli, as they did formerly. In remote parts the Akamba certainly still carry on elephant hunting secretly.

Opinions about the skill of settled African natives as hunters vary a great deal, even in the case of the same tribe, and one finds the most enthusiastic admiration side by side with rather contemptuous expressions of opinion. It is perhaps most correct to say that, just as among us there are good and bad hunters, so there is the same mixture among the natives. As far as the Akamba are concerned, I have heard nothing but good reports, and my own experience quite bears out the general good reputation they enjoy as hunters. Together with Mr A. Champion, District Commissioner of Kitui, I followed elephants in the bush towards Tana east of Ukamba for some weeks' time, and I had an opportunity of observing two experienced old Kamba-hunters and learned to estimate their capacities, their knowledge of the animals' habits, their acute sight and hearing and their skill in following a track. It was really a pleasure to see them study tracks and discuss them: Here the track is deeply impressed and the sand has been violently thrown up: the elephant has been frightened or for some other reason has begun to run. In another place, on the other hand, it is seen that the pachyderms are walking rapidly: they have probably scented us and consequently begun to move. This track, again, is that of an animal moving quite lazily, feeding on the leaves and bark of the trees. It is quite unaware of our proximity, and so on. A handful of sand serves to establish the direction of the wind. The Akamba also use dogs in hunting, and they are trained to follow the scent.

In order to attract the animals they also use call-notes but as far as I know only against rhinoceroses and in the case of boys hunting certain birds.

Traps.

Several traps of different construction and methods of use are called *ıkæŋgɔ*, as we shall see below. They are all, however, drop traps. The name is possibly formed from *kæŋga* 'to cheat, de-

ceive'. The words *kɪtæɪ* and *ɪtæo* also mean 'trap', perhaps in
a general sense (< *kutæa* 'to trap').

1. Drop trap (*kɪambu*[1]). A pole made of a hard species of
wood is pointed, coated with arrow-poison and fixed in another
pole, which in its turn is fastened in a log of wood. The whole
apparatus thus corresponds to an arrow with a head, loose middle
piece, and shaft. It is hung by means of a cord above an elephant track on a projecting branch; the cord is brought down to
the ground and there set as a trap. When the elephant comes walk-

Fig. 132. Trap for smaller beasts of prey.
a a ring made of plaited fibres near the end of the stock, whose length
is about 1,5 m. *b* stick fastened through the fibre ring.
c cord forming a loop at the extreme end of the stick *d*.
e fork stuck in the ground, in which the
cord rests. *f* bait (piece of meat) fixed
to the stick *d*. *g* The walls
of the trap.

ing along and releases the cord, the spear falls down on its back
and its point pierces it, while the remaining parts fall to the ground.
Traps of this type are also used for hyenas and leopards.

2. Drop trap (*ɪkæŋgə*) for killing smaller beasts of prey, such
as gennets and serval cats. A log, 1—2 metres long, is placed in
the position shown in fig. 132, built round at the sides with an
enclosure of twigs, etc. forming a narrow passage, on which the
log rests. A piece of meat (*f*) is used as bait. When the animal
touches this, the loop that the cord *c* forms round the extreme
end of the stick *d*, slips off. The released log then falls down.

---

[1] really = 'stopper, wedge of wood'.

3. The following trap is also set for smaller beasts of prey. A pit is dug in the ground with a sloping entrance. In the vertical back wall of the pit a hole is made and in it is placed a living hen, which is kept shut in by means of a grating made of sticks driven into the earth. The hen usually cries and so attracts small beasts of prey to the place. At the bottom of the pit is placed in a vertical position a running noose, which is fastened to a bow-

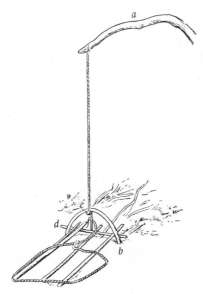

Fig. 133. Running noose (*mukwa*). From a photo by the author.

shaped bent switch. When the animal goes through the snare to the hen, it treads on the stick by which the snare is set in an unstable state of equilibrium. The released switch then becomes straight and the noose is drawn tight.

4. There are several types of running nooses for smaller game, sometimes intended to catch them round the neck, sometimes by the legs or body. Nooses of the former kind are set at the animals' drinking-places and in the fields, where they go to eat. The *mukwa* (fig. 133, 134) is a snare of the latter type. It is fixed to a stick thrust down in the ground, *a*, which is kept bent bow-shaped by the peg *c* placed on the noose and pressed

against the bow *b* (set in the ground) by the peg *f* wedged in unstable equilibrium between the bow and the stick *d*.

Another sort of running noose, called *ṇdɪndelo*, is only known to me by name.

5. Bird snare (*ɪkæŋgɔ*). This is made of sticks (fig. 135) and somewhat resembles in shape an arched lid of a box. The snare is placed edgeways resting against a stick, which is resting

Fig. 134. Running noose (*muḵwa*).

unstably between the prongs of another fixed in the ground and shaped like a fork. From the lower end of the first stick a cord runs to the ground, where it is fastened to a small stick lying beneath the outer part of a longer one, which in its turn extends in beneath the trap. Here are scattered grains of maize or other bait. When the bird touches the last-mentioned stick, the trap falls down like a lid.

These snares are made by the boys. The one reproduced here was used for catching partridges, francolins, pigeons, etc. For guinea-fowl they are made larger and heavier.

6. Hobley, who mentions four traps (Akamba, p. 30), speaks

Fig. 135 Falling bird snare.

of another kind of drop trap (*ıkæŋgə*) of a well-known type, »consisting of a flat slab of stone supported by a twig and baited with grain; the supporting twig is usually pulled away with a string. This is used »to catch birds and monkeys».

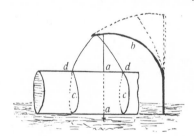

Fig. 136. Trap for catching moles. $^1/_6$ nat size.

7. Trap for catching moles (*kıtatı* or *kısuŋgula*). The mole, which in Ukamba is much bigger than the Swedish species, does a great deal of damage to the fields and the natives accordingly try to catch as many as possible. The trap consists of a cylindrical piece of wood (fig. 136), hollowed out except at one end. It is

placed with its aperture towards the moles' hole or in the mole run itself. Through the small holes *a* is drawn a cord, which is fastened to a stick in the ground and keeps the pliant stick *b* bent in a bow. The running nooses *c*, fastened to the stick, run through small holes *d* in the upper part of the cylinder and are hidden by being placed in recesses in the walls of the cylinder. In addition earth is strewn over the nooses at the bottom of the cylinder. On this are put grains of maize, etc. as bait. When the mole knocks against the cord running through *a* and is checked by it, he finds it suspicious and bites it through. The stick is suddenly straightened, draws the trap with it and the mole swings at *d*. The person who has set the trap remains near it and goes occasionally to see to it.

Formerly this trap was also used, although in a smaller size, for catching rats indoors, but nowadays, when cats are usually kept, it has almost entirely gone out of use for this purpose.

Moles are also caught in the following way: The natives observe the animal's wandering in its underground passages, and when they have discovered they proper place, they drive a pointed pole down with such accuracy that it blocks the way for the mole, which is then quickly dug out. A certain amount of skill is needed to see where the animal is and to place the pole so that is goes just through the passage.

*

No fishing is carried on, as the Akamba do not eat fish. Besides there are no waters with fish in them in Ukamba, no lakes at all and hardly any rivers except Athi, Tiwa and Nthua.

Chap. XXVII. **Domestic animals.**

1. **Myths about the origin of cattle.**

When one remembers that cattle are the negro's dearest possession in this world, it is not strange to find that he has pondered over the origin of these precious animals. While real myths of origin, as I have shown on p. 252, are almost entirely lacking among the Akamba, there are ideas about the origin of cattle in several of the people's myths, in their folklore and traditions[1]. To this subject I have found the following allusions.

1. In the myth of the origin of man (p. 252) the first cow and one of the first two human couples come out of a termite hole (*mupumbını*).

2. A myth that I heard in Kitui, which is possibly the same as the preceding one or a variant of it, is as follows:

The first human beings, who came up out of the termite hole, settled down in the neighbourhood of the mouth of the hole. They had no cattle, but increased and soon formed a whole village. One day they heard a voice from heaven — it was Ngai — saying: »On the seventh evening after this, when you go to rest, do not shut your craals!»

The seventh evening came, and some did as they had been requested, others, on the other hand, were afraid and carefully shut the entrances to their craals, before they retired to rest. They were awakened by a gentle, inexplicable sound from the big opening in the earth. It was the cattle coming up and going into the craals that were open. A little while later other and more shrill cries were heard from the hole. It was goats and sheep coming the same way as the horned cattle.

---

[1] Hobley declares (p. 20) that the Akamba have no legend as to the origin of cattle and other domestic animals.

Whe the sun rose, those who had left their craals open found
them full of cattle. Those on the other hand who had kept them
shut bitterly repented not having obeyed Ngai's exhortation. From
the former arose the Masai, from the latter the Akamba.

3. In the tradition about the common origin of the Akamba,.
Akikuyu and Masai (p. 353) the Masai are the first to keep
cattle. According to their own traditions as well[1], they consider
themselves as originally the sole owners of all cattle, and when
they set out on a plundering expedition, they are getting back,
according to their own view, only their rightful property and they
use this as an excuse, if they trouble to try to find any excuse
at all.

4. Among the numerous stories of the Akamba about animals there is one that treats of how the cow became a domestic
animal. She was originally a wild animal, »like the buffalo», but
harassed by beasts of prey, came to the villages of human beings
and asked to be taken in by them. In return for the protection
they gave her, she gave them her milk, and so they lived together
to their mutual satisfaction and profit.

5. In Muutha, East Ukamba, I heard this tradition: When
the first human beings, the Akamba, came out of the termite
hole, they had in their right hand a bow, in the left the products of the field[2]. Thus we see that they had no cattle, and it
was a long time before they got any. They maintained themselves instead principally by hunting. They shot elephants especially
and sold the ivory to the Suaheli traders, who came up from
the coast to meet them. They soon learned to go down to the
coast themselves, and on these journeys they got to know about
cattle and were especially pleased with their milk and with their
fat »to mix in their snuff». Then they exchanged ivory for cattle.
»This was the beginning of cattle.»

These traditions have little scientific value. At a hasty glance
they seem to contradict each other, but on closer comparison
this contradiction can be explained. The fourth in the series can

---

[1] See Hollis, The Masai, p. 268.

[2] The expressions »right» and »left» undoubtedly denote the distribution of labour, the difference between the man's and the woman's
occupations. Cf. p. 104, note 2.

at once be left out of the reckoning as being merely a *wanu*, a fairy-tale. Similarly we can eliminate nos. 1—3, which may be considered as probably having the same value as fairy-tales, and which are probably taken really seriously by few people except women and children. The fifth story, on the other hand, is connected in the beginning, it is true, with the myths about origin, but has afterwards a good deal of truth in it. It teaches us that the Akamba consider themselves originally a hunting people, who seem, however, to have been connected with the land to a certain extent. This short tradition is of a certain interest because it introduces us to a common problem concerning the way human culture has developed. We know the old customary path of cultural development from hunters to nomads and then to farmers. Against this division E. Hahn especially, and many others after him, have emphatically pointed out[1] that cattle and other domestic animals could only be produced by settled peoples, who were therefore at a comparatively high level of culture (through the attempts at cross-breeding of generations of different wild races). For this reason it is clear that after being a hunter and gatherer man first became a farmer, more or less settled, before he began real cattle-breeding.

What led me on to this topic was the fact that the last-mentioned Kamba tradition says that the people had the products of the field before they got to know about cattle. We may venture, perhaps, on account of this to state that this idea, even though it is unconscious, forms part of the primitive consciousness of the fact that agriculture is older than cattle-breeding.

2. Cattle-breeding.

The Akamba's cattle is of the same race as that which is kept by the neighbouring tribes and numerous other East African peoples, namely a species of zebu with rather short horns. With regard to the colour the cattle is black and white, light yellow or greyish, while brown animals are very rare. The stock was app-

---

[1] E. Hahn, Die Haustiere, Leipzig 1915, and, in concentrated form, in Demeter und Baubo, Versuch einer Theorie der Entstehung unsres Ackerbaus, Lübeck 1896.

reciably reduced by rinderpest and also during the last great famine, but is now, on the contrary, pretty considerable. There is a general tendency, even among those who possess only a small number of animals, not to keep them in the same place, but to divide them up into small herds in different craals with intervals between them, which, in the case of a rich man with many women to look after the animals, may be as large as a whole day's march or more. This is done chiefly for practical reasons, to prevent the spreading of cattle diseases, and in former times also as a protection against the attacks of the Masai. In either case the risk of losing the whole stock at once was, of course, decreased. Superstitious motives may also play a part. The natives are afraid of their neighbour's envy, the »evil eye» and other magic.

These precautions were, however, not always sufficient to save them from rinderpest. The great epidemic in 1891, the same one as decreased the Masai's herds so enormously, passed in Ukamba from village to village, and those, for instance, who owned 500 head .of cattle had only five to ten left.

The cattle are milked early in the morning, but are not driven out to graze before the dew has dried up, as the wet grass is not considered to improve their condition. They are watched by youths and boys, who do this work in regular turns. One sometimes sees an old man who has no sons at home minding his cattle himself. Although this is, as we see, the work of the men, there is nothing to prevent women doing it (among certain other Bantu peoples, Kafirs, etc. they are not allowed to do this), and they usually do it when the men are engaged with other things. The cattle-herd usually takes his place on a termite heap (*kıbumbu*), from which he can watch the animals. The boys pass the time with games and jokes, and the young men sit and polish their ornaments. In warm Kikumbuliu the cattle are taken to rest beneath some big trees during the hottest part of the day.

A number of cattle are pastured as a rule so far from the village that they cannot be driven home daily but are kept during the nights in an enclosure called *kıæygo* out at the grazing place. In it there is also a hut for those who are looking after the cattle.

The cattle are milked in the morning and evening by women.

A man living alone in the *kₗꞓŋgo*, however, milks them himself. The women milk standing, in a somewhat crouching position, with only one hand, as they hold the calabash in the other.

According to Hildebrandt, in his time the men did the milking. This seems to be a custom common for cattle-keeping tribes at an earlier stage, and if his statement is true, it is very interesting to see how the Akamba in late times have changed the original custom. In the beginning not only hunting but also cattle-keeping, and everything connected with it, is the work of the men.

To increase the supply of milk in cows and small cattle they are given certain plants, preferably those rich in milky sap, often the same as are eaten by women who are suckling their children and who have a deficient supply of milk. Such plants have been mentioned on p. 319. We may mention here, in addition, a decoction of *mwelₓa* or *kamwelₓa* (Croton?) and *ŋondu* (*ₓa*) *akaбι*, which is chiefly given to goats to drink.

When milking cows which have young calves, the calf is allowed to suck before the milking begins. If the calf dies, the mother stops giving milk. The Akamba then stuff the calf's skin with hay and put it by the mother, who then lets herself be milked, a practice that is also known among the Masai and Nandi.

Cows which do not care for their calves are given the excrements of the python to eat. It is said to have a good effect (for the various use of the excrements of this snake vide Index).

If an animal will not stand still or if it has the bad habit of kicking, a stand is made with tree trunks, to one pole of which the animal's head is fastened, and its hind legs to another.

Fierce cattle that wish to butt can be made harmless by the following process, which is undoubtedly of a magic character, though the mental procedure of the natives with regard to it is not so easy to understand. An *ιawɔ*, a sort of night-jar, is procured and its feathers and skeleton are burnt and the ashes put in water, which is given to the animal to drink. If eggs of this bird are found, they can be used for the same purpose. In this case it is only necessary to throw the eggs at the animal that is to be cured of its bad habit. To make animals tractable by a certain ceremony, by using certain magic means, is called *kuбoбₓa*. We shall find that the Akamba also take measures with their bees for the same purpose (p. 496).

To lead cattle leather straps are used. They are fastened round the base of the horns. To catch calves a long wooden crook (*mboloʒ*) is used, of the same type as that by which beehives are hung up. Cow-bells (*mbwi*) are used. They are made of iron, of the type usual in these districts and like those in Europe.

Cattle are castrated by having a red-hot awl stuck through the veins of the testicles. This is called *kuɓakua* in the case of horned cattle, *kutua* when sheep and goats are castrated.

Sheep and goats are killed by being strangled. The animal's mouth is kept closed and its neck squeezed.

Bleeding of cattle. Like the Masai, the Akikuyu and other tribes the Akamba now and then bleed their cattle, the blood being a favourite food. I have seen them seize an animal which was to be bled where it was grazing; this was done by suddenly seizing it by one of its hind legs and throwing it over. Then its legs are fastened tightly with leather straps, so that the animal cannot move. Another strap is fastened so tightly round its neck that the blood accumulates in the big blood-vessel and forms a swelling. A blunt arrow (*ndʑa*, see fig. 137) is shot with a short bow at the lump. The shooter stands close by the animal. The arrow does not stick in, but rebounds back. A stream of blood rushes out and is collected in a calabash. Some people then put their mouths to the hole and drink eagerly. One may even see boys busy picking lice from the animals' udders and putting them in their mouths. Then the animal is released, after the stream of blood has been stopped by smearing a little cow-dung or earth on the wound. It resumes its interrupted grazing as if nothing had happened. Another animal is then caught and treated in the same way.

The arrows that are used are kept in a leather quiver of the same type as the ordinary arrow quiver. For bleeding sheep and goats, however, they use arrows with shorter points. The arrows have no feathers, as the distance is only a few decimetres. The base of the arrow is bound above the notch, sometimes with sinews, sometimes with hair from the zebra's tail.

During famine they take the blood in this way once a month or more often. At other times bleeding is really used chiefly as a medical remedy, especially during the rainy season, when it is sometimes carried out, during an abundant rainfall perhaps twice. The natives maintain that during the rainy season the animals get constipation more easily than at other times, and bleeding is used as a remedy for this[1].

A difficulty that cattle-breeding has to overcome in many places in East Ukamba is the meagre supply of water during the dry season. It is then often very troublesome to procure water for the needs of human beings, and still more for cattle. Even the bigger rivers, such as the Tiva, dry up, and holes 1—2 metres deep have to be dug in the riverbed in order to reach the water

Fig. 139. Arrow for bleeding cattle. ⅓ siz. Riksmus. Ethn. Coll. Inv. 12. 7. 82.

Fig. 140. Cattle-bleeding.

The cattle are watered in some places only every other or every third day, and not more than one or two animals at a time are allowed to go down to the water, so that they shall not jostle together and stir up the water. To prevent this the waterhole is often also enclosed. I have often seen a man standing at the entrance of such an enclosure with his sheep and goats outside, waiting for them to drink. They go one by one down to the water, and it is interesting to see in what an orderly way this is done and how patiently the animals wait for their turn to come,

---

[1] The Masai also bleed their cattle, especially during the wet season, as a remedy for an illness that the animals get by eating big larvae that are found in the grass on the steppe (Merker p. 171).

although they are very thirsty. The man guides them merely by whistling. In Kikumbuliu I saw a kind of water reservoir consisting of living trees with their trunks broad, as it were swollen, at the bottom and hollowed out. During the rainy season water was collected in these hollows, out of which the goats were then allowed to drink.

It is usual to guide the cattle by whistling also, when they are driven to and from their grazing places. The Kamba herd controls his animals as skilfully as a thorough nomad, and his silent but certain demeanour has a salutary effect on one who is accustomed to the Swedish peasant's continual shouting and hallooing to his cattle. To whistle is called *kuusₜa mu̯ₓ*; no kind of superstition is connected with it.

The Akamba, like other cattle-owning people, are very fond of their cattle, as they are, of course, their real wealth. More than one man whom I jokingly asked whether he liked his cattle or his wife best took this question seriously and was unable to decide, leaving me without any answer. A herd of fine oxen is the special pride and delight of the Kamba man. A delight to the eyes is just the right expression, for the cows are there to give milk and fat, but the oxen »to grow fat», as one of my native friends expressed it. They seldom have the heart to kill an ox, except in cases of need and on ceremonial occasions. To kill a calf is almost unthinkable. The meat that the Akamba get from their herds is given for the most part by sheep and goats. To use oxen for any work appears ridiculous to them; besides »they grow thin from it and their flesh is spoiled». Thus the oxen lead a pleasant life, and only in their older days do they get killed for food.

This love for cattle has made many a coward show proofs of courage and daring, when at a Masai attack he had to recover a favourite ox. If a grazing herd was attacked, it was considered a great dishonour for the herdsman to abandon his cattle and try to save himself by flight. He had to fight as long as possible. Sometimes he was able to keep the Masai in check as long as his arrows lasted, and then, when they were all shot away, he would yield with dull submission and wait for death.

On the other hand this passion gives rise to endless quarrels. Most of the law-suits may be said to be in connection with cattle. They also cause avarice and dishonesty. It is not long since the Akamba enjoyed the doubtful honour of being regarded as prominent cattle thieves, even among themselves. While I was still living in Machakos, it happened that some men went over to the Kikuyu country and in the old traditional style drove off some animals. In former times it was not uncommon, when a man died, for someone to come to his heir and say: »Your father owed me an ox or so many goats». Young and inexperienced individuals were sometimes taken in by such deception. One of my friends answered such a claim very pertinently: »My father lay ill a long time before he died. Why did you not come while he was living?» They also imposed on the credulity of boys who were tending the cattle. A man would go, for instance, to the grazing place and say to the herdsman: »Your father told me to bring an ox home with me, as I had to pass this way.» He would then disappear with his booty.

Cattle and also goats and sheep often appear in the numerous riddles of the Akamba. Of about 120 riddles I have noted, 14 deal with these domestic animals.

3. Other domestic animals.

Besides horned cattle the Akamba keep very many sheep and goats. The former are a species of fat-tailed sheep. The he-goats become very tame, and one sometimes sees a he-goat following a woman like a dog on her way to and from the fields. The following plants are considered to be good food for goats: the leaves of *mupélea*, a low bush with lip-shaped, lilac flowers (2 stamina); the leaves of the tree called *mwæma nžæu* (Leguminosae, with small lilac flowers); the dry hard fruit of the *wa* (Acacia sp.).

They do not keep **asses**, but in former times these were found in certain places. Hildebrandt says about asses (p. 380): »They do not thrive well in Ukamba because of the dondorobo fly[1] [tsetse fly? — only found, however, in the south-east]. The

---

[1] A *dorobbo* is the Masai name for the tsetse fly (Glossina morsitans).

Akamba eat the tame ass after having first fattened them, a thing that I have not found among other East Africans».

Poultry is perhaps the most common domestic animal in Africa, and however mean a hut may be, it is never without some cocks and hens. The species is small and thin and lays small eggs, which are never used by the natives as food. This is due partly to a mere dislike of eggs, which are called »the hen's excrement» (maṱ ma ŋguḵu), but economic reasons are still more important. It is, of course, foolish to eat eggs and by so doing voluntarily prevent the increase of one's poultry.

Poultry must never be shot with arrows. A friend of the author had a great number of cocks and hens and often used to have a good meal of one of them, which, for the pleasure of the thing, he shot with his arrows. His poultry thrived excellently for a long time, but then they began to die, one after the other, and many were taken by kĭɓuṱ, probably a species of gennet or some small cat. The old men maintained that the cause of this was that he had killed poultry with arrows.

The poultry are very tame. I used now and then to buy a few, and when the natives let them loose at my tent, it was very amusing to notice how they were immediately at home and began to look for food. In the evening they crept into the tent without any fear and slept there. On my marches the bearers transported them in the usual cruel native manner, namely by tying their legs together and fastening them to a load. Often they were unable to get a foothold but hung down swinging from side to side. One meet natives daily carrying poultry in this brutal way. If a single person, however, is carrying a number of cocks and hens to market, he takes them in a sort of wicker basket on his head.

The Akamba have a story about the origin of domestic poultry. Like the cow they were originally wild beasts. The story is briefly as follows:

Long ago guineahens and barndoor fowls were brothers and sisters and lived together in the wilderness. Once during the rainy season they were very cold, and so the guineahen said: »Go to the Akambas' villages and fetch what they warm themselves with, fire!» The barndoor fowl raised objections and did not want to go, for she was afraid of human beings, but the guineahen drove her off. She came to a village, went into a hut and began to warm herself. When she was warm she crept in beneath a bed and went to sleep.

The guineahen waited in vain the whole night and was exceedingly cold. When it got light, she went out to look for the barndoor fowl, calling continually to her. Finally the fowl heard her, but she had found her new home much too pleasant to leave. Accordingly she cried at the top of her voice: »There is no fire here, there is no fire here!» The guineahen then went away but came back again the next morning, and the same thing was repeated. The guineahen then flew away in anger, never to come back again. »But the day they were cold the friendship between the barndoor fowl and the guineahen died and never came to life again».

Many of the Kamba dogs are undoubtedly of a mixed race, as many Akamba got pups from Europeans during recent years. The original race — I must leave the question unsettled as to whether there is really only one race — shows a great resemblance to our village curs, rather small animals with tails curling upwards. They often cut the tail off to improve the animal's appearance. Hildebrandt saw in his time a species of greyhound; I have, however, never come across any of these.

The Akamba are very much attached to their dogs, as they are to their animals in general, and treat them very well. Thrashing a dog may occasion severe hostility, even a life and death struggle. The native dogs are very afraid of Europeans, just as, on the other hand, the white men's dogs usually show a great dislike to the natives.

In Hildebrandts time there were no cats. Nowadays they have a number, obtained from the Europeans.

To keep wild animals as company or for amusement is not usual.

The different kinds of domestic animals are called with different cries. For dogs they whistle or call *su, su, su*. To goats they say *kæh, kæh, kæh*, to sheep a sort of buzzing *mah, mah* and to poultry a sort of clacking sound which it is difficult to express in writing. The cattle have names, and each animal is called by its name.

4. Names for domestic animals in the Kamba language.

Many of the African tribes that keep cattle have an extensive nomenclature for their cattle, having for instance different words for the same kind of animal at different ages, etc. and similarly an enormous number of technical terms in connection with cattle. My studies in the Kamba language have not given very great results with regard to these. The rather few terms I have found for domestic animals are as follows:

ŋombǝ cattle

ṇžau̯ bull

ṇdǣwa ox

kasau̯, kasalu calf

moṭ heifer, dimin. *kamolɩ*

mulaǫ calf that has finished sucking

ṇduṭ half-grown cattle

muᵽuku̯ (*kɩᵽuku̯*) hornless cattle (one occasionally sees such cattle)

ṇðata barren cow

ɩumbɩ grey cattle (apart from this the Akamba have no word for grey [1])

ŋgɩndǝ cattle with the horns bent forward and backward close to the head (they are loose and vibrate, as it were, when the animal moves)

ṃbuṭ goat

ṇðæŋgǝ he-goat

ṇdǣla, ŋgulata castrated he-goat

mwǫma female goat bearing young

ṃbaṭka young female goat, that has not yet had kids

ṇdǣna, katǣna kid

ŋgondu, ɩlondu sheep

ṇdamǝ ram

mwatɩ young female sheep not yet bearing

ŋguku barndoor fowl

ṇžokolo cock

mwǣla hen

ŋgɩtɩ, sulu, ɩkulu, ŋgulu dog

ṃbaka cat (Kisuaheli *paka*)

ɩŋoṭ donkey (onomatopoetic word)

ŋgamɩa camel (= Kisuaheli)

ṃblasɩ horse (Kisuaheli *farasɩ*).

We can scarcely expect a closer investigation of these words to give us any idea of the origin of the domestic animals among the Akamba. Experts in the Bantu languages have observed that most of them are pure Bantu stems. I have not found any resemblance to the Masai and Galla languages. In Kikuyu these expressions are the same as in Kikamba, making allowance, of course, for the differences due to sound laws.

---

[1] Cf. how the Hottentots have numerous terms for the colour of cattle, but not for colours on other objects.

The natives, especially the women who have to milk the cows, give names to the cattle. The sheep and goats also often get names. Examples:

mwœlu (dim. *kœlu*) 'the white one'

kaɪlu 'the little black one'

mutuna (dim. *katunə*) 'the red one'

katundumu (< *tunduma* 'to thunder')

kɪɓala: name of cattle with a white blaze on the forehead (lit. 'spot on the ground where no grass grows')

sɪo-nðɪa 'the mother of the duiker'. The name is given to a cow with a calf like a duiker (Cephalophus sp.)

sɪo-kutu: name of a cow that bore a calf with peculiarly shaped ears (*kutu* 'ear'). About the prefix *sɪo-* cf. p. 101.

A common name for dogs is *masáɪ*.

5. Rites connected with cattle=breeding.

To anyone who has the slightest knowledge of primitive ways of thought it must be obvious that cattle and cattle-breeding, which are so important in the Akambas' life, must have given rise to numerous rites. There are, as a matter of fact, an infinite number of such rites, especially of a preventive character, and they are discernible, among other places, in sexual life. Here and there in the preceding pages of this work we have come across examples of how in certain cases sexual connection brings good luck, is purificatory and is necessary to ritual, and on the other hand in other cases is inauspicious and must therefore be carefully avoided. This chapter gives us still further contributions to the same subject.

As long as the cattle are out at pasture and in the *kɪœŋgo*, the outlying farm, it is injurious to them and can cause their death if their owner has connections with his wife. If, however, this takes place, the herd must, on its return, be first purified with *ŋondu* and the craal and the entrance to it (*muɓɪa*) as well, before the animals are let in. The *ŋondu* that is used is described in pp. 295 ff., and is made from the hyrax (*kɪkɪla*). Even if no sexual intercourse has taken place, they sometimes sprinkle the cattle, on their return home, with ordinary *ŋondu* of the goat in order to be safe.

This strict demand for continence does not seem, however, to apply to the younger people. As far as I could understand, a fairly unrestricted freedom prevails among the young people during the time they stay out herding cattle[1]. I do not know the reason for this, but those of them, at least, who have not yet been circumcised are not real members of the community, and their behaviour is therefore of small importance.

In a case of infectious disease in a herd, it is rather common for the cattle-doctor (see below) to forbid the owner and his wife to have sexual intercourse for a time, sometimes for several months.

On the other hand, when newly-acquired cattle, the proceeds either of purchase or plunder, are brought home to the village, their owner has coitus with his wife in the hope that because of it the cows will »calve well», quite according to the old magic sentence that »like begets like».

If cattle die without an obvious cause, it may be due to magic or other things, but it may also arise from using utensils that are supposed to be injurious to the cattle, especially in connection with milk. The Akamba follow, for instance, the well-known African custom of fumigating the milk-vessels with some aromatic kind of wood. If some calves die, the wood hitherto used may be blamed for this, and it will be changed for some other kind. In a similar way they may change the spoon used to take the fat out of the calabashes that serve as butter-churns. If, for instance, they have formerly carved these spoons from the wood of the *mupæu* tree, they will afterwards make use of another kind of wood. In this way they try to prevent mortality amongst the cattle. They also use different kinds of *ɣondu* for cleaning the milkpails and for sprinkling on the cattle. Plants used for preparing such *ɣondu* are *waɩpu* (a red-flowered Compositæ with potato-like roots), *mɩlɩndɩtɩ* and *kɩoŋgwa* (Sanseviera sp.).

A Kamba man never counts his cattle, as this may bring bad luck. When they are driven into the craal of an evening, they look carefully, of course, to see that all the animals are there, but they do so without counting. They recognize the individual animals by their appearance[2].

---

[1] According to Hobley (Akamba p. 166) all herdsmen are exempt from this prohibition.

[2] Vide further Hobley, Akamba, p. 165.

We have seen that the boys of a family, regularly and with an equal number of days' interval between each, relieve each other in watching the cattle. A period of this kind is often six days, but it must never be as high as seven, or it will be disastrous for the cattle[1].

Rites for a twin-birth among cattle. We remember that the birth of twins both among human beings and animals is considered as an inauspicious event (see p. 38). If a cow has twins, both the mother and the calves are killed, but there is no danger in eating the flesh. It must be a really strong belief to make the Akamba kill cows and calves, as in normal cases they never do so[2]. There are, however, men — although very few in number — who know certain rites by which the danger can be removed without killing the animals. One of these men was the beforementioned *gondu* specialist Malata wa Kyambi, living near Machakos. He had learned the secret from a person who was now dead and whom he had consulted in a similar case. He had then used his art with good results (naturally) in the case of a brother-in-law of his, one of whose cows had given birth to twin calves.

As there is thus a way to ward off the loss, one might perhaps ask why this secret is not more generally known. The reason is presumably that cases of twin birth among horned cattle are rather rare, and when such a case occurs, it is too late to do anything in the matter, as an expert in the rite is not always at hand.

In order to show me a favour, Malata initiated me into this rite, which few men in Ukamba know. For this he demanded in return several calabashes of sugarcane, beer and two rupees in cash. The method of procedure is, according to his own words, which I took down in their original language, as follows:

---

[1] Cf. p. 58, note.
[2] Except in this case, or if a cow is barren, a private man cannot kill or dispose of cows. They are to a certain extent the property of the whole family, and the consent of all the adult males is necessary before any of them is allowed to take a cow away. The animals given when a wife is purchased are not an exception to this; they are, of course, only a deposit, as they go back to their owner, if the man does not want his wife any longer.

»If a cow gives birth to twins, its owner takes a bee-hive (i. e. a cylindrical wooden tube) and puts the calves through it (perhaps to symbolize a new birth). Another man receives them at the other end. The calves are taken back to the craal. When they have finished getting milk from their mother, one of them is sent away to another village, the other may stay behind with its mother. When the cow calves the next time, one takes *ǥondu* made of *mulalə, mutạ* and *waɪpu*, the two first of which are, perhaps, the most common of all *ǥondu* plants. The plants are crushed on a stone and put in a calabash shell with water (thus prepared in the usual way). A sheep's tail is taken and dipped in the *ǥondu*, the cow's tail is lifted up and the animal smeared with the *ǥondu* (first of all obviously the genitals). Now one may milk the cow (before this its milk could not be used). The first milk is taken far away and poured out. If anyone treads in this milk and then goes home and has intercourse with his wife, she will give birth to twins».

If a goat or a sheep has twins, they are allowed to live, but the young ones are given to another person. Presumably the birth of twins among these animals is too common for there to be anything remarkable about it.

6. **Cattle diseases.**

Just as the Akamba have a not inconsiderable experience in the treatment of human diseases, so they know and can cure various cattle diseases. Here too, of course, real knowledge is more or less indistinguishably bound up with magic rites and quackery. Of course every private person doctors his animals for ordinary ailments, but there are, in addition, special doctors for cattle diseases, a kind of veterinary surgeons after a fashion, who are not to be confounded with the medicine men (*awǝ*). Those of them who possess a reputation for skillfulness have an extensive practice and are called from distant places.

A common and rather severe illness, which I cannot however identify, is called *ǥgaɪ* (an external form of anthrax?). On the sick animals body are seen sores and swellings, on which the milky juice of *ɪkwapa* is rubbed for 4—5 days, after which the wound is burned with a redhot iron.

As a remedy for *ŋgaị* other plants are also used. The copious milky sap of *kịạp̌a* (a small tree with entire leaves — Euphorbiaceæ?), which can produce a burning pain in the face and eyes, is rubbed on the diseased places and burns away the evil[1]. Decoctions of several plants are given to the cattle as a drink. Such plants are *mubuabuị* (Araliaceæ, with flowers on a bare branch), *mutụla* (decoction made from the leaves), *muṗulụ* (Croton Elliottianus), the *ol marbait* of the Masai, the bark of which boiled together with meat and blood makes a strengthening soup.

The clan marks on cattle have already been discussed on p. 129 ff. I wish to add here that the X-shaped brands that are seen every now and then on cattle, must not be confused with these marks; they only indicate that the animals have been treated for the disease *ŋgaị*[2]. A brand with a similar use is seen in fig. 141. It is called *kịọ kịa mabuị* 'the brand of the lungs'; i. e. it is a mark to denote treatment for disease of the lungs.

Fig. 141.
Cattle brand (vide the text).

muŋutu or *muṗuṇị* is a skin disease. The skin gets sore and peels off and ultimately looks fungous, or as if it was overgrown with some sort of lichen. The diseased places are rubbed with the fat of Rhicinus.

A disease of an infectious nature is *ịkæṇə*. The symptom is »swelling of body and legs». If an animal dies from this disease, its flesh cannot be eaten — the Akamba do not despise the flesh of an animal that has died from natural causes — before one of the above-mentioned doctors has treated it. It is cut up, and the doctor pours a mixture, made from certain plants, on it. A sheep is killed and cut up into small pieces, which are mixed with the beef, and then this may be eaten. When it is all eaten up, the doctor puts medicine in the fire on the hearth in the hut, and then the disease cannot return.

A method commonly used by all these doctors to prevent the spreading of infection to a herd consists of burying certain

---

[1] The milky sap is so abundant that it almost spurts out when a branch is broken. It congeals pretty quickly and then grows black.

[2] Hobley (Akamba, p. 28) seems to take this brand as a part of a clan mark.

roots across the entrance to the cattle craal, so that the animals go over them as they pass in and out.

The infectious disease called *ndęlu* seems mysterious, reminding one of rinderpest, inasmuch as it is said to affect wild beasts as well, such as antelopes (the hartebeest for instance). Its symptoms in the animal are unknown to me, but if a human being eats the flesh of an animal that has died from this disease, »he vomits, his body begins to swell and his evacuations have a nasty smell, which makes others ill. At the swollen places his flesh becomes loose and falls off with a crack (!)». The disease is usually fatal, although the Akamba imagine they can cure it with certain herbs, which are mixed with the milk of the dead animal's mother and given to the sick persons to drink.

A good deal of superstition is obviously connected with this disease. The natives also believe that it always claims an odd number of victims, so that if, for instance, four people have died from it, they are certain that at least one more will follow.

I have unfortunately to confess that I do not know the name for rinderpest in the Kamba language, nor the symptoms of that disease. It is possibly one of the diseases mentioned here.

More ordinary cattle illnesses are stomach complaints and colds with subsequent diarrhœa, coughs and fever. For colds and diarrhœa in goats they use a decoction of the leaves of *kıluma*, a species of aloe with red, cylindrical flowers, for cough the leaves of *musoka soka*. In cases of fever the animals are washed with this decoction. For diarrhœa cattle are given a decoction of *mutumba-ŋgużo* or *mukuŋguni*, an Artemisia. *ŋdaż*, a bush-like plant with soft, herb-like branches filled with milky sap, is used for constipation in cattle. The sap is crushed out into water, which the animals drink.

For sore eyes on cattle the natives chew to pieces the leaves of the *mutula*, a plant used, as we have just seen, for *ŋgaż*, and put them on the eyes. Whether the leaves are chewed merely to break them up effectively or whether a healing effect is also ascribed to the saliva, I cannot say, as the latter possibility only occured to me while writing. A fact that supports this idea is that another remedy for eye-disease in cattle, namely the bitter leaves of the *ısıbu* bush (Capposidaceæ?), are also chewed before the compress is put on the eye[1]. If we turn, for the sake of comparison, to the remedy for eye-disease in human beings mentioned in Chap. XV, we find no support, for though I have certainly noted that a plant is »crushed» and placed on the eye, there is nothing said about how it is crushed. We can understand, however, from various details mentioned in previous pages that saliva is also considered among the Akamba to possess a beneficial (magic) power. The old man, for instance, who carries out circumcision spits out over the crowd of young men after the circumcision is accomplished.

In the rivers there is a sort of larvae or insects called *nðamba*, »narrow, as long as a finger» (leeches?), which, when the cattle are drinking, sometimes bites on to their tongues and make them bleed[2]. The animals are made to release their hold, if the cattle drinks a decoction of *mwɪnda-ŋguə*.

---

[1] The Masai spit milk in the animals' eyes in cases of eye-inflammation. Merker, Die Masai, p. 169

[2] According to Hofmann's dictionary the animal is a waterspider.

Chap. XXVIII. **Beekeeping.**

Beekeeping is widely spread in the Dark continent, and this seems to be especially the case in great parts of East Africa, where quite wild swarms of bees are always numerous. The main business of this, in many places very comprehensive bee-culture — if one can use the expression »culture» of these more than half-wild bees — is of course a pure plundering of the habitations of the bees. On account of a too ruthless persecution — they were smoked out wherever they were found — the number of the bees diminished, and they began to keep away from inhabited districts and to take refuge on the steppes, in bushes or in the primitive woods. Because of this presumably the negro came to think that he must tempt the bees in some way to come to him, and so he began to construct beehives. Among the Akamba these are of the type which, with inessential deviations, are found all over East Africa, namely a hollowed-out piece of a trunk of a tree of a half to one metre long. The ends are closed by thin pieces of wood (in the Machakos dialect called ꞯbǣngǣo, eastward ꞯbalaᴂ), which are fitted inside the rims of the cylinder and are supplied with two holes for entrances for the bees[1]. Such a beehive is called mwạtu in Kikamba. One end has on the side turned downwards its owner's mark (see p. 134). Only certain kinds of tree are used for the making of beehives. The mụku, kᵻ6utᵻ (Aberis precatorius) and kᵳumu (the wild fig-tree) are considered especially suitable.

Everywhere in East Africa one sees these beehives on the trees, not seldom a dozen on the same one. They are either

---

[1] Those of the amutǣᵳ clan, who live in Kikumbuliu, have only one entrance hole in their beehives, and that in the middle of the mark (seen in fig. 43).

placed on a fork or, more usually, hang down free from a branch.
Their suspension is carried out by fastening lianes or some such
substance[1] round the hives near their middle, so that the hive
hangs a little inclined. Through the lianes is threaded a wooden
hook (*mbolo*), the upper end of which also has a hook, turned
towards the lower one and hung on a branch. The beehives
are often placed so high up and so far out on the branches that
hanging them up really endangers life. Curiously enough, the
Akamba, unlike e. g. the Wataveta and Wadjagga, do not use
rope to hoist the hives up in the trees.

In Kitui, which is more rich in vegetation than Machakos,
there are also more beehives than in the latter place, and still
more in Ikutha. Here it is not unusual for a single person to
own two to three hundred. The hives sometimes hang far out in
the desert, many hours journey from the owner's village. I saw,
for instance, hives in a solitary baobob on the road from Machakos to Kitui about five hours march away from Kitui station.

To tempt the bees to a new beehive the latter is smoked
out before suspension with an aromatic kind of wood, the smell
of which appeals to the bees. The smoke of certain kinds of
wood is also used to keep snakes away from the hives. Herr
Gutmann, the missionary, says that in Kilimandjaro green tree-
snakes are found in beehives, where they, unmolested by the bees,
live on the honey[2].

The African bees are known for their fierce temper, of which
even many European travellers have had unpleasant experiences.
To lessen their fierceness, and consequently make it easy to gather
the honey, a beehive is treated in the following way: a kind of
lizard, *mbolo*[3], is put into it and a bit of honeycomb is rubbed
against a bit of mutton, after which the bees are ordered not to
be fierce but to behave as peaceably as the lizard. Both this
and the sheep being very harmless animals, the procedure is evidently a kind of homoeopathic magic. To make the bees gentle

---

[1] The creeper *mu* is commonly used for this purpose.

[2] B. Gutmann, Bienenzucht bei den Wadschagga, Globus 1909
(96), p. 206. B:s article gives a good glimpse into bee-culture among
an East African tribe.

[3] A lizard about 1 dm. long, grey-black, resembling a snake, with
four short, narrow feet and a short, thick tail.

in this way is called *kuḇoḇ̤a*. We have seen (p. 479) that they also used to *kuḇoḇ̤a* the real domestic animals, such as savage cattle[1].

It has been observed that the bees have a partiality for certain kinds of flowers, and similarly one knows that the quality of the honey changes according to the flowers from which it is got. The best kind, a clear, light sort, is said to be got from *kᶎuᶇgu*[2] and *mwondƏ*, the latter a red-flowered Malva species. The above-mentioned *muku* tree also gives very good honey. It has small short

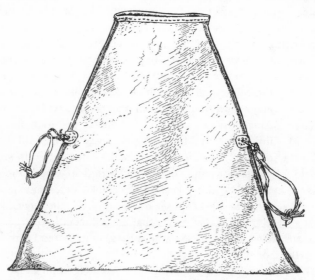

Fig. 142.　Leather bag for carrying honey. ¹/₆ nat. size.
Riksmus. Ethn. Coll. Inv. 12. 7. 33.

flowers with a sweet, pleasant smell. From millet (Penicillaria spicata), which the bees fall back on, probably during a scarcity of flowers, is got a darker honey, which is also considered good, but not so good as that obtained from the first-named flowers. A great deal of honey can be got from the acacia-like *mwaᶇgƏ* (big pale yellow or white flowers with long, red stamens), and where these trees are found, the beehives are suspended in them. The *kasalu* (Labiatæ) plant is also considered a good honey plant.

---

[1]　*kuḇoḇ̤a* is a technical term, which means 'to tame an animal by a special ceremony'.

[2]　Creeper with tendrils, pulpy, tripartite leaves and red fruit.

The honey is usually gathered after the fall of darkness. The extremely fierce and aggressive bees, according to the natives' statements, find it altogether too cold after the sun has set, and when they are expelled, their first thought is to find a new place of refuge as soon as possible. A beehive full of honey is a heavy article and the owner usually needs two helpers to take it down from its elevated place. That the bees shall not abandon the hive some honeycombs are usually left in it. After being gathered, the honey is placed in a flat triangular bag made of goatskin with loops at the sides (fig. 140), in which it is transported home.

Honey is extracted two to four times a year after the supply. According to what I was informed at Taveta, there also the honey is gathered atmost four times a year[1]. The Wadjagga, say, according to Gutmann, that the bees need three months to build their cells and a whole year to fill them.

To take honey out of the beehives is called *kutwa*, to look for wild honey *kulaka*. During my stay in Ukamba I never heard anything of the honey-indicating bird (Cuculus indicator) which is well-known in Africa, but Hildebrandt says that »it is followed very cautiously by the Wakamba, because it often only shows the way to the hiding place of a wild beast».

The honey which is gathered is kept in wooden cylinders (*kɩp̅ɛmbə*) with leather lids, a common type among numerous East African tribes; these cylinders are hung on the props which support the roof of the hut. As a rule the honey is very much mixed with wax and dead bees. Formerly the wax (*mawa*) was considered worthless, but now it is sold to the small Indian traders, who have their simple shops of galvanised iron here and there in the country. They carry on a by no means inconsiderable export of wax.

The Akamba like to eat honey and even empty honeycombs which are smeared with honey. The larvae of the bee are a delicacy, which, however, are not eaten by women. We have previously spoken about honey as food for pregnant women (p. 28). But the special importance of honey is for beer-making, especially in places such as the Kitui district, which are not rich enough in

---

[1] G. Lindblom, Anteckningar öfver Taveta-folkets etnologi, Ymer 1913, p. 166.

water to allow of the cultivation of sugarcane to any extent. Honey beer (*ukı wa nžukı*) is also more appreciated than sugar‑cane beer (*ukı wa kıwa*)[1]. A *mutumıa* (old man) likes to indulge in this privately and at night‑time so as not to have to share the prized beverage. And if he wishes company, he informs a few intimate friends of the matter with the greatest secrecy. Hospitality, or rather the prevailing custom, would make him share with his visitors, and such visitors would certainly not be lacking if it became known that he had plenty of honey beer at home.

*   *   *

As in the case of all important undertakings in the life of primitive people there are a great many things for the Kamba man to observe, when he intends to cut the honeycombs from the beehives. During this work he may not have coitus (sexual taboo). A man who has to have other people to help him, gets them to take an oath by the *kıpıtu* to abstain from sexual intercourse, saying, for instance, »If I have connections with a woman, may I be eaten by this *kıpıtu* before the end of the month». Certainly in such cases they do not use the *kıpıtu* described in Chap. XI. 4, but one of a less dangerous character. This prohibition seems to be in force for about ten days onward, or during the time which is considered to pass until the bees have again begun to bring honey to the hive. When this time is at an end the owner of the beehive has a look at his bees. If they have then abandoned their nest or have not begun to collect honey, he is certain that his assistants have broken their oath to abstain from coitus. He then prepares *ɣondu*, a purifying medium, and spreads it together with a bit of mutton on the beehive.

The rôle played by sexual intercourse during the time the honey is taken out of the hives is also shown by the following fact. They will not give the first lot of honey from new hives to anyone indiscriminately to eat, so as not to expose themselves to the risk of the person having already had intercourse. For this might cause the bees in the new hives to cease their work or the honey in them to become useless.

---

[1] Vide further the chapter Beermaking (p. 518).

Of the customs which are connected with the collection of honey we may finally mention that it is considered lucky for the community of bees if their owner, before the honey is taken out of the beehives, should get a goat as a gift from his father or uncle. Nothing special seems to be done with the goat, but the receiver incorporates it into his flock.

When an owner of beehives dies, his nearest relations proceed to his beehives and throw small stones or clods of earth against these to attract the bees' attention, saying: »Wake up, you bees! Your owner is certainly now dead, but because of that you must not cease to work and gather honey!» The Wataveta treat their bees in the same way after a death[1]. It appears from this as if the bees are thought to have a close personal relationship with their owner.

I have noted from Taveta another instance of how they talk to the bees. When a Taveta man hangs a new beehive up he unloosens the ring plaited from grass or banana leaves, on which he has carried the beehive on his head, saying: »Bees, wherever you are, it may be in Ukamba, Udjagga or elsewhere, come here!» By this untying of the ring used for carrying, the bees are also »released», i. e. this symbolic action is intended to bring them to the place. And B. Gutmann relates how the Wadjagga invite their bees to a newly-suspended hive by singing[2].

It happens very often that prayers and exhortations are adressed to the bees, and the not infrequently respectful tone in which such addresses are made is undoubtedly due partly to a real respect for the small creatures' touchy temperament, partly to admiration of their intelligence and other good qualities, which the natives with their keen power of observation have not neglected to notice. The author does not know how much the Akamba know about the life of the bee, but probably they possess as great knowledge as the Wadjagga, of whom Gutmann says that they know very well the various elements in a community of bees, the queen, the working bees, the drones, the different kinds of cells, etc.

---

[1] G. Lindblom, Anteckningar öfver Taveta-folkets etnologi, Ymer 1913, p. 166.

[2] B. Gutmann, Bienenzucht bei den Wadschagga, p. 206.

We have already read (p. 160) that it is considered a very serious crime to steal honey from the beehives. This does not, however, prevent the occurrence of such thefts, and, in order to protect his beehives which are often hung a long distance away, the owner applies various magical means, »medicine», to them; this is said to bring unpleasant surprises to a possible thief. Thus, for instance, the latter may find, when he wishes to climb down the tree, that his way is barred by a snake, which is coiled threateningly round the tree-trunk. Or else his hands are caught as he seizes the beehive, so that he cannot get free before the owner himself releases him. I heard of such a thief who was unfortunate and could not get free before the owner had spat three times on his hand which had been caught. It is, of course, to the interest of the bee-owners to spread the rumour that their beehives are protected by strong »medicine» and consequently dangerous to approach.

———

Chap. XXIX. **Agriculture.**

1. **The fieldwork and the harvest.**

Even though cattle-rearing is of very great importance to the Akamba, still agriculture is their principal occupation, as they maintain themselves chiefly by the products of the fields. This is due, as we have seen, not to scarcity in the supply of meat, but essentially to the fact that the natives do not care to slaughter their animals. Some decades ago, when the stock of animals could more easily be increased by plundering from the neighbouring tribes, and when hunting too was more productive than it is now, meat played a more important part as food than it does today. At least this was so in Ulu and the Kitui district, while in the more southern part of Ukamba, because of the Masais' and Gallas' plunderings, they had at that time smaller herds than now or even none at all. Krapf relates, for instance, how in his time the Akamba living at Jata, the now uninhabited plateau east of Athi, had no horned cattle at all, but only sheep and goats, so as not to attract the Galla there. And this observation of his concerning Jata could certainly be extended to apply to many other districts in the south-east. But this does not, however, necessarily imply that these Akamba had lost all their horned cattle, for just as, for instance, even at the present day the Akamba living in Kikumbuliu keep their animals away in the hills because of the tsetse fly, so in former times they might keep their animals in another place to protect them from being carried off.

The Akamba arrange their fields (sg. *munda*, pl. *m;unda*) preferably along the banks of rivers, in depressions in the ground and on the slopes of small hills, thus at the places that are best watered. Towards the east they also make clearances in the woods. They understand how to water the fields artificially by

Fig. 143.
Knife (*nẓoṃo*)
used for clear-
ing the fields.
¹/₂ nat. size.
Riksmus. Eth-
nogr. Coll.
Inv. 12. 7. 78.

making a network of narrow and shallow ditches (sg. *mutau*) in the fields, into which the water from the streams and the riverlets of the slopes is guided.

Agriculture is carried on almost exclusively by women, a relic of the distribution of labour at the time when the men were occupied in hunting, trading journeys and plundering expeditions. Of course they help nowadays in the agricultural tasks when it is necessary, but only one part of this work is carried out by men as a rule, namely the task of breaking up new ground for agriculture. This is usually done by means of fire; bushes etc. are cut down with a knife of a certain type (*nẓoṃo, kasoṃo*, see fig. 143), which can also be used for digging. The green-sward itself is then broken up with a long pointed pole, 2—3 metres long (*nde*), which is held with both hands. When a worthy father of a family goes to the field to carry out this work, one can see one of his minor wives walking behind him, carrying his digging pole and his snuff-bottle as well. The men have now done their part of the work and the women may proceed to loosen the soil, break up lumps of earth etc. with their hands (*kususṭa*), choppers and digging sticks. In Kikumbuliu I seldom saw land worked in this way; there they used chiefly burn-beaten land and sowed in ashes. There is no doubt that they understand the importance of ashes as a fertilizer, yet no other materials to improve the soil, such as manure, seemed to be used. Cattle-rearing and agriculture have, as a matter of fact, not the slightest connection with or influence upon each other. The burning of dry remains of plants, weeds and other rubbish, which always takes place before the old fields are put to rights, is thus intended just as much to fertilize the soil as to make the fields clean in a convenient way. The Akamba, like the Akikuyu, also understand the importance of letting the soil rest every now and then, but they do not let it lie fallow before they see the crop becoming poor. The fallow land may then rest undisturbed for 3—4 rainy seasons. They also usually change the grain sown at intervals of a few rainy seasons. If, for instance, they have had Cajanus indicus in a field for a couple of years, they then plant something else instead.

The form of agriculture carried on by the Akamba is what German ethnologists, beginning with Ed. Hahn, call »hackbau». No domestic animals are used in the field-work, the woman's only implement is her digging-stick (*mẹ*, *mwẹ*, dim. *kamolọ*). This is made of some hard species of wood, is 0,5—1 metre long, flattened and somewhat pointed (fig. 144). It is made by the men. The following trees, among others, are suitable because of their hardness: *mutandɪ* and *munoạ mapoḳa*, a species of acacia[1]. The fear of working at the fields with iron tools — there might in that case be no rain — has been mentioned in the chapter on magic.

The fields are got in order in good time before the rain comes (*kwɪma* 'to dig'), and when it seems to be coming, they are sown. The sowing is done by the woman making holes with her digging-stick, putting the grain in (putting down the cutting, if there is one), and then covering the hole over again with her foot. In the case of small seeds, like Eleusine, they content themselves with throwing them out with their hands (*kuɓanda* 'to plant', *kuɓwɪa* 'to sow'). During this time the women are kept fully employed and even youths and boys are allowed to help, on which occasions they cannot, of course, refrain from exchanging jibes with the girls.

When this work is done they have a quiet time until the plants begin to shoot up, when the fields have to be cleared of weeds (*kwɪa* 'to weed'). This is especially the girls' work, and friends and neighbours help each other at it. The fields present an animated aspect, often with a dozen girls in the same field,

Fig. 144. Womans digging-stick ¹/₃ nat. size. Riks-mus. Ethnogr. Coll. Inv.12.7.80.

---

[1] < *noa* 'to be tired'? An appropriate meaning would in that case be »that which makes the axes tired». The form of the verb, however, is against such a translation.

chattering and singing as they work. If there are no men about, they take their clothes off and toil away to their heart's content. They go forward over the field in a row, like soldiers in a firing-line, and in that way no weeds escape them.

Then the women have a little leisure from the field work. They merely look now and then at the crop and carry out various small tasks. When, for instance, the maize flowers, they remove the off-shoots of the flowers, stating as a reason that the produce will be better. It is obvious that the maize-cobs then will get more sun.

A busy times comes when the corn begins to ripen. This is in February. If one meets a woman during this time and asks her where she is going, in most cases the answer will be: »I am going to the field to frighten the birds away» (*kuṣa nɔ̰unɔ̰*). For

Fig. 145. The watcher of the fields takes his place on a sort of platform.

they have to keep parasites at a distance. In this category come, first and foremost, a great number of birds, but also other animals, such as wild boars, porcupines and in East Ukamba monkeys as well, especially baboons, which are serious thieves on account of their watchfulness. The fields are accordingly guarded against such enemies. This duty of watching is carried out to a great extent by children and young people. The watcher takes his place on a heap of earth or, even better, on a sort of platform built of posts, from which he has a view over the field (fig. 143). The birds are driven off by shouting and throwing stones, the boys also wield their slings with great accuracy. One sometimes sees long cords, with light objects (banana leaves, etc.) fastened on them, issuing from the look-out post, and when the birds settle down at a place, the watcher pulls the cord leading to it. Scare-crows consisting of objects that move in the wind are also used.

Where wild boars and porcupines are especially troublesome, watch is also kept during the night-time.

When harvest time comes, there is still more to do if the harvest is to be got in safely as early as possible. The grain is cut before it is so ripe that the seeds might fall off, and then it is spread out outside the village on the *pomə* to dry. Here or at some other hard place the grain is thrashed (*kuɓθa,* really 'to break to pieces'; *kɪɓuʐo* 'thrashing-place'). Standing in a row, like a line of soldiers, the woman work at the stalks with long sticks, keeping time to singing. The husks and other rubbish are then separated by putting the grain in a calabash shell, which is held up in the air and shaken. When its contents run out, the light chaff is carried away by the wind. This process is repeated until the grain is clean. This work is usually given to old women, who are not strong enough for other work. One never finds the Akamba letting cattle tread out the corn.

The harvest is then kept in the storehouses — we have spoken about these in our description of the Kamba village — each kind of grain in its own vessel, calabashes or large bulging vessels (*kɪʐga*), as much as 1 m. in height, made of soft grass, preferably *ɪlɑ,* a grass with reddish-brown panicles (Tricholæna rosea). They are made by the youths, one of the few useful things they do. The outside of these grass receptacles is thickly coated with cowdung as a protection against ants and other insects. A part of the maize is hung up on the ceiling of the hut. In Kikumbuliu I saw the maize intended for sowing hung up in large bundles in the trees, where it was thought to be best protected against rats.

Let us now see what the Akamba cultivate in their fields. The three most important kinds of grain are Sorghum (*muɓɪa*), maize (*mɓæmba*) and Penicillaria spicata (*mwǽ*). Eleusine (*wɪmbɪ*) is cultivated to a somewhat less extent. Several different species of leguminous plants are cultivated, of which by far the most popular is Cajanus indicus (*nʐu,* the plant itself is called *musu*), which takes two rainy seasons to ripen. We may also notice Phaseolus vulgaris (*mɓoso*), *nðoko* (probably haricot beans), *mbumbu* (Dolichos), *ggɪna* (presumably Phaseolus mungo), *ndulɪa,* a kind of red bean, and finally *nʐaɓɪ,* small beans with a white spot (Phaseolus lunatus?)

Among root-crops they cultivate the well-known sweet potatoes (*makwası*), yams (*kıkwa*), manioc (*mayga*) and Colocasia
(*matǫma*). There are several kinds of pumpkins and similar plants,
whose scientific names, however, I am unable to give: *malǣygǝ*
(Kisuaheli *tango*), *mǫygu* (Kisuaheli *mumunye* 'a sort of vegetable
marrow')[1], calabash (*kıkıu*).

One seldom sees a field with only one kind of crop. Sorghum and Penicillaria are usually sown together, and among Cajanus indicus is put, for instance, maize. When the maize is ripe,
a new lot is planted among the more slowly growing beans.
Calabash plants are also put in here and there.

Sugarcane (*kıwa*) is cultivated on low-lying ground along the
rivers. It is found especially in Ulu, in the drier east only in certain places. The irrigation channels are specially arranged with
regard to the sugarcane, which is very highly esteemed.

The banana (*ıĩu*) is also very much liked. It is, however,
not cultivated generally, as of course it too needs well watered
ground. There are several different varieties, namely *mulalu*, of
average size, which is the most delicious of them, *mutaɓatu*, a large
fat one with rather coarse pulp, *ndıɓı*, a small short one (from the
coast?) and *munžǎ,* a species from the Kikuyu country. The banana
is said to have been more widespread in former times than it is now.

The preparation and methods of using the various cultivated
plants for food will be dealt with in the chapter on »Food».

A rapid glance at the names in Kikamba of the plants used
for food shows[2] that they are practically identical with those in
Kikuyu, and to a great extent with those in Kipokomo (at the
upper Tana) and in Kidjagga (Kilimandjaro), thus with the names
in those dialects that are closely or fairly closely related to Kikamba. There seems to be no affinity with the Galla and Masai
languages in this respect.

Traditions about the origin of agriculture. Among many
peoples there are traditions to the effect that a certain cultivated
plant is of divine origin or has in some more or less wonderful
way been conferred upon mankind. The Akamba have no such

---

[1] E. Steer, A Handbook of the Suaheli Language, London 1908.

[2] See F. Stuhlmann, Beiträge zur Kulturgeschichte Ostafrikas,
Berlin 1909.

myth about the origin of special plants, but they have reflected about the origin of agriculture, and the tradition created in this way is rather interesting. We remember how the first human beings, who came up out of the termite hole, had various kinds of seeds in their left hands. The following tradition was then attached to this myth:

The first seed was put into the ground in small open places. They did not understand how to work at or loosen the ground. One year, when they wished to sow again, a huge tree had fallen and was found lying over one of the small »fields». With great efforts they succeeded in getting the tree away, and then they sowed the field. When the crop was ripe, it was found that the plants at the place where the big tree had fallen were much more vigorous than at other places, because the soil there was looser. There were also less weeds. From this arose the idea of loosening the soil with a stick, and in this way came the digging-stick.

2. Agricultural rites.

Any one who has read the foregoing part of this work will understand that rites and customs of a religious and magic nature are connected with the Akamba's agriculture. I have, however, not very much to offer concerning such rites, compared with what I succeeded in learning with regard to others. There is probably a good deal still to be discovered on this subject.

Sexual relations between man and wife, which, as we have already seen, are regulated by prescripts in connection with many different undertakings, have also to take agriculture into consideration. One might expect rites for producing fertility, based on homœopathic magic, such as ritual coitus between man and wife when the fields had been sown and planted. The state of affairs is, as a matter of fact, just the opposite: all sexual intercourse is considered to have an injurious effect on the crop before the buds have begun to appear. A possible explanation of this continence is to be found in the fact that the primitive mind sometimes tries to attain a result — in this case a good harvest — by using a means that is directly opposed to what might be considered the natural one. The prohibition applies only to the owners of the fields, the man and his wife, not to their children.

During the nights when a married couple keep watch in the fields to protect them against animals they may not have sexual intercourse, if the woman has children at home. It is believed that, if they do, these will fall ill, to become thinner and thinner and, perhaps, finally die (result of »ceremonial uncleanliness«?).

The growing crop is sprinkled with ordinary *ŋondu* so that the harvest may be good. The time for this treatment is apparently decided by Cajanus indicus (*nžu*), as the fields are sprinkled only after these beans have grown a little. The sprinkling is done by the old people of the *nžama* and *ʧpœmbo* (pp. 144, 220).

Cajanus indicus seems to be the only nutritive plant with whose cultivation additional special observances are bound up. During the time it is in flower the women may not make pottery; if they do the harvest of it would be spoiled. Similarly during this time the women are forbidden to make cords of *muʧi,* a species of acacia that is commonly used for twisting into cords. The old men, who keep good order and maintain the old customs, watch carefully to see that the prohibitions are observed, and, if a woman is proved to have offended against them, her husband has to give the goat that is demanded in order to purify the fields. The reason why it is just *nžu* that plays so important a part in the agricultural rites is possibly because it is the Akamba's favourite food. The fact that it is forbidden to make pottery and cords, i. e. material for plaiting bags, may be explained as due to an idea that it is dangerous to make preparations for bringing home the *nžu* (the bags) and to make receptacles for it (the pots) before the fruit has been formed.

The cultivated plant of the Akambas that is most interesting to the ethnologist is, however, Eleusine (*wɪmbɪ*), as it and the food prepared from it (*ŋgɪma* porridge) play a greater part in public rites and in magic than any other nutritive plant. Instances of this have been given in the preceding chapters, p. 33 (birth) — where, however, it is not necessarily a matter of ceremonial; p. 171 (cursing) and, still more clearly, p. 203. The special position of Eleusine in this respect is undoubtedly due to the fact that it is a very old cultivated plant among the negroes, perhaps the very first cereal they knew, although later on it was displaced by more productive plants. The traditions of several peoples point to this. The Nandi, for instance, are known to relate how the tribe formerly lived by hunting and did not know of agriculture. But one day some warriors found an Eleusine species growing wild and took the seeds of it home and planted them[1]. And Stuhlmann is certainly right in supposing that in former times Eleusine was cultivated more in East Africa than it is now, when in many places and especially in the regions near the coast it has had to give way to better tasting and more productive cereals (maize, sorghum)[2]. It would be interesting to investigate this question more closely, to find out whether Eleusine has been found in pre-historic settlements in Africa, etc. But the question does not really belong to this part of the subject, although I have called attention to it here. We shall now return to the question of »agricultural rites».

If some special event occurs that threatens the growing crop, extra precautions are taken. This is done if grasshoppers appear. A grasshopper is then taken to the sacrificial place (*ɩpæmbo*) and killed there, and at the same time they offer food to the spirits, slaughter a goat and pour its blood out at the base of the big tree. The fields are sprinkled with *ɡondu*. It is exspected that the grasshoppers will then disappear[3].

Although it does not come within the scope of this chapter, I take the opportunity of mentioning here how they try to extirpate ticks in the same way as grasshoppers. These are sometimes found in enormous numbers in the grass on the steppe and are a great plague both to man and beast[4]. A tick is taken to the *ɩpæmbo* and killed there; the ground is sprinkled with *ɡondu*.

Before the harvest is taken from the fields a goat and some corn are offered at the place of sacrifice. This sacrifice is not only carried out within the families but forms a public festival, a public sacrifice of the kind described in the chapter on Religion, p. 187.

The first thing that is eaten of the new harvest seems to be,

---

[1] Hollis, The Nandi, p. 120.

[2] F. Stuhlmann, Beiträge zur Kulturgeschichte Ostafrikas, p. 181.

[3] Methods of getting rid of harmful insects and vermin among other African tribes are given by Frazer in his study upon this subject in The Golden Bough 5: 2, vol. II, p. 274 ff.

[4] The author himself was ill with fever and slight blood-poisoning of the feet for three weeks, probably as a result of tick-bites.

at least to some extent, bound up with rites. When the first vegetables for the year are eaten, they are mixed with the contents of a goat's *kɩpatṇa* (the stomach that is used in the preparation of *ṇondu*), »so that the people shall not get coughs».

Finally observances of a prohibitive nature are bound up with the rain and thus intimately connected with agriculture. We have learned about these in the preceding part of the work, such things as the fact that an oath on the *kɩpɩtu* may not be sworn during the rainy season so as not to prevent the rain from coming (p. 171). Cf. also p. 181.

―――――――――

Chap. XXX. **Food.**

1. **Animal food.**

The products of the field form the basis of the Kamba people's food. As we already know, this is not merely a question of taste, but is due to the fact that they do not want to kill off their herds. In former times, when they were able to steal cattle and could hunt big-game without hindrance, they ate considerably more meat than now, when this article of food is seldom eaten by anyone who has not great herds, except on ceremonial occasions. That the Akamba like meat is shown by the fact that they unhesitatingly eat it raw and do not mind eating animals that have died from natural causes, even such as have attained an advanced state of decomposition. They seem even to be pretty well known as having a certain penchant to this, and examples are found here and there in descriptions of travels. I myself once found the remains of a wild boar, which had been torn to pieces by a lion and of which my bearers took with them the little flesh that was left. A. Arkell Hardwick relates, for instance, how his Kamba porters eagerly devoured an ass that had fallen ill and died[1]. I have also seen my porters take the bones after my own meals and carefully gnaw them clean. Their power of eating all sorts of things without being in any way famished is shown, among other things, by the fact that they roasted guineafowls' feet. During the great famine of 1898 and 1899 a few cases of cannibalism occurred, easily explained by the extraordinary conditions prevailing[2]. On the other hand I have no experience to support the idea that the Akamba eat lion and hyena flesh[3].

---

[1] An Ivory Trader in North Kenia, p. 138.

[2] H. R. Tate, Notes on the Kikuyu and Kamba Tribes of British East Africa. Journ. Anthr. Inst. 1904, p. 136.

[3] C. H. Stigand, The Land of Zinj., London 1913, p. 275.

By the side of this greediness of meat they sometimes show an amazing fastidiousness. I have, for instance, eaten zebra meat myself without feeling any dislike to it, while my negroes have refused to touch it, explaining that »it smelled badly». There was no religious motive present in this case. Nor will adults eat monkeys, which one sees the children doing, however; they catch long-tailed monkeys in traps.

Meat is usually boiled; out in the fields it is roasted over a grating made of sticks.

We already know that the blood of cattle is drunk. It is also mixed with milk, millet flour and fat, and this soup is stood in a sunny place before it is drunk. The blood is stirred with a *mupekæpɪ*[1], which is of the type usual in East Africa, namely a stick split at the end with two thin pieces of wood fixed in the fork and crossing each other (fig. 146). They also used a dorsal

Fig. 146. Wooden instrument to whisk blood with (*mupekæpɪ*).
¼ nat. size. Riksm. Ethn. Coll. Inv. 12. 7. 499

vertebra of a small mammal. The utensil is rotated between the hands, as in drilling fire. Soup, *kɪpuɪ*, is also cooked from meat.

Milk plays, of course, a large part as an article of food. Goat's milk is used almost only in those districts where there are no cows, such as Kikumbuliu. Fresh milk (*ɪpumo*) is, however, drunk only by women and children. They all prefer the sour milk (*ɪɪa*), and the men keep entirely to it. As in many other North East African tribes the milk calabash (*kɪkamɪ*) is fumigated, before milking, with certain kinds of wood, brands of which are thrust in the calabash. This is called *kutæa* and is thought to improve the smell and taste of the milk. One of the kinds of wood used for this is *mukaɪ*. The first milk after a cow has calved, the blestings, is called *kɪpana*.

From the sour milk butter (*maúta*) is churned. It is prepared in a calabash (*kɪpukɪ < kupuka* 'to make butter'), which a woman shakes and knocks against her thighs. Stones are also put in the calabash to accelerate the process. When the butter is ready,

---

[1] < *kupekæpa* 'to drill, bore'. *k. mwɑki* 'to drill fire'.

it is washed in water. To get it still more clean it is put in a pot with porridge and boiled. The melted butter is then poured off, while the dirt remains at the bottom together with the porridge and is eaten with it. Besides being used as a food, butter is also used to rub into the body and into leather garments. A person who is so poor as not to be able to get sufficient butter from his cattle uses the oil of the castor oil beans, which are humorously called »the poor man's cattle».

The Akamba bring considerable quantities of fat into the market, which is purchased by the Indian traders.

2. Vegetable food.

From the products of the field are prepared the following important dishes, several of which may be called the Akambas' national dishes:

ıs̗ıo, i. e. maize and *n̥z̥u*-beans (Cajanus indicus) boiled together; eaten practically every day without anything being added to it.

usu̥ is a gruel made of water or sour milk with the flour of *mwœ* (Penicillaria spicata) or maize. It is very well liked, has a sour taste and is really refreshing. At the same time it is very nourishing and thus serves as both food and drink. It is the most useful food when travelling. It is considered to be very good for sick people.

A sort of thick gruel (*kınḁ*) is boiled with milk and *mwœ* flour. It is very much liked by old people whose teeth are too poor to eat solid food.

ŋgıma is a porridge made of Eleusine flour and water, mixed with fat. It is eaten chiefly by women and small children. With its dirty dark brown colour it does not look very appetising. It is so thick and coherent that the children can run round holding their portions in their hands. This porridge seems to play a part in rites.

Another kind of porridge is *kıtœk̗ə*, which is prepared from the flour of Penicillaria or Sorghum, boiled in water. It has a very indifferent taste, especially because it contains no salt.

To prevent a pot from boiling over the women put some twigs in it. They stir with a stick flattened at the end, which has its place on the hearth among the cooking utensils. Of spoons

there are, besides large porridge ladles, also smaller and more elegant »tablespoons», usually made of red acacia wood. All the spoons
are without any decoration. The natives prefer to eat gruel with
the index finger, which is drawn along the edges of the calabash
vessel. To eat in this way is called *kusuna*, and the index finger
is accordingly called *kɩa kɩa* (*k*)*usuna* ('the finger to *kusuna* with') [1].

In preparing flour (*mutu*) the grain is first pounded with a
heavy pole, 2 metres or more long, *mupɩ* (< *pɩa* 'to grind, crush
into flour'), in wooden mortars (*nde*) fixed to the ground. Then
it is powdered still more between grindstones of the familiar type:
a large one, flat and hollowed out by wear, as the nether mill-
stone, and a smaller rubbing stone. The flour falls on to a piece
of skin at the side of the stone. The woman carries on the work
kneeling and leaning forward and usually sings at the same time.
When the grindstones become too worn and smooth, they are
sharpened by being rubbed with a piece of quartz.

From maize flour some natives prepare bread, which, on account of the method of preparation, contains numerous fragments of
stone. It is called *mukaɔ, mukatɔ* or *kɩmutu* (cf. *mutu* 'flour'), in
East Ukamba also *kɩkɩɔ* [2]. The two first names are identical with
the Suaheli word for bread (*mkate*), and this method of preparing
bread, which is not in common use, is no doubt borrowed from
without.

A favourite way of eating maize is to roast the spadices and
then nibble the grains off. It is called to *kuɓala*.

Turning to the vegetables, we find that taro, yams and manioc
are not cultivated to any great extent. The former, like all Aroids,
has in its fresh condition a sharp taste, and has therefore to
be boiled before being eaten. The commonly cultivated sweet
potato is boiled or roasted in the embers. A favourite food is
pumpkins (*malæŋgɔ*), which are eaten boiled, and as long as there
is a supply of them the natives scarcely eat anything else. They
say that they are »sweeter than honey». Their taste reminds one
of artichokes, and with some butter they taste excellent, even to
a European palate. The *nʑu*-beans, which are cultivated especially in Ulu, are even more liked. When natives who live there

---

[1] *kusuna* < *usu* 'gruel'?

[2] In certain places this word signifies 'gruel made from maize
flour'.

go to a place where this bean is not cultivated, as, for instance, the Kikuyu country, they miss this food more than anything else, and their friends sometimes send them some of the longed-for food.

. Both with regard to the quantity of the harvest and the number of different food-plants Ulu is the best circumstanced part of Ukamba. In Kikumbuliu the natives seem principally to cultivate only maize, Sorghum and *nḍoko*-beans, while neither pumpkins nor *nźu* are to be obtained there.

A number of plants are used for a sort of spinach, which is sometimes eaten by itself, mixed with fat, and sometimes used as an addition to other food. In this way are used the leaves of the *nḍoko*-bean, those of *nḍulu*, a Solanum species, which grows as a weed in the fields, and *wua*, another weed (Chenopodiaceæ?). The leaves of *kaunaæḅi*, a yellow-flowered Oxalis species, are chewed raw or boiled as spinach. They are considered to taste salty. Other plants are cooked together with certain dishes to improve their taste. This, for instance, is the case with *kɪloɣoɀo*, a leguminous plant with an aromatic smell resembling new-mown hay, which is cooked together with gruel.

Of fruit only the banana is cultivated, but it is not important as an article of food. There is not a single wild fruit of real value as food; how poor East Africa is in wild edible fruits, is well-known to every traveller. A person who had to maintain himself exclusively on wild fruits would soon starve to death. As, however, I took the trouble to collect them, I shall give here the names of some plants with fruit that the children eat or that the natives occasionally pick a few of when they come across them. As has been mentioned, they are of no importance to the household.

Among the best of these fruits are the yellow juicy ones of the *kɀua* tree, which are as big as a French plum and very refreshing. Several others resemble plums, such as the small yellow sourish ones of *muka-mbua* and the beautiful light-red ones of the little *kɪtula* tree, the skin of which, however, is very thick and tastes of prussic acid. They also eat the very sour fruit of the tamarind (*nḍumulạ*), the red, fleshy ones of *muḅulwa*, which are smaller than a cherry, and also the round fruits, flattened on one side, of the little *mutuŋgu* tree; the acorn-like ones of *mumụ*, those of *muɓa* (Vangueria edulis?), and the dry, sweetish berries of the *mutuɓa* bush (Turneraceæ?). The berries of the *muɓɪlɪŋgwa* bush (Cissus) are eaten by children, and also the red, fleshy berries or the low *muþumbu* bush and the small lilac sweet ones of the *muɓɪsaɓɪsɪ* bush (Labiatæ).

In times of famine, of course, they make more use of these fruits and also of a great many others, such as those of the baobab (*mwamba*) and the duṁ palm. The roots of the *ɡaþuɪ* (Leguminosæ) are eaten raw. From the extremely small seeds of the *ukuku* grass (Dactylotenium) flour is prepared. The small green flowers, placed in a head-like position, of *mukaɪuɪ* (a liana species?) are cooked by themselves with a little salt or are used to eke out the *ŋɡɪma*-porridge. Its taste somewhat resembles cabbage.

Mushrooms (*ɪkunu*) are not very common in Ukamba. Certain species are sometimes eaten by children.

Finally we may mention some things that are uneatable for Europeans, but which are, however, considered by many of the natives as delicacies. In the animal kingdom grasshoppers, ants and lice come into this category. Especially when the boys are looking after the cattle they are in the habit of catching grasshoppers and threading up a number of them living on a twig, just as Swedish children thread wild strawberries on a blade of grass. They then take one grasshopper at a time, pull its wings and legs off, and put the rest of the body in their mouths. They also roast them over a fire. The flying ants (*mɓa*), which are very numerous during the rainy season (*mbua ʐa uwa*), are similarly caught by the boys, who roast them on potsherds. Lice are eaten with delight, especially by elderly women, who catch them in their heads like monkeys or in the broad beaded belt which they wear round their waists and which harbours these vermin. Resin (*kɪþana*) is also a delicacy for many women.

Their supplies of salt the Akamba nowadays get for the most part from the Indian traders, who provide them with a very coarse kind. Apart from this they have from the earliest times obtained salt from saliferous soil, which they mix with water and then filter, the water being used for cooking. Thus they do not know of any real method of preparing salt. According to G. Kolb, in his time they sold the saliferous sand that they dug up from the riverbeds[1]. Women use more salt than men, and in former times the latter would not eat salt at all on certain occasions, such as, for instance, when they went out on a military expedition. They asserted that the salt had an injurious effect on the joints of the legs und hips, inasmuch as it reduced their mobility. The great power which salt is thought to possess and which mankind uses as a protection — of which numerous instances are found[2], although I cannot, to be sure, give any from the Akamba (cf. however p. 539) — this very power naturally causes people to act cautiously with it sometimes.

We have still to notice briefly the food that is given to babies. If the mother has a good supply of milk, the newborn child lives practically entirely on this for the first 6—8 months. When the mother has been out at work during the heat of the day, she washes her breasts, which have been exposed to the rays of the sun, with cold water before giving them to the child, because it is considered that otherwise the milk will be too warm. Besides mother's milk many babies are given uncooked fat at an early age. If the mother's milk is insufficient, they also begin very early to give the child gruel (usụ), which is done by letting it suck a finger dipped in the gruel. When the child is considered big enough to eat all kinds of food, it is weaned by the mother rubbing on her nipple something with a strong taste or smell such as snuff or pepper; the latter is bought from the Indian traders. As a rule they begin astonishingly early to give the children the same food as the grown-ups eat, much of which is particularly unsuitable and indigestible.

Finally a few words must be added about the eating of food by the different sexes at the same time and in common. As a general rule it may be said that women do not eat together with men, except in the narrower circle of the family. Thus a man and his wife may eat of the same vessel when they are alone at home, but if other men come on a visit, the woman may not eat in company with them. In the same way the man may not eat together with the women who come and call on his wife.

---

[1] Petermann's Mitteil. 1896, p. 230.

[2] See, for instance, Haberlandt, Das Salz im Volksglauben, Globus 1882, p. 265.

Chap. XXXI. **Stimulants.**

1. **Beermaking.**

The Akamba use an intoxicating drink (*ukɪ*), which is mostly made from the sugar-cane (*ukɪ wa kɪwa*), but in certain places also from honey. The latter drink is at least as well liked as the former, but honey is, of course, also particularly relished when eaten uncooked, and so in the districts where there are sugar-canes beer is usually made from them. It is certain, however, that the honey beer is the more primitive, the word for beer (*ukɪ*) clearly having the same root as the name for the bee (*ṇ̌žukɪ*) [1].

To make beer the sugar-cane is cut into pieces, which must not be too short. These are then pounded in a wooden mortar with long poles. This work is always carried out by the youths, *anakə*, who, singing rhythmically, thrust their poles in the mortar in a fixed order. There are often as many as ten at the same mortar, and it is interesting to see how they can pound rapidly without even colliding with each other, and letting their poles meet in the mortar. When all the sugar-cane is crushed, the pulp (*kɪtumbu*) is tied up with cords into bundles, out of which the juice is wrung with the hands into a large calabash shell (*ua*). It is to make it easy to fasten these bundles that the pieces of sugar-cane are not cut too short. A fork-shaped branch (*kɪkælə*), between the two prongs of which cords are stretched, is then placed across a large calabash vessel. A layer of grass is placed on the *kɪkælə* and above this the *kɪtumbu*. The juice of the sugar-cane is

---

[1] The Akikuyu distinguish between *njohi*, beer made from sugar-cane, and *uki*, made from honey and water. The sugar-cane is certainly not indigenous in Africa. When it came to East Africa is rather difficult to tell exactly, but the first Portugese found it cultivated on the coast. F. Stuhlmann, Beitr. zur Kulturgeschichte von Ostafrika, p. 159.

then poured through this filtering apparatus, during which process all the lees is stopped by the grass. This is called to *kukœla ukı*[1]. The beer is then poured into calabashes, which are placed in a warm place for a day or so. As a ferment dried pieces of the fruit of the *mwatınə* (Kigelia africana) cut into slices are added. Almost every family father keeps this fruit in his hut for this purpose. The following day the beer is ready to drink, and it must be drunk quickly as it does not keep. As the liquid is rarely diluted with water, it thus consists of pure sugar juice. Honey beer is also fermented with Kigelia fruit.

The top, frothy part of the beer (*kıɓuo*) is considered the best. It is said to belong to the host's family and is therefore always drunk by him or his father-in-law, if the latter is present. Because it is white and floats on top it is called *kıɓuo*, which means the white shells which, fastened to the hair, adorn the youths' heads.

It has been mentioned that the youths prepare the beer. Women are never allowed to do this or to take any part in making it; the old men would not drink beer brewed by women. At most they may carry the beer calabashes to the place where the carousal is to be held. Nor may they drink beer. Among the neighbouring tribe, the Kikuyu, the women may in some places also prepare the beer, and when Kamba men pay a visit to the Kikuyu, they adopt the custom of the place and drink their beer without raising any objection.

According to the old custom, beer-drinking is a privilege for the old men, the *atumıa*, while not only women but also young men and boys are forbidden to drink it. A violation of this rule is punished with a thrashing, in severe cases with the father's curse (see p. 182). Only after a young man has settled down and stopped running about with girls can he usually get permission from his father to drink beer. The old people say that the youths must choose between girls and beer. The sanction is purchased by the son with a present to the father, consisting of an ox, a sterile cow (equivalent to an ox) or, among those who are not so well off, a goat. To obtain a father's permission to drink beer by such means is called to *kuɓa* or *kuɓaıa* (derived from *kuɓạ*).

---

[1] Certainly the same verb as in the expression *kukœla nžıa* 'cross a path'.

This is probably a ritual act, as *kupa* really means 'to sacrifice, as shown by the phrase *kupaẕa aïmu* 'sacrifice to the spirits'.

This prohibition for younger men to drink beer may undoubtedly be looked upon as a case of a phenomenon that is not uncommon among primitive peoples, namely for the older

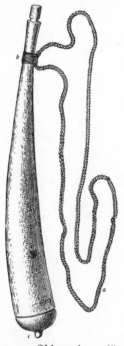

Fig. 147. Old man's snuffbottle made from the horn of the Eland. Worn by an iron chain (*a*) around the neck. *b* copper wire, *c* wood. ¹/₄ nat. size. Riksmus. Ethn. Coll. Inv. 12. 7. 237.

Fig. 148. Wooden snuffbottle, *a* stopper made by strings, *b, f,* brassrings, *c* copper wire, *d* copper plate, *e* tin plate, *g* chain made of copper wire. ¹/₂ nat. size. Riksmus. Ethn. Coll. Inv. 12. 7. 232.

people to reserve for themselves what is best in the way of luxuries. But there is in addition another very reasonable cause. They seem to realize quite clearly, as a matter of fact, that in the long run beer has an injurious effect on the body. »It settles in the legs», as the Akamba say. Now the younger married men and the unmarried men constitute, of course, the warriors, and it is important that they should keep in good condition so as to be in full fighting trim. Unfortunately, however, this good old custom seems to be decaying, and one now sees even young men drinking beer. This is caused by the fact that there are no longer any military expeditions. »What is the use of keeping nimble», say the warriors, »we can no longer begin a war with our neighbours without the Europeans interfering in it.»

Beerdrinking is the favourite occupation of the old men, and the way is never too long for them when it is a case of attending some beerparty. These are often held, as they take turns in inviting, and public carousals also take place, for instance, at sacrificial feasts. The drink is intoxicating, but considerable quantities seem to be needed to produce a complete state of intoxication. As the beer cannot be kept, this itself encourages excessive drinking. It is not at all uncommon to see those who are taking part in one of these festive gathering considerably the worse for liquor, on which occasions the *atumĭa*, generally so careful about their dignity, forget it, and sing, babble and gesticulate in a way that is very amusing to the spectator. Many of them get very wild when in liquor, and it may happen that the carousal finishes with a fight, when they attack each other with their sticks, and have recourse even to swords and arrows. A great number of lawsuits arise from such quarrels, and the only Akamba who have been disrespectful to the author were drunk. It is also probable that this immoderate drinking helps to make the men old before their time and to shorten the duration of their lives.

Fig. 149. Snuffbottle, attached to an armring. *a* horn of hartebeest, *b* brass nails, *c* brown wood. $^1/_4$ nat size. Riksmus. Ethn. Coll. Inv. 12. 7. 234.

2. **Snufftaking and smoking.**

The Akamba call tobacco *kumbato*, a very common name among the negro peoples. It is made from a red-flowered Nicotiana species, of which a small number are cultivated near the hut or grow practically wild on some refuse heap. To make the tobacco the leaves are plucked and placed to ferment between two layers of leaves, such as banana leaves, with stones and pieces of wood as a weight on top. When they have turned a yellowish-red colour, they are

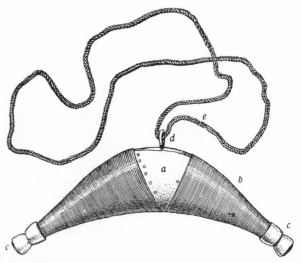

Fig. 150. Wooden snuffbottle of unusual type, with two mouths. *a* tin plate, *b* brass wire, *c* brass rings, *d* brass ring, *e* chain made of brass wire. ¹/₃ nat. size. Riksmus. Ethn. Coll. Inv. 12. 7. 233.

left for a day in the sun, after which they are lightly pounded in a mortar, without, however, being crushed. They are then put in a calabash, which is shut up and hung for a few days on the ceiling above the fireplace. The tobacco is then kept in a cool place until it is to be used. If an extra good mixture is wanted, pieces of banana or hydromel are added before the tobacco is placed out in the sun. To make snuff (*mbaki*), as great a quantity of leaves as is desired is then taken out and powdered between two grindstones, designed specially for this purpose, the upper one of which is almost spherical. They then add a little water and fat, and, as is common in East Africa, natron (*ɛ̱ɑ̱tɩ*, plur. *mɑ̱tɩ*, presumably < Kisuaheli *magadɩ*). The fat is intended to keep the snuff damp enough, the natron to make it stronger [1]. The snuff is now ready.

The natives assert that they can distinguish the different kinds of snuff, even at some distance, by their smell, and it is said to have happened that a person who had had his supply of snuff stolen and had afterwards been invited to take a pinch of it recognized his own snuff by the smell.

Natron is found in many places in East Africa, especially on the Masai steppes. It

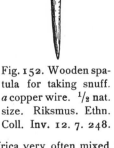

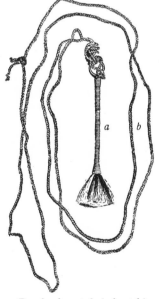

Fig. 151. Brush of goats hair for taking snuff. *a* copper wire, *b* brass chain. $^1/_2$ nat. size. Riksmus. Ethn. Coll. Inv. 12. 7. 247.

Fig. 152. Wooden spatula for taking snuff. *a* copper wire. $^1/_2$ nat. size. Riksmus. Ethn. Coll. Inv. 12. 7. 248.

---

[1] Even the smoking tobacco is in East Africa very often mixed up with natron, a custom also known from the upper Nile and other regions. F. Stuhlmann, Beiträge zur Kulturgeschichte von Ostafrika, p. 370.

is found in Ukamba, at least in Kikumbuliu. It is boiled in water until the water vaporises.

Like most of the natives of East Africa the Akamba are passionately fond of snuff, the women at least as much as the men. Even small girls have their own snuff-bottles. But the snuff is used differently by the two sexes: the men take snuff in the usual way, but the women chew it. They find it just as hard to do without snuff as, for instance, a Swedish farm-hand. »We cannot work if we do not have the snuffbottle within reach», they say themselves. During my marches I found out on more than one occasion that this statement was not exaggerated. It was much more difficult for my porters to march when their supply of snuff had come to an end, as they were accustomed to refresh themselves with a pinch during the halts. I consequently found it useful

Fig. 153. Smoking pipe, maize cob with reed shaft. $^1/_2$ nat. size. Riksmus. Ethn. Coll. Inv. 12. 7. 261, 262.

Fig. 154. Pipe head of black clay. $^1/_2$ nat. size.

to take a reserve of snuff with me myself on long marches. When the women have no snuff, they sometimes chew as a substitute the leaves of *mukandu*, a high verticillate.

Snuff is kept in the *kıaŋgı*, a snuff-bottle made of wood, but also of horn or, though exceptionally, of ivory. They also use bamboo tubes and small, beautifully shaped calabashes and the hollowed-out kernel of the fruit of the dum palm. The wooden ones are made preferably of ebony or some other hard species of wood such as the beautiful red wood of the *mupæu*, a species of acacia. The stoppers are cut out of rhinoceros or hippopotamus skin.

Great care is taken with the making of the snuff-bottles, and these elegant articles serve at the same time as ornaments for their owners. They are usually carried on a chain round the neck or fastened on the upper part of the arm. The women like to carry them on the beaded belt round their waists. Various snuff-bottles are reproduced here (fig. 147—150). A person who has a large quantity of snuff keeps it in a horn or some other utensil in his hut and then fills up his snuff-bottle when necessary.

When taking snuff a little is held in the hand and then raised to the nose with the fingers or with a little brush, which is also carried on a chain round the neck or fastened directly to the snuffbox (fig. 151). A wooden spatula is also used for the same purpose (fig. 152).

The Akamba are much more fond of taking tobacco as snuff than of smoking it. As a matter of fact they only smoke in rare

Fig. 155.   Smoking pipes with heads of clay and reed shafts.
$^1/_2$ nat. size.   Riksmus. Ethn. Coll. Inv. 12. 7. 259, 260.

cases, except among the younger generation, who, through contact with Europeans or Suahelis, have learned to make and smoke cigarettes. They smoke simple pipes (*ndoʐo*), the simplest type of which is a hollowed maize spadix (fig. 153). They also use, however, pipe-heads of burnt clay, some of which are reproduced here (fig. 154—155).

It is interesting to observe that the clumsy and coarse pipe-heads among those reproduced here were made by a woman, and the more graceful ones, on the other hand, by a man. The latter show obvious attempts at ornamentation and are remarkable as being the only pieces of pottery I saw among the Akamba that were executed artistically. I have unfortunately omitted to find out whether this difference in the pipes is only due to chance and is confined to exceptional cases, but if this should prove not to be the case, we should find in Ukamba confirmation of the experiences arrived at in other parts of Africa, namely: (1) that among all earthenware articles pipes are usually the most ornamented and artistically made, and (2) that these pipes are, as a rule made by men, not by women[1]. In connection with this I wish to make up for an oversight in the chapter on Decorative art and to mention that practically all the little ornamentation the Akamba possess, the carvings on the calabashes, etc. is carried out by the men. We have now arrived at the question of woman's talent for the free arts, but we must refrain from a discussion of this question and return to the subject of tobacco smoking.

The pipe is lit by putting charcoal in it, so that the smoker often inhales a good deal of carbonic oxide as well. The smoking tobacco, which is unpleasantly strong for these not accustomed to it, is kept and transported for sale in the way usual in these districts, namely in round packets made of banana-leaves. This trade in tobacco must in former times have been incomparably more widespread than now, to judge from Hildebrandt's statement that tobacco from Ukamba was sold to the Masai and even at the coast[2].

---

[1] Se H. Schurtz, Das Afrikanische Gewerbe, Leipzig 1900, p. 17.
[2] Hildebrandt, Ethnographische Notizen, p. 373.

Chap. XXXII. **Industries.**

A. **Metalwork.**

1. **Iron industry.**

The Akamba supply their requirements in iron ($k\underset{\sim}{\imath}a$) now-adays largely by imported wire, but also continue to get a certain amount from their own land. Many rivers contain ferriferous sand, a fact that can easily be proved, especially in the dry season when the waterless riverbeds shine black with iron sand. This has probably arisen from weathering of gneis containing iron mica. The iron is found less frequently in the form of lumps. The iron ore is called *kɪlea*. In former times the Akamba seem to have brought iron to their neighbours the Wanyika, who partly obtained iron from the Akamba, partly from the Arabs[1].

The author had no opportunity of seeing the Akamba's method of obtaining iron, but according to Hobley (Akamba, p. 29) »they separate the grains of iron ore from the silica by washing the sand in a dish made of a gourd in the same way as a prospector for gold would do». And he adds: »These are the only people in East Africa who appear to know this art». This method indicated by Hobley is presumably, however, identical with the one used by the Akikuyu and described in detail by Routledge (The Akikuyu, p. 81). Apart from these districts in East Africa, however, this preliminary preparation of the ore by working the iron-bearing sand in order to get rid of the sand and concentrate the mineral seems — as far as iron is concerned — to be practically unknown throughout the world. Professor Gowland of London, who is an expert on the subject, says that the method has not been described before (Routledge, Appendix IV). But a closer investigation would perhaps show that the method

---

[1] Vide Ch. Pickerings, The Races of Man, p. 199.

is not uncommon in East Africa, for R. Stern, the missionary, in a description of the iron industry among the southern Wanya-mwezi[1], says that they mix ferriferous sand and earth and then wash out the iron, and, according to Merker and Baumann, the Akikuyu and the Wapare carry out a preliminary cleansing of the ferriferous sand by repeatedly pouring water over it[2].

I am sorry to confess that I have not seen how the iron is smelted, but according to Hobley the Akamba use »a rude furnace of the Catalan type», and Routledge describes a similar method from the Akikuyu[3].

The Akamba's bellows consists of two sacks made of skin, sheepskin being considered best. They are thus of the type that the Germans call schlauch(sack-)-gebläse, as opposed to the vessel-shaped bellows (schalengebläse or gefässblasebalg), which is the most common type in Africa. Most investigators assume that the sack-shaped bellows, which within negroid Africa is most widespread in the east, has been introduced there by Moham-medans from the coast or has come from the Hamites in the north. Its appearance and method of use has been described so often (Frobenius, Ankermann, v. Luschan, Stuhlmann, etc.) that in the case of the Akamba I shall content myself with giving the main features.

The air-aperture, which is situated in its back end and is bordered by two ribs, closes when the bellows are pressed to-gether. At the front each arm of the bellows is bound round with a V-shaped pipe (*kɪ̯u*), made of a hard species of wood. This opens out into a clay tube, made of ordinary potter's clay, which leads in its turn into the fireplace. This earthenware nozzle gets burnt away at the end and becomes shorter and shorter.

Like the Akikuyu, Masai and other tribes, the Akamba forge their iron in the open air, in a shallow hollow in the ground at the *pǫmǝ*, the open place in front of the village. The bellows,

---

[1] Given as an appendix in F. Stuhlmann's Handtwerk und Indu-strie in Ostafrika (p. 152).

[2] O. Baumann, Usambara und seine Nachbargebiete, p. 232.

[3] One also gets a good picture of the Akamba's iron industry from the description of this industry on Kilimandjaro given by R. Andree, Die Metalle bei den Naturvölkern, p. 20.

which is managed by a helper[1], has an underneath of skin to protect it from rubbing against the sand. To keep it steady in its place four sticks are driven in the ground round the wooden pipe, and above it between the sticks is placed a stone as a weight.

In the hollow there is also a heap of charcoal (*maka*). The best coal is made from the *muku*, a cedar tree, and from the *kɟoa* and *mupau*, the latter a small tree with entire leaves and extremely small greenish-yellow flowers. Near the hearth sits the smith himself (*mutwι* < *kutua* 'to forge') at his anvil. This consists of a piece of iron, fixed to a block of wood lying horizontally on the ground, or quite simply of a stone. The only tools of the smith are a hammer (*kιɓa*, fig. 156) and a pair of tongs (*mwιɓælo* fig. 157)[2].

A person who wants a piece of work done by the smith must himself procure the coal and take it to him. The customer has not merely to order what he wishes. According to Rout-

Fig. 156. The smith's hammer.   Fig. 157. The smith's pair of tongs.
$^1/_{12}$ nat. size. $^1/_{12}$ nat. size.

ledge the same thing happens among the Akikuyu, and I think one may say that it is usual among many African people for the customer himself to procure the necessary material when he wishes to have a piece of work carried out.

When a smith hands over the completed article, he usually spits on it to bring good luck to it.

With regard to the smiths' position it may be observed that they form no special caste or clan, nor are they despised. Their skill, on the other hand, gives them a good reputation and they enjoy even a certain respect. No one dares to steal from a smith; he may without risk leave his belongings lying about on the ground. Thus there is the same respect for craftmanship

---

[1] If this helper is a casual one or a pupil of the smith, I have neglected to find out. The question about the position of helpers within the different professions is, however, of a certain importance for the study of the development of the professions. Cf. H. Schurtz, Das Afrikanische Gewerbe, p. 79.

[2] The Akikuyu have quite the same word, apart from differences due to sound laws: *mihato*, in Kinyamwezi *mwivatyo*.

as we shall soon see prevails with regard to stealing pots from
their makers[1].

We have already come across several examples in this work
of how on certain occasions objects may not be mentioned by
name by certain persons. Such observances apply also to smiths.
If they are to succeed in their work, they must never speak in
connection with it about *ua* 'skin' (referring to the bellows), *uumba*
'potter's clay' or *ŋgolıa* 'tongs' (cf. p. 532, chainmaking).

2. Other metals.

Iron is the only metal found in the country, but the natives
also manufacture trade wire of brass and copper, the old East
African Company's small copper money, and tin, which they also
get through the traders.

All wire is used in wiredrawing, which is done here in the
same way as over large parts of the Dark Continent, namely by
means of a drawplate fitted with holes of various sizes, through
which the wire is drawn. This is called in Kikamba (and also
in Kikuyu) *uta* 'the bow' and is an iron bar about 2 dm. long.
Nowadays, of course, the Akamba do this work exclusively with
trade wire, but originally the wire was made by hand and this
art is not extinct, even though, for practical reasons, it is rarely
used, although the Kikuyu smiths, on the other hand, still sometimes practise it.

The wire (*upuku*) is principally used in the Akamba's finest
metal work, chain-making, for which they are well known and
famed over the whole of East Africa. All the tribes use and
make chains, but none of them can compete with those of the
Akamba. Travellers also unanimously express their admiration
of their accomplishments in this craft. The chains are used exclusively as ornaments and are consequently manufactured by the
principal makers of such things, namely the young men. The
material is, as we have said, trade wire, but formerly home-made
wire was used.

---

[1] The Akikuyu consider the curse of a smith to be particularly
dangerous, and, to take another example, among the Nandi nobody
dares to steal anything from a smith, as the owner of the stolen article »will beat his furnace and, while blowing his bellows, will curse
the thief, who will surely die». Hollis, The Nandi, p. 37.

Chainmaking is carried out in the following way: First the wire is rolled spirally round another wire by means of the apparatus *kɪlɪŋgɪ* (fig. 158). This consists of a piece of rhinoceros hide (*a* in the fig.), in which is fixed a rather long stick (*b*) as a handle and another shorter one (*c*) fixed in beneath, with which the wire is wedged fast. The metal is seized by the thumb and index finger of one hand and the handle is twisted round by the other, so that one wire is rolled in a spiral shape round the other. The spiral can be made as long as is desired by taking the wedge out and drawing the finished spiral a little way down through the hole and the inner wire upwards. Formerly the whole apparatus was cut out of a single piece of wood.

In all East African chainmaking the wire is twisted round an iron rod, but other tribes use an iron resembling a knitting-needle, which is thicker than the wire, while the Akamba, as in the apparatus reproduced here, often have both of the same kind of wire. The principle is thus the same everywhere, but the Akamba have brought the technique to greater perfection than the other tribes.

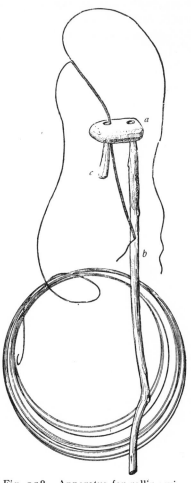

Fig. 158. Apparatus for rolling wire. 1/4 nat. size. Riksmus. Ethn. Coll. Inv. 12. 7. 88.

The spiral is afterwards cut into links, which are twisted S-shape, with their ends in different planes (fig. 159, 161 d), while in other East African chains the links are flattened out, giving the

chain the appearance shown in fig. 160. The Akamba keep the
finished links in a bamboo tube.

The artist makes his chains sitting on the ground with his little
kɪtɑ̰tɪ (fig. 161 a), on which the loose links are placed, put down
in the ground between his legs. With two iron rods resembling
knitting-needles — they are made preferably out of old umbrellas
which are sold by the Indian traders — the links are taken and

Fig. 159. Kamba chain.   Enlarged to show the composition.

joined to each other. With a pair of pincers (*ŋgolɪa*, fig. 161 b)[1]
they are squeezed together. Each of the ends of the pincers is
fitted, as shown in fig. 161 c, with an oblique groove, which makes
it easier to seize and hold the wire fast. The finished chain is
triangular.

Fig. 160. Kikuyu chain, the usual type in East Africa.
Enlarged.

One must admire the craftsmanship and taste shown in these
chains. The finest of them, used by the young men for leg ornaments, look at a few metres' distance like painting on their legs.
In my collection there are chains as narrow as 2 mm. It requires

---

[1] Certainly identical with Kisuaheli *koleo*. The fact that these
tongs are somewhat different from and have a different name from
those of the smiths gives rise to the suspicion that the Akamba's
chainmaking has been subject to foreign influences. The word for
chain, *munʐo*, gives perhaps also an indication of this. In Kisuaheli a
chain is called *mnyoro* or *mkufu* (I do not know the difference between
these two words) and in Kikuyu, where it is usually called *kirengeri*,
only a certain kind (I do not know which) is called *munyoro*.

extraordinary dexterity to join together the fine links of which they consist. Chains of different finenesses are seen in figs. 76, 77, 79, 80, 82, 89—92, 94—95, 145—149.

As has been just mentioned, the Akamba's chain are famous over the whole of East Africa. In many remote places there are small Kamba colonies, which have settled down there principally to manufacture and sell chains. Up at Lake Victoria, for instance, there are at Kisumu a number of Akamba who sell chains to the Kavirondo people.

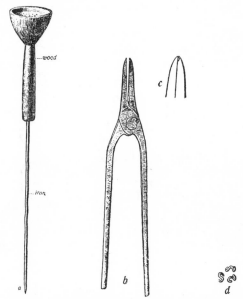

Fig. 161. Tools for chain-making. *a* the *kıtatı* (¹/₆ nat. size), *b* the pair of pincers (¹/₄ nat. size), *c* the ends of the pincers (¹/₂ nat. size), *d* links in nat. size.
Riksmus. Ethn. Coll. Inv. 12. 7. 90, 91.

Besides wire the Akamba also get tin, in the form of small bars, from the Indian traders. This is used exclusively for ornamental armrings, earrings, breast ornaments and fittings on snuffboxes. When they can get hold of it, they also collect the tin casing in old packing cases and biscuit boxes. The tin is melted and poured into a hole in the ground. In this way are made, among other things, massive armrings (fig. 87), in which pieces of brass or copper wire are also put as decorations.

Gold and silver are not found in any form. We have touched upon the treatment of metals in the chapter on ornaments (p. 374 ff.).

B. **Woodwork.**

Every head of a house makes the wooden articles that are needed, such as beehives, stools, spoons, snuff-bottles, handles of axes and knives, etc. Here, as in other places in East Africa, holes are bored in wood with a red-hot iron. All the larger objects are cut from a massive piece of wood with the ordinary wood-

Fig. 162. Woman's chair. ¹/₅ nat. size. Riksmus. Ethn.
Coll. Inv. 12. 7. 72.

axe (*ɩpoƙa*), whose iron blade is only about 4 cm. wide, sometimes still narrower. The coarsely made three-legged stools (*kɩɓɩla*) that are used in the huts (the same type as among the Akikuyu) are cut out of a piece of tree-trunk. Especially in Eastern Ukamba there is used a special stool for women (*kɩtumbɔ*), which is bigger than the ordinary stools (fig. 162). The stools (*mṵmbo*) which the *atumɩa* use as a special privilege (see p. 144) are, on the other hand, neat and comfortable, often real little works of art. Great pains are taken in making them, and they are usually adorned with copper or brass fittings. One of these is shown in fig. 163, where the seat and the feet are fitted with brass fastened with small tacks made of brass wire. This stool also shows how cracks in the wood are mended, namely with pieces of wire, which are driven in on both the upper and lower sides. There are also really splendid

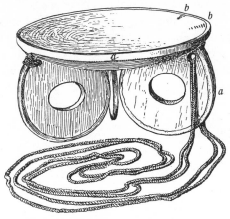

Fig. 163. Old man's stool. *a* brass, *b* mended cracks.
¼ nat. size. Riksmus. Ethn. Coll. Inv. 12. 7. 74.

specimens of this type of stool, as shown in fig. 76. The superior specimens, however, are made by specialists in this department.

The heavy work is thus done with the axe, after which the final cutting is done with the *ŋgomo,* a sort of chisel or adze with

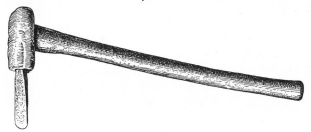

Fig. 164. The *adze ŋgomo.* ¼ nat. size. Riksmus.
Ethn. Coll. Inv. 12. 7. 78.

its blade almost at right angles to the handle (fig. 164). This, with the knife (*kaбʑo*), is used for all fine work and is one of the natives' most important tools. The base of the blade is fixed in a piece of rhinoceros hide surrounding the end of the handle; this gives greater stability and firmness to the whole.

The women, who only use axes for chopping fire-wood, have their own axes for this work and seem not to be allowed to use those of the men. The type is however quite the same.

The Akamba choose their wooden material with great care and with an eye to both the aesthetic and the practical. Thus for stools and for objects that have to be hollowed out, such as beehives etc., they take soft kinds of wood, as for instance *kıbutı* (Aberis precatorius); for snuff-boxes they usually take ebony, but when they are to be mounted, softer kinds as well. Spoons are made from the beautiful red wood of the acacia sp. *mupæu. mundwǝ* and *mupạ*, a small tree with large yellow flowers (Cassia sp.), are suitable for knife-handles and sword-hilts.

C. **Pottery-making.**

According to tradition it was a medicine woman who discovered and taught women the art of making pottery. Before this, it is said, people cooked in shells. Pottery-making is held in high esteem among the Akamba and it is by no means all women who understand the art. There is also a special clan, *mba-kıpumbǝ*, whose women are tabooed from making pottery as long as they belong to the clan. A girl from this clan who gets married is thus freed from this taboo, and, on the other hand, women from other clans are subject to it if they become the wives of men of the *mba-kıpumbǝ* clan.

The pots are made of a mixture of black and red clay. As suitable clay is not found everywhere, the women have, in many places, to carry the material a long distance home, and in some places they never have any opportunity of making their pots for themselves, but have to buy them from distant places. The process is as follows:

The clay is mixed with water in a hole in the ground and is then worked up with poles. The pot is shaped by hand, as is the case among all the tribes in these districts; the only tool used is a small oblong piece of calabash, with which the surface of the shaped pot is finished off, smoothed and polished. The pots are then placed in the sun to dry, and the dry season (*pạnu*) is considered most suitable for this purpose, so that they take the opportunity of making their pottery during this time of the year. After being dried, they are burnt, which is done by the well-known process of covering them with dry grass (preferably *ʋlʊ*, Tricholæna rosea) and twigs, which are set fire to on the windward side. The completely burnt pots have a pale reddish-brown colour.

The pots are very important articles in the native's life, as they make possible savoury and practical cooking of food, the source of all power and life. Their manufacture is consequently an important task, in which much caution has to be observed. For this reason the work is carried out preferably at a place where one is not exposed to strange looks (the evil eye). As an additional safeguard they also get the medicine man to protect the place by means of his arts, in the first place against possible enviers of the worker and against her enemies among the other women. For it is a good opportunity for such people, by means of magic, to give the pots pernicious qualities and so injure those who eat food from them. In addition the women abstain from sexual intercourse as long as they are working at making pots, and as they may be spoiled even by sexual intercourse on the part of outsiders, they are especially careful not to allow any men to approach the place where they are working. The fact that the latter is situated somewhat out of the way makes it more easy to carry out these observances.

In the discussion of agricultural rites it has already been shown that pottery may not be made during the time when the *nžʊ*-beans are flowering. I do not know any explanation of this idea, but it would be in accordance with primitive processes of thought to argue that by making pots, that is by making preparations for cooking these beans that are so much liked, one runs the risk of producing a result opposite to the one hoped for, namely a good crop of beans. This way of thinking is obviously closely related to that which, when children die in a family, causes the parents to give those born later repulsive names, so as to make the malignant spirits believe that they do not care for children, in consequence of which the spirits will not consider it worth while to take the children from them.

At Machakos I once came across some women who were making pots during the flowering time of the *nžʊ*. They did this very secretly, inside an enclosure, and had placed their daughters to look out and report if any outsider should approach. It would have been interesting to ascertain why they violated the prohibition in this way, as the women are, of course, usually extremely anxious not to offend any ritual prescriptions, especially when it concerns something within their own province.

The Akamba's pots, which are used exclusively for cooking in — beer, for instance, is preserved exclusively in calabashes — are very simple and all of the same shape: extended with short necks and rounded at the bottom, so that they cannot stand by themselves[1]. They never have ears, which I saw sporadically only in Ikutha. As the pots in general of the African Negroes never have ears or similar arrangements for taking hold of them, these must be considered as due to foreign influence. The women in Ikutha possibly imitated the pots they had seen in the kitchen at the mission station. The biggest pots I can remember having seen were 50 cms high; cooking pots are, on the average, rather less. A cooking pot in general is called *nẓuŋgu*, the big ones are called *kɪtænɔ*. There are also smaller ones, down to 20 cms in height. One of this size is the *munạ* or *kamunạ*, in which food is cooked for the father of the family alone, when he wishes to have some special dish. In a hut there are seldom more than four or five cooking pots.

In former times it is said that the natives made pots of such dimensions that the biggest could hold a human being. They were used during the happy time when there was a better supply of meat, that is when they had an opportunity of stealing cattle from their neighbours. The ordinary size was too small when they wished to hold a real feast with meat. In daily use, however, these large vessels were not employed, except possibly for keeping corn in.

No ornamentation is ever found on the pottery, but many of them have simple marks at the neck, which are carved there while the clay is still soft (fig. 165). They are a sort of trademark which are placed there by the woman who makes the pot. Our figures show some of these. Another consists of two stripes round the neck, which would certainly be interpreted as a decoration by anyone who did not know that it was a mark. It seems

---

[1] Vessels with flat bottoms seem to be extremely rare among the African peoples.

also as if the step from these marks to real decoration of the
pots were not far.

There are a number of observances with regard to the use
of pots. No male may eat out of a new pot before a woman
has eaten a little out of it[1]. Presumably before this they possess
a power that is dangerous to the men, who are unacquainted
with their manufacture. And if a cooking pot is going to break
when food is being prepared in it, and some of the food falls
out, it must not be eaten[2]. For if it were, they would be defeated
in the next campaign, presumably according to the old saying that
»like produces like». The women, on the other hand, may eat

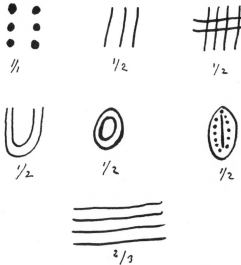

Fig. 165. Trade marks on pottery.

the contents of the broken pot without any risk, but they mix
salt with the food, probably as a sort of prophylactic. We are
reminded once more of the power that salt is generally considered
to possess, although I have not come across any other instance
of it than this one among the Akamba. Apart from this there
is no objection to the use of cracked pots.

---

[1] The Nandi observe the same thing (Hollis, The Nandi, p. 36).
Similarly among them no man may approach the place where pots are
made or watch the women at work.

[2] So also among the Nandi.

That the manufacture of pottery is considered to be a rather remarkable power seems to be indicated by the fact that no one would dare to steal pots from the woman who has made them from fear of being destroyed by her *kɩpɩtu*. For if she happens to be robbed, she makes a little jar and crushes it while uttering a curse to the effect that »the thief may be broken like the jar».

D. Making of strings and bags.

From the bark of certain trees the women make the strings (*ulɩ* pl. *ṇdɩ*) with which their brisk fingers plait bags. This is their most important use, but they are, of course, also used for a great number of different purposes, among other things for making necklets and other ornaments. The best strings are made of the baobab, and as this plant does not grow west of the Athi River, the people in Ulu get the desired material by barter from East Ukamba, whence it comes, made into bast, in long packages. The chief thing given in exchange is arrow poison, as the arrow poison tree (Acocanthera) is not found in the east. Besides the baobab a large number of other trees are used to make strings, such as the wild figtree (*mumo*), the acacia species *kɩpɩ* and the plants *mwondə* and *mwɩnda ṇguə* (Corchoras). I cannot remember whether the excellent fibre plants of the Sanseviera species, which occur abundantly here and there, are used by the Akamba.

The first stage in stringmaking is that the bark is chewed so that it shall become soft. It is not at all uncommon to meet a woman going along the path with a piece of bark in her mouth and with her jaws in regular motion. Sometimes even small boys are put to this work. When the fibre is soft, they twine the cords, which consist of two strings twisted together to the right. They are made with the flat of the hand against the thigh, and then they are wound into a ball (*kɩlɩṇga*)[1]. They use different sizes, varying from the coarsest down to the thickness of the finest pack-thread.

As has been shown, the strings are used especially for plaiting the sacks (*kɩondo*) in which the produce of the fields is carried home. The plaiting work occupies a considerable part of the women's time, and they even do it when they are on their way

---

[1] < *kulɩṇga* 'plait together, put together'.

from one place to another, just as in the country districts in
Sweden one can see old women taking their knitting with them
wherever they go. And during the pauses between their different tasks one can see the women sitting in groups outside the
village, talking and working at their bags at the same time. One
may say that a *kɨondo* is an inevitable appendage to a Kamba
woman during her work. When a wife is mentioned in the people's
numerous tales, it is almost always added in passing that she
was plaiting a bag (*kɨtuma kɨondo* < *kutuma* 'to plait') [1].

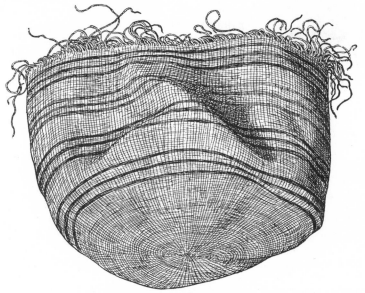

Fig. 166. Smaller bag (not yet finished) for carrying field products.
$1/4$ nat. size. Riksmus. Ethn. Coll. Inv. 12. 7. 27.

The bags are plaited with the fingers from two balls. The
Kikuyu women make them in the same way. So as to have one
hand free they often put one end between the teeth. The bottom
is made first and the bag is held with this upwards during the
work. The size varies from 50 cms in diameter down to quite
small wallet-like bags for small girls. The largest take a month
or more to make.

---

[1] The verb *kutuma* is also used for 'to sew', an art that the
Akamba themselves do not know.

There is never any ornamentation in the plaiting. Only in certain places in East Ukamba are the bags adorned with red and black lines (fig. 166), formed by the strings, which are rubbed with soot or red ochre.

On most bags there are leather straps to carry them (fig. 167),

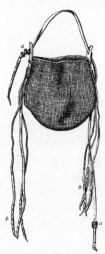

which are placed over the forehead. The Akamba, both men and women, carry loads in this way, and the length of the strap is so arranged that the load comes on the upper part of the back. Carrying is made easier by bending the arms up and catching hold of the straps. The usual method of carrying a load in Africa is, of course, by putting it on the top of the head, but this method is inconvenient in these districts, which consist to a great extent of thick bush with branches that hang down over the narrow paths. Even in the Machakos district, where the vegetation is now very sparse, they always carry their loads in the traditional way.

Fig. 167. Bag with leather straps for carrying. *a* blue glass beads, *b* brass beads. ¹/₈ nat. size. Riksmus. Ethn. Coll. Inv. 12. 7. 28.

On the smaller bags, which are called *nḑuŋgə*, hang as ornaments — as fig. 167 shows — some narrow leather straps, adorned with glass or brass beads. It is each girl's ambition, when she gets married, to bring one of these *nḑuŋgə*'s with long, pearl-adorned straps as a dowry; it is hung up on one of the posts that support her husband's bed.

The method of preparing straps and leather in general is described in connection with »Dress» (p. 372).

Chap. XXXIII. **Distribution of work between the sexes.**

Instead of illustrating the distribution of work by drawing up a table such as one often finds in ethnographical works, I prefer to let the natives themselves put forward their view on the matter, and, for this purpose, I have translated an extract from a Leipzig missionary's reading-book in Kikamba[1], written by a pupil at the mission's former station at Rabai, among the coast Akamba. It is curious to observe how many duties have been laid on the man's shoulders, and, to judge from the length of the description, he has a good deal more to do than his wife. But if one examines this formidable list of tasks, it is found to consist of a mass of details, all of which I have, however, not included. Instead of saying, for instance, quite simply »manufacture arrows» there is a host of minute details, such as: cutting the branches, trimming them, cutting the two parts of the handle, chewing and fastening the sinews, putting on the head, etc. In this way one gets the impression at a cursory glance that the poor man is overburdened with work, when, as a matter of fact, it is his wife that has the hardest part. The husband will not, however, admit this, except possibly in silence to himself. He enumerates with real devotion and self-satisfaction how much he has to do, and if the listener cannot repress a sceptical remark, he is greeted with severe disapproval. And with these few words we shall leave the native writer to speak.

1. **Woman's work.**

The woman's work is to powder maize, grind flour, chop wood, fetch water, look for vegetables and cook them, cook food

---

[1] Kitabu tja kutsoma, p. 7.

for her husband and to eat it herself (!) [1].   Her other duties are:
to milk the cows and churn butter, to dig (the field), sow and
plant, gather in the maize, thrash the millet and Penicillaria and
the *n̯ðoko* beans; to cut and carry home grass for thatching,
sweep the hut, shut the entrance to the craal and clean it after
the cattle (this is seldom done, however); to plait bags and mend
calabashes; feed children (a very important duty), suckle them,
look after them and bring them up (there is, however, no education in our sense of the word).

2. The man's work.

The man's work is to cut the *n̯ǵeti* (the framework of the
hut), peel off bark to make cords of, build racks to keep maize
on and other smaller ones to keep things on (they consist of
shelves beneath the ceiling in the hut); to chop material for the
fence around the craal, for the *mu6ịa* (the narrow entrance to
the craal) and for barricading the entrances with; to cut beams
to support the ceiling of the hut and wood for the sleeping-
places and to build the *wẹ* (the compartment in the back part of
the hut); to go to Ukamba and buy cattle, goats and ivory to
sell at the coast and then to buy clothes for his wife; to cut
posts that shall be driven into the ground to strengthen the hedge
round the craal; to make brooms to sweep the hut with; to make
the sleeping skins for the beds and the wife's skin dress and to
scrape the hair off this; to sew quivers, make bows and arrow-
shafts, arrowheads of iron and wood and to fix them on; to rub
the arrow poison on and find small bits of goatskin, rub these
very soft between the hands, bind them on the arrow-heads and
then fix the arrows in the quiver; to sew the ornaments of ostrich feathers on the quiver (*kịtuḳu*); to cut clubs, make swords
and sheaths for these, fix the hilts on and find a suitable strap to
fasten to the sword; to make straps for his wife to fasten bundles
of wood and water calabashes with; to hollow out beehives and
make the round lids to put on the ends, provide a wooden crook
to hang them up with and go to hang them up; to hollow out

---

[1] From many a cross husband I have heard the unjust opinion
that a woman is no use for much more than eating food and sleeping.

honey jars and make lids of skin for them; to make chains; to look after the cattle (if he has no children); to cut out snuff-bottles and make the tweezers for pulling out the hair of the beard and eyelashes.

The work of arranging all the different things is very many-sided.

―――――――――

P. VI.

ANTHROPOLOGY

Chap. XXXIV. **Mental Characteristics, etc.**

As I have now reviewed both the Akamba's spiritual and material culture, I shall, for the sake of completeness, add a description of their mental characteristics, an idea of which may, as a matter of fact, be obtained to a great extent from what has gone before. It is not my intention to make any scientific analysis of their spiritual life — it is, of course, beyond my power to do so — I content myself with describing them on the basis of my practical experience, to set forth the qualities that are most prominent among them.

It is very risky to generalize on such a subject, for it is unnecessary to emphasize the fact that even among primitive people there are, of course, individual peculiarities, exactly as is the case among those who are more civilized. One can, however, say, to begin with, that the Akamba are intelligent and, when they like, even easy to teach. Most travellers, missionaries and settlers will agree with this verdict. They have also a quick power of apprehension. For mission work their alert intelligence seems, however, to be of little use, a hindrance rather than an advantage. Among them mission work advances much more slowly than among the neighbouring tribes. When one thinks of the competency as regards education and the unprejudiced and practical view of their work that both the American and the German missionaries in Ukamba possess, it is quite astonishing to find that after 10 to 20 years' assiduous work they have obtained so little result, at least as far as one can see, with regard to religion. And yet there are many natives in the neighbourhood of the mission stations who attend divine service regularly and know the elements of the christian faith quite well, but seem to have no desire to live according to its teaching.

Besides intelligence the Akamba have also practical ability to carry out a thing, if they are properly instructed. When they wish to work — for they do not always wish to do so — they easily obtain places that the natives of many other tribes seldom attain to. Thus they compete with the Indians for places as firemen on the Uganda Railway's engines, and similarly on the steamers on Lake Victoria many of the firemen are Akamba, while members of other tribes have to be satisfied with less important posts, such as deck hands, etc. In smithies and workshops in Nairobi the Akamba are also superior to the other blacks with regard to craftsmanship.

A thing that one is struck by among the Akamba with regard to their work — and that is indeed characteristic of most negroes — is the onesidedness of the individuals. Everyone who has had native boys in his service knows what I refer to. They do their definite work pretty well, but only this, and object to doing other duties. Each becomes a sort of specialist at his own occupation. One is thus practically compelled to have a houseboy, a cook, a person to do washing, a groom, a gunbearer, etc. One notices the same tendency to specialisation among themselves at home. The medicine man, for instance, knows and can cure only one illness, a certain individual makes only chairs for sale, another only arrows, etc. In the same way different kinds of wood are often used only for certain kinds of work, for instance, to make knife handles. It is rather laughable to hear, when one asks what a certain bush with soft leaves is used for, that it is employed as toilet-paper for the babies.

The Akamba are popular as porters on Safari, and many travellers consider them the best of all their bearers, although they seldom carry as heavy burdens as bearers from many other tribes. »For all-round usefulness the Akamba are hard to beat», is A. Arckell-Hardwick's verdict on his Kamba porters after a long and adventurous journey from Nairobi to the districts far north of Kenia. And a German traveller, who has otherwise no great opinion of the Akamba, says about them as bearers: »I must admit that they differ from bearers from the coast and Wakikuyu in a way that is not to their disadvantage»[1]. To mention a Swedish investigator, Prof. E. Lönnberg has expressed to the author his great satisfaction with the Akamba who served

---

[1] A. Kaiser, Die wirtschaftliche Entwickelung der Ugandabahnländer, p. 56.

with his great zoological expedition in East Africa in 1910—1911. One could easily collect a great many of these favourable opinions from the abundant literature of travelling [1].

We thus see that the Akamba are not without the capacity to accomplish work, but for one kind of work that is of great importance to the white settlers they are not so useful, namely in cultivating the ground. This is perhaps due not so much to idleness as to the fact that they consider themselves too good to be in the service of the white man as workers. A number of them work at Machakos, but in Kitui it is, or at least it was in my time, very difficult to get any Kamba workers, and they had to take Akikuyu, although these are at least as lazy as the Akamba. The Akikuyu is the tribe from which is recruited the greatest part of the labour needed for the farms. Not a few of the Akamba keep Kikuyu workers themselves, while it would be unthinkable, under normal conditions, for the Akamba to go to the Kikuyu country to look for work.

This last point leads us naturally to a rather prominent feature of their character, namely their pride. Without doing them an injustice one may assign to them the position of the aristocrats among the Bantu tribes of East Africa. They have of old kept to themselves, and did not permit their women to marry outside the tribe. But the great famine, when many women had to seek for food among the neighbouring tribes, put an end to this, and now many Kamba women go to be the wives of Indians and Wasuahelis, among whom they get out of doing work and are called *bibi* (mistress).

They never appear grovelling even to Europeans, but, on the other hand, sometimes go too far in the other direction, and do not show them due respect. It sometimes happens, for instance, that they do not go to one side for a European when they meet on a path. This occasional unsympathetic stubbornness is undoubtedly due partly to the fact that the Akamba have never had chiefs to whom they have had to cringe, but it is unquestionably also encouraged sometimes by rather great indulgence on the part of the English authorities. This is not a criticism of the latter, as they must, of course, adopt the principles drawn up in England for the treatment of the natives in the colonies.

---

[1] Among others C. H. Stigand, The Land of Zinj, p. 202.

The Akamba are a cheerful people, rather loud and noisy in their demeanour. They have a mind open to humour and appreciate a good joke. A humorous word, produced at a suitable time, seldom fails to have its desired effect, and more than once I have seen ill-will and sullenness disappear before a joking rejoinder. I have used these tactics to advantage with my porters, and have been able, by means of some joke, to make them forget fatigue and the hardships of the road. In the same way I have also been able to divert opposition and grumbling and have made it all finish in a releasing laugh.

As is to be expected in a hunting people and in people in general who live in intimate contact with nature, their powers of observation are exceedingly well-trained, and they can understand very small details about animals or other objects, especially if it concerns something within their own circle of experience. Their rich treasure of riddles and proverbs, which in many respects give one a good insight into their psychology, show good instances of this. They also have an acute eye for the peculiarities of a person, what is typical both in his exterior and in his character, which is shown by the nicknames they have given to Europeans with whom they have come in contact.

The negro is generally a clever speaker and the Akamba too have a good command of language. Above all they are adepts at telling stories or describing the course of an event. There is feeling in their speech, their play of features and their gestures are picturesque. A number of onomatopoetic expressions give life and colour to the whole; when describing animals they imitate their cries, they reproduce the sound of the fire crackling on the hearth, the songh of the storm in the branches of the trees, etc.

Similarly they have a good power of adaptability. When they speak their language to a European, many of them try to talk more slowly and, from our point of view, more clearly than when speaking among themselves. On closer acquaintanceship they quickly form an idea of our knowledge of their language and choose, when speaking, words and forms known to us.

In their mutual relations to each other they are constant and helpful. This is, of course, especially the case with regard to relations and members of the same clan. A poor family who have no milk for their children can be almost certain of obtaining some daily from better situated kinsmen. The bond of friendship between unrelated persons is also strong, and for a friend they will make considerable sacrifices, even of a pecuniary nature. They sell things cheaper to him than to others and try, as far as is possible, to fulfil his wishes. When a friend or any or his family comes on a visit, a goat or a bull-calf is killed in the guest's honour. On Safari I have often had occasion to observe how my porters used to help each other with their loads and share their stores of food and water. I found that their mutual help was considerably greater than that, for instance, which Swedish conscripts show each other on the march and on similar occasions. And we have already shown how during military campaigns a man may, at the risk of his own life, try to check the enemy in order thereby to rescue a wounded friend who cannot fly because of his wounds.

The relations between neighbours are also usually good, and they help each other when necessary, as, for instance, in hut-building and in gathering in the harvest. If their neighbour is threatened with some danger, they try to help or at least to warn him. I heard of people who had been sentenced to death by the *kɨŋolɔ* (p. 176), being warned by their neighbours, who wished by this means to evade the unpleasant duty of taking part in the execution of the death sentence.

Their help is restricted, of course, chiefly to relations, friends and acquaintances, but they are often generous and hospitable even to strangers. Anyone who comes to a hut is almost always invited to have some milk or food, and they bring out a chair for him to sit on. Towards visiting Europeans they are also polite and hospitable, but never servile.

This custom, so pleasant to the observer, of showing hospitality to almost every stranger is not, however, entirely due to goodness of heart. It is simply a custom to do so, a custom that seems common to all people at a low stage of culture. It is practically necessary to show hospitality in a country where there are no inns; all travelling would otherwise be rendered difficult. It is thus in one's own interest to entertain a traveller, as one may be in need of the same favour oneself on another occasion[1].

[1] A. L. Kroeber, The Morals of Uncivilized Peoples, p. 441.

In many cases the motive for this is the desire to be on good terms with a stranger, who otherwise might perhaps take his revenge by *woʑ*, black magic.

They have also a certain delicacy in their dealings with each other. I often found that a person who had a claim on his neighbour and would like to have it paid did not care to remind him about it. It was considered unbecoming. And in the same way, if a man had lent an axe or some other tool to another person, who had kept it for a long time, he was slow to »remind him with his mouth» about it, even if he wished very much to have his tool back. Such sensitiveness appears exaggerated to us Europeans.

Almost all unspoilt primitive people have a good idea of right and wrong, especially when it concerns themselves. If a Kamba has committed a misdemeanour, he bears his punishment without murmuring. After this, in his opinion, all is well again, and he bears no ill-will to his punisher. But if he is of the opinion that he has been subjected to wrongful treatment, this feeling may remain and rankle in his mind for a long time and make him deceitful and revengeful.

An attractive feature in the Akambas' nature is their love for children, especially small children. A person who sees anyone treating a child brutally will rush wildly to its help, even if he has not the slightest idea whose child it is. It is not uncommon to see men, perhaps stern and powerful old men, take a child, even a strange child, on their knees and sit and prattle to it for long periods. It is, however, parental love that is, of course, most conspicuous. On entering a village I have often been received coldly, but when I turned to the small children, asked their names, praised their appearance, etc. the good people soon thawed and have sometimes even given me presents. »You have become friends with the children, you are also our friend», they have said.

Thus it is quite clear that the children are treated well, especially by their mothers, to whom they seem most attached, which is, of course, easy to understand in the case of a polygamous family. One sees the children creep up to their mothers and caress them with their small hands. The mothers, on their side, show their children all possible marks of tenderness. I have seen mothers and children kissing each other or rather »caress each other with the mouth», as kissing in our sense of the word is unknown to the natives[1]. Especially when a child dies the mother shows deep and sincere sorrow. I remember one woman who, after the loss of her son, could not bear the sight of his playmates, and when she saw his ornaments hanging on a post in the hut, she wept.

The parents' weakness for their children often, however, becomes excessive, and it is therefore extremely common for the latter, as soon as they have grown up a little, to be spoilt and disobedient. The young boys are the worst. It is true that they seldom directly oppose the injunctions given to them, but they prefer to say yes to everything, while at the same time they are often quite determined not to obey them. This is especially the case, as we have already seen, when the dances are proceeding at their height. Dancing is their life, and for it they will defy almost anything. During the dancing season they go from one dancing-place to another, from one district to another, where they eat and sleep with their relations and in addition always find people to show them hospitality. Generally speaking, however, the young people show respect for their elders, especially for the old men. Their answer to an old man's greeting is a long drawn a, an exclamation of respect.

Even though the young people thus enjoy great liberty, one may still say that the children are, to a certain extent, the objects of education. The boys are soon made to help in looking after the cattle, and while the girls are still quite small, they have to look after their still smaller brothers and sisters and to accompany their mothers to the fields to work there. The initiation rites must also be looked upon as a part of education. To be safe I should also add that chastisement of children also takes place, although it appears to be less frequent than among us[2].

---

[1] This is the case among most, if not all, negro tribes, but it is not uncommon for small children to caress their mothers with kisses. See, for instance, M. Meyer, Die Barundi, p. 112.

[2] With reference to education and the relations between parents and children in general among primitive peoples see S. R. Steinmetz's attempt at systematization in his essay Das Verhältnis zwischen Eltern und Kindern bei den Naturvölkern. Zeitschrift f. Social-wissensch. Berlin 1898, pp. 607 ff. H. Ploss's well-known work, Das Kind, also deals with this subject (Africans, p. 209).

In this chapter we shall also touch on public morals. In the sexual relations between men and women there exists no refined love; the whole thing consists of sexual intercourse. This does not exclude, however, the existence of a deep and sincere feeling, which may be so strong that a person will not live without the one he loves. More than one Kamba girl, sold by an avaricious father to some rich old voluptuary, has taken her life by hanging herself with her leather strap in her hut or on some tree. Although this is very rare, it is said, however, that the same thing has happened because of unrequited love[1]. We know that free love is permitted among the young people, but even the married women are not so particular about matrimonial fidelity. This is quite easy to understand when, as often happens, a rich old man has several wives — among them even young women whom he has procured in his old days — and has not time nor strength to attend to them all. They then keep lovers and meet them secretly. In the same way women who have been married against their will continue to remain in secret connection with the men they love. It is probably superfluous to add that a married man need not observe any greater fidelity towards his wife.

This free love among the yong people usually, however, leads to marriage. But with his practical disposition the native looks carefully to see that he gets an industrious wife. If the one he chooses is lazy, he continues his connection with her as long as it amuses him, but marries someone else.

Competition between the young men for the favour of the girls may be rather strong, and manifestations of jealousy are not infrequent. One has occasionally a good opportunity to observe this at the dances, which sometimes end with a fight. To be

---

[1] We thus see that suicide occurs among the Akamba, though not often. Another thing that causes it is when a girl has had intercourse with a man of the same clan and becomes pregnant, thus committing an uncommonly serious crime, and in despair over it and from fear of the results she takes her life. As a means poison is also used, usually *kilhamıbtı* (Jatropha sp.). Suicide occurs, although to a very slight extent, among many, perhaps most negro tribes, and the usual method is hanging. Routledge (p. 248) gives in the case of the Akikuyu also drowning and stabbing. It seems to be blameworthy, among some peoples, such as the Masai (Merker, p. 216), even a punishable offence, to try to take one's own life.

just one must, however, admit that nowadays they proceed calmly and peacefully, generally speaking. But the older men's recollections of the dances contain a good deal about combats. Merely because another person danced with his sweetheart a young man would challenge the real or supposed rival This was done by taking a handful of earth and throwing it at the hated competitor and then drawing one's sword. If any of their relations or any members of their clans were present, they were not slow to interfere and come to the help of their friends, and thus a big fight would arise.

Married men too are, of course, sometimes inveigled into committing deeds of violence because of jealousy, but the motive is at least as frequently a different one, namely that they consider that their right of ownership is violated, if anyone else tries to approach their wives. »They have not paid out their cattle for nothing», as they say themselves, meaning that, as they have bought and honestly paid for their wives with good cattle, no one else has a right to enjoy their pleasures. The lover who enjoys their favours for nothing is looked upon as a thief.

It cannot be too often emphasized that the negro's sexual morality, like his racial psychology in general, must not be measured according to the same standard as our own. And the numerous prescriptions regarding sexual life that are found — we have got to know a great many from the Akamba — are based less on moral than on other factors, such as practical experience, religious and supernatural ideas, etc.[1]

The Akamba are closely attached to their homes and their native district, and although, especially in earlier times, they travelled far and wide, they always long to be back and always find their native place better than other places. It happens sometimes that a girl refuses a suitor, whom she likes in other respects, merely because his village is so far away that she cannot go home often enough.

In comparison to the men the Kamba women are more conservative and more superstitious. We have seen that when they believe that their interests are threatened they are by no means submissive creatures, but can show proofs of great stubbornness

---

[1] H. Berkusky, Die sexuelle Moral der Naturvölker, Zeitschr. f. Social-wissensch. 1909, pp. 717 ff.

and in many cases get what they want. And when they get an idea in their heads it has to be carried out as soon as possible.

The verdict is given, especially in older descriptions of travel, that the Akamba are given to stealing. »They are very thievish», says von Höhnel, and Arckell-Hardwick's experience of his porters was that »the Wakambas' great weakness on the march was a penchant for stealing from the native villages whatever they could lay their hands on». I have heard similar opinions from British officials in Ukamba. It is also certain that they have acquired a name as desperate cattle thieves. To give merely one example, one of the scholars at the Leipzig mission, a Kamba youth, describes in his autobiography how a Kamba caravan, which he accompanied on a journey to the Giriama country, stole cattle on the way[1]. And the Akambas' wars were pure plundering expeditions to steal cattle, a thing which is, however, characteristic of all African warfare. It is only exceptionally waged for its own sake. We must remember, however, in this connection that such thefts must not be judged according to European morality, for they are usually committed against strangers, thus, according to the primitive point of view, against enemies. And when they took place within the country, they were directed against hostile districts. Thefts of cattle from strangers are, according to primitive morality, not stealing, but rather an honourable action, and consequently they find it very difficult to understand why the new masters of the country, the Europeans, do not allow them to continue with these praiseworthy deeds.

Thus, from the native point of view, a robbery takes place only when something is taken from members of tribes with whom one is living in friendly relations. From the chapter on judicial customs we know also that such robbery is severely punished. From my own personal experience I cannot call the Akamba thievish. I was never robbed by them during my stay among them, although my tent, which contained various things much desired by the natives, was completely unwatched for several hours each day, and once actually for three weeks at a stretch. At the mission station in Machakos they could, after the day's work was finished, leave hoes and other tools lying in the fields over-

---

[1] Erlebnisse eines Kambajungen, Verl. d. Ev.-Luth. Mission, Leipzig 1906, p. 10.

night. It ought perhaps to be added that both the missionary and I were on very good terms with the natives and enjoyed their confidence. If, on the other hand, they had thought that they had something to take revenge on us for, it is certain that our things would have disappeared.

That older travellers so often pronounce unfavourable judgements as a rule on the Akamba seems to be due to some extent to the fact that they know them less from their own experience than from the descriptions of the coast dwellers. The Akamba were in former times unpopular at the coast, the chief reason being perhaps that they tried in trading to avoid the dependence of the Wasuaheli, which aroused the jealousy and ill-will of the latter. Krapf, who had a better opportunity than any other of the white pioneers to become acquainted with the Akamba at home among themselves, speaks to some extent very well of them, although they often treated him without any consideration. He calls them courageous and persevering, enterprising, hospitable, and says that there was a certain grandeur about them.

One cannot rely on the Akambas' word very much. They readily make promises, but are not so careful to keep them, perhaps, on the other hand, determined from the beginning not to do so. This is especially so in the case of promises to Europeans. This is the experience of both missionaries and officials. I will mention as a typical case how an old man, who had promised to sell a drum to me, when reminded three times of his promise, answered each time that he would come »tomorrow», but never came. On the contrary I soon realized that he never intended to come.

Another typical feature of their character may also be stated. It appears, as a matter of fact, more or less markedly in all people. If the Akamba are exposed to something unpleasant, which rightly ought to fall upon others as well, they are very careful to see that the others are not allowed to escape it. Thus I have noticed several times that, when porters run away, their friends are very desirous that the names of the deserters should be posted up, so that afterwards they may be punished. And in fixing the hut tax, which, as we know, is arranged according to the number of wives, a man is rarely fortunate enough to »declare too low», as there are always people willing to inform the tax collector of the real state of affairs. In such cases there seems to be scarcely any feeling of solidarity among the natives against the white men.

Although it is not connected with their character, I will devote a few words in passing to the Akambas' aesthetic disposition. One must recognize that they have a certain amount of good taste and sense of beauty, shown, among other things, by their ornaments. The combinations of colours in their decorative objects, beads, etc. are always well chosen, never clashing. With regard to female beauty they seem to have about the same taste as we Europeans, at least when I asked the young men at the dances which girls they thought looked best, they usually pointed out those whom I myself would have decided for. Thick lips, for instance, are not considered beautiful. Only one detail in their conception of female beauty seems to be strange to European taste, namely their idea that long breasts on a woman are beautiful. This seems to be typical of negro women and so belongs to the beauty of the race.

It may also be added that they consider their own colour more beautiful than ours, which they compare to the colour of raw meat, a comparison which is not so much amiss in the case of white people in the tropics before they have obtained the sallow colour that comes from malaria and other illnesses. For this reason they originally did not call Europeans »white people» but »red people» (*andu atunɔ*).

If finally we should venture to attempt a summary of the scattered information brought together here, we can without hesitation say that the Akamba, like all people, possess both good and bad traits of character. It seems to me that older travellers are generally too severe in their conception of the Akambas' character, although none of them goes so far as the English official who stated quite categorically that, of the 33 negro tribes he visited, both in West and East Africa, the Akamba were undoubtedly the most faithless, the laziest, the most obstinate and the worst morally. One must admit, however, that the picture presented by the Akambas of our days, namely that of an obviously rather peaceful and harmless people, is not the original and genuine one. Fear of being called to account by the white men restrains them, but if an opportunity offered itself, most of them would certainly exchange the now prevailing calm state of affairs for the feuds and plundering expeditions of former times.

Chap. XXV. Somatic Characteristics, etc.

As the author is not a specialist in this subject, he has not attempted any anthropological investigations. Careful measurements were, however, taken of about 70 adult natives, according to a scheme drawn up by the Swedish anthropologist D:r G. Backman of Upsala, and they include 14 cranial measurements, 21 measurements of trunk and extremities, notes on flesh, hair, pigmentation (according to Martin), etc. A number of specimens of hair, drawings of the outlines of hands and feet, and fingerprints were also taken. Of the individuals investigated only a few are women, as it was almost impossible to persuade any of them to submit to the measurements. In addition a dozen skulls were collected[1]. The material was handed over to D:r Backman to be worked at, but he has so far had no opportunity to carry out this investigation.

The only investigation on the physical anthropology of the Akamba that, as far as I know, has been carried out (apart from my own and Hobley's measurements — ten individuals, see Hobley, Akamba p. 11) was published by N. M. Ley and J. A. Joyce under the title »Note on a series of Physical measurements from East Africa»[2]. In this note, however, we only find details as to five measurements, namely head length, head breadth, nasal length, nasal breadth and stature. With regard to the results it may be noted that the figures seem to indicate that »the Kenia tribes, the Kikuyu, Kamba and Embu, being, as it were, outposts of the Bantu, in a northerly direction, have mixed with the tribes across the border, and have thus acquired an affinity with the Baringo Nilotes, Suk and Kama-

---

[1] Hobley gives measurements of three Kamba skulls (Akamba p. 9). Another description of a Kamba skull is given by F. Shrubsall i A Study of Bantu Skulls and Crania, Journ. Anthr. Inst. 1898, p. 85.

[2] Journ. Anthr. Inst. 1913, p. 195.

sia, and the Nilotes of Kavirondo»[1]. Mess[rs] Ley and Joyce's measurements were carried out in Mombasa.

To a great extent there are found among the Akamba, as among most Bantu tribes, many different types from an anthropological point of view, from the »negro type» in the popular sense, with massive lower jaws and thick lips, up to higher types, many of which, who are certainly pure Akambas, remind one of Hamitic peoples, Masai or Galla. There is, however, various foreign blood as well among the Akamba, due to the fact that many mothers are captured Masai or Kikuyu and, in the East, also Galla women. If one asks individuals, for instance in Ulu, about their origin, one finds many whose mothers and even grandmothers are Masai women. After a little experience these half-Masai are not so difficult to recognize; their features are, in our opinion, more intelligent and bold, their noses narrower and more straight, etc.

The body is generally slim, the Kamba men being considerably more slender than the average Suaheli. For the weight of the body I have got an average of 117.56 lbs, based on the weight of 60 prisoners at the time they were put into the jail at the Kitui government station. The absolute minimum among these prisoners was 79.5 lbs., and the absolute maximum 133 lbs.

The rather slim build of the Akamba makes it impossible for them to carry such big burdens as the Wasuaheli and many other tribes. The 60 lbs. that the latter can easily carry for many days at a stretch, are, according to my own and others' experience, too much for most Akambas. There are, however, contrary opinions. One traveller says, for instance: »The Kamba possess wonderful power of endurance, though of small physique. Some of our men carried altogether 90 lbs. dead weight during one or sometimes two marches a day for weeks at a stretch, often on insufficient food and sometimes on no food at all»[2].

An abnormality that is not uncommon is the presence of too many fingers, each hand having six. The extra finger, which is not infrequently as much as 2 cm. long and has a completely developed nail, but no bone, proceeds from the base of the little finger, to which it is connected by a very thin connecting joint,

---

[1] Journ. Anthr. Inst. 1913, p. 202.

[2] A. Arckell-Hardwick, An Ivory Trader in North Kenia, p. 7.

so that it can be bent in all directions. Nothing is done to remove this rudimentary finger, but it often happens that it is cut
off when the child creeps about. The wound that is then made
heals and leaves a wart-like swelling.

In the same way a sixth toe is found. On one girl I saw
another variation, an extra toe on each foot close to the little
toe, but situated a little higher up on the foot itself and having bones inside. Children who are born with superfluous toes
or fingers always get the name *nḍula*. The phenomenon does not
seem to occur according to any fixed rules or to be connected
with certain families or clans. These superfluous fingers or toes
are also met with among the Akikuyu.

Another abnormality may be mentioned, namely the presence
of only one testicle. The natives say that in such cases the other
is »in the stomach», by which they mean, quite correctly, that it
is farther in.

A rather common deformation of the feet is caused by elephan-
tiasis, which seems to occur among all East African tribes[1]. The
well-known jiggers (chigoes) may also, if they are neglected, bring
about deformation of the feet; the loss of one or more toes especially is not uncommon. Nowadays, however, the natives are
very skilful in removing the jiggers without injuring them; this is
done with an acacia thorn or a nail. But before they had learned
to do this, many feet had been disfigured or destroyed. Children
especially who creep about on the ground often get jiggers in
their knees and hands. The author himself had one even on the
waist. The natives say that the whites brought the jiggers to
the country, an idea that is probably due to the fact that the
animals became numerous in these districts at about the time of
the building of the Uganda railway at the end of the 'nineties[2].
The jiggers, as is known, came with the ships from South America to the West Coast of Africa, whence they became spread
over the continent.

People whose toes »go in» are called *nḍagi* or *matæyɔ*. They
are considered to be good runners. This position of the feet
appears especially among older men and may possibly be due to

---

[1] Merker (p. 180), however, has not observed it among the Masai.
[2] According to Merker (p. 191) the jiggers came from Uganda to
the Masai steppe in 1897.

the narrow paths. The Akamba state, however, that it is congenital.

Cripples are very rare, which is certainly due, to a certain
extent, to the fact that the babies are carried on their mothers'
backs in the above-described baby-carrier made of skin (ŋgoʋ)
and because of this they are less exposed to the danger of falling to the ground. I can only remember having seen a single
cripple, a man, and his disability was congenital. It would not
occur to the Akamba to kill a child born a cripple or disabled
in any other way, so that the small number of these cannot be
ascribed to any such factor.

Cross-eyed and one-eyed people (nɗoŋgo) are more often met
with, but even they are relatively uncommon. They are considered, as is the case in many other parts of the world, to be
more shrewd than people in general, and when hunting they seldom miss. One-eyed people also play a prominent part in the
Akamba's folklore. I have only seen a single blind person (kılı-
lında), who was said to have been born blind.

The result of some simple investigations to find out the natives' power of moving their fingers and toes, opening and shutting one eye at a time, etc., may be added:

21 of the individuals whose anthropological measurements
were taken (including 5 women) were tested with reference to their
power of opening one finger at a time from the closed hand. Out
of these 16 could do this without any difficulty, 1 could do it
fairly well, 4 let the little finger open at the same time as the
ring finger, and 1, a woman, could not do it at all.

12 of these persons, of both sexes, attempted to take up a
stone with their toes and they all succeeded. They used the big
toe and the second toe.

31 of the measured individuals tried further to shut one eye
at a time. 13 of them were able to do this more or less without
trouble. A number of them could not open one eye at a time.
6 were unable to shut the right eye, while 5 could shut the left
one. Finally 7 were quite incapable of doing any of these things.

13 of them were also tested with regard to their ability to
move their ears. Only 6 of these could do so, 1 other could
move the right ear a little, all the others could not do anything.

Most of them could not move their scalps, several could not even wrinkle their foreheads.

As far as age is concerned the Akamba, like most exotic peoples, age prematurely and die comparatively young. By chance I was able to ascertain fairly exactly the age of one of the oldest people in East Ukamba, a woman. This was done by means of an event that was a memorable one for the natives, namely the arrival of the first white man in their country, that of Krapf the missionary at the end of 1849. The woman in question remembered him very well and was at that time a young wife carrying her third child on her back. With the help of this her age in 1911, when I met her, can be put at about 85. She knew only two of her *nǯukɔ* (age-class) in the district still living. The old woman was still vigorous and both her sight and hearing were good. In Kitui there was a man of about the same age. He »went to dances», i. e. he was a young man, in the time of the wellknown Kivui, the contemporary and friend of Krapf, and was present at Kivui's death in 1851. Both these people were looked upon by the other natives as very old.

The natives who reach a great age are able, if they marry early, to see several generations of their successors. Kituva, a very old man near Machakos, perhaps as old as the two individuals just mentioned, had a son and a grandson, both *atumia*. The latter had a son who was *nǯælə*, who in his turn had a young boy. Thus there were five generations living at the same time.

A few scattered details may finally be collected here:

The natives make water sometimes in a standing position, sometimes bent.

They have coitus lying on their sides.

When they beckon, as, for instance, when they beckon some - one to come to them, they do so with the flat of the hand turned towards the ground. The gesture is thus almost the same as when we ward off something.

When one asks a Kamba the way or some such question, he usually indicates the direction by stretching out his tongue. This can, of course, scarcely be because it is easier, but has probably arisen out of their custom of keeping their hands concealed beneath their blankets, from which they cannot often immediately draw them without a certain amount of trouble.

When resting they sit on the ground, when no stools are to be had; on such occasions the men sit bent with their knees drawn up towards the chin; the women, on the other hand, sit with their legs stretched straight out.

———

ADDENDA

Addenda.

P. 10. The Akamba's expansion in German East Africa.

Scattered and brief statements about this expansion are found in the earlier literature, from which it is seen that enclaves of them occured — and still occur in many places — here and there over great regions of the eastern parts of the German colony, especially in Upare, Usambara, Uguru (Unguru), Usagara, Useguha, Uluguru[1] and Usaramu. A fairly good account of these are given by Carl Peters, who mentions the following dwelling-places of the Akamba[2]: In Usambara at Buiti, Kalamera, Gonya, the River Mbaramu and the Mgandu Swamp. In addition from Kitivo northwest out to Lungusa in the Mehikui hills (Dara) south of Kitivo and in the north-eastern part of Uguru and northern Usagara.

According to Stuhlmann[3] the Wadoe have a tradition to the effect that the Akamba from Kerenge and the province of Gedja in the present Uguru pushed forward as conquerors to the coast and settled down between Bagamayo and Windi, which is situated north of the former town and south of Saadani. But the conquered people called in the help of the Wazaramo — these two tribes are said to be related to each other[4] — and with their united strength they drove away the Akamba, who returned to Kerenge, »in the neighbourhood of which small colonies of them are still found at the present day in south-western Uguru, Gedja, north-eastern Usagara as well as in Usaramo». In former times many Akamba are said to have lived there.

---

[1] Uluguru is a hilly country in Ukami, west of Uzaramo, thus situated down towards the middle course of the Rufidji.

[2] C. Peters, Das Deutsch-Ostafrikanische Schutzgebiet, pp. 38, 815 (see the index and map). See also F. Stuhlmann, Mit Emin Pascha ins Herz von Afrika, p. 425.

[3] F. Stuhlmann p. 38, 815.

[4] F. Stuhlmann p. 33.

R. Hartmann[1] also mentions this push of the Akamba to the coast, as he informs us that they are said to have lived formerly in »Schikiani at Sadan, opposite Zanzibar» (Sadan is probably identical with the harbour of Saadani), and he thus gives us another of their dwelling-places in these parts. He adds that these Akamba waged continual war with the Wadoe (Watutu), who formerly ruled over the whole district south of the River Pangani. In order to be able to wage war against so powerful a people the Akamba who lived here must certainly have been rather numerous. According to a tradition quoted by Hartmann the Akamba were not conquered but left these parts voluntarily. For, he says, as the Wadoe cooked and eat their prisoners and even killed Akamba, the latter were seized by such an aversion to the Wadoe that they went away from their country and looked for new dwelling-places in districts »that had been abandoned by the Galla».

The rumour that the Wadoe were cannibals seems to be quite undeserved and is probably due, according to Stuhlmann[2], to one of the religious rites in use among them, as at a certain time each year an entirely black man was eaten by special persons who were decided on for this purpose; these persons had been chosen from the same families for generations. The above-mentioned tradition seems accordingly, at least at first sight, scarcely probable. There is, however, the possibility to be taken into account that the cannibalistic rite is the remains of a cannibalism that was previously more wide-spread among the Wadoe. In this case a considerable period must have elapsed since they were cannibals. Hartmann does not state any time, but if we note his statement that the Akamba emigrated to parts »that had been abandoned by the Galla», we may perhaps find support from another quarter for the probability of the whole tradition. From the knowledge we already possess of the wanderings of the Galla we know that in late times they have not been much farther south than Sabaki. But Paulitschke has shown that some centuries ago they had already penetrated as far as the River Pangani, from which in the fifteenth century they were again driven back north-

---

[1] R. Hartmann, Abyssinien, p. 165.
[2] Mit Emin Pascha, pp. 33 ff.

wards »by the Masai and the Wakwafi»[1]. Yet in the 16th century they are said to have overrun the whole country around Umba River north of Tanga[2]. If we combine this statement of Paulitschke's with the tradition quoted by Hartmann, the latter, which by itself sounds quite like a legend, becomes not at all improbable. And then we should also be able to date the earliest known history of the Akamba as far back as the fifteenth century.

With this we shall continue our investigation of their distribution in German East Africa in modern times.

Stuhlmann gives[3] as one of their dwelling-places in Usagara Mangubugubu near Kidete (south-east of Mamboia). The Wasagara lived here originally, but they were driven out by the Akamba.

I know nothing about the Akamba in Usaramo, but their number seems to be not inconsiderable, as on several maps we find the name Wakamba and a place Mkamba in the hinterland of Dar-es-Salaam, about 70 km. south-west of this town[4]. Burton also came across Kamba villages at a distance of a three days' march in Bagamoyo[5]. In addition I may mention in passing that, according to him, the Wazaramo assert that they are related to the Akamba, because of which he calls them »a sub-tribe of the Wazaramo». There is nothing to support this relationship, either in the material culture of the Wazaramos — the usual coast culture with an Arabic admixture — or in their language as it has been noted down by Meinhof.

It may also be pointed out that even the name Ukamba is found on the maps of several writers as a term for a district north of the lower course of the River Wami (Uame), opposite Zanzibar[6].

---

[1] Ph. Paulitschke, Die Wanderungen der Oromo oder Galla Ost-Afrikas, Mitteil. d. Anthrop. Ges. zu Wien 1889, p. 175.

[2] A. C. Hollis, Notes on the History of Vumba, East Africa, Journ. Anthr. Inst. 1900, p. 281.

[3] Mit Emin Pascha, p. 821.

[4] See J. Pfeil, Die Erforschung des Ulanga-gebietes, Petermann's Mitteil. 1886 (pl. 18), and C. Peters' map in Das Deutsch-Ostafr. Schutzgebiet.

[5] R. J. Burton, Zanzibar, City, Island and Coast, I, p. 55.

[6] See A. Bloyet, De Zanzibar à la station de Kondoa, Bulletin de la Soc. de Géographie 1890, p. 469; W. Junker, Reisen in Afrika, vol. III (map); Petermann's Mitteilungen 1891, pl. 13.

The literature to which these maps belong does not, however, give any information as to this.

In their capacity of traders and elephant hunters the Akamba undertook expeditions still farther southward. The most southerly point of these excursions that I have found mentioned in the literature is given by J. T. Last, a missionary at Mamboia. He says that the Akamba in Nguru cultivated only very little land, just enough to supply them with the corn they needed. When the harvest was gathered in, they went on hunting expeditions, sometimes as far as the southern end of Tanganyika. They brought the ivory home, and when they had collected sufficient, »they make up a caravan for Mombasa, where they sell it» [1]. Even in these remote districts the Akamba thus retained their old fame as the foremost elephant hunters in East Africa. We have previously shown that the famines were the strongest factors in these wanderings, but it is possible that elephant hunting ought to be given the first place.

The Akamba seem as a rule not to have been popular among their neighbours, the tribes among whom they settled. Although in most cases they were probably numerically inferior, they were arrogant and inconsiderate in their conduct. In addition they were not infrequently cattlestealers. Last relates in his essay quoted above how they stole cattle from the Wakaguru and Wanguru in the district north of the Mamboia mission station. It is clear from what has been said above that they also carried out really warlike attacks.

P. 14. The origin of the Akamba.

An additional detail may be added in connection with the assumptions of the Akamba's having originated from the Kilmandjaro district, which have been previously given. The Wadjagga in the province of Ken-Ko-Towo have a tradition that the Akamba originate from there, more exactly from a place called Kirien [2]. It is possible, of course, that some Kamba clan does so or that in former times some Akambas have lived there.

---

[1] J. T. Last, A Journey into the Nguru Country from Mamboia, Proceed. R. Geogr. Soc. 1882, p. 150 (with a map).

[2] J. Schanz, Mitteilungen über die Besiedelung des Kilmandscharo durch die Dschagga und deren Geschichte, Baessler-Archiv, Beiheft IV, p. 5.

P. 19. The Wadjagga originating from the Akamba.

Several families of chieftains at Kilmandjaro say that they originate from Ukamba, from where their ancestors are said to have come. This is true of families of chieftains in the province of Useri on the eastern slope of the mountain, not far from the southern boundary of Ukamba (their ancestor is said to have been called Msei)[1]. The others are also situated in this district, namely Mkuu, Kenj (Ko Tengia), Mwika (ancestor Urio), and Marangu (Morán). The well-known chieftain Mareale said that his ancestors came originally from a place in Ukamba[2], Umón (cf. Mumono), which appears to be situated eastward from Nairobi. The second chieftain was called Ngovi, which is a genuine Kamba name. Of the names of provinces given above Mkuu and Mwika might very well be Kamba names (cf. *uka* 'age, clan').

In the province of Oru (Uru), situated somewhat farther to the west, it is said that the families of Wamaturu and Wandzau also originate from Ukamba (cf. Kamba *nžau* 'bull').

P. 22. Name of the Akamba.

R. T. Burton says that the people of Mombasa call the Akamba *Warimangao*, and Guillain has the same word, *M'rimangao* or *Ouarimangao* (sing. and plur. respectively), which he translates »gens qui vont nus»[3]. The meaning of these expressions is uncertain, but it is clear that the Suaheli word *nguo* 'clothes' forms part of Krapf's *Waumanguo*. *Warimangao* is perhaps a corruption of *wari manguo*, which might mean 'those who have no clothes'.

P. 22. Masai-*akιpoŋgo*.

It must certainly be called *akιpoŋgo*, not *kιpoŋgo*. Kisongo is the name of a country, namely the great Masai province that extends south-east of Kilimandjaro. The Masai are often called after the separate provinces, e. g. Kisongo-Masai, Loita-Masai,

---

[1] J. Schanz, Mitteil. über die Besiedelung des Kilimandscharo durch die Dschagga und deren Geschichte, pp. 4, 6, 7, 9, 11, 19, 20.

[2] Vide also C. Peters, Das Deutsch-Ostafrikanische Schutzgebiet, p. 121.

[3] R. T. Burton, Zanzibar, City, Island and Coast, II, p. 66 Guillain, Documents sur l'histoire, la géographie et le commerce de l'Afrique orientale, p. 216.

etc. As Merker has shown[1], earlier travellers misunderstood these terms and thought that they meant special tribes. The fact that the Akamba formerly called the Masai *akɩpoŋgo* indicates that they lived in former times near just the Masai of Kithongo, which undoubtedly supports Krapf's statement that they originally lived somewhere near Kilmandjaro (cf. p. 14).

P. 29. Geophagy.

R. Lasch especially has shown[2] that geophagy, even of a non-pathological nature and not only among pregnant women, occurs all over the world and not least in Africa.

P. 94. Women's language.

I give below the few words I found that were exclusively or almost only used by women:

mbunu 'Rhicinus' seeds	instead of the usual				*mbaɩkɩ*
kɩbwu 'water'	»	»	»	»	*manzɩ*
kɩsæbɔ 'wind'	»	»	»	»	*ŋgútanɩ*
kusonoka 'to be ashamed'	»	»	»	»	*kwɩwa ndonɩ*
ɩma (onomatopoetic ⎱ 'sheep'	»	»	»	»	*ɩlondu*
ɩsubɩa muɩo ⎰					
mbupæŋgɔ 'firewood' (used by old women only)	»	»	»	»	*ŋgu*
ukatɩ 'clitoris'	»	»	»	»	*uŋupu.*

ukatɩ really means 'horn' of goats or of cattle. As long as a girl is not yet circumcised her mother uses this word instead of *uŋupu.*

P. 95. Maternal uncle.

It may be worth while mentioning that among the Masai too there exists a sort of reciprocal power of taking property and that this applies especially to a nephew and his maternal uncle[3].

---

[1] Merker, Die Masai, 2nd ed., p. 9.

[2] R. Lasch, Ueber Geophagie, Mitteil. d. Anthr. Ges. in Wien 1898, p. 214.

[3] A. C. Hollis, Notes on the Masai system of relationship, Journ. Anthr. Inst. 1910, p. 473.

P. 97. Terms of relationship.

The terms in use among the Masai show no resemblance to those among the Akamba. Only the terms for 'so-and-so' are the same in both languages, namely *ŋganıa*. On the other I cannot help calling attention — without, however, venturing to draw any conclusions — to the fact that the Kamba word *ınıa* 'mother' is very similar to the Galla word *iná* 'mother', an honourable appellation given to every elderly woman.

P. 114. Clan (*mbaı*).

Without venturing to draw any conclusions I only wish to state that the word *mbaı* and its forms in other Bantu dialects remind one of the Arabic *banı* 'children, descendants' (hence 'clan, family').

P. 192. War-flute.

It would be interesting to make a comparison of the signalling flutes that are found scattered at different places in Africa. For instance the bushmen between Swakop and the Orange River have one of these flutes, the shrill notes of which can be heard in calm weather at a distance of two or three kilometres. A definite number of notes with short and long pauses means »The enemy is there», »There is water here», etc. [1]

P. 195. Burial of a warrior fallen in battle.

The Wadjagga did not bury those who had fallen, either, but put them in the dense bush if they had an opportunity. To bury them would be disastrous for their fighting comrades [2].

P. 210. Ancestral spirits (*aımu*).

It may seem very bold, but as I have never seen the comparison made before, I cannot refrain from stating the striking resemblance that seems to exist between the *aımu*, etc. of the Bantu peoples and the old Assyrian word *edimmu* 'ghost'. The

---

[1] Trenck, Die Buschleute der Namib, Mitteil. aus den Deutschen Schutzgebieten 1913, p. 3.

[2] B. Gutmann, Trauer- und Begräbnissitten der Wadschagga, Globus 1906, p. 199.

latter was also supposed to come back to earth for many reasons. It grew hungry and restless if its descendants ceased to pay it due rites or offer sacrifices on which it might feed.

P. 278 ff. The *ɩƥaƃu*-custom.

The meaning of the word *ɩƥaƃu* is unknown to me, but it represents the curious custom — known from practically the whole of mankind — of throwing stones or sticks by passers-by at a place where something has occurred[1]. The Kamba native who sees human excrement near a path puts a branch or a stone on it. A woman who is carrying a load and accordingly may find it difficult te get hold of a stone or a branch perhaps takes a handful of maize or beans from her food-calabash and throws it over. The excrement of hyenas is treated in the same way, according to the natives' statements, because the hyena »swallows everything he comes across» and its excrement might consequently contain things that are closely connected with some human being.

According to Hobley (Akamba p. 101), in former times each passer-by throw sticks or stones at one of these places »till quite a heap accumulated». The author has never seen or at least has never had his attention drawn to any such heaps of stones in Ukamba, but I have heard a place mentioned where there was a heap of this sort. It was a place in the wilds where a famous medicine man had died (by accident) and been buried. Everyone who passes throws a stone there.

The motives behind this custom often seem uncertain and it is clear that they are of various origins. They are undoubtedly so primitive that their original meaning has long ago been forgotten. In the last case mentioned we may possibly be concerned with a sacrifice, as it frequently happens that a person who passes an ordinary sacrificial place, which is often, of course, a grave, throws a stone on it, as has been previously mentioned. And Andree's exposition referred to above shows us that in many cases it is really a sacrifice.

---

[1] See examples from various places in R. Andree, Ethnographische Parallelen und Vergleiche, I, p. 46 ff. and D Kidd, The Essential Kafir, p. 263 ff.

I may add here that among the Wataveta from Kilimandjaro I found that a branch or a handful of grass is thrown not only on excrement but also on a broken object on or by a path, such as a jar that has been dropped there. One ought to avoid stepping over such objects, and this is especially dangerous in the case of a man whose wife is pregnant. If he does she may have a miscarriage.

Finally we may also add to the chapter on magic the following procedure, which is undoubtedly of a magic character, but which could not be conveniently arranged under one of the preceding main headings:

When a person has been wounded or killed by an accidental shot, for instance by an arrow shot during a hunt, the head man in the deceased's village takes the fatal arrow and touches the wound with it. He then carries the arrow out into the wilds and, with his eyes shut, he puts it into a hole or crack, saying something like the following sentence: »Thou who hast killed our man, mayst thou lie here and not kill again». He then covers the opening up.

This procedure is probably based on a desire to prevent the arrow or the power dwelling in it from doing an injury again, as, according to native ideas, an accidental shot may very well be due to the secret arts of some enemy. The reason why the man shuts his eyes is perhaps that the place shall soon be forgotten, as with the eyes shut he cannot quite know, of course, what he is doing. With regard to the custom of touching the wound with the arrow and then hiding the latter, this seems, if it is not identical with, to be very similar to, the cases of sympathetic and contagious magic dealt with by Frazer in The Golden Bough; cf., for instance, the following quotation given by him from Boas: »Among the Lkuñgen Indians of British Columbia it is a rule that an arrow or any other weapon that has wounded a man must be hidden by his friends, who have to be careful not to bring it near the fire till the wound is healed» [1]. The sympathetic connection that is assumed to take place between a wounded person and the weapon that has wounded him is also, according to Frazer, probably »founded on the notion that the blood on the

---

[1] The Golden Bough, I: 1, p. 201 ff.   London 1911.

weapon continues to feel with the blood in his body». This does not, however, explain our case above, where we are concerned with a dead man.

P. 329. Birds of prey and ostrich eggs.

I have not succeeded in finding any confirmation in zoological textbooks of the idea that certain birds of prey, as the Akamba state, break ostrich eggs with stones. But Charles Andersson, the well-known Swedish traveller, gives the same information from natives living by the Orange River. When in the middle of the day the ostrich leaves its nest in order to look for food, one often sees a white Egyptian vulture hovering in the air with a stone between its claws. It carefully investigates the ground beneath and then suddenly drops the stone [1].

P. 333. The use of animals in magic.

Many animals are also useful to the medicine men and in magic.

In the stomach of the lion there is said to be an object as big as a fist which the lion sometimes vomits. It is, however, very rare and very much sought after by the medicine men as a remedy.

ndundu, the ant-lion, is used as a remedy for women who do not love their husbands. The medicine man rubs the animal against their foreheads.

A man who is fond of a girl but has a favoured rival has to take the excrement of the *nẑımba* (»a striped animal like a cat, but smaller»), mix it with powder from certain trees and bury all this on the path leading to his rival's hut. »The latter will then cease to trouble about the girl».

ıawɔ, a sort of night-jar (cf. p. 479), is used to prepare medicine which makes a person who takes it invisible or at least very difficult to see. This medicine was formerly used by spies during military expeditions and by the caravans that used to take ivory from Ukamba down to the coast, so that they might escape the plundering Galla and Masaı, etc. Here we have a good example of homeopathic magic or of »like producing like», as this bird is

---

[1] Ch. Andersson, Sjön Ngami, I, p. 246.

so bewilderingly like the ground on which it usually perches that it is practically impossible to detect it.

P. 352. Slave trade.

In H. Drummond's map of the slave roads in Central Africa the Kikuyu country is given, probably with great exaggeration, as one of the principal districts of the slave trade[1]. Machakos is situated on the map just at the edge of the territory marked with red. It is, however, certain that the fort was first constructed so that the slave trafic between the Lake and the coast could be supervised. Kitui too was originally built and the district occupied to enable the Government to check slave caravans. Arab and Suaheli traders found this route a safer and more convenient one from the time the caravans of the East African Company and the Government began to traverse the main road from Mombasa to Uganda[2].

P. 440. Fire-drilling.

According to some the art of making a fire in this way was originally a secret of the medicine men.

P. 474. Catching birds.

The boys catch small birds on lime-twigs. The lime (*ulæmbwa, læmbwa*) consists of the sap of the wild fig-trees. It is sometimes boiled, so that it may be more viscous.

The boys are also very clever at catching birds with their hands. At Machakos — the district with its almost treeless vegetation on the borders of the steppe — they are in the habit of sitting on a termite hill or some other raised place of an evening and noticing where the birds seek places to sleep in the trees by the nearest river. When darkness has fallen a whole lot of the boys go out, some of them take up their positions by the different trees and the others shoo the birds, which, half asleep, make for the nearest tree, where the stationed boys try to catch them in their hands, which they sometimes succeed in doing.

---

[1] H. Drummond, Central-Afrika, p. 64.
[2] Directory of British East Africa, Uganda and Zanzibar, p. 68.

P. 560. Conception of colours.

The Kamba word for »colour», *ilaŋgi,* seems to be the Kisua-heli term *rangi.* Originally they had perhaps no special expression for »colour». In order to test their sense of colour I made experiments with colour charts and found only three colours, namely black, white and red. The terms for these are, as far as their roots are concerned, *-ıu, -æu (nǯau)* and *-tunǝ* respectively. Black is identical with soot (*mbuı*), white with a sort of lime (*ea*), and red with a sort of clay (*mbǫ*). Green and blue are called by them black, yellow is called red. Transitional colours are defined very hesitatingly; it seems as if they had never reflected about them. When asked, for instance, what they called yellowish-brown and light yellow, they said white.

Markets.

In former times the Akamba had a sort of unperiodical market or market day (*kıyaŋa*), when the women met together and exchanged their products, especially pottery, which not all women, of course, could make. Nowadays there is no trace of this, and the expression *kıyaŋa* has almost passed into disuse. Instead of this the natives take their goods to the Indian bazars at Machakos and Kitui or to the shops of the Indian traders, which are scattered here and there over the country.

Concluding remarks.

The author began his work on this monograph without any preconceived opinions and theories. There was only one respect in which the Akamba seemed to me to offer a greater interest than an average negro tribe of the Bantu race, namely as being one of the most north-easterly outposts of this race against the Hamitic peoples. Because of this one might have expected a considerable influence from the latter with their higher culture. If, however, we take a broad view of the material put forward by me, we shall not find this supposition fulfilled. We can instead very safely state that the Akamba have remained very free from foreign influences, both physically and as regards material and spiritual culture. This is probably due partly to the character of the people and to their national pride, partly to the fact that their contact with their neighbours has been chiefly of a hostile nature, and partly, finally, to their separation from their neighbours by more or less inaccessible wildernesses poorly supplied with water. But we shall see below, however, that an influence can to a certain extent be detected.

As I believe I have shown, the Akamba were originally a hunting people, with their native place probably somewhere in the Kilmandjaro district; it seems impossible to define it more closely. They seem to have been continually on the move, and we know how, chiefly as elephant hunters and ivory traders but also with the object of plundering, they have wandered about large parts of East Africa, from the districts at the southern boundary of Lake Rudolph and Abyssinia as far as the south end of Tanganyika. And in many places they have founded colonies. It will be clear without any further explanation that with this great geographical expansion they must have played a rather large role in East Africa, a part of the Black Continent that has, as a matter of fact, been the scene of so much wandering of peoples. It would be specially interesting to study the scattered Kamba colonies in German East Africa. It is fairly probable that a study of these would afford valuable information about the tribe as a whole.

It is also worth while noting the traditions and statements that are found among several neighbouring tribes to the effect that parts of them or certain families originate from the Akamba. Such statements are known from the Akikuyu, the Wataveta, the Wadjagga and the Watharaka. The Wakitu on the slopes of Kenia also state, according to Dr. Kolb, that they derive their origin from the Akamba. In addition he mentions the Wandui, who live to the west of Mumoni, as a »bastard tribe of the Wakamba»[1]. Both these tribes are unknown to me and the names probably refer only to the population of some small districts.

From a physico-anthropological point of view it is certain that the Akamba in the most western parts of Ulu have adopted some Kikuyu and Masai blood, but the extent of this admixture is difficult to determine without a more thorough investigation of

---

[1] G. Kolb, Von Mombasa durch Ukambani zum Kenia, Petermann's Mitt. 1896, p. 224.

the conditions. It is a rather unexpected result that Messrs Joyce and Ley arrive at in their above-mentioned measurements when they say that the Akamba have acquired an affinity with the Nilotes of Kavirondo and Baringo, while they make no mention at all of any resemblance to the Masai or Akikuyu, which one would rather have been inclined to expect. But they carried out their investigations in Mombasa, and although they do not indicate the native places of their subjects, it is very probable that they belonged to the coast Akamba or the eastern Akamba, among whom one can, of course, scarcely expect to come across the mixture of race we have mentioned.

If we take a rapid glance at the language we find that the dialect in Mumoni resembles Kikuyu and the languages to the north (Kitharaka, etc.) — among other respects in its vocabulary and by the occurrence of *r*, which does not occur in real Kikamba. In south-eastern Kikumbuliu isolated loan-words from Taita and Kigiriama may also be noted. Other isolated words indicate Hamitic influence from the north. Thus the curious word *sulu* or *ŋgulu* 'dog' may be of Hamitic origin, and also *ɩɓaʂ* 'arrow-poison'. Several terms for wild animals are the same in the Kamba and the Masai languages, but in this case it is tempting to assume that the Masai, who are of course immigrants and who do not hunt or eat the flesh of wild animals, have adopted the names used by their neighbours for a number of these animals. One or more additional words in the Kamba language of a suspicious character might be added, but to obtain any results from this material it would be necessary to have a knowledge of the Hamitic languages that the author unfortunately does not possess. For the sake of comparison I shall only mention Somali *miji* 'plain' and Kamba *wɩ̃ə*, Galla *chaka* 'forest' and Kamba *kɩɓæ̃ka* 'wilderness, forest', Afar *dûje* 'cattle' and Kamba *ŋduʂ* 'half-grown cattle'.

Finally a word as to Suaheli-Arabic influence. Trading caravans from the coast have, of course, from time immemorial crossed East Africa and purchased ivory from the inland tribes. But in the British East Africa of our days their influence from a cultural point of view has not extended far from the coast, since the traders have not founded colonies and trading stations here, as they did along their routes through German East Africa, for instance. We accordingly find that the Akamba still continue to be practically quite independent of the coast culture.

*   *   *

The brief indications of foreign influences given here can be eked out by additional information scattered here and there in the monograph. As this consists, however, of rather unessential small details, it seemed to me unnecessary to collect them here in detail. I content myself instead with pointing out once more that on the whole the Akamba have remained astonishingly free in all respects from any dependence on outside peoples, even though such dependence can in certain tracts and in certain cases be traced from their contact with their principal enemies, the Masai and the Galla, and from their more peaceful connections with their neighbours of the Bantu race, with which the Akamba are closely related.

If we turn to the material culture, we may venture to say that the Akamba have obtained at least a part of their stock of cattle from the Masai and in the east from the Galla as well. From the former they have probably borrowed their cattle-brands too and the custom of bleeding their cattle. The greyhound, which Hildebrandt came across in Ukamba, must also have come from the Hamites in the north. From the Galla they have, in addition, perhaps learned the operation, mentioned on p. 312, of removing the uvula, when it is swollen.

The ornamentation of the Akamba, although simple and undeveloped, also seems to have adopted some foreign elements, as the oval decorations on armlets (p. 381) presumably derive their origin from the Masai or the Galla.

Among musical instruments the fiddle (*mbæɓɔ*, Arabic *rebāb*) is undoubtedly a loan, but it is uncertain whether it, like the *ŋgoma*, the drum which is furnished with two skins, and which is found in the Kibwezi district, has come from the coast. On the other hand, one may safely say that the little toy flute called *nǧumalɪ* is, as its name alone shows, of Suaheli-Arabic origin.

The art of inlaying the men's small stools with metal wire is known by so few individuals that we cannot consider it as a native element in the Kamba culture. I cannot however, give any opinion as to the correctness of the statement that it is borrowed from the Wagiriama and other neighbouring tribes towards the coast (p. 369), as I do not know what are the attainments of these tribes in this respect.

Turning to the spiritual culture we have first of all to note the word *ŋgaʾ*, the term used for the Supreme Being. We attribute the use of this word and its notion to influence from the Masai. It is thus used most in West Ulu, the regions on the borders of the Masai steppe. In addition we note the many strange spirits that tempt the women. In the department of magic, especially black magic, we can also trace a number of borrowings from the Akikuyu and the neighbouring tribes to the north and south-east.

The use of grass as a sign of peace or for magic purposes which is sometimes found among the Akamba (see Index: grass) is perhaps of Hamitic origin. Throwing grass in the air is a sign of peace among the Masai, and some of the Galla throw grass at a lion when they meet one[1].

---

[1] C. G. Seligmann, Some aspects of Hamitic Problems in the Anglo-Egyptian Sudan, Journ. Anthr. Inst. 1913, p. 657,

List of works referred to.

Adams, Die Sprache der Banoho. Mitteil. des Seminars f. Oriental. Sprachen X: 3. Berlin 1913.

Andersson, Sjön Ngami. Stockholm 1856.

Andree, Die Beschneidung. Arch. f. Anthropologie 1881.

——, Ethnographische Parallelen und Vergleiche. Stuttgart 1878. Vol. II. Leipzig 1889.

——, Die Metalle bei den Naturvölkern. Leipzig 1884.

——, Ethnologische Betrachtungen über Hockerbestattung. Arch. f. Anthropologie 1907.

v. Andrian, Die Siebenzahl im Geistesleben der Völker. Mitteil. d. Anthr. Ges. in Wien 1901.

Ankermann, Die Afrikanischen Musikinstrumente. Berlin 1901.

——, Verbreitung und Formen des Totemismus in Afrika. Zeitschr. f. Ethnologie 1915.

Arkell-Hardwick, An Ivory Trader in North Kenia. London 1903.

Armit, Customs of the Australian Aborigines. Journ. Anthrop. Inst. 1880.

Ashe, Two Kings of Uganda. London 1889.

Backman, G. Lindblom: The Akamba of British East Africa. Ymer 1916.

Bartels, Die Medizin der Naturvölker. Leipzig 1893.

Barth, Reisen und Entdeckungen in Nord- und Central-Afrika. Gotha 1857.

Baumann, Usambara und seine Nachbargebiete. Berlin 1891.

Berkusky, Die Sexuelle Moral der Naturvölker. Zeitschr. f. Social-wissensch. Berlin 1909.

Bloyet, De Zanzibar à la station Kondoa. Bulletin de la Société de Géographie. Paris 1890.

Bourke, Scatalogic rites of all nations. Washington 1891.

Brehm, Vierzehn Tage in Mensa. Globus 1863.

——, Tierleben, vol. 5, Leipzig 1913.

Brutzer, Begegnungen mit Wakamba. Verl. der Ev. luth. Mission. Leipzig 1902.

——, Was Kamba-Jungen treiben. Leipzig 1905.

——, Der Geisterglaube bei den Kamba. Leipzig 1905.

Brutzer, Handbuch der Kamba-Sprache. Mitteil. des Seminars f. Oriental. Sprachen III. Berlin 1906.

——, Tierfabeln der Akamba. Arch. f. Anthropologie IX.

Bugeau, La Circoncision au Kikuyu (British East Africa). Anthropos 1911.

Bulletin de la Société de Géographie, Paris 1890.

Burton, Zanzibar, City, Island and Coast. London 1872.

Cayzac, La Religion des Kikuyu (Afrique Orientale). Anthropos 1910.

——, Witchcraft in Kikuyu. Man 1912.

Champion, The Thowa River. Journal of the East Africa and Uganda Nat. Hist. Society. London 1912.

——, The Atharaka. Journ. Anthr. Inst. 1912.

Crawley, The Mystic Rose. London 1902.

——, The Tree of Life. A study of religion. London 1905.

——, Cursing and Blessing, The Encyclop. of Religion and Ethics.

Culin, Mancala, The National Game of Africa. Report of the U. S. A. Nat. Museum 1894. Reprinted Washington 1896.

Dannert, Über die Sitte der Zahnverstümmelung bei den Ovaherero. Zeitschr. f. Ethnologie 1907.

Decle, Three years in savage Africa. London 1900.

Deniker, Les races et les peuples de la terre. Paris 1903.

Directory of British East Africa, Uganda and Zanzibar. Mombasa 1909.

Drummond, Central-Afrika. Stockholm 1890.

Dundas, K., Notes on the Origin and History of the Kikuyu and Dorobo. Man 1908.

——, Kikuyu Rika. Man 1908.

——, Kikuyu Calendar. Man 1909.

Dundas, Ch., History of the Kitui District. Journ. Anthr. Inst. 1913.

——, The Organization and Laws of some Bantu Tribes in East Africa. Journ. Anthr. Inst. 1915.

Eliot, The East African Protectorate. London 1905.

Erlebnisse eines Kambajungen. Verlag der Evang. luth. Mission. Leipzig 1906.

Evangelisch-Lutherisches Missionsblatt. Leipzig 1898 ff.

Frazer, Totemism and Exogamy. London 1910.

——, The Golden Bough. London 1911.

Frobenius, Die Masken und Geheimbünde Africas. Halle 1898.

——, Der Ursprung der Afrikanischen Kulturen, Berlin 1898.

——, Kulturtypen aus West-Sudan. Petermanns Mitteil. 1910.

Gedge, A recent Exploration up the River Tana to Mount Kenia. Proceed. R. Geogr. Soc. London 1892.

van Gennep, Les Rites de passage. Paris 1909.

Gerhold, Wandertage in Nordost-Ukamba. Verl. der Evang. luth. Mission. Leipzig 1903.

Gerland, Atlas der Völkerkunde (Berghaus' Physikal. Atlas, Abt. VII). Gotha 1892.

Germann (Alberti), Zauberglaube und Mannbarkeitsfeste bei den Wapare, Deutsch Ostafrika. Jahrbuch des städt. Mus. f. Völkerkunde. Leipzig 1913.

Goldenweiser, Review of S. Hartland, Primitive Paternity. American Anthropologist 1911.

Gregory, The great Rift Valley. London 1896.

Guillain, Documents sur l'Histoire, la Géographie et le Commerce de l'Afrique orientale. Paris 1856.

Gutmann, Trauer- und Begräbniss-Sitten bei den Wadschagga. Globus 1906.

——, Die Fabelwesen in den Märchen der Wadschagga. Globus 1907.

——, Die Stellung der Frau bei den Wadschagga. Globus 1907.

——, Fluchen und Segnen im Munde der Wadschagga. Globus 1908.

——, Die Zeitrechnung bei den Wadschagga. Globus 1908.

——, Die Gottesidee der Wadschagga auf Kilimandscharo. Globus 1909.

——, Dichten und Denken der Dschagga-Neger. Leipzig 1909.

——, Kinderspiele bei den Wadschagga. Globus 1909.

——, Bienenzucht bei den Wadschagga. Globus 1909.

Haberlandt, Das Salz im Volksglauben. Globus 1882.

Haddon, Magic and Fetishism. London 1906.

Hahn, Die Haustiere. Leipzig 1896.

——, Demeter und Baubo. Versuch einer Theorie der Entstehung des Ackerbaus. [Lübeck 1896.]

——, Von der Hacke zum Pflug. Leipzig 1914.

Hammarstedt, Röda och gula fjädrar. Fataburen 1909.

Hartland, Bantu, in Encyclopedia of Religion and Ethics.

Hartmann, Abyssinien und die übrigen Gebiete der Ostküste Afrikas. Leipzig 1883.

Hein, Armringe von Eibesthal in Nieder-Österreich und von Ukamba in Afrika. Sitzungsber. d. Anthr. Ges. in Wien 1898.

v. Held, Märchen und Sagen der Afrikanischen Neger. Jena 1904.

Hetherwick, Some Animistic Beliefs among the Jaos of British Central Africa. Journ. Anthr. Inst. 1902.

Heydrich, Afrikanische Ornamentik. Intern. Archiv f. Ethnographie. Leiden 1914.

Hildebrandt, Ethnographische Notizen über die Wakamba und ihre Nachbarn. Zeitschr. f. Ethnologie 1878.

Hobley, The Akamba and other East-African tribes. Cambridge 1910.

Hobley, Kikuyu Customs and Beliefs. Thahu and its connection with Circumcision. Journ. Anthr. Inst. 1910.
——, Further Researches into Kikuyu and Kamba religious beliefs and customs. Journ. Anthr. Inst. 1911.
——, Kamba protective magic. Man 1912.
——, Anthropological Studies in Kavirondo and Nandi. Journ. Anthr. Inst. 1903.
——, Kikuyu Medicines. Man 1906.
——, The Evolution of the Arrow. The Journ. of the East Africa and Uganda Nat. Hist. Society. Nairobi 1913.
——, On some Unidentified Beasts. The Journ. of the East Africa and Uganda Natural History Society. Nairobi 1913.
Hofman, Geburt, Heirat und Tod bei den Wakamba. Verlag der Ev. luth. Mission. Leipzig 1901.
——, Wörterbuch der Kamba-Sprache. (Kamba-Deutsch). (Type-written) 1901.
Hollis, History and customs of the people of Taveta. Journ. of the African Society. London 1901.
——, The Masai. Oxford 1905.
——, The Nandi. Oxford 1909.
——, Notes on the Masai System of Relationship. Journ. Anthr. Inst. 1910.
Hubert et Mauss, dans L'Année Sociologique, Vol. VII.
v. Höhnel, Zum Rudolph-See und Stephanie-See. Wien 1892.
v. Ihering, Die künstliche Deformierung der Zähne. Zeitschr. f. Ethnologie 1882.
Joest, Tätowieren, Narbenzeichnen und Körperbemahlen. Ein Beitrag zur vergleichenden Ethnologie. Berlin 1887.
Johnston, British Central Africa. London 1897.
Johnstone, Notes on the Customs of the Tribes occupying Mombasa sub-district. Journ. Anthr. Inst. 1902.
Junker, Reisen in Afrika. Wien 1891.
Junod, Les Baronga. Étude éthnographique sur les indigènes de la Baie de Delagoa. Neuchâtel 1898.
——, Bulletin de la Société Neuchâteloise de Géographie. Tome X.
——, The Life of a South-African tribe. Vol. I. Neuchâtel 1912, Vol. II 1913.
Kaiser, Die wirtschaftliche Entwicklung der Ugandabahnländer. Globus 1907.
Kanig, Dornige Pfade eines jungen Missionars in Ukamba. Verl. der Evang. Luth. Mission. Leipzig 1902.
——, Kambakinder. Verl. der Evang. Luth. Mission. Leipzig 1909.
Karutz, Ueber Kinderspielzeug. Zeitschr. f. Ethnologie 1911.
Kay, Travels and Researches in Caffraria. London 1883.
Keane, Ancestor worship, in Encyclopedia of Religion and Ethics.

Kersten, C. von der Deckens Reisen in Ostafrika. Leipzig 1879.
Kidd, The Essential Kafir. London 1905.
Kitabu tja kutsoma (Kamba reading-book). Ev. Luth. Mission. Leipzig.
Koch-Grünberg, Zwei Jahre unter den Indianern. Berlin 1910.
Kohler, Das Banturecht in Ostafrika. Zeitschr. f. vergl. Rechts-wissenschaft, Stuttgart 1902.
Kolb, Von Mombasa durch Ukambani zum Kenia. Petermanns Mitteil. 1896.
——, Im Lande der Wakamba. Evangel. Luth. Missions-Blatt 1898.
Krapf, Reisen in Ost-Afrika. 1837—55. Stuttgart 1858.
Kroeber, The Morals of Uncivilised Peoples. Amer. Anthropolo-gist 1910.
Laman, Lärobok i Kongospråket. Stockholm 1912.
Lasch, Ueber Geophagie. Mitteil. der Anthr. Ges. in Wien 1898.
——, Die Verstümmelung der Zähne in Amerika und Bemerkungen zur Zahndeformation im Allgemeinen. Mitteil. der Anthrop. Ges. in Wien 1901.
Last, A Journey into the Nguru Country from Mamboia. Proceed. R. Geogr. Soc. London 1882.
——, Grammar of the Kamba language. Polyglotta Africana 1885.
Le Roy, La Religion des Primitifs. Paris 1909.
Ley and Joyce, Notes on a Series of Physical Measurements from East Africa. Journ. Anthr. Inst. 1913.
Lindblom, Anteckningar öfver Taveta-folkets etnologi. Ymer 1913.
——, Krigföring och därmed förbundna bruk bland Kambaneg-rerna i Brittiska Ostafrika. Ymer 1914.
——, Öfvertro och liknande föreställningar rörande djur bland Ost-Afrikas negrer, speciellt bland Kamba-stammen. Fauna och Flora 1914.
——, Afrikanska Ströftåg. Stockholm 1914.
——, Outlines of a Tharaka grammar. Archives d'Études Orien-tales. Upsal 1914.
——, Notes on the Kamba language. Ibidem 1919.
——, En Kamba-saga. Hela världen. Stockholm 1917.
Lönnberg, Mammals collected by the Swedish Zoological Expe-dition to British East Africa. Uppsala 1912.
——, Några exempel från Ostafrika på övertro rörande djur. Fata-buren 1911.
MacGregor, English Kikuyu Vocabulary. London 1904.
Mackenzie, Ten Years North of the Orange River. Edinburgh 1891.
Meinhof, Grundriss einer Lautlehre der Bantusprachen. Leipzig 1889.
——, Afrikanische Religionen. Berlin 1912.

Merker, Rechtsverhältnisse und Sitten der Wadschagga. Petermanns Mitteil. 1902.
——, Die Masai. Berlin 1904. 2. Aufl. 1910.
Meyer, Die Barundi. Leipzig 1916.
v. d. Mohl, Praktische Grammatik der Bantusprache von Tete. Mitteil. des Seminars f. Oriental. Sprachen VII: 3. Berlin 1910.
Nassau, Fetichism in West Africa. London 1904.
Neligan, The Kijesu Ceremony of the Akamba. Man 1911.
Neuman, Elephant hunting in Eastern Equatorial Africa. London 1898.
Nilsson, Primitiv religion. Stockholm 1911.
Nürnberger Missionsblatt. Nürnberg 1887 ff.
Orde Browne, Circumcision Ceremonies among the Amwimbe. Man 1913.
Paulitschke, Die Wanderungen der Oromo oder Galla Ostafrikas. Mitteil. d. Anthrop. Ges. zu Wien 1889.
——, Ethnographie Nordost-Afrikas. Berlin 1893.
Peters, Das Deutsch-Ostafrikanische Schutzgebiet. München 1895.
Pfeil, Die Erforschung des Ulanga-gebietes. Petermann's Mitt. 1886.
Pickerings, The Races of Man. London 1850.
Ploss, Das Kind im Brauch und Sitte der Völker. Stuttgart 1876.
——, Das Weib in der Natur- und Völkerkunde. Leipzig (1891) 1915.
Post, Afrikanische Jurisprudenz. Leipzig 1897.
Preuss, Die geistige Kultur der Naturvölker. Leipzig 1914.
——, Die Ursprung der Religion und Kunst. Globus 1904, 1905.
——, Die Vorbedeutung des Zuckens der Gliedmassen in der Völkerkunde. Globus 1909.
Ratzel, Die Afrikanischen Bögen. K. Sächs. Ges. d. Wissenschaften. Dresden 1891.
Raum, Über angebliche Götzen am Kilimandscharo nebst Bemerkungen über die Religion der Wadschagga und der Bantuneger überhaupt. Globus 1904.
Reinach, Le gendre et la belle-mère. L'Anthropologie 1911.
Reuterskiöld, Sakramentala måltider med särskild hänsyn till totemismen. Uppsala 1908.
Roscoe, The Baganda, their customs and beliefs. London 1911.
v. Rosen, Träskfolket. Stockholm 1916.
Routledge, The Akikuyu of British East Africa. London 1910.
Rütimeyer, Über einige altertümliche afrikanische Waffen und Geräte und deren Beziehungen zur Prähistorie. Zeitschr. f. Ethnologie 1911.
Sachs, Reallexikon der Musikinstrumente. Berlin 1913.
Sartori, Über das Bauopfer. Zeitschr. f. Ethnologie 1898.
Säuberlich, in Jahrbuch d. Sächs. Missionskonferenz, Leipzig 1889.
Schachtzabel, Die Siedelungsverhältnisse der Bantu-Neger. Int. Arch. f. Ethnogr. Leyden 1911.

Schanz, Mitteilungen über die Besiedelung des Kilimandscharo durch die Dschagga und deren Geschichte. Baessler Archiv, Beiheft IV.

Schmidt, Zahl und Zählen in Afrika. Mitteil. d. Anthrop. Ges. in Wien 1915.

Schneider, Die Religion der Afrikan. Naturvölker. München 1891.

Schurtz, Das Afrikanische Gewerbe. Leipzig 1900.

——, Altersklassen und Männerbünde. Berlin 1902.

Schwanhäusser, Das Seelenleben der Dschagga-Neger. (Dissert. Erlangen) Amorbach 1910.

Schöeller, Mitteilungen über meine Reise nach Equatorial-Afrika und Uganda. 2 Bde. Berlin 1901.

Scrubsall, A Study of Bantu Skulls and Crania. Journ. Anthr. Inst. 1898.

Seligmann, Some Aspects of Hamitic Problems in the Anglo-Egyptian Sudan. Journ. Anthr. Inst. 1913.

Spencer and Gillen, The native Tribes of Central Australia. London 1899.

Stadling, Shamanismen i Norra Asien. Stockholm 1912.

Stapleton, in Journal of the African Society XVI. London 1904.

Starcke, Die primitive Familie in ihrer Entstehung und Entwickelung. Leipzig 1888.

Steere, Suaheli Tales. London 1891.

Steinmetz, Rechtsverhältnisse von eingeborenen Völkern in Afrika und Ozeanien. Berlin 1903.

——, Das Verhältnis zwischen Eltern und Kindern bei den Naturvölkern. Zeitschr. f. Socialwissenschaft, Berlin 1898.

Stigand, The Land of Zinj. London 1913.

Stoll, Das Geschlechtsleben in der Völkerpsychologie. Leipzig 1908.

Storbeck, Die Berichte der arabischen Geographen des Mittelalters über Ostafrika. Westasiatische Studien. Mitteil. des Seminars f. Oriental. Sprachen, Berlin 1914.

Strandes, Die Portugiesenzeit in Deutsch und English Ostafrika. 1899.

Struck, Das Chamäleon in der Afrikanischen Mythologie. Globus 1909.

Stuhlmann, Mit Emin Pascha ins Herz von Afrika. Berlin 1894.

——, Beiträge zur Kulturgeschichte Ostafrikas. Berlin 1909.

Söderblom, Översikt af allmänna religionshistorien. Stockholm 1912.

Tate, Notes on the Kikuyu and Kamba tribes of British East Africa. Journ. Anthr. Inst. 1904.

——, Further Notes on the Kikuyu Tribe of Brit. East Africa. Journ. Anthr. Inst. 1904.

Taylor, Vocabulary of the Giriama language.

Thompson, Through Masailand. London 1885.

Trenck, Die Buschleute der Namib. Mitteil. aus den Deutsch. Schutzgeb. 1913.

Tylor, Primitive Culture. London 1903.

Wakefield, Routes of Native Caravans from the Coast to the Interior of British East Africa. Journ. R. Geogr. Society, London 1870.

Watt, Vocabulary of the Kikamba language. Harrisburg U. S. A. 1900.

Webster, Primitive Secret Societies. New York 1908.

Weeks Anthropological Notes on the Bangala of the Upper Congo River. Journ. Anthr. Inst 1910.

Weiss, Die Völkerstämme im Norden Deutsch-Ostafrikas. Berlin 1910.

Weissenhorn, Tierkult in Afrika. Int. Arch. f. Ethnographie 1904.

Werner, Notes on the terms used for »right hand» and »left hand» in the Bantu languages. Journ. Afr. Society, London 1904.

——, The Natives of British Central Africa. London 1906.

——, Note on Bantu Star-Names. Man 1912.

Westermarck, The History of human marriage. London 1891.

Weule, Die Eidechse als Ornament in Afrika. Festschrift an A. Bastian. Berlin 1896.

——, Wissenschaftliche Ergebnisse meiner Forschungsreise in den Südosten Deutsch-Ostafrikas. Berlin 1909.

——, Negerleben in Ost-Afrika. Leipzig 1909.

——, Die Kultur der Kulturlosen. Stuttgart 1910.

Widemann, Die Kilimandjaro-Bevölkerung. Petermanns Mitt. 1899.

Wood, Natural History of Man. Africa. London 1874.

Zeitschrift f. vergleichende Rechtswissenschaft 1908, 1909.

List of illustrations.

Errata.

P.	14	l.	5	Kraft		for Krapf
»	18	»	5	p. 118		» p. 126
»	18	»	2 fr. below	a Bantu people and		» a Bantu people, and
»	35	»	9 »	(cf. p. 103)		» (cf. p. 108)
»	35	note 1		Ch. XII		» Ch. XIII
»	41	l.	7	Chap. VIII		» Chap. VII
»	46	»	13 fr. below	(p. 135)		» (p. 144)
»	61	»	2 »	(see p. 138)		» (see p. 144)
»	62	»	7	p. 103		» p. 108
»	62	»	12	(Chap. VI)		» (Chap. VII)
»	79	»	20	Chap. VII		» p. 121
»	114	»	19	*mba-mindele*		» *ba-mindele*
»	125	note 1		Chap. XII		» p. 224
»	128	»	1	Chap. XII: 1		» p. 212
»	128	»	2	Ch. XIII: 6, XIV: 3		» pp. 292, 326 ff.
»	169	l.	7	*mukulwa*		» *mukulwa* (Acalypha)
»	240	»	15	(cf. next chap.)		» p. 269
»	248	»	13	Chap. XIV. 5		» p. 290

» 253: the passage »Fresh and smooth wounds . . . . the Masai» to be excluded

»	312	l.	13	with a with thread		for with a thread
»	349	»	10	Akikuya		» Akikuyu
»	369	»	5 fr. below	clothes		» cloths
»	372	»	21 »	skin		» skins
»	373	»	24 »	the young		» that of the young
»	374	»	12 »	these		» these cylinders
»	374	»	8 »	or		» of
»	393	fig. 106		describel		» described

INDEX.